7th edition

Early Education Curriculum

A Child's Connection to the World

Nancy Beaver
Susan Wyatt
&
Hilda Jackman

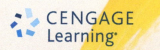

CENGAGE
Learning

Australia • Brazil • Mexico • Singapore • United Kingdom • United States

CENGAGE Learning®

Early Education Curriculum, A Child's Connection to the World, Seventh Edition
Nancy H. Beaver, Susan Skinner Wyatt, Hilda L. Jackman

Product Director: Marta E. Lee-Perriard

Product Manager: Cheri-Ann Nakamura

Associate Product Manager: Brady Golden

Content Developer: Lin Gaylord

Product Assistant: Chelsea Meredith

Content Project Manager: Rita Jaramillo

Art Director: Helen Bruno

Manufacturing Planner: Doug Bertke

Production Service/Compositor: MPS Limited

Text and Cover Designer: Jennifer Wahi

Cover Image: iStockPhoto.com/Peter Booth

Interior Images: Colorful paint set and brushes (image used next to H1-level heads): Antonova Anna/Shutterstock.com; Paint brushes: Val Lawless/Shutterstock.com; "Boy paints the sunshine" (sun painter, on cover, title page, plus sun picked up for TOC, COs, and Case Study box: iStockPhoto.com/Peter Booth

For product information and technology assistance, contact us at
Cengage Learning Customer & Sales Support, 1-800-354-9706.

For permission to use material from this text or product,
submit all requests online at **www.cengage.com/permissions.**
Further permissions questions can be e-mailed to
permissionrequest@cengage.com.

Library of Congress Control Number: 2016930882

Student Edition:

ISBN: 978-1-305-96063-3

Loose-leaf Edition:

ISBN: 978-1-305-96065-7

Cengage Learning
20 Channel Center Street
Boston, MA 02210
USA

Cengage Learning is a leading provider of customized learning solutions with employees residing in nearly 40 different countries and sales in more than 125 countries around the world. Find your local representative at **www.cengage.com.**

Cengage Learning products are represented in Canada by Nelson Education, Ltd.

To learn more about Cengage Learning Solutions, visit **www.cengage.com.**

Purchase any of our products at your local college store or at our preferred online store **www.cengagebrain.com.**

Printed in the United States of America
Print Number: 03   Print Year: 2018

I dedicate this to my daughter, Stephanie, the light of my life, and husband, Dom, who supported me with loving care through the revision of this textbook.

—NB

I dedicate this book to all my guys: Frank, Christopher, Patrick, and Brandon, who have never questioned or complained about my late nights and the bags of work I bring home on a regular basis. And also to my newest children, Sarah and Kara, and my multiple grandchildren who let me try out new ideas on them.

—SW

This book is lovingly dedicated to my granddaughters Cambria and Rachel and to the men in my life: my husband, Phil, my sons, Stephen and Larry, my brother, Rick… and, as always, to my nephew Jared.

—HJ

Brief Contents

Contents

Preface

Research confirms the value of early education for young children. Our early childhood profession continues to guide us with new and effective teaching applications, position statements, and developmentally appropriate practices. All three authors are colleagues **with 46 years of experience as teachers.** They have worked together as part of the Dallas County Community College District's Child Development/Early Childhood Education department. Our goal is to help students and developing professionals make informed decisions about curriculum content. To that end, the focus of *Early Education Curriculum: A Child's Connection to the Word, seventh edition,* remains the same: *the children* and the dedicated early childhood professionals who contribute daily to improve the lives of children everywhere.

Philosophies of This Book

We should listen to the children and concentrate our efforts on the development, needs, abilities, and interests of all children, including those with cultural, linguistic, and other diversities, as we plan our early childhood curriculum. In response to the needs of our students, the early childhood profession is dedicated to discovering new knowledge through research and new professional positions, and to establishing inclusiveness, equity, equality, and diversity through developmentally appropriate practices. It is the role of early education curriculum to integrate these insights into each classroom, from infancy through the early primary years.

In this seventh edition, the following interconnecting philosophies are underscored.

- The first advocates that curriculum be *child centered and child initiated*, that it is sensitive to, and supportive of, the development of young children, individually and in a group, emphasizing acceptance of each and every child. This includes acceptance of cultural, linguistic, gender, family orientation, and ability diversity in young children.
- The second focus is on the *curriculum* itself, which provides for all of a child's development by planning developmentally appropriate experiences that build on what children already know and are able to do. New findings inform us even more about early cognitive, physical, social, and emotional development. These facts help us to make connections as to how we teach and how children learn.
- The third philosophy of this text is to encourage children to *learn by doing*. This encourages experimentation, exploration, self-control, and the building of a positive self-image ("I can do it myself!").
- The fourth recognizes the importance of *cultural context* in the development and learning of young children. Growing up as members of families and communities, children come to us with rich backgrounds of cultural experiences. Now, more than ever, the curriculum should promote opportunities to support a child's cultural, linguistic, gender, family orientation, and diversity.
- The fifth belief advocates developing a learning environment that invites *creativity*. This provides opportunities for unevaluated discovery and activity, while promoting acceptance and respect for one another's creations. This also helps one to develop an awareness that the process of creative thinking is complex.

- The sixth concept involves reciprocal *relationships between teachers and families*. Positive communication between home and school is crucial to providing a consistent and beneficial experience for young children.
- The seventh philosophy recommends that curriculum facilitate *physical activity and play* by integrating movement within activities throughout the day. Each of these philosophies allows children to make choices and is nourished by play. With less time and opportunity for children to play, it is critical for us to encourage and support play in all our early childhood programs.

To best address these interconnecting philosophies, coverage in this edition has been expanded to all age groups through second grade and includes hot topics in Brain Research, reflective practice, intentional teaching, hands-on teaching ideas, and using the environment as a teaching tool. The research behind the techniques discussed has been further highlighted in this edition, whereas curriculum chapters will consistently include headings on "Technology" and "Diversity."

Intended Audience

This book is designed for a beginning student as well as an experienced teacher looking for current early childhood philosophies, research, curriculum resources and activities, and fresh ideas and insights. It can be used by those in two-year colleges or four-year university early education curriculum courses, graduate classes, mini/fast-track courses, distance learning, and workshop/seminar courses for continuing education of teachers. It is also applicable for students working toward the Council for Professional Recognition (CDA) credential or any professional working with children and families.

Chapter Changes and Highlights

The text remains divided into two parts. Part One, "Preparing for Learning through Assessment, Curriculum, and the Environment," presents the elements of the foundation of early education curriculum, and includes four chapters as follows:

- Chapter 1, *Starting the Process*, gives early childhood historical information, learning, and developmental theories of early childhood education; the importance of play in the lives of children; and communication with parents. The chapter has been thoroughly updated, including new standards and new references; outdated references and material have been deleted throughout. The Brain Research feature identifies how knowledge of brain development is crucial to an understanding of how to create curriculum.
- Chapter 2, *Observation and Assessment*, describes the purposes and process of observation and assessment; and also presents guidelines for assessment. This topic area is important because of the increase in reliance on the use of standards to guide our decisions about what and how we teach. These standards have been

updated and are based on the use of strong statistical data that help formulate our practices. Teachers have to have the ability to use appropriate observation and assessment techniques to create the data needed to begin the development of curriculum, experiences, and environments to support children's development and learning. A new feature of this chapter is about the use of technology in assessment.

- Chapter 3, *Creating Curriculum*, offers examples of curriculum models and programs; explains the process of curriculum development, including multicultural, anti-bias, and special needs considerations; and describes the development of concepts and skills, themes, specific lesson and activity plans. More coverage of the curriculum cycle and use of technology in assessment and curriculum planning has been added to this chapter.
- Chapter 4, *The Learning Environment*, reflects the continuing focus of this text on the learning environment. It describes developmentally appropriate early learning environments, indoor and outdoor; selection of equipment, materials, and supplies; and play guidance, including transitions. It also includes the first environment checklist that will also be included in Chapters 5 to 13. Those checklists will be on specific environmental areas that are described in those particular chapters. A floor plan was added to this chapter to accommodate the primary grades that were not covered in the previous edition.

These four chapters form the foundation for the remaining chapters.

Part Two, "Discovering and Expanding the Early Education Curriculum," explores each curriculum area in depth, taking into consideration the individual child, group of children, the process of setting up appropriate environments with a chapter checklist for use in observing environments, special subject content, information on the use of technology, more ideas to involve parents, meeting diverse needs, and integration of all curricula. Chapters 5 to 13 present developmentally appropriate activities for each age group and encourage self-esteem and creativity development. These chapters are organized to provide greater clarity and consistency to support better comprehension by the student.

- Chapter 5, *Language and Literacy*, describes the acquisition of languages with emphasis on dual-language learning. A major focus is teaching strategies and providing practical experiences and materials to support the development of language and literacy skills through literature. An additional activity plan has been add to extend the age range of activity plan samples through the primary grades. The brain research feature has added a description of new research related to the 50-million word gap by age 3 for low-income children. All references have been updated.

- Chapter 6, *Creativity: Art and Music*, describes the creative process with a specific emphasis on art and music. A focus of this chapter is how children discover their own original ways to explore forms of art and types of music and dance. Ideas are shared concerning the creation of an aesthetic environment and the use of the outdoors to foster creativity. Practical teaching strategies, experiences, and materials (including homemade instruments) support the development of creativity in diverse children. An additional activity plan has been added to this chapter to extend the age range covered to the primary grades. New and updated information has been added related to technology ideas for Music teachers. All references have been updated.

- Chapter 7, *The Child's World: Social Studies and Dramatic Play*, describes themes and appropriate content for social studies in the early childhood curriculum. The chapter includes developmental theories and research on the stages of play and types of social dramatic play. A thorough discussion of dramatic play includes the use of puppets and prop boxes and provides practical ideas for use in the classroom. The chapter includes a discussion of field trips as concrete experiences introducing children to the social world. The chapter includes additional information about multicultural play by including materials form different cultures. A new video "Multicultural Lessons: Embracing Similarities and Differences in Preschool Education" has been added to the MindTap digital platform. All references have been updated.

- Chapter 8, *Sensory Play*, discusses how the senses are used as learning portals and how every day, the early childhood classrooms should be filled with activities that involve multiple senses. Piaget's sensory motor period of learning, Goscoyne's continuum of fluid play process, and sensory integration are defined. A curriculum planning web for the book, *My Five Senses* demonstrates how to integrate sensory learning throughout the curriculum. The chapter discusses how to use technology and incorporate diversity into sensory play. New brain research on sensory development and an additional activity plan for 2- and 3-year-olds have been added to this chapter. All references have been updated.

- Chapter 9, *Science*, describes science for young children as engaging children in active construction of ideas and explanations to develop both inquiry and process skills. Categories of science to be explored identified by the National Research Council, are defined and the development of the brain's executive function is explained. The chapter relates the stages of child development to scientific learning and evaluates how the preparation of the environment supports that learning as children use the scientific process to make and test predictions, observe, solve problems, and make connections. The chapter contains many activity ideas for integrating science throughout the curriculum including explorations of earth elements such as water, ecology, animals, nutrition, and cooking. The use of technology in documenting science projects and the use of cooking experiences to explore diversity are discussed. New information on brain research has been added. There is an increased focus on nature in this addition, including the creation of outdoor classrooms that incorporate a variety of natural elements for children's play. An additional activity plan for 2- and 3-year-olds has been added to this chapter. All references have been updated.

- Chapter 10, *Math*, discusses the importance of providing hands-on, developmentally appropriate math experiences in a meaningful context that give young children opportunities to develop math awareness and understanding. The chapter contains a thorough explanation of mathematical terms and teaching strategies. There is a focus on how the environment is set up to provide opportunities for children to develop number sense and logical ways of thinking about time, space, and other mathematical ideas, as they discover math concepts through the process of play. New research on the use of technology has been added and the term *cardinality* has been added to key terms. An additional activity plan for primary grades has been added to this chapter as well. A new video titled *Using Read-Alouds to Develop Math and Literacy Skills* has been added to the MindTap digital platform. All references have been updated.

- Chapter 11, *Fine Motor and Manipulatives*, describes the different types of small muscle movement and coordination and how teachers can support the development of this coordination for different age children. The chapter describes how fine motor play is integrated throughout the curriculum with specific details on the importance of crossing midline and the use of scissor activities to develop cutting skills and pincer grasp. Suggestions for supporting each and every child's success address student diversity and activity ideas for parents to do at home are included in the chapter. All references have been updated.

- Chapter 12, *Large Motor and Outdoor Play*, explores how through large muscle and outdoor play children develop their eye–hand coordination, balance and coordination, large muscles skills, general health, a sense of freedom, an understanding of nature, creativity, social play skills, multisensory integration and learning, ability to explore and solve problems, and their imaginations. Different types of movement are defined and suggestions for equipment selection identified. Ideas are described for including motor development and physical fitness within activities

designed to target other curriculum areas such as music and art. New guidance on the crucial role of recess in school by The Council on School Health has been added as well as a new Brain Research feature that shows the relationship of physical fitness to better relational memory. A new video titled *2–5 Years: Gross Motor Development for Early Childhood* has been added to the MindTap digital platform. All references have been updated.

- Chapter 13, *Construction: Blocks and Woodworking,* describes well-planned block play and woodworking experiences where children create, build, construct, and stay engaged to facilitate children's development across domains in an engaging context. The unit block shapes and storage as well as the developmental stages of block play are visually represented to facilitate student understanding. A list of equipment and materials to use in woodworking is provided. The Brain Research feature discusses spatial reasoning and how to use technology in teaching construction play. New ideas for addressing diversity through block play and an additional activity plan for primary age children have been added in this edition. A new video titled *Preschool Stacking Activity* has been added to the MindTap digital platform. All references have been updated.

- Chapter 14, *Putting It All Together: Evaluation and Documentation,* examines the purpose, use, and process of evaluation including identifying standards for evaluation and ethical issues. The process used for creating a documentation plan is explored and methods for interpreting and using evaluation results are described. Types of evaluation including quantitative, qualitative, formative and summative evaluation are defined. Samples are provided to illustrate types of documentation used in evaluations. All references have been updated.

All chapters of the text are separate and complete, and at the same time connecting to other chapters to form curriculum as a whole for children from infancy to age eight. This allows each instructor to use the chapters in any sequence. This approach is helpful in meeting the individual needs of the teacher, the student, and ultimately the children.

New to This Edition

MindTap for *Early Education Curriculum: A Child's Connection to the World,* seventh edition, is a first-of-its kind digital solution with an integrated eportfolio that prepares teachers by providing them with the knowledge, skills, and competencies they must demonstrate to earn an education degree and state licensure, and to begin a successful career. Through activities based on real-life teaching situations, MindTap elevates students' thinking by giving them experiences in applying concepts, practicing skills, and evaluating decisions, guiding them to become reflective educators.

Updated and Revised Coverage

Early Education Curriculum takes an application-based approach that provides hands-on teaching tools, techniques, and tips for preschool and after-school programs through second grade. Building on the foundations of previous editions, the seventh edition has been thoroughly updated and revised:

- **Organization and Coverage:** The text has been updated, where needed, and the curriculum chapters (Part Two) continue to maintain a consistent chapter structure.
- **Case Studies:** Chapters 5 to 13 now have case studies to help apply the information in each chapter to different teaching setting situations. Each case study includes a "What Do You Think?" set of questions to get students to think critically about the case and what they would do in the classroom.
- **Brain Research:** Information on brain research related to the specific curriculum area appears throughout the textbook. While keeping seminal information about brain research that was in the sixth edition, the seventh edition includes new research:
  - Chapter 1 examines varying cultures roles in children's play.
  - Chapter 8 provides new research on the value of sensory experiences.
  - Chapter 9 research links young children's time in nature activities as having a large influence on the development of the child.
  - Chapter 10 describes the role of math activities on brain development.
  - Chapter 12 discusses the direct link between the level of child's physical fitness and memory.
  - Chapter 14 describes the Scientific Research-Based Intervention's (SPBI) system for evaluating data to assess progress toward learning goals.
- **Technology:** Each curriculum chapter contains a special section that focuses on the impact of technology related to the curriculum area discussed. This edition includes more information about the use of technology across the curriculum. Chapter 2 describes new technology in assessment that allows the teacher to better track a child's progress and to plan individualized instruction based on each child's needs and abilities. Chapter 3 identifies software that assists the teacher in lesson plan development and in the delivery of content throughout the curriculum.
- **Cultural and Linguistic Diversity:** The importance of culturally relevant curriculum appears throughout this edition and remains a continuing emphasis in the text. Chapters 5 to 13 each contain a section on how diversity impacts that chapter's specific subject

area. Teaching strategies for a diverse population are also included. New case studies also provide additional information on dealing with diversity in the classroom.

Chapter Pedagogy and Features

- **Student Learning Outcomes (SLOs):** Student learning outcomes have been updated to provide a clear road map of the major topics in each chapter and to allow for better assessment of student learning. SLOs have also been revised to focus on higher levels of thinking
- **National Standards:** National standards in literacy, mathematics, science, art, social studies, and music continue to appear at the beginning of each curriculum chapter as they relate to specific standards; they are also integrated before relevant chapter material as icons. Essential recommendations and position papers of the NAEYC and Association of Childhood Education International (ACEI) are included as well. In particular, NAEYC's Code of Ethical Conduct defines core values that are deeply rooted in the field of early childhood care and education. Also included are DEC Recommended Practices, Common Core State Standards, and InTASC Model Core Teaching Standards. The major standards (NAEYC, DAP, InTASC, and Head Start) have been compared to chapter content in a Correlation Chart located inside the covers. Additional standards more specific to a subject or group of students, such as DEC and ILA, are included in the chapters they relate to and in Appendix F.
- **Brain Research boxed feature:** This feature provides information about significant brain research targeted at the content of each chapter. New and updated research is found in Chapters 1, 8, 9, 10, 12, and 14.
- **Technology and Teaching boxed feature:** This feature discusses issues related to technology, including suggestions for the use of technology in the curriculum area discussed in the chapter. In some instances, it provides cautions related to its use. New information on using technology has been added to Chapters 2 and 3.
- **Appendix F** has been revised to include the standards that are specific to each chapter's content. Contact information for the Common Core and also contacts for the standards for states that have their own standards have also been included in Appendix F.
- **Videos:** TeachSource videos and questions have been moved to the MindTap digital learning platform under Activity 2 of the learning path.

More Features to Look For

Current and improved children's book lists—available as digital downloads in the Professional Resources section within MindTap—are included at the end of each curriculum chapter throughout the text. Expanded information is provided on themes, projects, webs, and developmentally appropriate activities. All of the features in this seventh edition are created to provide a resource of ideas, methods, suggested practices, and guidance goals that will give teachers and students guidelines to create and enrich their own curriculum.

Special Learning Features

This book is designed to help students build knowledge with each chapter. Concepts are introduced in a specific chapter and then reviewed for elaboration and application throughout the text. Topics are approached developmentally and placed appropriately within the curriculum area where students can benefit from their content. Each topic becomes a part of the entire curriculum.

In addition to the new features discussed previously, numerous learning aids appear in the text to help student comprehension:

- **Key terms** are bolded and listed as a running glossary in the text margins so that students are able to identify them as they read the chapters.
- **Sectional icons** visually highlight concentrated coverage that relates to developmentally appropriate practice, NAEYC standards, Head Start standards, and InTASC teaching standards. Depending on the topic of a chapter, additional standards icons have been added, such as ILA for language and literacy and NSES for science.
- **Chapter organization** is formatted around the student learning outcomes for that chapter.
- **Observation, Assessment Strategies, and Evaluation** guidelines, forms and suggestions provide effective tools to be used throughout the early childhood curriculum. Guidelines and forms are available as digital downloads in the Professional Resources section within MindTap.
- **Learning Environment Checklists** provide center-based checklist to assist students as they complete observations in the children's classrooms. These are also available as digital downloads in the Professional Resources section within MindTap.
- **Activity Plan Worksheets** provide detailed plans with guidance tips and assessment strategies, and are included as digital downloads in the Professional Resources section within MindTap.
- **Lesson Plan samples** provide guidance in weekly planning for different age groups
- **Appendices** are designed to give teachers practical information that can be used across the curriculum. Appendix A, My Self, is an integrated curriculum theme with developmentally appropriate activities. Appendix B, Additional Activities and Songs, is new and includes additional activities that can be used in curriculum development. Appendix C, Songs and Poems, is also new and provides songs appropriate for curriculum topics. Another new Appendix, D, Forms,

provides a collection of forms that can be used to support classroom activities. Appendix E, Resources for Teachers, includes updated and new useful resources. Appendix F, Additional Standards by Chapter including Common Core State Contact Information, describes additional early childhood standards and their alignment with the text content. Common Core State standards contact information is also included. Appendix G, Professional Organizations, includes updated and new useful resources.

- **Standards Correlation Chart**: A correlation chart of NAEYC Standards for Early Childhood Professional Preparation, DAP, InTASC, and Head Start is correlated to each chapter, and is included on the inside covers of this edition. The chart identifies how the content in this text aligns with these standards.

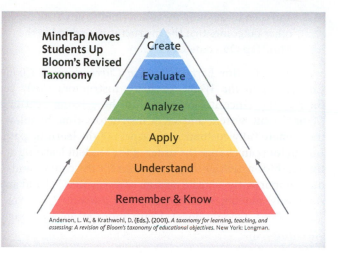

Anderson, L. W., & Krathwohl, D. (Eds.). (2001). *A taxonomy for learning, teaching, and assessing: A revision of Bloom's taxonomy of educational objectives.* New York: Longman.

Ancillaries

The following ancillary materials are available to accompany the seventh edition of *Early Education Curriculum: A Child's Connection to the World.*

Instructor's Manual and Test Bank

An online Instructor's Manual accompanies this book. It contains information to assist the instructor in designing the course, including sample syllabi, discussion questions, teaching and learning activities, field experiences, learning objectives, and additional online resources. For assessment support, the updated test bank includes true/false, multiple-choice, matching, short-answer, and essay questions for each chapter.

Cengage Learning Testing Powered by Cognero

Cognero is a flexible, online system that allows you to author, edit, and manage test bank content from multiple Cengage Learning solutions. Create multiple test versions in an instant and deliver them from your LMS, classroom, or wherever you want! No special installs or downloads needed. Create tests from school, home, the coffee shop—anywhere with Internet access.

MindTap™: The Personal Learning Experience

MindTap for *Early Education Curriculum: A Child's Connection to the Word* 7e, represents a new approach to teaching and learning. A highly personalized, fully customizable learning platform with an integrated eportfolio, MindTap helps students to elevate thinking by guiding them to:

- Know, remember, and understand concepts critical to becoming a great teacher.
- Apply concepts, create curriculum and tools, and demonstrate performance and competency in key areas in the course, including national and state education standards.
- Prepare artifacts for the portfolio and eventual state licensure, to launch a successful teaching career.
- Develop the habits to become a reflective practitioner.

As students move through each chapter's Learning Path, they engage in a scaffolded learning experience, designed to move them up Bloom's Taxonomy, from lower- to higher-order thinking skills. The Learning Path enables preservice students to develop these skills and gain confidence by:

- Engaging them with chapter topics and activating their prior knowledge by watching and answering questions about authentic videos of teachers teaching and children learning in real classrooms.
- Checking their comprehension and understanding through Did You Get It? assessments, with varied question types that are autograded for instant feedback.
- Applying concepts through mini-case scenarios—students analyze typical teaching and learning situations, and then create a reasoned response to the issue(s) presented in the scenario.
- Reflecting about and justifying the choices they made within the teaching scenario problem.

MindTap helps instructors facilitate better outcomes by evaluating how future teachers plan and teach lessons in ways that make content clear and help diverse students learn, assessing the effectiveness of their teaching practice, and adjusting teaching as needed. MindTap enables instructors to facilitate better outcomes:

- Making grades visible in real time through the Student Progress App so students and instructors always have access to current standings in the class.
- Using the Outcome Library to embed national education standards and align them to student learning activities, and also allowing instructors to add their state's standards or any other desired outcome.
- Allowing instructors to generate reports on students' performance with the click of a mouse against any standards or outcomes that are in their MindTap course.
- Giving instructors the ability to assess students on state standards or other local outcomes by editing existing or creating their own MindTap activities,

and then by aligning those activities to any state or other outcomes that the instructor has added to the MindTap Outcome Library.

MindTap for *Early Education Curriculum: A Child's Connection to the Word,* 7e, helps instructors easily set their course since it integrates into the existing Learning Management System and saves instructors time by allowing them to fully customize any aspect of the learning path. Instructors can change the order of the student learning activities, hide activities they don't want for the course, and—most importantly—create custom assessments and add any standards, outcomes, or content they do want (e.g., You-Tube videos, Google docs). Learn more at www.cengage.com/mindtap.

Acknowledgments

Our sincere and heartfelt appreciation is extended to the special friends and colleagues who, throughout the years, have inspired us through friendship, devotion to children, and commitment to students and the community. These generous friends, who have spent their professional lives pursuing all that is best for children and who are most willing to share their expertise. Specifically we want to thank **Janet Galantay**, **Jo Eklof**, **Bea Wolf**, and the students, faculty and staff of Eastfield College's Center for Child and Family Studies. THANK YOU!

Special recognition must go to Hilda Jackman's son, **Laurent Linn**, for his illustrations throughout all seven editions, which demonstrate his love and understanding of children and give depth and meaning to what we have tried to communicate in words.

Special thanks go to our husbands and families for their support, patience, and encouragement.

With deep appreciation and many thanks to professors, students, and colleagues who continue to use *Early Education Curriculum* in their classes.

To **Cheri-Ann Nakamaru**, product manager, and **Lin Gaylord**, senior content developer extraordinaire, for encouragement and guidance and to **Andy Miller**, **Timothy Kappler**, **Rita Jaramillo**, and the rest of the team at Cengage Learning, and Lynn Lustberg of MPS, a huge THANK YOU.

And finally, we appreciate the time, effort, and contributions that the following reviewers have given us:

Ann Barbour, Brandman University
Katy Basch, Kennesaw State University
Teresa Borchardt, Bates Technical College
Beverlyn Cain, Fayetteville State University
Lisa Cook, Navarro College
Renae Ekstrand, University of Wisconsin-Stout
Kristin Hommel-Miller, Rose State College
Sarah Huisman, Fontbonne University
Debra Johnston-Malden, Massasoit Community College
Dawn Kolakoski, Hudson Valley Community College
Sharon Little, South Piedmont Community College
Jane Loxtercamp, Eastern Maine Community College
Kerri Mahlum, Casper College
T Vail Shoultz McCole, Colorado Mesa University-WCCC Campus
Kerry Belknap Morris, River Valley Community College
Lynette Pannell, Anderson University
Ashley Simpson, Community College of Aurora
Cyndi Syskowski, Community College of Allegheny County
Sapna Thapa, University of Wisconsin-Stout
Loraine Woods, Mississippi Valley State University
Elaine Zweig, Collin College

Nancy H. Beaver, M.Ed., has worked 40 years in Child Care and Early Childhood Education. She holds a B.S. in Education from the University of Texas, and a M.Ed. in Early Childhood Education from University of North Texas. Currently, she is the program administrator of the Center for Child and Family Studies at Eastfield College, where she also teaches as an Adjunct Faculty in Child Development and Teacher Education. In addition, she teaches Early Childhood Education classes as an Adjunct Faculty for the University of North Texas at Dallas.

In her career, she has held a variety of early childhood roles from a consultant, providing training and technical assistance to Air Force Family Member Services program staff, to a Licensing Representative and Child Development Specialist for the state of Texas. She has also been the executive director of a nonprofit agency and has raised more than $5,000,000 for early childhood projects at nonprofit agencies and community colleges. She successfully led the Eastfield College Children's Laboratory School staff to earn NAEYC Accreditation in both 2008 and 2013. She worked on a faculty team to successfully earn NAEYC's Early Childhood Associate Degree Accreditation (ECADA).

Nancy Beaver, M.Ed.

She has a long history of involvement with the Dallas Association for the Education for Young Children (DAEYC) as president and many other board offices, Texas AEYC as vice president and secretary of the board and NAEYC as Academy validator, commissioner, and assessor. She is most proud of two awards: TAEYC Trainer of the Year (2005) and DAEYC Pat Kennedy Teacher Educator of the Year (2006).

Nancy has also served as president of the Associate Degree Early Childhood Teacher Educators, better known as ACCESS, in 2013 and 2014.

She is married to her college sweetheart, Dom, and has one daughter, Stephanie.

Dr. Susan Skinner Wyatt brings more than 40 years of experience in the field of early care and education to this book. She holds a master's degree in Child Development and Family Living and a doctor of philosophy in Child Development with an emphasis on Adult Education and Educational Administration, both from Texas Woman's University.

Her experiences include director of a child-care center, child-care teacher, public school teacher from elementary through high school, community college professor, and author. She currently serves as the chair of the Child Development/Early Childhood Education and Teacher Education departments at Eastfield College in the Dallas, Texas, area.

Susan has served on the boards of the Dallas Association for the Education (past president and treasurer), Texas Association for the Education of Young Children (Treasurer), Dallas Association for Parent Education (president), and Child Development Educator's Association of the Texas Community College Teachers Association (past president and secretary).

Dr. Susan Skinner Wyatt

Susan has received the Innovator of the Year for the Dallas County Community College District, Teacher Educator of the Year for the Texas Association for the Education of Young Children, and the Piper Professor Award for Texas. She has served as a validator for the NAEYC Center-based Accreditation and is currently a peer reviewer for the NAEYC Early Childhood Associate Degree Accreditation.

Susan is married and the mother of three adult sons.

Welcome to the world of early education. We are glad you are here. Our profession needs caring, committed individuals to encourage and support children through their early years.

Hilda L. Jackman brings to her authorship a background rich in experience and achievement as it relates to the education of young children. Long before she became professor emerita with the Dallas County Community College District and professor-coordinator of the Brookhaven Child Development/Early Childhood program, she pioneered children's television programming in the Dallas–Fort Worth area as a writer, producer, and puppeteer. She went on to earn a master of science degree in Early Childhood Education at the University of North Texas and for many years was a teacher of young children (infants through kindergarten) and director of several child development programs. During her 20 years at Brookhaven, besides writing curriculum and teaching, she helped establish the first certificate program in Texas to train nannies, developed multicultural/anti-bias curriculum courses, and consulted with business and industry on child care. Since retiring from college teaching, Hilda continues to act as a mentor, presents workshops and staff development seminars, consults, and stays active in professional organizations. She is also the author of *Sing Me a Story! Tell Me a Song! Creative Thematic Activities for Teachers of Young Children* (2005), also published by Cengage Learning.

Hilda is the proud mother of two adult sons and the very proud grandmother of twin granddaughters, shown with her in this photo.

Each of you has a different reason for wanting to be in an early childhood classroom. Some of you are just beginning. Others are experienced teachers. No matter what type of program or what age group you work with, it is important that you understand the development of young children, help them connect with the changing world of their families, and promote developmentally appropriate practices in early education environments and curriculum.

This text is designed to be a practical guide to help you develop a curriculum appropriate for young children. By learning about theory, underlying research, and developmentally appropriate activities found in this text, you can develop your own curriculum.

Use the resources that accompany this text to get started creating curriculum webs. Write lesson and activity plans using the digital forms as well. We hope these resources will help you develop appropriate curriculum for young children. Your experiences with young children are most important to your academic and professional development. We encourage you to use this curriculum text to stimulate your own creativity and knowledge of children. Mix and match, add to, and redesign the ideas and activities presented. Take the time to enjoy the uniqueness of each individual child, as well as the group of children, as they explore and interact with the curriculum.

It is also important to remember that professional ethics and confidentiality are concerns that are inseparable from all observation, assessment, and participation activities. It is crucial that you deal with each child or adult without prejudice or partiality and refrain from imposing your own views or values upon children or adults.

We hope this text will prove helpful to you as you strive to make a difference in the lives of young children and their families. We are all in this profession together, and, like the children, we too are growing and developing.

— *Nancy H. Beaver*
— *Susan Skinner Wyatt*
— *Hilda L. Jackman*

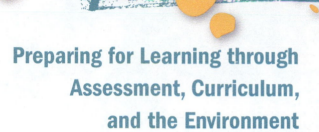

Part 1

Preparing for Learning through Assessment, Curriculum, and the Environment

"I stand outside the classroom, teacher,
At the doorstep to the world.
I want to see it all,
To hear and feel and taste it all.
I stand here, teacher,
With eager eyes and heart and mind.
Will you open the door?"

Janet Galantay
Reprinted with permission

1

Starting the Process

Standards Covered in This Chapters

 NAEYC 1a, 1b, 1c, 2b, 2c, 4b, 4c, 5c, 6b, 6d

 DAP 2, 3, 5

INTASC INTASC 1, 2, 7, 8

HEAD START
Domain: Approaches to Learning,
Domain: Perceptual,
Motor and Physical Development

 CEC DCC C12, C14, C15

Student Learning Outcomes

After studying this chapter, you should be able to:

- Analyze the importance of historical information and theories to the field of early childhood education.

- Identify developmentally appropriate practices as they relate to child development and learning; individual strengths, interests, and needs; and social and cultural contexts.

- Discuss the importance of play in the lives of young children, describe the developmental stages of play, and identify ways teachers foster play.

- Explain the value of the techniques for communicating with families.

Please think of the children first. If you ever have anything to do with their entertainment, their food, their toys, their custody, their day or night care, their health care, their education—listen to the children, learn about them, learn from them. Think of the children first.

These words of Fred Rogers (2003) are meaningful to us as students and teachers. Children must be at the center of all we do. As adults who genuinely care about them, we should honor the uniqueness of each child and the child's family. Give them teachers with commitment, training, experience, and knowledge about child development and how children learn. "Children come into the world eager to learn. … There can be no question that the environment in which a child grows up has a powerful impact on how the child develops and what the child learns" (Bowman, Donovan, and Burns, 2000, p. 1).

Research is showing in early and elementary education that "all children can and will learn when educational communities are ready for them … This requires a commitment that makes explicit the responsibility of education professionals to broaden their repertoires and hone their skills to create classrooms in which all children maximize their potential" (New, Palsha, and Ritchie, 2009, p. 3).

As you read this chapter, its focus on making the environment and the curriculum child centered will be apparent. This chapter extends this philosophy by studying historical aspects of early education, learning and developmental theories, developmentally appropriate practices (DAP), social and cultural contexts, importance of play for young children, curriculum planning, early childhood schedules and routines, and communicating with parents. Also included are ideas to enhance instruction and activities that respect a child's culture, language, and learning style. Additionally, in-depth attention should be paid to language development, cognition, physical development, and social and emotional competence.

Early Childhood Education

"The field of early care and education has changed profoundly in the last decade. In some ways, many long-time early childhood educators find it nearly unrecognizable. Standards and guidelines abound. Increasing numbers of early childhood programs are required to address state early learning standards (or guidelines) that will soon include three-year-olds and next, perhaps, even infants and toddlers (Freeman and Feeney, 2006, pp. 10–16)."

With this in mind, it is important to look back at our profession to see how changes produced new ways to help children and families. Historical information gives us an opportunity to see how past generations viewed children and their acquisition of knowledge, based on religious, ethnic, political, and economic pressures of the times. Almy (cited in Greenberg, 2000, pp. 6–10) believes that "it's most important not to leave behind everything we already know about children as we go on learning new things. … New knowledge should build on prior knowledge, not erase and replace it."

Exploring the storied history and philosophy of early childhood education presents us with significant individuals and far-reaching developments that have impacted and influenced our thinking. "The history of early childhood education is like a tapestry—woven of many influences. … The ingredients that early-childhood educators consider essential today—that care and education are inseparable, that teaching practices are developmentally appropriate, and that adequate funding is critical for success—all stem from historical events and people" (Gordon and Browne, 2011, p. 3).

The professional organizations mentioned in the timeline are all striving to improve the field of early childhood education. Their efforts emphasize the importance of advocacy, an attitude that encourages professionals, parents, and other caring adults to work together on behalf of young children.

Anyone who cares about children can be an advocate. Classroom teachers who work with school boards to change conditions for children and teachers are advocates. Caregivers who contact their elected officials to ask them to vote for child and family friendly policies are advocates. Professional associations who create opportunities to educate policy makers about problems that children face are advocates. Families that ban together to ask that the arts and music programs be returned to their school are advocates. Business leaders who form coalitions with early care and education caregivers are advocates. College students who support high educational standards so that they can be better teachers are advocates. Advocacy has many forms, and any person or group that is willing to stand on behalf of children is an advocate. (See Table 1-1.)

It is also essential for teachers to use every resource available to them, such as having membership in local, state, and national professional organizations. Attending meetings, workshops, and conferences offers opportunities for networking with other teachers. Reading professional journals keeps one up to date with current information as well. (See Appendix G for a comprehensive listing of professional organizations and their websites.)

Learning and Developmental Theories of Early Childhood Education

INTASC   DAP   HS   naeyc

As we continue to consider the influences that have contributed to the field of early childhood education, it is beneficial to review the developmental theories that examine children's growth, behavior, and process of learning. A **theory** refers to a systematic statement of principles and beliefs created to explain a phenomenon or group of facts that have been repeatedly tested or are widely accepted. All curricula should be based on our beliefs about how children develop and learn. These beliefs guide how we see teaching and supporting children as learners.

Following are a few of the most influential theories and information about the individuals who developed them.

Psychosocial Theory

Erik Erikson (1902–1994) made significant contributions to psychoanalysis, personality theory, education practice, and social anthropology over five decades.

Erikson recognized growth and development to be continuous throughout an individual's life. His eight **psychosocial** stages describe the interaction between an individual's social-emotional condition and the interpersonal environment. His stages of development help us understand the importance of allowing children to play out their feelings in an environment of acceptance. The first four stages are relevant to early childhood educators:

1. **Basic trust versus mistrust (birth to one year).** This developmental stage is important to an infant's learning that people can be depended on and that the child can depend on himself or herself. Love and acceptance are important for the child to learn that the world is a safe place in which to live. This foundation of trust will be developed if the infant's needs are met. This is observable when the infant babbles, coos, laughs, crawls, pulls up, and is comfortable with the environment.

2. **Autonomy versus shame and doubt (second year).** This stage helps a child develop a basic sense of self-control and independence. The child is growing rapidly. It is significant during this stage that the toddler has opportunities to do things for himself or herself. This is observable when a toddler feeds and dresses himself or herself, and generally has an "I can do it myself" attitude that is accepted and reinforced by the adults in his or her life.

theory: A systematic statement of principles and beliefs created to explain a phenomenon or group of facts that have been repeatedly tested or are widely accepted.

psychosocial: Erikson's eight stages that describe the interaction between an individual's social-emotional condition and the interpersonal environment.

TABLE 1-1:   Timeline of Early Education Historical Highlights

1000s Plato expressed the value of play.

1630s Locke emphasized importance of first-hand experiences as a means for learning. Children considered a blank page that could be molded by experience.

John Comenius, father of modern education, was first to recognize that play of childhood was learning and produced first children's picture book, *The World Illustrated.*

Jean-Jacques Roussueau proposed that children and adults think differently and children learn best through hands-on experiences.

1800s Johann Pestalozzi established the first school to teach preschool-age children.

1830s Froebel created the concept of kindergarten (children's garden) and Elizebeth Peabody organized first American Froebel union.

1840s Child Study movement created by G. Stanley Hall and Arnold Gesell.

1850s Nursery School for Children of Poor Women opened in cooperation with Children's Hospital of New York City.

1870s First public school kindergarten started in St. Louis.

1890s Hull House, a settlement house for immigrants, established a day nursery.

Piaget defined distinct stages of children's cognitive development.

1900s Patty Smith Hill created a curriculum that provided foundation for kindergartens in the United States, founded laboratory school at Columbia University Teacher's College as model for training early childhood educators and began a professional organization of early childhood educators.

Maria Montesorri opened Children's House in Rome.

1910s Nursery schools reflecting the principles of a child-centered approach were conceived and introduced in America by Margaret and Rachel McMillian (Gordon & Browne, 2001).

1920s At least one other adult living in home other than the parents. Nursery schools linked to child development and psychology and day nurseries focused on meeting the needs of poor and immigrant families were available (NAEYC, 2001).

1930s Depression produced economic and social crisis in the United States. Works Progress Administration (WPA) nurseries designed "to develop physical and mental well-being of preschool children in needy unemployed families or neglected or underprivileged homes resulting in almost 2,000 WPA nursery schools in operation by 1935"(NAEYC, 2001).

1940s Lanham Act allowed public funds to be used for child care while millions of women went to work for the World War II effort. Using Lanham Act funds, the Kaiser Shipyards opened child care centers that functioned 24 hours a day, year long and closed when the war ended (Gordon & Browne, 2011; NAEYC, 2001).

Reggio Emilia established in Italy influenced early childhood thinking around the world (Essa, 2011; Gordon & Browne, 2011).

B. F. Skinner proposed that children learn through experiences.

1960s High/Scope Perry Preschool Project began to serve at-risk children from impoverished neighborhoods. Based on landmark long-term study on the effects of high-quality early care and education on low-income 3- and 4-year-olds (Wiekart & Schweinhart, 2007).

National Committee on Nursery Schools (NANE) became National Association for the Education of Young Children (NAEYC) and now includes a membership of over 100,000.

Landmark court decisions established responsibility of states to educate children.

Project Head Start, part of the Economic Opportunity Act's "War on Poverty," was funded to counteract the effects of poverty among children.

1970s National Black Child Development Institute (NBCDI) was created to provide and support programs, workshops, and resources for African-American children, their parents, and communities (NBCDI, 2002).

Child Development Associate (CDA) created as part of the U.S. Department of Health, Education, and Welfare (NAEYC, 2001).

Education for All Handicapped Children Act, now know as Individual with Disabilities Education Act (IDEA), passed to include early childhood services.

1980s National Association for Family Day Care established.

Position statements defining and describing developmentally appropriate practice in early childhood programs serving young children published by NAEYC (Copple & Bredekamp, 2009).

San Francisco became first large city to require developers to set aside funds for child care space.

National Academy of Early Childhood Programs established by NAEYC voluntary accreditation of center based programs.

CDA Credentialing administered by NAEYC moved to Council for Professional Recognition (NAEYC, 2001).

U.S. Department of Education established Even Start, a parent education/literacy program.

1990s Association of Childhood Education International (ACEI) celebrated its centennial and is the oldest professional association of its type in the United States (ACEI, 2002).

National Association for Family Day care changes to the National Association of Family Child Care with a goal of providing assistance for developing leadership, professionalism, and quality for family child care providers (NAFCC, 2002).

T.E.A.C.H.Scholarship program enacted.

The Stand for Children Campaign begins.

2000s No Child Left Behind Act of 2001 placed more emphasis on program accountability and assessment in grades 3–8) (Essa, 2011; United States Department of Education, 2001).

Campaign launched to avoid SIDS in child care settings.

Operation Military Child Care started to address the child care needs of parents who were activated and deployed.

2010s President Obama called on Congress to expand access to high-quality preschool for every child in America through the Preschool for all initiative.

Every Student Succeeds Act replaces No Child Left Behind Act allowing states more control related to alternatives to high-stakes testing.

3. **Initiative versus guilt (3 to 5 years).** During this stage of life, children are becoming interested in exploring and are ready to learn. Children need to express their natural curiosity and creativity through opportunities in the environment. This stage of development is observable by watching how children demonstrate body control and motor skills while riding a tricycle and running. Initiative is reinforced when children are given freedom to engage in fantasy and other dramatic play activities. Social roles in dramatic play continue to show children identifying with adult roles. They enjoy making adult situations conform to their notion of the ways things are. Roles can be reversed and new roles can be tried out.

4. **Industry versus inferiority (6 to 11 years).** At this stage of life, the child is ready for challenges of new and exciting ideas. The child needs opportunities for accomplishment in physical, intellectual, and social development. This is observable by watching older children during creative dramatics activities. They improvise their own dialogue, play the scenes, and evaluate the results. This is informal and demonstrates individual and group imagination, problem solving, critical thinking, and cooperation with others.

The last four of Erikson's (1963) psychosocial stages follow the individual from the teenage years through the rest of the life span:

5. *Identity versus role diffusion (12 to 18 years).*
6. *Intimacy versus isolation (young adulthood).*
7. *Generative versus stagnation (adult middle years).*
8. *Ego integrity versus despair (older years).*

"Erik Erikson's work and wisdom have profoundly shaped the field of child development. What comes through most strongly in Erikson's work is his empathy and respect for children—and for their parents and the societies in which they live. . . . Erikson's work has more than withstood the test of time; it continues to inform and inspire the fields of child development, life-span studies, anthropology, history, sociology, and others (Stott, 1994, p. 43)."

Cognitive Development Theory

Cognitive development is described as the intellectual acquisition of information, facts, or data and includes reasoning, understanding, problem solving, and language acquisition. Much of what is known about cognitive development has come from the work of *Jean Piaget* (1896–1980). He introduced the study of children's thinking and was the first to describe how each child creates his own mental image of the world, based on his encounters with the environment. Piaget describes the system of thought that develops through common stages of all cultures goes through all children.

A careful consideration of Piaget's concepts, along with close observation of children, helps teachers provide appropriate environments and experiences. Piaget believed that **learning**, or change in behavior, occurs as children construct knowledge through active exploration and discovery in their physical and social environments. He also asserted that learning happens through the dual process of assimilation and accommodation.

Assimilation is a process that occurs when a child handles, sees, or otherwise experiences something, see **Figure 1-1**. He or she adds this information to existing schemata.

A **schema** (plural, *schemata*) is an integrated way of thinking or of forming mental images. "We constantly create, refine, change, modify, organize, and reorganize our schemata" (Essa, 2013, p. 116).

Accommodation occurs when a schema is modified as a result of experience. (See **Figure 1-2**.)

Equilibrium happens when there is a balance between assimilation and accommodation. According to Piaget, this continues until new information causes the process to begin again (Piaget, 1926).

---

cognitive development: The mental process that focuses on how children's intelligence, thinking abilities, and language acquisition emerge through distinct ages. Piaget's study of children's thinking, involving creating their own mental images of the world, based on encounters with the environment.

learning: Change in behavior or cognition that occurs as children construct knowledge through active exploration and discovery in their physical and social environments.

assimilation: Piaget's process of cognitive development, which occurs when a child handles, sees, or otherwise experiences something.

schema: An integrated way of thinking or of forming mental images.

accommodation: Piaget's theory of modification of existing cognitive information. Cognitive schemes are changed to accommodate new experiences or information.

equilibrium: A balance of one's cognitive schemes and information gathered from the environment; assimilation and accommodation.

A child has a concept for "ball" that fits all the balls the child has seen so far.

This child sees a football for the first time.

The football matches the "ball" concept, so the child adds it to the concept of ball.

Figure 1-1 Example of Piaget's concept of assimilation.

A child has a concept for "dog" that includes all animals with four legs.

This child sees a cat for the first time and calls it a "dog." When the child realizes the cat does not fit "dog," he may create a new category for "cat."

As the child matures, the process of accommodation will enable him to create a super-concept, or a broader category, which would include both the cat and the dog—such as "animal."

Figure 1-2 Example of Piaget's concept of accommodation.

Piaget divided cognitive development into four stages:

1. **Sensorimotor stage (birth to about 2 years)**. During this time, children grow from helpless newborns to children who are able to walk and talk. Infants begin learning through the use of their sensory system and reflexes. Gradually, these reflex behaviors are changed and new behaviors develop. Babies enjoy repeating behaviors. Often, something unexpected happens during repetitions and a new behavior is discovered. They then try to repeat the new behavior. Throughout the sensorimotor stage, infants are developing the concept of **object permanence**. According to Piaget's theory, a baby thinks that objects, including people, cease to exist the moment he or she stops seeing them. For example, if an object that has left returns, the infant considers it a new, though identical, object. As he or she develops, however, he or she begins to search for the missing object or person.

2. **Preoperational stage (about 2 to 7 years)**. Piaget believed that children's thinking during this stage is **egocentric**—that is, they think about the world only in relation to themselves. Along with this, the preoperational period is characterized by **symbolic thinking**. Symbols or mental representations are formed, allowing children to solve problems by thinking before acting. They begin to enjoy pretend play. As thinking emerges as verbal expression, language acquisition proceeds rapidly. Intellectual and language development blend together. The more a child uses all the senses and broadens his or her experiences, the more he or she has to think and talk about.

3. **Concrete operations stage (about 7 to 12 years)**. During this stage, children are developing concepts of numbers, relationships, and processes, as well as thinking problems through mentally. Logical thought requires actual physical objects or events. Piaget explains:

   " Manipulation of materials is crucial. In order to think, children in the concrete stage need to have objects in front of them that are easy to handle, or else be able to visualize objects that have been handled and that are easily imagined without any real effort. "

   " Children learn through the use of materials. They should be selected based on their ability to allow the child to become conscious of a problem and seek ways he/she can solve the problem. If the child generalizes too broadly, the teacher should provide additional materials to allow the child to refine his/her solution. "

4. **Formal operations stage (12 years through adulthood)**. The individual reasons logically and moves from concrete manipulations to abstract thinking. The ability to hypothesize and think about what might be rather than what is usually occurs during this stage.

Each of these stages involves a period of formation and a period of attainment. Each builds on the development of the preceding stage. Teachers and parents should provide appropriate environments and ask appropriate questions, moving from simple to complex and from concrete to abstract.

For exploration of other Piagetian concepts, see the section on play in this chapter and Chapter 10, "Math."

Sociocultural Theory

Over the past two decades, the educational theories of Russian developmental psychologist *Lev Vygotsky* (1896–1934) have been translated and made available in the United States. Vygotsky asserted that a child's learning development is affected by his culture, including the culture of family environment. He focused on the whole child and incorporated ideas of culture and values into child development, particularly the development of language and self-identity. "Because Vygotsky regarded language as a critical bridge between the sociocultural world and individual mental functioning, he viewed the acquisition of language as the most significant milestone in children's cognitive development" (Berk and Winsler, 1995, p. 20). It is from language that the child constructs reality.

object permanence: A mature state of perceptual development. According to Piaget's theory, a baby thinks that objects, including people, cease to exist the moment he or she stops seeing them. An older child starts to search for the missing object or person.

egocentric: A stage when individuals think about the world only in relation to themselves.

symbolic thinking: The formation of symbols or mental representations, allowing children to solve problems by thinking before acting.

Much of what a child learns comes from the culture around him. In addition, interactions with teachers, parents, and more experienced peers contribute significantly to a child's intellectual development. Vygotsky believed that a difference exists between what a child can do on his own and what he can do with help. Vygotsky called this difference the **zone of proximal development**. In other words, the "zone" is the range of potential each child has for learning, with that learning being shaped by the social environment in which it takes place. This potential ability is greater than the actual ability of the individual when the learning is facilitated by someone with greater expertise (Wertsch, 1991).

Vygotsky felt that children develop lower mental functions such as associative learning, simple perceptions, and involuntary attention through social interactions with people who possess more knowledge. Higher mental functions will eventually develop including problem-solving, moral reasoning, language, memory schemas, and logic.

For teachers of young children, the zone of proximal development may be used to provide a theoretical base from which to understand cooperative learning. In the culture of the classroom, this can translate into small-group instruction in which students work together to solve problems. This approach encourages children to construct their own knowledge while engaging in activities that build and rebuild, or construct, ideas based on previous experiences. In addition, the role of the teacher includes both designing an educative environment and collaborating with children by scaffolding their efforts to master new skills. Vygotsky-based teaching is activity-centered and encourages teacher to create opportunities for children to engage in culturally meaningful opportunities with the teacher's guidance. This kind of teaching emphasizes **scaffolding**, which occurs as the teacher (adult) continually adjusts the level of help offered in response to the child's level of performance. Scaffolding can help instill the skills necessary for independent problem solving in the future, and teachers must become experts in this experience. To do that, teachers must effectively utilize observation skills to learn each and every child's level of learning. Only then can they make a determination of the steps to take to meet each child's unique needs.

For exploration of another major Vygotskian concept, see the section on play in this chapter.

Multiple Intelligences Theory

Howard Gardner (1943–), a psychologist and professor at Harvard Graduate School of Education, is also a researcher who has studied the mind and brain with particular reference to learning and education. He has challenged the view that something called "intelligence" can be objectively measured and reduced to a single number or "IQ" score. In fact, Gardner's definition of intelligence is multifaceted. His ongoing research, Project Zero, at Harvard suggests that an individual is not born with all of the intelligence he or she will ever have. Rather, intelligence can be learned and improved on throughout a lifetime.

Gardner identifies his cross-cultural exploration of the ways individuals are intelligent as **multiple intelligences**. His philosophy also proposes that one form of intelligence is not better than another; all are equally valuable and viable. Gardner's theory also suggests that teachers should take seriously the child's individual differences. An understanding of each child's intelligence is critical in the development of curriculum to prepare children to learn in new situations.

The following explanations of Gardner's Multiple Intelligences are adapted from Gardner (1997), Hine (1996), and Nicholson-Nelson (1999):

1. **Verbal-linguistic intelligence:** From the babbling of infancy to the toddler's simple sentences, the ability to use language and words continues to grow throughout early childhood. Whether written or spoken, it develops with sensitivity to the order and rhythm of words. The learning environment should include a language- and print-rich classroom with opportunities for reading, writing, speaking, and creative writing. Children who are accomplished in verbal-linguistic abilities enjoy reading, writing, telling stories, playing word games, and communicating effectively.

zone of proximal development: The range of potential each child has for learning, with that learning being shaped by the social environment in which it takes place.

scaffolding: The adjustable support the teacher offers in response to the child's level of performance.

multiple intelligences: Gardner's theory, which proposes that one form of intelligence is not better than another; all nine are equally valuable and viable.

2. **Logical-mathematical intelligence:** Starting with babies inspecting their world and continuing on to toddlers recognizing similar characteristics of objects, the ability to categorize and to use numbers, patterns, sequencing, and cause and effect to solve problems develops and grows throughout early childhood. The learning environment should offer opportunities to relate math and science to real-life situations while providing activities that make math and problem solving fun, relevant, and challenging. Children who are adept in logical-mathematical abilities learn through asking questions in a logical manner, making connections between pieces of information, exploring, and developing strong problem-solving and reasoning skills.

3. **Musical-rhythmic intelligence:** Starting with the prenatal awareness of noises and rhythms and, later, imitations of sounds and pitches, a child soon develops the ability to produce and recognize simple and then complex songs and to perceive pitch, tone, and rhythmic pattern. He becomes immersed in the music and sounds of the world. The learning environment should provide opportunities for singing, listening, movement activities, sound awareness, and musical instrument appreciation and practice, while emphasizing cultural awareness through music. Children who are strong in musical-rhythmic abilities think in rhythms and melodies; enjoy listening to music, singing, dancing, humming, and playing musical instruments; and exhibit a sensitivity to environmental sounds.

4. **Visual-spatial intelligence:** From the infant's ability to discriminate among the faces around him or her to the toddler's first steps, the facility to perceive the visual world with a great deal of understanding continues throughout early childhood. Creating visual images with shape, color, and form opens up new understanding. The learning environment should be a graphic-rich classroom that encourages opportunities for visual processing as well as thinking and planning in three dimensions. Children who are highly capable in visual-spatial abilities think in images and pictures; like to draw, design, and create things; and often see things from different points of view. (See Figure 1-3.)

Figure 1-3   Creating visual images with shape, color, and form opens up new understanding for young children.

5. **Bodily-kinesthetic intelligence:** From an infant's looking for and grasping different objects to the strength and coordination of an older child, the ability to use the body for self-expression develops through information gained from muscles, sensations, reflexes, coordination, and movement. The learning environment should reflect opportunities for physical challenges throughout the day, not just outdoors but indoors as well. The classroom should facilitate tactile experiences and the use of manipulatives in math, science, and language arts. Children who are resourceful in bodily-kinesthetic abilities learn through moving, doing, and touching. They enjoy physical activities, such as those involving hand-eye coordination and hands-on experiments.

6. **Interpersonal intelligence:** From an infant's bonding with parents to the meaningful relationships with others outside the family, the ability to understand other people and their actions, moods, and feelings develops as young children deal with person-to-person relationships and communication. The learning environment should provide opportunities for children to relate to others by cooperatively participating, sharing, negotiating, and communicating in groups or with individuals. Children who show interpersonal abilities learn through listening, cooperating in shared projects, demonstrating leadership skills, seeing things from other perspectives, and organizing and negotiating group activities.

7. **Intrapersonal intelligence:** Starting with a baby's realization that he or she is a separate person from the mother, the child's ability to understand himself or herself grows throughout early childhood and at the same time helps in the identification of feelings, moods, strengths, and weaknesses. The learning environment provides plenty of space and time for self-reflection and working alone in a safe environment that encourages appropriate risk taking. Children who are accomplished in intrapersonal abilities learn through understanding their role in relationship to others, have a strong sense of self, and enjoy setting goals, planning, and working on self-paced projects, all of which involve having choices.

8. **Naturalist intelligence:** A child's interest in seeing, smelling, and touching a flower, reacting to the sound of a bird, or playing with the family pet demonstrates his or her ability to recognize important distinctions in the natural world. The learning environment should offer opportunities for exploring outdoors and bringing the outdoors inside by providing field trips, books, visuals, objects, and materials relating to the natural world. Children who show naturalist abilities learn through observing nature, being sensitive to all features of the natural world, and enjoying books, visuals, and objects related to the world around them. (See Figure 1-4.)

9. **Existential:** This ninth intelligence can be defined as the ability to be sensitive to, or have the capacity for, conceptualizing or tackling deeper or larger questions about human existence, such as the meaning of life, why are we born, why do we die, what is consciousness, or how did we get here. Children pose, and sometimes even answer, life's larger questions. Like: Why am I here? Why are we here? Can animals understand us, or do animals go to heaven? Where do we go when we die? These may be those children who can be described as "fully aware" of the cosmos—of its diversity, complexity, and wonder. Frequently, these are the children who persist in asking those "big" questions that adults cannot answer.

Figure 1-4   A child's interest in seeing, smelling, and touching a flower demonstrates the ability to recognize important distinctions in the natural world.

The Multiple Intelligences theory is a useful model for developing a systematic approach to nurturing and teaching children and honoring their individual needs and strengths within a classroom setting.

The concept of multiple intelligences does not require discarding previous ideas. Teachers can supplement current appropriate activities with new ideas that will reach even more of their students. In fact, Gardner contends that teachers need to guide students into using their combination of intelligences to help them learn whatever they want to learn, as well as what teachers and society believe they have to learn.

The multiple intelligences approach provides a framework for us to identify how children learn to build on their strongest assets, to help them become more intelligent by exposing them to a variety of ways of learning, to better individualize for their interests and needs, and to use teaching strategies that make learning more appropriate, successful, and enjoyable for all children. Examples of using Gardner's Multiple Intelligences theory in the classroom can be found in the curriculum content chapters of this book. For further application of this and other theories, see the curriculum models and programs in Chapter 3.

Developmentally Appropriate Practice

Developmentally appropriate practice (DAP), introduced more than 20 years ago by the National Association for the Education of Young Children (NAEYC), defines and describes what is developmentally appropriate for young children in childhood programs serving children and families, birth through age eight. NAEYC's current position statement "reflects both continuity and change in the early childhood field. ... DAP requires both meeting children where they are—which means that teachers must get to know them well—and enabling them to reach goals that are both challenging and achievable" (Copple and Bredekamp, 2009, p. xii).

Developmentally appropriate early education recognizes the social nature of learning, and it values cultural and linguistic diversity. Also included is the understanding that children need an environment that allows them to interact at their own level of development with a minimum amount of adult direction. (See **Figure** 1-5.) A strong emphasis is placed

developmentally appropriate practice: The curriculum planning philosophy expressed by NAEYC defines and describes what is developmentally appropriate for young children in childhood programs serving children and families, birth through age eight.

Figure 1-5   In a developmentally appropriate environment, teachers develop relationships with children that are consistent and supportive.

Brain Research: Brain Development

 According to recent brain research, we now understand that shortly after conception, the unborn child hears its mother's voice. The brain is already linking the circuits necessary to understand and reproduce language. There are "windows of opportunity" or critical periods in a young child's life when he or she can most easily acquire a new language. The language processing brain cells are being wired and are especially responsive to experiences. By the age of three, children's brains are twice as active as their parents.

Fleming (2002, www.nncc.org/release/brain.language .html) explains, "Each child has more than 50,000 nerve pathways that can carry sounds of the human voice from the ears to the brain. The brain encodes the words and actually rearranges its brain cells into connections or networks to produce language." Therefore, infants and toddlers need experiences with caring adults "who offer many one-on-one, face to face interactions with them to support their oral language development and lay the foundation for later literacy learning" (Neuman, Copple, and Bredekamp, 2000, p. 11).

Tomlinson (cited in Copple and Bredekamp, 2009, p. 200) adds, "The first five to seven years of life are a sensitive period for brain development. . . . The brain is more malleable than it will be later, making kindergarten an optimum time for learning and effective intervention with all children." Changes in the brain structure process are important because they influence how children interact with both people and with the environment.

Dr. Bruce D. Perry, M.D., Ph.D., is an internationally recognized authority on brain development and children in crisis. He is concerned about societal changes that may be impacting children's brain development.

"Our modern world is very different than the world that our brain is engineered for. In the world that human beings have lived in for centuries, there were many, many, many more people in our lives—aunties, grannies, extended family. We were in continuous relational interaction with each other. . . . The developing child under the age of 6 had at least, in those typical settings, four developmentally mature individuals who would help protect, enrich and nurture these kids (pp. 47–49)."

Thanks to the loving attention of many family members, Dr. Perry says, the part of the brain involved in relational interaction got lots of stimulation. This helped people grow up with a tremendous sense of empathy.

Dr. Perry's concerns point to the critical role that early childhood teachers play in supporting children's healthy brain development.

on children learning to think critically, work together cooperatively, and solve problems. Because developmentally appropriate classrooms are not only age and stage appropriate but also individually appropriate, they will not all look alike. To enhance the quality of educational experiences for young children, DAP is a framework for continuing to meet the diverse needs of all the children in our care. Kostelnik, Soderman, and Whirin (2014, p. 17) explain weaving the strands of age appropriateness, individual appropriateness, and sociocultural appropriateness into a cohesive philosophy requires deliberate effort and continuous reflections by early childhood practioners. Throughout this book, developmentally appropriate practice will be discussed in relation to chapter content.

Child Development and Learning

First, let us focus on what is developmentally occurring with young children, the variations in their development, and their developmental process for learning. **Development**, in relationship to early childhood education, can be defined as systematic and adaptive changes in the body and mind based on sequence and patterns of growth and maturity (Charlesworth, 2013; Swim and Watson 2013). "Developmental trends occur in a similar fashion for all children. This does not, however, imply uniformity. On the contrary, individual differences due to genetic and experiential variations and differing cultural and social contexts have strong influences on development" (Bowman, Donovan, and Burns, 2000, p. 5).

As we think about development and learning, it is important to remember that the areas of physical, intellectual, emotional, and social growth may overlap, even as age groups may. "Children's development and learning in one domain influence and are influenced by what takes place in other domains" (Copple and Bredekamp, 2009, p. 11).

development: Systematic and adaptive changes in the body and mind.

Infants

The early months of infancy are crucial in creating a foundation for all areas of development. Infants are actively involved with their world. They explore with all their senses (seeing, hearing, tasting, smelling, and feeling) and are acutely aware of their environment. Infants and the significant adults in their lives establish special relationships that involve getting to know each other and adjusting to each other. What adults do can modify how infants behave (Swim and Watson, 2014).

Infants learn about their surroundings by physically moving around, through sensory exploration, and by social interaction. (See **Figure 1-6**.) Gallagher (2005, p. 12) continues this thought, "A typically developing child needs frequent opportunities for movement and interactions with people and objects. Fixed pieces of equipment such as playpens, high chairs, and bouncy seats provide little opportunities for varied and active experiences." As they are learning, the sight of the adult who feeds, holds, and comforts the infant is reinforced when that adult shows pleasure in caring for the infant. Emotional attachment develops as the child learns to expect that special person to make him or her feel good. The infant then seeks more contact with that adult. Even after crawling and walking have begun, the child frequently asks to be held. Honig (2002, p. xi) explains further, "Research and clinical findings over the past decades confirm the connection to later emotional well-being of a secure attachment between each baby or young child and a warm, stable adult."

As teachers of the youngest children, we have a significant responsibility to the infants in our care. "Like dancers, the infant care teacher and infant synchronize their interactions, each responding to and influencing the other. The challenge is doing this with three, four, or five infants at once" (Copple and Bredekamp, 2009, p. 56).

As families and infants enter child care, it is most important that a solid relationship is built between each of them and the teachers. "Infant care teachers need to observe and learn from the experiences, knowledge, culture, and childrearing beliefs of family members" (Copple and Bredekamp, 2009). Daily communication between teachers and families is crucial. It fosters involvement and support and offers a culturally sensitive approach to dealing with caregiver/family member conflicts.

Decades of research by neuroscientists and others have found what we in early childhood education have been saying for years, namely, that a child's foundation for behavior

Figure 1-6   Infants are actively involved with their world.

and learning for the rest of his or her life is laid in the early years. The better the child's early nurturing, the better are his prospects for future development (Gabbard and Rodrigues, 2002).

Although it has been known for many years that most of a child's brain cells are formed in the prenatal stage, the brain is not completely developed at birth. Research indicates that important neural (nerve) connections, transferring information from one part of the body to another, occur and strengthen after birth. Formations of the connections depend on the relationships and experiences we are exposed to in our environments. Research continues to refine scientists' insight into brain development, such as "understanding of developmental periods of dramatic brain growth, information about regions of brain growth, and details on brain functions. We know that the brain has growth spurts during certain times of development, such as early childhood and adolescence" (Schore, cited in Gallagher, 2005, pp. 12–20). By using new research techniques, scientists are discovering that babies are aware of the world around them— more so than adults.

An important aspect of a young child's continued mental development is **self-regulation**, his or her growing natural ability to exercise control over physical and emotional needs in the face of changing circumstances. Self-regulation is visible in all areas of behavior and is the foundation of early childhood development. For example, by using consistent routines with infants, you are helping young children learn to self-regulate within the structure of a nurturing environment.

All of this, along with new and continuing exploration of brain function, from birth through the first 10 years of life, helps us understand more about the relationship between *nature* and *nurture*. The interplay between nurture (the nutrition, surroundings, care, stimulation, and teaching that are provided or withheld) and nature (an individual's genetic endowment) determines how humans develop and learn.

Figure 1-7   This is a time for rapid development as a toddler learns self-help skills.

Toddlers

Children aged 16 to 36 months grow and learn rapidly. (See **Figure 1**-7.) "The toddler is a dynamo full of unlimited energy, enthusiasm, and curiosity. ... The toddler begins this period with the limited abilities of an infant and ends with the relatively sophisticated skills of a young child" (Allen and Marotz, 2010, p. 111). This is a time for development in mobility, autonomy, and **self-help skills**, the child learning what can be done for himself or herself by his or her own effort or ability, such as washing and drying hands, and feeding or dressing himself or herself. "Perhaps one of the best ways to nurture good feelings about self is to encourage toddlers' already strong interest in doing things for themselves" (Gestwicki, 2014). They try many tasks that are often too difficult for them. At this time, the safety of the environment is critical. As a teacher, you should expect this newfound independence and allow for trial and error. Children love to repeat and use these new skills over and over again.

Toddlers are fascinated by words. As these active children become more independent, "their speech is limited, but their understanding of communication is beyond their speech. ... Toddlers learn a great deal through imitation and especially from observing demonstrations accompanied by a verbal explanation" (Charlesworth, 2011). Chapter 5 emphasizes language and literacy development.

> ❝Young toddlers are busy exploring the world from their new, upright vantage point. ... Once toddlers master walking, their motor skills grow by leaps and bounds. They learn to jump, tiptoe, march, throw and kick a ball, and make a riding toy go by pushing with their feet or perhaps even by pedaling (Copple and Bredekamp, 2009).❞

Appropriate teaching techniques require the building of trust between the children and the teacher and between the children and their environment. This can develop only if there are safe, consistent, and child-centered surroundings that encourage success for both children and teachers. There is more information on developmentally appropriate learning environments in Chapter 4.

self-regulation: A child's natural ability to exercise control over physical and emotional behavior in the face of changing circumstances.

self-help skills: In early childhood, a child's ability to care for himself or herself, such as dressing, feeding, and toileting.

Figure 1-8 Young children are full of enthusiasm and high energy.

Three- and Four-Year-Olds

The preschool years are special. "Now the preschool year or years before kindergarten are recognized as a vitally important period of learning and development in their own right, not merely as a time for growth in anticipation of the 'real learning' that will begin in school" (Copple and Bredekamp, 2009, p. 111). Three-year-olds have a distinct period of development with added skills and challenges. They are anxious to try new things but get frustrated when they cannot do what they set out to do. With an enlarged vocabulary, they engage in more extensive conversations; and although they can play along with other children, they often find it difficult to cooperate in a game. The 3-year-old enjoys fantasy and imaginative play, although the difference between fantasy and reality is not always clear.

Generally, the child's interest has become more sustained, but repetition is still important. He or she begins to enjoy looking at picture and storybooks and has a better understanding of verbal cues. There is a continued need for exploration and experimentation. Teachers of 3-year-olds need to respect their growing skills and competencies without forgetting just how recently they were acquired.

Four-year-olds are full of enthusiasm and high energy. (See **Figure 1-8**.) The ability to do more things without help, along with increased large and small muscle control, allows the children to develop a greater self-confidence. Children of this age enjoy learning to do new things and like to have an adult's attention. At the same time, because they are so eager to learn and learn so fast, they can use a higher level of language (more and bigger words) than they really understand.

The 4-year-old has broader and more diverse interests. He or she begins to understand the environment and benefits from field trips. His or her interest in others prompts him to ask searching questions about people and their relationships with others. He or she is interested in the letter carrier, the firefighter, the police officer, and everyone around him or her who performs various services.

The child is conscious of make-believe and begins to "be" other people or animals. He gradually builds a background for imaginative play. For fours, play is most often seen as a solitary activity. Even so, peers are becoming even more important to the fours. As a teacher, when you interact with these active children, you will be bombarded with questions. Sometimes they will insist on trying to do things that are too difficult for them. Help them find many things that they can do. Observe the children and set up the environment to match their skills. More information on play is provided later in this chapter.

Prekindergarten programs that support effective teaching practices and opportunities for 4-year-olds are available in approximately 40 states. Many school buildings have been created specifically for eligible preschoolers, which fills an expanding need for low-income children with disabilities (National Institute for Early Education Research (NIEER), 2015).

> "Teachers are encouraged to take a developmental perspective in implementing the Prekindergarten Guidelines. Teachers should "meet children where they are" and provide information and activities at a level that children can readily understand and engage with. This will mean building children's skills over time, working toward the school readiness outcomes step by step as children demonstrate mastery of beginning level skills. Teachers should have the outcome skills in mind, but will need to prepare children to meet these goals through scaffolding experiences and activities that are appropriate for individual children's current developmental levels and capabilities (University of Texas System and Texas Education Agency, 2008, p. 28)."

Five-Year-Olds

Five-year-olds are becoming more social; they have best friends and also enjoy playing with small groups of children. Their use of language, especially vocabulary, continues to grow along with the understanding that words can have several meanings. Experimentation with language is evident at this age.

Fives are more self-controlled, but family and teacher have the most influence on how they behave. They take responsibility seriously and can accept suggestions and initiate action. With the increase of large and small muscle abilities, 5-year-olds can run, jump, catch, throw, and use scissors, crayons, and markers easily. (See **Figure 1-9**.)

Exploration of the environment is important to these children. They are learning about the world and their place in it. They act on their own and construct their own meaning. Each of their actions and interpretations is unique to them. They are developing an understanding of rules, limits, and cause and effect.

"Kindergarten children are undergoing profound transformations—in their capacity to think rationally, persist in the face of challenge, use language, adeptly suppress impulse, regulate emotion, respond sympathetically to others' distress, and cooperate with peers" (Berk, cited in Gullo, 2006, KToday—Teaching and Learning in the Kindergarten Year, NAEYC). Children of this age also believe in their own abilities to master new skills.

The number of children attending child care and preschool programs continues to grow. Standards, guidelines, and academic demands continue to increase as well. These factors have transformed the role of kindergarten. Approximately 95 percent of children kindergarten age in the United States are enrolled in some type of kindergarten program. Kindergarten is now generally considered the first year of school (Copple and Bredekamp, 2009). The teacher's role is to create the appropriate environment, encourage curiosity, and learn along with the children. Kindergarten has to be a place for *every* child to grow and learn, in every dimension of development (Gullo, 2006).

Six-, Seven-, and Eight-Year-Olds

"The early grades are a time for children to shine. They gain increasing mastery in every area of their development and learning. They explore, read, and reason, problem solve, communicate through conversations and writing, and develop lasting friendships" (Copple and Bredekamp, 2009, p. 257). The body growth of 6- to 8-year-olds is slower but steadier, and physical strength and ability are important to them. Their motor coordination begins to improve, and playing games that require eye-hand coordination, such as baseball, becomes easier at this age. These children are able to think and learn in more complicated ways, both logically and systematically. They are developing the ability to concentrate their attention for longer periods of time.

The language and communication development in these primary-grade children is dramatic. They move from oral self-expression to written self-expression. They are becoming more independent and have strong feelings about what they eat, wear, and do. The six to eights are extremely curious about their world, and they actively look for new things to do, see, and explore. They are making new friends, and these peers play a significant role in their lives as they take into consideration the viewpoints and needs of others. "In order to make friends, certain skills are necessary: The ability to understand that others have different points of view, the ability to recognize that others have separate identities, and the ability to understand that each encounter is part of a relationship" (Click and Parker, 2009, p. 107).

They are becoming more empathetic by developing the ability to see things from another perspective. They are also very sensitive and their feelings get hurt easily. As these primary-age children try out their new independence, they need teachers' and parents' guidance, affection, encouragement, and protection as much as, if not more than, ever.

Including families in the program will encourage their support and provide you more insight into their children. Communication with family members is discussed throughout this book. Suggestions on how teachers can work in partnership with families and communities are discussed later in this chapter.

Figure 1-9 Young children playing outside can practice their newly discovered physical skills in a safe environment.

Diversity: Cultural, Linguistic, and Ability Differences

CEC **DEC**

Individual Strengths, Interests, and Needs

Now let us examine individual appropriateness, which involves adapting an early childhood environment to meet a child's cultural and linguistic needs, as well as his or her individual strengths and interests. This includes providing each child with the time, opportunities, and resources to achieve individual goals of early education. The teacher should support a positive sense of self-identity in each child. It is important for a teacher to provide many opportunities for teacher-child interaction. However, individual appropriateness should not result in the lowering of expectations.

Individual appropriateness requires the teacher or adult to try to put himself or herself in the place of the child in the classroom. It means asking questions, such as:

- What would make the environment comfortable for infants, toddlers, preschoolers, kindergarteners, early school-age children, or children with ability differences?
- What kind of adult support would be appropriate?
- What is planned to encourage parent participation?
- What is being done to develop a child's sense of trust, sense of self, and feeling of control over the environment?
- What should be happening to encourage positive self-concept development?
- What would I see if I were at the child's level?
- What kind of activities, supplies, and materials should be available?
- What is occurring to support a child's need for privacy or "alone time"?

In answering these questions, take into account what is known about how young children develop and learn, and match that to the content and strategies they encounter in early education programs. Being reflective and carefully listening to what children have to say is also important. As we continue through this book, the activities discussed in all curriculum areas will be developmentally appropriate, with an emphasis on meeting the needs of *all* children.

It is important to include opportunities for interacting with the child's family as well. Communication between home and school offers consistent and beneficial experiences for young children and their families.

Gestwicki (2015) says it clearly:

> "Developmentally appropriate practice does not approach children as if they were equal members of an age grouping, but as unique individuals… This knowledge [of specific uniqueness] primarily comes through relating and interacting with children and also their parents, who are important resources of knowledge about their children. Developmentally appropriate practice is based on parents' active involvement both as resources of knowledge and as decision makers about what is developmentally appropriate for their children."

By observing young children, gathering data about who they are, and developing awareness of their strengths, interests, and needs, you are starting to build a child-centered curriculum. You will discover that children benefit from being treated as individuals while being part of a class community. For curriculum and environments to be developmentally appropriate, they must be individually appropriate. We will study observation, assessment strategies, and evaluation of curriculum and environments in the ensuing chapters of this book.

Social and Cultural Contexts

DAP

Early childhood educators recognize the importance of cultural context in the development and learning of young children. Growing up as members of a family and community, children learn the rules of their culture—explicitly through direct teaching and implicitly through the behavior of those around them (Copple and Bredekamp, 2009). "Rules of development are the same for all children, but social contexts shape children's development into different configurations" (Bowman, 1994, pp. 218–225). To affirm these differences and similarities, an early education environment should encourage the exploration of gender, racial, and cultural identity, developmental abilities, and disabilities.

The ability to go beyond one's own sociocultural background to ensure equal and fair teaching and learning experiences for all is known as culturally appropriate practice. This expands DAP to address cultural influences that emphasize the adult's ability to develop a multiethnic perspective. To eliminate **bias**—any attitude, belief, or feeling that results in unfair treatment of an individual or group of individuals—and to create an **anti-bias** atmosphere, you need to actively challenge prejudice and stereotyping. **Prejudice** is an attitude, opinion, or idea that is preconceived or decided, usually unfavorably. **Stereotype** is an oversimplified generalization about a particular group, race, or sex, often with negative implications (Derman-Sparks and A.B.C. Task Force, 2012).

Literature by de Melendez and Beck (2012) explains further:

> "The Derman-Sparks antibias model presents and addresses cultural diversity content with an emphasis on promoting fairness and equality. It also refrains from using a tourist-like approach curriculum where the child 'visits' a culture and usually learns about its more exotic details. Such curricula only offer glimpses of cultures contributing little to development of awareness and knowledge about the daily life and problems people face in other cultures. "

The curriculum goals for an anti-bias approach are:
Every child will be able to:

- Construct a knowledgeable, confident self-identity.
- Develop comfortable, empathetic, and just interaction with diversity.
- Develop critical thinking skills.
- Develop the skills for standing up for oneself and others in the fact of injustice.

(Derman-Sparks and the A.B.C. Task Force (2010))

Early education classrooms today include children with learning, behavioral, or physical disabilities as well as those with multiple and diverse linguistic and cultural backgrounds. Each child needs to be appreciated by the teacher and other significant adults. He or she needs to experience an environment that reflects back to the child an awareness of and appreciation for his or her individual and cultural differences. The results of these positive influences will stay with the child for a lifetime (de Melendez and Beck, 2013).

bias: Any attitude, belief, or feeling that results in unfair treatment of an individual or group of individuals.

anti-bias: An attitude that actively challenges prejudice, stereotyping, and unfair treatment of an individual or group of individuals.

prejudice: An attitude, opinion, or idea that is preconceived or decided, usually unfavorably.

stereotype: An oversimplified generalization about a particular group, race, or sex, often with negative implications.

play: A behavior that is self-motivated, freely chosen, process-oriented, and enjoyable.

Importance of Play

naeyc

Play is at the core of developmentally appropriate practice. **Play**—a behavior that is self-motivated, freely chosen, process oriented, and enjoyable—is a natural activity for children. It allows them the opportunity to create, invent, discover, and learn about their world. It provides children joy and understanding of themselves and others.

Reflect On This

What happens if children aren't allowed to play?

Research has shown that children's play is present in every human society and the adults in all cultures support play with the manufacture of play toys and equipment. But play is different between cultures based on social and economic circumstances and attitudes about childhood and play. Children's rights and opportunities for play are seen to be constrained within some societies depending on stressors related to contemporary life, separation from nature and an increased view within educational circles that "more and earlier is better" (Whitebread, 2012).

Free, spontaneous, and self-initiated play was once the norm for young children. This is no longer the case. Both parents and early childhood educators, who once encouraged young children to choose their own activities, are being pressured to replace them with adult-directed games, sports, and academic instruction. When children have the opportunity to engage in true play, they are learning to consider options and make choices. The question then becomes, "Why are we trying to teach the elementary curriculum at the early childhood level?"

Children coming to early childhood programs and schools today typically have little time or opportunity to engage in informal play. Jambor stated:

> This situation is the result of concerns of neighborhood violence, changing family structures, elimination of recess due to academic pressures, increased vehicle traffic, squeezed residential play space, unsafe and unchallenging playgrounds, and an increase in sedentary lifestyle brought on by TV, videos, and, most recently, computers (2000, p. 308).

Now we can add video games, iPods, cell phones, and other new devices to the mix.

With less time and opportunity for children to play, it is crucial for those of us in early childhood education to keep focused on what we can do to encourage and support play in our daily programs. As with all aspects of early childhood growth and development, young children go through a series of stages in the development of play. Each new experience offers opportunities for play exploration. Some types of play are characteristic of children at identifiable stages, but children can use many of these stages in varying degrees of sophistication as they get older. (See **Box 1-1**.)

Developmental Stages of Play

Children's observable behaviors that reflect social development and participation in play were first identified by Mildred Parten in 1932. She provided this landmark study that is still considered valid today (Essa, 2013; Gestwicki, 2014; Miller and Almon, 2009; Sluss, 2005). These stages of social play are described as follows.

Unoccupied Behavior

Unoccupied behavior usually occurs during infancy and early toddlerhood. A child occupies himself or herself by watching anything of momentary interest. Sometimes the child may not appear to be playing at all.

unoccupied behavior: Refers to a child (infant or toddler) who occupies himself by watching anything of momentary interest.

BOX 1-1: Why Play Is Important		
Play	Inspires	Imagination
Imagination	Inspires	Creativity
Creativity	Inspires	Exploration
Exploration	Inspires	Discovery
Discovery	Inspires	Solving Problems
Solving Problems	Inspires	New Skills
New Skills	Inspires	Self-Confidence
Self-Confidence	inspires	Sense of Security
Sense of Security	inspires	More Play

Onlooker Play

Onlooker play is sometimes observed in young toddlers or in children introduced to new situations. This play focuses on the activity rather than the environment. Onlookers place themselves within speaking distance of the activity. Although passive, they are alert to the action around them.

Solitary Play

Solitary play surfaces first for a toddler. The child actually engages in play activity alone at home but is within "earshot" of mother or another adult. In an early education setting, the child plays independently without regard to what other children are doing.

Parallel Play

Parallel play can be observed in the older toddler and young 3-year-olds. A child this age is playing for the sake of playing. This child is within "earshot" and sight of another child and can be playing with the same toy but in a different way. Parallel play is the early stage of peer interaction, but the focus is on the object rather than another child.

Associative Play

Associative play finds the 3- and 4-year-old playing with other children in a group, but he or she drops in and out of play with minimal organization of activity. Two or three children use the same equipment and participate in the same activity, but each in his or her own way.

Cooperative Play

Cooperative play is organized for some purpose by the 4-year-old and older child. This type of play requires group membership and reflects a child's growing capacity to accept and respond to ideas and actions not originally his own. Group play (social play) is the basis for ongoing relationships with people and requires sharing of things and ideas, organizing games and activities, and making friends.

Another aspect of cooperative play is the emphasis on peers and moving away from the importance of adults in the life of a child. The 6- to 8-year-old extends cooperative and symbolic play to include detailed planning and rule making. Leadership roles begin to emerge as play becomes serious.

Theorists and Play

Erik Erikson (1963) emphasized the importance of play in helping children to develop cooperative relationships and gain mutual trust. He believed that children develop their "self-esteem and sense of empowerment by allowing them mastery of objects" (Tsao, 2002, p. 230). Play can also build ego. It fosters the development of physical and social skills that build a child's self-esteem.

According to the theory of Jean Piaget (1961), play provides opportunities for many types of learning in young children, with emphasis on developing representational language and thought. Piaget calls play during the first two years of life **practice play or sensorimotor play**, the stage in cognitive development during which the young child learns through repetitive sensory and motor play activities, also known as functional play.

In the beginning of Piaget's preoperational stage around the ages of two to four or five, **symbolic play** or **dramatic play** become observable in a young child by the way he or she spontaneously uses objects, images, and language. The use of the environment represents what is important to the child at that moment. This type of imaginative play allows the child to imitate realities of people, places, and events within his or her experiences, such as pretending to sleep while patting the baby doll to sleep, drinking "coffee" from an empty cup, and talking to imaginary friends. These imaginary friends allow children to work through anxieties in times of stress or change. In addition, symbolic play and language give children an outlet to practice new physical and mental activities for dealing with the world, such as practicing acceptable behaviors that they see around them so that they can act appropriately in different situations (Krissansen, 2002; Tsao, 2002). Superhero fantasy play is considered a type of symbolic play for a child. (Chapter 7 discusses dramatic play for young children in greater depth.)

onlooker play: The play of young children introduced to new situations that focuses on an activity rather than the environment.

solitary play: Independent play behavior of a child without regard to what other children or adults are doing.

parallel play: Observable play in the older toddler and young 3-year-olds that emphasizes being near another child while playing with an object rather than playing with a child.

associative play: An activity of a 3- or 4-year-old child playing with other children in a group; the child drops in and out of play with minimal organization of activity.

cooperative play: A type of play organized for some purpose by the 4-year-old and older child. It requires group membership and reflects a child's growing capacity to accept and respond to ideas and actions not originally his own.

practice play or sensorimotor play: The stage in cognitive development during which the young child learns through repetitive sensory and motor play activities.

symbolic play: A type of play that allows the child to transfer objects into symbols (things that represent something else) and images into people, places, and events within his experiences. Symbolic play occurs during Piaget's preoperational stage (2 to 7 years). Superhero fantasy play is considered a type of symbolic play for a young child.

dramatic play: Also known as symbolic play.

Piaget's third stage of play, ages 5 to 11, is characterized by games with rules. The roles of the children are clearly defined, the rules of the game are clear-cut, and behavior imitates reality (Sluss, 2005). With increased maturity, children arrive at a complete understanding of rules in both behavior and thought.

Lev Vygotsky's theory (1978) states that social experiences shape children's way of thinking and that social play offers children a way to interpret the world by focusing on rules that underlie all play activities and social interactions. Early imaginative situations created by very young children include social rules, although these rules are not laid down prior to participating in the situations. Supportive guidance scaffolds children's learning, which is required to move children to higher levels of cognitive development.

> "Psychological research has established that there are five fundamental types of human play, commonly referred to as physical play, play with objects, symbolic play, pretend or sociodramatic play, and games with rules. Each supports a range of cognitive and emotional developments, and a good balance of play experience is regarded as a healthy play diet for children. Some types of play are more fully researched than others and much remains to be understood concerning the underlying psychological processes involved (Whitebread, 2012)."

Play also provides children with important insights into themselves and the communities in which they live.

Fostering Play

Teachers have a responsibility to help children develop in their use of play. Play, particularly in preschool and kindergarten, needs to be an integral part of the educational process. Play is neurologically important. Scientific studies of the brain have shown that stress-free, fatigue-free, and anxiety-free environments foster neurological pathways. Play-based activities make connections, combine materials, repeat actions, take risks, extend skills, and create electrical impulses that help make connections and interconnections between neural networks. These connections extend children's capabilities as thinkers, communicators, and learners. Also, we should convey to parents the importance of play in the lives of young children. Play can be a valuable means of gauging a child's developmental progress. This information, in turn, can be communicated to parents. Other teacher responsibilities are to:

- Be aware of current research and resources that validate the importance of play.
- Create a positive and safe place for play.
- Provide open-ended play materials.
- Respect and encourage individual differences in play abilities.
- Have patience with children and give them time to learn new play skills.
- Introduce activities and materials appropriate for each child's age and stage of development.
- Take a sincere interest in learning discoveries.
- Provide a play environment that reflects attitudes and values of the surrounding culture.
- Offer appropriate props from a child's culture that will help him make connections as he plays.
- Make available culturally diverse materials for all the children to enjoy and learn from as they play.
- Encourage cooperation.
- Allow children time without scheduled or externally focused activity. This offers an opportunity for children to be internally focused so that imagination and creativity can take over.

- Take time to listen to children as they play and to observe how each child plays, what he plays with, who he plays with, and what the child *can* do.

It is also important to know the roles that teachers serve in children's play. These include (Jones and Reynolds, 2011):

- *Assessor:* builds on each child's strengths;
- *Mediator:* keeps play safe; teaches conflict resolution skills and solves problems to sustain play;
- *Planner:* pays careful attention to play to plan and support children's engagement and competence;
- *Player:* moves in and out of play to model, mediate, and encourage children to elaborate on their play;
- *Scribe:* represents children's play to help them communicate their ideas; and
- *Stage manager:* clarifies what is important and not important in the play, provides props and enough time for play.

The Association for Childhood Education International's (ACEI) position paper, "Play: Essential for All Children," sounds "A Call to Action" (2002). (See **Box 1-2**.)

Childhood play has a key role in the development of self and identity. Understanding this, you can help the children in your care develop to their fullest potential. As you continue through the chapters of this text, you will find specific examples of how curriculum planning and implementation influence and strengthen childhood play.

Elkind (cited in Koralek, 2004, p. 41) explains further:

> " As teachers of young children, we need to resist the pressures to transform play into work—into academic instruction. We encourage true play by making certain that we offer materials that leave room for the imagination—blocks, paints, paper to be cut and pasted—and that children have sufficient time to innovate with these materials. When we read to young children, we can ask them to make up their own stories or to give a different ending to the story they are hearing. Most of all we need to adopt a playful attitude that will encourage our children to do the same. "

BOX 1-2:   A Call to Action

ACEI believes that all educators, parents, and policy makers must take the lead in articulating the need for play experiences in children's lives, including the curriculum. To assume strong advocacy roles, it is imperative that all educators, parents, and policy makers who work with or for children from infancy through adolescence fully understand play and its diverse forms. Equally important is the ability to use that knowledge to achieve what is best for children in all settings. This paper has argued strongly for legitimizing play as an appropriate activity in schools and other educational settings. Therefore, educators, families, and policy makers can and should:

- Optimize brain functions by providing rich experiences that include a variety of learning materials, feedback, appropriate levels of challenge, and enough time to process information.
- Rethink and transform the nature of relationships and communication between adults and children.
- Make play a fundamental part of every school curriculum.
- Recognize, respect, and accept play in all its variations as worthwhile and valuable.

- Balance work and play to ensure that children reap the benefits of intrinsic motivation and experience sheer joy in their endeavors.
- Balance encouragement and opportunity to fulfill children's natural tendency and need to play; children will find the means to play if the environment affords an opportunity to do so.
- Create a climate of acceptance by respecting children's play choices, recognizing the cultural context in which play occurs, and providing many play options.

Communication with Families

As previously discussed in this chapter, it is the teacher's responsibility to keep the lines of communication open to families. It is the family's responsibility to be involved with their child's teacher and child care center or school. The following guidelines for DAP, which offer suggestions on how teachers can work in partnership with families and communities, are adapted from Copple and Bredekamp (2009) and Gestwicki (2014).

1. Success in the education of young children must be built on a foundation of teamwork involving both teachers and families. It is not the teacher telling the parent what needs to be accomplished. It is both teachers and family members cooperatively sharing knowledge and beliefs about educating children and developing common goals. These partnerships enrich relationships with children and bring together the expertise of both teachers and families for the benefit of the children. (See **Figure 1-10**.)

2. Families are the primary educators of their own children. It is imperative that teachers respect that crucial role by maintaining open communication with families, learning from them, and involving them in the education process.

3. There is a learning process that teachers and families always face in the educational experience. The teacher is learning from the children and their families about the children's world apart from the early childhood setting, while family members are developing knowledge about the principles and techniques of early childhood education. Both are necessary and important. With increased communication, mutual respect emerges.

4. Assessing the child's needs and progress must take into account the child's culture and environment. A teacher's failure to do so is likely to create a breakdown in the educational process.

5. A teacher is prepared to meet the special needs of individual children, including those with disabilities.

6. The early childhood teacher is in a unique position to be an advocate by recognizing the special circumstances of a child and his or her family and to help link up with whatever community resources are available and appropriate for helping them.

Figure 1-10 Encourage parents to share with you what they know about their children and what is important to them as parents.

Positive communication between home and school is crucial to providing a consistent and beneficial experience for young children. "Just as the teacher deals with each child as a unique individual by employing a variety of teaching guidance methods, so must a flexible approach be maintained in communicating with families to meet their individual requirements" (Essa, 2011, p. 72).

Children tend to see connections between school and home when their parents are involved. Children's positive attitudes increase when families are involved in the school which increases children's homework habits and attendance. In the busy and complex lives of parents and teachers alike, this connection between home and school is more important today than ever before.

Teachers and other staff members in early childhood settings should be responsive to cultural and language differences of the children and their families. Affirming and supporting diversity includes being perceptive about differences in caregiving, feeding, and other practices (Wortham, 2010).

Here are some additional suggestions for active communication with parents:

- Provide an infant daily report (see **Box 1-3**).
- Provide a toddler daily or weekly report (see **Box 1-4**).
- Create bulletin boards with information regarding health and safety issues, family meetings, guest speakers, community resources and referrals, and tips for parents.

BOX 1-3:   Infant Daily Report

(Morning input from parents to teachers.)

My Name: _____ Date: _____

When I last ate: _____ Food: _____ Formula/Milk: _____

Time I woke up today: _____ Time I went to bed last night: _____ Hours slept: _____

Last diaper change: _____ Medication: Yes ___ No ___ (must sign in)

How I feel today: (circle one) Great! OK Fussy Not well Feverish Upset tummy

Teething Diaper rash

Today, my teachers should know: _____

(Teachers, input to parents at end of infant's day)

Feedings: (Time & Description/Amount)	Naps: (Time Slept) (Time)	Changes: (My Diaper D W BM)
_____	_____	_____
_____	_____	_____
_____	_____	_____
_____	_____	_____
_____	_____	_____
_____	_____	_____

My day at school:

Supply needs: (circle one) Clothes Diapers Formula Food Wipes Other:

COMMENTS:

BOX 1-4:   Toddler Daily Report

Child's Name : _____   Date: _____   Teacher: _____

Morning input from parents to teachers:

(*Note:* Weekly menu is posted on parent bulletin board.)

MORNING SNACK:	Child Ate:	well ( )	fair ( )
LUNCH:	Child Ate:	well ( )	fair ( )
AFTERNOON SNACK:	Child Ate:	well ( )	fair ( )

NAP: _____

DIAPER CHANGES: TOILET USE:

ACTIVITIES:

ITEMS NEEDED FROM HOME:

COMMENTS:

- Provide family letters, e-mails, newsletters, on-line surveys, and web pages discussing the goals, objectives, themes, and classroom activities. Offer suggestions for activities families can do with children at home to extend or emphasize classroom experience.
- Encourage families to share with you what they know about their children and what is important to them as parents.
- Encourage families to visit the classroom. They should be as welcome as their child.
- Conduct parent-teacher conferences that focus on the accomplishments and needs of the individual child and that ensure privacy and confidentiality for the family.
- Provide multilingual written communications as needed.
- Provide opportunities for families to volunteer.
- Provide advisory committee meetings, trainings and family meeting.

Summary

1. **Analyze the importance of historical information and theories to the field of early childhood education.** Many influences, such as historical aspects of early childhood education, developmental theories, insightful educators, developmentally appropriate practices, and ongoing research have impacted and continue to impact our understanding of what is appropriate for the young children in our care. From them we learn that an early childhood program should be based on fulfilling the developmental needs of all children. It should be planned to meet each child's physical, intellectual, social, and emotional growth. Understanding the interrelationships among development, learning, and experiences is essential to providing the highest quality care and education for young children.

2. **Identify developmentally appropriate practices as they relate to child development and learning; individual strengths, interests and needs; and social and cultural contexts.** The program should be founded on the assumption that growth is a sequential process, that children pass through stages of development, and that children learn and grow through their play and by actively participating in the

learning experiences offered. It should adapt to the developmental, individual, and cultural differences of the children.

3. **Discuss the importance of play in the lives of young children, describe the developmental stages of play, and identify ways teachers foster play.** As teachers, we need to offer age, individually, and creatively appropriate experiences and activities for each child. We should assist each child in growing to his or her fullest potential by recognizing each stage of development; by providing an environment that encourages the success of each child; by respecting the culture, language, and special needs of each child; and by welcoming family participation in the program.

4. **Explain the value of and techniques for communicating with families.** As we plan for children and their families, we are saying: "Welcome! This environment is safe and appropriate. We care, we will listen, we will share, and we will nurture you and recognize your uniqueness."

Reflective Review Questions

1. If you are going to explain what you do in a classroom to families, colleagues, and administrators, then you need to have knowledge about the contributions of early childhood education history and theorists to the profession. Think about how this information gives you the confidence to express that what you know is based on hundreds of years of experience and research.

2. Why is the term *developmentally appropriate practice* a key concept that every person involved in early childhood should learn about, and how would you explain the concept to someone outside the early education field?

3. What are the distinguishing characteristics of Erik Erikson's *psychosocial theory*, Jean Piaget's *cognitive development theory*, Lev Vygotsky's *sociocultural theory*, and Howard Gardner's *Multiple Intelligences theory*?

4. David Elkind (2002, p. 41) said, "Free, spontaneous, and self initiated play was once the norm for young children. This is no longer the case. . . ." Think back to your childhood. How did you play as a young child? Why was playing important to you? Using the ideas from your reflective thinking about your childhood and the information from this chapter, do you think the nature of play and the opportunity for play has changed? In what way or ways has it changed? If you think play has changed, what might be some explanations for those changes?

Explorations

1. The number of early childhood programs has increased in response to the growing need for out-of-home care and education during the early years. Identify and discuss the indicators of the current need for child care and education, including changing lifestyles and family patterns. How is your local community responding to these needs of young children and their families? Give specific examples.

2. Describe what is meant by developmentally appropriate practice. Then, identify and describe at least three specific examples from your experiences and observations of young children that illustrate developmentally appropriate practice. In addition, it is important for you to read through NAEYC's updated *Developmentally Appropriate Practice*, 3rd edition, by Copple and Bredekamp (2009), to note the major areas discussed. Share this assignment with your classmates.

3. It is common to hear a comment about a young child such as, "Oh, he's just playing." The implication is that what he's doing is not important. From what you have learned about the developmental stages of play and from Parten, Erikson, and Piaget's theories

about the function of play for children, what is incorrect about this type of comment? Why do you think people tend to undervalue play?

4. Select a group of toddlers or kindergarten children. Observe them at play in their classroom and in their outdoor environment. Using the information on *play* in this chapter, describe what activities the children were involved in and what developmental stages of play you observed. How did the teacher plan for the children's play activities? Was it child-directed or teacher-directed play? Would you change anything if you were the teacher? Explain.

5. Visit an early childhood program. Select a classroom and look at its daily schedule and the routines within the schedule. Obtain a copy, if possible. Are the schedule and routines developmentally appropriate? Do they consider the needs of all the children? Explain your answers. Did the teacher follow the posted schedule and routines? What was changed and why? Would you change anything? Why or why not?

Observation and Assessment

2

Student Learning Outcomes

After studying this chapter, you should be able to:

- Compare uses or purposes for observation and assessment.

- Describe the process of observation and assessment, including various types of observations and assessments and guidelines for assessment.

- Evaluate the advantages and disadvantages of authentic assessment.

- Analyze the relationship between assessment and curriculum planning.

Standards Covered in This Chapter

 NAEYC 3a, 3b, 3c, 3d

DAP DAP 4

INTASC INTASC 6, 7

 CEC DCC C12, C14, C19

Curriculum and assessment drive our work with young children every day. If we do them well, we achieve positive outcomes for children. . . . We must also be careful not to confuse the role of ongoing assessment to support learning with assessment as part of program evaluation. The first uses information to guide decisions about each child's learning, while the second uses data to improve the program and prepare reports. . . . A comprehensive curriculum linked to a systematic assessment system leads to positive outcomes for children (Dodge and Bickhart, 2003, pp. 28–32).

Daily, teachers and directors make decisions related to the children they educate, the facility in which they work, and the curriculum they use. These decisions cannot be made without a firm understanding of the individual children, the workplace, and what their goals guide them to teach and how. To make these decisions, planning is required. A part of this planning process involves observation and assessment of each of these components.

Purposes of Observation and Assessment

INTASC **naeyc**

The purposes of assessment include providing information to stakeholders about expectations, helping teachers in planning instruction, helping administrators in improving programs, identifying children who may require special interventions, and providing information for program accountability. Meaningful assessment strategies include collecting data by observing children in a natural setting, using criteria that can assess children from birth to age eight at all ability levels, and categorizing observation results by curriculum content areas and developmental domains. Technical requirements of a meaningful assessment system are that it provides data on individual children that can be aggregated at the classroom program levels, provides descriptive statistics and gain scores, and is available in computerized and paper formats.

Teachers need to have a clear understanding of the purposes and benefits of observation and assessment to identify a child's current competency levels. We rely on observation of skills the child has mastered, which then informs our future planning. For children experiencing difficulties, we use the data to support early identification and referral for specific difficulties and the introduction of appropriate intervention strategies. The observation and assessment processes can also be used to identify the effectiveness of the environment, specific areas of the curriculum, specific activities, and the teaching strategies used. None of these can take place without prior observation and assessment of the current situation (www .sagepub.com/upm-data/9656_022816Ch5.pdf).

Child Outcomes

Before we start to plan for learning, we must first have a clear understanding of each individual child in your care. An *outcome* is defined as a benefit experienced as a result of services and supports received. Thus, a **child outcome** is what happens as a result of services provided to children. Child outcomes are measured by the attainment of different child development milestones or skills. To measure outcomes, teachers collect observational data on children's work in the areas of language and literacy, early math, social development, self-help, nature, science, and so on, and enter the information into a computer or log it onto a form.

child outcome: What happens as a result of services provided to children and that are measured by the attainment of different child development milestones or skills.

Data are collected at the beginning of the year to document skills the children have at entry. Teachers update the information as the year progresses and then enter data at the end of the year. This type of system gives teachers, parents, and administrators a comprehensive picture of the progress children are making over time in their early childhood program. Finding out what a child knows and is able to do helps teachers plan new experiences to advance learning.

Environment

The environment includes the organization of the space and furnishings, predictable daily routines, and responsive interactions between teachers and children. Although distinct, the interconnection of these components is critical for promoting effective teaching. Successful teachers know that the arrangement and management of the early childhood classroom have direct effects on the kinds of behaviors children exhibit as they live and work together.

The components of the physical space in an early childhood classroom include: traffic patterns, materials placed at the children's level, organized storage, adequate equipment and supplies, clearly delineated functional areas, coordinated placement of centers, small-group and independent work areas, and large-group areas. Infant and toddler environments will look different from environments for preschool, whereas primary environments will be planned differently and based on the program goals and developmental needs of the children served, but these basic components will be present in some fashion.

Classroom furniture should be child-sized, and labels and objects placed strategically where children can read them. The classroom should be clean, well maintained, interesting, and attractive. The classroom should be colorful and well lit and should consist primarily of examples of children's and teacher's work displayed at the child's eye level and when possible, supplemented with culturally and linguistically diverse posters, pictures, and books, depicting real people of differing abilities (*Revised Texas Prekindergarten Guidelines,* 2008; https://www.childrenslearninginstitute.org/Intro-TX-PreK-Guidelines-2008/index.htm).

Curriculum

The **curriculum** is the planned interaction of children with instructional content, materials, resources, and processes for evaluating the attainment of educational objectives. The curriculum outlines the skills, performances, attitudes, and values children are expected to learn. It includes statements of desired child outcomes, descriptions of materials, and the planned sequence that will be used to help children attain the outcomes.

According to the *Curriculum Review Cycle,* teachers need a systematic review cycle to ensure effective teaching and learning in every program. Four essential questions guide the review cycle:

- "What do children know and be able to do?
- How do you know that children have learned?
- What will we do when they haven't learned?
- What will we do when they already know it or can do it?

Curriculum review is a continuous process with adjustments made as necessary" (Seekonk Public Schools, *Curriculum Review Cycle,* 2009).

curriculum: The planned interaction of children with instructional content, materials, resources, and processes for evaluating the attainment of educational objectives.

observation: The process for taking in information and objectively interpreting it for meaning.

Plan of Observation and Assessment

Observation

Observation is the process for taking in information and objectively interpreting it for meaning. Watching children is not the same as observing them. Only by observing children can we truly understand them. We observe a child in order to understand the true nature of the child (see **Figure 2-1**).

Figure 2-1   Observe how each child plays, what each child plays with, and what each child can do.

Bentzen (2009) describes observation this way:

"Observation entails the noting and recording of "facts." We refine this meaning to include the idea of looking for something in a controlled, structured way. "Controlled" means that your observations are not random or haphazard. You know beforehand what you want to observe, where you want to observe, and essentially how you want to observe."

In this age of technology, video cameras are sometimes being used in the observation of young children. In doing so, as a teacher of young children, you should be aware that video cameras often change the behavior you want to observe. Children begin to "act" for the camera instead of continuing with whatever activity they were doing. It is difficult to observe just one child when all the children want to be part of the action. If possible, it would be helpful to have the video camera out of sight and operated by someone else who is knowledgeable in what you want recorded for later observation. Additionally, remember that permission from the family to videotape each child is required (see **Box 2-1**).

Bentzen further clarifies:

"We believe that under most circumstances in the professional lives of child care providers and early childhood educators, persistent and extensive use of a video camera would be unfeasible. . . . However, we recognize that some of you will want to use the video camera regardless of its disadvantages, real or imagined. In that event, we can recommend only that you use it judiciously and in combination with sound basic observational recording skills (2009, p. 84)."

Assessment refers to the collection of information for the purpose of making educational decisions about children or groups of children or to evaluate a program's effectiveness. In 2003, the National Association for the Education of Young Children (NAEYC) and National Association of Early Childhood Specialists in State Departments of Education updated their 1991 joint position statement on curriculum, assessment, and program evaluation. This statement is still valid today. Concerning assessment, they stated:

"Make ethical, appropriate, valid and reliable assessment a central part of all early childhood programs. To assess young children's strengths, progress, and needs, use assessment methods that are developmentally appropriate, culturally and linguistically responsive, tied to children's daily activities, supported by professional development, inclusive of families, and connected to specific, beneficial purposes: (1) making sound decisions about teaching and learning, (2) identifying significant concerns that may require focused intervention for individual children, and (3) helping programs improve their educational and developmental interventions (NAECS/SDE, 2003, p. 1)."

In most states early childhood educators are finding that state standards are guiding assessment. This has prompted early childhood educators to find better ways to assess children, particularly those with special needs. One way that has been shown to be valuable is called play-based assessment (Ahola and Kovacik, 2007). Play-based assessment is a developmental assessment that involves observation of how a child plays alone, with peers, or with parents or other familiar caregivers. These observations are conducted in free play or in special games. Because play is a natural way for children to show what they can do, how they feel, how they learn new things, and how they behave with familiar people, this type of assessment can be very helpful.

assessment: Collection of information for the purpose of making educational decisions about children or groups of children or to evaluate a program's effectiveness.

BOX 2-1:   Observing Young Children Guidelines

Reasons for observing children:
- To gain knowledge of age-appropriate behaviors.
- To gain knowledge of individual differences.
- To become aware of the total environment and influences on children.
- To identify specific strengths and difficult areas for individual children.
- To gather data to plan for individual children.
- To gain understanding of children—the stages of physical, intellectual, emotional, social, and language development.
- To gain an appreciation of young children—their abilities, interests, perceptions, and personalities.
- To gain knowledge of how children learn.
- To identify how individual children react/relate to a group situation.
- To become aware of positive (prosocial) and negative (antisocial) behaviors of young children.

Guidelines for recording the behavior of young children:
- Remember that all information is confidential.
- Observe quietly with little or no interaction with the child (children) being observed.
- Record objective observations in a clear, precise, and useful manner.
- Think of the child and respect her as she is, not as you think she should be.
- Be familiar as possible with the age group before beginning to observe.
- Use the speaker's exact words when recording conversation.

Guidelines for interpreting the behavior of a young child:
- To identify consistent patterns of behavior for a particular child over a specific period of time.
- To document patterns of behavior with specific examples of such behavior.
- To identify areas of difficulty and developmental delays as well as age-appropriate and accelerated development.
- To remember not to make assumptions about the child's family life as the cause of her behavior at school/center.
- To remember not to make assumptions about the child's behavior away from the school/center.

Developmentally appropriate practice emphasizes:

" [The] experiences and the assessment are linked (the experiences are developing what is being assessed, and vice versa); both are aligned with the program's desired outcomes or goals for children....In addition to this assessment by teachers, input from families as well as children's own evaluations of their work are part of the program's overall assessment strategies (Copple and Bredekamp, 2009, p. 22). "

The following methods for observing and recording are often used in the assessment and evaluation process.

Anecdotal Record

An **anecdotal record** is a brief, informal narrative account describing an incident of a child's behavior that is important to the observer. It may apply to a specific child or to a group of children. The anecdotal record process of assessment (observations written down in an organized way) is one of the developmentally appropriate ways teachers can evaluate a child's learning.

Use an anecdotal record/observation form to record your observations. Anecdotes describe the beginning and ending times of the observation, an objective, and a factual account of what occurred (telling how it happened, when and where it happened, and what was said and done). (See **Box 2-2.**)

Anecdotal records come only from direct observation, and are written down promptly and accurately (Essa, 2011). The anecdotal record allows us to view the child's behavior within the contexts in which it is happening and can be helpful in recording a specific episode that is

anecdotal record: A brief, informal narrative account describing an incident of a child's behavior that is important to the observer.

BOX 2-2: Anecdotal Record/Observation Form

CHILD'S NAME	LOCATION
DATE	TEACHER
TIME AT START OF OBSERVATION	DEVELOPMENTAL DOMAIN
TIME AT END OF OBSERVATION	
OBSERVATION	COMMENTS

Professional Resource Download

of particular interest or concern. Anecdotal records (notes) can be useful in parent interviews. Children of all ages should be observed using anecdotal records. When you keep these notes over an entire year, they provide an objective picture of how that child has grown or changed.

Use of an anecdotal record worksheet offers one way to take notes on what you observe. This should be done first without including your opinions. You can separate your subjective thoughts and include them in a separate column. The more you observe, the better an observer you will become. Information gained from this observation should be used to support the development of the child. Also, think about how to use your observations to effect changes in the classroom and the curriculum. (See Box 2-3.)

"Anecdotal records can be used alone or with other assessment methods such as documentation for checklists and parent interviews. Children of all ages should be observed for anecdotal records. Anecdotal records on *all* children should be kept for over a year and can provide an objective picture of how that child has grown or changed" (Charlesworth and Lind 2015, p. 39). Recording observations can become a habit and provides an additional tool in assessing children's learning and your teaching strategies. Anecdotes are also invaluable resources for parent conferences.

BOX 2-3: Anecdotal Record Worksheet

Date of observation	Observation (factual/objective)	Comments (opinion/subjective)
Beginning time:	(Suggestions of what to include: Date of observation. Description of the situation or activity. What is happening? Description of what the child is doing. Location of the child. Who else is near the child? Description of the child's body movements. What is the child, children, or adult saying? What changes occur between the beginning and the end of the observation?)	(Suggestions of what to include: your interpretations, opinions, and conclusions of what you observe. How interested is the child in what he is doing? Is the child really being included in what is happening? What do you think the child is feeling? Was any guidance, positive or negative, offered? Describe.)
Ending time of observation:		

Professional Resource Download

Checklist

A **checklist** is a record of direct observations that involves selecting from a previously prepared list the statement that best describes the behavior observed, the conditions present, growth and development; or the equipment, supplies, and materials available. Checklists can be used to reflect common activities and expectations in classrooms that are structured around developmentally appropriate activities and are based on national, state, and local standards. Checklists are easy to use and helpful in planning for individual or group needs. They eliminate the need to record all details of behavior.

Reflective Log or Diary

A **reflective log** or diary is a teacher's or administrator's record of the most significant happenings, usually made at the end of the day or during an uninterrupted block of time. This includes what stood out as important facts to remember for the day, written in as much detail as possible, and extends over a long period of time. The diary description is an informal method of observation; and it is considered the oldest method in child development (Wright, cited in Bentzen, 2009).

Case Study

A **case study** is a way of collecting and organizing all of the information gathered from various sources, including observations of and interviews with the child, to provide insights into the behavior of the individual child studied. Interpretations and recommendations are included. The main purposes for this detailed observational record are to discover causes and effects of behavior, to conduct child development research, and to plan for the individual child.

Portfolio Assessment

Portfolio assessment is based on a systematic collection of information about a child's ongoing development and the child's work gathered by both the child and teacher over time from all available sources. A portfolio is a collection of child-produced material, such as "works-in-progress," creative drawings, paintings, and dictated stories; lists of books and stories read; product samples showing a child's strengths and skills; samples of a child's self-initiated "work"; photographs, audio tapes and videotapes; teacher objectives for the child, observations and anecdotal records; developmental checklists; and family interviews and comments. Teacher comments on each portfolio sample can help document what the child knows, can do, and how she does it.

A **portfolio** can be a file folder or an accordion-type folder for each child (Batzle, 1992; Hendrick and Weissman, 2010). Portfolio information helps the teacher "construct a well-rounded and authentic picture of each child so you are better able to plan your program, to build on individualized strengths; and to support each child's growth….Because you want portfolios to be integrated into your daily program, they need to be within children's easy reach. Children enjoy looking back through their work, and browsing and reflection are important parts of this process" (Cohen 1999, p. 31).

Harris (2009, p. 82) adds: "Portfolios can foster continuous reflection and richer, deeper communication among all the members of the learning community—children, teachers, caregivers, administrators, and families."

Use of Technology in Assessment

Computers and software are used in assessment for entering data and reporting results (see **Figure 2.2**). Newer technology is allowing teachers to collect assessment data directly on mobile devices. In the absence of technology, teachers conduct an assessment with paper and

checklist: A record of direct observation that involves selecting from a previously prepared list the statement that best describes the behavior observed, the conditions present, growth and development, or the equipment, supplies, and materials available.

reflective log: A teacher's or administrator's record of the most significant happenings, usually made at the end of the day or during an uninterrupted block of time.

case study: A way of collecting and organizing all of the information gathered from various sources to provide insights into the behavior of the individual child studied.

portfolio assessment: A systematic collection of information about a child's ongoing development and the child's work gathered by both the child and teacher over time from all available sources.

Figure 2-2 Technology can be used by teachers in their curriculum planning.

pencil, and then score the results on the paper record form. Some assessments may have a paper report template that the teachers also complete. With technology, teachers enter data into the assessment's software package. The software then scores the assessment data and produces a report. Computerized scoring and reporting reduces potential for error. Newer technology is allowing teachers to collect assessment data directly on mobile devices, eliminating the need to transfer data from a paper form.

Some cutting-edge assessments are eliminating data entry altogether by having children respond to assessment items directly, typically on a mobile device's touchscreen. In the case of integrated curricula and assessments, computers and software are used to instantaneously assess, score, and report child outcomes, allowing for immediate data-based decision making (Hernandez et al. 2015).

Authentic Assessment

naeyc   DAP   INTASC

Art assessment can be described as authentic assessment because it visually documents a child's growth and development over time, using the child's art and explanations of the art in his or her own words. Each picture or piece of artwork shows where the child started at the beginning of the school year and where he or she is at the end of the year.

A **portfolio**, an assessment strategy discussed previously as a collection of work over time, works well in documenting children's artistic development by recording the child's process of learning—how he or she thinks, questions, analyzes, synthesizes, and creates (Gober, 2002). Portfolios come in many shapes and sizes, such as expanding, accordion-type files, file folders, cardboard boxes, scrapbooks, three-ring binders, or unused pizza boxes.

Nilson clarifies how children's artistic growth can be assessed:

portfolio: Collection of child-produced material.

❝ Portfolios, collections of the child's work and written observations are becoming an accepted form of documenting the child's progress. Written observations which are thorough, objective, regular, and done in the natural classroom environment are accurate measures of a child's progress (2013, p. 6). **"**

You need to work out a routine with the children as to how the selection process of what goes in the portfolio will work. Some suggestions include: (a) You can take one day per week, such as Friday, for the children to go through their weekly art and select one or two items they want to include. (b) You can also go through the art before or after the children have selected pieces to be included. (c) Art that is sent from home can be placed in each portfolio with date and explanation at any time. (d) It is important that children have an opportunity to choose and comment on each article of art because it promotes self-evaluation and self-assessment. It is also good for the child's self-esteem for him or her to focus on all the things he or she knows he or she can do. (e) Keep in mind that each child's portfolio should be respected and confidential. (f) There is no right way to do portfolio saving. You have to try different ways and decide on which is right for you and the children in your class. (g) Write an end-of-the-year summary that you will keep, and make a memory book of each child's artwork to send home.

You will find a portfolio checklist, a portfolio sample form, and file folder labels for organizing an individual child's portfolio online at this textbook's premium website.

Math assessment data on young children should be gathered through observations, interviews, and anecdotal records as children are actively involved in hands-on problem solving and investigation. Math assessment is an ongoing process to determine a child's strengths and needs, which supports teacher planning by using the information and insights you gain to evaluate your teaching techniques and curriculum:

> **"** Assessment is crucial to effective teaching....Child observation, documentation of children's talk, interviews, collections of children's work over time, the use of open-ended questions, and appropriate performance assessments to illuminate children's thinking are positive approaches to assessing strength and needs. Careful assessment is especially important when planning for ethnically, culturally, and linguistically diverse young children and for children with special needs or disabilities (NAEYC & NCTM, 2002, p. 9). **"**

As children work on projects, you will find yourself interacting with them on an informal basis. Listen carefully to children's concepts, and watch them manipulate materials. You cannot help but assess how things are going.

Recording your observations must become a habit. Making it routine can assist you later in assessing your teaching strategies and children's learning.

Chalufour and Worth (2004) offer two key elements to assessment that are helpful to documenting children's inquiry skills and growing understanding of science concepts:

1. *Collect data.* Spend at least 10 minutes three times a week collecting different kinds of data that capture children's level of engagement and understandings, including casual conversations, written observations, photographs, videotapes, audiotapes, and samples of their other work (see **Figure 2-3**).
2. *Analyze data regularly.* Time spent reflecting on your collection of documents will help you understand the growing skills and understandings of each child in your class. The more kinds of documents you have, the fuller the picture you will have of each individual.

Use assessment to support learning in the early childhood classroom (see **Figure 2-3**). Select useful information about children's knowledge, skills, and progress by observing, documenting, and reviewing children's language and literacy work over time.

Dodge, Heroman, Charles, and Maiorca wrote:

> **"** The most powerful outcome of ongoing assessment is the positive relationship teachers can build with each child. Every child is different, but the one thing every child needs is to feel accepted and appreciated....A system of ongoing assessment also helps the teachers build a relationship with each child's family (2004, p. 21). **"**

Figure 2-3   Portfolios are becoming an accepted form of documenting the child's progress.

Neuman, Copple and Bredekamp emphasize that:

"assessment should support children's development and literacy learning. Good assessment helps to identify children's strengths, needs, and progress toward specific learning goals.... Good assessment uses a variety of tools, including collection of children's work (drawings, paintings, writings), and records of conversation and interviews with children.... The core of assessment is daily observation. Watching children's ongoing life in the classroom enables teachers to capture children's performance in real activities rather than those contrived to isolate specific skills (2000, p. 104)."

Here are some suggestions for assessment collection of children's language and literacy activities and projects:

- Written language as collected in captions on drawings, labels, or child-made books
- Items that indicate a child's learning style and interests
- Spoken language as collected in anecdotal notes or on audio and videotapes
- Musical expressions such as made-up songs and dances
- Webs, lists of words, or other records of vocabulary
- Multiple examples of how a child expresses ideas
- Multiple examples of a child's self-portrait, even if it shows scribbling
- Multiple examples of anecdotal records of language and literacy skill development

(Adapted from Helm, Beneke, and Steinheimer, 2007; Gober, 2002; Santos, 2004; and conversations with early education teachers.)

Following is an example of an appropriate assessment checklist for recording young children's reading and writing development (see **Box 2-4**).

When recording your observations, it is critical that they be recorded objectively. Here are three guidelines for objective recording:

1. Record only facts.
2. Record every detail.
3. Do not interpret as you observe.

BOX 2-4:   Assessment Checklist

Child _____ Age _____ Grade _____

School _____ Teacher _____

What Child Can Do	Assessment Dates	Comments
Goals for Preschool: Awareness and Exploration		
• Enjoys listening to and discussing storybooks		
• Understands that print carries a message		
• Engages in reading and writing attempts		
• Identifies labels and signs in the environment		
• Participates in rhyming games		
• Identifies some letters and makes some letter-sound connections		
• Uses known letters or approximations of letters to represents written language		
Goals for Kindergarten: Experimental Reading and Writing		
• Enjoys being read to and retells simple narrative stories or informational texts		
• Uses descriptive language to explain and explore		
• Recognizes letters and most letter-sound connections		
• Shows familiarity with rhyming and with beginning sounds		
• Understands basic concepts of print, such as left-to-right orientation and starting at the top of the page		
• Understands that spoken words can match written words		
• Begins to write letters of the alphabet and some high frequency words, such as own name, family names, or words such as *cat, dog,* and so on		
Goals for First Grade: Early Reading and Writing		
• Reads and retells familiar stories		
• When comprehension breaks down, uses a variety of strategies, such as rereading, predicting, questioning, and contextualizing		

(continued)

BOX 2-4:   Assessment Checklist (continued)

What Child Can Do	Assessment Dates	Comments
• Initiates using writing and reading for his or her own purposes		
• Can read orally with reasonable fluency		
• Identifies new words through letter-sound associations, word parts, and context		
• Identifies an increasing number of words by sight		
• Can sound out and represent all the major sounds in a spelling word		
• Writes about personally meaningful topics		
• Attempts to use some punctuation and capitalization		
Goals for Second Grade: Transitional Reading and Writing		
• Reads with greater fluency		
• When comprehension breaks down, uses strategies more efficiently		
• Uses strategies more efficiently to decode new words		
• Sight vocabulary increases		
• Writes about an increasing range of topics to fit different audiences		
• Uses common letter patterns and critical features to spell words		
• Punctuates simple sentences correctly and proofreads own work		
• Spends time each day reading		
• Uses reading to research topics		
Goals for Third Grade: Independent and Productive Reading and Writing		
• Reads fluently and enjoys reading		
• Uses a range of strategies when drawing meaning from the text		
• When encounters unknown words, uses word identification strategies appropriately and automatically		
• Recognizes and discusses elements of different text structures		
• Makes critical connections between texts		
• Writes expressively in different forms, such as stories, poems, and reports		

BOX 2-4:   Assessment Checklist (continued)

What Child Can Do	Assessment Dates	Comments
• Uses a rich variety of vocabulary that is appropriate to different text forms		
• Can revise and edit own writing during and after composing		
• Spells word correctly in final written drafts		

Professional Resource Download

Do not record what you do not see—even if you know that a child can usually work a certain puzzle, if they cannot on the day you are observing, that is what you record.

Use objective words. Avoid words that draw assumptions like always, too, never.

Record facts in order. The sequence of behavior is important. There is a difference between a child who hit another back and a child who randomly hit another with no provocation.

Robertson (2010) suggests that the observer go through stages of observation like these:

- Act like a scientist and look for physical evidence or data, not opinion.
- Think of yourself as a detective and search out clues from the child's behavior, the environment, what happened before and after an incident or behavior.
- Be a garbage collector and sort out feelings or opinions from objective physical evidence you have observed.
- Be an advocate and look at the situation from the child's point of view and consider what caused a child to act in a certain manner.
- Act like an artist to paint a detailed objective picture of what you are observing.

As you review your observations to complete your assessment, ask yourself these questions:

- Are there cultural differences that impact the child's behavior?
- Is the child at any risk?
- Does the child have special needs?
- Was there a recent event that may affect the child's behavior or well-being?

As you record your observations remember to date items and entries, keep entries short, include everything (including the context of behavior, a description of behavior and outcome or child's explanation) and finally, stick to the facts (Robertson, 2012).

Assessment Guides: Curriculum Planning

naeyc **INTASC** **DAP**

Many educational programs are now applying state curriculum standards in their early childhood settings. Although they follow curriculum standards, they may not introduce skills in developmental order. Developmental order is essential for tracking learning and to help each child progress along the educational continuum. Without following developmental order, teachers and children can find themselves grappling with gaps in abilities and comprehension. In order to successfully support a child's learning, teachers need to know where that child is functioning according to developmental guidelines (Funk, 2012).

Through the process of assessment, teachers learn about children's knowledge, skills, and progress by observing, documenting, analyzing, and evaluating children's work over time.

This information then guides teaching. Thus, curriculum and assessment are linked in a continuous cycle (Dodge & Bickhart, 2003). Teachers' knowledge of each child guides them in planning a balanced yet challenging curriculum and to tailor teaching strategies that support each and every child's strengths and needs. "Systematic assessment is essential for identifying children who may benefit from more intensive instruction or intervention or who may need additional developmental evaluation. This information ensures that the program meets its goals for children's learning and developmental progress and also informs program improvement efforts" (NAEYC accreditation criteria, 2005). This type of child assessment forms the foundation for organizing and planning classroom activities and will set the stage for individualization and ongoing monitoring:

" The integration of curricula and assessments via technology is enabling practitioners to better track child progress and individualize instruction. Developers are building software packages that can capture assessment data, score it, and provide data-based instructional suggestions instantaneously. Results can be used to differentiate instruction to an individual child or aggregated across multiple children to form small groups. The technologies allow for objective data based decision making for instruction (Hernandez et al., 2015). "

Summary

1. **Compare uses or purposes for observation and assessment.** The purposes of assessment include providing information to stakeholders about expectations, helping teachers in planning instruction, helping administrators in improving programs, identifying children who may require special interventions, and providing information for program accountability.

2. **Describe the process of observation and assessment, including various types of observations and assessment and guidelines for assessment.** Assessment refers to the collection of information for the purpose of making educational decisions about children or groups of children or to evaluate a program's effectiveness. Different assessment methods include the following:
   - An anecdotal record is a brief, informal narrative account describing an incident of a child's behavior that is important to the observer. It may apply to a specific child or to a group of children.
   - A checklist is a record of direct observation that involves selecting from a previously prepared list the statement that best describes the behavior observed, the conditions present, growth and development, or the equipment, supplies, and materials available.
   - A reflective log or diary is a teacher's or administrator's record of the most significant happenings, usually made at the end of the day or during an uninterrupted block of time.
   - A case study is a way of collecting and organizing all of the information gathered from various sources, including observations of and interviews with the child, to provide insights into the behavior of the individual child studied. Interpretations and recommendations are included.

3. **Evaluate the advantages and disadvantages of authentic assessment.** Portfolio assessment, a form of authentic assessment, is based on a systematic collection of information about a child's ongoing development and the child's work gathered by both the child and teacher over time from all available sources. A portfolio is a collection of child-produced material, such as "works-in-progress," creative drawings, paintings, and dictated stories; lists of books and stories read; product samples showing a child's strengths and skills; samples of a child's self-initiated "work"; photographs, audio and video tapes; teacher objectives for the child,

observations and anecdotal records, developmental checklists; and family interviews and comments.

Careful assessment is especially important when planning for ethnically, culturally, and linguistically diverse young children and for children with special needs or disabilities.

4. **Analyze the relationship between assessment and curriculum planning.** Curriculum and assessment are linked in a continuous cycle. The teachers' knowledge of each child guides them in planning a balanced yet challenging curriculum and to tailor teaching strategies that support each and every child's strengths and needs. Systematic assessment is essential for identifying children who may benefit from more intensive instruction or intervention or who may need additional developmental evaluation. This information ensures that the program meets its goals for children's learning and developmental progress and also informs program improvement efforts. This type of child assessment forms the foundation for organizing and planning classroom activities and will set the stage for individualization and ongoing monitoring.

Reflective Review Questions

1. Careful observation and assessment of children is essential to planning appropriate learning experiences for them. However, isn't this just wishful thinking? How can teachers with a myriad of tasks to do every day possibly squeeze in observation and assessment of children? How will you accomplish (or do you accomplish) this when you are responsible for a classroom of children?
2. Describe the observation and assessment techniques that are most appropriate for each of the uses or purposes of observation and assessment.

Explorations

1. Interview a teacher from one of the model programs discussed in this chapter, such as Montessori, Head Start, or an accredited child care center. Ask the teacher to describe the philosophy of the school; how he or she develops curriculum to meet the abilities, interests, and needs of the children in her class; and how he or she assesses the development of the children and the program itself.
2. Interview a teacher who works at an accredited child care center about their experience with child portfolios. How do they collect items to go in the portfolio? How do they balance their role as a teacher/caregiver with that of being the person who collects the items for the portfolio?
3. Observe a child in a classroom for at least 30 minutes. Use the anecdotal record method to document what you observed. Read what you wrote and decide if you just included observation or did you also include some interpretations or value judgments. What could you have done to avoid interpreting what you saw while you observed?

3

Creating Curriculum

Student Learning Outcomes

After studying this chapter, you should be able to:

- Illustrate the process of curriculum development.

- Explain multicultural/anti-bias considerations in early care and education settings.

- Describe the development of curriculum based on themes, units, projects, and websites.

- Develop lesson plans appropriate for children of different ages.

Standards Covered in This Chapter

 NAEYC 4b, 4c, 5a, 5b, 5c

DAP DAP 3.

INTASC INTASC 1, 2, 7.

HEAD START Domain: Approaches to Learning

CEC DEC CEC DCC

As we progress through this chapter, focusing on how to create a curriculum appropriate for young children, we once again emphasize the interconnecting philosophies of this text:

1. Curriculum is child-centered or child-initiated while being sensitive to, and supportive of, the development, age, and experiences of young children, individually and in a classroom community.
2. Curriculum provides for all of a child's development by planning experiences that build on what children already know and are able to do.
3. Curriculum encourages children to learn by doing through experimentation, exploration, and discovery while building self-control and a positive self-image.
4. Curriculum includes appropriate supports and services for children with special needs in an inclusive environment.
5. Curriculum promotes opportunities to support each child's diverse cultural and linguistic heritage.
6. Curriculum invites creativity by providing opportunities for unevaluated discovery and activity while promoting tolerance and respect for each other's creation.
7. Curriculum facilitates physical activity and play by integrating movement within activities throughout the day.
8. Curriculum involves reciprocal relationships between teachers and families. Positive communication between home and school is crucial to providing a consistent and beneficial experience for young children.

This chapter illustrates how we develop an early education curriculum and all it encompasses, including classroom management techniques and appropriate practices for inclusion. Arrangement of indoor and outdoor space and selection of equipment and materials will be discussed in Chapter 4. The plan of observation, assessment strategies, and evaluation discussed in Chapters 2 and 14 will help determine if developmentally appropriate curriculum goals and content have been achieved.

Curriculum is a multilevel process that encompasses what happens in an early education classroom each day, reflecting the philosophy, goals, and objectives of the early childhood program. In an early education program, the philosophy expresses the basic principles, attitudes, and beliefs of the child care center, school, or individual teacher.

Goals are general overviews of what children are expected to gain from the program. Administrators and teachers consider what children should know, understand, and be able to do developmentally across the disciplines, including language, literacy, mathematics, social studies, science, art, music, physical education, and health (Copple and Bredekamp, 2009).

Objectives are specific teaching techniques or interpretations of the goals and meaningful descriptions of what children are expected to learn. They are designed to meet the physical, intellectual, cultural, social, emotional, and creative development of each child.

> "In DAP [developmentally appropriate practices], the curriculum helps young children achieve goals that are developmentally and educationally significant. The curriculum does this through learning experiences (including play, small group, large group, interest centers, and routines) that reflect what is known about young children in general and about these children in particular, as well as about the sequences in which children acquire specific concepts, skills and abilities, building on prior experiences (Copple and Bredekamp, 2009, p. 20)."

As we continue focusing on the process of curriculum development, let us remember that whatever we do, say, plan, or assess must concentrate on developing a child's positive self-esteem. Valuing each child's cultural background, experiences, interests, and abilities is critical. The "I can do it!" feelings of competence strongly influence learning ability. This is true for all children, from the youngest infant to the preschooler or the eight-year-old. (See **Box 3-1.**)

curriculum: A multileveled process that encompasses what happens in an early education classroom each day, reflecting the philosophy, goals, and objectives of the early childhood program.

goals: The general overall aims or overview of an early childhood program that consider what children should know and be able to do developmentally across the disciplines.

objectives: The specific purposes or teaching techniques that interpret the goals of planning, schedules, and routines, as well as meaningful descriptions of what children are expected to learn. These objectives are designed to meet the physical, intellectual, social, emotional, and creative development of young children.

As teachers of young children, we face many daily decisions that have moral and ethical implications. NAEYC's position paper *Code of Ethical Conduct and Statement of Commitment* (2005) defines core values that are deeply rooted in the field of early childhood care and education. The following are NAEYC's ethical core values:

- Appreciate childhood as a unique and valuable stage of the human life cycle.
- Base our work on knowledge of how children develop and learn.

- Appreciate and support the bond between the child and family.
- Recognize that children are best understood and supported in the context of family, culture, community, and society.
- Respect the dignity, worth, and uniqueness of each individual (child, family member, and colleague).
- Respect diversity in children, families, and colleagues.
- Recognize that children and adults achieve their full potential in the context of relationships that are based on trust and respect.

Process of Planning and Scheduling

DAP **INTASC** **naeyc**

Wonderful things don't just happen in your classroom. If you want them to happen, you must make wonderful plans.

Planning and scheduling are important in early education classrooms, including those with infants and toddlers. Detailed information about this process will follow in Chapter 4, but it is important to explore several guidelines at this point:

- As you create plans, you must set up goals and objectives. Goals can help describe the general overall aims of the program. Objectives are more specific and relate to curriculum planning, schedules, and routines. The goals you choose for your program should be valued for each child's nature, the values and goals of the community in which the children live, and your own values.
- Goals and objectives should involve developmentally, individually, culturally, and creatively appropriate practices. They should consider the physical, intellectual, social, and emotional development of the children you are teaching.
- The center or school in which you teach can offer a long-range plan that will help you see where you and the children fit into the total program.

Schedules and Routines

The schedule and routine components of planning can help create a framework of security for young children. "Children who are provided with a predictable schedule and secure environment are more likely to feel confident about exploring their world. ... Through these explorations, children strengthen their connections to the people and environment around them" (Klein, 2002, p. 11). The format becomes familiar to them, and they welcome the periods of self-selected activities, group time, outdoor play, resting, eating, and toileting. The establishment of trust that grows between teacher and parent is based on consistent daily contact and the well-being of the children.

All early childhood programs include basic timelines, curricula, and activities that form the framework of the daily **schedule**. The events that fit into this time frame

schedule: Basic timelines, curricula, and activities.

are the **routines**. The secret of classroom management is getting the children used to routines:

- **Arrival** provides interaction time for the teacher, parent, and child. It also offers a smooth transition from home. This early morning ritual reinforces the trust, friendship, and consistency necessary to young children and their families.
- **Departure** at the end of the day should also offer a relaxed transition for the child and family. This is another time for sharing positive feedback with the parents and provides a consistent routine for the child.
- **Mealtimes and snacks** are some of the nicest moments of the day when teachers and children sit down and eat together. This time should be pleasant and should focus on eating and be a social experience. Self-help skills are developed as well when children pour their own juice and milk and help themselves family-style during meals. If children bring food from home, teachers need to give the parents culturally sensitive and nutritionally sound guidance concerning what food is appropriate for the children to bring.
- **Diapering and toileting** are routines that are ongoing throughout the day as needed. The development of toileting skills and handwashing occurs as the young child matures. Adult handwashing and disinfecting diapering surfaces to prevent disease are other important daily routines.
- **Rest or naptime** runs smoothly if teachers make the environment restful, soothing, and stress free. Consistency in how this routine is handled each day provides security to the children. The use of soft music, dim lights, and personal books or blankets encourages children to rest or sleep on their mats or cots. Older children need a short rest-time, too. Sitting quietly with a book offers a quiet period during the day.
- **Transitions**, such as cleanup, prepare the environment for the next activity. These times are part of your lesson plan and should be based on the developmental needs of the children. (A complete discussion of transition activities is included in Chapter 4.)
- **Activity time** offers children a large block of time for them to self-select from a variety of activities. "A wide variety of well-planned activities should reinforce the objectives and theme of the curriculum. Each day's activities should also provide multiple opportunities for development of fine and gross motor, cognitive, creative, social, and language skills" (Essa, 2011, p. 222). In addition, appropriate times for solitary moments, small and large group activities, indoor and outdoor play, along with a balance of active and quiet activities, should be provided.
- **Outdoor activities** offer children many opportunities for growth and learning. To be developmentally appropriate, outdoor play requires the same planning, observation, and evaluation as indoor activities. Large blocks of outdoor time should be scheduled and planned daily.

Boxes 3-2 and 3-3 are examples of infant, toddler, and preschool schedules and routines appropriate for early education programs.

We should remember, too, that the physical classroom space should allow children to move from center to center, from large group to small group, and from small group to individual choice activities as well (Bobys, 2000). All of this is carefully orchestrated by the teacher, with selection of language and literacy activities by the children being the ultimate goal.

As with everything in an early childhood environment, the organization and focus is on creating a child-centered space. For infants and toddlers, the surroundings should be sensory-rich colors everywhere, the air full of soft music, words from around the world being spoken, songs being sung, books being read, drawings being scribbled, and textures within reach. (A complete discussion of environments will be found in Chapter 4.)

routines: The events that fit into the schedule.

BOX 3-2:   Infants

(3–18 months)
Very Flexible Schedule and Routines

7:00	Prepare for morning arrival.
	Greet parents and infants.
	Put away bottles, food, and diaper supplies.
	Spend individual time holding and talking to each child.
8:00–9:00	Provide snack.
	Younger infants: Individual cereal, fruit, formula, or juice
	Younger infants have individual schedules that include feeding, diapering, and sleeping.
	Older infants: Snack, cleanup, diapering, and looking at books
9:00–11:00	*Younger infants:* Individual play on floor, movement exercise, outdoor play, or take a walk in stroller
	Provide individual formula, juice, or water.
	Talk to each child throughout the day.
	Child sleeps when tired.
	Older infants: Individual or group play
	Visit toddler playground, walk around center, or play in indoor playroom, read books, incorporate dramatic play, manipulatives, art, music and movement, and finger plays.
11:00	*Older infants:* Lunch with formula, milk, juice, or water
	Talk to each child.
11:30–12:30	Cleanup and prepare for naps: Lights dimmed, soft music, quiet play.
12:30–2:00	Naptime
	Talk to and play quietly with infants who are awake.
2:00–3:30	Quiet play with books and toys, individual exercises with each child.
	Younger infants: Individual formula, juice, or water; soft snacks
	Older infants: snack
3:30–4:30	Individual play, group activities, outdoor play, walks.
4:30–5:30	Prepare for going home read books, play on floor, and so on. Talk to each parent.

Diaper changes: As needed after snacks, after lunch, before and after naps, before departure,
and changing of soiled diapers anytime during the day.
Note: All times are suggested and are sensitive to the needs of the children.

BOX 3-3:   Toddlers and Preschool

(18 months–3 years)
Flexible Schedule and Routines

7:00	Prepare for morning arrival.
	Greet children and parents, free play (children choose activities).
8:00–8:50	Center activities (art, manipulatives, blocks, dramatic play); spend individual time with each child or small group activity.
8:50–9:00	Clean up with song or poem or special individual time.
9:00–9:30	Bathroom time (wash hands, change diapers, toileting, etc.); talk to each child.
	Provide snack; allow time for washing hands and face.
9:30–10:30	Outdoor play.
10:30–10:40	Bathroom time (wash hands, change diapers, toileting); talk to each child.
10:40–11:15	Center activities
	Lead guided exploration.
	Lead large-group activity of a story, finger plays, language activities, or music.
11:10–11:30	Bathroom time, wash hands for lunch, and change diapers if needed.

BOX 3-3: Toddlers and Preschool (continued)

11:30–Noon	Lunch
Noon–12:30	Bathroom time, brush teeth, and change diapers if needed.
12:30–2:30	Quiet time with books and music while children finish in bathroom and get on their cots for naptime or rest.
2:30–3:00	Wake-up time (put away cots and blankets, toileting, diaper change, washing, put on shoes), free play.
3:00–3:15	Provide snack and clean up.
3:15–3:30	Group time with story, song, flannel board, or other language activity.
3:30–4:30	Outdoor play; spend individual time with each child.
4:30–4:45	Bathroom time.
4:45–6:00	Quiet activities (books, puzzles, music); spend individual time with each child, playing games, singing, talking; prepare to go home.

Note: This daily schedule is flexible, depending on the needs of the children and the weather. Times are suggested ones and are compatible with the needs of the children.

Curriculum Development

Policy makers, the early childhood profession, and other stakeholders in young children's lives have a shared responsibility to implement a curriculum that is (NAECS/SDE, 2003):

- Thoughtfully planned
- Challenging
- Engaging
- Developmentally appropriate
- Culturally and linguistically responsive
- Comprehensive across all developmental domains
- Likely to promote positive outcomes for all young children

The process of curriculum development is ongoing. It is both planned and impromptu, written or unwritten. "Creating a good curriculum for young children is not simply a matter of practicing curriculum planning. It is a matter of understanding the process: how children interact with people and materials to learn" (Gordon and Browne, 2013, p, 186). The selection of themes, projects, integrated curriculum areas, equipment, and materials is based on sound child development theories reinforcing the child's current stage of development and challenging him or her to move toward the next stage. As you begin this process of curriculum development, the first step is to set goals for learning based on the philosophy of the center or school and on the knowledge of the individual children in your classroom. Throughout this chapter and all the other chapters, we will be discussing the ongoing process of curriculum development, culminating in the selection of topics and activities, writing of objectives, and planning for observation, assessment strategies, and evaluation.

The use of the terms *inclusive curriculum, integrated curriculum,* and *emergent curriculum* in early childhood education explain further what is appropriate in developing curriculum for young children. **Inclusive curriculum** underscores the importance of individual differences, special needs, and cultural and linguistic diversity among young children,

inclusive curriculum:
Underscores the importance of individual differences, special needs, and cultural and linguistic diversity among young children.

allowing for children to learn at their own pace and style. **Integrated curriculum** encourages young children to transfer knowledge and skills from one subject to another while using all aspects of their development. Gestwicki (2014, p. 68) explains that "integrated curriculum helps children build meaningful connections when presented with new information, allows children to use knowledge and skills from one area to explore other subject areas, and allows teachers to negotiate the tricky balance between standards and developmentally appropriate practice." **Emergent curriculum** emerges out of the interests and experiences of the children. "In traditional teaching, teachers give instructions to children about what to do, and the children (preferably) do it. In emergent curriculum, teachers and children together decide what to do and teachers participate in learning alongside children, asking their own questions and conducting their own quest" (Jones, 1994).

The 2009 revision of NAEYC's position statement, "Developmentally Appropriate Practice in Early Childhood Programs Serving Children from Birth through Age 8," suggests these guidelines for planning curriculum:

1. Teachers plan curriculum experiences that integrate children's learning within and across the domains (physical, social, emotional, cognitive) and the disciplines (including language, literacy, mathematics, social studies, science, art, music, physical education, and health).
2. Teachers plan curriculum experiences to draw on children's own interests and introduce children to things likely to interest them, in recognition that developing and extending children's interests is particularly important during the preschool years, when children's ability to focus their attention is in its early stages.
3. Teachers plan curriculum experiences that follow logical sequences and that allow for depth and focus. That is, the experiences do not skim lightly over a great many content areas, but instead allow children to spend sustained time with a more select set.

In the last few years, there has been increased concern about measuring student achievement as mandated accountability requirements, particularly third-grade testing, exert pressures on schools and teachers at K–2 levels, who, in turn, look to teachers of younger children to help prepare students to demonstrate the required proficiencies later. As a result, the concepts of implementing an intentional curriculum that is research-based and the development of state and national standards, such as the Common Core math and language standards, have impacted curriculum planning and development.

An **intentional curriculum** designed for enhanced learning comprises three elements:

1. *Explicit learning outcomes,* which are what teachers and administrators want the students to know and be able to do
2. *Strategic learning design,* which is how teachers will develop learning opportunities to achieve learning outcomes
3. *Meaningful assessment,* which measures if children are learning what teachers want them to learn

An intentional curriculum incorporates explicit teaching strategies that build skills identified through research as resulting in better child outcomes in school, such as literacy skills in phonological awareness, knowledge of print, and writing.

Learning (or content) standards are intended to set the bar for student achievement. They can help create equity among learners by ensuring that each and every child is prepared to meet the challenges of an increasingly complex, demanding world. Although standards vary by state, they generally have similar broad goals for children in the primary grades (National Institute for Early Education Research, 2015). The Early Childhood Education Assessment Consortium of the Council of Chief State School Officers (CCCSO) defines early learning standards as:

> "Statements that describe expectations for the learning and development of young children across the domains of: health and physical well-being; social and emotional well-being; approaches to learning; language development and symbol systems; and general knowledge about the world around them (CCSSO, 2015, p. 8)."

integrated curriculum: Encourages young children to transfer knowledge and skills from one subject to another while using all aspects of their development.

emergent curriculum: A curriculum that emerges out of the interests and experiences of the children.

intentional curriculum: Curriculum that incorporates explicit learning outcomes, strategic learning design, and meaningful assessment.

Standards are not intended to limit creative teachers or to become barriers for learners with special needs. Instead, they can guide, support, and encourage enterprising and knowledgeable primary teachers to create intriguing and motivating educational environments and experiences that are developmentally appropriate for each child and optimize learning for all (NAEYC and NAECS/SDE, 2002).

Curriculum Planning Cycle

"Whether the early childhood program uses a commercially published curriculum or develops its own, the **curriculum planning cycle** is an ongoing process that links with child assessment (Dodge and Bickhart, 2013)."

Early childhood programs are accountable for ensuring that children are making progress. State and national educational standards give us measurable, realistic targets. To achieve them, teachers must choose a curriculum with goals and objectives that are compatible with these requirements and that address all aspects of a child's development. A systematic approach to assessment that helps teachers learn about each child, plan experiences that support each and every child's development and learning, and ensure that all children are making progress is essential. Teachers who understand how to implement their program's chosen curriculum and how to use ongoing assessment to make decisions about instruction are more likely to achieve positive outcomes for children (Dodge and Bickhart, 2013, pp. 28–32). Following is a planning cycle that can be revised to meet the needs of a variety of settings.

Planning for Assessment
- Know the goals and objectives of your curriculum.
- Develop a systematic plan for observation, documentation, and organization of your notes.
- Create a portfolio for each child.

Collecting Facts
- Observe children with curriculum objectives in mind.
- Document what you see and hear.
- Collect and date samples of children's work over time for portfolios.

Analyzing and Evaluating Facts
- Sort observation notes by developmental area for each child.
- Label each note and work sample with the number of each objective that applies to the observation.
- Review observation notes and portfolio items.
- Identify each child's progress in meeting the curriculum objectives.
- Enter information on an individual record that tracks each child's progress.

Planning for Each Child
- Summarize each child's progress on a reporting form.
- Meet with families to share information and jointly plan next steps.
- Implement your plan and continue to observe the child's progress.

Planning for the Group
- Reflect on the progress of your group.
- Decide which objectives to focus on for the whole group and for selected children.
- Plan strategies to support children's learning, including whole group and small group activities.
- Implement your plan and continue to observe children's progress.

curriculum planning cycle: an ongoing process that links with child assessment.

Reporting on Children's Progress

- Generate reports as needed.
- Identify aspects of the program that need strengthening and develop a program improvement plan.

(Revised from Dodge and Bickhart's 2013 recommendations to Head Start for planning curriculum.)

Examples of Curriculum Models and Programs

> "A curriculum model is a structure or organizational framework that is used to make decisions about everything from policies and priorities to teaching methods and assessment procedures (Crosser, 2005, p. 125)."

As a teacher of young children, you will find many early childhood curriculum models and theories available. It is important to identify curriculum approaches and resources that are based on the developmental and cultural needs and interests of the children in your classroom. Curriculum models are helpful to point out guidelines for planning and organizing experiences. However, keep in mind that no single model addresses all the developmental and cultural priorities, such as anti-bias, inclusion, emergent curriculum, and the project approach.

The following is an overview of curriculum model examples that were chosen because they continue to be identified by the early childhood profession, have been implemented in multiple locations, and contain an extensive literature, including content and structure, educational objectives, and assessment procedures. As teachers, we should continue to investigate other models and programs as well, looking for additional insights into early education curriculum.

Montessori (1870–1952)

Montessori programs are based on Dr. Maria Montessori's original ideas, materials, and methods, which were designed to meet the needs of impoverished children in Italy. The Montessori method is the second curriculum model created expressly for early education (Goffin and Watson, 2001). (The first model was created by Friedrich Froebel in Germany, who began the kindergarten, or "garden for children," in the mid-1800s.) In the United States today there exist wide variations and interpretations of the Montessori principles.

According to Dr. Montessori's philosophy, children learn best in a child-sized environment that is stimulating and inviting for their absorbent minds—an environment that offers beauty and order. The arrangement of the room offers low, open shelves holding many carefully arranged materials. Placed in that environment, the child may choose his or her own work—activities that have meaning and purpose for him or her. For example, to teach her students how to write, Montessori cut out large sandpaper letters and had the children trace them with their fingers and later with pencil or chalk. Soon, the 4-year-olds were able to write letters and then words by themselves. The Montessori classroom was one of the first to emphasize a warm and comfortable environment based on independent learning. "Many of [Montessori's] once radical ideas—including the notions that children learn through hands-on activity, that the preschool years are a time of critical brain development, and that parents should be partners in their children's education—are now accepted wisdom" (Gordon and Browne, 2016).

> "Montessori classrooms contain is an attitude of cooperation rather than competition in completing work. Children complete work independently and then check responses with the "control" material or ask other children for help. The teacher as the sole source of information in the room so the teacher's job is not to artificially "teach in" what the child lacks but rather to be a careful observer of each child's development (Gordon and Browne, 2016)."

After the child is introduced to the Montessori materials by a guide (teacher), he or she is free to use them whenever he or she likes, for as long as he or she wishes, undisturbed by others. The materials are self-correcting. If the child makes a mistake, he or she can see it for himself or herself, without the need for an adult to point out his or her errors. (See **Figure 3-1**.) Montessori materials are also didactic, designed to teach a specific lesson; focused on daily living practical tasks to promote self-help and environmental care skills; sensorial, planned to encourage children to learn through using their senses; and conceptual, or involving academic materials designed to develop the foundations of reading, writing, and math. Some examples of Montessori-type materials found in many early childhood classrooms today are:

> Puzzles—self-correcting
> Nesting or stacking cups, rings, or blocks—self-correcting
> Rough and smooth boards and fabrics—didactic and sensorial
> Containers and tops—self-correcting and practical life task
> Setting a table—practical life task
> Washing dishes—practical life task
> Sound or scent bottles—sensorial
> Sandpaper letters and numbers—sensorial and conceptual
> Measuring materials—conceptual

Figure 3-1 Self-correcting Montessori materials.

Head Start

Head Start programs are the largest publicly funded educational programs for infants and toddlers (Early Head Start) and preschool children. They include health and medical screening and treatment, required parent participation and involvement, and comprehensive services to families. "Today there are Head Start programs in every state and territory, in rural and urban sectors, on American Indian reservations, and in migrant areas" (Essa, 2011, p. 16).

From its inception in 1965, Head Start has sought to provide classroom-based and, most recently, home-based comprehensive developmental services for children from low-income families. Head Start's experience has shown that the needs of children vary from community to community and that to serve these needs most effectively, programs should be individualized, thus meeting the need of the community served and its ethnic and cultural characteristics (Head Start, 2014).

Developing a curriculum that continuously meets the needs of children is an important task for any Head Start program. The Head Start program performance standards define curriculum as a written plan that includes the following:

- Goals for children's development and learning
- Experiences through which they will achieve the goals
- Roles for staff and parents to help children achieve these goals
- Materials needed to support the implementation of a curriculum
- Support for children's first language while they acquire English
- Creation of a respectful and culturally sensitive environment

Head Start programs have a low child-to-staff ratio, with 10 percent of the enrollment in each state available for children with special needs. Head Start provides staff at all levels and in all program areas with training and opportunities, such as the Child Development Associate (CDA) credential, associate and bachelor's degrees in Early Childhood or Child Development, and related subjects at colleges and universities.

> ❝Many different programs have been developed and evaluated as part of Head Start. An essential part of every Head Start program is the involvement of parents in parent education, program planning, and operating activities. Head Start also addresses families' unmet needs (housing, job training, health care, emotional support, and family counseling) that may stand in the way of a child's full and healthy development. Much research in early childhood education has been undertaken in Head Start programs. Head Start has been beneficial not only to the millions of children who have attended programs but also to the profession of early childhood education (Brewer, 2001).❞

The original vision of Head Start has been improved and expanded for the new century as a model that challenges the effects of poverty and promotes physically and mentally healthy families. In 1994, Early Head Start was created to promote healthy prenatal outcomes, enhance the development of infants and toddlers, and encourage healthy family functioning while responding to the unique strengths and needs of each individual child and family. Head Start has created a highly comprehensive and detailed set of provisions for working with families.

Early Head Start fulfilled a growing need that developed during this same period. Research on brain development revealed how crucial the first years of a child's life are to healthy development, how the lack of infant and toddler care was desperately affecting most communities, and how welfare reform was creating new child care needs. As Early Head Start continues to serve diverse families across the United States, with both center-based and home-based support, it is strengthening developmentally appropriate and culturally sensitive services for infants and toddlers (Essa, 2011, p. 16; Head Start Bureau, 2005).

The U.S. Congress continues to address the ongoing needs and funding requirements of Head Start. As advocates for young children and their families, we should continuously stay abreast of new developments.

Bank Street

Founded in 1916 by Lucy Sprague Mitchell, this program continues to be an important model of early childhood education in the United States. Mitchell envisioned a new type of educational experience for all children, which essentially shifted the focus to child-centered learning, emphasizing individual children and how they learn. Now for nearly 100 years, Bank Street has utilized these ideas to influence the lives of children and the educational system.

Bank Street's developmental interaction method is dedicated to fostering all aspects of a child's development, the whole child, and not simply promoting specific learning. It also emphasizes the interaction between the child and the environment, as well as the interaction between the cognitive and affective areas of the child's development, thus underscoring that thinking and emotion are not separate but truly interactive.

Children are creators of meaning. They work to understand the world they inhabit. The creation of meaning is the central task of childhood; if this task is fostered by the adults who care for them, children will become learners for life (Bank Street School for Children, 2002). At Bank Street School for Children, teachers arrange the classroom environment into distinct learning centers such as math, science, art, dramatic play, blocks, group meetings, and music. These centers, along with a variety of materials and experiences, relate to the ages and interests of the children in the group to encourage integrating the curriculum, making choices, taking risks, and accepting help. The school provides numerous opportunities for children to experience democratic living. Schedule flexibility provides extended periods of time for children to explore the potential of materials, to become involved in expanding ideas and interests, to take a trip, and to work together. Teachers and children alike learn from and teach one another by building on shared experiences to develop meaningful relationships. This sharing extends to the families and communities.

The Bank Street approach is an open education approach. This refers to a program that provides a well-conceived environment that allows the children to better understand what they already know in depth rather than trying to teach the children many new concepts (Gordon and Browne, 2016).

High/Scope

Under the leadership of David Weikert, this educational approach began more than 30 years ago as an intervention program for low-income, at-risk children. The High/Scope Perry Preschool Study is a landmark long-term study of the effects of high-quality early care and education on low-income 3- and 4-year-olds that followed the children to 40-year-old adults (High/Scope, 2003). Today the High/Scope program serves a full range of children—infant, toddler, preschool, elementary, and early adolescent—adapting to the special needs and conditions of their group, their setting, and their community. The High/Scope program has been successfully implemented in both urban and rural settings in the United States and around the world.

Active learning, High/Scope's central principle for all age levels, emphasizes that children learn best through active experiences with people, materials, events, and ideas. Influenced by Jean Piaget and Lev Vygotsky's theories of cognition and social interaction, this cognitively oriented model assists children in constructing their own knowledge from meaningful experiences. Materials are organized in each activity area so that children can get them out easily and put them away independently. In this kind of environment, children naturally engage in key experiences—activities that foster developmentally important skills and abilities. (See **Figure 3-2.**)

A pioneer in conducting research and developing programs for young children, High/Scope implemented its first home visiting program for parents of infants more than 40 years ago. It continues to focus on the development and needs of infants, toddlers, and families, while creating infant and toddler key experiences for teachers of this young age group (High/Scope Educational Research Foundation, 2003).

Teachers in a High/Scope program give children a sense of control over the events of the day by planning a consistent routine that allows children to anticipate what happens next. Central to this curriculum is the daily plan-do-review sequence in which the children, with the help of teachers, make a plan, carry it out, and then recall and reflect on the results of their chosen activities.

Plan-do-review was developed to help play become more meaningful. Planning allows children to consider the what, where, when, how, and why of what they will be doing for the next time period. Doing means action, such as working with materials, interacting with other children, choosing, creating, and sharing, thus stimulating the children's thinking abilities through the application of skills to problem-solving tasks. Reviewing involves putting what one has done into words or pictures and sharing the representation with other children, teachers, or parents. Daily schedules provide for both large and small group interaction, a time for outside play, and time for the plan-do-review sequence of student-selected activities.

Figure 3-2   Children learn best through active experiences with people, materials, and ideas.

In addition to plan, do, review, the High/Scope approach emphasizes key experiences in which the children have plenty of time for active exploration in the classroom and accentuates the High/Scope *Child Observation Record* compiled from the daily recorded observations of the teacher. All of these are unique components of the High/Scope framework.

Reggio Emilia

Reggio Emilia, a small city in industrial northern Italy, established what is now called "the Reggio Emilia approach" shortly after World War II, when working parents helped to build new schools for their young children (New, 2000). Founded by Loris Malaguzzi, the early childhood schools of Reggio Emilia, Italy, have captured the attention of educators from all over the world. Inspired by John Dewey's progressive education movement, Vygotsky's belief in the connection between culture and development, and Piaget's theory of cognitive development, Malaguzzi developed his theory and philosophy of early childhood education from direct practice in schools for infants, toddlers, and preschoolers.

The teachers in Reggio Emilia are partners and collaborators in learning with the children and parents. The teachers become skilled observers of children to plan in response to the children. Each group of children is assigned co-teachers. There is no lead teacher or director of the school. A *pedigogista*, a person trained in early childhood education, meets with the teachers weekly. Every school has an *atelierista*, who is trained in the visual arts, working closely with teachers and children. The *hundred languages of children* is the term teachers use in referring to the process of children depicting their understanding through one of many

BOX 3-4:   Guiding Principles of the Reggio Emilia Approach

The following are some of the concepts of the Reggio Emilia Approach:

- The image of the child—the cornerstone of Reggio Emilia experiences conceptualizes an image of the child as competent, strong, inventive, and full of ideas with rights instead of needs.
- Environment as a third teacher—preparing an environment that acts as a third teacher carefully designed to facilitate the social constructions of understanding, and to document the life within the space.
- Relationships—seeing the importance of relationships physically in the way objects are displayed in the classroom; socially and emotionally in the interactions of the people in the environment; and intellectually in the approach to learning that is always seen in context and depends on co-construction of knowledge.
- Collaboration—working together at every level through collaboration among teachers, children and teachers, children and children, children and parents, and the larger community.
- Documentation—providing a verbal and visual trace of the children's experiences and work, and opportunities to revisit, reflect, and interpret.
- *Rrogettazione*—this difficult to translate Italian word means making flexible plans for the further investigation of ideas, and devising the means for carrying them out in collaboration with the children, parents, and, at times, the larger community.
- Provocation—listening closely to the children and devising a means for provoking further thought and action.
- One hundred languages of children—encouraging children to make symbolic representations of their ideas and providing them with many different kinds of media for representing those ideas.
- Transparency—creating transparency through the light that infuses every space and in the mirrors, light tables, and glass jars that catch and reflect the light around the classroom; and metaphorically in the openness to ideas and theories from other parts of the world, and in the availability of information for parents and visitors.

symbolic languages, including drawing, sculpture, dramatic play, and writing. Teachers and children work together to solve any problems that arise. Children stay with the same teacher and group of children for three years (Albrecht, 1996; Gandini, 1993; New, 2000).

In 1987, the NAEYC introduced the first presentation on Reggio Emilia at the annual conference. Since then, inspired by the exhibition "The Hundred Languages of Children" and supported by delegations of educators who have seen the city and its early childhood classrooms firsthand, U.S. interest in Reggio Emilia has grown at a remarkable pace (New, 2000). The Reggio Emilia approach is currently being adapted in early childhood classrooms throughout the United States, including many Head Start programs.

Bredekamp (1993, p. 13) concludes that "[t]he approach of Reggio Emilia educators is both old and new. Fundamentally, the principles of Reggio Emilia schools are congruent with the principles of developmentally appropriate practice as described by NAEYC, presumably because both sets of principles share some of the same philosophical origins." See **Box 3-4** for concepts of the Reggio Emilia approach. Throughout this book you will find suggestions for incorporating Reggio Emilia principles into the curriculum.

Multicultural or Anti-Bias Considerations

INTASC   naeyc   DAP   CEC DEC   HS

By 2050, Hispanic and African American children under age 5 will outnumber non-Hispanic whites in the United States. Spanish accounts for almost 80 percent of the non-English languages, but more than 460 languages are spoken by English language learners nationwide. The dramatic rise in ethnic and linguistic diversity in the United States means more and more children in kindergarten and other early childhood programs speak a language other than English as their first language (NAEYC, 2007).

You are, and will continue to be, an important person in the lives of these children. Your ability to understand and address their individual needs will help determine whether they have the knowledge and skills to succeed in school (Colbert, 2007). Each time you set up an appropriate, warm, supportive environment for young children, much of what you do is familiar to you. At the same time, if you are exploring new ways to encompass each child's uniqueness, you may find many things that are unfamiliar to you. Exploring gender, culture, race/ethnicity, and different-abledness offers opportunities to develop new insights about yourself and the children in your care. You may feel comfortable and uncomfortable at the same time. It is important to understand that exploring and implementing a multicultural/anti-bias curriculum becomes a continuous journey of growth and change. As a teacher of young children, you should take, as one of the first steps in your exploration of multicultural education, the task of discovering your own cultural uniqueness. By reflecting on the culture and race or ethnicity of your family, you learn about yourself and about the culture of others as well.

Exploring your feelings about individuals who differ from you culturally or racially or individuals with special needs or disabilities is another step in the anti-bias curriculum development process. Discovering and coming to terms with your own feelings and attitudes will help you when these children join your group. Thus, **anti-bias** is an attitude that actively challenges prejudice, stereotyping, and unfair treatment of an individual or group of individuals. The inclusion of all children, whether they are differently abled or not, is a supporting principle of the anti-bias rationale. Ask yourself the following questions and then evaluate yourself: Which of these issues have surfaced? What have I already accomplished? On what areas do I need to work?

- What differences among people or children make me feel uncomfortable?
- Do I have strong reactions to children from certain economic backgrounds, cultures, or races?
- How do I feel when children do not conform to my expectations about appropriate or acceptable behavior?
- Do I generally tend to prefer children of one sex?
- How do I react to families who have lifestyles that are different from my own, and do these reactions influence my relationships or feelings about their children?
- When have I experienced or witnessed bias in my life, and how did I respond?
- How did I become aware of the various aspects of my identity and culture?

The *Anti-Bias Curriculum*, developed by Derman-Sparks and the A.B.C. Task Force (1989), is a comprehensive curriculum that offers helpful guidelines, activities, and materials that create an early education environment rich in possibilities for valuing differences and similarities. "Through anti-bias curriculum, teachers enable every child to achieve the ultimate goal of early childhood education: the development of each child to her or his fullest potential" (Derman-Sparks and Edwards, 2010, p. 2).

It is imperative that we remember that the center of each child is his or her culture. We must be sensitive to and respectful of the cultural background of each family member. The home and the center or school should develop a partnership to enable children to make an easy transition from known to unknown. We must support and retain the language and culture of the family as we add the language and culture of the early education program to each child's experiences.

Many children today are bicultural and bilingual (see **Figure 3-3**). The number of multiracial babies born since the 1970s has increased more than 260 percent compared to a 15 percent increase of single-race babies. West (2001, p. 27) explains further, "Third culture children whose lives span two cultures, so-called for the third culture created within them, may hold two citizenships or hold citizenship in only one country but be born of parents representing two different races or ethnic groups." Increasing diversity means that as teachers and caregivers, we must become more observant of individual children.

Figure 3-3   At the center of each program is the child, and at the center of each child is culture.

anti-bias: An attitude that actively challenges prejudice, stereotyping, and unfair treatment of an individual or group of individuals.

As teachers we must also be aware that some cultures emphasize a child's relationship to his or her group with group problem solving, rather than independence, individualism, and competition. In addition, some cultures value learning by active participation, whereas others encourage learning by observing and listening.

> "A simple but sometimes problematic cultural difference involves personal space. In cultures where people are often in crowded groups, children may sit and stand very close, touch a lot, and bump up against each other. This behavior may feel aggressive to children who aren't used to so much closeness and may require some guidance from the teacher. … It takes real sensitivity on the part of teachers and providers to decide how to handle behavior that is acceptable to one child within his family but considered aggressive by other children or by a teacher (Gonzalez-Mena & Shareef, 2005, p. 34)."

Therefore, we must give young children time to develop independence and accept responsibility within their own cultural framework. As teachers we should recognize our own defensiveness, continue to work on understanding, appreciating, and respecting differences, and developing patience with ourselves and the children. "The diversity of life is astounding, and the world is more complex than ever before. Our children will experience more new ideas, people, and change than any other generation in history" (Perry, 2002, p. 47).

Culture Is Learned

No one is born acculturated. You must learn the beliefs of your culture. Anthropologists and educators consider culture to be something that is learned and transmitted from generation to generation. Another dimension is the concept that culture is something that members of a group share in common. You are born to a group with rules. However, groups borrow and share with other groups. As a result, culture is ever-changing rather than static and fixed.

> "Culture is a glass prism through which we look at life. Like a prism, culture has many facets. Early childhood educators need to be cognizant and aware of these various angles that help explain the behavior, reactions, and manners of children in the classroom (de Melendez and Beck, 2010)."

Culture, then, is the sum total of a child's or family's ways of living: values or beliefs, language, patterns of thinking, appearance, and behavior. It includes the set of rules that govern a family's behavior and that are passed or learned from one generation to the next. However, as we learn about cultures other than our own, we should be careful not to assume that just because children or families are from a specific ethnic or racial group that they necessarily share a common cultural experience. Recognize differences within cultures and within families (Marshall, 2001).

A multicultural/anti-bias curriculum is one that actively challenges prejudice and stereotyping and represents an opportunity for the development of mutual respect, mutual sharing, and mutual understanding. It is crucial to establish an early education environment that enables children to make connections to their own reality as well as to the larger world, to develop positive self-esteem, and to receive approval, recognition, and success.

Irvine (2009) believes "[a] culturally relevant pedagogy builds on the premise that learning may differ across cultures and teachers can enhance students' success by acquiring knowledge of their cultural background and translating this knowledge into instructional practice." Therefore, as teachers we need to use the strengths that our children bring to the classroom—a rich language, a strong culture, and a remarkable history.

As you continue to study curriculum development in this book, you will understand how the anti-bias approach can flow through every element of the early childhood curriculum. Expanding learning experiences to include others helps young children develop values, respect, and a cultural sense of belonging. Suggestions for integrating multicultural/anti-bias content and materials into specific curriculum areas can be found in Chapters 5 through 13. (See **Box 3-5**.)

culture: The sum total of a child's or family's ways of living: their values or beliefs, language, patterns of thinking, appearance, and behavior. These are passed or learned from one generation to the next.

BOX 3-5: Guidelines for a Multicultural Anti-Bias Environment

The following guidelines can help you provide a developmentally appropriate, multicultural/anti-bias environment for young children.

- Be sensitive to, and respectful of, each child's cultural learning style without stereotyping. Include content about ethnic groups in all areas of the curriculum.
- Use differences in language and culture as a foundation for learning. Identify staff members or other adults from the community to serve as role models to help develop language learning and cultural activities.
- Communicate with parents to clarify home and school values about socialization and children's cultural and racial identities.
- Involve parents in the planning and implementation of activities.
- Model acceptance and appreciation of all cultures.
- Adapt curriculum materials to make them more relevant to all your children, and offer accurate information about different cultural groups in contemporary society.
- Ensure that the environment contains abundant images that reflect diverse abilities and current racial, ethnic, gender, and economic diversity.
- Make the necessary instructional and environmental adaptations (when possible) to meet the needs of children with special needs.
- Discuss cultural, racial, physical, and language differences *and* similarities honestly with children. Children are aware of differences in color, language, gender, and physical ability at a very young age.
- Provide opportunities for children to reinforce and validate their own racial and ethnic identities. Help children develop pride in their language and in their skin, hair, and eye color. Place value on the uniqueness of each individual.
- Help children find alternative ways or words to deal with racism and racial stereotypes.
- Focus curriculum material about cultures on similarities *and* differences, such as food, clothing, shelters, celebrations, and music. Global awareness of similarities and differences builds understanding and respect.
- Provide opportunities to ask children questions about the activities/materials to assess their knowledge and help them to construct new knowledge. Allow time for children to practice changing perspectives.

Themes, Units, Projects, and Webs

INTASC **naeyc** **DAP** **HS**

You will find that the core of curriculum development is your capability, as a teacher of young children, to integrate the children's needs, interests, and abilities with your conceptual plan for implementing goals and objectives. As discussed previously in this chapter, emergent curriculum themes actually emerge from the interests of the children and adults in the program with no specific time frame for the learning to unfold (Essa, 2012; Jones and Nimmo, 1994). Themes, units, projects, and curriculum webs will aid you in developing a child-centered, emergent curriculum approach.

Themes and Units

Thematic curriculum is curriculum that focuses on one topic or theme at a time. This is a process for managing curriculum while achieving developmental appropriateness. Integrated curriculum is intertwined with the thematic approach and enables the teacher to tie in the observations, interests, and abilities of the children to major content areas of language and literacy, dramatic play, art, sensory play, music and movement, math, science, and social studies with curriculum direction and expansion initiated by the children.

Many educators use the terms *theme* and *unit* interchangeably. This book presents a **theme** as a broad concept or topic, such as "Magnificent Me," "Seasons," "My Community," "Friendship," and "The Environment." This approach can be used to introduce children to activities that require active exploration, problem solving, and acquisition of a specific concept or skill. A **unit** is a section of the curriculum that you determine to be important for the

theme: A broad concept or topic that enables the development of a lesson plan and the activities that fit within this curriculum plan.

unit: A section of the curriculum based on the unifying theme around which activities are planned.

children to know more about and is based on the unifying theme around which activities are planned. This is often offered as an activity planned for a particular learning center.

Developing a list of themes is usually the first phase. This is useful as you move toward developing a lesson plan and the activities that fit within this plan. Remember to remain flexible and responsive to the children, including being adaptable to the varying developmental stages, special needs, and experiences within the group. Your theme planning should merge play with child-directed and teacher-initiated experiences.

Here are some examples of themes that have proven to be favorites. These can be modified to fit any age group:

- Magnificent Me
- My Family and Me
- My Community
- Families
- Friendship
- Caring and Sharing
- The Seasons
- Weather
- My Five Senses
- Colors and Shapes in Our World
- Textures
- Things That Grow
- The Environment
- Plants and Gardening
- Animals
- Pets
- Cars, Trucks, and Buses
- Airplanes, Trains, and Tracks

Basic Concepts for Developing Thematic Curriculum

1. Themes and activities should reflect the philosophy suggested by the (NAEYC for developmentally appropriate practice (DAP) in Early Childhood Programs, such as: the critical role of teachers in understanding and supporting children's development and learning; the concept of classrooms or groups of children as communities of learners; the importance of each child in the group; and the significant role of families in early childhood education.
2. Themes and activities should take into consideration the age, stage of development, and experiences of young children.
3. Themes and activities should emphasize and integrate different aspects of development and learning.
4. Themes and activities should be developmentally appropriate and underscore the importance of individual differences and cultural and linguistic diversity among young children. This allows children to learn at their own pace and style.
5. Themes and activities should encourage the development of positive self-esteem and a sense of "I can do it" in young children.
6. Activities should be easily adaptable to large group, small group, or individual instruction.

See Appendix A for an example of an integrated curriculum theme with activities: *My Self*.

Projects

A **project** is an in-depth investigation of a topic worth learning more about. This is usually undertaken by a small group of children within a class, sometimes by an entire class, or individually by an older child. This approach involves children applying skills, asking questions, making decisions and choices, and assuming responsibility. Projects may last for a few days or for extended periods of time. The less first-hand experience children have in relation to

project: An in-depth investigation of a topic.

the topic, the more dependent they become on the teacher for the questions, ideas, hypotheses, information and so forth that constitute the essence of good project work.

Some examples of project work include drawing, interviewing experts, reading, recording observations, and writing. The information gathered by the child is then summarized and represented in the form of charts, diagrams, drawings, graphs, models, murals, paintings and other constructions and reports to peers and parents. In the early years, an important component of a project was dramatic play in which new understanding was expressed and new vocabulary was used.

The first phase in beginning the project process is to choose a topic, such as pets, cars, flowers, or the grocery store. Sometimes children have ideas for a topic, and sometimes a teacher chooses a theme based on the children's experiences (Gandini, 1993). The teacher uses these personal experiences and recollections to review their actual knowledge of the topic. The teacher can also develop a topic web as a visual approach to the project. This web can also provide assistance for documenting the progress of the project. The topic should allow the integration of a range of subject areas, including social studies, science, and language arts, as well as literacy and math skills.

Chard (2001, http://www.projectapproach.com) suggests the following criteria be used "to discriminate among different possible topics of study that depend on how children learn best, the basic social values we expect children to live by, and what we understand the role of the school to be in educating children." These criteria can be expressed in the form of questions about the value of studying any given topic. For example, how can study of this topic:

- Build on what children already know?
- Help children to make better sense of the world they live in?
- Help children to understand one another better?
- Enable children to understand the value of literacy and numeracy in real-life contexts?
- Encourage children to seek sources of information outside school?
- Facilitate communication with parents? (Chard, 2001.)

Progressing to the second phase involves gaining new information, especially by means of firsthand, direct, real-world experience. The children develop and expand the topic by their investigation and exploration of objects or events of the project while collecting data, making observations on field trips, making models, and using Internet resources.

In the third phase of the project process, as interest reaches its maximum point, end the project by reviewing what you and the children have learned and participate in a culminating group activity. Throughout the project process, families act as partners in the children's learning. With you as their guide, everyone takes part in an exciting exploration together.

Helm and Katz's (2010, p. 3) use of the project approach explores how early childhood professionals can apply project work to meet the challenges they encounter in their classrooms. They offer these comments:

- Projects provide contexts in which children's curiosity can be expressed purposefully, and that enable them to experience the joy of self-motivated learning.
- Teachers and children embark on these learning adventures together.
- Parents also become involved and interested in the children's projects.
- The use of technology by teachers and children during the project is beneficial.
- Projects are helpful to children who are learning English and native-English-speaking children who are learning second languages. Children get meaning from hands-on experiences, demonstrations, and role-playing, as well as from language.
- Projects can be done in classrooms where children have special needs, both in self-contained classrooms and others with full inclusion. Teachers determine interests through observation, encourage verbalization from children who are not verbal, and support children by offering a multitude of ways to investigate.

Finally, Chard (2001) extends our understanding of the project approach further:

" The inclusion of project work in the curriculum for young children addresses the four major learning goals of all education: the construction and acquisition of worthwhile knowledge; development of a wide variety of basic intellectual, academic, motor, and social skills; strengthening of desirable dispositions [organizational skills]; and engendering of positive feelings about self as a learner and participant in group endeavors. **"**

Webs

A **curriculum web** integrates various learning activities. This visual process offers flexibility for you and the children. You can move in different directions, design learning activities that integrate various curriculum areas in special ways, and extend the thematic planning or project chosen. "Webbing" helps develop the scope and content of the theme.

To produce a thematic web, you have the choice of brainstorming a single idea or topic by yourself, with a colleague, or with the children. Then record the ideas in an expanding web. This becomes a visual illustration of what could be included in a theme or unit or project approach to the curriculum. You can then put the elements of the web into planned daily activities, with the children actively investigating, initiating, questioning, and creating. For an infant, toddler, or child with special needs, have the individual child be the center of the theme (web) to plan activities for that child.

Buell and Sutton (2008, p. 100) explain their approach to emergent curriculum planning for young preschoolers by using the child-centered webbing:

- Write each child's name in the center of a separate sheet of paper.
- Circle each child's name.
- Observe each child during play.
- Record interests observed on the right side of each child's web.
- Record developmental needs observed on the left side of each child's web.

Then, review each child's interests and create activities for the children that focus on the identified needs and goals.

To make the program inclusive, Buell and Sutton found this child-centered approach meets the Individualized Education Plan (IEP) and the Individualized Family Services Plan (IFSP) goals.

Figure 3-4 is an example of a curriculum-planning web.

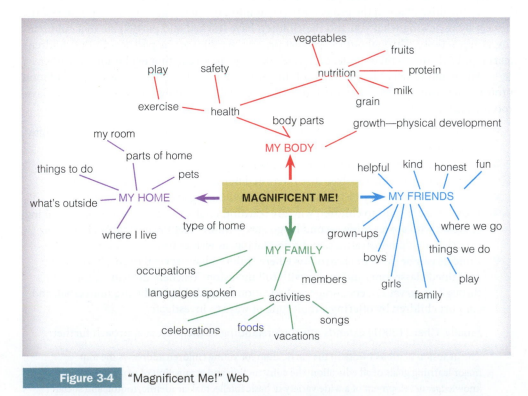

curriculum web: A visual illustration or process that integrates various learning activities and curriculum areas.

Figure 3-4   "Magnificent Me!" Web

Use of Technology in Curriculum Development and Instruction

Curricula frequently use computers and traditional software to deliver content to children. More cutting-edge curricula feature web-based materials in the form of software that is an online service. Instructional tools are intended to assist practitioners with direct instruction, often with the ability to engage multiple children at once. Examples of instructional tools include interactive whiteboards and multi-touch tables. Teachers can use interactive whiteboards to involve children in interactive lessons provided by curriculum developers. They can also use whiteboard software to develop their own lessons. The touch-activated nature of interactive whiteboards and multi-touch tables are particularly engaging for young children (Hernandez, et al., 2015).

Additionally, tablets are being used more frequently in classrooms. In a study conducted by Northwestern University's Center on Media and Human Development in collaboration with the Fred Rogers Center and the National Association for the Education of Young Children (NAEYC), teachers reported having significantly greater access to tablets in the classroom in 2014 (55 percent) compared to 2012 (29 percent), and interactive whiteboards (26 percent versus 22 percent). Access decreased for televisions and DVDs (71 percent from 80 percent) and digital cameras (88 percent from 92 percent), which is likely a sign that tablets are replacing those technologies (Wartella, 2015).

"A model of good practice for using technology in planning and implementing curriculum is outlined by the five e-words coined by Martin Blows, a consultant and formerly a director of online learning at the U.K.'s National College for School Leadership:"

- Exchange: swapping traditional ways of doing things with ICT (technology)
- Enrich: engaging learners with a richer mix of media
- Enhance: encouraging deeper learning through the use of ICT
- Extend: encouraging students to take their learning further
- Empower: giving students control over their own learning

It is not the technology itself that is important, it is how it is used. And this requires investment not just in equipment but in giving teachers the confidence and competence to exploit it.

And it also requires rethinking the way we teach if we are to make the most of the opportunities presented by technology (Morrison, 2014).

Lesson Plans

The **lesson plan** is an outgrowth of theme selection, brainstorming or webbing, and selection of projects and activities. This involves making a series of choices based on the developmental stages, learning styles, and interests of the children; the goals and objectives of the program; and the availability of materials, supplies, and resources.

As you plan for the weekly, biweekly, or monthly period, think about the following:

- A classroom that is well planned, attractive, and organized provides an environment that facilitates learning and becomes a part of the learning program itself.
- It is helpful to schedule a specific teacher planning time during each week. This allows you time to reflect on your observations of the children, what is working, what needs to be changed, and what additional materials and supplies are needed.
- It is helpful to develop a planning form, such as a written lesson plan worksheet. This will clarify your thinking and aid you in articulating your rationale for what you plan to do. It can also be posted for parents, teacher-assistants, and substitute teachers to see and refer to. (See **Figures** 3-5, 3-6, and 3-7 for lesson plans of infants, toddlers,

lesson plan: An outgrowth of theme selection, brainstorming/ webbing, and selection of projects and activities. Involves making a series of choices based on the developmental stages, learning styles, and interests of the children; the goals and objectives of the program; and the availability of materials, supplies, and resources.

SAMPLE **INFANT LESSON PLAN** (12-18 Months)

TEACHER(S):   DATES: THEME: Magnificent Me!

CENTERS & ACTIVITIES	MONDAY	TUESDAY	WEDNESDAY	THURSDAY	FRIDAY
SENSORY: ART, MUSIC, TACTILE ACTIVITIES	Scribble with multicultural crayons. Make banana/raisin snack.	Sing "Name Song." Use large soft blocks.	Sing "If You're Happy and You Know it" with jingle bells.	Watch or chase bubbles floating to music. Play with play dough.	Cover table with white sheet & use non-toxic markers.
COGNITIVE & LANGUAGE ACTIVITIES	Sing "I Have Two Ears" and read **Yellow Ball.**	Show and talk about family pictures. Read **My Family**	Play "Pat-a-Cake" with jingle bells. Read the book **Pat-a-Cake**	Play "Peek-A-Boo" and read the book **Peek-A-Boo.**	Play "Where's ____? There s/he is!"
SMALL MUSCLE & LARGE MUSCLE ACTIVITIES	Push & pull toys	Roll ball back & forth, crawl on soft rug	Drop (wooden) clothespins into a container one at a time	Crawl up soft foam incline	Stack bean bags
SELF-AWARENESS, SELF-HELP ACTIVITIES	Make faces into a mirror	Play Peek-A-Boo in mirror	"Jack Frost," fingerplay naming parts of body	Sing "Rock-a-Bye Baby" with soft babydolls.	"This is the Way We Wash Our Hands"
SPECIAL ACTIVITIES	Take stroller walk	Play on a quilt outdoors	Hang wind chimes near window or vent and listen to them.	Sing or chant "Roll the ball to ____. Roll it back to me.	Visit from grandparents (if possible)
BOOKS OF THE WEEK	**Peek-a-Boo** (Ahlberg), **Pat-a-Cake** (Kemp), **Yellow Ball** (Bang), **I Hear** (Isadora), **I See** (Isadora), **I Touch** (Oxenbury), **My Family** (Ostarch), **Baby Says** (Steptoe)				
SPECIAL NOTES	Dramatic play with soft multicultural baby dolls and blankets. Multicultural music and song tapes.				

Figure 3-5   Infant Lesson Plan Worksheet.

SAMPLE **TODDLER LESSON PLAN**

TEACHER(S):

DATES: THEME: Magnificent Me!

CONCEPTS: I am special & wonderful! I'm learning to do many things. **SKILLS:** Self-Help, Language, Social

DAY	LARGE GROUP ACTIVITIES	SMALL GROUP ACTIVITIES
MONDAY	Sing "I'm a Special Person and So Are You"	Practice dressing with dress-up clothes
TUESDAY	Read **A Baby Just Like Me** while sitting on a cozy quilt	Bathe baby dolls in warm soapy water (use no-tear baby shampoo), pat dry
WEDNESDAY	Read **My Feet** Wiggle toes together	Take off and sort shoes, then put your own back on
THURSDAY	Read **Caps For Sale** while wearing caps from dramatic play	Add caps to the pile of shoes, sort, put on, then look in the mirror
FRIDAY	Read together "Una Casita Roja (A Little Red House)"	Use small, unbreakable hand mirror "_____, _____,who do you see?"

SENSORY ACTIVITIES
Sand box toys
Colored water in water table
Play dough in various skin colors

DRAMATIC PLAY / HOME LIVING & PUPPETS
Play kitchen with dishes, aprons, dress-up clothes include hats, full-length mirror, family puppets

MOVEMENT / OUTDOOR ACTIVITIES
Chase bubbles
Push and pull toys, trikes
Climbing structure

MUSIC ACTIVITIES
Sing "Rock-a-Bye Baby" to dolls
Sing "If You're Happy & You Know It..."
Listen to multicultural music & dance.

SELF-AWARENESS, SELF-ESTEEM, SELF-HELP ACTIVITIES
Dress self, put on shoes and caps
Serve and pour at meals

SMALL MUSCLE / MANIPULATIVE ACTIVITIES
Cut & tear paper in tactile table
Puzzles of babies & families
Small figures & doll house

ART ACTIVITIES
Scribble on sheet-covered table
Put torn paper on sticky-backed paper
Foot & hand prints with paint

LANGUAGE ACTIVITIES
"Humpty Dumpty" finger play
Discuss torn paper: color, feel, sizes
Flannel board 'Una Casita Roja'

TRANSITIONS
"If your name is _____, then go to _____, (the door, etc.)"
"Name Song"

BOOKS OF THE WEEK:
Here Are My Hands. To Baby With Love, Making Friends, Where's the Baby? On Mother's Lap, The Napping House

ACTIVITIES / NOTES:
Take a walk in the neighborhood
Visit from grandparents (if possible)
Cut up apples and eat.

Figure 3-6 Toddler Lesson Plan Worksheet.

SAMPLE **PRESCHOOL LESSON PLAN**

TEACHER(S):

DATES: **THEME:** Magnificent Me!

CONCEPTS: I am unique, special, and part of a family

SKILLS: Prewriting, writing, measuring, graphing, problem-solving, and-awareness of similarities/differences

CENTERS & ACTIVITIES	MONDAY	TUESDAY	WEDNESDAY	THURSDAY	FRIDAY
MORNING GROUP ACTIVITY	Sing "Good Morning." Introduce "My Body."	Take individual instant photos. Introduce "My friends."	Read **On the Day You Were Born.** Introduce "My Family."	Make breadsticks formed initials. Introduce "My Home."	Healthy snack chart: finish & discuss.
AFTERNOON GROUP ACTIVITY	Identify body parts and what they do.	Animal friends: share stuffed animals and/or pets	Chart birthdays of the children and family members.	Read **How My Parents Learned to Eat.**	Bring and share something about yourself.
LANGUAGE & LITERACY	Begin "All About Me" books.	Write about photo and put into "Me" book with photo.	Add family photo to book. Write or draw about photo.	Write class story about field trip experience.	Finish "All About Me" books and share. Finish class story.
ART	Make life-sized self-portraits.	Make thumbprint and footprint pictures.	Make puppet papercup family pop-ups.	Make kitchen gadget puppets.	Mix playdough to match skin color.
MUSIC & MOVEMENT	"Name Song" Body parts move to music.	Sing "I'm A Special Person and So Are You" and "Friends Go Marching."	Beanbag toss and Kitchen marching band	Sing "So Many Ways to Say Good Morning" and dance.	Dance in hats with streamers to music.
DRAMATIC PLAY HOME LIVING	Home living center with a full mirror and baby pictures of children.	Add phones, paper, and pencils for message-taking.	Bathe baby dolls in warm sudsy water. Add stuffed animals to area.	Add a Wok and other cookware to center.	Add hats to dress-up clothes.
MATH MANIPULATIVE	Measure and record height of each child.	Graph the children's heights.	Use puzzles of family celebrations.	Gather items from home and play "What's missing?"	Estimate number of pennies in a jar, then count them.
SCIENCE & DISCOVERY	Listen to heart with stethoscope. Examine picture or model of skeleton.	Magnifying glasses to see thumbprints. Exploring shadows.	Food colors, eye droppers, and ice trays	Weigh on scales for "Me" book. "What's That Sound?"	Magnets and what sinks, what floats?

BLOCKS
Add: people figures, animal figures, boxes, houses, cars

SENSORY CENTERS
Water table with warm, soapy water
Multicultural skin colored playdough.
Healthy snacks "Tasting Tray"

SOCIAL STUDIES
Invite family members to visit.
Field Trip to grocery store.
We are all alike. We are all different.

OUTDOOR/LARGE MUSCLE
Nature walk: obstacle course on playground
Hop, run, skip, jump

TRANSITIONS
Puppet helper of the day
Variations on "Name Song"

BOOKS OF THE WEEK
My Five Senses, Big Friend, Little Friend, Mommy's Office, William's Doll

SPECIAL ACTIVITIES & NOTES
Week-long project: Field trip to grocery store. Children decide which healthy snacks to buy. Explain decisions. Make chart or diagram re: food groups. Prepare and eat snacks. Write class story.

Figure 3-7   Preschool/Kindergarten Lesson Plan Worksheet.

and preschool/kindergarten children.) The activities included in these plans are in Chapters 5 to 13. Blank lesson plan worksheets can be found online on this text's premium website, along with additional lesson plans and in Appendix D. There are also examples of lesson plans for individual children. For weekly planning in the first through third grades, teachers usually use the forms provided by the school district. Generally, the morning focus is on math and the afternoon is on science, reading, and social studies.

- The lesson plan allows for planning the emergent curriculum theme or unit, concepts to be explored, skills to be developed, individual activities, and large or small group activity times to be created, integration of the learning centers and curriculum areas, and preparation for special activities or field trips. (See **Figure 3-7**.)

- It is helpful for you to develop a "things to remember" form for writing down items or materials to prepare or gather before the children arrive. It also allows you to write down ideas that come to mind to be used at another time. You will find that many new or remembered ideas come to mind during this special planning time.

- Remember to plan for "a rainy day." Unexpected events, such as bad weather, can require you to have on hand materials and supplies for new activities to be implemented at a moment's notice. A new puppet, a book, a game, a flannel board story, a song, and an art activity are examples of items you can put in a special box to use for such an occasion (see **Figure 3-8**).

- As you plan, develop a checklist for yourself that includes the following questions:

  1. What do the children already know? How can I build on that? What have they thought of?
  2. Is the theme or activity appropriate for the age and stage of development of the children?
  3. Are the selections too general or too broad?
  4. Are there too many or too few activities?
  5. Are multicultural and anti-bias activities included?
  6. Is the lesson plan flexible enough to allow for unexpected events or spontaneous moments?
  7. Is there a wide selection of books, songs, finger plays, and so on?
  8. Are the units of instruction open-ended, allowing for exploration and learning opportunities to occur?

As the children learn at their own pace about the world around them, they are organizing, manipulating, experimenting, communicating, and trying out different roles. To help children initiate their activities, trust the value of play experiences and spontaneous moments. If all of this is happening in your early childhood environment, then independent thinking and creative responding will happen.

Using an activity plan format as you set up learning centers will help you clearly describe the activity, learning outcomes, concepts, skills, space, and materials needed; step-by-step procedure; guidance and limits for expected behavior; assessment strategies; and follow-up.

The presentation of an activity works on many levels. When teachers lead activities, present materials, and guide discussions, it makes an enormous difference in how children think and whether they use thought, feelings, expressions, or independent thinking. We hope each activity will encourage children to solve problems, complete a project, and develop an eagerness to learn more.

When writing measurable child learning outcomes for an activity, "Describe the precise quality of change in knowledge, behavior, attitude, or value that can be expected from the learner upon completion of the learning experiences" (Marotz, 2014, p. 296). For example, the child will be able to demonstrate math concepts such as one-to-one-correspondence, counting, and measuring. The key word in this objective is *demonstrate*. Child outcomes should align with relevant state standards.

Reflect On This

Why isn't this an appropriate objective for an activity plan? The child will learn to be empathetic.

Figure 3-8   The lesson plan offers opportunities for small group activity times.

Other examples of measurable terms can be found on Bloom's Taxonomy in **Box 3-6.**
The activity plan worksheet is a suggested format that can be used to help you plan activities. Multiple activity plan examples are included in Chapters 5 through 13 and can be found online at this text's premium website.

BOX 3-6:   Bloom's Taxonomy

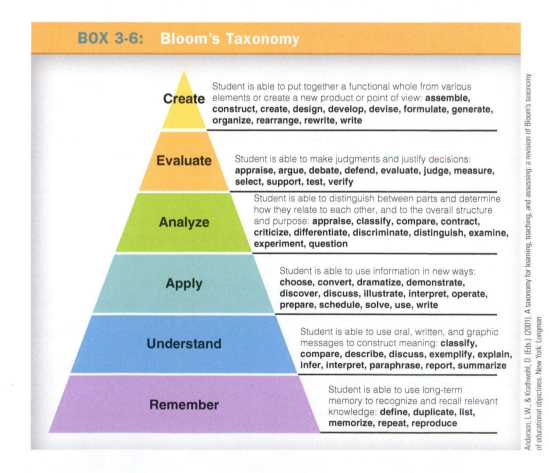

Create — Student is able to put together a functional whole from various elements or create a new product or point of view: **assemble, construct, create, design, develop, devise, formulate, generate, organize, rearrange, rewrite, write**

Evaluate — Student is able to make judgments and justify decisions: **appraise, argue, debate, defend, evaluate, judge, measure, select, support, test, verify**

Analyze — Student is able to distinguish between parts and determine how they relate to each other, and to the overall structure and purpose: **appraise, classify, compare, contract, criticize, differentiate, discriminate, distinguish, examine, experiment, question**

Apply — Student is able to use information in new ways: **choose, convert, dramatize, demonstrate, discover, discuss, illustrate, interpret, operate, prepare, schedule, solve, use, write**

Understand — Student is able to use oral, written, and graphic messages to construct meaning: **classify, compare, describe, discuss, exemplify, explain, infer, interpret, paraphrase, report, summarize**

Remember — Student is able to use long-term memory to recognize and recall relevant knowledge: **define, duplicate, list, memorize, repeat, reproduce**

Anderson, L.W., & Krathwohl, D. (Eds.). (2001). A taxonomy for learning, teaching, and assessing: a revision of Bloom's taxonomy of educational objectives. New York: Longman

Activity Plan Worksheet Template

Children's age group: _____

Number of children in this group: _____large group _____ small group

Learning center to be used: _____

Name of Activity and Brief Description

Child Outcomes for Activity

Concepts, skills, awareness, or attitudes you have designed the activity to teach or develop. Describe in measurable objectives. These should align with your state curriculum standards.

Space and Materials Needed

Procedure

Step-by-step description of the activity. Tips for getting started: describe what you will say or do to get the children interested in the activity, and let them know what they will be doing.

Describe the activity in the sequential order you will use with the children. Where will this activity take place? Plan for ending the activity. How will you help the children make a smooth transition to the next activity?

Guidance

Establish necessary limits for behavior and boundaries of activity. Anticipate problems that may develop during this activity and consider ways to handle them.

Assessment and Follow-Up Strategies

Were child outcomes met? _____Yes _____ No

What was the children's response? What worked well? What didn't work? How could this activity be changed to make it more effective or more appropriate? List possible activities that would extend or give practice to the objectives of this activity.

⌄⌄ Professional Resource Download

Summary

1. **What is involved in the process of curriculum development?** The children acquire the skills, concepts, and knowledge of the curriculum through rich and varied interaction with peers, teachers, and materials. As a teacher, you prepare and organize a developmentally, individually, and culturally appropriate curriculum plan and environment to provide children with a range of high-quality learning experiences. This is based on curricular goals and objectives, age-appropriate practices, children's interests and instructional needs, and appropriate observation, assessment, and evaluation.

2. **What are some multicultural/anti-bias considerations to consider in early care and education settings?** As we know, young children develop and learn in a variety of ways. As teachers we have the responsibility to understand the cultural influences and developmental characteristics of young children, to extend and support children's ideas and interests, and to provide appropriate learning activities and guidance techniques to meet their needs. Effective early education classrooms involve children in multisensory and multicultural experiences in a variety of settings, including independent activities, small group activities, and large group projects. Children are encouraged to talk about and share their experiences with their peers and adults.

3. **How is the development of curriculum based on themes, units, projects, and webs?** Themes, units, projects, and curriculum webs are tools that will aid you in developing a child-centered, emergent curriculum approach. A theme is a broad concept or topic around which active exploration, problem solving, and acquisition of a specific concept or skill can be planned, whereas a unit is a section of the curriculum that you determine to be important for the children to know more about and is based on the unifying theme around which activities are planned. A project is an in-depth investigation of a topic worth learning more about, usually undertaken by a small group of children within a class, sometimes by an entire class, or individually by an older child. This approach involves children applying skills, asking questions, making decisions and choices, and assuming responsibility. A curriculum web

integrates various learning activities. This becomes a visual illustration of what could be included in a theme or unit or project approach to the curriculum. You can then put the elements of the web into planned daily activities, with the children actively investigating, initiating, questioning, and creating.

4. **How can teachers develop lesson plans appropriate for children of different ages?**
A developmentally appropriate lesson plan should give children the opportunity to select activities from a variety of curricular experiences that are interesting and meaningful and allow the children to create situations using both the real world and their fantasy world to solve problems and express creative ideas. Activities should provide a balance of child initiated and teacher directed activities in small and large groups as well as in self-selected learning centers and outdoors. The selection of open-ended materials for these activities encourage children to freely explore, experiment, and create, while taking into account the age and individual ability of each and every child.

Reflective Review Questions

1. If curriculum is inclusive, integrated, emergent, child-centered, and child-directed, then what is your responsibility in planning curriculum? Explain your answer in a written format.
2. Many Americans take the position that this country is a *melting pot*, and that immigrants should quickly assimilate with the culture of the United States. Is this position consistent with a multicultural/anti-bias curriculum in an early childhood setting? Why or why not?
3. In a short paragraph, summarize the history and background of each curriculum model you were introduced to in this chapter, including significant individuals who were involved in the creation of the model. Can you identify some similarities and differences as you compare them? If you had a choice, which curriculum model would you choose?

Explorations

1. Research the Individuals with Disabilities Education Improvement Act of 2004. Study the IFSP and the IEP, which are requirements of this law. How would this information affect how you plan your curriculum?
2. Interview a teacher from one of the model program discussed in this chapter, such as Montessori or Head Start. Ask the teacher to describe the philosophy of the center or school and how he or she develops curriculum to meet the abilities, interests, and needs of the children in his or her class.
3. Keep a journal or notebook for one week on multicultural/anti-bias and inclusion activities you observed or culturally related activities that you personally experienced. List the date, event, and what you learned or experienced for each entry. Your listings can report your observations in an early education classroom; present a synopsis of articles you read in newspapers, magazines, or journals; or describe ethnic events you attended, new ethnic foods you ate, or a multicultural resource center or museum you visited in your community. Turn in your journal or notebook to your instructor, and discuss your findings with your classmates or colleagues.

The Learning Environment

Student Learning Outcomes

After studying this chapter, you should be able to:

- Plan the management of the learning centers, both indoors and outdoors.

- Evaluate the equipment, materials, and supplies needed for indoor and outdoor learning environments.

- Develop appropriate guidance techniques, including transitions.

Standards Covered in This Chapter

naeyc NAEYC 1c

DAP DAP 2

INTASC INTASC 3

HS HEAD START
Domain: Approaches to Learning

CEC DEC CEC DCC C1, C5, C6, C8

Early childhood environments are more than just the rooms where child learn, play, and are cared for. Attention has to be paid to the actual learning areas included that assist in play. Careful attention is also given to the contents of each area of the classroom both indoors and outdoors and the materials and supplies used to teach children.

The environment also includes how the adults guide the children individually and in groups and the transitions they use to maintain order as children move and explore.

Managing the Early Childhood Environment

naeyc   DAP   HS   INTASC

Arrangement of the Learning Environment

The indoor environment should invite you to "come on in." If you do not feel a positive welcoming, it is a signal that something probably needs changing. "It is important to remember, however, not to change everything at once. When making changes, think about what will appeal to you and the children and see where it takes you. Also think about the various areas and materials in the classroom and the type of behaviors and activities you wish to foster. If something is not functional or attractive, be brave enough to let it go" (Klein, 2007).

The classroom will be a "home" where children and teachers spend a large part of their day, so the environment should have homelike qualities. A homelike classroom is:

- Filled with images of children, families, and teachers.
- Includes living things such as plants and pets.
- Contains softness—rugs, soft furniture, pillows, curtains, and tablecloths.
- Provides richness of texture and color without being overwhelming.
- Contains beauty—artwork, flowers, order, and symmetry.
- Reflects the values and culture of the children, families, and teachers.
- Reflects the surrounding community (Bullard, 2014, p. 116).

Arranging appropriate indoor and outdoor areas in an early education program is significant to curriculum development. This is an extension of classroom management and part of a teacher's strategy to accomplish the learning goals and objectives. Organization of the outdoor environment, like the indoor classroom, should set limits with reasonable, appropriate rules that are consistently reinforced to promote appropriate behavior. Teachers and children spend many hours in the classroom and on the playground. The extra time you spend to organize, plan for the needs of the children, and plan effective and efficient use of space will aid you in creating a developmentally appropriate learning environment. (See **Figure 4-1**.)

Indoor Learning Environment

Many people see the environment as a tangible thing including equipment and materials and other items contained there. In fact, the environment is more intangible than tangible. It is the way it looks and the way it smells and sounds. It is not only whether it is warm or cold but also if it encourages us to stay and play or to pass through quickly. The environment is how a room feels in its entirety and sets the stage for a child's primary aesthetic experience.

Children need to feel that they belong. The environment should tell the children, "We care about you." For example, have a personal space or "cubby" for each child with his or her name or photo. In a shared space, each child needs to know there is one place that belongs to him or her. Display children's art, special projects, pictures, and bulletin boards at their eye level. These wall areas should be a visual extension of what is happening in the classroom. Ideas suggested by the children and their involvement in the final product should be part of the creative process of assembling the bulletin board. Reflect the interests of the children in all that you do.

Figure 4-1   Selection of appropriate materials and efficient use of space stimulates children's interest and learning.

Think about how you use color in the classroom. Try to express an anti-bias atmosphere. Primary colors and colors of the rainbow are used most often, but you should be sure to include brown and black as well. Many times we send a message that these colors are not aesthetically equal to other colors (Thomson, 1993). Children can get overloaded with too much use of color. Keep the background neutral or pastel and use color for accents and to focus children's attention on materials.

A characteristic of a responsive, organized classroom is the presence of a variety of well-defined **learning centers**, sometimes called interest centers, zones, clusters, or activity centers, where materials and supplies are combined around special groupings and common activities. These centers support children's learning and enable them to explore, experiment, and interact with the environment at their own rate of development.

Arranging and organizing the space for preschool, prekindergarten, kindergarten, and primary classes becomes more specific and complex. The following learning centers are suggested for early education classrooms and outdoor areas (many of these can be combined or expanded):

- Books, language, literacy, listening, and writing center
- Dramatic play, home living area, or puppet center
- Art center
- Sensory activities with water, sand, and mud play
- Blocks and woodworking
- Music and movement
- Science, discovery, cooking, and nature
- Math and manipulatives
- Social studies or multicultural
- Computers or technology center

When planning the arrangement of these centers in your classroom, think of your space as having four zones: dry, wet, active, and quiet. Combining these qualities can be an effective way to arrange learning centers. Think of the activities that take place in each center.

learning centers: Interest centers, zones, clusters, or activity centers where materials and supplies are combined.

Where would it fit best? Is it a learning center where active wet, messy play happens and perhaps water is needed, like the sensory table or art center? Is it a wet, but quieter learning center such as science that still might need access to water, but also might need natural light for plants or an electrical plug for a fish tank? Is it a quiet, dry learning center like the library, manipulative, or computer center? Finally, is it an active dry center like music, blocks, or dramatic play?

By grouping learning centers with like qualities together in the different zones of the room, children can play and work more easily without disrupting the play of others. In addition to these zones for centers, an entry area where children store their personal items in cubbies, lockers, or shelves allows for easier transitions in and out of the room. Although toddlers may not have as many centers as older children, the same zones can be used to arrange their space. Spaces for infants also have the same zones, but the materials included will be different. For example, the wet area would include diapering and feeding, the dry area would have play materials on low shelves, the quiet area would be rocking and sleeping, and the active area would be for crawling, climbing, and active play.

An additional factor to consider when designing your indoor space is having clear pathways that go from the front door of the classroom to different parts of the room. Avoid large, open spaces that invite children to engage in rough-and-tumble play or long "runways" that invite running. Many teachers use the block center, which should be large and enclosed on three sides, to accommodate several builders, as the place for circle time and other large-group activities. This allows the library area to remain small and cozy to invite reading and exploring books.

Learning centers involve hands-on experiences with a variety of materials. These materials and supplies have a direct correlation to a particular objective, theme, lesson plan, or concept being introduced. Well-planned, continuous introduction and rotation of new materials stimulates interest. The learning centers make possible individual and small group instruction while providing an opportunity for the children to make choices in many different areas.

The placement of the centers is important for balancing the number of noisy and quiet activities. How many of the areas are used at the same time depends on what is happening in relationship to schedule, routines, and lesson plans. Sometimes specific learning centers may be closed to allow for expansion of other centers, for reasons relating to guidance and discipline, or because the size of the room necessitates rotation of activities.

Also, the ages of the children and regulatory requirements will affect the numbers and types of learning centers available in an early education setting. Chapters 5 through 13 offer specific curriculum activities and a rationale for each learning center.

> "Children are sensory motor learners, so it is important to create environments where they can experiment and learn with their physical being as they move their bodies through classroom space (Duncan & Salcedo, 2015)."

The clearly arranged spaces and classroom design assist children in setting their own pace and making choices that will help them to be more self-directed, which, in turn, will improve their self-control. (See **Figures 4-2, 4-3,** and **4-4** for suggested room arrangements for infants, toddlers, and preschoolers/kindergarteners.)

For developmentally appropriate primary grade classrooms (grades one, two, and three), many of the components of the preschoolers/kindergartners are the same. Cubbies will become lockers, usually in the hallway, and the majority of the seating in the classroom should be tables or clustered desks. A teacher's desk may be used, but is best situated in a corner rather than being the center of attention. Learning centers may change but common ones for this age group are reading, writing, math, computer, social studies, and science. A project area with shelving, table and chairs, moveable whiteboard, and a smart board will allow the teacher to incorporate ongoing topics into the curriculum.

The environment tells children how to act and respond. Children are more likely to follow classroom rules when the environment reinforces these. For instance, if it is important for reasons of safety that children not run inside, classroom furnishings should be arranged in a way that makes walking, rather than running, natural (Essa, 2011; Isbell, 2007).

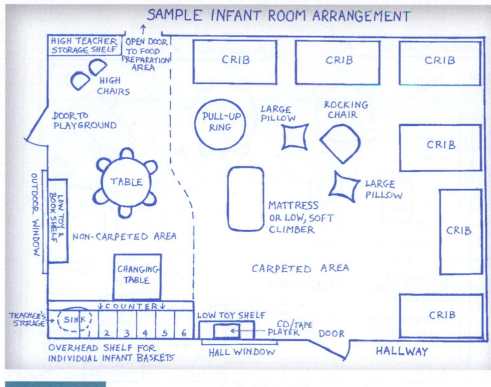

Figure 4-2 Room arrangement diagram for infants.

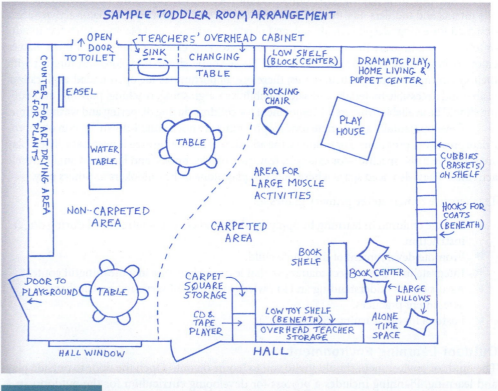

Figure 4-3 Room arrangement diagram for toddlers.

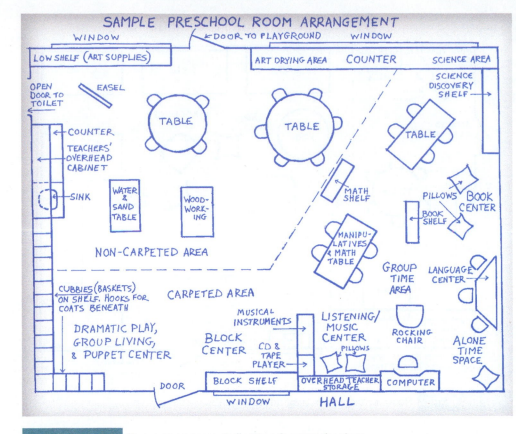

Figure 4-4   Room arrangement diagram for preschoolers.

Exploring their physical environment comprises a great deal of the curriculum for mobile infants and toddlers. For them, a safe and healthy environment offers major activity areas designed for eating, sleeping, diapering, and playing. Caring for and playing with a few infants or toddlers at a time are the focuses of these areas. Rocking chairs or gliders are a must. Babies enjoy rocking while being fed or comforted. These young children explore and interact with their environment through their senses; therefore, opportunities for open-ended exploration, visible and accessible materials, and safe possibilities for grasping, reaching, pushing, and pulling should be available. Mirrors add enjoyment for children during diapering and washing time.

Developmentally appropriate toddler programs are not a scaled-down version of appropriate preschool programs. For toddlers, the addition of a toileting area is necessary. Their play areas can be more specific—for example, featuring blocks, books, and large and small muscle activities. They also need space where they can play alone or be onlookers as others play.

Teachers use centers in the primary grades to:

- Engage children in learning by applying skills and concepts introduced during direct instruction.
- Promote development of the whole child.
- Integrate multiple subject matters so that learning happens in a meaningful context.
- Assess child's understanding and knowledge through observation and authentic assessment practices.
- Foster a love of learning (Stuber, 2007).

Outdoor Learning Environment

The outdoor environment should invite you to "come on out." Open the door to outside play and learning. Planning includes a process for developing curriculum for the outdoors in a way that parallels what teachers do indoors. Outdoor space should have zones that include areas for active physical play, nature exploration, gathering spaces, digging, sand, and water as well as dramatic play.

To be able to plan a varied and balanced outdoor environment, it is beneficial to being able to understand children's perceptual motor development, Incorporating outdoor activities into lesson plans and regularly alternating the outdoor environment are key strategies for enhancing skill development. Many outdoor activities can also encourage independence and socialization.

> "Simple experiences with nature can be very powerful opportunities for teaching and learning with very young children. Observing and talking about the many sensory aspects of nature—the sounds and smells of wind and rain, changing colors of the seasons, the tastes of fruits, vegetables, and herbs—inspire interest and appreciation of the beauty of nature (Torquati and Barber, 2005, p. 40)."

An outdoor space for infants can be as simple as placing a blanket or mat in an unused section of a larger playground, or it can be an area with appropriate infant-sized equipment. It is important that infants have access to the outdoors where they can experience the change in temperature, color, smell, sounds, and textures.

As a part of learning, children explore and test the environments, and so the playground, like the indoor classroom, must have limits. Fences, mandated by licensing requirements, set the parameters, and the teacher sets reasonable and appropriate rules that are consistently enforced. For example, "We sit on the slides and come down feet first."

Safety is the first priority. At least two adults should be supervising the playground at all times. McCracken (2000) advises, "Outdoor time requires adults who are playful, have sharp senses and quick reactions, and who will closely observe children. Save reading, resting, parent conferences, team meetings, and even casual conversations with other adults for more appropriate occasions. Your attentive eyes can prevent an injury." (See the safety checklist for indoor and outdoor environments in **Box 4-1**.)

BOX 4-1:   Indoor and Outdoor Areas Safety Checklists

Indoor Areas Safety Checklist

1. A minimum of 35 square feet of usable space is available per child.

2. Room temperature is between 68°F and 85°F (20°C and 29.4°C).

3. Rooms have good ventilation.

   a. Windows and doors have screens.

   b. Mechanical ventilation systems are in working order.

4. There are two exits in all rooms occupied by children.

5. Carpets and draperies are fire-retardant.

6. Rooms are well lighted.

7. Glass doors and low windows are constructed of safety glass.

8. Walls and floors of classrooms, bathrooms, and kitchen appear clean; floors are swept daily, bathroom fixtures are scrubbed at least every other day.

9. Tables and chairs are child sized.

10. Electrical outlets are covered with safety caps or safety plates.

11. Smoke detectors are located in appropriate places and are in working order.

12. Furniture, activities, and equipment are set up so that doorways and pathways are kept clear.

13. Play equipment and materials are stored in designated areas; they are inspected frequently and are safe for children's use.

14. Large pieces of equipment (e.g., lockers, piano, bookshelves) are firmly anchored to the floor or wall.

15. Cleaners, chemicals, and other poisonous substances are locked up.

16. If stairways are used:

   a. Handrail is placed at children's height.

   b. Stairs are free of toys and clutter.

BOX 4-1:   Indoor and Outdoor Areas Safety Checklists (continued)

c. Stairs are well lighted.

d. Stairs are covered with a nonslip surface.

17. Bathroom areas:

   a. Toilets and washbasins are in working order.

   b. One toilet and washbasin is available for every 10–12 children; potty chairs are provided for children in toilet training.

   c. Water temperature is no higher than 120°F (48.8°C).

   d. Powdered or liquid soap is used for handwashing.

   e. Individual or paper towels are used for each child.

   f. Diapering tables or mats are cleaned after each use.

18. At least one fire extinguisher is available and located in a convenient place; extinguisher is checked annually by fire-testing specialists.

19. Premises are free from rodents and/or undesirable insects.

20. Food preparation areas are maintained according to strict sanitary standards.

21. At least one individual on the premises is trained in emergency first aid and CPR; first aid supplies are readily available.

22. All medications are stored in a locked cabinet or box.

23. Fire and storm/disaster drills are conducted on a monthly basis.

24. Security measures (plans, vigilant staff, key pads, locked doors, video cameras) are in place to protect children from unauthorized visitors.

Outdoor Areas Safety Checklist

1. Play areas are located away from heavy traffic, loud noises, and sources of chemical contamination.

2. Play areas are located adjacent to premises or within safe walking distance.

3. Play areas are well drained.

4. Bathroom facilities and drinking fountain are easily accessible.

5. A variety of play surfaces (e.g., grass, concrete, sand) are available; there is a balance of sunny areas and shady areas.

6. Play equipment is in good condition (e.g., no broken or rusty parts, missing pieces, splinters, sharp edges, frayed rope).

7. Selection of play equipment is appropriate for children's ages.

8. Soft ground covers are present in sufficient amounts under large, climbing equipment; area is free of sharp debris.

9. Large pieces of equipment are stable and anchored in the ground

10. Equipment is placed sufficiently far apart to allow a smooth flow of traffic and adequate supervision.

11. Play areas are enclosed by a fence at least four feet high, with a gate and a workable lock for children's security and safety.

12. There are no poisonous plants, shrubs, or trees in the area.

13. Chemicals, insecticides, paints, and gasoline products are stored in a locked cabinet.

14. Grounds are maintained on a regular basis and are free of debris; grass is mowed; broken equipment is removed.

15. Wading or swimming pools are always supervised; water is drained when not in use.

⌄⌄ Professional Resource Download

Outdoor play is an essential part of the overall primary grade curriculum. Play reflects and enhances all areas of children's development, yet outdoor recess today is in jeopardy in many schools. Recess is increasingly viewed as the most useless of activities. Nonetheless, available research suggests that recess can play an essential role in the learning, social development, and health of elementary schoolchildren. Recess may be the only opportunity for some children to engage in social interactions with other children. According to Louv (2008, p. 35), "One U.S. researcher suggests a generation of children is not only being raised indoors, but is being confined to even smaller spaces. ... [T]hey spend more and more time in car seats, high chairs, and even baby seats for watching TV. When small children do go outside, they're often placed in containers—strollers—and pushed by walking or jogging parents."

As you continue to plan outdoor spaces for play and learning, think back to when you were a child. What were your favorite outdoor play settings? They probably included dirt, water, flowers, trees, places to be alone, places to climb, places to hide, places to build, and plenty of unstructured playing time with your friends. As teachers, we have the opportunity to give the children in our care these same activities in safe, creative, stimulating, and developmentally appropriate play environments. Chapter 12 also suggests other activities for outdoors.

Inclusive Environment

CEC DEC

Establishing an inclusive environment in an early childhood program should reflect and be sensitive to the cultural and linguistic diversity of all the children and their families. Each child, whether with special needs or not, should be viewed as an individual with unique characteristics, strengths, and needs. Materials should include dolls, pictures, books, block play, people figures, and other materials that represent a variety of cultures in a natural, realistic manner. Multicultural instruments and dramatic play cooking utensils also add depth of cultural understanding. Material should be labeled in the home languages of the children. Use a different color for each language consistently throughout the room, such as blue for English and red for Spanish.

For children with special needs, additional environmental conditions should be considered. Children are all children regardless of their abilities. Even though children have the same needs, the needs of many may be more pronounced. Here are some examples:

- *Create an environment for moving about safely.* An environment free from clutter, slippery floors, or rumpled rugs contributes to the safety and security of every child. For children with limited vision or physical problems, an environment free of obstacles protects against serious injury. (See **Figure 4-5**.)

Figure 4-5   Wide pathways help all children move comfortably around the classroom.

- *Minimize clutter and confusion.* This enhances the ability of all young children to concentrate on the tasks at hand. For children with attention or learning disorders, reducing distractions may be the best way to promote learning.
- *Be a teammate with families.* Do not try to work alone in educating their children. Together, you and the family can help their child reach his or her full potential.
- *See the whole child.* Do not fear or worry about having a child with special needs in your classroom, center, or school. See the child as a unique, complex individual; don't just focus on the hearing impairment, the cerebral palsy, or the autism. Remember, they are just kids (Ray, Pewitt-Kinder, and George, 2009).

Equipment, Materials, and Supplies

DAP

"Children are sensory motor learners, so it is important to create environments where they can experiment and learn with their physical being as they move their bodies through classroom space (Duncan & Salcedo, 2015)."

The selection of indoor equipment (furniture and other large and expensive equipment), materials (smaller items such as puzzles, books, toys), and supplies (consumables such as paint, paper, glue) should be developmentally appropriate for the children in each classroom. Items must be child-size, nontoxic, aesthetically appealing, sturdy with rounded corners and edges, easy to maintain, and not easily broken. Many activities can be done on the floor, so the floor covering must be "child-proof" and made of linoleum, tile, or carpeting that can take spills and hard wear. Tables can serve as art, manipulative, and eating places. Boys and girls need experiences with the same kinds and variety of learning materials. Soft toys, big and comfy pillows, and furnishings that fit the children's size, abilities, and interests should also be included.

Arrange the environment to allow children access to materials, supplies, and learning centers. Make sure children's play choices are clear, and they can see where to put up materials independently. Word and picture labels on containers and shelves, signs, and other kinds of print around the room offer visual guidance for children.

The Bank Street College of Education (1992) emphasizes the importance of including sensory materials in the selection for young children, especially toddlers. They use tactile materials and make it a full-body experience, as they will have shaving cream up to their arms or fingerpaints they use with their hands instead of brushes.

In the outdoor area, play structures are lower and wider for those young children who need time to climb up or down. The design should (1) offer novelty, variety, and challenge; (2) allow a wide range of movement; (3) stimulate the senses; and (4) be safe and comfortable. The selection of outdoor equipment and materials emphasizes safety, durability, and age appropriateness for all children. The outdoor space should contribute to physical, intellectual, creative, emotional, and social development and offer a variety of stimulation for play and exploration. The design should also offer ramps and tracks that accommodate wheelchairs and adapted vehicles, giving proper attention to slope, width, types of surface, and direct and safe accessibility to play and structures. The surfaces should offer various textures and colors, such as a hard-surfaced area for games and wheeled toys, a large soft grassy area with trees, a garden area, organic loose material such as play bark/wood chips and pine bark mulch, inorganic loose material such as sand and pea gravel, and rubber or foam mats.

The following are suggestions for equipment selection:

- Permanent climbers
- Take-apart climbers for older children to rearrange
- Sturdy wooden crates and barrels

- Tire swings with holes punched in several places for drainage (steel belted tires are not appropriate)
- Slides
- Balance beam
- Tricycles, wagons, and other wheeled toys
- Plastic hoops
- Balls of various sizes
- Mounted steering wheel
- Sturdy cardboard boxes
- Equipment and materials that eliminate head entrapment points

With recess in many public schools still being reduced or eliminated, it is more important than ever that we, as teachers of young children, plan additional activities outdoors. Also, sharing activity ideas with parents will help ensure that children get more opportunities to experience the world of nature. Louv (2008, p. 35) emphasizes why children *need* to spend time outdoors with access to nature:

" As the nature deficit grows, another emerging body of scientific evidence indicates that direct exposure to nature is essential for physical and emotional health. For example, new studies suggest that exposure to nature may reduce the symptoms of Attention Deficit Hyperactivity Disorder (ADHD) and that it can improve all children's cognitive abilities and resistance to negative stresses and depression. "

Learning Environment Checklist

_____ 1. Is the purpose of each learning center or interest area evident and well defined (furniture, walls, or rugs separates each area)?

_____ 2. Are boundaries between centers movable so they can be changed as needed?

_____ 3. Are activities that share common materials located adjacent to one another (e.g., blocks and dramatic play)?

_____ 4. Is furniture arranged to prevent long and wide-open spaces that encourage roughhousing and running?

_____ 5. Are learning areas arranged so that activities in one area do not interfere with activities in another (e.g., blocks located near the reading center)?

_____ 6. Are there places in the classroom for children to be alone?

_____ 7. Is the classroom furniture arranged so that all children can be observed or supervised from all vantage points in all areas of the classroom, including corners and cubbies?

_____ 8. Are all learning centers located near resources (e.g., CD player and cooking area near electrical outlets and art, water play, and cooking activities near a water source), or are provisions made for needed resources?

_____ 9. Is commercial display material limited to those relevant to a topic of study or an activity area (e.g., alphabet in writing center and book center and photos of bridges and building in the block center)?

_____ 10. Are nonstereotypic materials and displays used that reflect a range of roles, special needs, and the social or cultural contexts of the families in the classroom and beyond?

_____ 11. Does every child have a cubby or a safe place to store work and personal belongings that is labeled with the child's name and photograph?

_____ 12. Are materials stored on low shelves where children can take them out independently for play and return them when finished?

_____ 13. Are the centers large enough to accommodate the number of children and the activity occurring in each center?

_____ 14. Does the classroom have good lighting, softness, variety of textures, quiet, cozy spaces, homelike touches, and living things to make the classroom comfortable and attractive?

_____ 15. Are materials well maintained and in good condition?

_____ 16. Does the environment adapt space and modify materials to accommodate specific needs of children with disabilities and to make it possible for these children to be included in most activities?

_____ 17. Are materials labeled and identified where they belong by using pictures, photos, and written words?

_____ 18. Do traffic paths allow clear access to a door or fire escape?

_____ 19. Are traffic paths wide enough to accommodate a child in a wheelchair?

(continued)

Learning Environment Checklist (continued)

_____ **20.** Is the classroom inviting and aesthetically pleasing?

_____ **21.** Are transitions used to move children smoothly from one activity to another and in small groups as much as possible?

_____ **22.** Is there an abundance of materials so that children do not have to wait or get stymied in their attempts to create?

_____ **23.** Are there places in the room to gather comfortably as a group?

_____ **24.** Are transitions used as an opportunity to teach concepts and skills?

_____ **25.** Is there an abundance of opened-ended materials?

_____ **26.** Are materials developmentally appropriate, providing challenges but not being so difficult that children become frustrated?

_____ **27.** Do children know how to use the materials?

_____ **28.** Are there materials for a wide range of developmental levels?

_____ **29.** Is the entry space welcoming for parents, children, and staff?

_____ **30.** Are displays that consist primarily of children's original artwork and writing samples at the children's eye level on the walls or room dividers?

_____ **31.** Are photographs of children with their families displayed at the children's eye level in the classroom?

∨∨ Professional Resource Download

Managing the Environment with Appropriate Guidance Techniques

naeyc **DAP** **INTASC** **CEC DEC** **HS**

Management in early education, including infant and toddler programs, is a direct result of understanding child development, establishing a philosophy, determining goals and objectives, and applying appropriate guidance techniques. This includes the personal philosophy of the teacher and the overall philosophy of the early education program. Inclusion of both indoor and outdoor environments is involved. The **environment** represents all the conditions and surroundings affecting the children and adults in an early childhood setting. "The environment is the stage on which children play out the themes of childhood: their interests, triumphs, problems, and concerns" (Gordon and Browne, 2011, p. 158).

The arrangement of indoor and outdoor space requires planning for each individual child and group of children, understanding prior experiences and development of the children, and supporting the formation of trust, independence, and creativity in the children. If the children feel they belong and their needs are being met, appropriate behavior usually follows.

Set clear, consistent, and fair limits for classroom and playground behavior; guide younger children toward appropriate ways to relate to others and to function in a group environment; and help older children set their own limits. Setting limits means security for young children. It is appropriate to remind children of the rules and listen when they express their feelings and frustrations. The National Association for the Education of Young Children, in the brochure "Helping Children Learn Self-Control" (NAEYC brochure, 2000), suggests, "The rules should be kept simple, few in number, clear, truly necessary, and reasonable for the age of the child." Whenever possible, explain the reason for the rule. For example, "The water stays in the water table so the floor will not be wet. Someone could fall on the wet floor." Remember, too, that as a teacher, you should model good behavior. You must follow the rules you expect the children to follow.

Miller (2010) suggests that we can use the following guidelines to determine the appropriateness of children's day-to-day behaviors and help them learn the difference between right and wrong:

- Behavior must not infringe on the rights of others. (Be kind! Wait for your turn.)
- Behavior must not present a clear risk of harm to oneself or others. (Be safe! Go down the slide feet first.)

environment: All of the conditions and surroundings affecting the children and adults in an early childhood setting.

- Behavior must not unreasonably damage the environment, animals, objects, or materials in the environment. (Be neat! Put your paper towel in the trashcan.)

Many times children experience intense and dramatic emotions. A part of early education management is to help children deal effectively with the outward expression of their feelings. Help the individual child identify what he or she is feeling, place a limit on his or her behavior, and give the child an appropriate outlet for that feeling. For example, "I know you are angry with Jared, but I cannot let you hit him. You may hit the play dough instead." "Use your words to tell Maria how you feel."

Try to explain a child's behavior to another child. "I think Larry wants to play with you." "I think Stephen needs to play by himself for a while." Also, try to use suggestion or redirection rather than the word *don't*. It is helpful to say, "Sand stays in the sandbox!" rather than, "Don't throw the sand!" Tell children what you expect them to do in a positive manner. (See **Table 4-1**.)

Handle spills and mishaps as a natural part of a child's day. By saying, "Juanita, please get some paper towels to clean up the milk," and, "I'll help you clean that up," you preserve a child's self-concept while allowing him or her responsibility for his or her actions.

The following guidance techniques are additional suggestions to think about as we deal with challenging behaviors of children in our classrooms.

- Remember to address the behavior, not the child, when a behavior occurs that is not appropriate. Our goal should be to help guide the child from inappropriate behavior to appropriate behavior. Redirection, getting them interested in something else, is a nonthreatening way to achieve this.
- It is important to identify and stop bullying behavior immediately. Lipman (cited in Riley and Boyce, 2007; p. 3) explains that "[b]ullying is not an occasional unkind act. Bullying is distinguished by repeated acts of aggression and unequal power between bully and victim." Make sure the children in your class know that any type of bullying is never acceptable. Help the children learn to manage their own behavior; help

TABLE 4-1:	**Appropriate Verbal Guidance with Young Children**

Practice saying "DO," not "DON'T." Focus on the positive. Use clear, short, meaningful phrases that encourage and offer positive suggestions to the child.

Say This:	Instead of Saying:
"Thank you for sitting down when you slide."	"Don't stand up when you slide."
"Please keep the puzzle on the table."	"Don't dump the puzzle pieces on the floor."
"Please turn the book pages carefully."	"Don't tear the book!"
"Thank you for talking in a quiet voice."	"Don't shout!"
"Please wipe your brush on the side of the paint cup."	"Don't drip paint on the floor."
"It's time to go inside. I have something to show you."	"Shall we go inside?"
"You need to turn off the faucet after you wash your hands."	"Don't waste the water."
"Please give me the ball to hold while you're climbing."	"Don't climb with that ball."

them to learn how to cope with difficulties; and limit aggressive behavior firmly and consistently. Hanish (cited in Copple and Bredekamp, 2009, p. 122), said:

> "Children may use their improved cognitive and language skills as tools to intentionally hurt others' feelings. (*"You can't come to my birthday party," "Your hair is ugly."*) This relational bullying, as well as physical bullying, may be seen toward the end of the preschool years having potentially negative effects on both the bully and the bullied child."

- Teachers, parents, and child care providers quite often are trapped by the idea that if something does not work the first time, then it will never work. Children eventually change a behavior when they finally comprehend and remember that the action will quickly and consistently be stopped or redirected. As teachers, we should remind ourselves that for children to behave appropriately, there must be consistency in both our expectations and our applications of rules (Miller, 2013, p. 308).
- Shidler (2009, p. 88) reminds us to be mindful of what we intend to teach:

> "It is evident from my observations in more than 100 classrooms over the last 15 years that children's behaviors are influenced by their teacher's behavior and use of language. . . . When we choose how we will interact with children, we choose what we will teach them."

- Remember to communicate with parents. Teacher–family interaction creates a consistent and beneficial experience for young children. Our cultural values profoundly influence our perceptions about what guidance practices are most appropriate for children. Parents oftentimes assume that other parents naturally share the same underlying beliefs about how children should be disciplined (Miller, 2010). It is important that you, as the teacher, clarify what appropriate behavior is expected of the children in your care. If a child's behavior creates problems, open discussions between home and school are important.
- Model expected behavior and demonstrate self-control. Name feelings. Teach acceptable ways to express feelings. All of these actions can further show children how to be kind to and considerate of others.
- As a teacher, you need to develop a support system for yourself. Create a teaching team whose members can help each other when children have crises or long-term needs.
- Look for additional guidance suggestions throughout this book.

Setting limits, anticipating, and preparing for behavior difficulties are only part of a teacher's responsibility. Ensuring safety and preventing accidents in the environment for young children must also be considered at all times and in everything we do with and for young children. An integral part of every program should be health and safety. No matter the excuse, such as physical or curricular constraints, financial limits, or staffing, health should be a critical part of daily planning and program activity. Indoor and outdoor safety is essential for all children. Preparation and prevention are critical to child safety. When staff turn their full attention to implementing goals and objectives, the program has already addressed issues of safety, prevention of problems, and the meeting of needs.

Transitions

Transitions are activities or learning experiences that move children from one activity to another. They are both teaching and guidance techniques. A sensitive teacher determines in advance the transition times in the daily program so that the children avoid lining up or waiting their turn, and the change of pace will not be jarring or interruptive to them.

There will be times when transitions do not seem to be working. Think about why the children are engaging in some form of challenging behavior:

> "Challenging behavior is more likely to occur when there are too many transitions, when all the children transition at the same time in the same way, when transitions are too long, and when there are not clear instructions. . . . Perhaps it is the child's first experience in a group setting or the classroom rules and routines are different than at home (Hemmeter, Ostrosky, Artman, and Kinder, 2009, p. 18)."

transitions: Activities and learning experiences that move children from one activity to another.

Children need time to adjust to change; therefore, as a teacher you should use a transition activity to direct children from:

- A self-initiated to a teacher-directed activity
- An active to a quiet activity or from quiet to active play
- Cleanup and toileting to snack time
- Lunch to naptime
- Outside to inside or inside to outside play

In addition, for the younger child, transitions can be used to help them adjust to arriving and then separating from mommy or daddy, learning to listen, sitting down, and joining in a small group activity for a brief time. For older children, transition activities can be used for getting attention, giving directions, gathering the group, and helping them understand the sequence of events or when events change without warning.

When the children get used to the schedule and routines of the day, the number of transitions used can be reduced. Children who are free to choose their play and activities will develop their own natural transitions as their interests and curiosity direct.

Transition Activities

- Use a CD, or sing a song such as "The Hokey Pokey," in which children can join the group as they finish with cleanup.
- Provide opportunities for supporting social skills and emotional competencies. Encourage children to work together. ("Look at all of you cleaning up!" "Cambria, can you help Rachel get her coat on?")
- After group time, ask all children who are wearing red to stand up. Continue calling various colors until all the children are standing. Then give directions for the next activity.
- Prepare a set of flannel circles with each child's name on one. Place them name-side down on a flannel board, and take them off one at a time while saying each child's name. When a child's name is called, he or she chooses a song, finger play, or activity for the group to do.
- Use rhythm instruments to accompany a song you are singing. Let the children take turns using these instruments. As each child finishes a turn, he or she chooses a learning center to go to.
- Children gather quickly when you play the autoharp, guitar, or other instrument. Let a few children strum the instrument while you are waiting for others to gather.
- Pretend that one child is the engine on a train. As that child "chugs" around the room, other children join the train by putting their hands on the shoulders of the child ahead. When all children are part of the train, then "chug" along outdoors.
- Play Simon Says. On the last direction, Simon says, "Sit down." You are now ready for a story or other quiet activity.
- Play directional games such as "Touch your nose, turn around, sit down." Start with simple directions and get more complicated as the children are able to follow through on two and three directions.
- Gently remind children when it is time to begin to complete their activities. A simple blinking of the overhead lights will let them know it is time to clean up.
- Help children move toward closure of the daily activities. Put things away and gradually close down the centers. Then read or tell a story until all the children have been picked up.

Summary

1. **How can you manage the learning centers, both indoors and outdoors?** The environment should have a personal space or cubby for each child with his or her name or photo. Display children's art, special projects, pictures, and bulletin boards at their eye level. Have a variety of well-defined learning centers that involve hands-on

experiences with a variety of materials. Arrange the environment to allow children access to materials, supplies, and learning centers. The selection of outdoor equipment and materials emphasizes safety, durability, and age appropriateness for all children.

2. **Evaluate the equipment, materials, and supplies needed for indoor and outdoor learning environments.** The selection of indoor equipment (furniture and other large and expensive equipment), materials (smaller items such as puzzles, books, toys), and supplies (consumables such as paint, paper, glue) should be developmentally appropriate for the children in each classroom. Items must be child-size, nontoxic, aesthetically appealing, sturdy with rounded corners and edges, easy to maintain, and not easily broken. Many activities can be done on the floor, so the floor covering must be "child-proof" and made of linoleum, tile, or carpeting that can take spills and hard wear. Tables can serve as art, manipulative, and eating places. Boys and girls need experiences with the same kinds and variety of learning materials. Soft toys, big and comfy pillows, and furnishings that fit the children's size, abilities, and interests should also be included.

   The selection of outdoor equipment and materials emphasizes safety, durability, and age appropriateness for all children. The outdoor space should contribute to physical, intellectual, creative, emotional, and social development and offer a variety of stimulation for play and exploration. The design should also offer ramps and tracks that accommodate wheelchairs and adapted vehicles, giving proper attention to slope, width, types of surface, and direct and safe accessibility to play and structures. The surfaces should offer various textures and colors, such as a hard-surfaced area for games and wheeled toys, a large, soft grassy area with trees, a garden area, organic loose material such as play bark/wood chips and pine bark mulch, inorganic loose material such as sand and pea gravel, and rubber or foam mats.

3. **What are some appropriate guidance techniques, including transitions?** Set clear, consistent, and fair limits for classroom and playground behavior; guide younger children toward appropriate ways to relate to others and to function in a group environment; and help older children set their own limits. Model expected behavior and demonstrate self-control. Name feelings. Teach acceptable ways to express feelings. Try to explain a child's behavior to another child. Use suggestion or redirection rather than the word *don't*. Remember to address the behavior, not the child, when a behavior occurs that is not appropriate.

   Children need time to adjust to change; therefore, use a transition activity to direct children from a self-initiated to a teacher-directed activity, an active to a quiet activity or from quiet to active play, cleanup and toileting to snack time, lunch to naptime, and outside to inside or inside to outside play.

Reflective Review Questions

1. Children with special needs provide challenges in designing a developmentally appropriate classroom. What are the challenges, and how can you overcome those challenges?
2. Select three different themes. For each one, suggest an appropriate transition and identify the purpose of the transition you selected.

Explorations

1. Use the Learning Center Environment Checklist in this chapter to conduct an observation of an early childhood learning environment.

   - Beside each statement, place an X if the classroom you observed met the statement.

- On a separate sheet of paper, describe what you actually observed related to each statement.
- On a separate sheet of paper, for each statement that you did not check as met, describe what you would do to improve that classroom so that the statement would be met. Be sure to put the number of the statement first.
- Submit this with the name of the location you observed and the age group.

2. Select a child's book. Brainstorm all of the ways you can use that book in an early care and education classroom. Make a curriculum web with the title of the book at the center.

3. Based on the information from this chapter and from observing in an early education classroom (infant, toddler, preschool, prekindergarten, kindergarten, or primary), generate a list of guidance techniques you have observed teachers using with a group of young children. Were any of the children you observed children with special needs? Did any of the children display challenging behaviors? Was each guidance technique developmentally appropriate?

Part 2

Discovering and Expanding the Early Education Curriculum

> "A child is sunshine,
> Sparkling in every step she takes.
> A child is laughter,
> Filling the air with sounds he makes.
> A child sees beauty,
> Wonder, and excitement everywhere
> And freely offers
> A vision of joy, to treasure, to share."
>
> —Hilda Jackman
> Reprinted with permission

Standards Contained in Each Chapter of Part 2

naeyc Program Standards

5a: Understanding content knowledge and resources in academic disciplines: language and literacy; the arts, music, creative movement, dance, drama, visual arts; mathematics; science, physical activity, physical education, health and safety; and social studies.

5b: Knowing and using the central concepts, inquiry tools, and structures of content areas or academic disciplines.

5c: Using own knowledge, appropriate early learning standards, and other resources to design, implement, and evaluate developmentally meaningful and challenging curriculum for each child.

DAP Developmentally Appropriate Practice (DAP) Guidelines

2: Teaching to Enhance Development and Learning.

INTASC Interstate Teacher Assessment and Support Consortium (InTASC)

Standard #4: Content Knowledge. The teacher understands the central concepts, tools of inquiry, and structures of the discipline(s) he or she teaches and creates learning experiences that make the discipline accessible and meaningful for learners to assure mastery of the content.

Standard #5: Application of Content. The teacher understands how to connect concepts and use differing perspectives to engage learners in critical thinking, creativity, and collaborative problem solving related to authentic local and global issues.

Standard #8: Instructional Strategies. The teacher understands and uses a variety of instructional strategies to encourage learners to develop deep understanding of content areas and their connections, and to build skills to apply knowledge in meaningful ways.

5 Language and Literacy

Standards Covered in This Chapter

 NAEYC 5a, 5b, 5c

DAP 2.

INTASC 4, 5, 8

HEAD START
Domain: Language and
Communication,
Domain: Literacy

ILA 1, 2, 3, 4, 6, 12

CC English Language Arts Standards

NAEYC, DAP, and INTASC standards
described on Part II introduction page

Student Learning Outcomes

After studying this chapter, you should be able to:

- Define and give examples for key terms related to language and literacy development and literature for children.

- Discuss language development in young children and relate stages of child development to literacy development.

- Evaluate various components of planning and preparation of literacy environments, including the selection of appropriate literature.

- Create literacy activities appropriate for young children.

- Identify various ways to use technology in a literacy environment.

- Distinguish ways to incorporate diversity into literacy experiences.

- Describe ways to develop partnerships with families that support child literacy.

- Analyze the teacher's role in promoting literacy in the classroom.

As human beings, we have the desire to communicate with others. We do this in many ways. A smile communicates a friendly feeling; a clenched fist transmits anger; tears show happiness or sorrow. From the first days of life, a baby expresses pain or hunger by cries or actions. Gradually, the infant adds expressions of pleasure and smiles when a familiar person comes near. Then, the little one begins to reach out to be picked up.

A baby eventually learns the words of his or her parents. If the parents speak English, the baby will learn to speak English. If the baby spends a lot of time around significant adults who speak Spanish, Japanese, Hebrew, or any other language, the infant will learn the language of the people around him or her.

The process of acquiring a language is important. It is one of the most important skills a child develops and requires interaction with other language speakers to develop naturally. Usually, a child learns the rules of language at an early age without formal instruction. A child learns language by listening and speaking and through modeling by teachers. He or she learns language by using it. Learning to talk, like learning to walk, requires time for development and practice in everyday situations. During the first few years of life, listening and speaking constitute a large part of a child's experience with language.

Literacy, the ability to read and write, gives one the command of a native language for the purpose of communicating. This involves skills in listening, speaking, reading, and writing. The excitement of learning to read and write, we hope, will be as rewarding as a child's first words and first steps.

In 2009, the National Council of Teachers of English (NCTE) redefined literacy for the twenty-first century by making it clear that further evolution of curriculum, assessment, and the teaching practice itself is necessary.

Literacy is seen as a collection of practices, both cultural and communicative, that binds together particular group members. Literature, just like technology and society, are in a state of constant change. Because of the complex nature of the technology, a literate individual must process a wide range of literacies.

Getting children to interact through books and other technologies help us enfold literature into language and literacy development. The language of literature provides children with vivid, imaginative, well-ordered words—words to think about, to listen to, to try out and make their own. Oral language relates to reading and writing. It is a part of the development of both. The child who hears stories all through childhood learns language and structure and develops attitudes and concepts about the printed word (Morrow, 2014).

Early education emphasizes reading and writing opportunities *across the curriculum.* Sawyer (2009) explains further, when literature is observable in each of the learning areas, logical connections are made between the program and classroom. This stability in a child's environment is a critical component of their education during the early years (Sawyer, 2009).

Children's literature is a wondrous and exciting part of the early education curriculum. Most of us can still recall favorite childhood stories that were read or told to us by a loving adult. Books have a way of connecting us to others. They put us in a different time and place and capture our imaginations and our hearts.

literacy: The ability to read and write, which gives one the command of a native language for the purpose of communicating.

language: Human speech, the written symbols for speech, or any means of communicating.

language development: Developmental process of a predictable sequence that includes both sending and receiving information. It is related, but not tied, to chronological age.

emergent literacy: A process of developing awareness about reading and writing before young children can read or write.

Language, Literacy, and Literature Defined

INTASC DAP HS

Language can be defined as human speech, the written symbols for speech, or any means of communicating. In each person's culture, language is their means of expression that has multiple facets and uses. **Language development** follows a predictable sequence. It is related, but not tied, to chronological age. This developmental process includes both sending and receiving information. It is important to remember that language is learned through use.

Emergent literacy in young children is a process of developing awareness about reading and writing before they can actually read or write. Their emergent literacy skills are the building blocks for later reading, writing, and communicating.

Helping you, the teacher, promote appropriate language and literacy environments is the intent of this chapter. Understanding language and literacy development in young children, encouraging family support, and setting up a developmentally appropriate environment to strengthen and extend this development will also be examined.

Literature, in its simplest sense, is all the writings (prose and verse) of a people, country, or period, including those written especially for children.

Children's literature can be defined in many ways. By looking at purposes, values, types, and genres of books for early education, we can define what literature is for young children. The material comes from many sources in both language and illustrated materials.

Naturally, we use books to teach children to read and to teach children about the world, math concepts, science, and social studies. Books also help children learn how to make things, develop multicultural understandings, and explain topics of personal interest.

Young children develop visual literacy skills even before they can read. As teachers, we can encourage this by helping them to use illustrations to decode meaning from the text and to challenge them to describe, compare, and value both visual and written communication. Furthermore, by starting with the literal and concrete, children begin to think about what they see in an illustration and, in turn, describe what they think will happen next in the book they are reading. Aesthetics can be emphasized to young children when teachers focus on line, color, and shape, as well as evaluate the illustrations for strength, mood, and feeling.

According to Strickland (2002), today's informed early childhood educator should understand and be able to build on the following principles to support young children's literacy development:

- Children's language and culture have a direct influence on their learning.
- Learning to read and write is a complex process.
- Language and literacy development are interdependent and interactive. What children know about communication through talk is used to build understandings about reading and writing.
- Children learn best when teachers understand and address the variability among them.
- Children learn best when teachers understand the developmental continuum of reading and writing, are skilled in a variety of strategies to help children achieve, and know how to monitor children's learning in terms of challenging but achievable goals.

Literacy development also can be encouraged by using Vygotsky's (1986) theory of *scaffolding*. This occurs as the teacher (adult) continually adjusts the level of help offered in response to the child's level of performance. For example:

Shared work: The teacher, in a leadership role, selects and shares a book with the children.
Guided work: The teacher guides and encourages the children on an as-needed basis as they explore children's literature, such as helping them to draw illustrations of stories read to them.
Independent work: By this time, children are embarking on their own responses to literature that interests them, the teacher being only minimally supportive, such as 5-year-olds doing a puppet version of a favorite story.

Purposes and Values of Children's Books

As we explore the many purposes of including children's books in early childhood classrooms and homes, it is crucial to understand their fundamental role in the learning experience. Because learning is basically the process of associating that which is new with that which is already known, stories can be a powerful tool to accomplish it. A book introduces a child to something new, which can give him or her greater understanding of the world and create an excitement to know more.

Books in children's lives provide them time to reflect on real-life experiences and help them develop curiosity about life and learning. Through books, children have the ability

literature: All the writings (prose and verse) of a people, country, or period, including those written especially for children.

to reread parts enjoyed or for increased understanding. To provide a foundation for math, children develop processes and skills that help them focus on skills for predicting outcomes, drawing conclusions, and solving problems. With experience, children learn to enjoy books and how to provide for their care and use.

It is important for teachers and parents of young children to share with each other what they think the purposes are of creating an environment filled with books as part of a child's life. Open communication can offer a partnership to enrich relationships for everyone.

Developmental Stages of Language and Literacy

Long before babies can speak, they listen to sounds and words. They hear differences in voices and sounds. Infants will turn their heads in the direction of a particular sound. Friendly verbal interaction with and encouragement from nurturing adults help a baby form his or her first words out of randomly babbled sounds. An infant learns quickly that communicating is worthwhile because it results in reactions on the part of others.

Just as babies are introduced to behavior of people and to the emotions of trust and love, babies learn language as a part of a communication system they will use the rest of their lives (Gestwicki, 2014).

Language Development of Young Children

Children learn language through predictable stages of development. As with many other aspects of child development, individual differences are apparent in the development and use of language.

Baby's cry (birth to 3 months): This form of communication varies in pitch and intensity and relates to stimuli such as hunger, discomfort, or fear. Just as adults respond differently to a baby's cry (some touch, some talk), the baby's response varies as well. An infant can stop crying and then smile or laugh in reaction to an adult's facial expression, to words spoken, or to being held.

Cooing (birth to 3 months): These are the sounds made when an infant's basic needs are met and he or she is relaxed, content, or stimulated by what is seen or heard. A baby derives a great deal of pleasure from practicing and listening to his or her own gurgling and cooing.

Smiling and laughing (birth to 3 months): Babies seem to be smiling when they are only a few days old. Some smile in their sleep, possibly through inner motivations. Adult facial, auditory, or motor stimuli can also be sources of smiles. Infants tend to incorporate hoots, howls, squeals, grins, and giggles into their early laughter.

Babbling (4 to 6 months): These early random sounds made by an infant are a repetition of sequences of clear, alternating consonant and vowel sounds. This vocalization will eventually be combined into words, such as *baba* for bottle and *wawa* for water.

Association (6 to 9 months): A baby begins to get some idea of the meaning of a few words at about 6 to 9 months. An association between the sounds an infant makes and the meanings of these sounds starts to become clear. When an adult begins to recognize and interpret these sounds, another level of communication has been reached. Playing "peek-a-boo" and "pat-a-cake" are fun to do and help the child develop an association between sounds and meanings.

By the end of the first year, babies limit their utterances to only those that are significant in their environment. Babies in Germany will use the guttural sounds

Figure 5-1 A child is developing an awareness of reading and writing before he can actually read or write.

they hear and babies in Mexico will trill the r sound. English-speaking babies will not learn either of these sounds because they are not commonly heard in their environment. All of these babies will eventually combine sounds to mean something specific and then to develop greater communication skills.

One-word usage (12 months): Many first words are completely original, private words of the child. They may be sequences of sounds or intonations used on a consistent basis. For progression during this stage, the physical organs need to be able to function in perfect unison. The child must also have attained a certain level of maturity. The speech centers are then ready to produce the first words. In the early stages of language development, a word, such as *hot* or *no*, often stands for a whole object or an experience. The one-word stage also uses a word to get something or some action from others, such as *go*, *down*, or *mine*. Getting the appropriate response, approval, and smiles from adults encourages the child to make the sounds again and again. Language is a two-way process. Reaction is an important feedback to action. Although a child can speak only in "one-word sentences," he or she can understand more complex sentences and can react to what others are saying. From this point on, the child has progressed from **receptive language**, that is, listening and understanding, to the period of **expressive language**, that is, speaking. (See Figure 5-1.)

Recall (7 to 12 months): A child's ability to remember an object named even when the object is not visible is helped by the touching, grasping, and tasting of the object. Responding to his or her name, identifying family members, and watching, pointing to, and naming an object usually occur toward the end of the first year. Recall is sometimes called "sign-language" communication, such as when a child holds up his or her arms to be picked up.

Telegraphic speech (1 to 2 years): The two-word sentence is the next step in the development of language of the young child. This speech helps a child express wishes and feelings and to ask questions. Because of a child's limited ability to express and remember large pieces of information, many words are often omitted in telegraphic speech. The child repeats words over and over, such as *all gone*, *drink milk*, or *throw ball*. It is important to talk and listen to a toddler. This is a critical language-growth period because the young child is processing, testing, and remembering language. (See Table 5-1 for toddler language characteristics.)

Multiword speech (3 to 4 years): When a young child reaches the stage of adult-like speech with longer sentences and almost all of the words present, he or she asks questions and understands the answers. The child can express feelings and tell others what he or she wants. At the same time, the child can understand the words of other people and absorb new knowledge. The child's vocabulary increases, and the repetition of songs, stories, and poems comes more easily. Words become important tools of learning, and they help a young child grow socially. Children talk together, and friendships grow. Thus, it becomes obvious that oral language is the foundation of early literacy.

Our knowledge of the language acquisition and development of young children will help us understand that speech and language irregularities come and go and appear to be self-correcting unless the child is pressured. We also need to be aware of early warning signs that a child could be having some difficulty.

Children become aware of the written word as a way of documenting what is spoken, around 5 or 6 years of age. Language development has reached its end when print and literacy emerges.

Literacy Development of Young Children

DAP   **COMMON CORE**

receptive language: Listening and understanding.

expressive language: Speaking.

As previously indicated, literacy development is a lifelong process that begins at birth and includes listening, speaking, reading, and writing. Listening is a prerequisite to speaking. Learning to speak is an important step toward learning to read.

Brain Research: Brain-Based Literacy Learning

 Research shows that infants start out able to distinguish the sound of all languages, but that by 6 months of age they are no longer able to recognize sounds that are not heard in their native tongue. As infants hear the patterns of sound in their own language, a different cluster of neurons in the auditory cortex of the brain responds to each sound. By 6 months of age, infants will have difficulty picking out sounds they have not heard repeated often.

Children's vocabulary skills are linked to their economic backgrounds. By 3 years of age, there can be a 30-million word gap between children from the wealthiest and poorest families. A recent study shows that the vocabulary gap is evident in toddlers. By 18 months, children in different socioeconomic groups display dramatic differences in their vocabularies. By 2 years, the discrepancy in vocabulary development has grown significantly (Fernald, Marchman, & Weisleder, 2013). Vocabulary use at age 3 is strongly associated with language skill at ages 9 and 10. In studies following both English- and Spanish-learning toddlers over several years, they found that children who are faster at recognizing familiar words at 18 months have larger vocabularies at age 2 years and score higher on standardized tests of language and cognition in kindergarten and elementary school.

Hart and Risley found that differences in the size of children's vocabulary first appear at 18 months of age, based on whether they were born into a family with higher education and income or lower education and income. By age 3, children with college-educated parents or primary caregivers had vocabularies two to three times larger than those whose parents had not completed high school. By the time children reach school, children of parents with lower education are already behind their peers unless they are engaged in a language-rich environment early in life.

Windows of opportunity for language development occur throughout life. For example, the window for syntax or grammar is open during the preschool years but may close as early as age 5 or 6, whereas the window for adding new vocabulary never closes completely (Shiver, E., 2001; Hart, B., and Risley, T., 1995).

TABLE 5-1:	Toddler Language Characteristics
• Uses two- to five-word sentences. "Baby down." "Baby boom boom." "No like." "No like kitty." "Me drink all gone." "See me drink all gone."	• Uses negatives. "Don't wanna." "He no go."
• Uses verbs. "Dolly cry." "Me going." "Wanna cookie."	• Runs words together. "Allgone," "gotta," "gimme," "lookee."
• Uses prepositions. "In car." "Up me go."	• Asks questions. "What dat?" "Why she sleep?"
• Adds plurals. "Birdies sing." "Gotta big doggies." "Bears in dat."	• Does not use letter sounds or mispronounces spoken words. "Iceam," "choo" (for shoe), "member" (for remember), "canny" (for candy)
• Uses pronouns. "Me big boy." "He bad."	Sings songs.

(continued)

TABLE 5-1:	Toddler Language Characteristics (continued)	

● Uses articles. "The ball gone." "Gimme a candy."	Tells simple stories.
● Uses conjunctions. "Me and gamma."	Repeats words and phrases.
	Enjoys word and movement activities.

SOURCE: Machado, 2010

To better understand the development of literacy, it is important to understand that reading and writing do not always develop at the same speed. One may progress more quickly than the other. Whatever the timetable, the goals of literacy learning are the same:

- To be able to make sense of and convey meaning of written language by becoming efficient and fluent readers and writers;
- To be able to review and analyze information by becoming thinkers and communicators;
- To enjoy writing and reading; and
- To use literacy successfully for a variety of purposes.

Researchers also believe children learn about reading and writing through play. As a teacher of young children, you see this happening every day. You have observed children learning to talk, read, or write when they are playing "peek-a-boo," engaging in nonsense speech play, listening to and singing familiar jingles and rhymes, scribbling, pretending, and using objects as symbols. Because literacy is a continuous process, children are working on all aspects of oral and written language at the same time.

> " Because the brain uses the innate language pathway to learn to read, the development of language is an essential precursor to reading. ... Speaking is a natural development, reading is not. Reading is an acquired skill (Nevills and Wolfe, 2009, p. 46). "

Understanding what is developmentally appropriate for young children can help you recognize what is important in the development of oral and written language. Here are the skills identified by the National Institute for Literacy (2009) as most important for children's development of literacy:

- Knowing the names of printed letters
- Knowing the sounds associated with printed letters
- Manipulating the sounds of spoken language
- Rapidly naming a sequence of letters, numbers, objects, or colors
- Writing one's own name or even isolated letters
- Remembering the content of spoken language for a short time

The following terms help us understand language and literacy development:

Phonics is the relationship between the letters of written language and the sounds of spoken language. Phonics emphasizes the sound–symbol relationship through "sounding out" unfamiliar syllables and words.

As teachers, you can emphasize the sounds of language by providing opportunities for children to practice with the **phonemes**, the smallest unit of speech, as well as helping them write the letter–sound relationships they know by using them in words, sentences, messages, and their own stories.

When children sing nursery rhymes, jingles, and songs, they are playing with and exploring the sounds of language. **Rhyming** is the ability to hear two words that end the same way, a beginning concept of **phonological or phonemic awareness**, which is the awareness

phonics: The relationship between the letters of written language and the sounds of spoken language.

phonemes: The smallest units of speech.

rhyming: The ability to auditorily distinguish two words that end the same way.

phonological or phonemic awareness: The ability to hear and identify individual sounds and spoken words.

and the ability to hear and identify individual sounds and spoken words and the development of listening skills.

Becoming attentive to the sound of language—becoming phonologically or phonemically aware—is a skill of the ear as opposed to phonics, which is a relation between sounds and letters in written words.

Another important aspect of language development is **vocabulary**. This refers to the words we must know to communicate. Teachers need to recognize the importance of expanding children's vocabulary as the child explores topics of interest. For example, when children study community helpers, they learn words such as *doctor, ambulance, firefighter,* and *siren*.

Through shared reading experiences, writing their names, and playing games related to their letter discoveries, they are developing literacy skills at their own pace. You are building on what children already know and can do, while creating a developmentally appropriate language and literacy environment, when you:

- Talk to children, even while diapering or feeding them.
- Talk to children in standard spoken language—not baby talk. Speak clearly and give simple explanations.
- Reinforce a child's native language. Understand that every child's language or dialect is worthy of respect as a valid system for communication.
- Speak in a voice that helps children listen—not too fast or too soft.
- Encourage children to talk to you.
- Enable children to use language to communicate their thoughts about ideas and problems that are real and important to them.
- Listen when children talk to you. Give children your full attention when they speak. Be on their level and make eye contact. Use nonverbal communication, such as eye-to-eye contact, smiling, and holding a child's finger or hand to reinforce that you are listening. Be patient.
- Use children's names frequently.
- Allow time and opportunity for children to listen and talk freely without interruption.
- Play music for children to listen to. Provide different types of music in the environment, such as tapes or CDs of lullabies, songs from many cultures, and classical music.
- Sing songs. Make up songs with the children.
- Play finger plays, which offer a combination of stories, poems, directions, songs, and hand movements. Finger plays also offer a transition into a story or activity.
- Give simple multiple-step directions for activities. Read or tell stories to children to help them build the brain structures they will need to read.
- Select a variety of books.
- Read books that expose children to a varied and rich vocabulary.
- Expose children to a variety of print features. Take walks and listen to the sounds of the environment. Talk about what you see and hear. Write down what the children say and then put their words in a classroom book or on a large sheet of paper posted on an easel or a wall.
- Play listening games to develop sound awareness, such as clapping hands in a fast or slow tempo; then have children repeat the clapping as they heard it. Audio tape the games, and then play them back to the children to see if they can associate the taped claps with the ones they did.
- Select books in a variety of languages, including Braille and sign language. (See **Figure 5-2**.)

Literacy experiences should be prevalent in every early childhood classroom and be incorporated into every area of the curriculum.

vocabulary: This refers to the words we must know to communicate.

Figure 5-2 Sign language poster (copyright School Specialty Publishing, used with permission).

The more we practice a new skill, the better we get at that skill and the more we enjoy it. This is also true of children learning to read. Additional and specific examples of language and literary developmental activities are presented later in this chapter and in Appendix B. As stated previously, in a developmentally appropriate setting, speaking, listening, reading, and writing are integrated into or combined with other curriculum areas. You will find examples of this throughout the chapters of this book.

Planning and Preparing the Environment

Reading and writing skills develop simultaneously and are interconnected. Focusing on just one of these, distracts from the importance of the other. Progress in one increases the development of the other.

As previously discussed, throughout a child's life, listening, speaking, reading, and writing are a prominent part of a child's world. As significant adults in a child's life, we should ensure that the environment surrounding each child is the best it can be—developmentally, individually, and creatively. When this occurs, children use and expand their language in almost every activity and curriculum area in which they participate.

Where you place the book center in your classroom, whether it is for two children or a special, private place for one child, indicates how much importance you place on a child's interacting with books and stories. When and how often you read a book to the group or an individual child points this out as well. Is it always at the same time each day or in the same location? Are you spontaneous? Sometimes do you just *feel* like telling a story, reading a book, or developing an activity? Being flexible and creating on-the-spot activities using children's suggestions are just as important and worthwhile as having planned activities. As you plan the physical space for the language and literacy activities, you should keep in mind that how you design this area will affect the choices children make in their selection of activities. This part of the environment, sometimes called the language arts center, should be arranged so children can use this area independently or in small groups.

You will find the language arts center is most effective when it:

- Is set in a part of the room that is quiet with little traffic but is accessible from any other center.
- Invites the children to use every inch of table, floor, and wall space.
- Displays things at the children's eye level.
- Attracts them to listen, look, think, write, draw, and read.
- Includes materials, supplies, and equipment that offer explorative and developmentally appropriate hands-on experiences for young children.

The language arts center should be an environment that is soft. This can be accomplished by having a carpet, rug, or carpet squares on the floor; by adding large pillows and beanbag chairs; and by adding some "creative spaces," such as enormous stuffed animals with large laps for children to sit on or an old-fashioned bathtub filled with pillows of all sizes and colors for an individual child to spend some alone time in reading a book or listening to a CD.

The center also should have good lighting and easy access to child-size tables, chairs, and bookcases that are arranged for group or individual use. Include both "stand-up" (chalkboard, easels, murals, window, clipboards) and "sit-down" (tables, lap desks, floor) writing places.

Setting up the Writing Environment

Children should have access to listening, reading, and writing materials in every learning center. Many of the items usually placed in the language arts center can be duplicated in other centers. For example, telephone message pads can be placed in dramatic play, graph paper can be put in the science center, and big pieces of paper with blue markers can be included in the block center for making "blueprints" of constructions. When children want to write, copy, or draw, the "tools" should be available.

Encourage children to learn written language in the same energetic and interactive ways they learn oral language. Learning the alphabet should begin with the letters in children's names rather than with worksheets or the letter of the week (Martin, 2008). Invite children to experiment with language in any way they choose and accept whatever the child "writes," such as lists, creative calendars, children's dictation, posters, signs, labels, songs, and "creative" spelling.

Materials should be available at all times for children to use for writing. They should be separated into appropriate, brightly colored containers to make it easy for children to choose what they need. The use and care of the materials should be discussed each time something new is added to the learning center.

The classroom should also be print-rich. Identification of words in the environment appears to be one of the first steps in learning to read. Signs, logos, and labels can be used as valuable literacy learning tools. Include environmental print in children's home language as well as English. Young children are aware of logos or trademarks of their favorite fast-food restaurants, the products they eat or use, and the signs around their neighborhoods. Environmental print can be used as a valuable springboard for learning phonics and phonemic awareness.

Types and Genres of Books for Children

Before a teacher, parent, or other significant adult selects books for children, understanding about the many *types* and *genres* of books available is essential. **Genre** is a category used to classify literary works, usually by form, technique, or content. A book's **format** is the overall arrangement, or the way the book is put together, involving factors such as size, shape, paper quality, colors, and content of each page. Isbell and Raines (2007), Machado (2010), and many other children's literature professionals believe that teachers and parents should select books from a wide variety of genres and types. This is fairly easy when you are working with adult literature, which falls into familiar categories, such as fiction, nonfiction, poetry, and prose. But with children's literature in all of its many varieties, the labeling is much more difficult.

Although several systems are used to group children's books, educators do not always agree on how a given book might be labeled or placed. Many books do not neatly fit any category, or they may fit more than one. Nevertheless, most books relating to children's literature fall into the categories that follow. The types of literature are listed with specific characteristics that identify each kind of book. For clarity and organization, the types or categories of children's books are arranged in alphabetical order.

Alphabet Books
Alphabet books are books based on the alphabet that:

- offer simple stories;
- present letter identification and one-object picture association;
- offer paired words and objects with matching illustrations;
- have a consistent theme; and
- present opportunities to discover names and association of alphabet letters that are easily identified.

An example of an alphabet book:

Pearle, I. (2008). *A child's day: An alphabet of play.* Orlando, FL: Harcourt.

Beginning-to-Read Books
Beginning-to-read books may also be referred to as easy-to-read books. These books:

- present words that are simple and repetitive;
- have short sentences;

genre: Category used to classify literary works, usually by form, technique, or content.

format: The overall arrangement of the way a book is put together, such as by size, shape, paper quality, colors, and content of each page.

alphabet books: Simple stories based on the alphabet that present letter identification and one-object picture association.

beginning-to-read books: Predictable books that are easy to read and present words that are simple and repetitive.

- are usually predictable; and
- are designed to be read by the emergent reader.

An example of a beginning-to-read book:

Rylant, C. (2008). *Annie and snowball and the pink surprise.* Illustrated by S. Stevenson. New York: Simon & Schuster Books for Young Readers.

Big Books

Big books may also be called oversized, giant, or jumbo books. Big books:

- present extra-large text and illustrations; and
- allow teachers to share books with a group of children easily.

An example of a big book:

Wood, A. (1984). *The napping house.* Illustrated by Don Wood. Orlando, FL: Harcourt Big Books.

Board Books

Board books are usually the first books for infants and toddlers because they are made of heavy cardboard and are laminated. Board books:

- offer ease of page turning for children learning to handle books;
- are sometimes referred to as mini books because they are small and can easily be picked up by a young child; and
- have simple illustrations.

An example of a board book:

Hamm, D. J. (2008). *Rock-a-bye-farm.* Illustrated by S. A. Natchev. New York: Little Simon.

Concept Books

Concept books have been identified as a young child's first informational book. These books:

- present themes, ideas, or concepts with specific examples;
- identify and clarify abstractions, such as color or shape;
- help with vocabulary development; and
- include alphabet and counting books as favorite types of concept books.

An example of a concept book:

Gibbons, G. (2007). *The vegetables we eat.* New York: Holiday House.

Counting Books

Counting books are books based on counting and numeral recognition. These books:

- describe simple numeral and picture association;
- often tell a story;
- offer one-to-one correspondence illustrations;
- show representations of numbers in more than one format; and
- vary from simple to complex.

An example of a counting book:

- Seeger, L.V. (2008). *One boy.* New York: Roaring Brook Books.

Folk Literature

Folk literature may also be called folk tales, fairy tales, fables, tall tales, myths, and legends. These tales:

- come from the oral tradition of storytelling;
- appeal to the child's sense of fantasy;

---

big books: Oversized books that present extra-large text and illustrations.

board books: First books for infants and toddlers made of laminated heavy cardboard.

concept books: Books that present themes, ideas, or concepts with specific examples. They also identify and clarify abstractions, such as color or shape, and help with vocabulary development.

counting books: Books that describe simple numeral and picture associations and often tell a story. They show representations of numbers in more than one format and vary from simple to complex.

folk literature: Tales that come from the oral tradition of storytelling that appeal to the child's sense of fantasy.

- teach value systems;
- offer language that is appealing to children and create strong visual images; and
- connect with other cultures and countries because they retell traditional stories that are shared from generation to generation.

An example of folk literature:

Wolff, F., and Savitz, H. M. (2008). *The story blanket*. Illustrated by E. Odriozola. Atlanta: Peachtree.

Informational Books

Informational books offer nonfiction for emergent readers. They also:

- explore new ideas;
- answer "why" and "how";
- stimulate and expand individual or group interest; and
- give accurate facts about people (biographies) and subject matter.

An example of an informational book:

DK Children. (2007). *See how it's made*. New York: DK Publishers.

Interaction Books

Interaction books are sometimes called novelty, toy, or participation books. These books:

- use some device for involving young readers, such as pop-ups, foldouts, scratch and sniff, pasting, puzzle pictures, humor, and riddles;
- stimulate imagination; and
- can be designed in different sizes and shapes for exploring and touching.

An example of an interaction book:

Johnson, T. (2009). *My little red fire truck*. New York: Simon & Schuster Books for Young Readers.

Mother Goose and Nursery Rhymes

Mother Goose and **nursery rhyme books** are often a child's first introduction to literature. These books:

- are known by children all over the world;
- are passed from generation to generation;
- offer varied illustrations of the rhymes; and
- appeal to infants and toddlers.

An example of a Mother Goose and nursery rhyme book:

Ross, T. (2009). *Three little kittens*. New York: Henry Holt.

Multicultural Books

Multicultural books are also referred to as cross-cultural or culturally diverse books. These books:

- develop awareness of and sensitivity to other cultures;
- increase positive attitudes toward similarities and differences in people;
- offer accurate portrayals and rich details of individual and group heritage; and
- can extend to seasonal and holiday books.

An example of a multicultural book:

Brown, M. (2007). *Butterflies on Carmen Street/Mariposas en la calle de Carmen Street*. New York: Piñata Books.

informational books: Books that offer nonfiction for emergent readers by providing accurate facts about people and subject matter.

interaction books: Books used to stimulate imagination by using some device for involving young readers, such as pop-ups, fold-outs, scratch and sniff, pasting, puzzle pictures, humor, and riddles.

Mother Goose and nursery rhyme books: Books passed from generation to generation and known by children all over the world. These are often a child's first introduction to literature.

multicultural books: Books that develop awareness of and sensitivity to other cultures. They also help to increase positive attitudes toward similarities and differences in people.

Picture Books or Picture Story Books

Picture books are often referred to as the most popular type of children's literature. These books:

- are written in a direct style that tells a simple story;
- offer varied illustrations that complement and associate closely with the text;
- are written especially for adults to share with children; and
- are uniquely appropriate for the young child.

An example of a picture book:

Yolen, J. (2009). *The scarecrow's dance.* Illustrated by B. Ibatoulline. New York: Simon & Schuster Books for Young Readers.

Poetry

Poetry is overlooked many times as part of children's literature. Poetry:

- can be one book, one poem, or a collection of poems;
- contributes imaginative rhyme, rhythm, and sound;
- is another way to present culture, country, and language; and
- stimulates imagery and feelings.

An example of a poetry book:

Yolen, J. (2007). *Here's a little poem.* Cambridge, MA: Candlewick Press.

Predictable Books

Predictable books contain familiar and repetitive sequences. These books:

- describe events that are repeated or added to as the story continues;
- permit successful guessing of what happens next; and
- supply opportunities for children to read along.

An example of a predictable book:

Barton, B. (1993). *The little red hen.* New York: HarperCollins.

Realistic Literature

Sometimes called bibliotherapy or therapeutic literature, **realistic literature** deals with real-life issues. These books:

- help children cope with common, actual experiences;
- offer positive solutions and insights;
- encourage talking about a child's feelings; and
- are often tied in with anti-bias literature that relates to children with special needs.

An example of realistic literature:

Heelan, J. R. (2000). *Rolling along: The story of Taylor and his wheelchair.* Rehabilitation Institute of Chicago.

Reference Books

Reference books emphasize individualized learning through special topic books, picture dictionaries, and encyclopedias. They also encourage older children to find a resource that answers questions.

An example of a reference book:

Ajmera, M. (2008). *Children of the U.S.A.* Watertown, MA: Charlesbridge.

Series Books

Series books are often written for primary-grade children. These books:

- are built around a single character or group of characters;
- can introduce the concept of books written in chapter form; and
- can be related to television characters that are familiar to children.

picture books: Books written in a direct style that tell a simple story with illustrations complementing the text.

poetry: A form of literature that contributes imaginative rhyme, rhythm, and sound.

predictable books: Books that contain familiar and repetitive sequences.

realistic literature: A form of literature that helps children cope with common, actual experiences by offering positive solutions and insights.

reference books: Books that emphasize individualized learning through special topic books, picture dictionaries, and encyclopedias.

series books: Books written for primary-grade children and built around a single character or group of characters.

Examples of series books:

Amelia Bedelia books. New York: Greenwillow.
The Magic Treehouse books. New York: Random House Books for Young Readers.

Teacher- and Child-Made Books

Teacher- and child-made books are a part of developmentally appropriate early education classrooms. These books:

- encourage self-esteem, creativity, and sharing ideas with others;
- reinforce group learning;
- develop children's understanding of authorship by seeing their names in print;
- encourage children to articulate experiences;
- invite children to use their imagination; and
- include parents in the process of reading and writing with their children.

  Examples of subjects for individual or class-made books:

  My Family

  My Friends

  My Community

  My Favorite Things to Do

Wordless Picture Books

A young child develops language, reading skills, and meaning through the illustrations with **wordless picture books**, sometimes called stories without words. These books:

- help develop building blocks of language;
- offer visually appealing illustrations;
- present sequential action from page to page;
- promote creativity by encouraging a child to talk about experiences; and
- invite older children to write a story about what is seen, with character descriptions and dialogue.

  An example of a wordless picture book:

  Lee, S. (2008). *Wave.* San Francisco, CA: Chronicle.

Selection of Books for Young Children

Because of the growing diversity in the country and the increasing integrated global economy, it is important for children to have experiences with literature that provide windows to the world and a view of other peoples. Lifelong experiences with literature help people gain an understanding of how all people are alike and different. This expresses why it is so important for us, as teachers and parents, to be most vigilant when we select the books to share with young children.

Many developmentally appropriate books are available for use in early education. The following criteria should be considered when making selections for young children:

- Select books for enjoyment.
- Select books that encourage a child's capacity for laughter.
- Choose durable books. Books are to be handled and used by children. (See **Figure 5-3.**)
- Select books with different styles of illustrations.
- Consider the length of the story. Books should be age and developmentally appropriate.
- Pick books that appeal to children and relate to their experiences. (See **Figure 5-4.**)

teacher- and child-made books: Books made by the teacher and child that encourage self-esteem, creativity, and the sharing of ideas. They also encourage children to articulate experiences.

wordless picture books: Books that tell a story with visually appealing illustrations. These books promote creativity by encouraging a child to talk about experiences and use his or her imagination.

Figure 5-3   Choose durable learning books. Books are to be handled and used by children.

- Choose books that have an appealing story and style. Children like sound, rhythm, and repetition in their stories.
- Avoid overly frightening, confusing stories.
- Offer children a variety of writing styles and languages, especially those spoken by children, families, and staff in the child care program or school.
- Choose books that appeal to a young child's senses. Especially enjoyable are books with descriptive words that make children taste, smell, and feel, as well as see and hear.
  - Use literature as a stimulus for activities that require children to use their senses in discovery or exploration.
  - Pick books that help children develop positive self-esteem by emphasizing the capabilities children have.
  - Share books that promote feelings of security.
  - Choose books that show characters seeing themselves positively.
  - Select books in which characters show emotions common to young children.
  - Read several books on the same topic to provide more than one perspective.
  - Introduce books that will expand vocabulary.
  - Present books that reinforce concepts already being acquired.
  - Select books that may help clarify misconceptions.
  - Select stories that have a plot in which there is action; for example, stories that tell what people did and what they said.
  - Enrich a child's experiences with literature by providing poetry selections and books of poems.

Books that Reflect Diversity

Multicultural books for children should introduce a variety of family compositions, including single parents, grandparents who play key roles in nurturing children, and extended families who share a home and each other's lives. Teachers of young children should use multicultural literature to discuss issues of diversity, to talk about differences, and to discuss why recognizing and celebrating differences is important:

Figure 5-4   Select books that appeal to children and relate to their experiences.

- Include a wide variety of multicultural/anti-bias books. There are many that present the uniqueness of a present-day culture as seen through the eyes of a child.
- Select books that do not stereotype people according to gender, ethnic background, culture, age, or types of work. Choose books that present accurate images and information with no overt or covert stereotypes. Minority characters should be shown as independent thinkers who can face challenges and solve problems. Select books with well-developed characters that show a range of occupations and income levels that support and supplement the diversity present in the center or school. Illustrations should not use stereotypical caricatures of a group's physical features.
- Look for accuracy in stories.
- Share literature from other countries to expand children's global awareness.
- Select books that challenge unfairness and prejudice.

The Reading Is Fundamental (RIF) organization (2009) suggests the following guidelines in the selection of books that include children with special needs:

- Choose books that show differently abled people in active and interactive roles. Be sure that some books have a person with special needs as the main character.
- Read those books that regard children with disabilities as children first. Pick those that approach children with special needs as being more like other children than different.
- Make positive reading experiences a priority for children with disabilities. Read books to children, which have characters with disabilities similar to theirs.
- Make use of technology by individualizing instruction for each student and match programming to student learning styles.
- Partner with families on reading strategies. (See **Table 5-2.**)

TABLE 5-2:   **Selecting Books that Reflect Diversity**
Suggested multicultural/anti-bias books for young children.
• Addasi, M. (2009). *The white nights of Ramadan.* Illustrated by N. Gannon. New York: Boyds Mills.
• Adoff, A. (2002). *Black is brown is tan.* New York: HarperCollins.
• Aston, D. H. (2009). *The moon over star.* Illustrated by J. Pickney. New York: Dial Books for Young Children.
• Cheltenham Elementary School Kindergarten. (1991). *We are all alike … We are all different.* New York: Scholastic.
• Cumpiano, I. (2008). *Quinito, day and night/Quinito, día y noche.* Illustrated by J. Ramirez. San Francisco: Children's Book Press.
• Ichikawa, S. (2009). *My father's shop.* New York: Kane/Miller.
• Isadora, R. (2008). *Uh-oh!* Orlando: FL: Harcourt.
• Joosse, B. M. (2008). *Grandma calls me beautiful.* Illustrated by B. Lavallee. San Francisco: Chronicle.
• Jules, J. (2009). *Duck for turkey day.* Illustrated by K. Mitteer. Morton Grove, IL: Albert Whitman.
• Katz, K. (2004). *The Color of us.* New York: Henry Holt.
• Murphy, M. (2008). *I like it when … Me gusta cuando ….* Translated by F. I. Campoy & A. F. Ada. Orlando, FL: Harcourt.

Thematic Selection of Children's Books

Many teachers find that using a thematic approach to literature selection gives them more individuality in curriculum development. The thematic strategy leads children to activities that suggest active exploration, problem solving, and the acquisition of specific concepts or skills. For example, when studying frogs, children could explore the life cycle of a frog by raising tadpoles in an aquarium, learn sequencing as they note the stages of frog development, use counting as they fish for plastic frogs with a net, and experience subtraction and phonological awareness as they sing "Five Little Speckled Frogs."

You can introduce new themes weekly, biweekly, or monthly. Select the theme that relates to the children in your class according to their experiences and their age and stage of development. Then, select the literature that will emphasize, explain, and extend the theme. Glazer (2000) suggests considering a variety of titles but focus on those that best fit your purpose.

Children's Book Awards

An understanding of who gives awards for outstanding children's literature and the nature of each award provides a guide to choosing books.

The Caldecott Award is awarded annually to the artist of the most distinguished picture book for children. It is named in honor of the English illustrator Randolph Caldecott (1846–1886), a nineteenth-century pioneer in the field of children's books. The selection is made by a committee, the members of which are either elected or appointed from the ranks of children's and school librarians who are members of the Association for Library Services to Children, a part of the American Library Association.

The Caldecott Award is presented at the same time as the Newbery Award. Named for John Newbery (1713–1767), the first English publisher of children's books, and established in 1922, the Newbery Award is for "the most distinguished contribution to American literature for children" published the preceding year. It honors the quality of the author's writing and is usually a book appropriate for older children who are more mature readers. Both the Caldecott and Newbery Awards are presented at the annual conference of the American Library Association.

The Hans Christian Andersen Medal, established in 1956, is given by the International Board on Books for Young People. This award is presented every two years to a living author and an illustrator in recognition of their entire body of work.

The International Reading Association Children's Book Award is given to new authors.

The Coretta Scott King Awards are presented to an African American author and illustrator for "outstanding inspirational and educational contributions to literature for children." In addition, the National Jewish Book Awards and the Catholic Book Awards add to the list of more than 100 awards made annually to recognize authors and illustrators of literature for children.

In 2004, the American Library Association established the Theodor Seuss Geisel Award, named in honor of "Dr. Seuss." This is given annually (beginning in 2006) to the author(s) and illustrator(s) of the most distinguished contribution to the body of American children's literature known as beginning reader books published in the United States during the preceding year. Use award books as a starting point for selecting literature. Personal evaluation and knowledge of individual children, their interests, and their needs should also be criteria for selection.

Recommended Books

A listing of recommended books is included at the end of the chapter and has been divided into topics related to age or use.

The Language Center

In addition to language and literacy being apparent in all of areas of the classroom and learning centers, it is important that the environment contain a literacy center specifically designated for literacy learning. It is also important to have a variety of materials that the children can use to create their own books. (See **Table 5-3**.)

The actual physical environment plays a large role in enhancing literacy development. A checklist is provided that can be used to evaluate the literacy environment in your own classroom or classrooms that you observe.

TABLE 5-3: Language Arts Center Materials and Supplies	
• Pencils, pens, and chalk of various sizes and colors	• Large and individual chalkboards, dry erase boards, and magic slates
• Crayons of various sizes, colors, and thicknesses	• Carbon paper
• Markers of various colors; fine-tipped, thick-tipped, washable; permanent, and scented	• Finger paints
• Magnetic letters and numbers	• Pencil sharpener
• Typewriter	• Rulers
• Computer	• Tape
• Toy or nonworking telephone	• Glue
• Toy microphone	• Scissors
• Paper of various sizes, colors, and textures; lined and unlined paper; drawing paper; construction paper; and scraps	• Stapler
	• Stickers
• Cardboard and poster board	• Date stamp and pad
• Stationary	• Other donated office stamps and pads
• Journals	• Paper clips
• Note pads	• Hole punch
• Index cards	• Brads
• Envelopes	• Maps and globes
• Graph paper	• Pictionaries and dictionaries
• Post-its	• Message board
• Order forms	• Folders and notebooks
• Business forms	• Old newspapers and magazines

Literacy Environment Checklist

_____ 1. Does the literacy center include written materials in English and all other languages spoken by the children in the class?

_____ 2. Is the center aesthetically pleasing?

_____ 3. Are books included in at least five learning centers?

_____ 4. Is a picture dictionary available?

_____ 5. Do the books represent a variety of cultures and families?

_____ 6. Is attention drawn to letters, words, concepts of print (i.e., top to bottom), author, illustrations, and book-handling skills?

_____ 7. Are books in good condition?

_____ 8. Is there a variety of writing materials such as wipe-off boards, notepads, envelopes, chalkboards, appointment books, and receipts?

_____ 9. Does the literacy area include a variety of books such as nursery rhymes, storybooks, alphabet, and informational and picture books?

_____ 10. Is an author's chair available?

_____ 11. Are books read to children in large or small groups and individually?

_____ 12. Is there adequate lighting around the literacy areas?

_____ 13. Do books have quality illustrations, award-winning authors, and interesting stories?

_____ 14. Is there a computer with writing software and a printer?

_____ 15. Are digital recorders available for children to record their own stories?

_____ 16. Are the alphabet and word walls displayed at child's eye level?

_____ 17. Is the literacy center available as a choice activity daily?

_____ 18. Does the literacy center include storytelling props such as puppets, flannel boards, story apron, or magnetic boards?

_____ 19. Is literacy apparent through labeling, names on cubbies, daily schedules, job charts, dictation about artwork, and recipes?

_____ 20. Do teachers write with children and encourage children to write?

_____ 21. Is a listening area provided that includes books with CDs or audio tapes, MP3 players, digital recorders headphones, or CD player?

_____ 22. Are the tapes or CDs and props stored together in plastic bags or baskets?

_____ 23. Does the literacy area include a variety of furnishings and materials such as a child-sized rocker, carpeted floor, beanbags, and large pillows where children can look at books?

_____ 24. Is the literacy center clearly defined and separated from the rest of the room?

_____ 25. Does the literacy area include a bookshelf with books facing out that can hold at least 25 books?

_____ 26. Are the books developmentally appropriate for each of the children in the classroom?

_____ 27. Does the literacy area provide a table with chairs for writing and a shelf for writing materials?

_____ 28. Are book-making supplies available?

_____ 29. Can children store and easily retrieve their writing?

_____ 30. Do the children share their writing with others through mailboxes, message boards, bulletin boards with experience stories, and child-created stories in the reading area?

_____ 31. Is the literacy center in a quiet area of the classroom?

_____ 32. Does the literacy area provide a variety of materials to write on and a variety of materials to write with such as clipboards, lined/unlined paper, stationary, journals, pens, pencils, markers, and chalk?

_____ 33. Can the center accommodate at least five children?

_____ 34. Are new books and props added on a regular basis?

_____ 35. Do at least three learning centers in the classroom include newspapers, charts, magazines, lists, and cookbooks?

≫ Professional Resource Download

Integrating Language and Literacy into the Curriculum

Strategies to Support Reading

DAP **naeyc** **INTASC** **HS**

No matter the age of the child, books are an important tool for introducing children to the pleasure, rhythm, power, and beauty of language through print and pictures. They can encourage children to ask questions and use their imagination. Stories can help children to see themselves as part of a larger world in which people are both alike and different from themselves.

Infants

When you hold an infant in your lap and share a special story or book, you are making a difference in that child's life. When you set up the special places in the infant room for reading or telling a story or for singing a nursery rhyme, include pillows, stuffed animals, quilts, and mats. It is important for infants to interact with the books. For them, that means chewing on the pages, touching and looking at them in unique ways, and making them a part of their "personal turf."

Toddlers

The special place for story time in the toddler room should be surrounded with colorful pillows, carpet squares, and other comfortable spots available for these young children to listen to, participate with, and enjoy books. Small groupings offer the children a chance to turn the pages, point, and identify things, while sharing their choice of books with the teacher and each other. For those toddlers who enjoy one-on-one time with a teacher and a favorite book, sitting in a rocking chair fulfills this need in a special way.

Story time outdoors on a big quilt, under a tree, and surrounded by grass can be exciting and appropriate for toddlers, too. Physically enjoying the story is important for these children.

Three-, Four-, and Five-Year-Olds

The story center, library, or book center should be one of the most inviting and exciting learning centers or curriculum areas in a classroom for these children, with many comfortable reading spaces provided, such as a soft rug; a big, empty "refrigerator-size" box with pillows to sit on and "windows" cut in the box to look out of; and child-size tables and chairs set up with a variety of books, magazines, catalogs, newspapers, books with CDs, blank paper, and writing instruments.

As teachers, you should read aloud to your 3-, 4-, and 5-year-olds every day and plan activities that integrate listening, speaking, reading, and writing. It is also important for you to continue to read to individual children if they ask you to because the children still need this special time with a significant adult. For example, they will benefit from hearing predictable books. These books help children practice decoding words, to develop the concept of story structure, and even create their own theme story. Book reading is enhanced when children are on a lap and become active participants when they turn the pages, point to things in pictures, make comments, and ask questions.

Six-, Seven-, and Eight-Year-Olds

Computers, cell phones, movies, television shows, video games, and music videos pose a challenge to teachers, librarians, and parents trying to capture the reading attention of 6-, 7-, and 8-year-olds. As a result, literature for this age reflects the addition of topics grounded in real-life issues. Illustrations are more complex and artistic, and a greater diversity is available.

As a teacher, you should provide many opportunities and motivations for reading and writing in the early childhood classroom. During this time, most children become real readers. The more emphasis you place on the importance of books in the lives of 6-, 7-, and 8-year-olds, the more important literature will be to the children. As with all ages, read aloud to them as often as you can. Let them tell you and others about what they have read, and encourage open-ended questioning by everyone. Special time should be regularly set aside for children to choose and read books on their own. Also, when visitors come to your classroom, have them tell a story or read to the children. Inviting parents, grandparents, community volunteers, other teachers, or staff to read provides another dimension. Keep a well-stocked reading corner that is regularly infused with new books. (See **Figure 5-5.**)

Figure 5-5 Select books with well-developed characters that support and supplement the diversity present in the center or school.

Integrating Literature into Other Curriculum Areas

The connection between literature and the other curriculum areas can be enhanced by using a variety of books and expanding them into child writing, drama, and art. Literature integrated units can be developed around a single book, such as *In the Tall, Tall Grass* by Denise Fleming. This book allows children to explore a backyard environment such as weather and things that live in the grass. The focus may also be in a content area, such as science, social studies, or basic concepts.

Other ways of connecting books to areas of the curriculum are by taking the responses of children to literature and having them reproduce those responses in their own language using art, music, and drama. This effectively teaches children to recognize and organize story elements.

Repeating structural patterns called *motifs* or *themes* are used throughout literature to emphasize a point the author wants to make. Papic, Mulligan, and Mitchelmore (2011) found that learning that focuses on pattern and structure can not only lead to improved generalized thinking but also create opportunities for developing mathematical reasoning.

Putting literature around the room can be done realistically by creatively decorating containers for books with bright contact paper, wallpaper, or children's drawings and by placing baskets of books in every learning activity center. For example, books relating to houses and buildings can be put in the block center; those dealing with shapes and colors can be put in the art center; and books concerning gardening, fish, and turtles can be near the sand and water table.

There are many techniques you can use to place items promoting language and literacy around the room. Some we have already discussed in this chapter. The following suggested activities are additional ones that teachers of young children have found to be developmentally and multiculturally appropriate, as well as lots of fun to do.

Flannel Board Activities

Often, teachers hear a child say, "Tell it again." One of the ways to tell or extend a story effectively is with the use of a **flannel board**.

Young children's symbolic play signals the development of representational thought (Piaget) and has been recognized as critical in the development of abstract thought (Vygotsky). As children use flannel board activities to retell a new or familiar story they represent oral and written language in picture form, thereby gaining structures for later abstract thinking. Using flannel boards with early childhood children provides a natural connection to process writing. Children enjoy writing and rehearsing their own scripts.

A good flannel board activity serves as a visual prop for a story, song, or poem, particularly for one that does not have illustrations. It also improves communication and dramatizes concepts. A good flannel board has the following characteristics:

- It attracts attention.
- It stimulates interest.
- It is flexible in use.
- It frees a teacher's hands.
- It adds texture to the activity.
- It is a visual prop for a story, song, or poem that does not have illustrations.
- It improves communication.
- It dramatizes concepts.
- It is easily made and easily stored.

Other important aspects of this type of activity are as follows:

- The children can help the teacher tell the story by placing the pieces on the board at the appropriate time in the story.
- After the teacher tells the story, the flannel board and character pieces can be placed in any activity center or curriculum area.
- The children or individual child can then tell the story to each other or make up another story to relate to the flannel board pieces.
- Flannel board figures can be touched, held, and moved, forming a bridge between the real and the abstract.

flannel board: Used as a prop to tell or extend a story effectively.

You can purchase a commercial flannel board or you can make your own. Select plywood, masonite, or any wood-based board for durability. Styrofoam board, heavy cardboard, display board, and pre-stretched artist's canvas are more lightweight and easier to carry but not as durable. The board may be freestanding or placed on an easel, on a chalkboard tray, or on a chair. Smaller, individual boards can be placed in the language arts center for children to use by themselves or with a friend.

Flannel cloth is usually the best material to use for covering the base. It has excellent adhering qualities and is lightweight and colorful. Felt cloth also can be used with good results, as can most fuzzy textured material. Velour (material used for making house robes and blankets) stretches slightly to cover the board, maintains its texture, and is available in an assortment of colors. (See **Figure 5-6**.)

An almost unlimited variety of materials to use with flannel board characters and activities are easily available and inexpensive. The most commonly used items are nonwoven interfacing material from the fabric store, felt, and heavy flannel. When selecting materials to be used for flannel board activities, it is important to be sure the adhesive quality of the material is great enough to support its own weight or the weight of the item to which it will be attached.

Some of the resources for finding flannel board poems, stories, and figures are: teachers of young children, commercial activity sets, and shapes and figures traced from books, magazines, photographs, illustrations, pictures, and drawings. (For puppet and flannel board characters introduced in this text, go to Chapter 5 in Mindtap and Appendix E for a listing of teacher resources.) Be creative and draw some yourself.

Color can be added to the flannel board set pieces with permanent felt markers, crayons, and paints. It is fun to accent the figures with wiggly eyes and imitation fur fabric. You will find it helpful to trace with tissue paper. For easy storage, use a folder with pockets, a large mailing envelope, a manila folder with the story stapled inside (make a pocket of tag board or construction paper to hold the pieces), or large plastic household bags. (See **Figure 5-6**.)

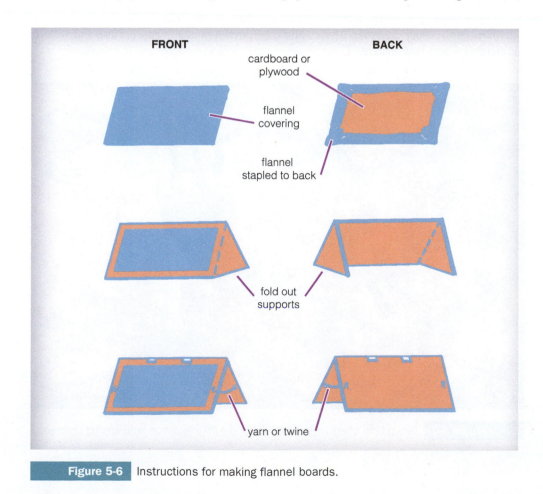

Figure 5-6 Instructions for making flannel boards.

Group Time Activities

Group time presents an opportunity for listening, speaking, vocabulary development, and cognitive and social activities. Here are a few helpful hints for successful group time activities (see **Figure** 5-7):

- Organize activities ahead of time, plan carefully, and think about what is going to happen before, during, and after.
- Have realistic expectations of the children and be flexible.
- Select a time and place where a few children can be involved or where others can join in when they finish cleaning up. Be able to accommodate the entire group.
- Select developmentally and culturally appropriate activities that relate to the children's experiences.
- Guide children in and out of group time with appropriate transitions.
- Change the pace often and include a variety of activities.
- Encourage listening and discussing skills. Respond to a child's meaning even if the words are not correct words. Model the appropriate words when you clarify what was said.
- Anticipate problems and take steps to avoid them by explaining expected behaviors to the children.
- Acknowledge and reinforce appropriate behavior.
- Give clear, simple directions.
- Respond to each individual child as well as to the group.
- Maintain physical and emotional closeness.
- Anticipate a "good" stopping point, or stop before the children lose interest.
- Be prepared with an extra activity in case what you have planned does not work or the activity time needs to be extended.
- Evaluate and make needed changes for next time.
- Enjoy the children.

Appropriate group time activities are finger plays, poetry, songs, stories, flannel board activities, and sensory activities. These should be developmentally appropriate and reflect multicultural/anti-bias content.

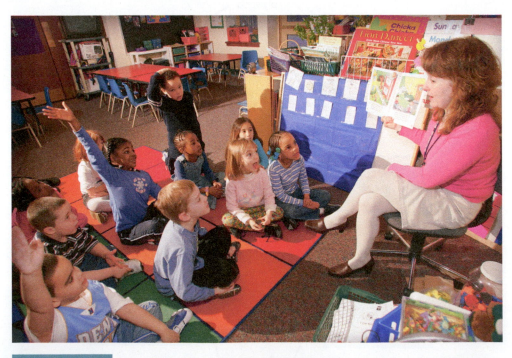

Figure 5-7   Group time offers an opportunity for quality interaction time among children.

The activity "HOP-HOP!" (see Appendix B) illustrates a musical finger play activity that toddlers and preschoolers enjoy doing.

The story of *A Little Red House (Una Casita Roja)* (see Appendix B) is an example of another appropriate group activity. It can be told in group time and then repeated by using flannel board pieces (online at this text's premium website). Follow-up activities can be: Put the flannel board pieces and the written story in the language arts center, have a special cooking center set up so children can find their own "little red house," and then make applesauce.

A **rebus chart** is another way to integrate literacy into the curriculum. The rebus chart offers visual picture signs and directions to help children make sense of any activity, that is, read left to right, top to bottom, and recognize letters and symbols. This helps put children in charge of their own learning. For older children, placing the rebus chart in a learning center helps them work independently without teacher direction.

Puppets

"In the digital age, the need has never been greater for teaching tools that are high-touch—that foster a bond between young and adult, [as well as] emotive intelligence, creativity, freedom, and individuality. . . . [Puppets can help] teachers reach all kinds of learners in ways that: activate and employ the hands; create powerful experiences for learners to help them articulate, express, and remember what they learn; foster socialization and civic values; employ upbeat and imaginative group dynamics; and build upon innate learning skills and strengths (Peyton, 2009, p. 7)."

The theory behind multisensory education is to provide each child the advantage of lessons taught through multiple senses that would increase the likelihood of the child absorbing the material. In more complex terms, instruction targeting multiple senses stimulates more neural pathways within the brain (Christie, 2010). Timeless Wisdom from Fred Rogers:

"No matter how helpful computers are as tools (and of course they can be very helpful tools), they don't begin to compare in significance to the teacher-child relationship which is human and mutual. A computer can help you learn to spell HUG, but it can never know the risk or the joy of actually giving or receiving one (Rogers, 2003)."

It is helpful to brainstorm ideas for high-touch teaching tools with colleagues and classmates, but here are a few suggestions to stimulate your creativity:

- Puppets can speak in any language. This shows that all languages are valued. For example, Mister Number is a puppet that can count from 1 to 20 in many languages. Another puppet says only *yes* and *no* or *hello* and *goodbye*, but does so in 10 different languages. Multicultural puppets can also be used to introduce cultural celebrations.
- Expand the language arts center by adding puppets and props. A puppet with a microphone can encourage creative play. Puppets can even interview other puppets. Because the characters can be human, animal, or "Mr. and Ms. Anything," they can ask questions about families, feelings, favorite foods, where you come from, or where you live. For older children, the questions can also concern current events, nutrition, math, science, or ecology.
- Encourage storytelling with sock puppets representing *The Three Billy Goats Gruff* by P. C. Asbjørnsen and J. E. Moe, *The Little Red Hen* by P. Galdone, or characters from *Winnie the Pooh* by A. A. Milne and *The Velveteen Rabbit* by M. Williams. Use finger puppets or hand puppets to read the storybooks *Corduroy* by D. Freeman, *Leo the*

rebus chart: Visual pictures, such as signs, illustrations, and directions, to help children make sense of any activity.

Late Bloomer by R. Kraus, or *Horton Hatches the Egg* by Dr. Seuss (T. Geisel). Relating puppets to familiar stories can extend the retelling.

- A puppet "helper of the day" can offer you a unique way to reinforce cooperation, cleanup rules, and problem solving. The puppet can ask the children questions, leading them to solve a problem themselves, instead of needing you to solve it. This puppet character can help defuse many disputes and difficulties that occur in an early childhood setting.
- Introducing a "listening puppet," one with big ears, can help you emphasize the importance of listening. One puppet might talk to or answer children only in song or verse. Perhaps another only dances. A shy puppet who will not talk can learn to do so with help from the children.

Word Walls

In early childhood classrooms, a **word wall** is a tool that children can use to discover new words while practicing and expanding their language skills. Word walls are ongoing displays of words or parts of words used to teach letter-sound correspondence, spelling, reading and writing strategies, and more. The word wall is an alphabetically arranged display or chart of words that children have experienced. These words should be reviewed regularly to help the children internalize them. As teachers, we should collaboratively build word walls with the children. They choose words from meaningful contexts such as shared reading materials and oral language experiences, thereby reinforcing their growing vocabulary and special interests they have explored in each previous unit of study (Houle and Krogness, 2001).

Neuman, Copple, and Bredekamp (2000) emphasize the importance of distinguishing letters of the alphabet and sounds in reading: "To read, children must be able to distinguish the letters of the alphabet and to connect letters and letter clusters with sounds. To become proficient readers they need to be able to recognize many familiar words at a glance as well as decode words they don't know by sight."

Creating a Word Wall

The following are a few tips for teachers for creating word walls from Houle and Krogness (2001):

- Create the wall at the children's eye level in an accessible and highly visible area.
- Keep the wall simple and uncluttered for easy reference.
- Make sure there is ample room to add new words.
- Encourage children to help build the wall with words they wish to spell or words they know and want to add.
- Make your word walls interactive by attaching key words with Velcro strips, sticky tack, or pockets. This allows the children to go to the wall, remove a word, use it, and return it.

Strategies to Support Writing

COMMON CORE   DAP

Offer pressure-free experimentation with writing, and encourage children to write often. Playing with written language is the first step in learning to communicate. Remember that children's first writing attempts appear as scribbling. Help them when you feel they need it. For example, "This is how I write your name. How do you write your name?"

Emergent writing "means that children begin to understand that writing is a form of communication and their marks on paper convey a message" (Mayer, 2007, p. 35).

word wall: An alphabetically arranged display or chart of words that children have experienced throughout the school year.

Emergent writing progresses along a developmental continuum. Reading and writing develop simultaneously and are interrelated. The relationship between reading and writing is bidirectional such that reading facilitates writing abilities and learning how to write, in turn, improves reading ability (Mayer 2007). Thus, progress in one fuels development of the other. Research suggests that letter-writing instruction and letter-writing activities may improve emerging literacy skills (Puranik, Lonigan, and Kim, 2011).

Emergent forms of writing include drawing, scribbling from left to right, creating letter-like forms, or creating random strings of letters, all used—sometimes even simultaneously—in the child's attempt to communicate an idea through print.

Early writing experiences during the preschool years should introduce and reinforce meaningful and authentic opportunities for the children in your classroom. The following activities provide a wide range of writing activities:

- *Writing with Water:* Take a bucket of water and several large and small paintbrushes outside. The children can "write" on or "paint" the sidewalk, the building walls, the tricycles, the wagons, and the fence. This activity helps develop large muscle control, and at the same time provides the beginnings of literacy development. It is easy and fun, too.
- *Labeling:* Encourage the children to label things in the classroom as well as outdoors. Start the labeling yourself and let the children help. Listen to the children and let them label what they think needs labeling. This will help them "read the room." (The children love to use Post-its to label things, and they can change them whenever *they* want to.) It is also fun to make floor signs, such as traffic signs, that say "enter," "exit," "stop," and "go."
- *Writing to Others:* Have the children write thank-you letters or notes to community members who visit the class and to those they have visited during field trips.
- *Story Starters:* Have the children tell you a story about when they were babies, or what happens when the wind blows, or what sounds they hear and sights they see. Use an audio or video recorder to capture their storytelling. Older children can write and illustrate their own big book based on the story.
- *Birthday Celebration:* Create a birthday celebration center once a month that lasts a week. Stock it with paper to make birthday cards; markers and crayons; old birthday card fronts; and scraps of lace, yarn, fabric, stickers, and birthday words. Use *happy birthday* in other languages, such as *joyeux anniversaire* (French) and *feliz cumpleaños* (Spanish). Children can make cards for family members and classmates. This is a wonderful way to promote thoughtfulness, socialization, language, writing, reading, and creativity. Extend this activity by making a "Birthday Book" of the class. (If a child's family does not celebrate birthdays, the child does not have to visit this particular learning center.)
- *Journal Writing:* Motivate the children to write about their day, record things they want to remember, jot down words from the word wall, or copy the words of the titles of books, songs, finger plays, and recipes in their journals. These journals can be used in any learning center in the classroom.
- *Dictionaries:* Promote opportunities for the children to go for "word walks" around the classroom and copy words from labels, books, and so on. They learn name recognition by writing their classmates' names in their dictionary. This helps the children to become more aware of print and identifies early alphabetizing or sequencing. Also have actual dictionaries around (Bobys, 2000).
- *Graphic Organizers:* Graphic organizers help children to see relationships between several pieces of information. Story maps, word wheels, and K-W-L (a chart or graphic representation that reflects "What I know, What I want to know, and What I just learned") work well with kindergarten children and first-graders (Schiller and Willis, 2008).

Activities that Encourage Children to Become Authors and Illustrators

Children can also benefit from dictating stories, which preserves their oral language in print and supports their understanding of the connection between oral and written language (Tunks and Giles, 2009). One of the most stimulating child-centered activities a teacher can use is having the children write original books or one-page stories. You can help the youngest children put their artwork together in the form of a book, using string or rings to do so; for older children, pair them as "book buddies" or "book partners" to write and illustrate their own books. Some teacher preparation or assistance may be needed or requested. Machado (2010) presents the values of books authored by children or their teachers:

- They promote interest in the classroom book collection.
- They help children see connections between spoken and written words.
- The material is based on the interests of both the children and the teacher.
- They personalize book reading.
- They prompt self-expression.
- They stimulate creativity.
- They build feelings of competence and self-worth.

You can encourage children's (and teachers') roles as authors and illustrators in many ways. Having children make book covers for their books can affirm the importance of all books. In the writing or art center, provide paper, wallpaper, or contact paper that will cover a child's favorite book. The child can decorate the cover and write the title, author, and illustrator as well.

How about a "Let's Pretend Book"? In the dramatic play area, have a camera (digital, video, or disposable type) ready for children to take pictures of what is going on in the grocery store, pet shop, post office, or whatever the area represents for that week. You can then place these images on sheets of paper to be made into a book together. The children can tell or dictate the story of who they were pretending to be. Visually and concretely, this helps children understand that their words and actions make stories and books.

Reading Is Fundamental (RIF 2009) suggests that looking at and understanding both words and pictures demands a higher cognitive level than merely seeing that words and pictures are there. Teachers should develop many opportunities for children to further develop cognitively. One such way is to encourage older children to become illustrators by using the following techniques:

- Have children author a book without illustrations and then author the same story, including illustrations.
- Have children develop a traditional storybook in which the text and illustrations are mutually supportive.
- Encourage children to try their hand at authoring and illustrating a wordless picture book.
- Help children see the relationship between a book's meaning and its art.

As with any child-directed activity, the teacher prepares materials and space in advance and is available to offer assistance. Suggestions for putting the book together can come from the teacher as well, with the children putting the book together with yarn, staples, masking tape, metal rings, or brads. The size and shape of the cover and pages of the book can be another creative element, such as books shaped to match the current curriculum theme or children's interests. For example, books can be in the shape of a bird, butterfly, car, bus, animal, fish, vegetable, and so on.

Keep in mind that however and whenever you mix and match literature with other curriculum areas, all activities should benefit the children developmentally, individually, and creatively. Family involvement in children's learning is also important in promoting children's love of literature. One way to encourage a family to contribute is to give each child a chance to take home one of the books he or she made individually or with a classmate. Many times, the family does not know that their child is the author and illustrator of a book.

Encourage family members to participate in the process by asking them to extend the story that their child began in school. Send the book home in a bag with index cards so family members can write the next part of the story. To make this a family activity, suggest that family members use the children's words when continuing the story. Primary-age children can write the words of the story on the cards themselves.

When the child brings the book back to the class, all the children can enjoy the story. This literacy project can go on until the child or the family decides to stop.

Reflect On This

How can you tell if a child is really involved in story time?

Teachers as Storytellers

In every culture in the world, people have told stories. The oral tradition was once the primary method for passing history and culture from one generation to the next. As Western nations embraced new technologies, however, oral traditions became unpopular. A story—whether written or oral—is one of the means by which children make sense of their world and organize events, experiences, and facts. A teacher telling a story without a book and using changes in pitch, tone, and dramatic flair; using puppets, props, toys, songs, flannel board pictures, and finger plays; or drawing a story while it is being told can captivate and entertain a small or large group of children. This unique way of presenting children's literature encourages children to tell their own stories or retell the stories back to the teachers.

"Storytelling is perhaps the most powerful way that human beings organize experience" (Engel, 1996/1997, p. 3). Im, Parlakian, and Osborn (2007, pp. 52–53) tell us, "Adults can tell stories through language, but infants and toddlers tell their stories with a flick of their eyes, the point of a finger, or a coo. . . . Remember that much of infant and toddler communication is nonverbal. Very young children need patient and willing listeners who can accurately read their cues . . . and respond appropriately."

It is helpful for the teacher to select stories with simple plots and small numbers of characters for the younger children. Older children like the challenge of remembering a complex plot with multiple characters.

Poetry

Teachers should read poetry to children often. Kindergarten and primary children can memorize a few poems of their choosing. Not only is this an enjoyable activity, but it is also a valuable way to develop phonemic awareness and cognitive skills. Appreciation for poetry develops slowly, but the time and place for poetry is any time, any place.

Have snack time become a "poetry break time." Start by reading a poem to the children during their snack. Then, on following days, let the children read or tell a poem to each other and the teacher after snack time. Adding a musical background, recorded or live, offers a different dimension to poetry reading.

Other activities that develop poetry time can be to act out a poem, draw an illustration for a poem, include poetry at group time, pick a theme and make an illustrated booklet or exhibit of poems that relate to the theme, and create a "Poetry Line" (clothesline or thick yarn) stretched across the back of the room with poems attached.

"Tongue Twisters for Young Children," is a different kind of poem. Children learn about language with this fun activity. The following section on activity plans provides examples of poems appropriate to share with young children.

Activity Plans

As suggested in Chapter 3, using an activity plan worksheet will help you clearly describe the activity, objectives, concepts, skills, space and materials needed, step-by-step procedure, guidance and limits for expected behavior, and assessment and follow-up strategies. These should align with your state curriculum standards. The following activity plan worksheets are examples for developmentally appropriate activities for infants; toddlers; 3-, 4-, and 5-year-olds; and kindergarten children.

Activity Plan Worksheet | Developmentally Appropriate Activities for Young Children

AGE: Toddlers (18 months–3 years)

Name of Activity and Brief Description

Sharing nursery rhyme books with individual children

These are the books we will share:

Hoberman, M. A. (2003, Sing Along Stories). *Mary had a little lamb.* Illustrated by N. B. Westcott. New York: Little Brown Young Readers.

Fox, M. (2008). *Ten little fingers and ten little toes.* Illustrated by H. Oxenbury. Orlando, FL: Harcourt.

Wells, R. (2001, Board Book). *Twinkle, twinkle little star.* New York: Scholastic.

Child Outcomes of Activity

- Listen to a short story for the development of listening skills.
- Look at books and rhymes.
- Recognize and point out objects and familiar animals.
- Turn pages.
- Say words and sing rhymes.

Space and Materials Needed

Rocking chair, floor, pillows, and books

Procedure

The following activities are mainly inside ones, carried on next to the bookshelf while the child sits on the adult's lap, on the floor, or in a rocking chair. These activities can also be taken outside and done while you are sitting on a blanket.

1. Let the child choose a book from the low shelf.
2. Read the book to the child. Point to what is going on in the pictures. See if the child will try to say a word or part of a word with you.
3. Do the finger plays for the rhymes, such as "Twinkle, Twinkle Little Star."
4. Repeat these finger plays or songs often during transition times.

Guidance

Usually, this is a one-on-one activity, but other children in the group are welcomed to look at the pictures and encouraged to do the finger plays, too. If other children want a book read to them at the same time, have enough books on the shelf or nearby so they can look at them. Keep the stories short.

Assessment and Follow-Up Strategies

These nursery rhyme books are popular with the infants, and so are the follow-up activities. Sing the nursery songs and do the rhymes often to encourage language and motor development. Play dough makes a great "Pat-a-Cake." Have a tea party for "Polly Put the Kettle On." Use cotton balls to make "Mary Had a Little Lamb." Eat muffins to relate to "Muffin Man," and do exercises (sit, stand up, and fall down) with "Humpty Dumpty." To achieve effectiveness in this activity, keep the stories short and do not mind when a child turns the page before you finish the rhyme. However, be sure there are plenty of books available, because a child this age does not share easily.

⌄⌄ Professional Resource Download

Activity Plan Worksheet	Developmentally Appropriate Activities for Young Children

AGES: 3-, 4-, and 5-year-olds

Name of Activity and Brief Description
Group time story and cooking activity
Here are the books we will share:
DK Preschool. (2005, Board Book): *Lift the flap: Things that go.*
    New York: DK Publishing.
Priddy, R. (2002, Big Board Book). *My big truck book.*
    New York: Priddy Books.
Ziefert, H., and Baruffi, A. (1992). *Where Is Mommy's truck?*
    New York: HarperCollins.

Reading a book about trucks or things that go offers a large format that brings images to life. Teacher and children can spend a few minutes together talking about the people who drive cars and trucks, big and small. Sometimes mommy and daddy drive a truck to work. Mommies and daddies go to many different kinds of jobs. By asking open-ended, short questions, toddlers can spend time one-on-one with the teacher and the book. After reading the book, the teacher will explain the art activity: car and truck painting. This activity will be available for any child to do with minimal assistance from the teacher, if needed. The children should direct the process.

Child Outcomes of Activity
- Practice small muscle skills.
- Practice hand-eye coordination.
- Demonstrate cause and effect.
- Practice color recognition.

Space and Materials Needed
Indoor (or outdoor) table with or without chairs, individual sheets of paper, washable paint on a tray, and small cars and trucks.

Procedure
1. Place cars and trucks on a tray with paint.
2. One child at a time (wearing a painting smock) rolls the cars and trucks through the paint and then "car paints"

on his sheet of paper. (If possible, have several places set up for this activity.)

3. The teacher talks to the child and asks questions throughout this activity, such as: "Can you drive the car and make some tracks?" "Show me how you can drive on the paper." "Does your car make some sounds?" "What color is your car or truck or the road you're making?"
4. At the end of the activity for each child, the teacher can say: "Your paper is full of roads and tracks." "Show me how you can wash your hands and hang your smock up." "Thank you."

Some children will participate in this activity in their own way. That is all right. It is the process that is important, not the product.

Guidance
Anticipating what a toddler might do, the teacher can easily use her words to guide the child. This encourages the child to use his or her words. Examples: "Your car drives on the tray or on the paper." "Show me how you can sit on your bottom on the chair." "Your paper is so full of roads; now it is another friend's turn." "Would you like another piece of paper?"

It is helpful to have another teacher or teacher assistant guiding the other children into activity centers while the teacher at the art table works one-on-one with a child.

Assessment and Follow-Up Strategies
Were all the objectives met? When an older toddler is participating in the art activity, the teacher can suggest placement of the car on the tray or paper, such as back-and-forth or up-and-down. And at this point, other paint colors on additional trays can be added. This helps a child see how one road can cross another. To further extend the activity, add puzzles of cars and trucks to the manipulative center. Sing songs such as "Little Red Wagon" or "The Wheels on the Bus."

⌄ Professional Resource Download

AGES: 3-, 4-, and 5-year-olds

Name of Activity and Brief Description

Group time story and cooking activity

These are the books we will share:

Heloua, L. (2007). *Tangerine and Kiwi visit the bread baker*. Illustrated by N. LaPierre. New York: Owlkids Books.

Levenson, G. (2008). *Bread comes to life: A garden of wheat and a loaf to eat*. Photographed by S. Thaler. Berkeley, CA: Tricycle Press.

Morris, A. (1989). *Bread, bread, bread*. Photographs by Ken Heyman. New York: Lothrop, Lee & Shepard.

Paulsen, G. (1998, reprint edition). *The tortilla factory*. New York: Voyager.

Reiser, L. (2008). *Tortillas and lullabies/Tortillas y cancioncitas*. Illustrated by C. Valientes. New York: Greenwillow Books.

Share the books with the children. (Place the ones you do not read to them in a basket in the home living area.) After reading one of the books, invite the children to go to the snack table. The teacher has provided a "tasting party" of different types of bread. Blunt table knives for spreading butter or margarine and jam or jelly are available for the children.

The teacher (with her teacher assistant) explains how she plans to let any child who wants to help with the cooking activity.

Child Outcomes of Activity

- Introduce the concepts that people all over the world eat bread and that bread comes in many different shapes, sizes, and colors.
- Recognize that some families serve bread for various festivities and ceremonies.
- Ask open-ended questions about the type of bread each child eats at home, such as: "Which is your favorite type of bread?" "Have you ever eaten corn bread?"
- Introduce children to different ingredients.
- Provide opportunities for measuring, pouring, sifting, stirring, and baking.
- Practice a cooking activity and involve children in the process of doing, thinking, talking, and asking.

Space and Materials Needed

Large low table, small chairs, mixing bowls, ingredients, measuring cup, measuring spoons, large spoon for stirring, muffin pan, paper muffin cup liners, oven tray, blunt plastic knives, butter or margarine, jam or jelly, variety of breads to taste, recipe, and book to introduce activity.

Procedure

1. At group time, read either *Bread, Bread, Bread* or *Bread Comes to Life*.
2. Ask open-ended questions about the families shown in the photographs in the book, the children's families, what kind of bread they eat at home, and which is their favorite.
3. Children go to the large table for snack time. They taste all kinds of bread, margarine, and jam.
4. The teacher explains the activity choices for the day. Making corn bread muffins is one of the activities. Three children and the teacher will make the first batch. Later the teacher will make some more corn bread with another three children. The corn bread muffins will be the afternoon snack.
5. The children and the teacher wash their hands and the table, put on smocks, put out the cooking utensils and ingredients, and read the recipe together. (The teacher has printed the recipe on a large poster with both illustrations and words.)

Corn Bread

1. 1 cup flour
2. 1 cup cornmeal
3. 1/4 cup sugar
4. teaspoons baking powder
5. 1/2 teaspoon salt
6. 1 egg
7. 1 cup milk
8. 1/4 cup cooking oil

Sift together flour, cornmeal, sugar, baking powder and salt. Add egg, milk and oil. Beat until smooth. Pour into a greased pan and bake for 20 minutes at 425 degrees.

Guidance

Before any cooking activity, the teacher should check the ingredients to make sure there are no foods that the children might be allergic to. That food should be eliminated or an alternative ingredient should be used. Anticipating what could occur, the teachers prepare to help children understand why they cannot taste the ingredients that are measured to go into the corn bread. There will be time when the muffins are cooking for them to taste the ingredients. (Put some ingredients aside for small tastes. Exclude the raw egg. Then, talk about pre- and post-baking.) Remind the children of safety factors when using utensils. Supervise closely. Provide sponges and soap and water for cleanup and child-size brooms for sweeping.

Assessment and Follow-Up Strategies

After this specific activity, the children participate with open-ended questions.

Other extended activities might include:

- Read other books about bread.
- Take a field trip to a bakery or bagel shop.

- Relate bread to nutrition and the food groups.
- Bake other breads, such as tortillas.

Tortillas

| 2 cups masa | 1 cup water |

Mix together. Roll into 1-inch balls. Press flat, using waxed paper to keep from sticking. Cook in a greased electric skillet at 350 degrees. Turn when you can "slip" a spatula under, and cook on the other side until done.

CORN BREAD

Sift together:

One cup flour, one cup cornmeal,

¼ cup sugar, 4 teaspoons baking powder,

and ½ teaspoon salt.

Add one egg, one cup milk and

¼ cup cooking oil. Beat until smooth.

Pour into a greased pan and bake for 20 minutes at 425 degrees.

Tortillas

Mix these ingredients in a bowl:

Two cups masa and one cup water

Roll into 1 inch balls.

Press flat using waxed paper to keep from sticking.

Fry in a greased electric skillet at 350 degrees.

Turn when you can "slip" a spatula under and cook on the other side until done.

Activity Plan Worksheet	Developmentally Appropriate Activities for Young Children

AGES: Kindergarten

Name of Activity and Brief

Group time story, writing invitations, and making no-bake cookies

These are the books we will share:

Carmi, G. (2006). *A circle of friends*. New York: Star Bright Books.

de Regniers, B. S. (1999). *May I bring a friend?* Illustrated by Beni Montresor. New York: Atheneum.

Hallinan, P. K. (2005) *A rainbow of friends.* New York: Ideals Children's Books.

Wilson, S. (2008). *Friends and pals and brothers, too.* Illustrated by L. Landry. New York: Henry Holt.

This is an introduction for the theme "Friends and Families." After reading one of the books, continue discussing friends, the ones in the book as well as the friends in the class.

The teacher explains how, during the week, each child can write an invitation to his or her friend in the classroom to come to the party on Friday during afternoon snack time. Another activity will be to make cookies to share with their friends at the party.

Child Outcomes of Activity

- Introduce concepts that friends can be people or animals and that friends are kind to each other.
- Recognize that everyone can *be* a friend and *have* a friend at the same time.
- Provide opportunities for cooperation, sharing, and kindness.
- Practice math skill development: counting, measuring, number value, and quantity.

Space and Materials Needed

Book to introduce the activity; various colored and textured papers; markers and crayons; pencils; scissors; paste; tape; rulers; large, low table; small chairs; mixing bowls; small plastic bags; rolling pins; cookie ingredients; recipe.

Procedure

1. At group time, read *one* of the books.
2. Ask open-ended questions about the book.
3. Explain the activity choices for the day. Making invitations for the "friend party" on Friday is one of the activities, and this center will be open for two children at a time until Thursday afternoon.
4. On Friday morning, the children give the invitations to their friends. (The teacher has asked each child to make just one invitation without a name on it.) The teacher then puts all of the invitations in a sack, and the children close their eyes and reach in to select one. Part of the fun is to see if the children get their own invitation or one that someone else made.
5. The no-bake cookies will be an activity choice for Friday morning. Two children at a time will make no-bake cookies until everyone has made some. (The teacher has printed the recipe on a large poster with both illustrations and words.)
6. The children and the teacher wash their hands and the table, put on smocks, put out the cooking utensils and ingredients, and read the recipe together.

Graham Cracker No-Bake Cookies

1/2 cup raisins	2 tablespoons honey
1/2 cup chopped dates	graham crackers

Let the children pour raisins, dates, and honey into a mixing bowl. Place several graham crackers in a plastic bag. Children can crush these with a rolling pin. Add to honey-fruit mixture. Mix until dry enough to roll into balls. Eat at snack time!

Guidance

By limiting the number of children at the writing table and having fewer at a time participating in the cookie making, the teacher has limited many of the problems that could occur. This is a time when the teacher can talk about sharing and taking turns with friends.

As with all cooking activities, provide sponges, soap, and water for cleanup. It is helpful to have the teacher assistant moving around the room to supervise the other learning activities. This will give the teacher an opportunity to have some special one-on-one time with the children involved in the cookie-making activity.

Assessment and Follow-Up Strategies

Were all the objectives met? Extended activities might include:

- Place the recipe poster in the writing center. This gives the children an opportunity to write out the recipe to take home.

● Make fingerprint paintings. Children can look at their own and those of their friends. Use the magnifying glass to look at the fingerprints. Are they alike? Are they different? How?

GRAHAM CRACKER NO-BAKE COOKIES

Pour ½ cup raisins,

½ cup chopped dates and

two tablespoons honey in

a mixing bowl. Place

several graham crackers in

a plastic bag. Crush crackers

with a rolling pin. Add to

honey—fruit mixture until dry

enough to roll into balls.

EAT AT SNACK TIME!

Technology in Language and Literacy Development

Technology has now found its place in the early education environment along with books, flannel boards, finger paints, markers, play dough, and other media. As a result, the use of technology in an early childhood setting requires that each of us, as early childhood educators, continue to learn as much as we can about technology issues and trends (**Figure 5.8**).

In the National Association for the Education of Young Children (NAEYC)/Fred Rogers Center Joint Position Statement, "Intentional and Appropriate Use of Technology Tools and Interactive Media" (2012, p. 5), author Chip Donahue states the position that:

Figure 5-8 Technology, especially computers, can bring learning experiences to the language and literacy curriculum.

> "Technology and interactive media are tools that can promote effective learning and development when they are used intentionally by early childhood educators, within the framework of developmentally appropriate practice, to support learning goals established for individual children."

> "Children's experiences with technology and interactive media are increasingly part of the context of their lives that must be considered as part of the developmentally appropriate framework."

Computers, along with developmentally appropriate software, whiteboards, inexpensive cameras, digital cameras, mini-cams, age-appropriate/nonviolent video games, interactive CDs, DVDs, and audio recorders, can make a unique contribution to the education of young children. As with any learning resource available, how technology is used is more important than *if* technology is used at all.

Technology, especially computers, can bring different learning opportunities to the language and literacy curriculum. Children from families with little technology in the home, will need to develop technology skills at school.

Technology & Teaching: Using Guidelines

The AAP (Oct 2011) Policy Statement says that babies and toddlers should learn from play and not from screens.

The following guidelines for using and selecting technology for preschool and primary-aged children are adapted from Buckleitner, 2009; Deiner, 2010; and Wardle, 2007.

1. Provide a computer center as one of many equally valued learning centers in the classroom. Allow use, access, and choices as you would any other center.
2. Link technology activities with hands-on classroom materials.
3. Encourage children to work on the computer in pairs. Place two chairs by each computer. If your child-care center or school offers wireless laptop computers, it is even easier to bring Web-based experiences to children in the context of their play or project activities.
4. Allow children lots of time to explore how to use a computer: what can or cannot occur, and simple exploration of the medium or literacy software or websites.
5. Young children need interactive programs they can gain control over. They need to learn cause-and-effect reasoning and that they can cause the computer to do something.
6. Don't try to formally "teach" technology skills and competencies. Instead, set the stage for successful experimentation by providing the materials, introducing them, and offering support.

Technology & Teaching: **Using Guidelines**

7. Do carefully evaluate all software, both for developmental appropriateness and for nonsexist, nonracist, nonstereotypical, and nonviolent material. Do not accept software brought from home without a similar evaluation.

8. New software is being developed daily. Many school districts have qualified individuals to assist teachers with this evaluation process. Many times funds are limited; this is another reason to select your language and literacy software carefully. You will be able to use the software longer if each selection meets the curriculum goals you have set.

9. Provide ways for children with special needs to use computers; encourage individual education plans (IEPs) that use technology to address specific learning disabilities.

10. Encourage children to use digital cameras to expand their language and literacy activities.

In some classrooms, interactive whiteboards (IWB) have replaced traditional whiteboards or flipcharts, or video/media systems such as a DVD player and TV combination. Even where traditional boards are used, the IWB often supplements them by connecting to a school network digital video distribution system. Many companies and projects now focus on creating supplemental instructional materials specifically designed for IWBs. One recent use of the IWB is in shared reading lessons. PowerPoint can be used to develop literacy activities for children with disabilities who are at high risk for having problems learning to read and write (Parette, Hourcade, Boeckman, and Blum, 2008).

Early childhood children are adding digital and media technology to the literacy curriculum. This age of child is drawn to technology and loves a good story. This combination creates a powerful educational tool. One way to support this literacy experience is to supply the tools to make a digital story—using a computer, a digital camera, a scanner, a printer, and software. A digital story mixes still images (photos or artwork), voice narration, and music to tell a story. Teachers should have the learning experiences with the technology first. This will enable them to become enthusiastic and ready to share digital storytelling with the children. It is also important to remember that the *story* is the starting point and the finishing goal. For this activity to be successful, all aspects must be developmentally appropriate for the children in the classroom.

Researchers have pointed out that care needs to be taken in selecting lively, animated multimedia titles. Although such software may increase children's attention span, this attention may not result in better learning. Okolo and Hayes (1996) determined that children spend four times as much time "reading" the book in a high-animation format. However, students who read the book with an adult obtained the highest scores on comprehension questions. Therefore, Okolo and Hayes have suggested that when such animated software is used, teachers must closely monitor children's use of software and offer support and guidance. (See **Figure 5-8** on the values of technology in the language and literature curriculum.)

Diversity in Language and Literacy

"In the 21st century, the United States is seeing a new wave of immigration carrying with it many languages. Migration within the country is also compounding the number of languages. Early childhood programs are caring for and teaching many more children whose home language is not English. It is becoming essential that these programs find ways to support children's home language as a component of respecting and integrating home cultures into each of their programs."

Research has found that students learning a second language move through five predictable stages: Preproduction, Early Production, Speech Emergence, Intermediate Fluency, and Advanced Fluency. How quickly students progress through the stages depends on many factors, including level of formal education, family background, and length of time spent in the country. The following stages of second language learning are adapted from Bank Street (2002); Hernandez (1995); Hickman-Davis (2002); and Espiritu, Meier, Villazana-Price, and

Wong (2002). These stages are not represented in any specific age group but occur when the child is introduced to a second language.

- *The Preproduction or Silent Stage:* A child's initial response to a new language is to listen to or "take in" the language rather than to speak it. He or she is trying to make sense of what goes on around him or her. Many times the child will imitate what other children do in the class, pretending that he or she understands. The length of this particular stage will vary from child to child. During this period, music, movement, dramatic play, and art activities are appropriate. Reading books aloud to the child can offer a one-on-one experience with a teacher as well. Do not rush children through this nonverbal period.

- *Early Production Stage:* At this stage, children have limited verbalization and growing comprehension. Occasionally asking questions that require a *yes* or *no* answer from the child will give a teacher an informal assessment of what the child is understanding. Speech can also be encouraged by asking questions that request the labeling of familiar objects ("What is this?") or finishing a statement ("We are eating …"; "The color of this crayon is …"). This can be accomplished easily in informal conversations with the child. Group time, classroom games, outdoor play, and one-on-one activities will provide ample opportunities in which you can guide children through this stage. At the beginning, English language learners will have to mentally translate the question into their native language, formulate a response, and then mentally translate the response back into English. This takes time. During this period, children may begin to use a mixture of words from both languages. This is referred to as *code switching*.

- *Expansion of Production Stage:* This is the speech emergence and expansion stage. With this comes increased comprehension and the ability to speak in simple sentences. Encourage the child to talk about his family and friends. Motivate him to describe, using his words, what he is experiencing with his five senses. The child may experiment more with a new language when he is with peers than with adults. Observe your students interacting with other children. This will give you information about the extent of his vocabulary and fluency. Finger plays, songs, and rhymes are useful in stimulating the child toward using his new language.

In acquiring a new language, remember that children may start school at different stages and may not progress at the same rate. You should appreciate the countless ways in which children learn and do not rely on a set curriculum for teaching oral language or literacy. Instead, know each child and adapt the curriculum based on the differences between each.

> " Real language acquisition develops slowly, and speaking skills emerge significantly later than listening skills, even when conditions are perfect. The best methods are therefore those that supply "comprehensible input" in low anxiety situations, containing messages that students really want to hear (Krashen, 2003, p. 7). "

Comprehensible input includes using gestures, facial expressions, voice tone, and props when speaking and planning hands-on multisensory experiences to illustrate concepts and provide a context for new vocabulary. The analogy of the "affective filter" describes how when the filter is high (smaller mesh) because of stress, little learning input gets through, but when the filter is low (larger mesh), more input can penetrate the brain.

Throughout the history of education, many different terms have been used to describe or characterize children whose second language is English. Some of these are limited English proficiency (LEPs), English is a second language (ESLs), and second-language learners (SLLs).

Currently, educators refer to these children as one of the following:

- English-language learners (ELLs)
- Dual-language learners (DLLs)
- Emergent bilinguals (EBs)

(Bank Street, 2009, 2002; NAEYC [2009]; Genishi and Dyson, 2009.)

It is essential that teachers see second-language learners as children with prior knowledge and experience about language learning.

Reflect On This

How does an early childhood teacher show that a child's bilingual and bicultural world is respected?

Observation will guide future decisions about targeted instruction for language development. Essential questions to answer include:

- How much home language does the child bring with him?
- What kind of language learning exposure and opportunities does the child experience at home?
- How can the child's knowledge in his home language be activated and applied to the task of learning English?
- How can you as the teacher promote the child's growth in both English language development and maintaining his home language? (Magruder, E. S., Hayslip, W. W., Espinosa, L. M. & Matera, C., 2013.)

Be sensitive and encourage each child to communicate in his or her own way during social interaction with other children. Emphasize the child's strengths, and help to build his or her positive self-concept. Provide consistent and continual modeling of English, and whenever possible, allow the child to speak the primary language as well as English.

It is important to understand that accepting a child's language is part of accepting a child. The children in the classroom will model your behavior. Children can be accepting and caring of each other. They communicate by gestures or by taking a child's hand and leading him or her to an activity, many times without your guidance.

"Families' insights into code switching, family language strategies, the sequence of second language acquisition, social and emotional development, and language transference and development help teachers create a welcoming and supportive setting for children who are dual language learners" (Michael-Luna, 2015).

Children will feel more successful if you involve their parents and families in activities and understand the different learning styles each child may have. Create an atmosphere in which sharing cultures is valued. The celebrations of many cultural holidays at the school that include the family members of *all* the children in your class offer positive reinforcement. Invite them to visit the classroom and share their language with the children. Activities in which parents directly teach their child, such as showing children how to write words, are linked to children's ability to identify letters and connect letters to speech sounds (Haney and Hill, 2004).

Maintain personal contact with the child's family throughout the year. When families feel comfortable and understand how important they are to their child's success, a strong relationship results.

Parents can help you identify some basic words used in the child's language, especially those that are important to the child. Be sure to use the child's correct name and not an "Americanized" one. Use the name often and pronounce it correctly. (Listen carefully to the parents' pronunciation and imitate it.)

At first, if possible, have a family member or someone who speaks the child's native language available to help the child learn the routines and expectations, as well as the new language. If another child in the class speaks the language, interaction between the two should be encouraged (Essa, 2011).

Creating Partnerships with Families

naeyc   DAP   HS

As previously stated, family members are a child's primary teachers of language. They are the first people a child hears speak, the first adults spoken to, and the most important people a child will communicate with throughout life. Research indicates that when parents are sensitive and responsive to their children's emotions, children are more likely to become socially competent and show better communication skills (Connell and Prinz, 2002). Awareness of the importance of parents and other significant family members to a child's language and literacy development is one of the first steps in working with parents. It is also helpful to let family members know how valued their efforts are. Express to them how much you appreciate their interactions with you. Let them know what you are doing in the early childhood program. Point out ways they can contribute to or extend language and literacy development at home with their child.

Research has also found that parents who maintain direct and regular contact with the early educational setting and experience fewer barriers to involvement have children who demonstrate positive engagement with peers, adults, and learning (McWayne, Hampton, Fantuzzo, Cohen, and Sekino, 2004). Here are some guidelines for establishing positive relationships with parents.

Developmentally appropriate early childhood programs establish and maintain collaborative relationships with each child's family to foster children's development in all settings. For example, welcome and encourage all families to be involved in every aspect of the program. Talk with families about their family structure and their views on child rearing and use that information to adapt the curriculum and teaching methods to the families served. Parent–child activities are culturally influenced so that activities that are characteristic of one ethnic group might not be characteristic of another (Arzubiaga, Ceja, and Artiles, 2000).

For example, teaching letters, words, songs, and music is more characteristic of black non-Hispanic groups, whereas reading and telling stories is more typical of white non-Hispanic groups (Nord, Lennon, Liu, and Chandler, 1999).

Use a variety of strategies to communicate with families, including family conferences, new family orientations, individual conversations, telephone calls, and emails, and provide program information—including policies and operating procedures—in a language that families can understand (NAEYC, 2009).

In addition, some teachers find it helpful to send notes or emails home periodically. Here are some suggestions for "Language Links" from you to the parents:

1. Read to your child. Read books, stories, magazines, comic strips, and poems. (See **Figure 5-9**.)
2. Have children's books around the house for your children. Some can be purchased and some can be checked out from the library.
3. Read books to children often, and add to them regularly. These are the books we are reading in class this week.
4. Have a regular story time before or after meals or at bedtime.
5. Read all kinds of signs, labels, restaurant menus, and calendars to your child. Point out print on home equipment and products and items of print used in your daily life. Point out signs when you are out riding together.
6. Let your child see you reading newspapers, magazines, books, and letters.
7. Do activities together and then talk about them.
8. Surround your child with opportunities to play with words.
9. Provide a variety of things to write with: chalk, crayons, pencils, markers, and all kinds of paper. Encourage your child to draw.
10. Tell family stories. Encourage your child to ask questions. Let him or her tell a family story of his or her own.
11. Post your child's scribbles and drawings on the refrigerator or the wall in his or her room.
12. Write to your child. Put notes in lunchboxes, in book bags, under pillows, in pockets, or on the refrigerator.

Figure 5-9 Reading a book with daddy is a favorite language activity for a young child.

Case Study: Dual-Language Learners

Naomi is a Pre-K teacher in a San Diego Early Childhood school. She realizes that many of her children come from homes where English isn't normally spoken with the children. Naomi reflects on her own early literacy experiences with her Nana, when she climbed on the bed with her sister and listened to Nana read book after book as she moved each completed one from the pile of books on the right to the pile on the left.

She remembers stories in the Little Golden Books and pictures of landscapes and strange animals. As the books became bigger, the length of time to complete them became longer. She also remembers learning the power of words and the ability to create her own picture in her mind as Nana continued to read.

Naomi knows that this early reading in the home is critical for children's future reading ability and love of books, and she wonders what she can do to more incorporate the families of the children she teaches.

What Do You Think?

1. How can Naomi integrate and build on home language experiences?
2. How can she find out from the families what the child's reading experiences have been at home?
3. What strategies can she use to support dual-language learners?

The Teacher's Role

Guidance for Language and Literacy Play

The following guidance techniques can be helpful to use during story time:

- When a child wants to leave the group during story time, gently encourage the child to stay, but do not insist. Sometimes a reassuring arm around the child will help.
- Young children are easily distracted. Listening as part of a group is a skill they must learn. Begin with books that have only a few pages.
- Asking a child a question about what might happen next will help direct his or her attention back to the story.
- While telling the story, whatever has to be said or done to handle a problem should be as brief an interruption of the story as possible. (Sometimes interruptions can be an important part of the literature experience, if they offer focused discussion of the story or book.)
- Be sure that the children have elbow and knee room. Be sure that everyone can see. For the habitual nudger or distracter, catching his or her attention might be achieved by inserting his or her name as part of the story.
- It is helpful to include the children in the process by having them retell the story using their own words, joining in to repeat lines, or letting them add the flannel board pieces as you tell the story. Using a puppet is effective in guiding the children through the story.

TEACHING TIPS Reading to Children

A common teacher misconception is that sharing picture books is a separate activity to be reserved for a story time of a few minutes a day. Actually, teachers who are successful in promoting literacy infuse picture books into their entire program by making their classrooms and centers places where books are shared, recommended, connected with all curricular areas, and supportive of the goals of diversity (Jalongo, 2004).

When reading aloud to a group of children:

- Start the process by selecting an appropriate piece of literature for your age group.

- Read through the story several times before reading aloud to the children. Practice your presentation.
- Plan the appropriate time, place, and purpose for the story time. Alternate small group and large group activities.
- Make sure everyone is comfortable.
- Show the cover and read the title, author, and illustrator of the book.
- Introduce that book in a way that connects it with children's background knowledge.

TEACHING TIPS Reading to Children

- Suggest things the children can look for or listen for during the story.
- Try to maintain as much eye contact with the children as possible while you share the story.
- Sit on the floor with the children or on a low chair.
- Hold the book to the side facing the children so that everyone in the group will be able to see the page while you read. The use of big books can be effective.
- Use different voices for different characters. The children will enjoy your involvement with the story, and these "voices" help children to distinguish between characters.

- Ask children to make predictions about the plot, the characters, and the setting.
- Allow children to ask questions or make comments during the story.
- Ask questions about the story after you read it. Give all the children time to answer your questions and then to ask some of their own.
- After you read the story, provide opportunities for children to act out, retell it using props, or review the sequence of the story.

Professional Resource Download

Summary

1. **What are some key terms related to language and literacy development and literature for children?** Literacy, language, language development, emergent literacy, literature, receptive language, expressive language, phonics, phonemes, rhyming, phonological awareness, and vocabulary. Why is it important to know these terms? To understand the process of language acquisition and literacy skills. How can early care and education teachers use each term in their teaching? (1) To plan experiences that embed these concepts and (2) to reference the key terms as they are discussing literacy so that children will become familiar with the terms while they are learning the concepts.

2. **How does language develop in young children?** Children learn language through predictable stages of development. This developmental sequence generally follows these predictable stages (crying, cooing, smiling/laughing, babbling, association, one-word usage, recall, telegraphic speech, and multiword speech). Why is it important that we guide children through each of these stages? Each of the stages of language development builds on the previous stage.
   How does language development relate to literacy development? Literacy development is a lifelong process that begins at birth and includes listening and speaking, which are part of language development, as well as reading and writing.

3. **Why is it important to plan for a literacy center within classrooms for young children?** Although children use and expand their literacy in almost every activity and curriculum area in which they participate, creating a child-centered language arts area focuses on the importance of literacy as a central core of the curriculum. If there is a literacy center in the classroom, what are the values of also including literacy materials throughout the room? Including focused literacy materials in different learning centers enriches the curriculum domain specific learning.

4. **Books are essential in enabling a child to learn how to read, but they serve many other functions as well. What are they, and why is each important?** Books develop a child's imagination, reinforce discoveries about the world, focus on predicting outcomes, drawing conclusions and solving problems, and encourage a child to develop a curiosity about learning and life.

5. **What criteria should be used when selecting books?** Criteria should include selecting books that (1) are durable, (2) have different styles of illustrations, (3) are age and developmentally appropriate, (4) are length-appropriate, (5) have rhythm, sound, and repetition, (6) have a variety of writing styles and languages, (7) have characters

that show emotions common to children, (8) expand vocabulary, and (9) reinforce concepts already being acquired.

6. **If adequate books are in a classroom, why should literacy activities also be planned?** Planned literacy activities help make books come alive and can focus on specific concepts such as rhyming and letter recognition, as well as exploring the functions of print such as signs and writing notes. Planned experiences integrate literacy into exploration of curriculum themes. Shared writing activities help children make the connections between oral and written language. What are some items other than books that should be included in a literacy environment? The literacy arts center should include lots of books; materials to retell stories (such as flannel boards and puppets), a listening center, and a writing center. The writing center should include alphabet manipulatives and a variety of things to write with and to write on.

7. **What are some ways to integrate technology to support literacy development?** Computers, along with developmentally appropriate software, whiteboards, digital cameras, video cameras, age-appropriate/nonviolent video games, interactive CDs, DVDs, and audio recorders, can make a unique contribution of the education of young children. How can you select appropriate technology? Carefully evaluate all software, both for developmental appropriateness and for nonsexist, nonracist, nonstereotypical, and nonviolent material. Do not accept software brought from home without a similar evaluation. Select language and literacy software carefully. You will be able to use the software longer if each selection meets the curriculum goals you have set.

8. **Why is it important to consider diversity of the children in a particular group when planning environment and activities that foster literacy?** Many children are learning English as a second language. Other children may need special materials, equipment, and strategies to access language learning. Materials from a variety of cultures allow children and their families to feel respected and to explore differences in our diverse world. What areas of diversity should be included in an early childhood classroom? The areas of diversity that should be included are language, culture, abilities, and gender roles. Why should a larger view of diversity of the world be evident in classrooms? Often, the world is not represented in the classroom, just those that are evident. For instance, a classroom with only Anglo children may not have any diversity representing other cultures.

9. **Why are partnerships with families important in literacy development?** Parents are their child's first teachers. Sharing literature helps parents understand that when reading books is a regular part of family life, they send their children a message that books are important, enjoyable, and full of new things to learn. What are some ways to develop partnerships with families? The following suggestions have been successful for some teachers of young children:

- Give parents addresses of local libraries and list the story times.
- Send home a list of the books that are going to be or have been read to the children.
- Set up a parent-lending library at your school or center.
- Read more than books. Use grocery shopping to encourage reading. Read whatever is close at hand.

10. **What is the teacher's role in promoting literacy in the classroom?** Teachers who are successful in promoting literacy infuse picture books into their entire program by making their classrooms and centers places where books are shared, recommended, connected with all curricular areas and supportive of the goals of diversity. Why is it important that the teacher be familiar with and use positive guidance? We want children to love reading and writing, so experiences should be positive. Knowing appropriate techniques can help children focus on the activity and learning to be more effective.

Reflective Review Questions

1. A new student to a classroom of 4-year-olds recently arrived from Honduras and speaks virtually no English. Although he listens to and watches everything going on around him, he says nothing for days. Is this fairly normal behavior for a child in his situation? What strategies should his teacher pursue in helping him?

2. You have been asked to set up a language and literacy (language arts) center in a pre-K classroom. Using paper and colored pens, pencils, or markers, design the learning center. What criteria will you use? Think about how this center will relate to the other learning centers in the classroom. How does this language arts center support the emergent reading and writing development of the children?

3. You are opening a new child care center and need to order books to go in classrooms for children of different ages. Identify specific sources you would use to select quality books. What would you look for when deciding whether or not a particular book would be appropriate for children?

4. Any adult can read aloud, but reading aloud to children involves special preparation and skills. What are six important guidelines that you might advise a new teacher to follow when reading to the children?

5. Reflect on what you should consider when choosing a book to read aloud to a group of young children. Select three books you would like to read to a class of kindergarten or primary age children. Why did you select these specifically?

6. How would you answer a parent who asked, "Of what possible value could a book be to an infant? She can't read or even understand what the pictures are about. Shouldn't you wait to expose her to books when she is older?" How would you go about explaining to the parent why infants should be exposed or introduced to books? How would you encourage the parent to do the same?

Explorations

1. Select and plan a language activity for young children. Specify which age group this activity is planned for: infants, toddlers, preschoolers, or primary-age children. In writing, list objectives, materials needed, step-by-step procedures for presenting this activity, follow-up activities, and evaluation guidelines. (Use the activity plan worksheet in Appendix D.) Prepare this activity and demonstrate it during class or with a group of children.

2. Select a classmate or colleague as a partner. Share ideas on games and activities to extend a child's vocabulary. Discuss ways to use or adapt these games to extend the vocabulary of children who speak other languages or dialects. Then, develop one activity that helps a child learn new words and appropriate language usage. If possible, share your activity with a group of young children. Evaluate its appropriateness and effectiveness. Did it accomplish your objectives? Explain.

3. Create a book for young children. Complete an Activity Plan Worksheet, such as the one in this chapter; then read the book to a small group of young children. Observe their responses. What age group did you select? Was your book developmentally appropriate for that age group? Explain your answers and your assessment and follow-up activities.

4. Based on the information in this chapter and on your observations of early education environments, design a pre-K language and literacy learning center. Using paper and colored pens, pencils, or markers, design the learning center showing where materials, supplies, and equipment are placed. What criteria will you use? Think about how this center will relate to the other learning centers in the classroom. How does this language arts center support the emergent reading and writing development of the children?

5. Use the Literacy Environment Checklist in this chapter to conduct an observation of an early childhood learning environment.

- Beside each statement, place an *X* if the classroom you observed met the statement.
- On a separate sheet of paper, describe what you actually observed related to each statement. Place the number of the statement first and then your observation.
- On a separate sheet of paper, for each statement that you did not check as met, describe what you would do to improve that classroom so that the statement would be met. Be sure to put the number of the statement first.
- Submit this with the name of the location you observed and the age group.

Language and Literacy Books for Young Children

Suggested books for infants

Brown, M. W. (1991, First Board Book Edition). *Goodnight moon.* Illustrated by C. Hurd. New York: HarperCollins.

Carle, E. (2007). *Baby bear, baby bear, what do you see:* New York: Henry Holt.

Fox, M. (2008). *Ten little fingers and ten little toes.* Illustrated by H. Oxenbury. Orlando, FL: Harcourt.

Kubler, A. (2002, Board Book). *Head, shoulders, knees, and toes.* New York: Child's Play International.

Rescek, S. (2006). *Twinkle, twinkle little star and other favorite nursery rhymes.* New York: Tiger Tales.

Shaw, C. G. (1993). *It looked like spilt milk.* New York: HarperCollins.

Suggested books for toddlers

Baker, K. (2008). *Potato Joe.* Orlando, FL: Harcourt.

Emberly, R. (2000). *My colors/Mis colores.* Boston: Little, Brown & Company.

Smith, C. R., Jr. (2008). *Dance with me.* Illustrated by N. Z. Jones. Cambridge, MA: Candlewick Press.

Thompson, L. (2008). *Wee little lamb.* Illustrated by J. Butler. New York: Simon & Schuster Books for Young Readers.

Wood, A. (2000). *The napping house.* Illustrated by D. Wood. New York: Red Wagon Books.

⌄ **Professional Resource Download**

Suggested books for three-, four-, and five-year-olds

Cote, N. (2008). *Jackson's blanket.* New York: Putnam.

Emberly, R., and Emberly, E. (2009). *Chicken little.* New York: Roaring brooks.

Gravett, E. (2009). *The odd egg.* New York: Simon & Schuster Books for Young Readers.

Heap, S. (2009). *Danny's drawing book.* Cambridge, MA: Candlewick Press.

Katz, K. (2007). *The colors of us.* New York: Henry Holt.

Martin, B., Jr., & Archambault, J. (1988). *Listen to the rain.* Illustrated by J. Endicott. New York: Henry Holt.

Van Fleet, M. (2009). *Cat.* Photographed by B. Sutton. New York: Simon & Schuster Books for Young Readers.

Suggested books for six-, seven-, and eight-year-olds

Bruchac, J. (2009). *Buffalo song.* New York: Lee & Low Books.

Giovanni, N. (2005). *Rosa.* Illustrated by B. Collier. New York: Holt.

Naylor, P. R. (2008). *Eating enchiladas*. Illustrated by M. Ramsey. New York: Cavendish.

Paratore, C. M. (2008). *Catching the sun*. Illustrated by P. Catalanotto. Watertown, MA: Charlesbridge.

Williams, V. B. (2009). *A chair for always*. New York: HarperCollins.

Zemach, K. (2008). *Ms. McCaw learns to draw*. New York: Arthur A. Levine.

Suggested poetry books for young children

Baker, K. (2009). *Just how long can a long string be?!* New York: Scholastic.

Barrett, J., and Moreton, D. (2003). *I knew two who said moo: A counting and rhyming book*. New York: Aladdin.

Howe, A. (2008). *Come and play: Children of our world having fun with poems by children*. New York: Bloomsbury.

Prelutsky, J. (2002). *The frog wore red suspenders: Rhymes*. Illustrated by P. Mathers. New York: Greenwillow.

Scieszka, J. (2009). *Truckery rhymes*. Illustrated by D. Shannon, L. Long, and D. Gordon. New York: Simon & Schuster books for Young Readers.

⌄ **Professional Resource Download**

Creativity: Art and Music

6

Student Learning Outcomes

After studying this chapter, you should be able to:

- Define and give examples for key terms related to art and music development for children.

- Discuss art and music development in young children and relate stages of child development to art and music development.

- Evaluate various components of planning and preparation of art and music environments.

- Create art and music activities appropriate for young children.

- Discuss various ways to use technology in an art and music environment.

- Distinguish ways to incorporate diversity into art and music environments.

- Describe ways to develop partnerships with families that support child art and music.

- Analyze the teacher's role in promoting art and music in the classroom.

Standards Covered in This Chapter

naeyc NAEYC 5a, 5b, and 5c

DAP DAP 2

INTASC INTASC 4, 5, and 8

HS HEAD START Subdomain: Creativity

 NVAS 1, 2, 3, and 4

 NSME 1, 2, 3, 6, 7, and 8

NAEYC, DAP, and INTASC standards described on Part II introduction page

135

The arts are creative works that express the history, culture, and soul of the peoples of the world, both past and present (Koster, 2009). As we begin this chapter, it is important to understand that a child's art—or artwork, as some educators call it—belongs to the child. His or her awareness that he or she can produce something is critical to a child's development of a sense of self (Baghban, 2007). No adult interpretations or descriptions can, or should, describe what a child has created. This is part of the child's own process of communication and creativity.

When children bring something they made through effort, desire, and originality to a significant adult in their life, that child is attempting to initiate a relationship that is the core of living. When bringing to you their "creation," however strange or simple, the child is saying, "Here is a part of myself I am giving you."

The first time a child makes a mark with a crayon, dips a brush into paint, or glues colored circles onto paper is the birth of a creative process. A child's blank sheet of paper soon becomes a creation that never existed before. This sensory event involving paints, crayons, and glue enables the child to freely experience the sheer pleasure of getting to know himself or herself in a new way—through self-expression.

Art is fundamental to the growth of a child and an integration of many skills and basic experiences that begin at home and are continued and expanded in early childhood programs. Art is *visual* communication through the elements of color, line, shape, and texture instead of words. Art is developmental, and its contributions can be seen in physical, cognitive, social, and emotional development.

Coates (2002) observed that 5- and 6-year-olds draw, pretend, and converse while labeling real or imaginary events or objects as they stimulate one another.

Creativity is the process of doing or bringing something new and imaginative into being and includes openness or flexibility, autonomy, motivation, curiosity, and divergent thinking. By encouraging creativity in children, we can help them become adults who can solve problems creatively.

The creative arts provide an avenue for learning and experiencing in a way that is uniquely different for each child. The inclusion of the creative arts during the early years establishes a foundation that adapts to change, provides joy, and inspires involvement.

For those in early education, Gordon and Browne (2016) extend this point of view even further by explaining that the roots of creativity reach into infancy. Each individual's unique and creative process to explore and understand the world around them helps them in searching to answer larger questions such as "Who am I?" "What and where am I?" and "Where am I going?"

We should offer encouragement by providing opportunities for creativity to be expressed and by showing that we genuinely respect its expression. Children need to be in an inspiring environment, one that they help create and interact with. A teacher who does not appreciate either the creative act or the child who expresses the act can destroy creativity.

Creative development is fostered when a teacher allows children to be self-directed and go at their own pace in a relaxed atmosphere. The learning environment should also eliminate conditions that promote stress and enforce strict time limits. The child who is creating or attempting to create should be valued and be provided many opportunities for his or her creation.

creativity: The process of doing or bringing something new and imaginative into being.

physical development: Type of development involving children using large muscles, manipulating small muscles, developing eye–hand coordination, and acquiring self-help skills.

cognitive development: The mental process that focuses on how children's intelligence, thinking abilities, and language acquisition emerge through distinct ages; Piaget's study of children's thinking, involving creating their own mental image of the world, based on encounters with the environment.

Art and Music Defined

naeyc **INTASC**

Physical development involves children using large muscles (gross motor development) in activities such as easel painting or clay pounding; manipulating small muscles (fine motor development) in actions such as finger-painting or cutting; developing eye–hand coordination (using eyes and hands at the same time) through involvement with all types of materials; and acquiring self-help skills (gaining control over what the body can do) by freely manipulating materials to create expressions in art.

Cognitive development relates to children making art forms that represent and clarify how they see the world; finding new ways to problem solve with art materials and supplies; experimenting with cause and effect by asking, "What happens if?"; comparing sizes and shapes; and predicting outcomes through their involvement with art activities. All of these projects actively stimulate cognitive development for young children.

Social and emotional development in art consists of children developing positive images of themselves; expressing personality and individualism; representing imagination and fantasy; establishing enjoyable relationships with others; and expressing feelings by using paints, paper, pencils, chalk, clay, fabrics, and other media as their "vocabulary" while participating in developmentally appropriate art activities.

Language development is included in cognitive and social development as children clarify color, size, shape, texture, and patterns while talking about their art and the art of others. For example, when a toddler picks out a piece of velvet from the art materials box and asks you to "'sof' it," in her stage of telegraphic speech she is saying to you, "Touch it and feel how soft it is!" Older children are introduced to new words when they pound the clay, make brush strokes, create a design, and make an arrangement of lines and patterns. Koster (2011, p. 6) believes that "the arts are the child's first language. Through the arts, children's minds can demonstrate their concepts of the world long before they can put their constructs into spoken and written words."

Perceptual development occurs when children use their senses to learn about the nature of objects, actions, and events. Perception refers to the ways a child knows what goes on outside his or her body. A child perceives through systems: touch, taste, smell, hearing, and sight.

Teachers need to provide experiences that are sensually rich and varied and that require children to use their perceptual abilities in many different ways. Observational and visual perception skills are heightened as children use their senses to study the patterns, colors, textures, and shapes found in nature and in the artwork of others (Koster, 2009).

As we continue through this chapter, we will look at how the developmental stages relate to specific art activities for infants, toddlers, preschoolers, kindergarteners, and primary school children. Creating an environment that values artistic expression and encourages children's creativity and experimentation is the focus of your role as teacher, facilitator, and observer. As one child suggested, "Let's do some arting today!"

Music is a language, a means of communication. It is communicated through tone, rhythm, volume, range, tempo, and movement. Music can communicate feelings to children even when its cultural origin and language is foreign to them. Children are acquainted with music from birth. The tone of a mother's voice, the rhythm of a rocking chair, and the chanting of nonsense syllables are basic to a child's life. Before he or she knows words, an infant experiments with vocal sounds and understands tones and rhythms. Children are learning both language and music simultaneously. A child's involvement with music includes listening; creative activities related to singing, body movement, playing, and making instruments; and aesthetic examination. (See **Figure 6-1**.)

> " Music and movement are intertwined. They reinforce and strengthen each other. A child hears music, and she moves in response. A child's physical maturation process motivates her to move naturally in response to internal and external stimuli. Children exposed to creative movement are becoming more aware of their own natural resources. They are expanding their concepts of creativity and of how they can use their own bodies. Research has shown that a developmentally appropriate music and movement program can positively affect jumping and dynamic balance of preschool children (Zachopoulou, Tsapakidou, and Derri, 2004, p. 63). "

In this chapter, we explore the ways music and movement can introduce concepts, foster growth in motor skills, reinforce and develop language skills, nourish positive self-esteem, encourage self-expression, explore diversity, and connect to other curriculum areas and chapters of this book.

Figure 6-1 A developmentally appropriate and creative classroom for young children has music and movement experiences woven into the daily curriculum.

social and emotional development: Type of development consisting of children developing positive images of themselves, expressing personality and individualism, representing imagination and fantasy, establishing enjoyable relationships with others, and expressing feelings.

language development: Developmental process of a predictable sequence that includes both sending and receiving information. It is related, but not tied, to chronological age.

perceptual development: Type of development in which children use their senses to learn about the nature of objects, action, and events.

Developmental Stages of Art and Music

"Stages in artistic development do not have discrete beginnings and endings in the developmental sequence, but rather children exhibit a tendency to move back and forth between stages as they learn and grow" (Taunton and Colbert, 2000, pp. 67–76).

A teacher can recognize characteristics that are identifiable to help in understanding the needs and interests of the children in an early childhood program. Understanding how the child has previously developed helps in knowing what to look for as the child matures.

Isbell and Raines (2013) discuss Howard Gardner's theory of multiple intelligences that says that children may be talented in specific areas and learn in different ways. For some, art may be the way they learn the best. For others, it may be a new way to experience the world.

Art Development

Infants and Toddlers

Art is a sensory experience for infants and toddlers. The child uses his or her entire body when interacting with the art materials, which stimulates large and fine motor skill coordination. The enjoyment for the child comes from this exploration.

Think about safety and appropriateness when selecting supplies and materials for this age. Younger children may be overwhelmed or overstimulated at first by too many choices, so start slowly and add items a few at a time. Crayons, finger paints, paints, paper, play dough, and water play should be available. The child needs opportunities to poke, pat, pound, shake, taste, smell, and scribble.

Transitions into and out of art activities are important. The younger the child, the more verbal and visual clues are needed to help him or her move from one activity to another.

Flexibility, both inside and on the playground, is needed. This age child loves to water paint on the floor, table, brick wall, and sidewalk. Opportunities for experiencing color

Brain Research: Creating Art

The cognitive event identified as "creating art" appears to have an impact on the brain development of human beings, especially children. Neuroscience research demonstrates that the preschool and elementary school child's brain is at a crucial stage of development. The neural synapses of the brain are growing rapidly and changing at this point in life. Research shows that the younger the child is exposed to an arts education, the more the development of the brain is impacted. A child's early years are a crucial time for exposure to the arts (Flohr, Miller, and DeBeus, 2000). Timing is important because the child's brain is making neural connections at a rapid rate. When children play they sing, draw, and dance. These are natural art forms. These activities engage all the senses and wire the brain (Rauscher, Shaw, and Ky, 1993).

The brains of the infant, toddler, and preschooler are genetically programmed to develop most effectively when exposed to an environment that includes language exposure, social experiences to understand self-awareness and our role in society, as well as endless opportunities for physical play, imaginative play, and creativity. Over the last two decades, these types of experiences, so crucial for appropriate brain

development, have been usurped by television and other electronic media. The fact is that when children watch television or play electronic games they are not engaging in other important activities for cognitive and social development.

Fantasy play is critically important for brain development, since this type of play leads to understanding symbolism, which is the cornerstone of reading and mathematical skills. The ability of a child to fantasize, to create alternative scenarios and to explore "other realities" ultimately creates a brain that can think outside the box to achieve novel solutions to problems and creative ways of responding to real life and academic challenges later in life. Creative play creates a comfort zone in which a child is able to learn from trials and errors and become more comfortable with the option of failure.

None of this activity takes place if a child is engrossed in television where fantasies are spoon-fed and provide no opportunity for alternative explanations. Since preschoolers usually have difficulty in differentiating between fantasy and reality, their understanding of what constitutes the real world can be strongly, and often wrongly, influenced by what they observe on television.

(add food coloring to the water or play dough), texture (art materials box or texture board), and temperature (warm water, cold play dough) can encourage a child to participate.

Scribbling begins around age 2, but as with all developmental stages, it can begin earlier or later. The important thing is to supply the opportunity. Scribbling is the foundation of children's art. From the moment children discover what it looks like and feels like to make lines on paper, they have found something they will never forget. In the process of scribbling, a child finds art (Kellogg and O'Dell, 1967).

For toddlers, repeat activities over and over and allow toddlers to make one or many art projects. The more they create, the more they learn. If it will not work today, try it tomorrow. Being flexible, supportive, and nurturing is the key to working with toddlers. Toddlers, while rubbing a crayon on paper or making lines in sand, learn that their actions can create marks on a surface. The pleasure they experience as they recognize their abilities motivates them to continue to explore scribbling.

Expect an older infant and toddler to explore and manipulate art materials, but do not expect them to produce a finished art product (Copple and Bredekamp, 2009).

Preschoolers, Prekindergarteners, and Kindergarteners

From her research of 2 million pieces of children's art from 30 countries (Baghban, 2007), Rhoda Kellogg (1959) found that these scribbles are meaningful to a child and that they should be valued by the adults in their environment. Kellogg's "20 basic scribbles" (vertical, horizontal, diagonal, circular, curving, waving, zigzag lines, and dots) continue to be discovered by preschoolers. (See **Figure 6-2**.) Their art also shows them passing through the Placement Stage (definite patterns of scribbles placed in the left half, right half, center, or all over the page), into the Shape and Design Stages (combinations of scribbles forming definite shapes and designs), and then into the Pictorial Stage (structured designs that begin to look like something adults have seen before) around ages four and five (Kellogg and O'Dell, 1967).

Children enjoy exploration and manipulation of materials. Watch for a younger preschool child painting her hands, for example. An older child still enjoys sensory experiences but will demonstrate this by experimenting with the materials in new and unusual ways. It is important for the child to develop control over the process. A child might even tear up his work during the process.

Art represents feelings and perceptions of a child's world. Children draw pictures and write to organize ideas and construct meaning from their experiences (Baghban, 2007). They create what is important to them. They use colors that please them, and these colors may bear little relation to the actual colors of the objects created. An older preschooler creates forms and shapes, chooses materials carefully, and looks at the materials in new ways.

> "The teacher demonstrates his/her respect for children's way of learning when she provides open-ended materials such as clay, paint and a variety of tools (Isbell and Raines, 2013, p. 141)."

Children enjoy using their imagination. Copying a model changes their whole experience. A child who has used coloring books tends to lose the capacity to create naturally and individualistically. (See **Figure 6-3** for Kellogg's 20 scribbles.)

Primary Grade

The child at this stage becomes more serious and focused in the art process. The child's early concrete experimenting and learning-by-doing art activities become a bridge to complex thinking. Realistic color and proportion are evident in the child's finished art. Careful planning is also becoming more apparent as part of the process.

The opinion of the adult observer becomes important. The child feels his or her art must be recognizable in both content and subject matter to the viewer. Often, the child offers critical evaluation about his or her own work. Once children enter the primary grades, the focus often moves from art to

Figure 6-2   Scribbling with crayons is more enjoyable with a friend.

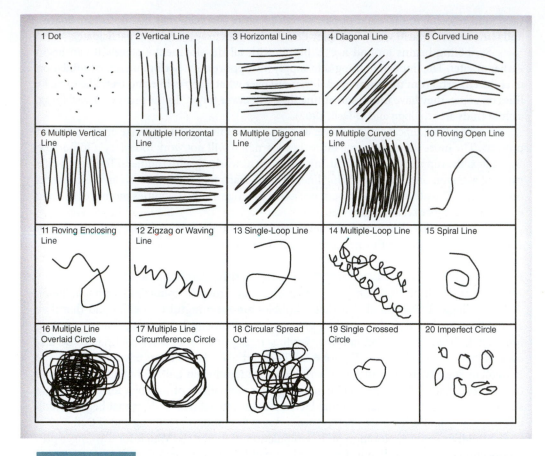

Figure 6-3 Representations of the 20 types of scribbles identified by Rhoda Kellogg. (Source: Isbel and Raines, 2013, p. 110)

other subjects such as literacy, math, and science. It is important to remember that children do benefit from frequent experiences through integration of art activities and techniques and specialized instruction. Children at this age should experience complex and meaningful art activities such as making storyboards for making videos and creating their own book (Copple and Bredekamp, 2009).

The Chinese view is that creativity will emerge after children have been taught essential drawing skills. The U.S. view has been that children's drawing skills emerge naturally and that directive teaching will stifle children's creativity. The research showed that Chinese children who had more opportunities to draw and who received more guidance in drawing were more advanced in their drawing (Huntsinger, Jose, Krieg, and Luo, 2011).

Music Development

naeyc   INTASC

Children are uninhibited performers and love music and movement. Both of these enrich children's lives and learning in many ways. As with art, there should be a focused part of the day for music and movement, and it should also be integrated with all of the content areas (Copple and Bredekamp, 2009).

Findings demonstrate that students who practiced school readiness skills through music, creative movement, and visual arts classes demonstrated higher levels of achievement and greater receptive vocabulary than a control group (Brown, Benedett, and Armisteas, 2010).

Music makes children want to clap hands, tap toes, beat drums, and dance. Children learn best through acting on what they experience. Moving can be fun for its own sake and a way to enjoy music even more. Children express the music's aesthetic qualities through the movement of their bodies as they listen to, perform, and create music. The child can express what he/she perceives in the music, how he/she feels about the music, and what he/she understands simply by using the body. Smith (2002, p. 90) expands this thought even more:

> " Every child learns by moving, and every teacher can teach by moving with the children. In dance, children interpret ideas and feelings through the use of their bodies in an open-ended search for a unique movement vocabulary. Children are able to create their own dances just as they create their own stories. "

For young children in early education settings, including infants and toddlers, music and movement activities nurture the development of minds, bodies, emotions, and language. As you plan developmentally appropriate goals and objectives to encourage music and movement experiences, consider the following:

1. Include physical development activities that can help children gain increasing control over their large and small muscles, experiment with the movement of their bodies, and experience success in movement. Play, as discussed in Chapter 1, is the most developmentally appropriate activity in which young children engage. Researchers (Elkind, 2009; Erikson, 1963; Parten, 1932; Piaget, 1961) have validated this again and again. Brown (2009) emphasizes that rich, developmentally appropriate play experiences can develop a person's personal resilience, emotional control, continuing curiosity and social competence. Play is who and what we are.

2. Incorporate intellectual growth activities that can stimulate children to experiment with how sound is created through their voices or musical instruments, to recognize songs, and to explore melodies by varying tempo, rhythm, tone, and volume.

3. Include listening activities that make music a part of the daily environment by asking for a response, remembering a song or parts of a song, recognizing musical instruments, focusing on sound, and developing auditory discrimination. Every time a child engages in a music experience, he or she is listening.

4. Provide children with socially and emotionally responsive activities that energize, soothe, and enhance children's expression of feelings and sharpen their awareness of feelings for others. Music and movement experiences can also help children know and appreciate themselves and promote cultural identity and pride in themselves and others.

5. Include musical language development activities that encourage the acquisition and use of language to extend vocabulary, to learn word and sound patterns through singing and listening, and to describe musical happenings that can help children develop an appreciation for the music and language of diverse cultures. "The songs and music of childhood are a part of our cultural heritage. The folk songs and ballads that have survived to the present day and the regional tunes parents and teachers offer are part of each child's cultural literacy" (Machado, 2010, p. 171).

6. Take advantage of music and movement opportunities that stimulate children's creativity and uniqueness. Give children musically creative group time by offering each child the opportunity to add to songs and finger plays and to create new movements for action songs. Each musical creation adds to the creativity of the whole group.

All children need the opportunity to use the creative process in discovering their own original ways to move and in using their bodies to communicate their emotions and ideas. However, as they grow they also need to learn how to control their bodies and match their movements to rhythms, music, and the movements of others by participating in simple dances from our own and other cultures (Koster, 2011).

Reflect On This

Coloring books are not creative art. How would you handle a parent who brought in coloring books that are advertisements from the company where she works?

Planning and Preparing the Environment

Art Environment

DAP

As you plan or redesign your visual art environment, provide time, space, and materials that allow children to work at their own pace without interference. The area should be large enough to accommodate the easels and art table. The art center should be a free-choice area. The National Art Education Association (NAEA) states, "We believe that children construct and reconstruct their own learning as they interact with their environment. This constructivist point of view places as much importance on *how* children think as on *what* children think" (quoted in Aulthouse, Johnson, and Mitchell, 2003, p. 3).

When entering an integrated, open-ended arts program, the observer will not notice an art corner. There will not be art projects of the day posted around the room. What will be seen is a variety of art activities embedded in many places throughout the environment.

The location within a classroom where major art materials and equipment will be located requires a great deal of thought and planning. Art activities that require some degree of "messiness" will need to be close to a sink for easy cleanup. A bucket or tub of warm soapy water near the area will also help. The water does need to be changed often. An uncarpeted area is also useful to protect the floor, but plastic sheeting or a shower curtain secured to the floor will serve the same purpose. To keep the art materials and spaces clean, children should be made aware of their responsibilities for the use, care, and cleaning of this area.

Sponges and paper towels need to be handy for the children to use. Pre-planning to protect the environment and the children will allow the children freedom to create without worrying about making a mess. Smocks, aprons, or donated men's shirts can serve to protect children's clothes.

It is important to think about safety in selecting exciting and appropriate supplies and materials for use as art materials. Always select only nontoxic materials. Using recycled materials is encouraged but can also be dangerous. Used Styrofoam, even if it has been washed, can still carry dangerous bacteria. Most grocery stores will give you new Styrofoam trays at little or no cost.

Finished art needs a safe location to dry. Hanging racks or clotheslines across the room can provide that needed space while bringing the beauty of children's art to the environment.

If possible, place an art area near a window so children can see outside while they are creating. The children can stand or sit at tables or spread out large sheets of paper on the floor for art activities.

Art materials need adequate space on low open shelves. Items need to be labeled so that the children can become independent in choosing the materials for their art experiences.

Outdoor Environment

Take it all outdoors! Children enjoy the space and freedom offered by outdoor art activities. Take the easels, a table, long sheets of butcher paper, paints, and clean-up buckets outdoors. Let the children use chalk on the sidewalk; explore rocks, shells, flowers, trees, birds, and butterflies; go for walks and look for colors, textures, and shapes; and gather leaves for making rubbings or prints or for using as materials on paintings and collages.

Nature walks can inspire creativity in artwork as children draw or paint pictures about their experiences. Collections of natural materials such as dried wheat stalks for tracing; seeds, acorns, and pebbles for collages; and berries for dyes can be used to create masterpieces.

If your playground has a chain link fence, it can be used as a drying area. Clothespins easily attach the paintings or murals to the fence. A safe drying area can also be arranged inside a large cardboard box. Plan for cleanup with buckets, hoses, and lots of paper towels.

Chapter 9 offers additional ideas for outdoor activities with sand, water, and woodworking.

Aesthetic Environment

Greenman (1987) captures the essence of environmental aesthetics when he describes a room containing bright splashes of color provided by not only items in the room but also small moving bodies. Sunshine is captured through reflections on objects such as a prism. The walls and carpet provide warm and muted hues. Cool, dark corners flow into shadows, indirect light, and patches so bright that cause the observer to squint. Baskets of plants sit low on the floor and hang from ceilings that provide the sights, textures, and fragrances of nature.

We can actively create such an **aesthetic environment** for children, one that cultivates an appreciation for beauty and a feeling of wonder and excitement of the world in which we live.

Creating an Aesthetic Environment

- Design indoor and outdoor environments that emphasize beauty, attention to detail, color, shape, textures, lines, and patterns in carefully thought-out space and arrangements.
- Allow time for looking at and talking about all kinds of art.
- Provide beautiful books with all types of illustrations.
- Introduce children to fine art by displaying prints of paintings and sculptures in the classroom (the water gardens of Monet, the mothers and children of Cassatt, the ballerinas of Degas, and the splashed action paintings of Pollock) and by visiting local galleries and museums.
- Encourage the aesthetic display of children's art in a classroom "museum," which offers an opportunity for the children to take turns being the curator, the person who decides what art to display and how to display it (Fox and Diffily, 2001).
- Hang up objects that play with the light, including mobiles made of cellophane, papers, and children's art Fox and Schirrmacher (2015).
- Include art, wall hangings, weavings, and tapestry from diverse cultures as part of the aesthetic room environment.
- Expose children to nature by allowing time to watch a spider spin a web or to look closely at a wildflower.
- Support children's self-expression and creativity as they reflect the world around them.
- Involve and inform parents how art production and appreciation are integrated into curriculum areas and inviting them to participate in museum trips.

Additionally, Epstein (2001, p. 38) emphasizes that:

> " [T]oo often, early childhood practitioners limit art education to the making of art. But being artistic in the fullest sense also involves developing a sense of aesthetics. Enabling young children to appreciate art gives them another mode of learning through direct encounters with people (artists) and objects (the work they create). "

Art Environment

A checklist that can be used to help you evaluate the art environment in your own classroom or classrooms that you observe follows.

Music Environment

Musical Instruments

Instruments of all kinds have value in the musical environment of young children. They should be encouraged to listen to the instrument, touch it, and experiment with making sounds and music on it. Provide instruments of good quality that are well cared for, such as tambourines, wooden maracas, woodblocks, rhythm sticks, drums, finger cymbals, bells, triangles, and rain sticks. Teacher and child-made instruments should always be included, as well as wind chimes, gongs, and music boxes.

aesthetic environment: An environment that cultivates an appreciation for beauty and a feeling of wonder and excitement of the world in which we live.

Art Environment Checklist

_____ 1. Do all art materials encourage creativity?

_____ 2. Are the art materials and displays age appropriate?

_____ 3. Is the art center located in a quiet area of the classroom?

_____ 4. Does the art displayed reflect children's artwork and artists?

_____ 5. Is there enough space for large projects and for children to work together?

_____ 6. Can the children use the art materials and easel independently?

_____ 7. Is there enough storage for materials and ongoing projects?

_____ 8. Are there pictures and displays to provide inspiration?

_____ 9. Is there adequate light, both artificial and natural, around the art center?

_____ 10. Are all art displays at the children's eye level?

_____ 11. Is the art center easy to clean?

_____ 12. Are there authentic materials and tools for use in the art center?

_____ 13. Is diversity apparent through all art materials?

_____ 14. Are art materials on low, uncluttered shelves for easy access by the children?

_____ 15. Is there a variety of art materials for children to use in a variety of ways?

_____ 16. Are all materials nontoxic?

_____ 17. Is the art area protected from traffic?

_____ 18. Are their adequate reference materials on art and current themes?

_____ 19. Is the art center near a water source?

_____ 20. Is the artwork displayed attractively?

_____ 21. Is there a table with four to six chairs where the children have a hard surface on which to work together?

_____ 22. Do materials encourage children to create their own artwork (no patterns, coloring pages, stencils, cookie cutters)?

_____ 23. Is the art center available as a choice activity daily?

Professional Resource Download

Usually the first instrument sounds a child hears and experiments with are those created in the home, such as banging on pots and pans (drums), jingling two spoons together (castanets), shaking a ring of metal measuring spoons (tambourine), banging two wooden spoons together (rhythm sticks), and crashing two lids or metal pie pans together (cymbals).

It is important for early education programs to encourage young children to continue this exploration of sounds and to broaden their understanding of musical instruments and the sounds they make. Percussion instruments are the ones most widely used in an early childhood setting. (See **Figure 6-4** for a list of musical instruments.)

Musical instruments have many more uses than just entertainment and can be found in almost every culture. They can play large roles in war, communication, religion, politics, and celebrations.

Drums are used in the music and dances of many cultures, including African, American Indian, Korean, and Thai (hand drums, tom-toms, and long drums carried on one shoulder with a strap). Maracas and claves sticks (short, polished hardwood sticks) are part of the Mexican and Caribbean musical heritage.

Other instruments also have been a part of ethnic music for centuries, such as the flute from American Indian and African cultures and the bamboo flute from Chinese, Japanese, and Korean cultures. Stringed instruments, such as the Japanese _samisen_ and _koto_ (a type of harp), and the Thai _so sam sai_, add beautiful sounds to music selections (Allen, McNeill, and Schmidt, 1992).

Ask parents and community musicians to visit your class and share their music and musical instruments with the children. The combination of personal experiences and hands-on involvement with percussion, string, woodwind, and brass instruments will enrich the children _now_, during their formative years.

Making Musical Instruments

Young children enjoy making their own musical instruments with materials collected from home, including:

- Rolls from bathroom tissue and paper towels
- Aluminum pie plates

Percussion Instruments	String Instruments
Drums	(bowed)
Triangle	Viola
Cymbals	Cello
Tambourine	Bass
Xylophone	Violin
Chimes and bells	(plucked)
Castanets	Guitar
Maracas	Mandolin
Claves	Ukulele
Glockenspiel	Harp
Piano	Banjo

Wind Instruments	Brass Instruments
Flute	Trumpet
Piccolo	Cornet
Oboe	Bugle
Clarinet	Trombone
Bassoon	French horn
Saxophones (soprano, tenor, and baritone)	Tuba

Figure 6-4   List of musical instruments.

- Paper plates
- Salt, cereal, and oatmeal boxes
- Large, round ice cream cartons
- Bottle caps
- Spools
- Embroidery hoops
- Wooden blocks

The process of making musical instruments further extends the children's self-expression, their knowledge of how sounds can be made from their environment, and the possibilities for hands-on experiences. This activity also combines language, art, science, math, social studies, and sensory learning opportunities (younger children will need guidance and supervision from the teacher). Some easy-to-make instruments include the following.

Drums

Children can make drums from salt or cereal boxes or from large ice cream cartons. Glue the lid to the box or carton and decorate with markers and paint. Drums can be played by hitting or tapping with fingers or with soft drum sticks made from pencils covered at one end with felt. (See **Figure 6-5**.)

Tambourine

Take an aluminum pie plate or a heavy paper plate, punch several holes on the rim, and tie small bells or bottle caps with thin wire, string, or pipe cleaners to the plate in such a way that the bells hang freely. Then, shake to the musical beat. (See **Figure 6-5**.)

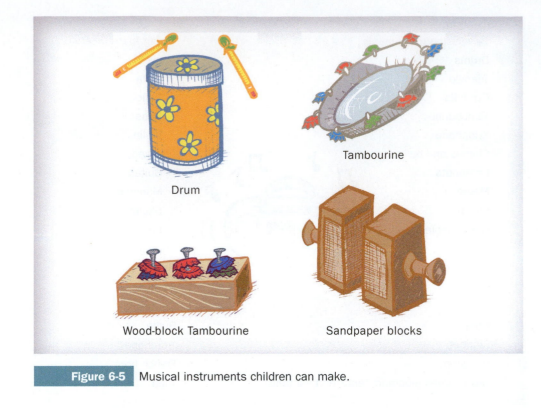

Figure 6-5 Musical instruments children can make.

Wood-Block Tambourine

The materials needed to make a wood-block tambourine are one block of wood (approximately ¾ inch by 1½ inches by 6 inches), six or more bottle caps, and nails with wide heads. Hammer a nail through the bottle caps partway into the wood block. (See **Figure 6-5.**) Be sure the hole in the bottle cap is wide enough so the cap will slide freely along the nail. Any number of nails and bottle caps can be used.

Sandpaper Blocks

Glue, staple, or thumbtack sandpaper to two wooden blocks (approximately three inches by two inches by one inch) on one 3-inch side of each block. On the opposite side, glue a spool or a small drawer handle. (Alternatively, drill a small hole in the block and screw a handle to the block; then glue sandpaper over the opposite side of the block.) Try experimenting with sandpaper squares of different coarseness. Rub the sandpaper blocks together to make interesting sounds (when the squares wear out, replace them with fresh sandpaper). (See **Figure 6-5.**)

Shakers

Young children can make shakers from small boxes or clean plastic milk jugs of various sizes (the handles are easy to hold onto). Place clothespins, small pieces of wood, pebbles, dried beans, or birdseed in the container. Another type of shaker is made with paper plates. Take two paper plates and decorate them with crayons, markers, or paint. Place pebbles, dried beans, or birdseed between the two paper plates. Staple the plates together or sew them together with brightly colored yarn. Then, shake and shake to the rhythm of the music! (See **Figure 6-6.**)

Wind Chimes

Wind chimes can be made from many different materials, such as various sizes of nails, scraps of metal, pieces of bamboo, or old silverware. Tie various lengths of string, evenly spaced, to a coat hanger or embroidery hoop. Tie nails to the strings, and adjust string lengths so that

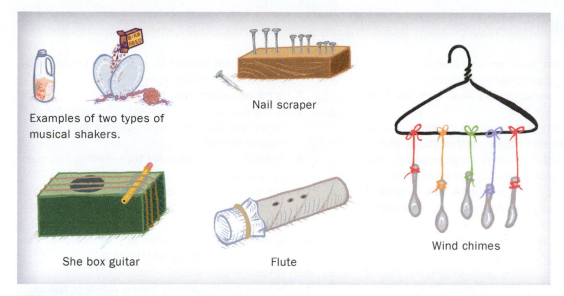

Examples of two types of musical shakers.

Nail scraper

She box guitar

Flute

Wind chimes

Figure 6-6 Musical instruments children can make.

the nails strike each other when blown by the wind or gently swayed. For a variety of sounds, use items of several different sizes, and substitute silverware, pieces of bamboo, or scraps of metal for the nails. (See **Figure 6-6**.)

Nail Scraper

Materials needed to make the nail scraper are a block of wood about two inches by two inches by eight inches and nails of different sizes. Hammer a few nails of the same size into a block of wood so that they are all the same height. Leave a large space and then hammer some other size nails into the wood, making these all the same height. Continue placing nails in the wood until there is no more room. To play this instrument, take a large nail or threaded rod and run it quickly along the row of nails. The different lengths of the nails will make different sounds. (See **Figure 6-6**.)

Shoe Box Guitar

This instrument is made by taking a shoe box and cutting a 2-inch oval hole on the top of the box. Stretch strong rubber bands lengthwise around the box. Place a pencil at one end of the top of the box under the rubber bands. Move the pencil to get different tones as the shoe box guitar is strummed or plucked with the fingers. (See **Figure 6-6**.)

Flute

The children can make their flutes from bathroom tissue, paper towel, or wrapping paper cardboard tubes. Cut a circle of tissue paper or waxed paper and place over one end of the tube. Attach with a rubber band. Cut several small holes on the side of the tube. The children can hum into their flutes while they place their fingers on the holes to change the sound. (See **Figure 6-6**.)

Storing and Caring for Instruments

All instruments, including those made by the children, should be treated with care. Guide the children into understanding that each instrument is to be handled carefully and valued. Musical instruments are not to be used as toys or weapons.

Rules (limits) should be developed and explained when you introduce musical instruments to the children. For example, "treat the instruments gently," "be careful not to touch anyone else with the instrument, stretch both arms out until you don't touch anyone else—this is your personal space," and "be careful not to hit instruments on the floor or anything else."

Music Environment Checklist

_____ 1. Does the room have an uncluttered area with space for music movement activities?

_____ 2. Is the music center located away from the quiet area?

_____ 3. Is there a variety of instruments (triangles, drums, step bells, chorded zithers, rhythm sticks, fretted instruments, finger cymbals, gongs, electronic keyboard instruments, cymbals, jingle bells, xylophone-type instruments with removable bars, resonator bells, and assorted instruments) representing a variety of cultures?

_____ 4. Is there noise reduction through earphones and absorbent materials on floors, ceilings, and walls?

_____ 5. Are all four content standards (singing and playing instruments, creating music, responding to music, and understanding music) represented through materials and activities?

_____ 6. Is instrument storage in areas that provide easy access for the children?

_____ 7. Is the equipment easy to operate?

_____ 8. Is there a variety of musical collections for children's use that represents diverse cultures and musical styles?

_____ 9. Is there sound equipment that children can operate themselves?

_____ 10. Are their materials for preschool and early elementary children so that they can write their own music?

_____ 11. Is there a variety of music to play music with, to listen to, and to move and dance to?

_____ 12. Is there written music?

_____ 13. Is there music available from a variety or historical time periods, genres, and cultures?

_____ 14. Is there high-quality, award-winning music?

Professional Resource Download

Each type of instrument should be stored in a special storage place. They should never be dumped into a cardboard carton or be piled on a shelf or in a basket. These practices can destroy good instruments and affect the attitudes of children for them. Accessible storage should be provided for the instruments that allow the children to use them independently. All damaged instruments should be discarded.

A checklist that can be used to evaluate the music environment in your own classroom or classrooms that you observe follows:

Integrating Art and Sensory Play into the Curriculum

INTASC   **naeyc**

Visual arts have a powerful ability to communicate. Teachers can facilitate this by observations and conversations about the creative art in the environment such as ceramics, paints, photographs, sculpture, and other media.

Try connecting art to everything you do. For example, children can listen to music and draw or paint in rhythm to the music. They can express in their creations how the music makes them feel. Verbal and nonverbal language is expressed through art. As pointed out previously in this chapter, children learn to include an art vocabulary into their everyday conversations with other children and adults. They express and represent what they know through their art. "Looking, talking, and creating together turns an art activity into a social activity in which children can learn from each other" (Mulcahey, 2009, p. 107). The art activities discussed in this section also give children an understanding of themselves and others. Their study of artists and their visits to art galleries and museums help them relate to their community and to the world.

Koster (2009) and Williams (1995) suggest that math and art content can be combined on a regular basis. For example, the math concepts of problem solving, inventing patterns, measurement, sorting, and classifying relate to the art concepts of awareness of line and shape, decoration of line and pattern, and awareness of texture and changing shape.

Reflect On This

Is it art or a craft? How can you tell if an activity is truly creative?

Fox and Schirrmacher (2015) point out that children quantify art materials, equipment, and supplies by counting the number of brushes and jars of paint that are in use and by deciding which brushes have longer handles, which crayons are fatter, and which geometric shapes are being used in their art creations.

Many scientific principles have already been discussed in this chapter, including:

- Discovering what a specific material can do and what the child can do to control it.
- Observing what happens when colors are mixed together.
- Noticing what happens when flour and water are combined.
- Experimenting with thick paint and thin paint.
- Discovering what happens when you press down hard or lightly with a brush or crayon on paper.
- Observing what happens when paint is brushed over a crayon picture.
- Determining what occurs when different ingredients are mixed together.
- Setting up a "discovery table" with art materials such as paper of different shapes and colors, clay, and other art media that can be integrated into any subject that is being discussed in the classroom.

Use of Food in Art Projects

Using food in art activities with children is a continuing topic of discussion between teachers and administrators who are divided on this issue. We have found that not using food works better for the following reasons:

- It is difficult to justify using food when many parents are working long hours to put food on the table for their families. Food is expensive. Also, the casual use of food in art when many are homeless and hungry can be upsetting to some adults.
- The use of food in an art activity may offend some cultural groups who use that food item for religious or ethnic celebrations Fox and Schirrmacher (2015).
- Many children are severely allergic to some food items, such as milk, wheat, soy, eggs, and peanuts.
- It is important *not* to use foods for art because toddlers are developing self-regulatory skills and must learn to distinguish between food and other objects that are not to be eaten (Copple and Bredekamp, 2009).
- Children become confused when they are told that they can eat one art material but not another one that seems similar (Koster, 2011).
- Using cornstarch, flour, salt, and food coloring is acceptable because these are used in small amounts as additives to make play dough and other recipes for art.
- There are other alternatives for art projects. For example, instead of using macaroni, string together paper shapes with a hole punched in the middle or paper straws cut in various lengths. Sand or buttons can be glued instead of rice. Use cotton balls, Styrofoam, or toothpicks instead of beans for collages and textured art. It is fun to come up with other creative choices.

You will need to decide for yourself whether you want to use food in art projects or not. Consider your own values, economic factors, and the policies of your center or school.

Involving Children in All Forms of Art

Children involved with art develop sensory awareness, aesthetic appreciation, self-expression, and improved visual and motor coordination. The process of experimenting with and creating two- and three-dimensional projects from a variety of media connects children to other facets of their world such as their community, family, animals, and self.

We see, time and again, a young preschooler put one color of paint on the easel paper and then place another color exactly on top of the first, and then continue this process until the result is a mass of "indescribable" color. The color is beautiful to the child, and he or she has created it. This newfound ability to change color is important and exemplifies learning for the child. The older child paints masses of color next to each other and may surround the color with dots and shapes. Both exemplify the process of making art.

The emphasis throughout this chapter is on allowing appropriate time, space, and flexibility for creating; to give permission and responsibility to the children; and to nurture and value their creativity. This will provide children with many opportunities to move beyond investigation to using these materials in unique, imaginative, and individually creative ways.

Tearing, Cutting, and Gluing

Tearing, cutting, and gluing offer individual activities to young children and provide small muscle development and tactile experiences; offer opportunities for controlling scissors and direction of cutting for creative purposes; provide discovery of form, shapes, colors, sizes, and textures; develop eye–hand coordination; and encourage verbal communication and sharing.

Let the children do the tearing, cutting, and gluing. Use white glue, school paste, flour and water paste, glue sticks, masking tape, and clear tape. Pour white glue into small plastic squeeze bottles or pour small, individual amounts of glue into jar lids, small bowls, or other containers. Children can use cotton swabs or their fingers to manipulate and spread the glue. Supply a wet paper towel for each child to have at his or her place, or moisten a sponge that several children can share to wipe their fingers.

Children can tear and cut tissue paper, construction paper, fabric scraps, old greeting cards, wallpaper samples, newspapers, and catalogs. Glue these materials to construction paper, corrugated paper, any sizes of paper plates, index cards, box lids, brown wrapping paper, foil, or gift-wrapping paper.

During an art activity of tearing, cutting, and gluing, children discover they are making a **collage**. "This art activity, making a picture containing glued-on objects or paper, is very popular with young children.... Children are extraordinarily free of restraints as they become immersed in the creative process of making a collage" (Koster, 2011, p. 241).

Painting

Expression of ideas and feelings can be found in every painting in the world. Instead of using talking and writing, paintings rely on colors, arrangements, shapes, and lines to relay its message.

Painting, in all its forms, provides sensory experiences, allows for coordinated use of many body muscles, encourages language development, helps with the judgment of spatial relationships, provides an opportunity for manipulation and experimentation, develops form perception, is often a two-handed experience, and develops skill in handling a brush and other art materials and tools.

Painting develops skills that are used in reading and writing. The curves, patterns, and lines that children make are similar to letters and words. The awareness of spatial relationship and configurations on the page relates to reading skills. Distinguishing painted forms, lines, and patterns from the background requires the same discrimination as reading. When you read, you separate, or "pull out," letters from the background.

Organizing the art environment for painting will help make the activities successful for children. When finger-painting, children can use the paint directly on the table top, on a table that is covered with butcher paper, or on individual pieces of paper. For younger children, place a spoonful or two of finger paint into plastic bags. Close the bags carefully and seal with tape to prevent leaks. Each process offers a different experience for children. They have direct sensory contact with the material. They create changeable patterns, designs, and shapes in a short amount of time while maintaining their interest for a long time. To preserve a table-top painting, blot the finger-painting with a piece of butcher paper to get the reverse design that the child can keep.

Finger paints in many colors are commercially available. Selecting skin-tone colors offers young children another way to develop self-esteem. They often choose paint that

collage: An art activity that involves making a picture containing glued-on objects on paper.

matches their skin colors. This reinforces the anti-bias approach that all colors are beautiful. Other items to use as finger paints are toothpaste, cold cream, hand lotion, or wet sand.

Easel painting is popular with young children. Easels can be placed indoors or outdoors. If several are set up, place them close together. This encourages interaction and conversation between the painters. Easels should be the correct height for young children, washable, and sturdy, and should have a tray for holding containers of paint. You could also tape the easel paper to a wall indoors or a fence outdoors.

Furnish large sheets of easel paper or paper cut into different shapes, brushes (one for each color being used) in a wide variety of sizes, and a choice of colors. For younger children, it is helpful to start with one color at a time. Have them use the primary colors of red, blue, and yellow; the secondary colors of orange, purple, and green (the colors obtained by blending pairs of primary colors); and black, brown, and white. Mixing black or white with primary colors teaches pastel tints and grayed tones. Children quickly discover for themselves what happens when colors are mixed together.

To thicken paint, add liquid starch or cornstarch (children will need large brushes to paint with thick paint). A teaspoon of alcohol added to each pint of paint or a drop or two of oil of wintergreen will prevent the paint from souring.

Before children start to paint, you may have to remind them to put on a smock or apron. After the children are through, let them wash the brushes with soap and water, shape them, and place them brush-end up in a container to dry. Additional tools that can be used as brushes are paint rollers, pot scrubbers, sponges, feathers, toothbrushes, and fly swatters.

String painting is another art activity that young children enjoy doing. It involves moving a string dipped in paint around on paper to make a design. You might first attach a button to one end of the string so that the children can hold the button to manipulate the string more easily.

They can also dip short lengths of string or yarn into bowls of paint mixed with a small amount of white glue (holding the string with a clothespin can help those children who do not want to get their fingers in the paint). They then lay the yarn or string onto a piece of construction paper to form a design. Children can vary the lengths of yarn, string, or twine to add texture to the painting.

Children can fold a sheet of paper in half, then open it and place the paint-wet string on one side of the paper. Fold the other side of the paper over and hold it with one hand. Then gently pull the string through while holding the folded paper in place with the other hand. To complete this activity, younger children may need assistance from you or another child.

Children enjoy experimenting with object or gadget painting. Provide items such as kitchen utensils, forks, corks, sponges, pieces of wood, combs, and cookie cutters for dipping into paint or a paint pad (made by pouring thick tempera paint onto several layers of paper towels or a thin sponge). The children press the object down onto a piece of manila or colored construction paper. A unique print is the result.

Painting with feet offers another sensory experience for children. (See **Figure 6**-7.) This is an extension of hand painting. Begin by covering the floor or outdoor sidewalk with newspaper, and then place long pieces of butcher paper or brown wrapping paper over the newspaper. Tape the corners so that the paper will stay in place. The children remove their shoes and socks and then stand at one end of the paper. Help them step into containers or tubs you have prepared with tempera paint. Paint is slippery, so you may need to assist some children as they walk on the paper. At the other end of the paper place a tub of warm, soapy water and some towels. After the children make their "feet design," they will end up by stepping into the tub of water. This project makes a wonderful mural. This is a fun activity to do with parents as well. I still remember the first time I did feet painting, when my oldest child was in preschool. It was a parent–child activity during an open house. I have used it many times since with children, parents, and teachers.

Other types of painting for young children are fingerprint painting (walking fingers dipped in paint across paper), sand mixed with paint (gritty paint), salt and paint (sparkle paint), flour and paint (lumpy paint), ball or marble painting (dipped items rolled over paper placed in a box), painting on rocks, and painting with watercolors.

string painting: A type of painting that involves moving string dipped in paint around on paper to make a design.

Figure 6-7 The feet painting process.

Figure 6-8 Chalk provides an interesting type of drawing experience for young children.

crayon rubbings: Duplicating an object of texture by placing it under paper and rubbing over it with a crayon.

Drawing with Crayons, Markers, and Chalk

According to Koster (2011, p. 229), "Drawing is the most basic of all the visual arts. It is usually the first art experience young children have and is the first step toward literacy." Crayons and markers are familiar to most young children. They have used them at home and other places, such as at restaurants that welcome children to color on the paper table covering or on the children's menu. *Caution:* Young children should use only water-based markers because permanent markers may contain toxic solvents. Chalk provides another type of drawing experience. All these materials are ready to use, easy to store, and require little cleanup.

When using crayons, markers, and chalk, children use different types of muscular coordination than those they use to control a paintbrush or a finger. They also encourage exploration of what colors can do, provide an excellent prewriting experience, develop hand-eye coordination, and stimulate the imagination. (See **Figure 6-8**.)

Scribbling, as discussed previously in this chapter, is important to young children. Crayon scribbling is usually one of the first activities children enjoy doing over and over again. It is easier for children to control crayons when they are sitting down. They often use pressure to make marks on the paper, so having large, less breakable crayons available for younger children works well. Older children prefer the small crayons.

By starting with large sheets of paper, then moving on to all sizes, shapes, and textures of paper, you can extend the crayon scribbling and drawing activities. Using crayons on colored paper teaches children what happens when one color is applied to another.

Crayon rubbings can be introduced early in the school year, then continued as the variety of objects to be rubbed changes throughout the year. To make a crayon rubbing of a texture, children place an object under newsprint or other type paper and rub with a crayon. (You might need to tape objects down on the table at first.) Rubbing the side of a peeled crayon across the paper usually works best. Suggestions of objects to be rubbed: cardboard squares, circles, rectangles, triangles, and ovals; coins and leaves of various sizes and shapes; different textures of wallpaper; and bricks, tree bark, and sandpaper. (Let the children discover these and others.)

A favorite art activity of toddlers and preschoolers is to "draw a child." For the young ones, you can draw around each child lying on a large piece of paper. Older children can choose partners, and they can draw around each other. Then each child can color himself or herself. He or she can add a face, hair, clothes, and shoes with additional materials from the art materials scrap box.

Crayon resist is an interesting art activity for school-age children. They can draw a picture on paper with light-colored crayons, then cover the picture with watercolors or thin tempera paint. The paint will cover all but the crayon markings. A variation of this project is for the children to place waxed paper over a sheet of white paper and draw on it with a pencil, pressing wax lines and design into the bottom paper. They then remove the waxed paper and brush thin paint over the wax lines on the paper. A design of white lines will appear on the painted surface.

For a wet chalk project (wet chalk provides an interesting texture different from dry chalk), guide the children into dipping the chalk in a cup of water before writing on paper. Another way to do this is for the children to wet the paper, including paper plates, instead of the chalk. For big pictures and designs, sweep the sides of the chalk across the paper. Children soon discover that they can mix the colors together by blending them with their fingers or with a tissue.

Three-Dimensional Materials

The sensory experience of handling and shaping a variety of materials encourages young children to experiment, explore, and discover original ways to create three-dimensional art. These activities can help children release emotional tensions and frustrations, work with their hands, develop small muscles, and provide opportunities to manipulate, construct, and learn about spatial relationships.

Three-dimensional art (having depth as well as height and width) is demonstrated through the use of play dough, clay, and "goop." These materials should be used on a surface that is easily cleaned and is large enough for children to have plenty of "elbow room." They should be soft enough for the children to manipulate easily, neither too wet nor too dry. Placing individual amounts of these materials on a tray, linoleum square, or manila folder for each child helps the children identify limits and gives them personal space. It is helpful to provide a bucket of water for the children to wash their hands in when they are finished with the activity. This will keep the residue of the materials out of the sinks.

Play dough, clay, and goop are extremely valuable because the children are able to use the materials with their hands without having to learn how to manage a tool, such as a paintbrush. (Younger children do better with play dough because it is softer and easier to manipulate.) The children are concerned with managing the material and learning what they can do with it. You can add rolling pins, cookie cutters, or other accessories after the children have had a lot of time to handle and experience the feel of the clay or dough. Many classrooms have both commercially prepared clay and play dough. In others, the teachers prefer to make these materials themselves. You might want to supply both to the children.

The following are recipes for play dough (*do not eat*) and goop.

Cooked Play Dough	
1 cup flour	1 tablespoon cooking oil
½ cup salt	2 teaspoons cream of tartar
1 cup water	

crayon resist: A type of art for older children that involves drawing a picture in light-colored crayons then covering the picture with watercolors or thin tempera paint. The paint will cover all but the crayon drawing.

three-dimensional art: An art form that has three sides. Play dough and clay are examples of three-dimensional materials.

Mix the ingredients. Heat and stir over low heat until the mixture forms a ball. Remove from heat and wrap in waxed paper to cool. Knead it well and store in an airtight container. The dough will last much longer if kept in the refrigerator. Add food coloring, if desired. You can make this first and then give it to the younger children. You and the older children can make it together so they can see the process. Some teachers put the food coloring in before cooking; others add color after cooking so the children can see the change from white, to marbled, to the final color. For more play dough, just double the recipe.

The following is the recipe for uncooked play dough (do not eat). For younger children, give it to them already made. Let the older children make it with your guidance.

Uncooked Play Dough	
1 cup flour	food coloring (optional)
½ cup salt	1 tablespoon salad oil
1 cup water	

Mix flour and salt. Add oil. Slowly add water until the mixture sticks together but does not feel sticky. Add more water if too stiff, add more flour if too sticky. Knead it well and store in airtight container.

GOOP
½ box to 1 box of cornstarch

Water

Add water slowly to cornstarch until it is semi-firm. Mix it with your hands or let the children do it. They can feel and see the changes in the texture. Store covered in the refrigerator. As it becomes dry from storage and handling, simply add more water.

Other three-dimensional works of art can be made into the form of sculptures by adding materials such as the following: toothpicks, Styrofoam, boxes, pieces of wood, egg cartons, paper towels, and toilet paper rolls.

Integrating Music Play into the Curriculum

"Play is the primary vehicle for young children's growth, and developmentally appropriate early music experiences should occur in child-initiated, child-directed, teacher-supported play environments" (Music Educators, 1994). We should provide numerous music and movement activities that invite and encourage children to move around, especially because many children live in confined spaces. Integral to the success of these activities is well-planned space that is adaptable to a number of uses. Consider sound levels that will not interfere with the simultaneous activities of other groups or individuals. These spaces should not be confined to the outdoors or a large motor room but integrated into portions of the general classroom. Classrooms should be arranged (or rearranged) to accommodate music and movement activities.

By promoting music and musical activities, you are also promoting mathematical thinking, according to Scholastic Magazines (2016):

> The very first patterning activity that a child encounters is musical. When a parent or teacher comforts a crying child they may pat, rock, or bounce the child using a steady beat or a rhythmic pattern. They may even sing them a simple song when they do this. … The goal for using music to support mathematics should be to provide infants, toddlers, and preschoolers with a stimulating and interactive environment. Next time you are looking for a way to engage children's mathematical mind, try a song—any song, and then ask the children to talk about the beat, rhythm, tempo, or melody. We think the children will surprise you with what they know about mathematics through music.

Music and movement are vital components of an early education environment. They contribute to language curriculum by introducing vocabulary, sound patterns, and literacy skills.

TABLE 6-1:	Basic Musical Terms
Beat	An accent of sound or a continuing series of accents
Melody	A sequence of tones of varying pitches organized in a rhythmically meaningful way
Pitch	The highness or lowness of a tone on a musical scale
Rhythm	A sense of movement and patterns in music created by beats, the duration and volume of sounds, and the silences between sounds
Tempo	A senses of slowness or rapidity in music
Timbre (TAM-bur)	The unique tone quality of a voice or musical instrument
Tone	An individual musical sound
Volume	The softness or loudness of sound

Simple songs, such as question-and-answer songs or name games, can help children make the transition from speaking to singing. Examples of this are included in the songs in Appendix C.

Additionally, music and movement can support social studies by bringing into the classroom music, musical instruments, and dances from around the world and creating a vibrant early childhood setting. Use the suggestions discussed in this chapter to stimulate your curriculum.

Types of Music

Music education for young children involves a developmentally appropriate program of singing, moving, listening, creating, playing instruments, and responding to visual and verbal representations of sound. The content of such a program should represent music of various cultures in time and place (National Association for Music Education, n.d.).

The basic sources of music are the human voice, instruments, environmental sounds, and music from radio, television, DVDs, and CDs. As you use these sources to plan music experiences for young children, remember to connect them to their life experiences. (See Table 6-1 for basic terms.)

Songs and Singing

Young children love to sing. Beginning in infancy and continuing on throughout their childhood, they are experimenting with their voices and the sounds that they can make. Billhartz (2007) helps us understand this even more:

    "A young child will first attempt to sing by isolating parts of words or selected words from a larger song. If provided a rich array of singing experiences, children will begin with spoken and singsong inflection as toddlers, and then move to matching pitches and singing entire songs as older preschoolers. Although many children will not sing in a group setting or in front of another child or adult, they will sing during playtime. This is a perfectly developmental way for young children to respond. As children become more comfortable with their singing voices, they will begin to join in group singing activities."

Here are a few more points to think about:

- Singing can be experienced alone or shared with others.
- Songs encourage the children to make up new words and to move with the music.
- Singing with children throughout daily routines nurtures important learning connections.
- Enthusiastic teacher participation in singing encourages the development of children's innate musical ability.

"There is a whole generation that doesn't know nursery rhymes or traditional tunes. You and I have the responsibility and privilege of passing on our musical heritage and putting music back into children's lives. ... Just open your mouth and SING (Feldman, 2002, pp. 6–7)."

There are many delightful and fun-filled songs to sing, such as the ones included in the developmentally appropriate activities at the end of this chapter and the following ones:

- Songs that offer repetition and chorus, such as "Polly Put the Kettle On," "Mary Had a Little Lamb," and "Here We Go Round the Mulberry Bush."
- Songs with repeated words or phrases that can be treated like an echo, such as "Miss Mary Mack" and "She'll Be Comin' 'Round the Mountain."
- Songs that ask children to supply sound effects or animal noises, such as "If You're Happy and You Know It" and "Old MacDonald Had a Farm."
- Ballads or songs that tell a story, such as "Hush Little Baby," "Humpty Dumpty," and "Little Bo Peep."
- Question-and-answer songs or name games that help children make the transition from speaking to singing, such as "Do You Know the Muffin Man?"

Songs can be extremely important to a young child, and songs with words can easily lead to spontaneous play. When music is integrated into a child's life, it becomes central to all of a child's play. Through play, children are integrating new concepts and music can provide the anchor children require to remember and repeat what they learn (McGraw, 2002).

Introducing Musical Sounds and Instruments

We know that music is a spontaneous and joyous part of young children's lives. They hear it in the world around them and they respond by cooing, babbling, singing, dancing, and interpreting it in their individual ways from infancy onward. How we gather and keep the energy and interest of the children depends on how we include music in our daily curriculum. (See **Figure 6-9**.)

Bea Wolf, composer and performer of children's music, suggests the following activities for sharing musical experiences with young children:

Figure 6-9 Combining music with dramatic play.

- Introduce musical recordings that children can sway to. Have the children close their eyes and move their arms to the music. Ask them, "What do you hear?" Listen to their responses. Suggest that they sway their bodies with the music. A waltz tempo is easy to begin with, by swaying on the beat of 1 (1–2–3, 1–2–3, 1–2–3, etc.).
- Select a favorite song and have the children clap to the rhythm of the music. They can clap their hands together, clap hands on knees, and clap hands on the floor. Often, they will continue this activity on their own by humming, singing, and clapping to themselves throughout the day.
- Wind chimes offer a delightful way to have the children focus on soft sounds. Group time can be a special time for children to listen closely as you share the sounds of several different kinds of wind chimes. Have the children listen closely to what these sound like. Then let them play the chimes gently by themselves.
- Music boxes offer other unique sounds for children to listen to. Bring in several different sizes and types for the children to explore. Ask them to bring ones from home, too.
- It is helpful to introduce musical instruments one at a time before combining all the instruments in conjunction with musical recordings. The *triangle* extends listening skills and shapes awareness. Shaking the *maracas* (use only one at first) invites children to shake their own rhythm, as does shaking the *jingle bells*, tap-tap-tapping and then rub-rub-rubbing with wooden sticks, shake-shake-shaking the tambourine, and beat-beat-beating the drums. Try having the children play the instruments to this beat: *sshhh-sshhh/ssh-ssh-ssh/sshhh-sshhh/ssh-ssh-ssh or 1–2/1–2–3/1–2/1–2–3.*

- Jingle bell instruments are fun to play along with the song "Jingle Bells," even in the month of June. Other fun songs to play bells with are Stephen Foster's "Oh, Susanna" and lively folk songs such as "This Ole' Man" and "She'll Be Comin' 'Round the Mountain."
- Children 5 years and older enjoy discriminating between sounds and listening to the vibrations of various instruments. Introduce gongs and give the children time to experiment with them. Wooden sticks offer vibrations that sound differently. Place the serrated stick flat against the floor and rub it with the other stick. The floor becomes the amplifier. You can hear different sounds when you place sticks on a carpeted floor and then on a noncarpeted floor.

Move with Scarves Activity

Moving with scarves (or any lightweight material) is another way for children to practice their creativity by moving and swaying to music. Take this activity outdoors for a change of pace. Scarves can encourage children to create stories through movement and act out stories using these and other props. The children are also practicing manipulative movement skills. Krull (2009) offers the following ideas for getting the children started:

- Throw the scarf in the air with one hand and catch with the other.
- Toss and try clapping once or twice before catching the scarf.
- Hold the scarf together with a friend as you move together around the classroom.
- Toss the scarf in the air, spin around, and catch it before it falls to the ground.
- Catch and toss with a partner.
- Dance with the scarf to music.

Play "Follow the Leader" where the child at the head of the line does a movement with the scarf and all children will copy that movement. Do this activity until every child has a chance to be the leader. Use music or musical instruments to accent the beat of each action.

Using the Voice

The voices of children are expressive as they speak, chant, and sing. When young children experiment with their voices and tongues, they can sound like musical instruments, animals, and the wind. Encourage the children to make some of these sounds:

whisper quietly	cluck
talk softly, then loudly	buzz
whistle	growl
sneeze	bark
purr	snore
hum	cry

Choosing Classical Selections

Research tells us that classical music stimulates musical responses from young children. Whether they are "conducting," relaxing, listening, or moving creatively to these recorded musical works, children enjoy and can get caught up in them. Children's tastes vary greatly. Because of this, teachers should introduce music and then let the children select pieces they like. This can be done by providing a wide variety of instrumental and orchestral pieces. CDs are available in libraries or stores under many different labels and performing artists. Here are a few children's favorites:

- Britten/*The Young Person's Guide to the Orchestra*
- Copland/*Rodeo*

- Dukas/*The Sorcerer's Apprentice*
- Grofé/*Grand Canyon Suite*
- Mozart/*Concerto for Flute, Harp, and Orchestra*
- Prokofiev/*Peter and the Wolf*
- Rimsky-Korsakov/*Flight of the Bumble Bee*
- Rossini/*William Tell Overture*
- Saint-Saëns/*Carnival of the Animals*
- Strauss, R./*Till Eulenspiegel's Merry Pranks*
- Stravinsky/*The Firebird*
- Tchaikovsky/*The Nutcracker Suite*
- Tchaikovsky/*The Sleeping Beauty*

For infants and toddlers, gradually introduce classical background music into the environment. As you plan your music curriculum for all the developmental stages, think about when and why you want to have music playing, and then choose it carefully. For all ages, research by Parlakin and Lerner (2010, pp. 14–19) has shown that classical music has a significant effect on the brain. "Thoughtfully planned music experiences can support and nurture each of the domains of development—social-emotional, physical (motor), thinking (cognitive), and language and literacy."

Children should be offered a whole musical picture even though they might be too young to understand it. During the first years, children learn and understand a great deal more than we think they can. We never think of not speaking to infants and toddlers just because they cannot speak. It is the same with music. Teachers should offer a wide variety of musical experience long before they are able to sing.

Activity Plan Worksheet | Developmentally Appropriate Activities for Young Children

AGES: 2-, 3-, 4-, and 5-year-olds

Name of Activity and Brief Description
Tissue Collage Suncatcher: Use torn colored tissue to make a collage on wax paper.

Child Outcomes of Activity
- Develop the pincher grasp.
- Create a design using their imagination.
- Develop eye–hand coordination.
- Create secondary colors when tissue overlaps.

Space and Materials Needed
Colored tissue, wax paper, liquid starch or mixed water and glue, cups, brushes, a table, a drying rack or space, a window to hang the finished art

Procedure
This can get messy, so I like to put vinyl placemats or shallow trays to contain the wax paper.

1. Give each child a piece of waxed paper and a brush.
2. Set cups with the starch or watery glue mixture so each pair of children or each child has a cup near him.
3. Place sheets and random sized pieces of tissue in the center of the table.
4. Encourage children to tear the paper and place it on the waxed paper to create whatever design they want.
5. Encourage children to put glue/starch both under and on top of the tissue until it is soaked through (colors may run).
6. Allow collage to dry and then hang in a window.

Guidance
Do this art activity with a small group of children or individually. Allow children to stand while working, if they are more comfortable. Prepare for clean-up and spills by having paper towels nearby.

Assessment and Follow-Up Strategies
Talk to the children as they are creating. Ask them to predict what will happen if they glue a piece of tissue on top of another. Observe to assess children's eye–hand coordination and use of the pincher grasp, as well as their stage of artistic development, such as whether they create representational or abstract art.

⌄ Professional Resource Download

Activity Plan Worksheet
Developmentally Appropriate Activities for Young Children

AGES: 3-, 4-, and 5-year-olds

Name of Activity and Brief Description

Paper Plate Twist: Use a recording of Chubby Checker's "Let's Twist Again." Get each child two paper plates to use. They will stand on them to twist to the music and pick them up to do hand motions.

Child Outcomes of Activity

- Develop listening skills.
- Develop body control and coordination.
- Practice balance.
- Support cross lateral and vestibular development.
- Follow directions.

Space and Materials Needed

CD or mp3 player, floor, recording for "Let's Twist Again" and paper plates

Procedure

To prepare, practice the movements to the song so you are familiar with them.

1. Give each child two paper plates to stand on and twist.
2. Remind the children to listen for your instructions.
3. Demonstrate the movements, including twisting while standing on the plates, picking them up, holding a plate in each hand as they swing their arms in front of their body to the right, to the left and up and down, moving their hands in a circle in front of their body, and clapping the plates together. Do all movements twice in a row.
4. You can do as many of the gestures as you feel your children are ready for, starting with twisting while standing on the plates. Younger-than-threes may just like to twist on the plates.
5. Suggest movement sequences start with twisting, then pick up plates and swing to right and left twice, when lyrics say "round and around and up and down we go" move plates accordingly, then clap plates together slowly (two beats = one clap), put plates down and twist when he sings "Twist again." Repeat

Guidance

Allow children to stand on the plates and start twisting immediately while you get the music set up. Model movements for children as you do them yourself. Encourage children to move freely.

Assessment and Follow-Up Strategies

As children are moving to the movement, observe to assess children's ability to follow directions, development of physical skills, stamina, coordination, flexibility, position of their body in space, and ability to cross midline. Integrate movements that cross midline and require balance into other music and movement activities.

⌄⌄ **Professional Resource Download**

Technology in Children's Art and Music

Technology & Teaching: Children's Art and Music

The use of technology in conjunction with art expands the classroom environment and creates new expressions for children's art. Aulthouse and colleagues (2003) suggest the following:

- *Overhead projector:* Children can place color paddles, colored tissue paper, or cellophane on the overhead projector to find out what happens to light and color.
- *Cameras:* Digital or inexpensive disposable cameras can immediately document children's art activities. Taking photographs is yet another way for children to explore their world. Computers, printers, and scanners streamline this process and allow for flexibility with image size. Jacobs and Crowley (2010, p. 92) expand the use of cameras this way: "Children can take photographs, study them, and then try to recreate the image with paint, crayons, play dough or other media."
- *Photocopier:* Children and teachers can also enlarge photographs on a color copier to display the pictures taken of their art.
- *Videos:* Video of children's activities can show not only how children are engaged in art but also how art can be integrated into all learning centers.

- *Computer technology:* Older children can use computers for word processing as they write and illustrate books. When selecting computer tools to use with art, it is important to use software that allows a child to design the art and control the creation of the pictures or illustrations. There are paint programs available for young children. Be sure to view computer art as only one component of your art program. They shouldn't replace the hands-on art experiences.

Isbell and Raines (2013, p. 151) help us understand how to choose appropriate software for art, especially with many different computer programs available for children.

1. The child is able to determine what will be drawn.
2. Options are available for creating lines, forms, colors, and making changes.
3. Different drawing tools can be used to change the texture, size, and proportion of the drawing.
4. The child's name and title or description can be added.

Different types of software have different effects. Open-ended programs, such as those that do not expect children to just answer predetermined questions with only one correct answer, foster cooperation and collaboration, which in turn encourage children to be active participants. The pace should be set by the child and not the software program (Mayesky, 2011). Always preview a program before offering it to children. It is important for the software to be developmentally appropriate and meet your educational objectives.

Digital technology can help involve students in performing, creating, and analyzing music. There are two major reasons to use technology in teaching music: Some students will be more motivated to learn when technology is used appropriately, and there are some learning experiences in music that are much more feasible when technology is used. Also, state and national standards require that students use technology in all subject areas.

So...what are some ways to start using technology in the music classroom? Using MIDI and audio files to accompany singing, playing, and movement, as well as using software for instruction. Slide show software such as PowerPoint can be used to create multimedia listening guides. The Internet is a great tool for finding information about music. Computer software for music learning may be in the form of multimedia CD-ROMs that are installed on a computer, networkable software, downloaded software, or programs that are free on the Web.

Diversity in the Creative Arts

Multicultural and Anti-Bias

Art activities are developmentally appropriate for children when they are encouraged to become more aware of and appreciate art present in their own culture and communities and beyond. Displaying prints of fine art; books that include art reproductions, including community artists; and taking field trips to performances, museums, and galleries are all excellent ways to bring art into the classroom:

> "Using reproductions of art in the curriculum is surprisingly easy and provides a broad range of benefits for children. Introducing artwork to young children allows them to construct their own knowledge, teaches appreciation of diversity, encourages storytelling, and fosters imaginative and critical thinking skills (Mulcahey, 2009, pp. 107–112)."

In our global society, it is necessary that we encourage children to look at art from different cultures as a way to see the world. This requires teachers to choose carefully the art reproductions that children will explore. Select from various forms of art, geographic locations, time periods, and cultures. This will give children a window into the diverse traditions of the art world.

Multicultural art materials should always be available to young children. Just as each culture brings its own richness to our world, so do the projects and creations of each child bring richness and beauty to our classrooms and communities.

Guide children to discover projects that reflect both ancient and modern cultures. Ancient cultures produced some of the most beautiful art and exciting artifacts ever created. Many of these techniques have passed from generation to generation:

> "When children see the art of their heritage displayed and honored, they feel valued as people. When they see the art of others treated with respect, they learn to value people who are different (Koster, 2011, p. 170)."

The following example of an activity can get you started in introducing an appreciation of color in a fun and simple way. A book, first introduced in 1955, that is one of the most popular ones for both children and teachers is Crockett Johnson's *Harold and the Purple Crayon*. You can use this imaginative story as a springboard for many art activities related to multicultural and anti-bias curriculum in an early childhood program. For example:

- Read the book to the children at group time. Ask the children to think of other things Harold can do with his purple crayon. At the next group time introduce a flannel-board story that has Harold as the main character doing some of the things the children suggested.
- In the art center place only purple items, such as crayons, markers, and construction paper. This is a creative way to introduce children to all the different shades of purple. Let the children experiment with paints and problem solve which ones to mix together to make purple. Also have purple play dough available for creative play.
- For their snack, you can serve purple grapes, or introduce the children to eggplant or other purple foods.
- The children will also suggest other purple things to do.

Activities for Children with Special Needs

It is important to explain to the family of a child with special needs how their child participates in art activities.

> "Because of the open-ended nature of well-designed art activities, children with special needs can participate fully in most art programs, often without many modifications. If necessary, changes can be made in the tools and environment to allow active participation. The other children also need to be encouraged to accept and support those with special needs (Koster, 2011, p. 127). "

For example, Koster (2011), Fox and Schirrmacher (2015), and special needs educators suggest putting trays across wheelchairs or providing wheelchair-height tables. Placing a stool under the table so that a child sitting in a regular child-size chair who cannot reach the ground will be able to rest her feet on the stool and stabilize his or her body, thus being able to more easily use his or her fine motor skills. Art tools such as crayons, markers, pencils, and brushed can be wrapped in foam hair curlers to improve grip.

Paper can be taped to the table to keep the paper smooth and to prevent it from moving while the children are using it. Contact paper or other sticky paper can be used as backing for collages to eliminate the difficulty of bluing and pasting. The child only has to put things on paper.

Easels can be lowered and used with a chair for those who cannot stand and assistive technology can be incorporated for successful inclusion. Adaptive peripherals such as special switches or hardware are available for children unable to use a mouse or keyboard.

Creating Partnerships with Families

Another part of the teacher's role is to help parents understand that the many pages or examples of art the children bring home are the results of creative and imaginative processes—all of them from the children. If families understand *why* art is valued in the early childhood setting, they can more easily offer support to their child at home.

You can also guide the parents into setting up a special place at home for their child to continue experimenting and creating with art. Send home suggestions and lists of what materials and supplies are appropriate as well as explanations of what he or she has been doing in the classroom. Interpret the child's developmental progress to the parents, not what the child's art is or is not.

As you share the children's art and activities with the families, ask each family to share with you. Invite them to bring in any of the art their children create at home. Some may want to take photographs at home showing the child and family member involved with the activity. Start a "Family Art" section on your parent bulletin board.

The content of **Figures 6-5** and **6-6** on making musical instruments would be excellent to include in your family newsletter so that they can reinforce musical activities at home.

Parents like to see their children's art experiences but sending home DVDs of their children participating musically can also carry creativity experiences to the home.

The Teacher's Role

Guidance for Art and Music Play

When designing an environment in which young children can integrate visual art into all areas of the classroom, you should consider how the surroundings, organization, and storage will affect the children. Clarify your goals and objectives for the art area and each art activity. Relate them to the theme and lesson plan when appropriate. Establish rules with the children concerning the care and use of art materials and limits within the art area or areas. Guide them toward assuming responsibility for the use, care, and cleaning of materials and tools by showing them where they are kept, how the children are to take them, where to use them, and how they are to be returned.

Help children and their parents deal with being messy. Being messy is okay! Supply smocks or aprons. The children can be responsible for getting a smock, putting it on during an art activity, and putting it back when they have finished. Continue to repeat rules of the art areas when necessary.

As you introduce each new activity or group of materials or supplies, explain the appropriate ways to use them. Help each child learn to respect his or her own art and the art of others. Many times a cooperative art activity, such as painting a mural with each child having his or her own space on the paper, will demonstrate to a child how to focus on his or her own creation to work together as a team with others.

Bring order to the environment by setting up the structure of space, time, and materials to reflect your educational goals. Make sure the environment includes space where children can discover, process, experiment, and explore. (See **Figure 6-10**.)

Arrange the materials and space so that the children can gain independence in self-selecting what they need and returning them when they are finished with them.

Arrange the environment so that there is adequate open space for movement with music, space for listening independently to music CDs, and for storage of musical instruments.

Figure 6-10   Make materials available where children can create in an undisturbed environment.

Case Study: Art Activities

Suzie is a first-year teacher in a kindergarten classroom at Park Meadows Elementary School in Portland, Oregon. Easter is coming and she has been looking on Pintrest for some art activity ideas. She has found an "Easter Basket" craft project she thinks is cute.

She has created a model to show the children what the finished basket should look like. She has dye-cut bunnies and eggs for the children to use to decorate their baskets.

What Do You Think?

1. Is this an appropriate art activity? Explain.
2. What do you think the children are learning from this activity?
3. How could Suzie change it to make it more appropriate?

TEACHING TIPS   Art and Music

When you were young, you probably had experiences, some that were positive but some that were negative, concerning what teachers thought about *your* art. You should strive to be the kind of teacher the children in your care will remember as a positive and supportive influence in their lives.

In this chapter, as in all chapters of this book, you are asked to view what a child has created with different eyes than perhaps you have used before. Do not focus on the outcome or product: Look at the process. Is the child participating, interacting, experimenting, exploring, and getting involved "up to the elbows"? This is what you should be observing as you plan, initiate, and evaluate the art center and art activities.

Your role as teacher is one of facilitator and observer. You set up the developmentally appropriate environment, furnish a variety of safe materials and supplies, provide opportunities for child-directed art experiences, and offer support and encouragement to the children as you observe their unique creations.

Approaching children's art from the perspective of facilitator can take any real or imagined pressures off of you and the children. For example, let the children decide whether to talk about their art or not talk about it. If they freely describe it and want you to write down a description, do so—otherwise, do not.

Many times, we try to get some response from the children and ask them to "Tell me about your picture" or "Tell me a story about what you're painting." This puts stress on the child to say what he or she thinks you want to hear. I overheard one child emphatically tell a teacher, "This is not a story! This is a picture to look at!" (That answer certainly made the teacher reflect on what she had asked the child.)

Some suggestions of what you could say should describe what you observe. Talk about the children's actions: "I see you used different colors in your picture." "You're feeling the finger paint, aren't you?" "You have a lot of dots on your paper today." "I see you covered the whole page." These statements and others like them do not ask for the child to "come up with an answer." This type of response from you offers affirmation and encouragement and avoids vague and extremely judgmental types of praise. "This is 'ART TALK' that infers 'show me' instead of 'tell me'" (Aulthouse, 2003, p. 136).

Another part of your responsibility as a facilitator is to make materials available where children can create in an undisturbed environment. As you decide which activities and materials are appropriate, try them out yourself before you put them out for the children. This will enable you to introduce new supplies or materials comfortably and show the children how to use them appropriately. Once this is accomplished, step back and allow the children to investigate, explore, and try out the materials for themselves. (See Figure 6-10.)

The following are some additional thoughts that teachers should consider when establishing an art environment:

- Develop an awareness that the process of creative thinking is complex.
- Understand that there is no right or wrong way of doing things, only possibilities.
- Recognize that some children are more creative in one area than another.
- Recognize that creativity may reflect an ability to think divergently or seek multiple solutions rather than a single solution to problems.
- Arrange an appropriate classroom space for children to leave unfinished work to continue the next day.
- Encourage children to engage in creative processing as they manipulate and play with objects, while remembering that it may not result in a finished product.
- Help parents to appreciate their child's creative abilities, with or without a finished product.
- Offer encouragement for, and acceptance of, a certain amount of messiness, noise, and freedom.
- Continue to experiment and test alternatives to determine what is best for your children and your classroom situation.
- Understand that creative expression should flow through the entire curriculum.
- Relate your goals and objectives for the art area or areas to the theme and lesson plan when appropriate.
- Encourage the children to participate in all phases of an art activity, including preparation and cleanup.
- Add several drops of liquid dishwashing soap to tempera paint. It washes out of clothes more easily and also prevents paint from chipping off the children's art when dry.
- Balance art activities: new with familiar, messy with clean, indoor with outdoor, large muscle and small muscle.
- Attract children to the art area by including activities that promote color, texture, shape, and design.
- Make sure the activities you plan are developmentally appropriate for each child. Mastery of these art activities will help them to feel confident that they can master more complicated ones.

Tips for Displaying Children's Art

As you send the children's art home, remember to save some of the creations to place around the classroom—with the child's permission, of course. The early education environment should reflect the children, and a wonderful way to do this is to display their art. (This also actively creates an aesthetic environment, as previously discussed in this chapter.)

Displays show the parents what is happening in their child's classroom. Provide a place with wall and table displays outside the classroom in a hall or lobby for parents' enjoyment.

Art should be displayed at the child's eye level. Frame children's art attractively in a variety of ways using colored paper, wallpaper, or gift wrap as a background; rick-rack, fabric, or yarn to outline pictures; and a large group finger-painting to serve as a mounting for individual art. Taking the time and effort to mat and frame the children's art is another way to show that you value what they have done.

Display all kinds of children's creations (clay models, Styrofoam structures, mobiles, wood sculpture, and collages). These kinds of art can be displayed on tables or shelves and arranged attractively on brightly colored paper. Change the art displays frequently. Let the children help decide when to change the selections and what to put up next. Arrange art in different kinds of groupings, such as several art items belonging to an individual child, several pictures that share the same colors, pictures with the same theme created from different media, and art connected to the theme or lesson plan of the week.

> "An art kiosk is a workable solution to limited wall space. A kiosk is a self-standing display with three or more sides. It can be constructed of panels of sturdy cardboard, wood, or stacked cartons. It is space-efficient in that many pictures can be simultaneously displayed on a number of sides in a few feet of floor space Fox and Schirrmacher (2015)."

The following are some final suggestions to help you share and enjoy music and movement with children:

- Invite parents to participate in your music experiences. Ask the parents to think about songs that hold special cultural and family memories—songs they learned from their parents and grandparents when they were younger. Encourage them to bring musical instruments and music that are a part of their cultural heritage and share them with the children.

- Use a variety of approaches in introducing songs. Use flannel-board characters, puppets, books, or simple props. Know the songs well yourself and sing them to the children several times while they listen. New songs should be sung to the children in their entirety, not phrase by phrase. Children pick up the tune and words naturally without having to be taught them. Incorporate simple actions into the songs. This offers visual clues to help children remember the words.

- Ask children to provide sound effects for a story. The more music and rhythm is used and the more complex listening is experienced, the broader the foundation laid (Shore and Strasser, 2006).

- Observe and listen to the children. They will let you know what is working and what is not.

- Enjoy singing songs, playing musical instruments, and participating in movement activities. Be involved! Be part of the activity! The children pick up on your enthusiasm (or lack of it). Do not be concerned about your singing voice. Young children are not critical! They will be so happy that you celebrate music with them.

- Children need music every day and every year of their learning lives, and the more complex, the better! Continuing to listen to complex music throughout childhood and even adulthood is as important for brain development as learning to read letters and words. Music has much to offer our educational settings, even beyond simply touching our feelings. Music can touch our minds (Shore and Strasser, 2006)!

Summary

1. **Define and give examples for key terms related to the arts for children.** Creativity is the process of doing or bringing something new and imaginative into being. An aesthetic environment is one that cultivates an appreciation for beauty and a feeling of wonder and excitement of the world in which we live. Types of art activities includes collage (an art activity that involves making a picture containing glued-on objects on paper), string painting (a type of painting that involves moving string dipped in paint around on paper to make a design), crayon rubbings (duplicating an object of texture by placing it under paper and rubbing over it with a crayon), crayon resist (a type of art for older children that involves drawing a picture in light-colored crayons then covering the picture with watercolors or thin tempera paint which will cover all but the crayon drawing), and three-dimensional art (an art form that has three sides such as play dough and clay).

2. **Discuss artistic development in young children.** Stages in artistic development do not have discrete beginnings and endings in the developmental sequence, but rather,

children exhibit a tendency to move back and forth between stages as they learn and grow. A teacher can recognize characteristics that are identifiable to help in understanding the needs and interests of the children in an early childhood program. Understanding how the child has previously developed helps in knowing what to look for as the child matures.

3. **What would be included in the preparation of an environment that supports creative exploration?** As you plan or redesign your visual art environment, provide *time*, *space*, and *materials* that allow children to work at their own pace without interference. The area should be large enough to accommodate the easels and art table. The art center should be a free-choice area. When entering an integrated, open-ended arts program, the observer will not notice an art corner. There will not be art projects of the day posted around the room. What will be seen is a variety of art activities embedded in many places throughout the environment.

   The location within a classroom where major art materials and equipment will be located requires a great deal of thought and planning. Art activities that require some degree of "messiness" will need to be close to a sink for easy cleanup. A bucket or tub of warm soapy water near the area will also help. The water does need to be changed often. An uncarpeted area is also useful to protect the floor, but plastic sheeting or a shower curtain secured to the floor will serve the same purpose. To keep the art materials and spaces clean, children should be made aware of their responsibilities for the use, care, and cleaning of this area.

4. **How would you integrate creative activities appropriate for young children?** Try connecting art to everything you do. For example, children can listen to music and draw or paint in rhythm to the music. They can express in their creations how the music makes them feel. Verbal and nonverbal language is expressed through art. Children learn to include an art vocabulary into their everyday conversations with other children and adults. They express and represent what they know through their art. Art activities also give children an understanding of themselves and others. Their study of artists and their visits to art galleries and museums help them relate to their community and to the world. Math and art content can be combined on a regular basis. For example, the math concepts of problem solving, inventing patterns, measurement, sorting, and classifying relate to the art concepts of awareness of line and shape, decoration of line and pattern, and awareness of texture and changing shape.

   Children quantify art materials, equipment, and supplies by counting the number of brushes and jars of paint that are in use and by deciding which brushes have longer handles, which crayons are fatter, and which geometric shapes are being used in their art creations.

   Music and movement are vital components of an early education environment. They contribute to language curriculum by introducing vocabulary, sound patterns, and literacy skills. Simple songs, such as question-and-answer songs or name games, can help children make the transition from speaking to singing.

   Additionally, music and movement can support social studies by bringing into the classroom music, musical instruments, and dances from around the world and creating a vibrant early childhood setting. Use the suggestions discussed in this chapter to stimulate your curriculum.

5. **How can technology be used in an environment that supports creative exploration?** The use of technology in conjunction with art expands the classroom environment and creates new expressions for children's art. Ways that technology can be used include:

   - Place color paddles, colored tissue paper, or cellophane on the overhead projector.
   - Document children's art activities with a digital or inexpensive disposable camera. Taking photographs is yet another way for children to explore their world. Streamline the process with computers, printers, and scanners.
   - Display the pictures taken of children's art by enlarging photographs on a color copier.

- Show how children are engaged in art and how art can be integrated throughout the classroom through the use of videos.
- Select computer tools to use with art that allows children to design art and control its creation.

6. **How can diversity be incorporated into creative activities?** Art activities are developmentally appropriate for children when they are encouraged to become more aware of and appreciate art present in their own culture and communities and beyond. Displaying prints of fine art; books that include art reproductions, including community artists; and taking field trips to performances, museums, and galleries are all excellent ways to bring art into the classroom.

   In our global society it is necessary that we encourage children to look at art from different cultures as a way to see the world. This requires teachers to choose carefully the art reproductions that children will explore. Select from various forms of art, geographic locations, time periods, and cultures. This will give children a window into the diverse traditions of the art world. Multicultural art materials should always be available to young children. Just as each culture brings its own richness to our world, so do the projects and creations of each child bring richness and beauty to our classrooms and communities.

   Guide children to discover projects that reflect both ancient and modern cultures. Ancient cultures produced some of the most beautiful art and exciting artifacts ever created. Many of these techniques have passed from generation to generation.

7. **How can partnerships with families be developed that support children's exploration of creativity?** Part of the teacher's role is to help parents understand that the many pages or examples of art the children bring home are the results of creative and imaginative processes—all of them from the children. If families understand *why* art is valued in the early childhood setting, they can more easily offer support to their child at home. Teachers can also guide the parents into setting up a special place at home for their child to continue experimenting and creating with art. Sending home suggestions and lists of what materials and supplies are appropriate as well as explanations of what he or she has been doing in the classroom can connect the parents more with the classroom. As teachers share the children's art and activities with the families, each family should be asked to share with you. Invite them to bring in any of the art their children create at home. Some may want to take photographs at home showing the child and family member involved with the activity. Start a "Family Art" section on your parent bulletin board.

8. **What is the teacher's role in promoting creativity in the classroom?**

   - When asked to view what a child has created with different eyes than perhaps you have used before, do not focus on the outcome or product: *Look at the process*. Is the child participating, interacting, experimenting, exploring, and getting involved "up to the elbows"? This is what you should be observing as you plan, initiate, and evaluate the art center and art activities.
   - Facilitate and observe. Set up the developmentally appropriate environment, furnish a variety of safe materials and supplies, provide opportunities for child-directed art experiences, and offer support and encouragement to the children as you observe their unique creations.
   - Approaching children's art from the perspective of facilitator can take any real or imagined pressures off of you *and* the children. For example, let the *children* decide whether to talk about their art or not talk about it. If they freely describe it and want you to write down a description, do so—otherwise do *not*.
   - Many times we try to get some response from the children and ask them to "Tell me about your picture" or "Tell me a story about what you're painting." This puts stress on the child to say what he or she thinks you want to hear. I overheard one child emphatically tell a teacher, "This is not a story! This is a picture to look at!" (That answer certainly made the teacher reflect on what she had asked the child.)

- Some suggestions of what you could say should describe what you observe. Talk about the children's actions: "I see you used different colors in your picture." "You're feeling the finger paint, aren't you?" "You have a lot of dots on your paper today." "I see you covered the whole page." These statements and others like them do not ask for the child to "come up with an answer." This type of response from you offers affirmation and encouragement and avoids vague and extremely judgmental types of praise: "This is 'ART TALK' that infers 'show me' instead of 'tell me'" (Aulthouse; 2003; p. 136).

- Another part of your responsibility as a facilitator is to make materials available where children can create in an undisturbed environment. As you decide which activities and materials are appropriate, try them out yourself before you put them out for the children. This will enable you to introduce new supplies or materials comfortably and show the children how to use them appropriately. Once this is accomplished, step back and allow the children to investigate, explore, and try out the materials for themselves.

Reflective Review Questions

1. We often hear an adult asking a child about a painting by saying such things as "What is this?" or "Tell me about your picture." True, the adult is giving attention to the child and the painting, but are these appropriate questions? What might the adult say that would be more appropriate? Why?

2. Describe how a classroom's art environment and materials might be altered to make it more suitable for children with special needs.

3. What do outdoor arts activities mean to you? Why is it important to take art outdoors? What difference will it make to a group of young children? Are there ways of planning an arts activity for outdoors that differs from art done indoors? Explain.

4. Name and describe five different ways to make musical instruments that young children could enjoy playing. How would you introduce these to the children? Explain.

5. Choose a classical music selection from this chapter and plan how you would share it with a group of kindergarten children. Describe your plan in writing.

Explorations

1. Select an early childhood classroom. Observe for at least one hour. In writing, describe any music and movement activities you observed. Did the children or the teacher initiate these activities? Describe some examples of how the children spontaneously approached these activities.

2. Select an early childhood classroom. Observe for at least one hour. In writing, describe any art activities you observed. Did the children or the teacher initiate these activities? Describe some examples of how the children spontaneously approach these activities.

3. Create a book for young children. Complete an Activity Plan Worksheet, such as the one in this chapter; then read the book to a small group of young children. Observe their responses. What age group did you select? Was your book developmentally appropriate for that age group? Explain your answers and your assessment and follow-up activities.

4. Based on the information in this chapter and on your observations of early education environments, design a pre-K art center and a pre-K music center. Using paper and colored pens, pencils, or markers, design the learning center showing where materials,

supplies and equipment are placed. What criteria will you use? Think about how this center will relate to the other learning centers in the classroom. How does the art and music center support the creativity of the children?

5. Use the Art Environment Checklist and the Music Environment Checklist in this chapter to conduct an observation of an early childhood learning environment.
   - Beside each statement, place an X if the classroom you observed met the statement.
   - On a separate sheet of paper, describe what you actually observed related to each statement. Place the number of the statement first and then your observation.
   - On a separate sheet of paper, for each statement that you did not check as met, describe what you would do to improve that classroom so that the statement would be met. Be sure to put the number of the statement first.
   - Submit this with the name of the location you observed and the age group.

Creativity Books for Young Children

- Carle, E. (2002). *The art of Eric Carle*. New York: Philomel.
- Jenkins, S., & Page, R. (2003). *What do you do with a tail like this?* Boston: Houghton Mifflin.
- Lee, S. (2008). *Wave*. San Francisco, CA: Chronicle.
- Lionni, L. (2006). *A color of his own*. New York: Alfred A. Knopf.
- Reynolds, P. H. (2003). *The dot*. Cambridge, MA: Candlewick.
- Sayre, H. S. (2004). *Cave Paintings to Picasso: The inside scoop of 50 masterpieces*. San Francisco: Chronicle.
- Scieszka, J., & Smith, L. (2005). *Seen Art?* New York: Viking.
- Weitzman, J. P., & Glasser, R. P. (2002). *You can't take a balloon into the Museum of Fine Arts*. New York: Dial Books.

Children's Books and CDs featuring Music and Movement

Books

- Aliki. (2003). *Ah, music!* New York: HarperCollins.
- Bassett, C. (2003). *Walk like a bear, stand like a tree, run like the wind: Cool yoga stretching and aerobic activities*. New York: Nubod Concepts.
- Krull, K. (2003). *M is for music*. Illustrated by S. Innerst. New York: Harcourt.
- Kubler, A. (2002). *Head, shoulders, knees, and toes*. Auburn, ME: Child's Play International.
- Kubler, A. (2005). *Sign and sing along: Itsy bitsy spider*. Auburn, ME: Child's Play International.
- Moss, L. (2001). *Our marching band*. Illustrated by B. Bluthenthal. New York: Putnam.
- Moss, L. (2003). *Music is*. Illustrated by P. Petit Roulet. New York: Putnam.
- Shulman, J. (Adapter). (2004). *S. Prokofiev's Peter and the Wolf: With a fully-orchestrated and narrated CD*. Illustrated by P. Malone. New York: Knopf Books for Young Readers.
- Turner, B. C. (2000). *Carnival of the animals: Classical music for kids*. Illustrated by S. Williams. New York: Henry Holt.
- Wagrin, K. (2004). *M is for melody: A music alphabet*. New York: Sleeping Bear Press.
- Wenig, M. (2003). *Yoga kids: Educating the whole child through yoga*. Photographed by S. Andrews. New York: Stewart, Tabori, and Chang.

⌄ Professional Resource Download

CDs

- Disney. (2005). *Here come the ABCs*. New York: Disney Production.
- Eklof, J. (2000). *My favorite animal/Mi animal favorito; So many ways to say "good morning."* Dallas, TX: Miss Jo Publications.
- Palmer, H. (2000). *American folk, game, and activity songs*. New York: Folkway Records.
- Sesame Workshop. (2003). *Songs from the Street: 35 years of music*. New York: Sony/Wonder.
- Sesame Workshop. (2008). *Platinum all time favorites: Sesame Street*. New York: Koch Records.
- Verve/Various Artists. (2004). *Jazz for kids*. New York: Verve Music Group.

≫ Professional Resource Download

7

The Child's World: Social Studies and Dramatic Play

Standards Covered in This Chapter

 NAEYC 5a, 5b, 5c

DAP 2

INTASC 4, 5, 8

HEAD START
Domain: Social Emotional
Development, Subdomain:
Creativity

 NCSS Social Studies
Standards Themes 1, 2, 3, 4

CEC DEC CEC DCC C4, C5

Student Learning Outcomes

After studying this chapter, you should be able to:

- Define and give examples for key terms related to social studies and dramatic play development for children.

- Discuss social studies and dramatic play development in young children and relate stages of child development to social studies and dramatic play development.

- Evaluate various components of planning and preparation of social studies and dramatic play environments.

- Create social studies and dramatic play activities appropriate for young children.

- Discuss various ways to use technology in a social studies and dramatic play environment.

- Distinguish ways to incorporate diversity into social studies and dramatic play environments.

- Describe ways to develop partnerships with families that support social studies and dramatic play.

- Analyze the teacher's role in promoting social studies and dramatic play in the classroom.

Social studies is a developmentally appropriate link in the early childhood curriculum chain. Social studies emphasizes ways to provide care and education for each child by focusing on the child, the child's family, the community, the nation, and the world. Young children are enthusiastic as they gain understanding of the many aspects of their cultural and environmental world.

To become functioning citizens of society in the future, it is important for children to be prepared for this role. The field of social studies is the best way for children to obtain the required knowledge, skills, and attitudes. They experience the functions of small democracies in their own neighborhoods, school settings, and homes on a daily basis to prepare them their future participation.

Children today are aware at a young age about aspects of all the social sciences. They are experiencing moving to and living in different places or knowing family members and friends who have. Many travel on a regular basis and have access to the Internet, television, video games, movies, books, and magazines that introduce them to an ever-changing world.

With all of this in mind, your role as an early childhood teacher continues to be nurturing, valuing, and accepting of the children and families in your care, both individually and as a group. Supportive adults in a supportive environment allow children to release their feelings, ask questions and expect appropriate answers, solve problems, and resolve conflicts. As you continue through this chapter, you will understand how social studies follows the path through the preschool years of a child's own life, to those of his or her family, school, neighborhood, then branching off during the primary years to his or her nation and then to the larger world or global community.

Play is the natural language of the child. It helps a child observe and respond to his or her relationship to others and to the world in which he or she lives. Play is at the core of developmentally appropriate practice. Dramatic play helps to expand this important self-motivated behavior that will serve each child throughout his or her life.

From pat-a-cake to peek-a-boo, a baby watches others and then copies them. "The infant year is spent in close and intense observation of the human species. The baby learns to read every expression and gesture of the important adults around her. Toward the end of that first year, imitation begins" (Miller, 2002, p. 25). The more you can play such pretend games with an infant, the more the infant learns. As the baby coos and babbles, your smiles and hugs give encouragement. When you say a word over and over, the baby will try to say it, too. An infant's awareness of human expression, gestures, and sounds is the beginning of creative thinking.

Toddlers love the world of pretend. They will use dishes and pretend to eat and drink. "Toddlers have object hunger. They love objects of all kinds and use them in every conceivable way. This shows up in their early pretending. As long as the toy looks like an object they have seen, even if it is not exact, the child will use it in the intended way" (Miller, 2002, p. 26). They enjoy pretend hellos and goodbyes. As you talk and enter such play, you are helping them learn about the real world. Children learn by repetition. Your willingness to do the same thing over and over is the key that opens the door to their learning. Although toddlers may pretend for short periods of time alone, they need other children and adults to give words and some direction to their play.

Dramatic play is one of the most valuable forms of play in children. "Early childhood educators know the value of dramatic play with preschoolers. Children learn empathy as they practice literally putting themselves in someone else's shoes. Language is enhanced as their play characters express themselves to their peers and social relationships are strengthened" (Miller, 2002, p. 25). Preschool children love to have stories read to them. They will retell the stories as they play. A few props will get them going on the story. They may give their own twist to the story each time they "play the role." They're trying out new ways to solve problems as well as "trying on" being adults.

Children are fond of imitating people they have seen at the grocery store, the doctor's office, the service station, and the restaurant. Preschoolers like to emulate family members as well as define their own relationships with them. Home relationships are intense, and in dramatic play children graphically show their varying relationships to different family members. This creative play reveals children's pressing needs at the moment. They may seek in play the warmth and affection they fail to get at home. If they are consistently urged toward mature behavior at home, they may seek infantile roles in their role playing.

Play also handles a child's uniqueness of being little in a world of big people. Through dramatic play, a young child can indicate confusion or misinterpretation of facts, as well as possible fears and attempts to master these fears. "Dramatic play can help children grow in social understanding and cooperation; it provides a controlled emotional outlet and a means of self-expression" (Deiner, 2010, p. 107).

Primary-age children enjoy creating their own activities. They may make them up as they go along. You will see familiar stories in most of their dramatic play. Children's group play usually has "the bestest good guys" and "the baddest bad guys." The good guys will win and often invite the bad ones to be good and win with them.

Children will play out their ideas of death, marriage, parenting, daredevil escapades, superheroes, and everyday life. Although the plots may be complicated, the theme remains the same. That theme of "everything turns out right" adds to a child's feeling of security. The dramatic play area offers a safe haven for children to act out their fears and anger, knowing that the teacher will be there to respond to their individual needs.

A 2002 study by Elias and Burk tested Vygotsky's assumption that sociodramatic play in early childhood contributes importantly to the development of self-regulation. Findings are consistent with Vygotsky's theory and suggest that sociodramatic experiences may be especially advantageous for impulsive children, who are behind their peers in self-regulatory development (Elias and Berk, 2002, pp. 216–238).

We will also appropriately plan and prepare the early childhood environment to integrate this fantasy play into the learning centers and curriculum, as we encourage the development of the children's cooperative interaction skills. When children are engaged in dramatic play, one of the things they are learning is how to transfer what they learned in one setting and apply it in another.

social sciences: The core of social studies: anthropology, sociology, history, geography, economics, and psychology.

anthropology: The study of the way people live, such as their beliefs and customs.

sociology: The study of group living, cooperation, and responsibilities.

history: The study of what has happened in the life of a country or people.

geography: The study of the Earth's surface, resources, and the concepts of direction, location, and distance.

economics: The study of the production, distribution, and consumption of goods and services.

psychology: The study of the mind, emotions, and behavioral processes.

dramatic play: A type of creative, spontaneous play in which children use their imaginations to create and dramatize pretend characters, actions, or events.

Social Studies and Dramatic Play Defined

Social studies, like math and science, needs to be experienced firsthand by the children. To have this happen, children need to be taken out into the world of people as well as have the world brought to them in the classroom (Feeney, Moravcik, and Nolte, 2015). Through interactions with children's families and the community, you can assist children in learning about the core of social studies—the **social sciences**. Individually they are the following: **anthropology**, the study of the way people live, such as their beliefs and customs; **sociology**, the study of group living, cooperation, and responsibilities; **history**, the study of what has happened in the life of a country or people; **geography**, the study of the Earth's surface, and resources, and the concepts of direction, location, and distance; **economics**, the study of the production, distribution, and consumption of goods and services; **psychology**, the study of the mind, emotions, and behavioral processes; and other areas of study such as environmental science, art, and current events.

Dramatic play is free play of the very young child in which he/she explores his universe, imitating the actions and character traits of those around him/her. Dramatic play is spontaneous and can be expanded or repeated over and over again just for the fun of it.

With **sociodramatic play**, the highest level of symbolic play, young children create their own happenings based on their experiences. They imitate the actions and people that they have experienced in their play. They repeat, solve problems, and relive these experiences (Isbell and Raines, 2007). Gordon and Browne (2011, p. 78) provide an additional explanation:

> " Sociodramatic play happens when at least two children cooperate in dramatic play. Dramatic play provides the means for children to work out their difficulties by themselves. By doing so, they become free to pursue other tasks and more formal learning. [This]type of play involves two basic elements: imitation and make-believe. "

Researchers believe the fantasy element of dramatic play is quite useful. It enables the child to discharge or accomplish through imagination what he or she is unable to do in reality. Fantasizing relieves tensions and offers a way to interpret and put together the pieces of the complex puzzle that is a child's world. For example, animal play releases aggression, but this is not the only function of this type of dramatic play. A child will often impersonate animals when feeling shy or insecure about verbalizing.

I remember such a child, a 3-year-old named Michael. He came into the classroom growling like an animal. His hands were in the position of paws. Michael entered freely into dramatic play with other children as a dragon, tiger, or wolf. Many times he got the attention of several children when he played the big bad wolf. Morning after morning, "The Three Little Pigs" was played out. The other children, laughing and chattering happily, hid under the tables to escape the wolf. Michael was capable of expressing himself verbally, but he didn't. Instead, he found peer acceptance in dramatic play. Later, when he was ready to talk and enter into other dramatic play activities, he did so. (See **Figure 7-1**.)

Figure 7-1 A young child invites a teacher to join in his fantasy play.

sociodramatic play: The highest level of symbolic play in which young children create their own happenings based on their experiences.

Developmental Stages of Social Studies and Dramatic Play

Theorists, researchers, and educators emphasize the importance of developmental stages of dramatic play in varying ways. As discussed in Chapter 1, Mildred Parten (1932) categorizes six stages of social play: unoccupied behavior (infants), onlooker behavior, solitary play, parallel play (toddlers), associative play (young preschoolers), and cooperative play (older preschoolers, kindergartners, and primary-age children).

Brain Research: Pretend Play

Pretend play requires the ability to transform objects and actions symbolically. This ability is furthered by interactive social dialogue and negotiation and it involves role taking, script knowledge, and improvisation. Many cognitive strategies are exhibited during sociodramatic play, such as joint planning, negotiation, problem solving, and goal seeking. A number of researchers have studied the relationship of play to specific cognitive strategies such as self-regulation, narrative recall, divergent problem solving, and rule understanding. When children lack opportunities to experience sociodramatic play, their long-term capabilities related to metacognition, problem solving, and social cognition, as well as to academic areas such as literacy, mathematics, and science, may be diminished. These complex skills involving many areas of the brain are most likely to thrive in an atmosphere rich in high-quality pretend play (Bergen, 2012).

Reflect On This

Should children be allowed to have imaginary friends?

Types of Play

Jean Piaget's research (1962) has helped us understand play in terms of cognitive development by presenting play in three stages:

1. **Practice play** takes place during the sensorimotor stage of development (infancy to 2 years), in which infants explore the sensory qualities of objects and practice motor skills. This is observable through a child's physical movements and interactions with objects in the environment.
2. **Symbolic or dramatic play** takes place during the preoperational stage of development (2 to 7 years), when we see children transfer objects into symbols, things that represent something else. Symbolic thinking is observable during dramatic play when realistic objects such as pots and pans are used for "cooking soup," a block becomes a "real" telephone and the child "talks" into it, and older children, using gestures and actions, pantomime props when there are none.
3. **Games with rules** take place during the concrete operations stage of development (7 years and older), in which children's spontaneous play develops into games involved with perfecting physical skills and organizing games with rules that are both physical and cognitive. This type of play is observable when it demonstrates children making up their own rules for the games they play, their ability to accept and relate to another person's point of view, and their ability to understand rules to a game that cannot be changed.

Sara Smilansky (1968) divides play into four types of sociodramatic play:

1. **Functional play** (infancy through early years) occurs when a child takes on a role and pretends to be someone else. This type of play embodies sensory and motor exploration of the environment and the people in the environment. This is observable when children play in "dress-up clothes" or use props to identify the person they are portraying.
2. **Constructive play** (toddlers and preschoolers) helps children understand their experiences. This type of play can occur alone or with others as the child plans the manipulation of objects or people to create a specific experience. This is observable when a child puts keys in a pretend car, starts the motor, adds the sound effects ("Vroooom"), and lets others ride in the car with him or her.
3. **Dramatic play** (toddlers through primary-age children) involves pretending and make believe. This represents a higher level of play behavior and is observable when two or more children take on related roles and interact with one another. "Rules that children follow in make-believe play teach them to make choices, to think and plan about what they will do, to show willingness toward self-restraint, as children learn to follow the social rules of pretend play. This is important preparation for real-life situations" (Gordon and Browne, 2011, p. 78).
4. **Games with rules** (older preschoolers and primary-age children) require children to behave according to preexisting rules. This is observable when children play board games and many outdoor sports.

Understanding Fantasy and Reality in Young Children

Dramatic play experiences help young children sort out what is make believe and what is real. "Human beings have a gift for fantasy, which shows itself at a very early age and then continues to make all sorts of contributions to our intellectual and emotional life throughout the lifespan" (Harris, 2002). "Children need ample supplies of fantasy and reality. Gradually children learn to separate fantasy and reality, identify which is which, and travel between them purposefully" (Vail, 1999, p. 20).

It is both appropriate and developmentally important that young children try out ways to differentiate fantasy from reality. The younger the child, the more dramatic play is rooted in fantasy. Children confuse fantasy with reality because they believe what they think is true,

practice play: During Piaget's sensorimotor stage (infancy to 2 years), infants explore the sensory qualities of objects and practice motor skills.

symbolic or dramatic play: A type of play that allows the child to transfer objects into symbols (things that represent something else) and images into people, places, and events within his experiences. Symbolic play occurs during Piaget's preoperational stage (2 to 7 years old). Superhero fantasy play is considered a type of symbolic play for a young child.

games with rules: Children's spontaneous physical and cognitive play that occurs during Piaget's concrete operations stage of development (7 years and older).

functional play: Play that occurs when a child takes on a role and pretends to be someone else.

constructive play: Play that helps children understand their experiences. Involves planning or manipulation of objects or people to create a specific experience.

whether or not it is true in reality. Children need help and time to make the distinction between reality and fantasy without having to reject their fantasies. They have a right to imagine and to create fantasies as well as a need to learn to identify reality.

At age 5 or older, children understand when they are pretending and when they are in the real world. Their understanding is sometimes sophisticated. "Rather than try to force understanding, which is usually in place by the end of kindergarten, encourage children to use language as a tool to ask questions and explore their thinking. . . . 'Do you think that could really happen?'" (Vail, 1999).

Planning and Preparing the Environment

Dramatic play offers many opportunities for supporting a young child's growth and development. Dramatic play produces sheer joy and delight. A child's total being is involved in the activity. His or her body, face, language, and emotions mirror enthusiasm for life. To support all of this, you should provide unstructured time, adequate space, flexible materials, and uninterrupted opportunity for the children to enjoy dramatic play. Most important, let the children have input! The environment should say, "Pretending is welcome here!"

If you see that a child is not ready to enter freely into dramatic play, your understanding is vitally important. This child needs sufficient time to watch and learn and proceed at his or her own pace. Perhaps if you pretend with the child at first and then gradually pull away, this will be all he or she needs.

> " It takes time to conjure new ideas, and it takes a welcoming and accessible environment for children of all abilities to explore and express the content of their imaginations. . . . [W]hen children know they have an uninterrupted stretch of time, they are more likely to try new roles, take emotional risks, negotiate rich worlds and stories, build tall towers and learn about the properties and possibilities of materials and objects in their environment (Haugen, 2002, p. 36). "

The following guidelines should help to define the teacher's role in children's dramatic play. Here, as in other curriculum areas, the teacher's role is primarily that of facilitator, so that dramatic play remains a child-initiated activity:

- Provide stimulating props, unstructured time, and adequate space for dramatic play.
- Create curtains, windows, a fireplace, and real plants to make the area home-like, comfortable, and welcoming.
- Monitor the dramatic play area so all children have the opportunity to participate.
- Assist children in learning acceptable kinds of social interaction.
- Allow children to solve their own problems as often as possible.
- Encourage creativity in language and play.
- Keep in mind the children's developmental capabilities.
- Value this type of play.
- Allow children opportunities to "try on" adult roles, both male and female.
- Limit the number of children in the area at one time.
- Introduce props to small groups of children.
- Select props that are authentic and can be used naturally and safely.
- Change props frequently and include ones that reflect different cultures.
- Avoid props and activities that are sexist or racist.
- Serve as a facilitator rather than teacher so dramatic play remains a child-initiated activity.
- Select dress-up clothes and outfits that are simple, durable, and easy to get on and off.

Some teachers keep the home living (housekeeping) area intact as a permanent center and set up a second dramatic play area that expands the theme of the lesson plan or project in which the children are involved. Others, who are limited in classroom space, may choose to have a dramatic play center that changes periodically and sometimes will include the kitchen area or another room in the home. Still others take the dramatic play center outdoors to take advantage of the additional space available. Outdoor dramatic play often incorporates wheel toys, wagons, and trikes into the play to create scenarios like an ambulance rushing to help sick people, a gas station, a drive-through car wash on splash day, and much more:

> "Indoors, as children get older, change the scene regularly to integrate the theme of study. Put all the chairs away. Bring in large moving boxes. Hang sheets like a stage curtain, a maze, or a tent. Change rooms with another class. . . . Create discovery kits to take along when you explore new environments. Include a magnifying glass, collecting bags, cameras, and so on (Haugen, 2002, p. 37)."

The basic equipment for the home living/dramatic play center should be: child-sized furniture made of wood or sturdy plastic including tables, chairs, rocking chair, and shelves; a "play" sink, stove, and refrigerator; and a full-length mirror. Dolls of both sexes representing differing cultural features and skin coloring, a doll bed or cradle, and two sturdy, nonworking telephones should also be included.

Sometimes, the most creative and appropriate dramatic play area is one that has little in it and does not have a specific theme. When a special "soft area" is created by adding some pillows, beanbag chairs, and a soft area rug, it becomes a totally child-directed dramatic play area. The children feel relaxed and safe, free to be creative and imaginative. The pillows become props, as needed, or the children can bring in props from around the room.

Clothes for the Dramatic Play Center

Clothing that helps children "dress up" in various roles is an important part of dramatic play. The clothes should be easy for children to put on and take off, as well as being attractive, durable, and washable. Wash and dry donated clothing before sharing them with the children. Hem the garments to make sure the children can wear them comfortably and safely. Remove long rope belts, or stitch them into place so they cannot be used around children's necks. Replace back zippers with Velcro hook-and-loop fasteners. Teenager-sized clothes are useful for young children, or (if you do not sew) perhaps there is a parent who will be willing to make some new "dress-up" clothes for the class.

There should be a special place where clothing is displayed or stored. A cardboard box "closet" with a rod placed across at the children's height can hold clothes on hangers. Clothing hooks or a shortened clothes or hat rack is also appropriate. Whatever you select will help the children understand that after they have used the article of clothing it should be placed back where they found it. Hanging labels that children can use to match with the real article of clothing can help children clean up and provide opportunities for one-to-one correspondence.

A variety of cultures should be represented by using clothing made of fabric that is tie-dyed and batiked and clothing made from madras prints and kente cloth. The clothing styles should include saris, kimonos, serapes, ponchos, grass skirts, and dashikis (Allen, McNeill, and Schmidt, 1992). You should research many cultures and consult with parents as you develop your dramatic play center.

Imbedding Multicultural Materials in Learning Centers

It is important to recognize that people from different cultures are different in a variety of ways, including: ways of looking at things, dressing, and expressing personality. Permeate daily classroom life through frequent hands-on activities that explore similarities and differences, beginning with but not limited to who is represented in class.

Children can be introduced to these intriguing differences and similarities by including multicultural materials throughout the classroom. The ideas given here are adapted from a presentation by Zacariah and Griffin of Indiana University, 1972.

Art center: Posters of art/artifacts, multicultural paints, markers, crayons, and construction paper, origami paper, rice paper, gourds, coconut, beans, seeds, leaves, feathers, clay, beads, yarn, ethnic fabric, straw, raffia, shells, fish scales, and coral.

Literacy center: Folktales, books with diverse characters demonstrating differing ethnicity and lifestyles, alphabet and counting books of other cultures, magazines and newspapers in different languages, classroom books made by children about themselves and their families, and recordings of ethnic background music. Display picture postcards, posters, and real-life photographs of people from different cultures throughout the room.

Block center: Photos or posters of different types of homes and buildings, bamboo sticks, straw mud and small boxes to make adobe bricks for building (can be done outside), sets of family and community helper figures and materials that depict diversity in race, ethnicity, gender, physical abilities, and occupations.

Music and movement: Folk songs, ethnic vocal and instrumental music from all over the world, multicultural instruments such as drums, spin drums, horns, conch shells, maracas, gourds, shakers, tambourines, marimba, and flutes.

Dramatic play center: Photographs that depict men and women in a variety of work and family roles. Represent various family compositions and lifestyles. Include varieties of bags, baskets, fake foods from different countries and different eating and cooking utensils, multiracial dolls, clothing, shoes, hats, scarves, belts, rugs, and mats from different cultures.

Manipulative center: Puzzles that show diverse ethnicity, ability difference, and nontraditional work and gender roles, games from other cultures, board games, sets of graduated wooden dolls for sequencing and foreign coins, shells, dried beans, ethnic fabric or quilt squares for sorting activities.

Puppets

Puppetry, like a dramatic play learning center, can be a way that children can pretend and make believe. Whether you offer a puppet center or puppets in every center, make it possible for the children to select and interact with any puppet they want to make or play with. The children should feel the freedom to move the puppets to another location to best meet their needs. Children are more likely to use puppets if the guidelines for use are clearly explained and if the puppets and puppet materials are organized and displayed attractively and accessibly.

At first, some children prefer just to examine the puppets and try them on to see how they feel. Others enjoy making puppets, and still others just like to play with ready-made puppets. Allow for individual and developmental preferences. (See **Figure 7-2**.)

For the creative and spontaneous use of puppets, a stage is not necessary. As mentioned previously, you, as a teacher, do not need to use a stage, and neither do the children. If you feel you need a creative boost, you can use a story apron. Tying on the story apron signals that it is time for puppetime to begin. The apron serves as a visual background for the song, story or poem. The pockets hide the props and puppets until the storyteller is ready to use them.

"This is an ideal costume for you to wear as a puppeteller. It signals that Puppet-time is about to begin, it provides a background for your story, poem, or song and it hides puppets and props until you are ready to use them. . . . A general all-purpose story apron can be made by adding pockets to a store-bought apron or by creating your own custom-apron from selected fabric."

If the children insist on needing a stage for their puppets, here are some easy ways to provide one:

- Construct a puppet stage from a large packing carton. Cut the center out of the box to form a "stage opening."
- Drape a cloth over a piece of rope suspended horizontally.

puppetry: The art of making or operating puppets or producing puppet shows.

Figure 7-2 Some children prefer to examine the puppets, try them on, and then play with the puppets while giving them personalities.

- Turn a small, sturdy table on its side so the children can "hide" behind it and show only the puppets, or use a table top draped in front with a sheet.
- Using a shower curtain rod, hang a piece of fabric low across an open doorway.
- Place two adult-size chairs back to back at a short distance. Drop a curtain or cloth over a yardstick placed between the chairs.
- Use a "gutted TV" (a television set from which the insides have been removed). This offers another dimension to a child's puppet play.

The following are ideas for puppet storage that many teachers use. They are suggested by Hunt and Renfro (1982), Raines and Isbell (1994), and the author's personal preferences:

- Hang a clothesline along a wall at child's eye and arm level, and use clothespins to clip the puppets to the line.
- Clip the puppets to a multiple-skirt hanger.
- Store finger puppets in egg cartons.
- Store puppets in tiered hanging baskets.
- Use a shoe bag or shoe rack to organize puppets.
- Place shoe boxes or clear plastic boxes on low shelves.

A child might like to make a home for his or her special puppet. Select a box into which the puppet will fit. Have the child decorate the box any way he or she chooses, including adding windows and a door. A scrap of soft material inside the box makes a bed for the puppet friend. The box can be placed in or near the child's cubby.

Easy-to-Make Puppets

Many puppets are stuffed animals with an opening at the bottom for inserting a hand to control the puppet. Others can be made using just a few inexpensive materials.

Hand Puppets. **Hand puppets** come in many types and varieties and are easy for young children to make and manipulate. Starting with finger puppets, the child gains ownership right away. It is fun to put two eyes, a nose, and a mouth on the child's thumb and fingers with a felt-tip pen. You will find some children do not want to wash their fingers after this activity. They like their puppets and want to keep them. (See **Figure 7-3**.)

Another kind of simple finger puppet can be made out of felt. Glue the two pieces together (as shown in the three-step illustration of **Figure 7-3**). Place eyes, a nose, and a mouth on the puppet. These can be easily manipulated by younger children and offer an unusual small muscle activity.

Other finger puppets can be made easily to illustrate shapes, numbers, nursery rhymes, or other concepts. You can first introduce them at group time and then put them in the manipulative center for the children to play with. By placing two fingers in one of these, the child can add "legs" to make the puppet walk and dance. (See **Figure 7-3**.)

Basic hand, glove, and mitt puppets provide a close link between the puppet and the puppeteer. Toddlers, especially, enjoy this type of puppet. There are many commercially made examples, but the ones the teacher and children make are the most fun.

Figure 7-3 illustrates an easy-to-make basic design. The hand can be the whole body, with two fingers as the arms and one or two fingers operating the head. This hand puppet can be made easily from two pieces of felt or other fabric glued or sewn together and cut to fit a child's or an adult's hand. Eyes, nose, mouth, ears, hands, and hair can be attached with Velcro, glued, or sewn to the fabric. Felt squares of tan, beige, cream, brown, peach, and black can be used so a child can make a puppet that has his skin tone.

Rubber household gloves, which have a smooth surface, and garden gloves, which are available in many colors and designs, can be used to make another kind of hand puppet. This variety allows you to move all five fingers, independently as separate characters. Use double-stick tape on the rubber glove or sew small pieces of Velcro to the fingertips of the garden glove. Place the same kind of material on matching story pieces. This gives you and the children flexibility in creating hand puppets. Ready-made mittens or household hot pad mitts can also be used to create another variety of hand puppets. Commercially crocheted puppets,

hand puppets: Puppets that are put on the hand, come in many colors and varieties and are easy for young children to make and manipulate.

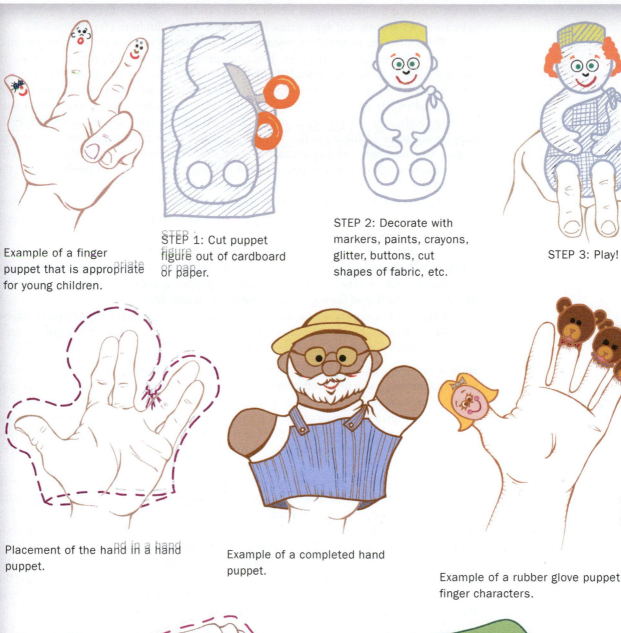

Example of a finger puppet that is appropriate for young children.

STEP 1: Cut puppet figure out of cardboard or paper.

STEP 2: Decorate with markers, paints, crayons, glitter, buttons, cut shapes of fabric, etc.

STEP 3: Play!

Placement of the hand in a hand puppet.

Example of a completed hand puppet.

Example of a rubber glove puppet with finger characters.

The hand position for a sock puppet.

Example of a sock puppet.

Figure 7-3 A variety of hand puppets.

usually representing animals, and sets of puppets are also available. Evaluate these carefully to be sure they are safe and appropriate for use with young children. (See **Figure 7-3**.)

Think of all the finger plays, poems, songs, and stories you and the children can share with each other using sock puppets. These are probably the easiest puppets to make and use. Ask parents to donate unneeded children's socks in all sizes and colors. Once a child puts the sock on his hand, the puppet will "come to life." Add eyes made from buttons, commercial wiggly eyes, or anything you wish. Hair, made from yarn, string, steel wool, or cotton balls, and ears give extra personality to the character. Paper plate and paper bag puppets are some of the most fun to make and use. They are inexpensive, children can create more than one, and they are easily remade if they get torn. You and the children will design many kinds of paper puppets, but to get you started, a few examples follow. (See **Figure 7-3**.)

Staple two paper plates together, leaving the bottom portion open for the puppeteer's hand. (You will find thin plates are easy for the children to handle.) Decorate this puppet, and it is ready to use!

For a paper-bag, floppy-mouth puppet, use a small- or medium-size bag. Draw a puppet face on the bag or cut and glue one from a magazine. Use crayons, markers, paints, glue, yarn, cotton balls, or other material to finish the puppet. It is easy to work by placing your fingers inside the flap of the bag and moving them up and down.

Other paper puppets can be made from products such as paper cups or pudding, oatmeal, or small cereal boxes. Add these to the other creative materials in your puppet center for the children's exploration and experimentation.

Stick or Rod Puppets. **Stick or rod puppets** are controlled by a single stick, such as a tongue depressor, dowel rod, paper towel roll, craft stick, or ice cream stick. An even smaller character might be placed on a paper straw. The figure itself can be cut from magazines, catalogs, and wrapping paper; traced from a pattern; or drawn by hand. Then it is glued to the stick or straw. Many card shops or toy stores have paper plates in the shape of animals. These make wonderful puppets when stapled to a dowel rod. These can be reinforced with tagboard and covered with contact paper or laminated.

A wooden spoon makes another delightful puppet. The bowl of the spoon makes a perfect head, and the handle becomes the body. Use felt-tip markers, crayons, or paint to make the face.

The "stick people puppet" is made out of cardboard or tagboard and then attached to a stick or dowel rod. Encourage children to add eyes, a nose, a mouth, hair, clothes, and shoes. Multicultural or skin-toned paints, crayons, and construction paper should be available for the children to use. This promotes self-awareness and positive self-esteem. Another variation of the stick people puppet is one depicting a face. The children can cut out the eyes and then add a nose, a mouth, and hair. Attach a straw or craft stick to create a stick puppet or mask. Primary-grade children enjoy this activity (see **Figure 7-4**).

Marionettes. **Marionettes**, controlled by strings, offer an extra range of expression and full body movement. As teachers, we should appreciate the sophisticated skills needed to make and operate a marionette. In encouraging a school-age child who wants to make this type of puppet, the first question a teacher should ask is, "What do you want it to do?" It is important to think through and plan each step in the creation of a marionette. The "airplane control" is the simplest design to manipulate, usually with one string to the head and a string to each of the hands. (See **Figure 7-5**.) Children need time to experiment and to experience the frustration of the puppet not working the first time it is tried. It is important to support them through the frustration. The failure and success of making and manipulating a marionette is part of their process. Maintenance and care of the marionette is also part of the experience. To avoid tangling the strings, it should be hung after it is used. Hanging marionettes make a distinctive classroom decoration.

Shadow Puppets. **Shadow puppets** offer a visual dimension to puppetry that other types do not. Shown in a darkened room, they are held from below by rods against a translucent screen lit from behind. Puppeteers manipulate flat, cut-out silhouettes that the audience can see on the other side of the screen as moving figures. One of the simplest shadow animal puppets, a flying bird, can easily be made with a single light source, such as a standing or desk

stick or rod puppets: Puppets controlled by a single stick, such as a tongue depressor, dowel rod, paper towel roll, craft stick, or ice cream stick.

marionettes: Puppets controlled by strings that offer an extra range of expression and full body movements.

shadow puppets: Puppets held from rods against a translucent screen lit from behind. These puppets offer a visual dimension that other types do not.

STEP 1: Cut out people puppet shape from cardboard.

STEP 2: Decorate with paint, markers, crayons, cut shapes of paper, fabric, etc.

STEP 3: Glue stick to back of finished puppet.

STEP 1: Cut face shapes from cardboard or paper.

STEP 2: Decorate with paint, markers, crayons, cut shapes of paper, fabric, etc.

STEP 3: Glue stick to back of decorated face shape.

STEP 4: Let it dry and then play!

Figure 7-4 Stick or rod puppets.

Figure 7-5 Example of a marionette.

lamp with the shade removed. Interlock the thumbs and slowly flap the hands. Pass them between the light source and a blank wall to form the shadow of a bird in flight.

Progression from this simple example to more complex shadow puppets will occur as older children discover creative ways to investigate and make these puppets. (See **Figure 7-6**.)

Materials for Puppet Making

All of the various types of puppets can be made from a wide variety of materials. (Puppet patterns for teachers can be found online at this textbook's website with new puppet patterns added.) An easy way to collect these is to place a box in the classroom simply labeled, "Materials for Puppet Making." This keeps it visible for parents and children while reminding them that all kinds of things are needed. (See **Table 7-1** for a list of what needs to be gathered.)

" Making a puppet should not be a one-time activity but something the child will return to again and

Figure 7-6 Example of a shadow hand puppet.

TABLE 7-1:   Materials for Puppet Making

- boxes—especially small cereal and salt boxes
- buttons and wiggly eyes—especially the larger ones
- clothespins
- cloth scraps—felt, lace, cotton, towels, and washcloths in tan, beige, cream, brown, peach, and black
- cotton balls, steel wool, sponges, pipe cleaners, corks, and hair curlers
- crayons, markers, pencils, pens, and paints
- egg cartons
- feathers
- gloves—cloth, garden-type, and rubber
- leather scraps
- magazines, catalogs, and newspapers
- office supplies—scissors, envelopes, paper clips, glue, brads, rubber bands, gummed labels and stickers, stapler and staples, and rulers

- paper products—cardboard; sandpaper; all sizes of paper bags, plates, and cups; towel and bathroom paper rolls; crepe paper; wrapping paper; tissue paper; wall paper; waxed paper; foil; straws; and construction paper in all colors representing skin tones, including tan, beige, cream, brown, black, and peach
- socks—especially those that will fit a child's hand and soccer socks for making adult-size puppets
- spools
- sticks—tongue depressors, ice cream sticks, craft sticks, yardsticks, toothpicks, and dowel rods
- Styrofoam balls and scraps
- tape—clear, masking, and double-stick types
- wooden spoons
- wood scraps—preferably already sanded smooth
- yarn, string, ribbons, and shoelaces

Reflect On This

If there are only Anglo children in a classroom, why is it important to have representation from many cultures in all areas of the early childhood classroom?

again in order to create a character or persona with which to face the world. After introducing puppet-making supplies at the art center, they should be available on a regular basis for whenever a child wants or needs to create a puppet (Koster, 2009, p. 386). ”

The physical environment plays a large role in enhancing social studies and dramatic play experiences. A checklist that can be used to evaluate the social studies and dramatic play environment in your own classroom or classrooms that you observe follows.

Social Science/Dramatic Play Environment Checklist

_____ 1. Is the dramatic play center a well-defined area from the other centers?

_____ 2. Does the center contain appropriate items that allow children to recreate their experiences?

_____ 3. Is there enough space for at least four to six children to play at a time?

_____ 4. Do dramatic play materials reflect multiple areas of diversity such as different family groupings, cultural materials and assistive devices?

_____ 5. Is the dramatic play center located next to the block area for shared play to increase the movement of materials between the two centers?

_____ 6. Does the dramatic play center contain clothing or pieces of fabric for children to expand their creativity?

_____ 7. Is the dramatic play center aesthetically pleasing?

_____ 8. Are there full-length mirrors available?

_____ 9. Is parallel play supported through duplicates of props?

_____ 10. Are rich play opportunities supported with a variety of props?

_____ 11. Is appropriate dramatic play equipment such as a toy stove for a home living center available?

_____ 12. Are changes and additions made as needed to sustain rich play opportunities?

_____ 13. Are authentic math props included?

_____ 14. Is the dramatic play center available as a choice activity on a daily basis?

_____ 15. Are authentic and appropriate literacy props available?

_____ 16. Do child-sized home furnishings and dolls, dress-up clothes, and accessories represent the children's families?

_____ 17. Are some loose parts included so children can develop what they need?

Social Science/Dramatic Play Environment Checklist (continued)

_____ **18.** Is there the ability to throughout the year to create new settings for dramatic play?

_____ **19.** Are props and clothing available and organized?

_____ **20.** Is the dramatic play center organized with labeled shelves, drawings, or silhouettes of utensils on pegboards, and dress-up clothes on hangers or pegs to promote independent use of materials?

_____ **21.** Are there home-like touches in the dramatic play center such as curtains, tablecloths, pictures, and dolls with clothes?

_____ **22.** Are there a variety of materials to help children learn more about people and how they live, such as career-related props, books about different

cultures and families, class rules, job displays, play money, cash registers, and family pictures?

_____ **23.** Are there a variety of materials to help children learn about spaces and geography such as, maps, road signs, or games that children use independently to explore directionality?

_____ **24.** Are there opportunities for children to care for the environment?

_____ **25.** Are there opportunities for children to see and explore similarities and differences among people and cultures?

_____ **26.** Are naturally occurring opportunities used to expand geographic thinking?

⌄⌄ **Professional Resource Download**

Integrating Social Studies and Dramatic Play into the Curriculum

DAP

Goals of Early Education Social Studies

❝ A curriculum is not an end in itself but a means, a tool for accomplishing educational goals. These goals are learner outcomes—the knowledge, skills, attitudes, values, and dispositions to action that one wishes to develop in students (Brophy and Alleman, 2013, p. 56). ❞

The social studies curriculum emphasizes basic goals that encourage children to become self-reliant, contributing members of their society—namely, in their families, in the classroom, and in the community, while developing an awareness of being a part of the world. These goals encourage children to make choices, act independently, and develop a sense of responsibility and respect for themselves and others. In the _Curriculum Guidelines for Social Studies Teaching and Learning_ (2008, p. 1), the National Council for the Social Studies (NCSS) states, "The primary purpose of social studies is to help young people develop the ability to make informed and reasoned decisions for the public good as citizens of a culturally diverse, democratic society in an independent world."

The following goals help us focus on the core of the social studies curriculum. They are adapted from various sources (Mayesky, 2009; Seefeldt, Castle, and Falconer, 2010; Taylor, 2004) and from conversations with early education teachers.

- _To develop a child's positive self-concept:_ A child's understanding and appreciation of himself or herself must come first, before learning to appreciate and relate to others. From infancy on, a child is learning to adjust and accept himself or herself in the family and the larger community. Curriculum activities to emphasize this goal should relate to a child's developing sense of autonomy and his or her place in the world.

- _To further an understanding of a child's role in the family:_ As the child learns about himself or herself, he or she is also learning about his or her family. Knowing about the family history, where family members lived before, and the family's values, attitudes, customs, celebrations, and occupations contributes to a child's sense of belonging. That, in turn, helps him or her to solidify a positive self-concept. Activities should offer opportunities for a child to talk about and identify things about himself or herself and his or her family.

- *To develop an awareness of a child's own cultural heritage as well as the traditions of others:* Continuing in the classroom what the child is experiencing in the home environment requires a teacher to communicate openly and often with the child's family. It also means that a teacher should start where the child is with his or her language, customs, traditions, and values and build on his or her growth toward self-understanding and acceptance.
- *To provide an inclusive, multicultural classroom environment:* This should reflect the *lives* and interests of the children, families, and teacher who live in the immediate environment, as well as foster a respect for people everywhere. Social studies activities should blend this diversity into themes, lesson plans, and daily activities throughout the year. An appreciation of different ideas, physical appearances, ways, and behaviors will result.
- *To understand the need for rules and laws:* Starting with the rules of the family, the child begins to understand the limits placed on him or her within his environment at a young age. Conflicts often occur as the child's sense of independence clashes with the rules of the home and classroom. To minimize these encounters, the child should participate in setting the rules.

Using a developmentally appropriate practice model (Copple and Bredekamp, 2009), teachers can develop a natural social studies curriculum, as suggested by Mindes (2005, p. 12):

- Build on what children already know. Use children's familiar, everyday experiences as the foundation for their social studies learning.
- Integrate children's development of social skills with their knowledge of social studies.
- Develop concepts and processes of social studies rather than focusing on isolated facts. Integrate with other learning domains.
- Provide hands-on activities.
- Use relevant social studies throughout the year.
- Capitalize on child interest.
- Tap into primary-grade children's experiences that extend to other parts of the country and even beyond (through travel, immigration, or technology).

> " Foster children's understanding of democratic processes and attitudes in concrete experiential ways that young children are able to understand, such as making and discussing rules, solving together the problems that arise in the classroom community, and learning to listen to others' ideas and perspectives (Copple and Bredekamp, 2009, p. 317). "

Social Studies and Thematic Strands

Written in 1994 and currently under revision, the NCSS curriculum standards are organized into 10 thematic strands based on the social sciences and designed to act as a framework for social studies curriculum while guiding the development of worthwhile learning experiences in early education. The following explanations of the 10 themes are adapted from Kostelnik, Soderman, and Whiren (2007), Mindes (2005), and Wortham (2010).

- *Culture*—Through activities in the classroom, children develop knowledge of their own culture and the culture of others. A child's culture is a fundamental building block in the development of a child's identity. During the preschool years children explore the concepts of likenesses and differences to help them understand themselves and others.
- *Time, continuity, and change*—Important to the lives of young children is their personal history and that of their family. The social studies curriculum should include experiences that provide for the study of ways human beings view themselves in and over time.
- *People, places, and environments*—Where things are in the children's near environment is important information for them to have as they move further from home. Younger children draw on immediate personal experiences as a basis for exploring geographic concepts and skills. They are also concerned about the use and misuse of the environment. (See **Figure 7-7.**)

Figure 7-7   Dramatic play as birds flying.

- *Individual development and identity*—The self, the family, and the community are most important to young children. A sense of belonging, and the ability to take care of themselves and their own needs impact children in the early years. For the youngest citizens, infants and toddlers, content focuses on self-development in the social world. In the preschool and primary years, social studies offer a structure for broad theme-based content.
- *Individuals, groups, and institutions*—Children belong to many groups—family, class, after-school activity groups, congregations, and so forth. This NCSS standard is better suited to study by older children.
- *Power, authority, and governance*—Children should be exposed to experiences that provide for the study of how people create and change structures of power, authority, and governance. This standard is also better suited for the older grades to investigate. The concepts are too abstract for young children.
- *Production, distribution, and consumption*—Children can be made aware of the diverse kinds of work adults engage in by talking to them and observing them at work. Prekindergarten and kindergarten children can develop an understanding of how goods and services are produced, distributed, and consumed through social studies projects.
- *Science, technology, and society*—Social studies for young children can introduce the concept that technology influences their lives and their families through household appliances, television, smart phones, computers, automobiles, trucks, railroads, airplanes, and ships. Activities that encourage further study can be accomplished individually or with small or large groups.
- *Global connections*—This NCSS curriculum standard is designed for older children to show the interconnectedness of the world. Global education is abstract, so it is less appropriate for young children. For primary-grade children, Copple and Bredekamp (2012) emphasize, "As our society becomes ever more global, knowledge of the interconnected relations between groups of people as well as between nations becomes increasingly vital for our children's generation."
- *Civic ideals and practices*—Children have opportunities to practice aspects of democratic living when they learn to understand the rules that govern the classroom and when they become involved in making some of the rules themselves.

Figure 7-8 Social studies is connected to all learning centers in an early education environment.

The social studies curriculum is connected to all learning centers in an early education environment. (See **Figure 7-8.**) Rather than create a separate center for social studies activities, the teacher needs to integrate these projects into all other learning centers. When using the project approach, children are building on what they know. At the same time, they are practicing cooperative learning; developing opportunities for observation, reading, writing, interviewing, and inquiry; and using multiple learning domains. Many of the activities described in the other chapters can become part of the social studies curriculum. The following are some additional suggestions to get you started:

- Appropriate *themes* to encourage the development of authentic self-esteem are "Magnificent Me" or "All About Me." Extensions of this can be "Me and My Family," "Me and My Friends," or "Me and My Community." (See Appendix A for a complete thematic, integrated curriculum for "My Community.")

- Children can dictate stories about themselves to the teacher or create an "I Like" book from drawings and pictures they cut from magazines. These meaningful activities can be introduced at group time and continued in the language and art centers.

- Plan for the social studies curriculum to include topics that relate specifically to children's families. For infants and toddlers, creating an atmosphere that makes them feel safe, secure, and special while they are away from home is most important. Activities for all children can include creating an individual or class scrapbook with photographs of family members and pets and magazine pictures depicting toys and home furnishings. Preschoolers can make craft stick puppets, coloring and designing one puppet for each family member.

- It is important for children to feel good about themselves and their families. As you continue to prepare your classroom to reflect this attitude, consider the following: What members are in a child's family? How many family members (or others) live in a child's home? What ages are they? What are the roles of family members, both inside and outside the home? What do family members do together? What holidays or events do they celebrate? How are they celebrated? What is the family's history and ethnic background? What changes has the family experienced?

- An exciting social studies theme can be "Homes." Stretch your and the children's interest and creativity by investigating information about all kinds of shelters for humans and animals. What types of habitats do the following live in: birds, rabbits, turtles, dogs, horses, and cows? Think of all the residences people live in, such as apartments, houses, duplexes, trailers, hotels, Navajo hogans, and tents. What are they made of, besides wood, brick, and stone? Examine what climate and location have to do with determining how a house is built. Gather books, pictures, computers, and computer software to illustrate concretely what you are talking about. The children can even experiment with building models of some of these residences with blocks, pieces of fabric, scrap wood, boxes, adobe bricks, and other materials.

- Taking a social studies viewpoint can become a process you can apply to most curriculum themes. Some people suggest a multicultural approach to learning about and caring for pets that could include the following activities and topics:

Animals communicating with each other
Communicating with pets
Cooperative care of a classroom pet
Different ways that animals feed, clean, and care for their young
Diversity of pets
Friendships, despite differences, between people and pets
Learning about pets belonging to people in the classroom
Names of animals in other languages

Pets in other places
Protecting the rights of pets
Similarities among all pets
Working to change conditions that are harmful to animals
(See **Figure 7-9**.)

This social sciences and social studies approach can also be used with other topics, such as different ways of cooking and eating, types of clothing, kinds of occupations and work roles, weather conditions, and how people in the world are transported from one place to another.

Figure 7-9 Cooperative caring for pets in the classroom teaches children social responsibility.

- This social studies activity relates to maps or place awareness. The main objective is to introduce children to a map as a picture that shows places and things, where they are located, and how to get from one to another. Young children can usually understand this concept by working with puzzles or by drawing maps of their rooms at home, the classroom, or the playground. Map making is an abstract concept, so the activities should be fairly simple. Keep a globe and other types of maps available to provide visual answers to children's questions about places in the world. Children can use these also as props in their dramatic play activities. To introduce this mapping project, share the following book and its illustrations with the children:

Sweeney, J. (2000). *Me on the map*. Illustrated by A. Cable. New York: Dragonfly Books.

- Another type of mapping relates to children's literature. Story maps can be a useful tool to introduce mapping skills. They can also increase comprehension of a story and the key elements of a story. Story mapping teaches students multiple modalities to learn and show what they have learned, and, in many cases, how to work cooperatively with other children. When introducing story mapping to children, it is useful to:

1. Choose a book that you have previously read to the children.
2. Discuss and chart the different places the main character goes.
3. Have the children illustrate the locations.
4. Label and cut out each picture.
5. Glue the illustrations on a large piece of paper in sequential order of the locations. This becomes a graphic way to introduce children to a map of the locations reached by the main character of the story.
6. Children can begin to start thinking in terms of sequence and chronology with the use of timelines. This technique is used to represent data in chronological or sequential order and offers visual aids for the children. Primary-aged children can be introduced to timelines by creating personal time lines starting with the year they were born through the present. For each year, the child will include at least one event that happened in the world or in his or her personal life. This can be an activity to be shared with families. The children can bring photographs from home relating to each year or ask their parents to write about what they remember from each year.

Brophy and Alleman (2007, p. 177) suggest:

"co-constructing learning resources, a strategy in which the teacher and students work together to construct interactive timelines … Teaching about developments in transportation, for example, can be built around a timeline that begins with people traveling by foot and is structured around key inventions such as boats, wheeled vehicles, and engine powered vehicles."

Use a large piece of paper and draw a line horizontally to make a timeline. Then, use cut-out pictures, drawings, and teacher sketches to help illustrate the transportation timeline.

As the students continue, they can incorporate information and graphics from the Internet and social studies software available. This approach encourages the children to use what they have learned to create something new (Brophy and Alleman, 2007).

The following examples of dramatic play centers, and the prop boxes to accompany each, have proven to be successful in early education curriculum. They represent developmentally appropriate play areas and offer creative opportunities for individual or small groups of children.

In setting up areas for infants and toddlers, change little from what they are used to. Add props or change the room arrangement slowly. The children will guide you by what they will or will not play with. Older children will help you decide when to change areas, when to add additional props and materials, and what areas of the room need to be expanded for more dramatic play.

Appropriate Dramatic Play by Age Groupings

Dramatic Play for Infants

- *A doll corner:* Select sock or soft dolls (depicting many cultures) that are easy to launder and simple cardboard beds for the dolls. The clothing on the dolls should be washable and easy to take off and put on.
- *A home living area:* Choose washable household items that the infant can grasp, such as pots, pans, lids, boxes, plastic cups, bowls, and baskets. These will encourage the child to bang, stack, squeeze, and put the objects together.
- *An area (indoor and/or outdoor) for push-and-pull toys:* This should include doll buggies, wagons, wheelbarrows, and trucks.
- *An area for crawling and climbing:* Provide a rocking boat, short tunnel, and climbing steps.

Dramatic Play for Toddlers

- *Home living area:* In addition to all types of dolls and child-size furniture, add empty food boxes of all sizes and shapes that represent what the children eat at home. This should include empty food boxes with print in different languages on them to represent foods from diverse cultures.
- *Dress-up clothes:* Include items that relate to community helpers (e.g., police officers, firefighters). Toddlers love sunglasses with plastic lenses, gloves, purses, and clothing that fits them.
- *Prop box:* Fill it with shopping bags, lunch boxes, toy telephones, keys, pots, pans, small cars, and trucks. (Miniature animals and people can be added to the block center prop box as well.)
- *A corner for puppet and mask play:* This should offer glove puppets, finger puppets, and people puppets; as well as animal masks with eyes, mouth, and nose cut out and a handle under the chin for easy manipulation.
- *A beauty/barber shop:* Provide washable black, brown, blond, and red wigs, both male and female styles; curlers; empty plastic shampoo bottles; and old hair dryers with the plugs and cords cut off. (*Note:* Wash or spray wigs and hats often with diluted bleach—one-half teaspoon bleach to one quart of water.)

One prop, such as a red wig, can encourage a young child to act out his or her favorite fairytale or create a new character to add to the story. (See **Figure 7-10**.)

Dramatic Play for Preschoolers

The dramatic play center in the 3-, 4-, and 5-year-old classroom can start with one specific theme. The concept can be expanded to include adjacent space as more children become involved.

- *Travel agency:* Set up a ticket counter and chairs. The prop box for this activity can include tickets, maps, brochures, posters, pens, pencils, flight schedules, boat schedules, and car and hotel information. The tickets, maps, schedules, and information sheets can also be made by the children.

Figure 7-10 One prop, such as a red wig, can encourage a young child to act out his or her favorite fairytale or create a new character to add to the story.

- *Ship:* All it takes is a balance beam becoming the gangplank, cardboard boxes becoming the outer part of the ship, and "water" (painted by the children) surrounding the ship. Let the children help you add to this adventure by deciding where the ship will land. This is a wonderful opportunity to expand the dramatic play into various ports and countries, such as Hawaii, Africa, Mexico, Alaska, and the Caribbean. Set up prop boxes for each country. Selecting what goes in each is both creative and educational and helps children develop problem-solving skills. Packing small suitcases or briefcases with clothing for warm climates (straw hats, beach toys, suntan lotion, sunglasses, and short-sleeved shirts) and clothing for colder areas (gloves, earmuffs, mufflers, stocking caps, and sweaters) helps start this dramatic play.

- *Train station and train or airport and airplane:* This can expand the travel agency dramatic play or add to the lesson plan relating to transportation. As with the ship theme, develop a prop box for each, including appropriate clothing. Plan the destination with maps and brochures.

- *Supermarket/grocery store/farmer's market/mercado:* Fill the prop box with a toy *cash register*, calculator, play money (or money the children make), price tags, sales slip pad, empty food containers (some with print in different languages on them to represent foods from diverse cultures), artificial fruit and vegetables, grocery boxes, shopping bags, small shopping carts, brown paper bags, telephone, coupons, and shopping lists. Make signs in several languages and with pictures to explain what is for sale.

- *Picnic:* This is fun for indoors or outdoors and is an excellent dramatic play activity to plan for snack or lunchtime. The children decide what to take on the picnic and place the items in a picnic basket. They can wear "dress-up" clothes and use props from the prop box, such as plastic or paper cups, plates, tableware, tablecloth, napkins, eating utensils, aprons, and blankets.

- *Ants at a picnic:* Put several large picnic baskets in the dramatic play area. Add play food. Then make a tunnel by taking the ends out of boxes. Line the boxes up, and tape them together to form a tunnel. You can use a cloth tunnel, if you already have one, to have more than one tunnel for the "ants." The children can pretend to be ants taking the "food" from the picnic basket to their home through the tunnels. Continue to add items that the children want to use.

Other suggestions for dramatic play centers are restaurant, florist shop, pet shop, post office, library, book store, music shop, musical instrument store, recording studio, health center, doctor or dentist office, gymnasium, camp site, shoe store, fix-it shop, and apartments in the loft and lower level of the dramatic play area.

Dramatic Play for Primary-Grade Children

Any of the dramatic play suggestions listed for the preschoolers can be expanded or adapted for older children. Give them the list of acceptable themes and allow them the freedom to make choices and select their own activities (see **Figure 7-11**). For example, if they choose to visit another country as they play, the children may "discover the rain forest" or "go on a safari in Africa." This child-initiated form of dramatic play encourages the older child to take an interest in the wider world, and it is exciting to watch as it unfolds. Some children get involved with one aspect and tackle it as an independent project. Others make the theme a special event or a cooperative venture.

The following are a few examples of other dramatic play exercises and activities that are appropriate for school-age children:

- *Rag doll, tin man, and marionette:* Have the children perform simple warm-up exercises by being as limp as a rag doll; they can bend from the waist and bob up and

Figure 7-11   Costumes can transform a child into a flying princess.

Reflect On This

How can a center or school connect children to the community if it doesn't have the ability to take field trips?

down and swing their shoulders. As stiffened tin men, let them discover how their movements change. Expand this activity and have the children choose a partner. One becomes a marionette and the other becomes the puppeteer. The puppeteer stands in front of the marionette and moves the strings attached to the various parts of the marionette's body. The marionette responds with the proper movement.

- *The imaginary machine:* First, one child will form a "machine-part shape" with his or her body and add a made-up sound to fit that shape. Each successive child connects to the shape last made with his or her own unique shape and sound until all of the children are involved in the imaginary machine. Slow the machine down and speed it up. To demonstrate the importance of the parts on the whole, "break" one of the parts. What happens to the machine?
- *Mirror images:* Each child chooses a partner. They face each other, always keeping each other in full view. One child becomes a mirror that reflects what he or she sees his or her partner doing. Perhaps the child puts on clown makeup, exercises, or puts on a tie. After a while, the partners change places, with the other partner becoming the mirror.

Dramatic Play and Other Learning Centers

Dramatic play lends itself to every aspect of the curriculum. As an example, dramatic play doesn't first have to be initiated by reading a book, but many teachers like to integrate dramatic play into other learning centers using this method.

Language and literacy development, socialization, exploration of feelings and fears, and problem solving are ongoing components of these activities. Music and rhythmic movement become dramatic and creative when a child makes use of them to become someone or something other than himself or herself.

Math and science concepts apply to many dramatic-play situations. Charlesworth and Lind (2016, p. 275) offer some examples:

- One-to-one correspondence can be practiced by exchanging play money for goods or services.
- Sets and classifying are involved in organizing each dramatic play center in an orderly manner.
- Counting can be applied to figuring out how many items have been purchased and how much money must be exchanged.
- Comparing and measuring can be used to decide if clothing fits or to determine the weight of fruits and vegetables purchased.
- Spatial relations and volume concepts are applied as items purchased are placed in bags, boxes, or baskets and as children discover how many passengers will fit in the space shuttle or can ride on the bus.
- Number symbols can be found throughout dramatic play props, such as on price tags, play money, telephones, cash registers, and scales.

As you select the theme, brainstorm using the curriculum planning web worksheet in Chapter 3. Develop your lesson plan, integrate the learning centers, and gather supplies and materials to discover how to meet your goals and objectives through the use of dramatic play.

Making Prop Boxes

A vital part of the planning and preparing process for dramatic play activities is the creation of prop boxes. A **prop box** is a collection of actual items related to the development and enrichment of dramatic play activities focused on a specific theme or lesson plan. These items should be collected for easy accessibility and placed in sturdy boxes that can be stacked for storage. Empty cardboard boxes with lids make great prop boxes.

Label each prop box clearly for identification. A picture or drawing on the outside can suggest what is inside. Cover the boxes with colored contact paper to give them an uncluttered and uniform appearance. (See **Figure 7-12.**)

prop box: A collection of actual items related to dramatic play activities that focuses on a specific theme or lesson plan.

The props selected for the dramatic play areas should stimulate interest, encourage creative expression, create opportunities for problem solving, relate to and expand the experiences of the children, and represent many cultures. These props can be found anywhere and everywhere: in the families' and staff's closets and garages; at surplus stores, thrift stores, and garage sales; and at local businesses and offices that have used and throwaway items. Invite the children to bring appropriate props from home that represent their interests, their hobbies, their lifestyles, or the current theme. Share with families the learning possibilities that prop boxes provide. Invite them to visit the classroom to see how the children use the different contents of the prop boxes. Guide them into making prop boxes at home with their children.

Hanvey (2010, p. 30) offers other learning opportunities for children with an outdoor prop box:

> When I introduced the prop box to the children, we discussed how they were responsible for bringing the prop box outside with them each day, returning the props to the box at the end of play, and bringing it back to a designated area. . . . This outdoor prop box experience not only enabled children to practice and extend academic skills they were learning indoors, but also enhanced their social skills. We observed the children using conflict resolution techniques when trouble arose. The kindergartners took turns with the materials and learned what it meant to be responsible as they restored the prop box each day and put it back where it belonged.

Fill a plastic tub or crate with many different items for the children to take outdoors—items that will encourage exploration outdoors. For example, you might include ping-pong balls, tennis balls, marbles, blocks, books, magnifying glasses, chalk, small buckets to be filled with water, brushes, measuring tape, bubbles, wind socks, and blankets. The outdoor boxes should be different from the indoor prop boxes. This will help keep the children interested and involved.

Figure 7-12   Prop boxes for dramatic play.

Field Trips as Concrete Experiences in Early Education

Another way of connecting the child to the community is through taking field trips with the children in your class. Such trips are an enriching part of early education curriculum that adds a special dimension to classroom learning by providing firsthand experience that books, pictures, or discussions alone cannot provide. Young children need to see, hear, feel, taste, and touch their world to connect words and ideas to locations and people within their community. (See **Figure 7-13**.)

Figure 1-13   Connect children to the community by taking enriching field trips.

Types of Field Trips

There are different types of field trips to consider. Leipzig (1993), Seefeldt, Castle, and Falconer (2014), and some early childhood classroom teachers suggest the following.

- *A walking trip around a familiar room.* This trip offers infants and toddlers an opportunity to notice and learn the names of everything in the room. It can then be extended to another room until the children feel comfortable exploring and noticing things in the entire building or house.
- *A walking trip around the neighborhood.* This is the natural extension of the room walk, and there are advantages to neighborhood field trips. They are free, and you do not have to arrange for cars or buses. They are short in duration and less tiring for the children. There is not a rush to meet schedules, so the children can make discoveries, their questions can be answered, and learning can occur. Repeated trips around the neighborhood offer chances to learn something new each time you visit the same places. (First take a walk without the children. Look at things from a child's point of view. Find connections that can be natural outgrowths of classroom activities.)
- *Taking a small group of children at one time on a mini-field trip.* Once the children become used to taking turns, go on a mini-trip. There are frequent opportunities to do so. There usually is no difficulty in planning trips for a specific purpose with a small group of children.
- *Specific-purpose field trips.* This type of field trip can be as simple as a neighborhood walk to go bird watching or to record sounds around the neighborhood. It can be a short trip to the grocery store to get carrots and celery to go into the vegetable soup the children are making or down the block to see the new house being built.
- *Major field trips.* These are often taken by the entire class to a community location. This type requires additional adults and travel arrangements for cars, a van, or a bus. (This type of field trip is discussed in more detail as you read through the rest of this chapter.)

Planning for a Successful Field Trip

Many child-care centers and schools are not taking as many field trips as they once did for reasons that include tightening of the budget and shortage of staff. For those of you who are still planning field trips, careful planning is most important.

Making decisions about what an appropriate field trip should provide, selecting the site, visiting the location, planning for the trip, taking the trip, preparing follow-up activities, and evaluating the trip are all parts of the *process*. Think about the following guidelines as you plan field trips for young children.

Appropriate field trips provide:

- Opportunities to clarify misconceptions young children have about places and people in the community
- Concrete experiences for the children
- Sensory activities outside the classroom
- Occasions to discover firsthand examples of real-life work settings
- Contact with adult work models
- Opportunities to gather information and observe multiple environments
- Reinforcement and extension of concepts already learned, while developing new concepts
- A common core of experiences for play and problem-solving activities

An appropriate site should:

- Be safe for young children to visit.
- Be fairly close by so that the children have only a short car trip or bus ride.
- Not be too fatiguing for the children.
- Not be too crowded or noisy.
- Offer the children sensory experiences.
- Offer genuine learning experiences through participation.

Before you step out of the classroom door with the children, you should:

- Visit the field trip site yourself.
- Talk to the contact person who will be there on the day you and the children visit and call that individual for verification the day before the field trip.
- Explain how many children and adults will be coming and the ages of the children; arrange for a time when the site is not too crowded.
- Explain the children's need to be able to explore, see, and touch.
- Find out the site's rules and regulations.
- Find out where the bathrooms are located.
- Find out accommodations for children with special needs, if applicable.
- Determine arrangements for lunch or snack.
- Walk around the location and look for dangerous places.
- Set up the length of the visit, date, and time.
- Get brochures, posters, and any other information to share with the children during pretrip discussions.

Prepare the children for the trip:

- Give them an idea of what to expect.
- Read books; showing videos, pictures, and posters; and talk about the planned trip.
- Involve them in the planning of the trip.
- Remind them of the rules of expected behavior.
- Remind them that during the field trip they are not to talk to or go with anyone other than the people on the field trip.
- Select a partner or buddy for each child and explain how important it is to stay with their partner.
- Tell them what to do if they get separated from the group.

Prepare the parents for the trip:

- Have the parent or guardian sign a walking field trip permission form at the beginning of the year, so that you can take the children on spontaneous walks around the neighborhood. (An example of a walking trip permission form can be found in Appendix D.)
- Have the parent or guardian sign a field trip form for major types of field trips a week before the trip is to be taken. (An example of a field trip permission form can be found in Appendix D.)
- E-mail or send information home to parents explaining the field trip, its purpose, and other details.
- Involve parent volunteers to accompany you and the children (one adult for every two or three children is advised. For older children, one adult for every five or six children seems to work well. You will need to decide what child-to-adult ratio is best for you and the children).
- Explain the emergency procedures and assure them that all of the adults going on the trip understand the procedures.
- Explain that arrangements have been made for any child who does not have permission to go on the trip to visit another class during the duration of the field trip.

Taking the Field Trip

Consider the following guidelines when you and the children take the field trip:

- Take at least one fully charged cell phone with you.
- Be sure that the drivers of cars, vans, or buses have a map with simple, precise directions on how to get to the field trip location.
- Prepare a trip kit containing bottled water and paper cups, a basic first-aid kit, and several wet washcloths in individual, self-seal bags.
- Keep the most apprehensive children close to you.
- Take the time to see things along the way.

- Listen to the children to find out what they do and do not know. Talk to them; ask open-ended questions and answer their questions.
- Count "heads" often throughout the trip.
- It is helpful if the children wear T-shirts or name tags with the center's or school's name on them. It is best not to put the child's name where it is visible because a stranger calling the child's name could pull him or her away from the group.
- Enjoy the field trip!

Follow-Up to and Assessment of the Field Trip

There should be many opportunities for follow-up activities. Here are a few suggestions:

- Have the children write thank-you notes or draw pictures to send to the parent volunteers and the field-site guides or managers who helped make the field trip successful.
- Encourage group discussions with the children on what they liked best or what they remember about the trip.
- Expand lesson plans to include follow-up activities.
- Deepen the children's understanding and recall through follow-up activities: dictate or write stories, draw pictures, create songs and poems, make puppet characters, and draw maps. Add related props and materials to the dramatic play, block, and other learning centers.
- Clarify and build on what the children have seen, heard, experienced, and shared.
- Get written evaluations from all of the adults participating in the trip. Did the activity fulfill the trip's goals and objectives? How could the activity be changed to make it effective or more appropriate?

Suggested Field Trips

"Children's museums provide a safe harbor in a scary, busy, and complicated world. They offer children the gift of playing freely in an inviting and complex environment and of playing with new things and people in time-tested ways. These positive play experiences are changing children's lives, not merely by what they learn during a museum visit, but by helping them believe in their own powers to learn, to succeed, to make their own choices, to get along with other people, to make their own discoveries, and to know that they are interesting people with good ideas (Sinker and Russell, 2000, p. 3). (See **Figure 7-14**.)"

Figure 7-14   A field trip is all about discovery!

TABLE 7-2:	Field Trips: Suggestions of Places to Visit	
Aquarium	Farmer's market	Puppet show
Arboretum	Fire department	Science museum
Art museum	Library	Sports field or arena
Bird-watching site	Museum of natural history	Wildlife sanctuary
Children's museum	Newspaper	Zoo
Children's theater	Pet shop	
City Hall	Planetarium	

It is interesting to note that as psychological, sociological, and physical spaces for children have decreased, the number of children's museums has increased. At the turn of the twentieth century (1899), the first museum for children opened in Brooklyn, New York. Now, in the twenty-first century, there are about 250 children's museums, with approximately 100 more in the planning stage. There are more than 400 children's museums around the world.

The national goals of a children's museum work hand in hand with each local museum. A children's museum is a place dedicated to children, their families, and educators, where children learn to be proud of their own families and heritage and develop a better understanding of their classmates' and neighbors' cultures. It also serves as an extension of the classroom for educators and a place for parents to "get down on the floor" and play with their children while spending time together.

It is helpful to have a checklist to complete on the day of the field trip. This should be filled out completely by you. Not only will this give you an opportunity to double-check all of your preparations, but it is also written documentation that you are in compliance with state or school requirements for taking children away from the center or school. (See Appendix D for a checklist of Field Trips.)

Additional Developmentally Appropriate Activities

DAP

A map-making project of the center or school can help children learn about the program and understand where they belong in this larger community of learners. Start with mini fieldtrips to different parts of your center or school and have the children interview staff such as the director/principal, teachers, cook, or janitor about what they do. Lauren McCann recalls, "During these visits, I ask the children questions to help them become more aware of their environment, such as, 'How long did it take us to walk here?' Or 'Is this room bigger than our room?'"

Children can make field drawings of different locations such as the playground and work in small groups to draw the final maps (McCann, L. A., 2014). Primary children might want to make a 3D model of their school. Another map activity that recognizes classroom diversity is to identify where the children were born or their family moved from and, with children's help, put pins in the map marking those locations, running a string from the various places to the location of your program.

The following song and activities ("Humpty Dumpty" by Bea Wolf) show how a fingerplay activity that is developmentally appropriate for toddlers and 3-year-olds can be expanded to a dramatic play activity appropriate for 4- and 5-year-olds. The "Humpty Dumpty Song" is provided in **Box 7-1**.

BOX 7-1:   Humpty Dumpty*
(finger play activity with song)
(suitable for toddlers and 3-year-olds)

Before attempting this activity, read or recite the rhyme to the children on several occasions so they become thoroughly familiar with it. If possible, find a colorful illustration to stimulate their interest. The teacher asks the children questions while pointing to various features of the illustration:

Teacher: Who is this?
Children: Humpty Dumpty!
Teacher: What is Humpty Dumpty sitting on?
Children: The wall!

   (If children are too young to answer, teacher supplies the answers.)

Teacher guides the children in identifying articles of clothing worn by Humpty Dumpty, points out the horses and soldiers and anything else of visual interest. If children are old enough to understand, some discussion may take place about the fact that Humpty Dumpty is an egg and eggs can break. Children are prepared for the activity when they appear well acquainted with the rhyme.

Teacher: Now we're going to tell the story of Humpty Dumpty with our hands. First, make a wall, like this: (*Teacher
                holds forearm as though looking at a wristwatch.*)
                Now, make a fist with your other hand. This is Humpty Dumpty! Set him down on the wall. Is he happy there?
                Let him sway back and forth. (*Sway fist as though rocking back and forth on forearm.*)
Teacher: Now everyone sing (or say):
                Humpty Dumpty sat on a wall.
                Humpty Dumpty had a great fall—Boom!

(Bend wrist down so that Humpty Dumpty drops off wall. Establish a rhythm by beating hands on thighs to simulate horses galloping. Sing or chant the next lines to this rhythm:)

   All the king's horses and all the king's men

   Couldn't put Humpty together again—

   Couldn't put Humpty together again!

   Why? (*Extend hands outward in a large shrug.*)

(During the next phrase extended hands slowly rise to meet over head, simulating an egg shape. Fingers meet on the word egg.)

   Because he was an egg!

(This activity provides a good opportunity to point out that an egg is oval shaped and to practice shaping ovals using fingers, hands, and arms.)

Review the nursery rhyme. Conduct a group discussion based on the fact that, once broken, an egg can never be put together again. Many children will have their own experiences to relate regarding this subject.

Announce that we are about to dramatize Humpty Dumpty. Explain that the word *dramatize* means to act out.

Guide the children in "falling" safely from a seated position to a lying down position on the floor. For this practice, children should already be seated on the floor so there is very little distance to fall. Explain that this is a fake fall, that we are acting, and that everyone must fall softly so as not to be hurt. Allow a very short time for fake fall practice (two or three falls should do it). Then guide children in pretending to be soldiers or king's men on horseback. Let them pretend to hold reins and gallop about for a short time; then announce that everyone seems ready to dramatize the story.

Divide the class into two groups. Group 1 consists of Humpty Dumptys, and group 2 of king's men. Instruct the king's men to wait quietly in a designated area until they hear their cue, which is the galloping rhythm the teacher will clap at the appropriate time. Instruct the Humpty Dumptys to sit on their wall, which can be a line on the floor. When everyone is ready, start the Humpty Dumptys swaying back and forth as all sing or say the first two lines of the rhyme. On "had a great fall," all Humpty Dumptys fake-fall on the floor and lie still. The teacher then claps the gallop rhythm. All the king's men then gallop over to the fallen Humpty Dumptys,

BOX 7-1: Humpty Dumpty (continued)

dismount, and pat them gently, trying to put them together. On "Why?" the Humpty Dumptys sit up and all the children shrug with hands out. On "Because he was an egg," all slowly form an oval shape with arms above heads, fingers meeting on the word egg. Repeat the dramatization, with group 1 switching roles with group 2.

HUMPTY DUMPTY SONG*

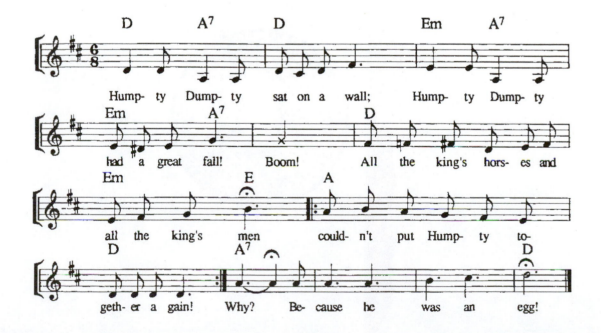

The song and dramatic play activity "The Doughnut Shop" by Bea Wolf is appropriate for 4- and 5-year-olds. Think about how you could use it for other age groups. "The Doughnut Song" is provided in **Box 7-2**.

BOX 7-2:   The Doughnut Shop*

(dramatic play for 4- and 5-year-olds)

(entertainingly illustrates the concept of subtraction)

This activity requires the following cast:

1. A group of children who act as doughnuts
2. A group of children who each purchase a doughnut
3. A cashier or shopkeeper

Begin by selecting the shopkeeper. The teacher can fill that role herself, delegate the role to a child who has earned a special privilege, or select the shopkeeper in some impartial way.

The children who act as doughnuts are seated in a row, on chairs or on the floor, in a designated area. The purchasers, each equipped with an imaginary or simulated coin, sit or stand in a different area. The shopkeeper sits near the doughnuts and operates an imaginary cash register.

The song is sung as many times as there are doughnuts lined up. Each time it is sung, a different child is named from the group of purchasers. That child walks over to the "shop," pays the shopkeeper, and selects a doughnut to take "home" (back to the purchaser area). Between each repetition of the song the teacher asks, "Now, how many doughnuts are left in the shop?"

After the last doughnut has been purchased, children usually wish to repeat the activity, with the groups switching roles.

THE DOUGHNUT SONG*

---

*Reproduced by permission of B. Wolf—1995
Copyright B. Wolf—1993

BOX 7-2: **The Doughnut Shop** (continued)

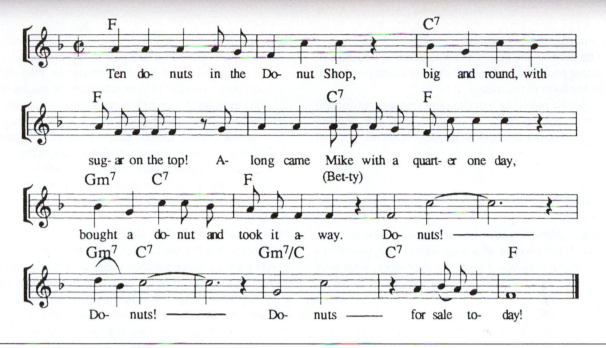

*Reproduced by permission of B. Wolf—1995
Copyright B. Wolf—1993

Elias, C. L., and Berk, L. E. (2002). Self-regulation in young children: Is there a role for sociodramatic play? *Early Childhood Research Quarterly,* 17(2), 216–238.

Books and stories can be used to integrate all areas of the curriculum, including dramatic play. The selection of a familiar story such as *The Three Billy Goats Gruff* or *The Three Little Pigs* can be the first tale to be acted out. Then add another book, such as *Brown Bear, Brown Bear, What Do You See?* by Bill Martin Jr. (1983), *Gilberto and the Wind* by Marie Hall Ets (1978), or *The Talking Vegetables* by Won-Ldy Paye and Margaret Lippert (2006). Put the book away once you and the children are familiar and comfortable with the story. This gives more freedom to add to or change the basic story as you go along. Simple props and settings can add to the dramatic play. Once the children experience the enjoyment of this kind of activity, they can then expand the activity.

Activity Plan Worksheet   Developmentally Appropriate Social Studies Activity

AGES: pre-kindergarten, kindergarten, and primary-age children

Name of Activity and Brief Description

The Our Classroom Map activity is designed for children to create a three-dimensional map of their classroom on a miniature scale as they work together using a large piece of cardboard, markers, and collage materials to construct a map of their own classroom.

Child Outcomes of Activity

- Encourage cooperative problem solving.
- Develop math concepts, such as one-to-one correspondence, proportion, and size.
- Use materials such as: pipe cleaners, Styrofoam pieces, small counting cubes, crayons, markers, glue, and various types and colors of paper.
- Strengthen eye-hand coordination.
- Develop small muscles.
- Explore map making.

Space and Materials Needed

This can be done on the floor in the classroom or outside. Put down butcher paper and set a large piece of cardboard on top to use as the base of the map.

Suggested materials include: pipe cleaners, Styrofoam pieces, small counting cubes, crayons, markers, glue, and various types and colors of paper or whatever the children want to use.

Procedure

- Read books to children about maps. Discuss how maps are made.
- Bring in different types of maps to look at and discuss. Discuss the concept of a map legend. Ask children to think about making a map of the classroom. What symbols might they use in their legend? Help children decide on the scale of their map.
- Let the children create the map.
- Ask questions about their map and point out details in the room they may want to include.

Guidance

- Limit the number of children based on the size of the cardboard you are using to create the map. Different children may want to help with different stages of creating the map. Act as a resource to discuss possible solutions to construction problems and conflicts the children cannot resolve without support. Be sure to allow the children to guide the direction and flow of the play. This activity may take several days or weeks to complete. Let the children make the decision as to when it is time to stop working on and playing with this activity.

Assessment and Follow-Up Strategies

Take photographs of the map in progress. Work with the children to create a documentation board or class book using the photos to develop a timeline and have the children describe what they were doing in the pictures. Create a KWL chart or web with the children to document what they knew before starting to build, what they wanted to learn about maps, and what they did learn in this activity.

⌄ Professional Resource Download

AGES: 2- and 3-year-olds
Dramatic Play Center

Name of Activity and Brief Description—Baby Care

Encourage children to practice nurturing family roles as they pretend that they are taking care of the baby dolls.

Child Outcomes of Activity

- Demonstrate family roles through pretend play.
- Demonstrate empathy and caring for others.
- Recreate caregiving tasks in pretend play.
- Express ideas and feelings about caring for babies.

Space and Materials Needed

Baby dolls, blankets, bottles, cups, bowls, plates, spoons, baby bed (it can be a box), chair or rocker, doll stroller.

Procedure

1. Set up dramatic play center with materials for baby care.
2. Explain the activity to children.
3. If needed, suggest scenarios for children to play out, such as the baby is sick or hungry.
4. Describe children's actions as they play using vocabulary that they may not regularly say.

Guidance

Provide duplicates of most materials. Offer additional props, if needed. Suggest different roles for individual children should conflicts arise.

Assessment and Follow-Up Strategies

Were child outcomes met? Yes___ No___
What was the children's response?
What worked well? What did not work?
How could this activity be changed to make it more effective or more appropriate?

Technology in Social Studies and Dramatic Play

Technology & Teaching: WebQuest

Children can use the Internet or the teacher can develop a WebQuest, which is an inquiry-based series of lessons that supports K–2 students' learning and technology competency, to research social studies or dramatic play topics such as puppets or different types of bread around the world. A WebQuest uses tasks that lead students to collate, analyze, and transform online and offline information.

In their everyday lives, children come across barcode scanners in supermarkets, mobile telephones, portable computers, cash dispensers, and parking lot ticket machines, all of which confront them with modern technology and can be integrated into their dramatic play scenarios. Photos or videos taken by student's families on vacation can be integrated into lessons about different cultures and countries. Dramatic play by any age can be videoed and viewed by the participants.

Cristol, D. and Gimbert, B. (2004). Teaching curriculum with technology: enhancing children's technological competence during early childhood. *Early Childhood Education Journal*, 31, 207–216.

Diversity in Social Studies and Dramatic Play

Using traditional and modern clothing, fabric pieces, and authentic props from different cultures can facilitate imaginative play and make it more meaningful. As teachers, we are daily role models for young children. By incorporating the goals for social studies into our activities, we can create a supportive environment for the children and their families. We can emphasize an anti-bias approach that influences children to respect and appreciate differences and similarities among people. Ideas for including cultural diversity have been imbedded throughout this chapter. Some ideas for including each and every child follow.

Each and every child, whatever their developmental level and differences, have individual interests and special capabilities. The following suggestions, from Deiner (2013), Isbell and Raines (2013), and Mayesky (2015), are intended to help teachers include children with special needs in dramatic play:

1. Apply only those rules that are really needed for the child to play safely.
2. Let the child take the lead. This may involve some patient waiting for the child to choose something to do.
3. To encourage the child to play with others, define the space where the children can play, and keep it small at first.
4. If a child wants to play with another child or a group of children but does not know how to join in, encourage him or her to gradually become involved, and then slowly lessen your own involvement.
5. Encourage verbalization during play by asking questions and encouraging communication with other children.
6. Offer dramatic play materials that are familiar and part of a child's daily life experiences.
7. Set up the dramatic play area in a variety of different ways. If children want to play through medical experiences, set it up as a doctor's or dentist's office.
8. Use puppets as a way for children to talk indirectly about experiences.

9. Provide some dress-up clothes that are simple to put on or take off.
10. Sharing ideas with peers helps children with developmental delays see how things work and how they are to be done.
11. Provide a lot of props. Be sure that at least some of them give obvious cues (tactile as well as visual) about the activity going on.

Some children with developmental delays fatigue very easily. Make sure that the child has supportive seating. Some children need chair inserts or standing.

Creating Partnerships with Families

As you establish partnerships with families, it is important to continuously assess their needs and interests and use this knowledge to involve the parents as active partners in the lives of the children at the center or school. The families of today offer new challenges to early childhood educators. In a lifetime in the profession, teachers will find many families that don't resemble them in family style, relationships, structure or values. As the United States grows, teachers need to continuously prepare themselves to recognize, appreciate, and work with these diverse families.

Knowing this, we should relate to the families of our children with a commitment to accept their individual differences. We should acknowledge and respect children's home language and **culture** (National Association for the Education of Young Children [NAEYC] 2005). We should maintain positive interactions with them while communicating our goals of a child-centered, developmentally appropriate curriculum.

Get parental and family input as you plan activities and services. If the parents help to set the priorities and agenda, your planned activities will better meet their needs. "Teachers need to be prepared to build partnerships with several parents and family members who are active in a child's life in different configurations and are concerned about the child's development, education, and future" (Rockwell, Andre, and Hawley, 2010, p. 34). The following are some examples of how to communicate with parents to maximize their involvement:

- "Parents are the most important people in their child's life. They know their child well, and their preferences and choices matter. Excellent teachers work hard to develop reciprocal relationships with families, with communication and respect in both directions" (Copple and Bredekamp, 2009, p. 45).
- With parents of an infant or toddler, you will need to spend a lot of time making them feel comfortable in leaving their child with you. It is most important to build a sense of trust, and this takes time. Show them that you will communicate with them through daily notes and conversations. Let them know that there will be a period of adjustment for their child as well as for them. Explain that during this time, it might be helpful if their child brought a "security" toy or blanket. The parents can also call or visit during the day to check on how their child is doing, if this will help them feel more at ease. All these suggestions can open lines of communication between you and the family members.
- Place a parent bulletin board or information sheet on the door of your classroom. For family members who bring and pick up the child each day, this offers a consistent place to look for messages and items of interest. Change materials often.
- Post weekly lesson plans on the classroom door to keep the parents up to date on the curriculum. This sends a signal that you want the parents to be fully aware of the daily activities of their children.
- The weekly menu of lunch and snacks should also be posted for parents to see, as required by licensing regulations in most states.
- An email newsletter, in the family's language, is another way to get parents involved. Some enjoy receiving it, whereas others are interested in taking the responsibility for writing it or collecting information to be in the newsletter. The teacher can contribute

culture: The sum total of a child's or family's ways of living: their values or beliefs, language, patterns of thinking, appearance, and behavior. These are passed or learned from one generation to the next.

facts about what is happening in the classroom, as well as suggestions for children's books and videos, parenting articles, and children's art.

- The program's governing or advisory groups include family as members and active participants in the program.
- Have a family breakfast, potluck supper, or picnic on the playground. Food always adds to the welcoming environment of family–school activities.
- An open house or family meeting is a time for sharing with parents what their children are doing and what they are learning. This is an excellent opportunity to talk about the importance of play and other developmentally appropriate learning experiences. Be prepared to answer questions. Give family members an opportunity to take part in some of the activities the children have been doing. Set up materials and supplies in each learning center so that they can "learn by doing," the same as the children. Read a story to the parents or have them participate in a music and movement or social studies activity.
- Once or twice a year, plan individual parent–teacher conferences to discuss each child's developmental progress. Plan both day and evening conferences to accommodate the parents' work schedules.
- Invite family members to share their interests, talents, and occupations with the children in the class. This offers another way to make parent involvement special. Work together to plan events.

> "[W]hen teachers and families create real partnerships, their spheres of influence overlap and form a caring community around students. The Harvard Family Research Project refers to the need for complementary learning for children to be successful, an array of linked learning supports around them, including families, early childhood programs, health and social service agencies, businesses, libraries, museums, and other community resources (Caspe, López, and Wolos, cited in Gestwicki, 2013)."

Creating partnerships with community members and resources can be helpful. One of the most important groups of individuals to invite into your classroom consist of older members of the families of children in your class as well as senior adults in the community. Intergenerational programs offer many ways to connect young children with the history and family customs of their own or other cultures.

Family Quilts

Connect the social studies curriculum to the theme of "Self and Family" to assist children in learning the values, cultural traditions, and history of families.

An effective way to accomplish this goal is to introduce children to quilts. Throughout the history of many countries, you will find quilting, an ancient craft. In U.S. pioneer days, families and friends got together to make quilts for special occasions, such as weddings, births, and farewells to families moving West. This tradition continues today, and the act of quilting brings many adults together in friendship and sharing.

The term *quilt* "refers to a fabric sandwich made of a top, a bottom or backing, and a soft filler [batting] in between. The top consists of blocks arranged in a pattern. Each block may be a patchwork, that is—pieces of fabric cut in squares, rectangles, and other shapes and sewn together to form the block" (Parks, 1994, p. 22).

Invite a quilter to visit your class. This individual can bring some handmade quilts and also show the children the three unfinished parts of a quilt—top, batting, and backing.

"The fascinating tradition of quilt-making can become an inclusive, engaging experience for children when the early childhood teacher considers a cross-curricular approach" (Helm, Huebner, and Long, 2000, p. 44).

Your children may enjoy making a friendship quilt of single pieces of fabric or paper. To further illustrate this activity, there are several books that give information about family quilts. These selections offer opportunities for literature-based integrated curriculum. As you read one of the books during group time, pass a quilt around the circle of children. This is a tangible example of the abstract story you are reading. (Older children will be able to read the books by themselves or read them to younger children.)

These books, when shared with family members, stimulate the telling of family stories and, many times, the discovery of family quilts. The stories relate not only to families but also to the multiple relationships within a family.

After you read the story, encourage the children to retell it by acting out the parts in small groups. You can extend the quilt to many learning centers. There are many projects that can promote the development of large and small muscle skills, as well as problem solving, socialization, cognitive development, language, and literacy abilities. The following are suggestions for these extended activities:

- Develop a story or sequencing chart that diagrams the story line of the book. This can be a way of developing how the story can be reenacted.
- Ask the children open-ended questions, such as, "Do you have a quilt at your home?" "Would you like to make a paper quilt in the art center?" "Do you want to write your story about a quilt in the writing center?" "Would you help me collect fabric to make new squares for our class quilt?" "How do you think we can find the fabric?" "Who should we ask to help us?" "Would you like to make a quilt for the doll bed?"
- Explore color in the science center. Children can mix colors, look through kaleidoscopes, or dye their own fabrics (Helm, Huebner, and Long, 2000).
- Place a "quilt box" in the manipulative area containing an assortment of fabric squares (all the same size) with snaps or Velcro on each corner (top and bottom). A child can snap pieces together to make his or her own quilt, or several children can do this activity together. Some of the squares should have different patterns and shapes on the fabric.
- Each child can design and paint a paper square for the classroom quilt. Patch the painted squares together with clear tape. Then place the completed quilt on the wall outside the classroom to share with the parents and other children.
- Put washable paint of skin-tone colors into individual shallow aluminum pans, and let each child make a single handprint on a piece of paper. Cut out each handprint and glue it onto a precut, individual square of construction paper. Let each child label his or her handprint with his or her name. Make holes in the corners of each square and use brightly colored yarn to lace the squares together. Hang this "quilt" in the classroom so that the children can daily enjoy seeing their art displayed.
- "Our Classroom Family Quilt" in the form of a bulletin board can be made by mounting photographs of the children on squares of fabric. Add the children's dictated comments to the squares. A variation of this bulletin board can be to make a "Family Tree," with the photographs added as leaves of a tree.
- During group time, discuss with the children activities that they enjoy doing with their families. They can draw pictures of what they like to do best.

Making the Class into a Neighborhood

Another, more complex social studies theme and series of activities is making the entire classroom into a neighborhood. This can be a creative follow-up to a walking trip around the neighborhood. It requires careful planning with the children to decide on how to do this, which will then indicate to the teacher what supplies, materials, and props will be needed for each area. Each learning activity center can be restructured into a part of the neighborhood, such as a home, construction site, fire station, grocery store, or other business establishment in the community. This all-encompassing plan benefits the physical, intellectual, social, emotional, and language development of all the children. The neighborhood concept connects children to their immediate world and brings about a feeling of community.

Daniel Red Stick is a Native American second-grade teacher at William Jennings Bryant elementary school in Lincoln, Nebraska. Daniel is preparing a social studies unit but is concerned about how Native Americans are portrayed in a stereotypical way in most resources that he typically uses and the message his second graders are receiving about other cultures.

What Do You Think?

1. How can Daniel use his state standards in social studies as a guide is planning this unit?
2. How can Daniel incorporate a learning experience that depicts how different tribes of native people lived in the past and how they live now?
3. What type of activities can be utilized to help the children better understand cultural similarities and differences?

The Teacher's Role

Guidance in Social Studies and Dramatic Play

Two issues that teachers are concerned about during social play are rough-and-tumble superhero play and exclusionary behavior based on difference in race, gender, and social status. The following can help in guiding superhero play:

1. Show children that superheroes are not special just because they are physically powerful. Point out when superheroes show kindness and helpfulness to others, and show appreciation to the children when they do the same.
2. Talk about real heroes and heroines with children. Introduce them to people such as Helen Keller and Martin Luther King Jr., and discuss how everyday people can demonstrate acts of courage and goodness.
3. Help children build on their interests through superhero play. Watching a segment from *Star Wars* may lead to learning about space travel, whereas a scene from the *Spiderman* movie or comic book may lead to exploring the world of insects. Always keep your eyes open to learning opportunities for children (NAEYC, 1997).

The appearance of television or movie heroes, such as Spiderman or Wonder Woman, may change children's dramatic play. When you hear these heroes' names, you will want to observe the children's play more closely. Sometimes the stunts on television and in movies are dangerous when children try to do them. Rough play may become too much a part of the play as they pretend to be superheroes. Your observation will give you an opportunity to teach better ways to solve problems without aggressiveness. Besides open discussions with the children, teach conflict resolution skills and invite real, healthier role models (such as community helpers and family members) to visit the classroom. Help children regain control of their play by changing it from imitative play to creative, imaginative play. And importantly, work with parents, other teachers, and the early childhood community to understand and support each other's efforts to deal with the marketing of violence to children.

Early childhood educators wonder how to counter the negative stereotypes children see and hear on television, in the movies, or with their friends or family. When talking to children, keep their age and developmental stage in mind, so use words and descriptions they can understand, but be certain not to dismiss their inquisitiveness. If a child senses an open climate in the early childhood setting, he or she will be more able to share concerns with you. By immediately taking the time to discuss questions and concerns with young children in an age-appropriate manner your interest says that what concerns you concerns me, your response helps clear up inaccuracies and erroneous generalizations and talking with children helps to make them more comfortable with the differences they see. In addition, your dialogue gives them the vocabulary needed to talk positively about differences themselves.

Both parents and teachers can be embarrassed by the questions children ask and may tell children, "Don't say that" or "That isn't very nice." Others may think it best to deny differences, believing that to ignore them is to raise a color-blind or bias-free child and may simply ignore a child's questions about observed differences. Although you may mean well, you in fact, confuse the child who already clearly recognizes that we are all quite different:

> "We must respond to differences in a positive way and speak up when we encounter bias and prejudice. Children take their lead from the behavior of the adults around them. If someone makes a disparaging remark in front of you and you say nothing, the child assumes that you agree with that person's comment. If you disagree, make a point of saying so. A simple statement of disagreement with those who may make unkind, negative, or disparaging comments will give the children in you care a true sense of what you believe (Kupetz, 2008, p. 2)."

TEACHING TIPS Culture and Dramatic Play

Multicultural teaching strategies for infants and toddlers include:

- Conduct a home visit before the infant begins in the classroom.
- Incorporate things from baby's home into the classroom (favorite book, music, other materials).
- Post family pictures on wall or crib.
- Record favorite stories or songs sung together at home and bring to classroom.
- Incorporate foods, activities, and finger plays from home.
- Learn how routines are handled at home.
- Have a basket of pictures of child's family and pets.
- Make a classroom holiday or home events timeline border in classroom.
- Share pictures of children and babies of all races and cultures.

Beaty (2009, pp. 83–84) suggests there are both positive and negative aspects of children's imitation of superheroes:

> The superhero is a good character who is good-looking, strong, loyal, helpful, unselfish, ready to fight against evil, and always the winner. The bad character is evil-looking, strong, selfish, disloyal, underhanded, sneaky, always challenging the good character, and always the loser .... Children are going to attempt superhero play whether or not it is allowed .... [S]uperheroes are powerful symbols, indeed, to young children. When you understand that such symbols can represent positive values in our society, then you may want to consider allowing superhero dramatic play in the classroom if it can be controlled and directed into prosocial channels.

Additionally, superhero play can offer children a way to deal with their real fears and anxieties and answer the "big questions about the world such as 'what is right and wrong, what is good and bad, what is fair and unfair, what is life and death, what is a boy and a girl, and what is real and fantasy'" (Hoffman, cited in Gordon and Browne, 2016, p. 78).

Let us think about how we can deal effectively with the superhero characters in an early education setting. One of the first things to do is to become familiar with *what* is available for the children to watch on television, videos, and movies. Second, think about *why*

the children are imitating these characters. Ask questions of the children and talk to them about other, more appropriate, choices for play. It's important to establish limits ahead of time.

Children have very little real-world experience by which to evaluate the relation of media violence to real life. Because of this, they can benefit greatly from discussing these connections with adults. "Teachers sometimes think they have to solve these problems for children. In a classroom community, a better alternative is a group problem solving" (Dodge, Colker, and Heroman, 2008, p. 114).

In the position statement *Valuing Diversity for Young Children (p. 3)*, the Southern Early Childhood Association (SECA) offers the following tips for teachers:

- Include diverse individuals in wall and room decorations. When children see themselves reflected in classroom materials, they understand that who they are is valued, accepted, and deemed important. This simple, yet deliberate act can make the difference in how well children are motivated to learn.
- Use language with children that demonstrates an acceptance of all cultures. Word choices indicate acceptance of and often determines behavior in children. Choose words carefully and avoid those that would convey a negative connotation when none is intended. Life is given to words when we speak them, and children usually try to live up to our characterizations of them. Expect the best from all children and communicate that expectation to them in positive and motivating ways.
- Consider field trips that are taken and who the guest speakers are. If all field trips are reflective of one culture, students never have an opportunity to see themselves or individuals in their communities as something of value. Guest speakers should represent as many diverse individuals as possible. When all speakers come from one group, the message sent to children is that individuals from their particular group have little to share with them.
- Look at cultural celebrations and when they are celebrated. Contributions of many cultures should be shared throughout the year and not only at specified times during the year. Each culture has its own beliefs, customs, rituals, religions, and business and academic achievements that make it both unique and great. Celebrate them.

Summary

1. **What are examples of key terms related to social studies and dramatic play for children?** Social sciences, which are the core of social studies: anthropology, sociology, history, geography, economics, and psychology; anthropology, which is the study of the way people live, such as their beliefs and customs; sociology, which is the study of group living, cooperation, and responsibilities; history, which is the study of what has happened in the life of a country or people; geography, which is the study of the Earth's surface, resources, and the concepts of direction, location, and distance; economics, which is the study of the production, distribution, and consumption of goods and services; psychology, which is the study of the mind, emotions, and behavioral processes; culture, which is sum total of a child's or family's ways of living: their values or beliefs, language, patterns of thinking, appearance, and behavior; dramatic play, which is a type of creative, spontaneous play in which children use their imaginations to create and dramatize pretend characters, actions, or events; sociodramatic play, which is the highest level of symbolic play in which young children create their own happenings based on their experiences; and symbolic or dramatic play, which is a type of play that allows the child to transfer objects into symbols (things that represent something else) and images into people, places, and events within his experiences.

2. **How do social studies and dramatic play relate stages of child development in social play?** Jean Piaget's research (1962) has helped us understand play in terms of cognitive development by presenting play in three stages: Practice play in infancy, symbolic or dramatic play in preschool, and games with rules during the primary years. Sara Smilansky (1968) divides play into four types of sociodramatic play: functional play (infancy through early years), constructive play (toddlers and preschoolers), dramatic play (toddlers through primary-age children), and games with rules (older preschoolers and primary-age children).

3. **What should be considered in the planning and preparation of socially supportive and dramatic play environments?** Provide unstructured time, adequate space, flexible materials, and uninterrupted opportunity for the children to enjoy dramatic play. Select props that are authentic and can be used naturally and safely. Change props frequently and include ones that reflect different cultures. Avoid props and activities that are sexist or racist. Select dress-up clothes and outfits that are simple, durable, and easy to get on and off.

   The basic equipment for the home living or dramatic play center should be: child-size furniture made of wood or sturdy plastic, including tables, chairs, rocking chair, and shelves; a "play" sink, stove, and refrigerator; and a full-length mirror. Dolls of both sexes representing differing cultural features and skin coloring, a doll bed or cradle, and two sturdy, nonworking telephones should also be included.

4. **How can you integrate and create social studies and dramatic play activities appropriate for young children?** The social studies curriculum emphasizes basic goals that encourage children to become self-reliant, contributing members of their society—namely, in their families, in the classroom, and in the community, while developing an awareness of being a part of the world. These goals encourage children to make choices, act independently, and develop a sense of responsibility and respect for themselves and others. The social studies curriculum should include topics that relate specifically to the children themselves, children's families, including pets, the classroom as a community, and the local community and state. It should also foster understanding and respecting differences in culture, gender, and abilities. This social sciences or social studies approach can also be used with other topics, such as different ways of cooking and eating, types of clothing, kinds of occupations and work roles, weather conditions, and how people in the world are transported from one place to another. Include field trips that provide firsthand knowledge that connect children to their community.

5. **What are some ways to use technology in a social and dramatic play environment?** Children can use the Internet to research social studies or dramatic play topics such as puppets or different types of bread around the world. In their everyday lives, children come across barcode scanners in supermarkets, smart phones, portable computers, cash dispensers, and parking lot ticket machines, all of which confront them with modern technology and can be integrated into their dramatic play scenarios. Photos or videos taken by student's families on vacation can be integrated into lessons about different cultures and countries. Dramatic play by any age can be videoed and viewed by the participants.

6. **How can you incorporate diversity into social and dramatic play?** Emphasize an anti-bias approach that influences children to respect and appreciate differences and similarities among people. Ideas for including cultural diversity include providing soft dolls representing different cultures, "play" food and utensils from various cultures, both male and female clothing, clothing made of fabric that is tie-dyed and batiked, and clothing made from madras prints and kente cloth. The clothing styles should include saris, kimonos, serapes, ponchos, grass skirts, and dashikis. Plan activities in a way that children of all abilities can easily participate.

7. **How can you develop partnerships with families that support a child's social awareness and dramatic play?** Acknowledge and respect children and family's home language and culture. Get parental and family input as you plan activities and services, such as what cultural items to put into the dramatic play center and how to present their culture to children in a way that does not include stereotypes. Communicate with parents about children's social play and the values of dramatic play through daily notes and conversations, bulletin boards, newsletters, social events, and open houses. Ask parents to share with the children about their cultural traditions.

8. **What is the teacher's role in promoting social studies and dramatic play in the classroom?** One form of dramatic play that all children explore as they deal with issues of power and control is superhero play. NAEYC suggests that teachers show children that superheroes are not special just because they are physically powerful. Point out when superheroes show kindness and helpfulness to others, and show appreciation to the children when they do the same. Help children regain control of their play by changing it from imitative play to creative, imaginative play. Have open discussions with the children about heroes, conflict, and differences. Teach conflict resolution skills and invite real, healthier role models, such as community helpers and family members, to visit the classroom.

Reflective Review Questions

1. What, from a social studies standpoint, is the value in making maps? How might this type of activity be integrated into other areas, such as art, science, or math?
2. Reflect on the teacher's role in supporting children's dramatic play. Is the dramatic play theme part of the lesson plan? How much input should the children have in deciding what to play? What types of limits are placed on children during dramatic play?
3. Why is it both appropriate and developmentally important that young children try out ways to differentiate fantasy from reality?
4. Relate dramatic play to four other learning centers. Be specific in the ways that dramatic play would help teach concepts in these other learning areas.

Explorations

1. Select an early education classroom and observe for at least one hour. Describe, in writing, several dramatic play activities the children were involved with at the time

of your observation. Describe the activities, which learning centers were part of the activities, how props were used, who initiated the play, and how many joined it.

2. Discuss children's dramatic play on the playground. What are some of the activities that take place? What limits does the teacher place on outdoor activities? Are they different from indoor dramatic play activities? Explain.

3. Select and plan a social studies or dramatic play activity for young children. Specify which age group this activity is planned for: infants, toddlers, preschoolers, or primary-age children. In writing, list objectives, materials needed, step-by-step procedures for presenting this activity, follow-up activities, and evaluation guidelines. (Use the activity plan worksheet in Appendix D.) Prepare this activity and demonstrate it during class or with a group of children.

4. Use the Social Studies and Dramatic Play Environment Checklist in this chapter to conduct an observation of an early childhood learning environment.
   - Beside each statement, place an *X* if the classroom you observed met the statement.
   - On a separate sheet of paper, describe what you actually observed related to each statement. Place the number of the statement first and then your observation.
   - On a separate sheet of paper, for each statement that you did not check as met, describe what you would do to improve that classroom so that the statement would be met. Be sure to put the number of the statement first.
   - Submit this with the name of the location you observed and the age group.

5. Based on the information in this chapter and on your observations of early education environments, design a pre-K dramatic play-learning center. Using paper and colored pens, pencils, or markers, design the learning center showing where materials, supplies and equipment are placed. What criteria will you use? Think about how this center will relate to the other learning centers in the classroom. How does this language arts center support the emergent reading and writing development of the children?

Social Studies and Dramatic Play Books for Young Children

Caseley, J. J. (2002). *On the town: A community adventure*. New York: Greenwillow.

Gilliland, U. H. (1990). *The day of Ahmed's secret*. Illustrated by T. Lewin. New York: Lothrop, Lee & Shepard.

Gresko, M. S. (2000). *A ticket to Israel*. Minneapolis: Carolrhoda Books.

Heiman, S. (2004). *Mexico ABC's: A book about the people and places of Mexico*. Illustrated by O. Todd. New York: Picture Window Books.

Bolton, J. (1994). *My grandmother's patchwork quilt. A book and pocketful of patchwork pieces*. New York: Doubleday Book for Young Readers.

Bourgeois, P. (2003). *Oma's Quilt*. Illustrated by S. Jorisch. New York: Kids Can Press.

Flournoy, V. (1985). *The patchwork quilt*. Illustrated by J. Pinkney. New York: Dial Books for Young Readers.

Franco, B. (1999). *Grandpa's quilt*. New York: Children's Press.

Hopkinson, D. (1993). *Sweet Clara and the freedom quilt*. Illustrated by J. Ransome. New York: Alfred A. Knopf.

Jonas, A. (1994). *The quilt*. New York: Greenwillow.

Polacco, P. (1988). *The keeping quilt*. New York: Simon and Schuster Books for Young Readers.

Ransom, C. F. (2002). *The promise quilt*. Illustrated by E. Beier. New York: Walker Books.

Root, P. (2003). *The name quilt*. Illustrated by M. Apple. New York: Farrar, Straus & Giroux.

Wallace, N. E. (2006). *The kindness quilt*. Tarrytown, NY: Cavendish.

Waterstone, R. (1999). *The too much loved quilt*. Clarksville, TN: First Story.

⌄ **Professional Resource Download**

8 Sensory Play

Standards Covered in This Chapter

 NAEYC 5a, 5b, 5c

 DAP 2

 INTASC 4, 5, 8

HEAD START
Domain: Scientific Reasoning

Student Learning Outcomes

After studying this chapter, you should be able to:

- Define and give examples for key terms related to sensory play for children.

- Discuss sensory play in young children and relate stages of child development to sensory play.

- Evaluate various components of planning and preparation of sensory environments.

- Create sensory activities appropriate for young children.

- Discuss various ways to use technology in a sensory environment.

- Distinguish ways to incorporate diversity into sensory play.

- Describe ways to develop partnerships with families that support child sensory play.

- Analyze the teacher's role in promoting sensory play in the classroom.

We are born with two essential skills in life: our reflexes and our senses. This means that from the start, children learn about their world through their senses. It is through our sensory experiences that we develop much of our brain in the early years. The more children's senses are engaged in meaningful ways, the more easily learning can occur. Ultimately, the senses act as learning portals. All raw information enters the brain through those learning portals. Our challenge is to help children make meaning from that information and connect it with previous experiences and past knowledge. (See **Figure 8-1** on learning about the world through the senses.)

Children naturally learn through their senses every day as they observe changes in nature such as observing shadows, ice melting, dew on the grass, and the wind in their hair. Although it is important to engage children in these spontaneous sensory activities, planned sensory play provides the perfect medium for teaching many scientific concepts, such as cause and effect, making predictions, comparing, exploring, and using scientific tools.

Young children learn best through sensory experiences that offer them opportunities for free exploration in a variety of curriculum areas and through repeated explorations. The sensory area gives them multiple possibilities to do this. The importance of sensory activities for young children cannot be overemphasized and are critical for the brain development (Essa, 2014).

As you read this chapter, focus on how children see, hear, feel, touch, and taste the world around them. Observe carefully how the children in an early education setting make choices and react to the environment. The quality of the environment also contributes to the sensory development of children. Ask yourself if the classroom is "their room." Is it set up so that they can claim ownership? Is it giving them hands-on knowledge about their world? (See **Figure 8-2** related to sand play as a unique sensory activity.)

Figure 8-1 These children are learning about their world through the senses of sight, smell, and touch.

Figure 8-2 Sand play offers children a unique sensory activity that lets them experience their world in a different way.

Sensory Play Defined

Why is sensory play important? Sensory play supports the whole child in developing skills necessary for learning and life. Children have the ability to take in and make sense of information obtained from their senses: *visual*—to see, *auditory*—to listen, *olfactory*—to smell, *tactile*—to touch, and *gustatory*—to taste. We have discussed this previously, and this chapter uses that information as a foundation on which to build additional developmentally appropriate experiences. The main sensory centers in the early childhood curriculum—water-sand-mud play, blocks, woodworking, and cooking experiences—can be indoors or outdoors, separate from, or a part of other learning centers. These areas can be changed easily as the children's developmental needs change and the children's sensory involvement with their environment changes as well.

sensory experiences:
Experiences that use the senses and offer opportunities for free exploration in a variety of curriculum areas.

"Children and adults inhabit different sensory worlds. Imagine a young infant's world of touch and taste—a world where you see and hear more than you look and listen—where you, in effect, think with your body and actions, and your whole body is your only means of reacting (Gestwicki, 2015)."

Every day, the early education classroom should be filled with sensory activities that are sticky, squishy, slippery, smooth, heavy, light, soft, loud, crunchy, colorful, aromatic, and flavorful. Sensory experiences are exciting because each child can use the materials differently while involving multiple senses. **Sensory awareness**, the use of the senses, promotes self-discovery. It is another way the body gives the mind information (Gordon and Browne, 2016). In addition, children learn to cooperate and work together around the sensory table and the sand box.

> "Daily interactions with young children should be peppered with statements and questions that show the wonder and value of the sensory qualities of the environment. Adults cannot verbalize these qualities to the children if they do not experience them themselves (Koster, 2015)."

As you continue through this chapter, sharpen *your* sensory awareness and observe how the sensory centers interact and interconnect with the total curriculum.

Developmental Stages of Sensory Play

DAP

Piaget believed all children pass through phases to advance to the next level of cognitive development. In each stage, children demonstrate new intellectual abilities and increasingly complex understanding of the world. Piaget's first stage, sensorimotor, begins at birth and lasts until 18 months to 2 years of age. This stage involves the use of motor activity and the senses to explore and learn about the world. Knowledge is limited in this stage because it is based on physical interactions and sensory experiences. Infants cannot predict reaction, and therefore must constantly experiment and learn through trial and error. Such exploration might include shaking a rattle or putting objects in the mouth.

In her research on sensory play, Sue Goscoyne identified a three-stage sensory play continuum of fluid play process. For young children, the first stage is about exploration; What is the object? What is it like? The feeling of discovery as each sense is employed to explore the properties of the object in question is enough to keep a child entertained for hours. As children get older, they tend to play in a more complex way, combining objects and other resources to ask, What can I do with it? What can it become? This most creative stage of play inspires the imagination. In the third stage of the continuum, adult facilitation can be employed to alter and adapt the realms of play. As children grow, play becomes increasingly elaborate with their age, developmental level, or familiarity with the resources. Children frequently move from single object play to more complex play with multiple objects.

sensory awareness: The use of the senses.

Brain Research: Sensory Integration

The child collects information and sensations through the senses. The first level of development is sensory motor skills. Sensations of movement and gravity help him to develop postural security and motor planning. Information from his joints and muscles help him develop an awareness of both sides of his body and reflex maturity. Visual, olfactory, gustatory, auditory, and tactile experiences foster his ability to screen input. All of these sensations and experiences allow him to develop body scheme.

Sensory experiences are crucial to a child's development. Movement such as rocking helps organize the brain. A young child learns to integrate the sensation of gravity, sensations from the muscles and joints and sensations received

through his hands and knees, mouth, and ears. Eventually, the child will use these sensory integrations for speech, play and learning, and to master motor skills (Family Child Care Academy, 2014).

The brain is a plastic, growing organ connected to the five base senses through which all initial knowledge is gained. Sensory integration is vital for the more complicated life skills to develop. Proprioceptive senses (or place in space), vestibular senses (movement knowledge), and tactile, auditory, visual, and olfactory input must all integrate successfully. Through sensory integration, the body–brain connection builds the lifelong knowledge it will need to form lasting reasoning, social, emotional, and endurance skills (Cummons, J. (2010).

As practitioners, this means taking a different approach to unstructured play opportunities, altering the assortment of resources, and varying their levels of inter-action and involvement in guiding the play or suggesting activities. (See **Figure 8**-3.)

Sensory play supports the whole child in developing skills necessary for learning and life. Sensory play is therapeutic. Who does not love to climb into a hot bath after a hard day at work or wiggle toes in the sand at the beach? Water and sand are soothing to children as well as adults. Time alone at the sand and water table can help a child who is out of control.

Children develop strength in their large muscles by pouring, carrying, and listing activities. They strengthen small muscles and strengthen their pincer grasp by using the sum and index finger to pick up an item and by pouring, measuring, scrubbing, grasping, and squeezing. They develop eye-hand coordination by focusing and coordi-nating eye movement and visual input to control and direct the hands when reaching for objects underwater, pouring, ladling, digging, and using eye droppers. They develop bilateral coordination by using both hands together to perform a task such as picking up a big bucket of sand, wrist rotation and wrist stability as they hold and twist objects when pouring, and finger dexterity by moving individual fingers in isolation. Sand and water play facilitates the use of the trunk and arms while at the same time maintaining coordination of the body and overall balance.

Eye-hand coordination and fine motor skills such as shoulder stability, forearm rotation, wrist control, and hand grasp skills needed for future writing are facilitated by sand and water table play. Playing and digging with shovels, funnels, and scoops in the sand or water provides resistive activity, which supplies the muscles and joints in the hands and arms with information that is sent to the vestibular and proprioceptive sections of the brain (Gibbs, 2012).

Children develop cognitively as they explore scientific concepts such as the proper-ties of water and stand by gaining experience in measuring, comparing, observing, problem solving, classifying, comparing, determining cause and effect, and evaluating. They gain con-ceptual understanding of volume and measurement, and construct explanations and under-standing through reasoning and logical thinking.

Children develop language as they discuss their actions informally or evaluate activity with the teacher. Sand and water play naturally encourage cooperation and social interaction as children work together and share materials (Beaver, 2002).

Figure 8-3   Give each child unstructured time to spend experimenting with a variety of materials.

Reflect On This

Why do some children play in the sink in the bathroom?

Planning and Preparing the Environment

When setting the stage for sensory play, support children's exploration by providing space for messy activities and materials that can be fully explored without concern about waste (Feeney, Moravcik, and Nolte 2010). Structure the centers so children have interesting and challenging materials to stimulate their water and sand play. Depending on the type and size of the area used for the water and sand activities, decide when and if you should limit the number of children playing at one time. Have smocks, aprons, and changes of clothes available for the children!

Sensory play can take place indoors or outdoors. The best place indoors is near the art area where floors are not carpeted and can be mopped or swept easily. If the sensory play area is carpeted, the floor can be protected with a sheet of vinyl from the hardware store. Towels or newspaper can be put down on the floor to absorb water spills. The sensory table should be placed so that all four sides are accessible for the children to use. For toddlers, who cannot share and spill a lot, separate trays or dishpans placed on a table covered by towels or newspapers works well. Another set up for this age group is to use a low sand and water play table or large plastic container set on towels placed on the floor. This allows toddlers to kneel so the smock covers to their knees and their shoes do not get wet or full of sand. Messy materials such as cornstarch and water or

Silly Putty will generally be put in smaller containers and placed on tables or inside the larger sand and water play table.

Outdoors the sand and water table is best placed in a shady area that can be easily supervised. When placed near dramatic play structures, play in both areas can be integrated. Placing the sandbox away from the building entrance can reduce the amount of sand tracked indoors. A sturdy cover is needed for the sandbox, and the sandbox should be covered when not in use. Water play tables should be cleaned and sanitized at least daily, and after each use by a classroom group of children unless the water play structure uses running water, which can drain out of the structure. Outdoors is a good place to do big messy projects such as washing and scrubbing the classroom chairs, setting up a car wash for the tricycles, washing doll clothes and hanging them up on a clothesline, or using hoses or buckets to study the effects of erosion in the sandbox.

Props and Materials

Props and materials should be stored on a low, accessible shelf or in bins under the water play table. Wet props should be cleaned and sanitized along with the water play table and allowed to air dry before they are put up. The following is a suggested list of props and materials to include in water, sand, and mud play. It is best to use dry, finely textured sand (available at toy stores and lumber, building, or garden supply stores). Use plastic props and containers, if possible, because metal will rust. "Take note of which materials the children seem to use most and start with just a few simple props, such as plastic bottles or dolls to wash. Gradually add props to introduce a range of new possibilities" (Dodge, Colker, and Heroman, 2008, p. 409). (See **Table 8-1**.)

TABLE 8-1: Props and Materials for Water, Sand, and Mud Play	
Suggested Props	
Basters	Rotary eggbeaters
Eyedroppers	Spray bottles
Funnels	Cookie cutters
Measuring cups and spoons	Gelatin molds
Scoops	Salt shakers
Sieves	Scale
Colander	Sand timer
Straws	Sand combs
Slotted spoon	Spoons and shovels
Buckets, pails, and tubs	Bowls and pitchers
Magnifying glass	Paintbrushes
Plastic tubing	Sponges
Child-size brooms and dust pan	Pulleys
	Bubbles

TABLE 8-1: Props and Materials for Water, Sand, and Mud Play (continued)

Suggested Containers

Sand and water table	Outdoor sand pile
Wading pool	Wash tubs
Dishpan	Boxes
Bathtub	Infant tub

Suggested Substitutes for Sand

Aquarium gravel	Cork pieces
Small pet bedding (avoid cedar and pine materials because of allergies)	Styrofoam pieces
Seashells	Birdseed
Washed gravel	

The Learning Environment

naeyc

The actual physical environment plays a large role in enhancing sensory development. (See **Figure 8-4**.) A checklist can be used to evaluate the sensory environment that you observe in your own classroom or classrooms.

Figure 8-4 Whisking liquid in a bowl is a fun sensory activity.

Sensory Environment Checklist

_____ 1. Are sensory activities available as a choice activity on a daily basis, either indoors or outdoors?

_____ 2. Is the water clean and fresh?

_____ 3. Does the sensory table allow for child access from all sides?

_____ 4. Is sand and water play available daily, either indoors or outdoors?

_____ 5. Are the floors easy to clean?

_____ 6. Is there adequate storage for materials to use?

_____ 7. Are there a variety of props for water play such as whisks, buckets, squirt bottles, cups, funnels, water wheel, or floating toys?

_____ 8. Is the sensory area near a sink or other water source for easy clean up?

_____ 9. Is there a sufficient amount of sand and materials for digging sifting, molding, and pouring?

_____ 10. Are long-sleeved, waterproof smocks easily accessible to the children?

_____ 11. Is the water bleach free?

_____ 12. Does the sensory center provide a variety of interesting props?

_____ 13. Is the floor cleaned when spills occur?

_____ 14. Are literacy materials included in the sensory center?

_____ 15. Is water emptied after each group of children is done playing?

_____ 16. Are tubs and toys washed and sanitized daily?

_____ 17. Does the classroom avoid materials that pose a choking hazard?

_____ 18. Are children with cuts, scratches, and open sores excluded from using the sensory table?

_____ 19. Do children and adults wash their hands both before and after playing in the sensory table?

⌄⌄ Professional Resource Download

Integrating Sensory Play into the Curriculum

INTASC

Water, sand, and mud play can be an individual or a small group activity. Projects can be done indoors and outdoors. There is no right or wrong way to play with these multisensory materials. They are used in many different ways by the children using them. Even young children enjoy splashing, pouring, squishing, and mixing. Water, sand, and mud can relate to any theme, lesson plan, or curriculum web. (See **Figure 8-5** on curriculum planning web.)

Water play can be lively and at the same time relaxing. Young children enjoy running through a sprinkler, playing at the water table, bathing dolls in a plastic tub, filling and emptying water containers, and watering plants. It is fun, and children are naturally drawn to water play.

Stephenson (2001, p. 10) clarifies the importance of outdoor water play for toddlers:

> " Looking through George's eyes revealed to me the wonder of this strange sloppy substance that uncontrollably slides through fingers and disappears irretrievably into sand. Babies spend many hours handling solid objects yet have relatively limited opportunities to experiment with liquids, so it is not surprising that water is such a deeply fascinating material. "

Sand play is irresistible to young children. Starting with dry sand in the sand pile, sand tray, or sand table, children can spoon, pour, measure, dig, and shovel. They add props as

Figure 8-5   A curriculum planning web using the children's book *My Five Senses* by Aliki.

they construct cities, farms, and airports, and they love to drive trucks through and over sandy roads. (See **Figure 8-6** on sand play.)

Adding water to sand creates opportunities for additional sensory learning to take place. Combining props such as sunglasses, hats, towels, and an umbrella can turn the outdoor sand area into a beach. Have you tried adding live small crabs in a sand bucket to the "beach?" The children will be fascinated.

Mud play is a sensory activity like no other. After a rain, the playground takes on an added dimension. It is special. What you and the children do with the mud offers many possibilities. Try experimenting with a bucketful of mud. Make mud pies or "pizza," for example. Mix the mud to make paint. Brush the mud on different textures of paper. Dirt taken from different areas of the playground shows different pigmentations, which the children themselves will point out to you.

Nimmo and Hallett (2008, p. 32) offer another suggestion for exploration with mud:

“Gardens by their very nature involve mud—a phenomenon that simultaneously inspires delight in young children and a wonderfully interesting reaction from adults. Mud

Figure 8-6 Sand play is irresistible to young children. They can spoon, pour, measure, dig, and shovel this fascinating substance.

inspires children to wonder about the transformation of passive dirt into an almost sinister substance. It resists muscles when a child is in the thick of it and speaks to the child's need to explore nature. "

This child-centered activity of mud play offers children another way to experience their world. As we are spending so much of our time on concrete, it is important to remember to save a spot of earth for our growing children.

Jensen and Bullard (2002, p. 16) reminisce about the pleasures of creating mud pies and mud sandwiches and holding tea parties with a variety of mud treats. "We [remember] the deep sense of satisfaction in baking mud pies for the entire neighborhood. . . . Our children are affected by traffic, lack of space, and schedules that allow little time for outdoor play. . . . [As a result,] the idea of a mud center outdoors [at a child care center or school] emerges from the interests of both children and adults."

Purposes and Objectives
naeyc

When you plan opportunities for children to grow developmentally and practice skills in the water, sand, and mud learning centers, you are providing relevant meaningful learning experiences. Encourage children to do the following activities.

Develop Inquiry-Based Learning
Investigate to gather information about water, sand, mud, and rocks. Ask questions. How does water get into the faucets? What is mud? What is a rock? Why are some rocks big and others little? What makes sand? What makes sand gritty? According to Ogu and Schmidt (2009, p. 12), "Because inquiry is such an intrinsic human learning strategy, it makes sense for teachers to use an inquiry-based approach in their curriculum."

Perform Simple Experiments
Predict whether objects will sink or float in plain water—try rocks, marbles, Styrofoam, ping-pong balls, coins, corks, and sponges. Add salt to the water to see whether the objects will sink or float. Explore various types of sand with magnets by running the magnet through the sand to see whether any grains stick to the magnet, or search for hidden metal objects buried in the sand. Discover how long it takes for water to evaporate outside on a hot or a cold day. Examine dirt using magnifying glasses and sifters.

Measure, Compare, and Problem Solve
Provide empty cardboard milk cartons, such as half-pint, pint, quart, and half-gallon containers, for children to pour from one carton to another to discover how much water each one holds. Measure equal amounts of wet and dry sand and put them on opposite sides of a balance scale to determine which is heavier. After a rain, ask the children to problem solve how to get the water out of a mud puddle.

Play Creatively
Provide soapy water, food coloring in the water, sponges, and washable toys for the children to clean. Experiment with sand molds and determine whether dry sand or wet sand works best. Have boat races with children, problem solving how to get their boats across the water-filled tub. (*Hint:* Children can either blow on the boats to make them move or pull them across with a string.) Make designs in the sand with sand combs made from pliable plastic

containers such as clean bleach or detergent bottles. Put out buckets and sponges to scrub the playground equipment. Set up a "truck wash" for sand box construction toys. Build underwater cities with Legos.

Develop New Vocabulary
Introduce words such as *pour, fill, flow, spray, squirt, splatter, empty, full, shallow, deep, measure, absorb, droplets, sift, sink, float, evaporate, melt,* and *dissolve*.

Demonstrate New Concepts
Demonstrate how gravity causes water to flow downhill through tubes and funnels, how water takes the shape of its container, and how the liquid form of water can change into a solid by freezing in ice trays, paper cups, or milk cartons. Offer indoor and outdoor water play often.

Activities in the Five Senses
The following activities involve all the senses. They are included in the curriculum web and are appropriate for young children to do.

Making Sandpaper
Provide cardstock, watery glue, paintbrushes, and containers of sand of various grades. Children first paint on one side of the cardstock with watery glue. Then they choose a grade of sand and sprinkle it on the card. Allow to dry overnight. When dry, the cards can be examined and touched by the children to compare how the different types of sand feel.

Whip It Up
Using a hand rotary eggbeater, dish pan, and liquid dishwashing detergent, children can turn the beaters and whip up bubbles in the individual dishpan or the sand and water table.

Indoor Rainbow
Fill a clear glass jar with water and set on a windowsill in the bright sunlight. Place white paper on the floor to "capture the rainbow." The children can paint rainbows with watercolors.

Sensory Texture Box
You *can* make this for the infants and toddlers *or* you and the older children can make one. Use an appliance box at least three-feet square. Put several pounds of sand or gravel sacks in the bottom of the box to stabilize it. Close the box and tape down the flaps. Paint or decorate the box. Glue textured materials securely to the four sides of the box. Use sandpaper, cotton balls, egg cartons, kente cloth, silk flowers, foil, twigs, and other textured materials. This is a different kind of "texture board" for you and the children to enjoy in the classroom (adapted from Parks, 1994).

Make Place Mats
Make place mats for use at snack and mealtime. Cut out colorful labels from food packaging, magazines, or construction paper. Glue these on a piece of paper and laminate. The children can share these, or each child can use the one he or she made.

Let's Use All Our Senses
Set up a special "tasting tray" with foods that taste sweet, sour, salty, spicy, and bitter. Create "smell cards" using different spices and herbs secured to cards with white glue. (The glue does not have any odor.) Make "sound cans" by placing paper clips, beans, and so on in small, empty plastic containers. Make a "feely box" or "feely bag" filled with different items that emphasize shape and softness. Let the children feel an object and tell you what it feels like and what they think the items are without looking. Then they get to see if they guessed correctly or not.

As suggested in Chapter 3, using an activity plan worksheet will help you clearly describe the activity, objectives, concepts, skills, space and materials needed, step-by-step procedure, guidance and limits for expected behavior, and assessment and follow-up strategies. The following activity plan worksheet is an example for a developmentally appropriate sensory activity.

| Activity Plan Worksheet | Developmentally Appropriate Sensory Activity |

AGES: pre-kindergarten, kindergarten, and primary age children

Name of Activity and Brief Description

The Sand City activity is designed for children to explore their world on a miniature scale as they use measurement, tools, and blueprints to construct their own town or neighborhood out of sand in the sandbox.

Child Outcome of Activity

- Encourage cooperative problem solving.
- Develop math concepts, such as one-tone correspondence, counting, and measuring.
- Use tools such as: molds, scoops, shovels, and buckets.
- Strengthen eye-hand coordination.
- Develop small and large muscles.
- Dramatize adult career roles.
- Explore building and construction.

Space and Materials Needed

This can be done in the sandbox or sand table.

Suggested materials include: Toy trucks, bulldozers, and other heavy construction equipment; shovels, scoops, and trowels (blunt-ended); small boxes or other rectangular molds for making bricks; sprinkler cans or spray bottles for moistening sand; props such as construction hats, carpenter's apron or belt, lunchbox, small wheelbarrow, and metal tape measure; pieces of cardboard to brace excavations; sticks or dowels, string or surveyors tape; books with pictures of construction activity such as *Roxaboxen* by Alice McLerran and Barbara Cooney or *Mike Mulligan and His Steam Shovel* by Virginia Lee Burton; engineer's or architect's blueprint; large pieces of paper and blue Crayons for making blueprints; craft sticks, pieces of smooth the wood, small to medium sized cans or plastic containers for molding the sand, and leaves, stones and other items to add to sand buildings.

Note: This activity can be done with fewer materials, but the more variety of props, the more complex the play will become.

Procedure

- Read books to children about building and construction work. Discuss what construction workers do.
- If possible, take a field trip to a construction site.
- Show the children an engineer's or architect's blueprint and discuss how they use it. Discuss with the children what they want to build and then have them draw blueprints.
- Discuss various jobs involved in constructing buildings or roads and ask the children which roles they would like to play. (If this activity becomes a long-term recurring play theme, roles may change as the play progresses.)
- Discuss safety rules and let children develop their own.
- Help children map out the construction site using a metal tape and marking it with dowels in string or survey or tape.
- Let the children start digging and building.
- Make this activity a long-term project that children can return to by covering the sandbox daily to protect the children's work.

Guidance

Limit the number of children based on the size of the sand table or sandbox and remind the children that the sand should stay in the sand table or box. Act as a resource to discuss possible solutions to construction problems and conflicts the children cannot resolve without support. Be sure to allow the children to guide the direction and flow of the play.

Assessment and Follow-Up Strategies

Take photographs of the construction in progress. Work with the children to create a documentation board or class book using the photos to develop a timeline and have the children describe what they were doing in the pictures. Create a what I know, what I want to know, what I learned (KWL) chart or web with the children to document what they knew before starting to build, what they wanted to learn about their city and construction, and what they did learn in this activity.

Activity Plan Worksheet | Developmentally Appropriate Sensory Activity

AGES: 2- and 3-year-olds
Sand and Water Play Center

Name of Activity and Brief Description—Gourds and Goopy Stuff
Encourage children to explore the textures of gourds, pumpkins, and messy materials in the sensory table.

Child Outcomes of Activity
- Uses senses to explore and sensory language to describe properties of natural materials
- Examines and describes the texture of materials

Space and Materials Needed
Sensory table or dishpans, variety of size and shaped gourds and pumpkins, 1 box cornstarch, ½ to ¾ cup of water, 2 to 3 drops of food coloring, cups and scoops, smocks

Procedure
1. Show the children the pumpkins and gourds, and let them feel and describe the surfaces of them.
2. Let children help you make the goop mixture from cornstarch and water, adding a little food coloring, if desired.
3. Place the gourds and pumpkins in the sensory table.
4. Have children help you pour the goop mixture over the gourds and pumpkins.
5. Encourage children to rub and explore the feel of the gourds covered with the goop.
6. Describe children's actions as they play, using vocabulary that they might not regularly say.
7. Ask children questions about the texture of the materials.

Guidance
Make sure all the children have smocks on. Limit the number of children at the table to two to four so children have plenty of space to play. Have cleanup materials on hand. Remind children to keep the goop and the gourds in the sensory table.

Assessment and Follow-Up Strategies
Were child outcomes met? Yes___ No___
What was the children's response?
What worked well? What did not work?
How could this activity be changed to make it more effective or more appropriate?

⌄ Professional Resource Download

Technology in Sensory Play

Technology & Teaching: Sensory Play

The use of digital and video cameras that can capture children's sense of wonder and discovery as they interact with sensory materials can enhance their learning by letting children revisit their explorations, discuss the discovery process, and document their experiences. Light tables or boxes enhance the visual impact of explorations. A light box can be used with children to explore objects with the added dimension of upward facing light and can be brilliant for investigating silhouettes, color mixing, X-rays, and patterns. An inexpensive light box can be made out of an opaque, under-bed storage tub, two strings of white Christmas lights, large sheets of white paper to diffuse the light, and two-sided tape to secure the paper to the box lid.

Diversity in Sensory Play

Sensory processing (sometimes called sensory integration, or SI) is a term that refers to the way the nervous system receives messages from the senses and turns them into appropriate motor and behavioral responses. Whether you are biting into a hamburger, riding a bicycle, or reading a book, your successful completion of the activity requires processing sensation or "sensory integration."

Sensory processing disorder (SPD, formerly known as sensory integration dysfunction) is a condition that exists when sensory signals don't get organized into appropriate responses. Although not recognized by the American Academy of Pediatrics as a separate diagnosis, pioneering occupational therapist and neuroscientist A. Jean Ayres, PhD, likened SPD to a neurological "traffic jam" that prevents certain parts of the brain from receiving the information needed to interpret sensory information correctly. A person with SPD finds it difficult to process and act on information received through the senses, which creates challenges in performing countless everyday tasks. Motor clumsiness, behavioral problems, anxiety, depression, school failure, and other impacts may result if the disorder is not treated effectively.

One study (Ahn, Miller, Milberger, and McIntosh, 2004) shows that SPD affects at least 1 in 20 children's daily lives. Another research study by the Sensory Processing Disorder Scientific Work Group (Ben-Sasson, Carter, and Briggs-Gowen, 2009) suggests that 1 in every 6 children experiences sensory symptoms that may be significant enough to affect aspects of everyday life functions. Symptoms of SPD, like those of most disorders, occur within a broad spectrum of severity. These symptoms range from oversensitivity to sounds, taste, or light; lack of coordination; not being able to tell where their limbs are in space; and inability to engage in conversations or play. Although most of us have occasional difficulties processing sensory information, for children and adults with SPD, these difficulties are chronic, and they disrupt everyday life.

How Can Teachers and Families Help?

- Observe the child's response to various types of sensory stimuli during everyday activities that impact behavior.
- Provide sensory rich opportunities such as music, play, or varied textures throughout the day to support sensory needs.
- Encourage active play such as on playgrounds and limit sedentary activities such as television and computer games.
- Seek advice from an occupational therapist, including someone with specialized training in sensory integration if appropriate, to determine further need for evaluation and intervention.
- Consult a physician, when appropriate, for a referral to an occupational therapist that is knowledgeable about sensory processing approaches.
- Consult with your school district's special education team to determine whether the child is eligible to receive school-based occupational therapy services (Roley, Bissell, and Clark, 2009, p. 825).

sensory processing: The way the nervous system receives messages from the senses and turns them into appropriate motor and behavioral responses.

sensory processing disorder: Condition that exists when sensory signals don't get organized into appropriate responses.

Creating Partnerships with Families

Sensory play is messy, and parents often worry about things like wet or dirty clothing and sand in the hair. Be sure to explain in your parent policies or newsletter about your use of sensory play materials and the guidelines you use to protect children's health and safety, such as covering the sandbox while not in use, asking parents to bring a extra set of clothing, including a shower cap for children who don't want to get sand in their hair.

PBS.org has many resources that you can share with parents including an article "Developing and Cultivating Skills Through Sensory Play" by Danielle Steinberg that includes a few examples of easy, inexpensive, and creative ways to suggest to parents to engage children in sensory play at home. Some examples follow.

Touch

- Play games that require the use of muscles: jump on the bed, crab walk, make a fort or an obstacle course, play leapfrog or hopscotch, catching games using different objects like stuffed animals, water balloons or bean bags, and play tug-of-war.
- Include your child in chores that encourage the use of muscles: let him or her push a laundry basket or grocery cart or clean together (wiping the counters, sweeping, mopping . . . every parent's dream come true).
- Make use of stimulating textures or objects around your house. Go on a texture scavenger hunt, sip seltzer, or drink through a straw.

Sight

- Experiment with light around your home: play by candlelight, play flashlight tag, make shadow puppets, and wear sunglasses.
- Explore with colors: Add food coloring to bath water, paint each other's faces, or tie-dye clothes or other fabrics.
- Test the sense of sight by playing catch, completing mazes or dot-to-dot puzzles, tracing your body or hands, or playing "I Spy," peek-a-boo, or a variation of hide-and-seek.

Hearing

- Play or listen to an instrument or sing songs, sit quietly and try to guess the sounds you hear, make a chart of things you hear outside, or talk about different animal sounds you've heard.
- Experiment with volume: Play with the stereo dial to investigate loud and soft sounds.

Smell

- Use your kitchen: cook with strong-smelling scents (e.g., garlic, ginger, cocoa, lemon, vinegar, vanilla, mint, lavender); match scents while blindfolded (in opaque containers).
- Make use of the great outdoors: go on a "smelly walk" (wet grass, fertilizer, bakery), plant flowers.
- Read scratch-and-sniff books.

Reflect On This

What would you do if a child in your care refused to touch mud or finger paint? Why do you think the child would respond this way?

Case Study: Messy Sensory Play

Mary Jane is the first-year lead teacher in the first grade classroom in the Oklahoma City Central Early Childhood Learning Center. Her principal is observing Mary Jane for her annual teacher evaluation. Although this is the first time she has been officially evaluated, the principal has observed her many times on random visits in the classroom. A concern the principal has talked to Mary Jane about in the past is the fact that Mary Jane doesn't like to incorporate "messy" sensory play as a regular activity.

Mary Jane is really concerned about neatness and getting messy and always wears aprons when her class is participating in activities in which she might get her clothes dirty.

She also doesn't think children learn anything from this messy play. The principal wants to talk to her about ways she can get more involved in sensory play.

What Do You Think?
1. What might be some possible causes for this teacher's aversion to sensory activities?
2. What could you tell this teacher about why sensory play is so important to children?
3. What are some strategies Mary Jane can use to set up an environment to make cleanup easier while still allowing children to fully explore the sensory experience.

The Teacher's Role

Guidance for Sensory Play

The following suggestions should be helpful to you in defining the teacher's role in water, sand, and mud play:

- Empty water after each group of children is done playing.
- Wash and sanitize the tub and toys daily.
- Make sure that children with cuts, scratches, and open sores do not use the table or that they wear disposable rubber gloves.
- Have children wash their hands both before and after playing in the sensory table.
- Avoid any materials that the children in your classroom might be allergic to.
- Do not use materials that pose a choking hazard if working with younger children.
- Clean up the floor when spills occur.
- Remember the safety and health rules of water, sand, and mud play: (1) Never leave children unattended around any type of water; (2) empty the water tub or table daily; (3) sanitize the water, wet sand toys, and tub each day with a fresh bleach solution of one tablespoon bleach to one quart of water in a spray bottle, and rinse with running water (Miller, 1994); and (4) check the sand and mud play areas each day for foreign objects, such as glass, that should be removed.
- Limit the number of children at the sand or water table usually to no more than four for preschool or school-age children.
- Remind children that the water or sand stays in the table, sandbox, or in containers to avoid splashing friends, carrying water across the room or emptying the sand onto nearby sidewalks.
- Cover the sandbox or water play table when not in use.

TEACHING TIPS Water Play

- Observe, ask open-ended questions, and make comments to show support and interest. "The children learn what it means to answer an open-ended question: there are no right or wrong answers, all ideas are accepted, valued, and appreciated and become part of the learning process" (Ogu and Schmidt, 2009, p. 17).
- Allow children to get messy. That is when true learning takes place as they become involved.
- Encourage children to talk about what they are doing and what is happening.
- Offer indoor and outdoor water play often. "The sensory table encourages children's development of skills through natural exploration and discovery. . . . Observing children play at the sensory table can give teachers more information about how individuals react to sensory stimulation" (Hunter, 2008, p. 77). (See **Figure 8-7**.)
- Take your cues from the children on what to change and when to change it.
- Discuss with older children the importance of water and the shortages that will arise if we do not work to preserve this resource. Get the children's families involved, too.

Figure 8-7 Offer indoor and outdoor water play often.

- Avoid using any food such as pudding, dried beans, uncooked rice or macaroni, and uncooked oatmeal in sensory play.
- Make cleanup part of the process by providing materials such as child-sized brooms and mops near the sensory play area.

Summary

1. **What are some key terms related to sensory play?**
   - **Sensory experiences** are experiences that use the senses and offer opportunities for free exploration in a variety of curriculum areas.
   - **Sensory awareness** is the use of the senses.
   - **Sensory processing** is the way the nervous system receives messages from the senses and turns them into appropriate motor and behavioral responses.
   - **Sensory processing disorder** is a condition that exists when sensory signals don't get organized into appropriate responses.

2. **What are the stages of sensory play?** The first stage of sensory play is about exploration. What is the object? What is it like? The feeling of discovery as each sense is employed to explore the properties of the object in question is enough to keep a child entertained for hours. As children get older, they tend to play in a more complex way, combining objects and other resources to ask, What can I do with it? What can it become? This most creative stage of play inspires the imagination. In the third stage of the continuum, adult facilitation can be employed to alter and adapt the realms of play. As children grow, play becomes increasingly elaborate with their age, developmental level, or familiarity with the resources. Children frequently move from single object play to more complex play with multiple objects.

3. **What are the components of planning and preparation of a sensory environment?** When setting the stage for sensory play, support children's exploration by providing space for messy activities and materials that can be fully explored without concern about waste. Structure the centers so children have interesting and challenging materials to stimulate their water and sand play. Depending on the type and size of the area used for the water and sand activities, decide when and if you should limit the number of children playing at one time. Sensory play can take place indoors or outdoors. The best place indoors is near the art area where floors are not carpeted and can be mopped or swept easily. If the sensory play area is carpeted, the floor can be protected with a sheet of vinyl from the hardware store. Towels or newspaper can be put down on the floor to absorb water spills. The sensory table should be placed so that all four sides are accessible for the children to use. For toddlers, who cannot share and spill a lot, separate trays or dishpans placed on a table covered by towels or newspapers works well. Another setup for this age group, is to use a low sand and water play table or large plastic container set on towels placed on the floor. This allows toddlers to kneel so the smock covers to their knees and their shoes do not get wet or full of sand. Messy materials such as cornstarch and water or Silly Putty will generally be put in smaller containers and placed on tables or inside the larger sand and water play table.

   Outdoors, the sand and water table is best placed in a shady area that can be easily supervised. When placed near dramatic play structures, play in both areas can be integrated. Placing the sandbox away from the building entrance can reduce the amount of sand tracked indoors. A sturdy cover is needed for the sandbox, and the sandbox should be covered when not in use. Water play tables should be cleaned and sanitized at least daily, and after each use by a classroom group of children unless the water play structure uses running water, which can drain out of the structure. Outdoors is a good place to do big, messy projects such as washing and scrubbing the classroom chairs, setting up a car wash for the tricycles, washing doll clothes and hanging them up on a clothesline, or using hoses or buckets to study the effects of erosion in the sandbox.

Props and materials should be stored on a low, accessible shelf or in bins under the water play table. Wet props should be cleaned and sanitized along with the water play table and allowed to air dry before they are put up. Use plastic props and containers, if possible, because metal will rust. Gradually add props to introduce a range of new possibilities.

4. **What are some guidelines for adding sensory activities to the curriculum?**
   ● Develop inquiry-based learning.
   ● Investigate to gather information about water, sand, mud, and rocks.

Perform Simple Experiments

● Predict whether objects will sink or float in plain water—try rocks, marbles, Styrofoam, ping-pong balls, coins, corks, and sponges.
● Measure, compare, and problem solve.
● Provide empty cardboard milk cartons, such as half-pint, pint, quart, and half-gallon containers, for children to pour from one carton to another to discover how much water each one holds.
● Provide soapy water, food coloring in the water, sponges, and washable toys for the children to clean.
   Introduce words such as *pour, fill, flow, spray, squirt, splatter, empty, full, shallow, deep, measure, absorb, droplets, sift, sink, float, evaporate, melt,* and *dissolve.*
● Demonstrate how gravity causes water to flow downhill through tubes and funnels, how water takes the shape of its container, and how the liquid form of water can change into a solid by freezing in ice trays, paper cups, or milk cartons. Offer indoor and outdoor water play often.
● Provide cardstock, watery glue, paintbrushes, and containers of sand of various grades.
● Using a hand rotary eggbeater, dish pan, and liquid dishwashing detergent, children can turn the beaters and whip up bubbles in the individual dishpan or the sand and water table.
● Fill a clear glass jar with water and set on a windowsill in the bright sunlight. Place white paper on the floor to "capture the rainbow." The children can paint rainbows with watercolors.
● Use an appliance box at least three-feet square. Put several pounds of sand or gravel sacks in the bottom of the box to stabilize it. Close the box and tape down the flaps. Paint or decorate the box. Glue textured materials securely to the four sides of the box. Use sandpaper, cotton balls, egg cartons, kente cloth, silk flowers, foil, twigs, and other textured materials. This is a different kind of "texture board" for you and the children to enjoy in the classroom.
● Make place mats for use at snack and meal time.
● Set up a special "tasting tray" with foods that taste sweet, sour, salty, spicy, and bitter.
● Create "smell cards" using different spices and herbs secured to cards with white glue. (The glue does not have any odor.)
● Make "sound cans" by placing paper clips, beans, and so on in small, empty plastic containers.
● Make a "feely box" or "feely bag" filled with different items that emphasize shape and softness. Let the children feel an object and tell you what it feels like and what they think the items are without looking.

5. **How can you use technology in a sensory environment?** The use of digital and video cameras that can capture children's sense of wonder and discovery as they interact with sensory materials can enhance their learning by letting children revisit their explorations, discuss the discovery process, and document their experiences. Light tables or boxes enhance the visual impact of explorations. A light box can be used with children to explore objects with the added dimension

of upward facing light and can be brilliant for investigating silhouettes, color mixing, X-rays, and patterns. An inexpensive light box can be made out of an opaque, under-bed storage tub, two strings of white Christmas lights, large sheets of white paper to diffuse the light and two-sided tape to secure the paper to the box lid.

6. **How can you incorporate diversity into sensory play?**
   - Observe the child's response to various types of sensory stimuli during everyday activities that impact behavior.
   - Provide sensory-rich opportunities such as music, play, or varied textures throughout the day to support sensory needs.
   - Encourage active play such as on playgrounds and limit sedentary activities such as television and computer games.
   - Seek advice from an occupational therapist, including someone with specialized training in sensory integration if appropriate, to determine further need for evaluation and intervention.
   - Consult a physician, when appropriate, for a referral to an occupational therapist that is knowledgeable about sensory processing approaches.
   - Consult with your school district's special education team to determine whether the child is eligible to receive school-based occupational therapy services.

7. **How can you develop partnerships with families that support child sensory play?**
   - Play games that require the use of muscles: jump on the bed, crab walk, make a fort or an obstacle course; play leapfrog or hopscotch, catching games using different objects like stuffed animals, water balloons or bean bags, and play tug-of-war.
   - Include your child in chores that encourage the use of muscles: Let him or her push a laundry basket or grocery cart or clean together (wiping the counters, sweeping, mopping—every parent's dream come true).
   - Make use of stimulating textures or objects around your house. Go on a texture scavenger hunt; sip seltzer, or drink through a straw.
   - Experiment with light around your home: Play by candlelight, play flashlight tag, make shadow puppets, and wear sunglasses.
   - Explore with colors: Add food coloring to bath water, paint each other's faces, or tie-dye clothes or other fabrics.
   - Test the sense of sight by playing catch, completing mazes or dot-to-dot puzzles, tracing your body or hands, and playing "I Spy," peek-a-boo, or a variation of hide-and-seek.
   - Play or listen to an instrument or sing songs, sit quietly and try to guess the sounds you hear, make a chart of things you hear outside, or talk about different animal sounds you've heard.
   - Experiment with volume: Play with the stereo dial to investigate loud and soft sounds.
   - Use your kitchen: Cook with strong-smelling scents (e.g., garlic, ginger, cocoa, lemon, vinegar, vanilla, mint, lavender); match scents while blindfolded (in opaque containers).
   - Make use of the great outdoors: Go on a "smelly walk" (wet grass, fertilizer, bakery); plant flowers.
   - Read scratch-and-sniff books.

8. **What is the teacher's role in promoting sensory play in the classroom?**
   - Empty water after each group of children is done playing.
   - Wash and sanitize the tub and toys daily.
   - Make sure that children with cuts, scratches, and open sores do not use the table or that they wear disposable rubber gloves.
   - Have children wash their hands both before and after playing in the sensory table.
   - Avoid any materials that the children in your classroom might be allergic to.
   - Do not use materials that pose a choking hazard if working with younger children.
   - Clean up the floor when spills occur.

- Remember the safety and health rules of water, sand, and mud play: (1) Never leave children unattended around any type of water; (2) empty the water tub or table daily; (3) sanitize the water, wet sand toys, and tub each day with a fresh bleach solution of one tablespoon bleach to one quart of water in a spray bottle, and rinse with running water; and (4) check the sand and mud play areas each day for foreign objects, such as glass, that should be removed.
- Limit the number of children at the sand or water table usually to no more than four for preschool or school-age children.
- Remind children that the water or sand stays in the table, sandbox, or in containers to avoid splashing friends, carrying water across the room, or emptying the sand onto nearby sidewalks.
- Cover the sandbox or water play table when not in use.
- Avoid using any food such as pudding, dried beans, uncooked rice or macaroni, and uncooked oatmeal in sensory play.
- Make cleanup part of the process by providing materials such as child-sized brooms and mops near the sensory play area.

Reflective Review Questions

1. What is meant by sensory experiences of young children? Why are these important in the sensory play?
2. Discuss why sensory activities can offer problem-solving experiences to young children. Identify by sharing examples of at least two activities.
3. Why should you avoid using food as a medium to explore in sensory play experiences that do not involve tasting? Identify some alternatives you could use.

Explorations

1. Select an early education classroom and observe for at least one hour. Describe, in writing, six sensory activities the children were involved in at the time you were observing. What did you learn from this observation? Did any of these activities explore diverse cultures?
2. As stated in this chapter, young children are attracted to water. They enjoy pouring, measuring, splashing, and siphoning water. Observe children involved in water play. Describe the learning experiences taking place. To which curriculum do they relate? Math, science, social studies, language, art? List the supplies and materials used.
3. Select and plan a language activity for young children. Specify which age group this activity is planned for: infants, toddlers, preschoolers, or primary-age children. In writing, list objectives, materials needed, step-by-step procedures for presenting this activity, follow-up activities, and evaluation guidelines. (Use the activity plan worksheet in Appendix D.) Prepare this activity and demonstrate it during class or with a group of children.
4. Use the Sensory Environment Checklist in this chapter to conduct an observation of an early childhood learning environment.
   - Beside each statement, place an X if the classroom you observed met the statement.
   - On a separate sheet of paper, describe what you actually observed related to each statement. Place the number of the statement first, and then write your observation.
   - On a separate sheet of paper, for each statement that you did not check as met, describe what you would do to improve that classroom so that the statement would be met. Be sure to put the number of the statement first.
   - Submit this with the name of the location you observed and the age group.

Language and Literacy Books for Young Children

Sensory Play Books for Young Children

Arnold, T. (1998). *No More Water in the Tub*. New York: Puffin Picture Books.

Locker, T. (2002). *Water Dance*. New York: Voyager Books/Harcourt, Inc.

Lopez, M., Wong, M. L., and Roos, M. (2009). *Mud Tacos*. New York: Celebra/Penguin.

Overback Bix, C., and Rauzon, M. (1995). *Water, Water Everywhere*. San Francisco: Sierra Club Books for Children.

Ray, M. L., Springer, L. (2001). *Mud*. New York: Voyager Books/Harcourt, Inc.

Ryan, P. M. (2002). *Mud Is Cake*. New York: Hyperion.

Winslow, M., and Blegvad, E. (2010). *Mud Pies and Other Recipes*. New York: Review of Books.

Ziefert, H., and Demarest, C. L. (2001). *Brothers Are for Making Mud Pies*. New York: Penguin Puffin Books.

⌄ **Professional Resource Download**

9 Science

Standards Covered in This Chapter

 NAEYC 5a, 5b, 5c

DAP DAP 2

INTASC INTASC 4, 5, 8

HS HEAD START
Domain: Scientific Reasoning
Domain: Cognition

NSES NSES

NAEYC, DAP, and INTASC standards described on Part II introduction page

Student Learning Outcomes

After studying this chapter, you should be able to:

- Define and give examples for key terms related to science for children.

- Discuss science for young children and relate stages of child development to scientific learning.

- Evaluate various components of planning and preparation of environments that support scientific exploration.

- Integrate and create science activities appropriate for young children.

- Discuss various ways to use technology in an environment that supports scientific exploration.

- Distinguish ways to incorporate diversity into science activities.

- Describe ways to develop partnerships with families that support children's exploration of science.

- Analyze the teacher's role in promoting science in the classroom.

The science curriculum in an early childhood environment should shout, "Please touch! Please explore!" We must nourish young children's excitement about learning and encourage them to ask, "What would happen if . . . ?" and then give them the materials to find out the answers. These active encounters help children define basic concepts and stimulate natural curiosity, exploration, and discovery.

As we discuss throughout this text, all children learn about the world around them through their senses. Infants and toddlers, as well as preschoolers and primary children, base their scientific knowledge on what they see, hear, taste, smell, and touch. A developmentally appropriate science curriculum expands on this basic fact of child growth and development by stimulating observation, inquiry, interest, and verbalization.

As a teacher, you will also observe, question, predict, experiment, and verify many scientific occurrences along with the children. That is what science in early childhood is all about: setting the environmental stage for finding out about the world. Encourage young children to want to know, "What's in *my* environment? What effect do *I* have? What changes can *I* make?" Attitudes are formed early. We should nurture young children's natural curiosity and their need to know *why*, which will, in turn, encourage future scientific exploration and enthusiasm.

As you brainstorm ways to make exploration and discovery take place, you will come to realize that to have a good science program, skillful integration into the total life of the classroom is required. Part of this encouragement can be to spontaneously and creatively change the physical environment (indoor room arrangement) when the children initiate and motivate the changes, and to take advantage of what is happening in the outdoor environment. Materials that can be manipulated and reconstructed should be included. Plenty of time should be allowed so that questions can be asked, assumptions can be explored, and ideas can be expanded. This can provide the spark for a lifelong love of science.

Continue to display your own enthusiasm for science and discovery in our world. Ziemer (1987, p. 44) offers us a stimulating way to do this:

> " When you look up to the highest branches of an oak tree on an early summer morning, you may not be thinking of scientific principles operating to get nutrients from the soil, up the trunk, and out to every newly forming leaf and embryo acorn. But you have an awareness of it, and guiding your small students to be aware also is part of teaching science. Ask wondering questions: "I wonder what makes the leaves so green." "I wonder how long it took this tree to grow so tall." . . . We may not be teaching facts, but we are teaching curiosity. "

Science in Early Childhood Defined

Science is a combination of both process skills and content or how children learn and what children learn. **Process skills** allow children to process new information through concrete experiences. These build on and overlap each other. These process skills are also known as **inquiry** skills. An inquiry is a questioning process that can be developed in young children. The opposite of rote learning, it encourages their natural curiosity and exploration.

In 1996, the National Research Council published the *National Science Education Standards*, which were designed to support the development of a scientifically literate society.

New theoretical ideas and empirical research show that very young children's learning and thinking are strikingly similar to much learning and thinking in science. Preschoolers test hypotheses against data and make causal inferences; they learn from statistics and informal experimentation, and from watching and listening to others (Gopnik, A., 2012).

> " From the earliest grades, students should experience science in a form that engages them in the active construction of ideas and explanations that enhance their opportunities to

process skills: The ability to process new information through concrete experiences.

inquiry: A questioning process that encourages curiosity and exploration. The opposite of rote learning.

develop abilities of doing science. Teaching science as inquiry provides teachers with the opportunity to develop student abilities and to enrich student understanding of science. Students should do science in ways that are within their developmental capabilities. . . . Full inquiry involves asking a simple question, completing an investigation, answering the question, and presenting the results to others (National Research Council, 1996, pp. 121–122). **"**

The science curriculum content for young children responds to their need to learn about the world around them. As teachers, you know that children learn by doing. Therefore, the best way to learn science is to do science. Teachers would create a large part of the curriculum based on child-initiated, child-centered experiences.

The core of all science is observation. From the starting point of observing, children continue their investigation by comparing, classifying, measuring, communicating, inferring, and predicting. As a teacher, you should teach less and experience more by observing how eagerly the children use their senses to discover, to think about their experiences, and to talk about what they have seen and done. You will be learning right along with the children as you reinforce their curiosity and natural interests. Children learn science through a context of both past experiences and present environment. Science teaching strategies require a cooperative environment where children and teachers interact in the problem-solving process as co-inquirers.

Essa (2013, p. 193) believes, "Science concepts need to be concrete and observable. A concept that is abstract and not within the realm of children's experiences is not appropriate." Children learn science concepts through social interactions. While observing and working with other children in learning centers, cooperative groups, and paired activities, children exchange ideas, engage in science projects, and discuss their findings. Accordingly, based on the National Research Council standards, the fundamental science concepts and knowledge should be determined by what the children see and do each day and their developmental growth. The suggested categories are:

science as inquiry: Offers frequent opportunities to question, investigate, clarify, predict, and communicate with others.

life science: The study of living things, people, plants, and animals.

physical science: The sciences (physics, chemistry, meteorology, and astronomy) that relate to nonliving materials.

chemistry: The science dealing with the composition and transformations of substances.

earth and space science: The study of Earth materials, objects in the sky, and changes in the Earth and sky.

geology: The study of the materials that make up Earth, such as rocks and shells.

meteorology: The science of weather and atmosphere.

- **Science as inquiry**—offers frequent opportunities for children to question, investigate, classify, predict, and communicate with others. "Teachers modeling the use of 'I wonder . . .', 'What if . . . ?', and 'How can we find out?' introduces children to the basis of science inquiry. When children pose a question, we can introduce the process of observing, researching, creating, and testing hypotheses, and collaborating to find answers" (Bosse, Jacobs, and Anderson, 2009, p. 10).

- **Life science**—the study of living people, plants, and animals, including the functions and parts of living organisms (a butterfly's transformation cycle, for example). "Life science investigations lend themselves to simple observations, explorations, and classifications" (Charlesworth and Lind, 2010, p. 450).

- **Physical science**—the study of nonliving materials. It includes the study of matter (solids, liquids, and gases) and energy (light, heat, sound, electricity, motion, and magnetism) and their laws, such as gravity (an infant dropping a spoon from a high chair), balance (a child building an unbalanced block tower that falls), and **chemistry**, the science dealing with the composition and transformations of substances (such as those that occur in cooking).

"Young children enjoy pushing on levers, making bulbs light, working with magnets, using a string-and-can telephone, and changing matter. This is the study of physical science—forces, motion, energy, and machines. . . . Keep in mind that children are growing up in a technological world. They interact daily with technology. It is likely that future lifestyles and opportunities may depend on skills related to the realm of physical science (Charlesworth and Lind, 2010, p. 466). **"**

- **Earth and space science**—the study of Earth's materials, objects in the sky, and changes in the Earth and sky. It includes **geology**, the study of the materials that make up Earth, such as rocks and shells (for example, comparing a container of dirt from the playground with a container of dirt from a child's backyard); **meteorology**—the science of weather and atmosphere; and **astronomy**—the study of the universe beyond Earth's atmosphere, such as the sun, moon, planets, and stars.

- **Science in personal and social perspectives**—a developing understanding of personal health, changes in the environments, and ways to conserve and recycle (National Research Council, 1996). This includes ecology.
- **Ecology**—the relationship between living things and their environment and each other (caring for classroom plants and animals helps young children understand this concept).
- **Science and technology** focuses on establishing connections between natural and manmade items. Simple tools such as a kitchen timer, an apple peeler, a potato masher, and a flashlight invite children's hands-on investigations of how technical objects operate. "Opportunities for children to use developmentally appropriate software and digital cameras can be catalysts for curiosity and wonder" (Bosse, Jacobs, and Anderson, 2009, p. 10).

"The visions of both state and national standards serve to validate our belief that science is an ongoing process that requires children to be able to construct their own knowledge. . . . Learning is not a race for information; it is a walk of discovery (Buchanan and Rios, 2004, p. 82)."

Give children many open-ended opportunities to investigate, self-discover, and problem solve. Use the "hands-on, minds-on" approach that Grieshaber and Diezmann (2000) suggest. Find out what children know at the beginning of any scientific investigation. Ask the children questions and listen carefully to their answers. Work with the children to identify particular areas in which they want to further their understanding about the topic. Then, in small groups, the children decide how the investigation will proceed. Continue by actually investigating, exploring, and discovering. Examples of observation and exploration activities follow:

- Sensory exploration outdoors can include touching the bark of a tree or the grass, seeing the birds building nests or leaves blowing, hearing the sounds carried by the wind or the honking of a car horn nearby, smelling freshly cut grass or the fragrance of flowers, and tasting the vegetables grown in the school garden they helped to plant.
- Investigating the properties of items can be done using a magnifying glass to examine shells, rocks, feathers, or objects discovered on a nature walk.
- Children can problem solve while predicting or guessing which items will float or sink in a container filled with water.
- Using their naturalist intelligence, children can discriminate among living things (plants and animals) as well as develop sensitivity to the features of the natural world (clouds, rock configurations). "Some people from an early age are extremely good at recognizing and classifying artifacts. For example, we all know kids who, at age three or four, are better at recognizing dinosaurs than most adults" (Gardner, 1997, p. 9).

Give children many open-ended opportunities to question, to compare similarities and differences, and to use trial-and-error to try out their theories. Experimentation, verification, and discovery activities follow.

- With a teacher's supervision, children can experiment with cooking and discover how certain foods change through the cooking process, as well as what happens when foods are mixed together.
- Tasting different foods gives children a hands-on experience and at the same time enables them to discover the similarities and differences of ingredients such as flour, salt, and sugar.
- Classifying leaves by comparing their color, type, and vein structure offers another way to distinguish the similarities and differences of nature.
- Investigate a varied assortment of magnets with the children. Supply enough for each child to have one. What happens when the children select a magnet and attempt to pick up items from a tray filled with toothpicks, plastic straws, marbles, pencils,

astronomy: The study of the universe beyond Earth's atmosphere, such as sun, moon, planets, and stars.

science in personal and social perspectives: A developing understanding of personal health, changes in environments, and ways to conserve and recycle.

ecology: The study of living things in relation to their environment and to each other.

science and technology: The focus on establishing connections between natural and manmade items.

crayons, pieces of paper, cloth, shells, hairpins, small screws, keys, scissors, buttons, brads, paperclips, and pebbles? Which items did the magnet pick up? Which ones did it not pick up? Sort them into two piles. Why did it pick up some and not others? What conclusions can the children draw from this experiment? (Magnets attract objects made of metal.) Was the horseshoe magnet stronger or weaker than the magnetic wand or other magnets? Add new items and ask the children to predict if a magnet will pick them up. Keep this activity in the science center for the children to continue with their investigation (Adapted from Allen, 2007).

Developmental Stages of Science Play and Learning

A child's cognitive or scientific development is about the child developing or constructing a mental model of the world and how it works. Jean Piaget was interested both in how children learned and in how they thought. Piaget believed that children think differently than adults and stated they go through four universal stages of cognitive development, three of which include the early childhood years. Development is biologically based and changes as the child matures. Cognition, or the way we think, therefore, develops in all children in the same sequence of stages.

The *sensorimotor stage* ranges from birth to about age 2. Infants learn mostly through trial-and-error learning. Children initially rely on reflexes, eventually modifying them to adapt to their world. Behaviors become goal directed, progressing from concrete to abstract goals. Objects and events can be mentally represented by the child (sometimes called *object permanence*). Science activities for infants and toddlers focus on the senses—exploring textures, tastes, smells, and sounds—and involve natural discoveries as they explore the real world. How does this gate open? How can I get this top off? What happens when I press this button? What will this feel like when I put it in my mouth or over my head?

The *preoperational stage* ranges about ages 2–7. Children in this stage can mentally represent events and objects, and engage in symbolic play. Discovery learning—Piaget's idea that children learn best through doing and actively exploring—is central to the preschool science curriculum. Good preschool science curricula use real three-dimensional materials and objects (water table, shells, etc.), observe and act on changes (size, shape, motion), notice similarities and differences (sort, measure, discuss, handle), ask open-ended questions (who, what, when, where, how), and experiment, problem solve, and use the senses.

Piaget considered the *concrete stage*, ages seven to eleven, a major turning point in the child's cognitive development because it marks the beginning of logical or operational thought.

Brain Research: Executive Function

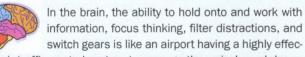

In the brain, the ability to hold onto and work with information, focus thinking, filter distractions, and switch gears is like an airport having a highly effective air traffic control system to manage the arrivals and departures of dozens of planes on multiple runways. Scientists refer to these capacities as executive function and self-regulation—a set of skills that relies on three types of brain function: working memory, mental flexibility, and self-control. Tests measuring different forms of executive function skills suggest that they begin to develop shortly after birth, with ages 3 to 5 years a window of opportunity for dramatic growth in these skills. Development continues throughout adolescence and early adulthood.

Center on the Developing Child at Harvard University (2011). *Building the Brain's "Air Traffic Control" System: How Early Experiences Shape the Development of Executive Function: Working Paper No. 11.* Retrieved June 28, 2016, from http://developingchild .harvard.edu/resources/building-the-brains -air-traffic-control-system-how-early-experiences -shape-the-development-of-executive-function/.

The child is now mature enough to use logical thought or operations (i.e., rules) but can only apply logic to physical objects (hence *concrete* operational). Children become less egocentric and better at conservation tasks. This means that the child understands that although the appearance of something changes, the thing itself does not. For example, if you take two pieces of string that are the same length and scrunch one up, a child will reply that the scrunched one is shorter, if conservation hasn't yet been reached.

Science activities for children in the concrete stage should involve children in the physical world by using equipment, getting messy, building and taking apart things, and using their hands. Children should be full participants by making decisions, helping to set up experiments, asking questions, trying new things, working together, talking about the process and their findings, evaluating results, and having fun. Their explorations and discoveries should teach how the world works, help children understand cause and effect, help children understand relationships, and relate to the child's personal experiences.

Recurring themes in the development of scientific understanding are individual learning, flexibility in the curriculum, the centrality of play in children's learning, the use of the environment, learning by discovery, and the importance of the evaluation of children's progress.

Because Piaget's theory is based on biological maturation and stages, the notion of "readiness" is important. Readiness concerns when certain information or concepts should be taught. According to Piaget's theory, children should not be taught certain concepts until they have reached the appropriate stage of cognitive development.

Within the classroom, learning should be child-centered and accomplished through active discovery learning. The role of the teacher is to facilitate learning, rather than direct instruction. Therefore, teachers should encourage the following in the classroom (McLeod, 2009):

- Focus on the process of learning rather than the end product of it (even scientists make mistakes).
- Use active methods that require rediscovering or reconstructing "truths."
- Use collaborative as well as individual activities (so children can learn from each other).
- Devise situations and experiments that present useful problems to solve.
- Evaluate the level of the child's development, so suitable tasks can be set.

Planning and Preparing the Environment

Reflect On This

How is a good science program skillfully integrated into the total life of the classroom?

We should prepare environments that allow the child to be actively engaged in the process of learning. The space should encourage investigations and be able to change as the demands of the active learners change.

Children notice everything in their world—icicles on the roof, the zigzag path of a ladybug, the dancing dust caught in the sunlight. As early childhood educators, we want to provide experiences that allow children to closely examine what interests them, although this often may mean rearranging instructional plans to take advantage of teachable moments.

Suggested Science Materials and Equipment

The science center should include a table where children can work and a shelf to hold displays, collections, and discovery materials. Provide a variety of tools such as magnifying glasses, balance scales, sieves, funnels, magnets, thermometers, containers, tweezers, tongs as well as materials to explore, such as plants, seeds and bulbs, pets, rocks, and soil. The center should also provide materials to investigate the physical properties of objects, such as pulleys, gears, wheels, mirrors, and flashlights. Materials should be organized on low open shelves, labeled and displayed so that children can use them independently.

Many materials in a science center can be donated and many can be recycled. Some equipment can be purchased inexpensively. (**Table 9-1** lists suggested materials and equipment that are appropriate for early education science investigations.)

TABLE 9-1:	Materials and Equipment for Science Investigation
Aluminum foil pans	Pine cones
Aquarium with contents and supplies	Pipe cleaners
Ant farm	Plants
Binoculars	Plastic bottles, jars, and trays
Batteries, wires, bulbs	Prisms
Birdhouse and bird feeders	Pulleys and levers
Collection boxes and collecting net	Rain gauge
Color paddles	Rock and seashell collections
Compass	Rulers, tape measure, and yard stick
Corks, plugs, and stoppers	Scales
Digital camera	Seeds and seed catalogs
Disposable cameras	Sieves, sifters, and funnels
Dried plants, such as flowers and grasses	Shallow pans
Eggbeaters and wire whip	Smelling jars and sound jars
Eyedroppers	Soil samples, such as clay, sand, and loam
Feathers	Stethoscope
Flashlights	Sundial
Food coloring	Recorders and CD's
Fossils	Telescope
Garden hose	Terrarium
Keys and locks	Thermometers, both indoor and outdoor type
Kitchen timer	Tongs and tweezers
Magnets, such as bar and horseshoe	Watering cans
Magnifying glasses and tripod magnifier stand, microscope, and slides	Waxed paper and foil
Observation sheets and science journals	X-rays (parents who are doctors or veterinarians often can give teachers old ones)

It is important to examine how materials and equipment are constructed. What they are made of and how they are put together will determine their durability when used by young children. Only some of the items will be appropriate for infants and toddlers, such as color paddles and measuring spoons and cups. You will need to be cautious in what you select, and close supervision is required when these objects are in use.

The actual physical environment plays a large role in enhancing science development. A checklist that can be used to evaluate the science environment in your own classroom or classrooms that you observe follows.

Science Environment Checklist

_____ 1. Does the science center have enough space to accommodate several children?

_____ 2. Is the science center located near a sink?

_____ 3. Are there a variety of types of tools such as magnifying glasses, balance scales, sieves, funnels, magnets, thermometers, containers, tweezers, and tongs?

_____ 4. Does the center arrangement encourage communication and cooperation?

_____ 5. Is the center organized with labeled shelving to store materials?

_____ 6. Are process skills stressed in the science center such as ask and reflect, plan and predict, act and observe, and report and reflect?

_____ 7. Does the center allow for uninterrupted work?

_____ 8. Is there adequate lighting in the science center?

_____ 9. Are there a variety of materials for exploring such as plants, seeds and bulbs, pets, and rocks and soil?

_____ 10. Does the center provide adequate work space?

_____ 11. Is the center near a window?

_____ 12. Are there a variety of materials for investigating the physical properties of objects such as sensory tubs, take-aparts, pulleys, gears, wheels, mirrors, and flashlights?

_____ 13. Does the center encourage children to develop "What if . . ." statements?

_____ 14. Is the center inviting?

_____ 15. Are there a variety of materials for actively investigating the life sciences?

_____ 16. Does the center encourage action rather than just looking?

_____ 17. Is specific content related to the topic being stressed?

_____ 18. Is there a bulletin board or other surface for posting information and findings?

_____ 19. Is the center built on current children' curiosity, interests, knowledge, background, and previous activities?

_____ 20. Are children allowed to use the center independently?

_____ 21. Do children represent their knowledge with the use of paper, graph paper, video/audio recorders, journals, recording sheets, clipboards, pencils, and markers?

_____ 22. Are open-ended materials or a variety of tasks at different levels provided to all for individual differences?

_____ 23. Are there a variety of materials for investigating the physical sciences?

_____ 24. Is there a clearly designated place for all items?

_____ 25. Are directions for the center available in pictures, written, recorded, or introduced at circle time?

_____ 26. Is there a variety of materials for exploring earth and the environment?

_____ 27. Are there resource materials available such as books, posters, videos, and computers?

_____ 28. Are there inquiry tools available such as magnifying glasses, microscope, Petri dishes, scales, eyedroppers, pulleys, tweezers, twine, clay for imprints, specimen bags and boxes, and nets?

_____ 29. Are all needed materials easily accessible to the children?

_____ 30. Are the materials arranged in a logical order or sequence?

_____ 31. Are the children encouraged to use scientific process skills such as explore, experiment, observe, reflect, describe, categorize, and record findings?

_____ 32. Are there opportunities for children to actively investigate life sciences?

_____ 33. Are there opportunities to explore physical sciences?

_____ 34. Are there opportunities for learning about Earth and its environment?

⌄⌄ Professional Resource Download

Integrating Science into the Curriculum

In an appropriate science curriculum, children learn to make and test predictions, observe, make logical connections, learn by trying things in a new way, have increased knowledge of the world, use the scientific process, solve problems, and apply knowledge gained from experiences.

Give children many open-ended possibilities to concretely demonstrate their discoveries. Reproducing and reworking what they observe and remember helps the children and the teacher learn together. Recording and communicating activities follow.

- Children's drawings, paintings, charts, audio recordings, or discussions can record their scientific experiences.
- Children can mark off days on a calendar as they watch the silkworms go through their life cycles or predict how long it will take acorns that they planted to grow.

- The children can then reflect on what they might do next.
- Church (2006) clarifies why it is so important for children to experiment. "This is when children test out their predictions and try out their ideas. The key to this step is to provide plenty of different materials and time to explore. Provide materials for free exploration in your science area so children can visit and revisit them on their own—which is how children conduct their own version of an 'independent study.' For example, How can we test if light will shine through a leaf? How many different leaves can we test? What places can we put plants to see if they will grow?"

Following are some additional ways to incorporate science into the curriculum.

Investigate Water

- Indoors or outdoors, place water in the water table or a large plastic tub. Let the children select which color they want the water to be. Add several drops of food coloring to the water. Also be sure to have plastic pouring and measuring containers, along with funnels and spray bottles. (See **Figure 9-1**.)
- Later add boats, corks, sponges, rocks, pieces of wood, large marbles, keys, feathers, and pine cones. What sinks? What floats? Guide the children in making a chart of what items sink and what items float. Ask the children why they think some things stay above water and others settle to the bottom. For example, the air holes in a sponge make it float. When the children squeeze the sponge under the water they can see bubbles of air come out of the sponge. What happens when they let go of the squeezed sponge? What other items can the children add?
- What happens to the items that sink or float in water when you add sugar, salt, oil, or sand to the water?
- Place plain water and one or two eggbeaters in the water table or tub. What happens when the children "beat the water"? Have them add liquid dish detergent, and then beat the water. Now what happens? (The water can then be used to wash the doll dishes from the dramatic play area.)
- Fill a sink full of water and notice how, when you pull the plug, the water always swirls down the drain in the same clockwise spiral. (This is because of the rotation

Figure 9-1 Children learn by doing. Therefore, the best way to learn science is to do science.

of the earth. South of the equator, it goes in the opposite direction.) This can be fascinating to young children. Follow up on this activity by looking at a globe and demonstrating how the world turns.

- Introduce the children to absorption and evaporation by having them dampen cloth rags and paper towels with water; then hang them in the sun to dry. What happens to the water? Does the cloth or the paper dry faster? Why?
- Making and blowing bubbles are delightful additions to water investigation. They float on air, glimmer with color, change shape, and pop! Why do bubbles pop? To make bubbles, mix one part liquid dish detergent into five parts water in a shallow tub or pan. Plastic circles on a handle or circles made with pipe cleaners work fine for making bubbles. Let the children experiment with blowing bubbles or moving the bubble ring in any manner they can think of to make bubbles. Try other bubble-blowing devises such as plastic berry baskets, child-size plastic hangers, or a bubble blower made from a Styrofoam cup and straw.
- See how water magnifies pebbles in a glass jar.
- Taste water, and then add salt or sugar or both. Discuss what this tastes like. What else will the children want to add?
- Examine how water takes the shape of the container it is in.
- Boil water in a pan on a hot plate (with close teacher supervision). Discuss the steam that forms.
- Guide children on how to change a liquid into a solid, and then reverse the process. First, place the water in a small, sealable plastic bag, and then freeze it. Next, let the children watch the ice melt. Encourage them to predict how long they think it will take the water to freeze and then how long to melt. Actively discuss the changes in the water.

Discover Rainbows

Set the scene for activities relating to rainbows by introducing a prism (a triangular piece of glass that breaks up a ray of light into a color spectrum). This can be purchased inexpensively. Glass beads can be used as well. (Parents may even have glass costume jewelry that can be used.) Whatever you choose, tape this "rainbow-making" glass onto a window of the classroom that faces the outdoors to catch the sunlight. Let the children locate the rainbow by themselves. This rainbow will mean more to them if they make the discovery. How many colors do they see? Have they seen a rainbow before? When? Do they remember how many colors it had? Encourage the children to draw the rainbow. What colors do they choose?

- Create other rainbows with the children by taking a shallow bowl of water out into bright sunshine.
- Place a drop or two of oil on the surface of the water. How many colors do the children see? Are they the same colors as the prism rainbow? If you stir the water with a stick, do the colors change?
- On a sunny day, you can help children find a rainbow by spraying water across the sun's rays with a garden hose or a spray bottle. The rays of the sun contain all the colors mixed together, but the water acts as a prism and separates the colors. Are they the same colors as the other rainbows the children discovered?

Explore Shadows

- What is a shadow? It is fun to find out what the children will answer. Can they offer suggestions about how to produce a shadow? Try out their predictions. Are shadows created? If they have difficulty, you might guide them by suggesting that one child holds her hand in front of a bright light. (Shade is a dark place that light cannot reach. A shadow is the shape cast by whatever is in front of the light.) The shadow of an object gets bigger when you move the object closer to the light. (See **Figure 9-2.**)
- Let the children experiment with different objects in the room to find out which ones cast shadows and which ones do not. They can make a chart of the items.

Figure 9-2 Look! Even snails have shadows!

- Extend "shadow play" into dramatic play or music and movement activities.
- The children can outline their shadows in chalk outside on the sidewalk. They can measure how long or how short their shadows are. Try this at different times during the day. Do the shadows change?
- Take the children on a nature walk and look for shadows that the plants, trees, buildings, or cars make. They can come back and create shadow drawings or write a story of what they discovered during their explorations.
- Here are some suggestions of books to read to the children and then place in the book center:

> Asch, F. (2000). *Moonbear's shadow.* (Revised ed.). New York: Aladdin.
>
> Berge, C. (2007). *Whose shadow is this?* New York: Picture Window Books.
>
> Dodd, A. W. (1994). *Footprints and shadows.* New York: Scott Foresman.
>
> Hoban, T. (1990). *Shadows and reflections.* New York: Greenwillow.

Focus on Nature

❝ *Childhood is a time of rapid physical, mental and emotional development. Time spent in nature provides a diversity of sounds, sights, smells and textures, and a variety of plants, animals and landscapes that children can engage with. This mental and sensory stimulation is important in human developmental processes.* ❞

Research commissioned by Planet Ark and Toyota Australia shows that time in nature helps us thrive as individuals—physically, intellectually, emotionally, mentally, and ethically. The results present a compelling business case regarding the value of nature and the multitude of benefits associated with green time including enhanced learning, concentration, healing, relaxation and recovery, to name a few. (For current research on benefits of nature, visit the PlanetArk website, planetark.org.)

❝ We're discovering that children know a lot more about the biological world than we ever thought. Even 3- and 4-year-olds are very interested in how the natural world works. Yet, in [U.S.]culture there's not typically a lot of exposure to the biological world. In a study where children received goldfish to care for and watched them live and die, children developed a sophisticated understanding of the way the natural world works. Likewise, other studies have shown that children on Indian reservations in Wisconsin—because of their environment and lifestyle—have deep understandings of the workings of the world and an intuitive sense of biology (Gopnik, 2016). **"**

For teachers, it is exciting to share the natural world with young children. The children are eager for active firsthand experiences.

If teachers hope children will use their senses to explore the natural world, they need to encourage real contact with the world. From the feel of oozing mud or jagged tree bark to the smell of freshly cut hay or decaying leaves; from the visual experience of a hovering hummingbird to the repetitive sound of a calling cricket; from the taste of a crisp, sweet apple to the bitter bite of a sour grape—nothing offers the variety in sights, sounds, tastes, textures, and smells as well as nature. (See **Figure 9-3**.)

Air

Can the children taste or see air? Can they feel it? How? On the playground, guide the children to experience how the wind (moving air) can come from different directions. Children can experiment with wind streamers, windsocks, wind chimes, and bubbles. You might read the following book as an introduction or extension to other activities relating to air:

Branley, F. (2006). *Air is all around you.* Illustrated by H. Keller. New York: Collins.

Nature Walks

There are opportunities for many discoveries to take place during a walk around the children's natural environment. Before you go for a walk, encourage the children to make binoculars. Tape together two toilet paper rolls or a paper towel roll cut in two. Place holes in one end of the rolls and attach a piece of yarn or string to make a neck strap. Looking for bird nests and watching butterflies or birds fly are only samples of the many things the children can do with their binoculars.

Figure 9-3 An early childhood science environment is everywhere.

Each child can also make an individual nature walk "collection bag." Construct it with folded construction paper or tagboard and lace it with yarn that is long enough to serve as a shoulder strap. Construct a classroom book with pages made out of sturdy cardboard and fastened together with rings. The children can glue or tape items that they find on the nature walk onto the pages. Then place it in the book center for the children to enjoy.

Humphryes (2000, p. 16) adds a special word for teachers. "Children have a tendency to want to take home everything they find. Explain to them that the balance of nature is very delicate and that everything in nature has a purpose (for example, a seed pod holds the seeds for next year's plants, a piece of bark may be home to many insects). … In general, *find, examine,* and *return.*" (See **Figure 9-4**.) Fresh leaves can be pressed easily by placing them between sheets of newspaper, which are then sandwiched between two pieces of cardboard and secured tightly with rubber bands. After a week, the leaves can be removed and glued into a scrapbook or displayed in other ways in the classroom.

Grow Grass

Go on a "science search" in which children look for different kinds of grass growing around their environment. In the classroom provide grass seeds for the children to plant. The quickest and easiest way to germinate the seeds is to place a damp sponge in a pie pan of water and sprinkle the seeds on the sponge. These seeds usually grow almost anywhere as long as they are watered regularly and have sunlight. (It is fun to cut the sponges into different shapes and watch the grass grow into a circle, triangle, or heart shape.) This is another way for children to observe nature firsthand. An alternative way to grow grass is to fill a plastic cup (which the children can decorate to look like a face) with dirt or potting soil. Sprinkle the grass seeds on the dirt, then water. The children really enjoy watching the "hair" grow.

Figure 9-4 Children are eager to investigate what nature has to offer.

Ecology in the Early Education Environment

Early involvement with the environment will help foster a sense of appreciation and caring in a generation of children who will then make a difference in how our future world is treated. Howard Gardner's theory of multiple intelligences includes his eighth intelligence, *naturalistic intelligence*, which emphasizes nature. Gardener (cited in Louv, 2008, p. 72) explains, "The core of the naturalist intelligence is the human ability to recognize plants, animals, and other parts of the natural environment, like clouds or rocks."

To help our children extend this eighth intelligence and guide them to explore environmental education, we, as teachers, need to help them notice things in the environment that others might miss; heighten awareness of and concern for the environment and endangered species; recognize characteristics, names, and categories of objects and species found in the natural world; as well as create and keep collections, scrapbooks, photos, specimens, logs, or journals about natural objects (adapted from Wilson in Louv, 2008).

As defined previously in this chapter, ecology is the study of living things in relation to their environment and to one another. The environment is everything that surrounds us. We human beings change the environment with our actions and reactions. In addition, everything in nature is constantly changing, and change in one area can cause changes in another.

There are several approaches you can take in your early childhood curriculum planning that will include the changing environment and what we can do to protect it. One suggestion is to select the theme "Things in Nature That Are Always Changing." Using the thematic method, you can introduce the children to changing seasons, specific weather changes, night changing into day, and the changes that take place with the individual child. Every curriculum should draw the children's attention to every part of nature, not only in the outdoor environment but also through finding meaningful ways to bring nature into the classroom.

Some activities that focus on ecology are offered next.

Plant and Garden at Different Times of the Year

In some places it is warm all year round, and plants there grow well at any time. In places where the ground freezes in winter, you will have to wait for warmer weather to garden outdoors, but indoor planting can work well. You can start plants in a collection of cans, grow a tree in a tub, or plant seeds in cracks in the concrete. Hachey and Butler (2009, p. 42) suggest, "Hang plants from the ceiling, place them on shelves and window ledges; use them to fill empty spaces on tables and furniture. . . . Just about anything can be used to hold plants, but be sure to use containers (with holes for drainage) that are big enough to hold plenty of soil and water." Children can plant an indoor garden (flowers or vegetables) in the sand and water table or in a window box. If there is a protected space outdoors, they can plant a garden there. This activity is another way to encourage children to take responsibility for living things. As a result, they develop a sense of pride by nurturing a seed into a plant. Discover with the children which plants grow well in your area and when are the best times to plant and harvest them.

Gardening and nature-based play encourages children's desire to question and seek answers. In addition, "Teachers learn to trust children with gardening jobs, understanding and accepting that they can't do the job the same way or as long as adults can" (Nimmo and Hallett, 2008, p. 33). (See **Figure 9-5**.)

Make a Compost Pile

The children can place leaves, plant cuttings, and food scraps in a compost bin or pile, along with worms to help "mix-up" the compost. Then they can use the compost when they plant a garden in the spring. This can be a cooperative experience with one or two other classes. Children enjoy participating with other children in the center or school.

Create an Outdoor Classroom

Intentionally designed spaces with natural elements encourage children to observe closely and take the time they need to really notice and appreciate the world around them (Jacobs, 2015). High-quality play spaces incorporate a variety of natural elements for children to play with

Figure 9-5 Plants in an early childhood environment give each child an opportunity to learn something about the growth and needs of plants.

such as trees, stumps, boulders, tall grass, water, pebbles, mounds, and slopes (Spencer & Wright, 2014). Learning takes place outdoors that differs from learning indoors, so it is important that outdoor environments be as richly equipped and thoughtfully planned to address the following challenges (Nelson, E. M., 2012):

1. Getting children outdoors and more active
2. Involving children in hands-on, loose-parts, and big body outdoor play
3. Creating opportunities to learn how to handle outdoor risks safely
4. Connecting children to nature in ways that encourage them to care and appreciate it more deeply
5. Teaching children about cause and effect through outdoor and shared activities
6. Planning a garden with children that allows them to experience the life cycle of plants as they plant seeds, weed, water, care for, and harvest plants
7. Providing rulers and other measuring tools for children to track plant growth
8. Furnishing areas with magnifiers and other tools needed to observe closely and use their senses

Catch Rainwater in a Container and Recycle It to Water the Plants

Filter rainwater through a fine sieve, such as a tea strainer. This will provide an opportunity for the children to see what pollutants rainwater collects, in addition to providing clean rainwater to water the indoor plants and vegetables.

Adopt a Tree or Plant a Tree

The children can select a tree on the playground or in a nearby park to "adopt" as their tree to take care of and to observe throughout the year. Sometimes children prefer to plant a tree of their own on the playground or in a tub. Whatever choice is made can lead to an environmental discussion when you ask the question, "What do you think the tree takes from the environment, and what does it give to the environment?"

It is helpful to invite a parent who knows a lot about trees or a professional gardener to visit the class to answer the children's questions and advise them in their selections. In addition, a field trip to a garden shop can motivate the children. Giving young children the responsibility of taking care of a tree can be a significant factor in encouraging them to take care of the environment.

After they select the tree and identify what kind it is, they can make drawings of it, take photos of their tree in different seasons, and compare it to other trees. They will also find it interesting to examine the bark, leaves, and bugs on the tree with a magnifying glass and observe and identify which birds like their tree. Children will enjoy hanging a birdhouse or a bird feeder in their tree and watching the activity it attracts.

Recycle and Conserve Materials and Natural Resources

The children can recycle newspapers, other types of paper, aluminum, glass, some plastics, and clothing. Find out about the recycling projects in your community and get the children and their families involved.

Try fixing broken items in the classroom instead of buying new things or throwing old things away. Encourage the children to stop wasting water. Have them turn off the water while brushing their teeth or washing their hands, instead of letting it run.

Use Grocery Sacks and Newspapers to Make Art

Provide one or both, along with paints, for the children to paint on. To make newspaper logs for the block center, take a section of newspaper and roll into a tight roll. Use tape to hold the "logs." These can then be used to build towers, fences, and so forth.

Stress the Importance of Not Littering

Trash should be placed in a trash container. Because littering can be dangerous and unhealthy, the children should be shown how to avoid littering and to participate in cleaning up instead.

Celebrate Earth Day, April 22

Make party hats out of newspaper and grocery bags. Bake an Earth Day cake decorated to look like the planet earth. Cut out eco-cookies in natural shapes, such as birds, leaves, and trees. Celebrate with an environmental musical band. Provide recycled materials for the children to make instruments, and have a parade!

Ask the Children Open-Ended Questions about the Environment

The following questions will help children think about why it is important to take care of our environment:

- What would happen if everyone threw trash on the ground?
- What do you think would happen if we poured polluted water into clean water?
- Why do we recycle?
- What would happen if we cut down trees instead of planting them?
- Why do you think plants are important to us?
- What are ways we can help the environment at home?
- Virtually all outdoors is science. This is where children become part of the natural world. … School yards, sidewalks, vacant lots, or any strip of ground can be an area for outdoor learning (Charlesworth and Lind, 2010, p. 478).

The following activities extend over a period of time. Participating in these will demonstrate to the children that many scientific investigations take time to evolve and that some are unpredictable. These experiments can also offer a concrete way to introduce the children to edible plant parts.

- Roots—Carrots, potatoes, turnips, radishes, and beets are the roots of plants.
- Stems—Celery and asparagus are examples of the stems of plants that connect the roots with the leaves.
- Leaves—Lettuce, spinach, cabbage, and parsley are the leaves of plants.
- Flowers—Broccoli and cauliflower are examples of the flowers of plants.
- Vegetables/fruits—Tomatoes and squash are examples of the "fruit" of plants.

Try the following activities.

Carrot Top Garden

After cutting the tops off of three or four carrots, the children can place them in a shallow pan or dish. The carrot tops should be sitting in one-quarter inch of water and be watered daily, a task that could be performed by the "plant helper" of the day. (A child can use a ruler to determine exactly how much one-quarter inch is.)

The children can predict how many days it will take the carrot tops to sprout new green foliage. Guide them to make a chart or graph that shows them how correct their predictions were. If some of the tops do not sprout, ask the children *why* they think they did not.

Rooting a Sweet Potato

This is another experiment that children enjoy doing. Push toothpicks halfway into a sweet potato. Then place the potato in a glass or jar of water with the toothpicks resting on the top rim. Be sure the end of the potato is immersed in water. The plant helper can be responsible to see that the bottom of the potato is always immersed in water. Place the potato where it will receive enough light. Put another sweet potato in a dark spot of the room so the children can see what happens to the potato's growth without adequate light.

The children can create a group art activity by drawing the sweet potato and adding to it over the time it takes for roots to grow out of the sides and bottom of the potato and the leaves to grow out of the top. A "before and after" drawing is interesting, too.

Thirsty Celery

This science experiment demonstrates how plants get their water. Fill two tall, clear plastic glasses with water. Let the children put a few drops of red food coloring in one glass and a few drops of blue food coloring in the other. Put a piece of celery into each of the glasses, being careful to make a fresh cut at the base of the celery stalks before you place them in the water. Ask the children to watch the celery and record what happens. They can do this with a drawing or verbally with a voice recorder. Over the next few days, the colored water should travel up the stalk and into the leaves. Ask the children what happened to the celery. Why do they think this happened?

Mini Greenhouse

This indoor gardening activity can expand children's understanding of how things grow. The needed materials are: one egg carton per child, six cotton balls per child, and seeds—birdseed, radish seeds, or grass seeds. Guide the children to put the cotton balls in the carton. Place three seeds on top of each cotton ball. Saturate the cotton with water and close the lid. Set in a warm spot. Check daily and use an eyedropper to wet the cotton. When green leaves appear, keep the lid of the egg carton open. What has happened? What will happen next? What should be done to keep the plants alive? Provide blank books for children to use as observation logs, and encourage them to record plant growth through drawing. They can use the classroom camera to take photos to show what is happening day by day or week by week.

Seeds

Several weeks before you plan to introduce this activity, gather all kinds of seeds. Encourage the children to place the seeds in a line from the smallest to the largest. Discuss the texture of the seeds. Try to sprout some seeds in damp paper towels and some in dry ones to find out whether seeds need moisture to sprout. Ask children to guess what would grow from the seeds if they were planted? Make a rebus chart for planting seeds. Give each child a small planting pot. Then ask each child to fill it with the potting soil you have provided, and water it. Each child should put several seeds into her planting pot. Place a number on each pot for identification. During the next few weeks, the children will take care of the plants, as well as measure the growth of each one and make a graph showing the progress. During this time, you and the children can try to figure out what kind of plants you have planted. Look up the leaf structure on the computer or in a gardening book. To expand this project, have the children place their planted seeds in various lighting conditions to observe the differences between plants grown in sunlight and those left in the dark. Water some of the plants and leave some dry. Encourage children to examine the contrast between the plants grown under different conditions and discover for themselves that plants do need water and sunlight. This activity can be the starting point for a project approach (an in-depth investigation) of seeds by several children or an individual child. (See **Figure 9-6**.)

Here is another activity that can extend the focus on seeds. Set up a tray with different fruits and vegetables, such as apples, cucumbers, oranges, plums, and green peppers. Allow the students to manipulate the items on the tray. Cut open one fruit and one vegetable. Ask the children what is inside these that is the same? (Seeds) Cut open the rest of the fruits and vegetables. Place each fruit and each vegetable seed on a separate paper plate labeled with a picture of each. Give the children a small taste of each fruit and each vegetable. Have they tasted any of them before? In what ways are seeds of each different? Both you and the children will continue asking and answering questions. Days later, the children may think of something else they want to know. You are actually planting "seeds" of interest and inquiry with all of these explorations.

Orange Juice

To reinforce the science of nutrition, have the children make their own orange juice. This helps the youngest ones connect the actual fruit with the juice. Many children think that orange juice always comes in a carton or bottle at the grocery store. Ask each child to place one-half of an orange in a resealable bag. Zip the seal closed. Have the children squeeze the orange. (You may have to help.) This will produce juice. Then, they can open the bag and take out the half, being careful not to spill the juice. Close the bag, leaving only enough of an opening for the child to insert a straw into the bag. Then, he or she can drink and enjoy the juice.

Figure 9-6 Children develop responsibility when they take care of their plants.

Animals in the Early Education Classroom

The world of animals inspires wonder and curiosity in young children. You can guide the children into drawing pictures of their experiences with animals, moths, butterflies, and ants. Extend this by making puppets of the animals they draw.

For language development, the children can bring in their favorite stuffed animals and talk about them during group time. Play music and have a parade of stuffed animals. Read books aloud, and place those that relate to animals, moths, butterflies, and ants in the book center. (See **Box 9-1**.)

BOX 9-1:   The Animals in Our World

As an animal lover and a wildlife rehabilitator, I have come to the conclusion that there are two categories of animals—not good or bad, but rather, touchable and untouchable. Touchable are those we know and with whom we have a relationship. I have spent many wonderful hours with my very special domesticated animals. We have learned to love and trust each other. I have the responsibility to see that all their needs are met.

Untouchable animals are those we do not know, who will probably be frightened of us and will do whatever they need to do to protect themselves. These animals, which are not domesticated, are born to be free. It is not fair to put them in a cage. They deserve to live as nature intended them to live. Because they are not used to people, they will be frightened and potentially very dangerous. They can also have diseases that you, the children, or your pets can catch, such as distemper or rabies. Enjoy watching and listening to them, but LEAVE THEM ALONE!

Occasionally, one comes upon an animal that looks as though it needs help; either it is injured or in some way unable to care for itself. It is important to know when and when not to rescue it. As an added precaution, even domesticated animals that we do not know (such as dogs in the neighborhood) should be classified as untouchable also.

What Not to Do

- *Do not* "rescue" an animal that does not need help. Most "orphaned" animals are not orphaned at all. The parent is usually hiding nearby, afraid to attend to its offspring when people are present. If you can see a nest from which a baby has fallen, it is best to place the baby back in the nest. Despite myths to the contrary, the scent of human hands will not disturb the parents, and they will usually care for their returned offspring.
- *Do not* be tempted to raise an orphaned animal yourself. Federal and state laws prohibit the possession of most nondomesticated animals—and with good reason. These creatures need special care, far different from domestic animals. Wildlife rehabilitators are trained to provide that care.

What to Do

- *Do* rescue an animal if the parent is known to be dead and the baby is too young to survive on its own, or if the animal is injured or in obvious danger. Emergency care can be given if you have determined that the animal really needs care. Put on a pair of gloves before you touch it. For your safety and the animal's well-being, handle it as little as possible. Place it in a covered box with air holes for ventilation. The box should be just a little larger than the animal. Put the box in a dark, quiet room away from the children (and pets), and free from drafts.
- *Do* resist the urge to feed an animal or give it liquids. The wrong food or wrong feeding method can do more harm than good. These animals have special diets and, as babies, must be fed often. For example, some baby birds must be fed every 20 or 30 minutes during the day and some baby mammals must be fed during the night.
- *Do* contact a wildlife rehabilitator immediately. Wildlife babies need to learn from their parents what kind of animal they are and how to take care of themselves (just like human babies). You can find a rehabilitator through your state parks and wildlife department or other private organizations in your community. Rehabilitators have been trained to care for wildlife orphans during the early stages of life and to reintroduce them to their natural environment.

We, as teachers of the future citizens of the world, have opportunities every day to instill in our children a love and respect for themselves and for all the people, animals, and plants with whom we share our world.

There are many interesting animal-related learning exhibits you can have in your classroom. While visiting classrooms, I have seen some wonderful science centers with plants and animals, but I have also been saddened by sights of animals being poorly fed or improperly housed. Before you get any animal, be sure you understand and are prepared to meet its needs. Get answers to the following questions:

- What kind of enclosure should it have?
- What kind of food does it require?
- What temperature must it have?
- Does it need any kind of special light?
- Should it be kept with another animal?

BOX 9-1: The Animals in Our World (continued)

- Is it safe for children to handle it?
- Does it need any special veterinary care?
- Does it meet your state licensing requirements? (Some states require documentation that shows that animals requiring vaccinations have been vaccinated according to state and local requirements. Some also require that parents must be advised when animals are present in the classroom or school.)

In addition to animals that are commonly found in centers that can be displayed safely and effectively (small rodents, such as gerbils and hamsters, frogs, fish, birds, and turtles), you might try some of the following:

- *Earthworms*—You'll need a large plastic or glass jar, sand or loose moist soil, cloth cover, damp leaves or grass, and a dozen or so earthworms. (You can look for earthworms after a spring rain or buy them from a local bait shop.)

Place a layer of pebbles in the jar; then fill it with sand or loose moist soil. Put in some earthworms. Keep the soil moist but not wet. The children can feed the worms damp leaves and grass clippings. Be sure to cover the container with a dark cloth to shield the worms from light, because they are used to being in the dark ground.

The children can observe how the worms burrow tunnels in the soil. They can also carefully place a worm on a table to watch its movements (with teacher supervision). Note the difference between its back and underside. Using a magnifying glass, count the rings on its body. Notice the worm's reaction to various stimuli: light, sound, types of food, and soil.

After viewing the worms for a while, the children can return them to their garden or playground. Earthworms are important for healthy soil. They loosen it so that air and water can get to plant roots. They also fertilize the soil.

- *Silkworms*—You will need a terrarium, mulberry leaves, and silkworm eggs or larvae. Many early childhood centers and schools store the eggs laid in one season in a small bottle in a refrigerator until the next season. When the mulberry leaves are on the trees, these eggs are placed in a terrarium with the leaves. (Network with other colleagues to get a supply of silkworm eggs or order a supply from Insect Lore Products, http://www.insectlore.com.)

The silkworm (like all other moths and butterflies) undergoes a complete metamorphosis. There are four stages of development: egg, larva, pupa, and adult moth. One female silkworm moth can lay from 300 to 400 eggs. In about 10 days, cream to light-green colored caterpillars hatch from the eggs and eat voraciously on mulberry leaves for about 30 days. Be sure you have access to mulberry leaves that

Opportunities occur every day for children to discover the beauty of butterflies.

have not been sprayed with insecticide. (Often, parents can help supply the mulberry leaves.)

Each silkworm will then construct a cocoon from a single fiber of silk, which could be up to a quarter mile long! It takes about three days to complete the cocoon. Inside the cocoon, the silkworm metamorphoses into a cream-colored moth, which will not eat, rarely flies, and lives only a few days. One ounce of silkworm eggs produces 30,000 larvae, which can spin approximately 100 pounds of silk! (As you can see, you need only a few eggs to get started.) Introducing children to silkworms offers a special way to help them understand what a life cycle is.

- *Butterflies*—The following company will ship butterflies directly to your center or school. Butterfly Garden is available from Insect Lore Products (http://www.insectlore.com). Children can watch the metamorphosis of larva into chrysalides into butterflies and then have the fun of releasing the butterflies back into nature.
- *Ants*—Commercially sold ant farms are widely available in stores selling educational materials. It is fascinating to watch these little creatures dig tunnels, drag food, and interrelate with each other.

—By Jo Eklof (2003)

Jo is an educator, wildlife rehabilitator, songwriter, and performer. Many of her songs are shared with you throughout this book.

Nutrition and Cooking Experiences in Early Education

Why do you think nutrition education in an early childhood classroom is necessary or important? Essa (2013, p. 296) comments, "Because food is a basic human need and so often provides great pleasure, nutrition education and cooking experiences should be an integral part of the curriculum. . . . You will need to tailor nutrition concepts to the ages and ability levels of the children, your own knowledge about nutrition, and the depth in which you plan to approach the subject." Introducing nutrition concepts at an early age can influence a lifetime of food choices and balances.

Nutrition

Nutrition is the study of food and how it is used by the body. Nutrients are substances found in foods that provide for the growth, development, maintenance, and repair of the body (Robertson, 2010). The body has three main uses for nutrients: as sources of energy, as materials for the growth and maintenance of body tissue, and to regulate body processes.

Additionally, Marotz (2009, p. 484) offers the following nutritional concepts relating to young children:

- Children should have food to grow and to have healthy bodies.
- Nutrients come from foods. It is these nutrients that allow children to grow and be healthy.
- A variety of foods should be eaten each day. No one food provides all of the needed nutrients.
- Foods should be carefully handled before they are eaten to ensure that they are healthful and safe.
- Snacks should contribute to the child's daily food needs and educational experiences.

Children should be exposed to and encouraged to accept a variety of foods from each of the food groups suggested by the US Department of Agriculture (USDA) My Plate Guide. This guide was created by the USDA to help children improve their food intake choices and the amounts needed to help them meet nutritional guidelines. The USDA offers a wealth of information designed to introduce children to food and its impact on the body. Visit the USDA website at http://www.myplate.gov.

The importance of good nutrition in the lives of young children has become a national issue. There has been a great deal in the news recently about how obesity is affecting many children:

> "Obesity in young children cannot be ignored. Prevention is always the most effective method. However, promising results can also be obtained by taking action when a child is young and still in the process of establishing lifelong eating and activity habits (Marotz, 2014)."

What is obesity? The American Academy of Pediatrics (AAP) explains that obesity is an excess percentage of bodyweight as a result of fat, which puts people at risk for many health problems. In children older than 2 years of age, obesity is assessed by a measure called the body mass index (BMI). A pediatrician is the best source for information regarding BMI and its application. For more information, visit the AAP website at: http://www.aap.org.

The USDA and the AAP guidelines recommend that children, teachers, and families find a balance between food intake and physical activity. They advise that older infants and toddlers should be provided with at least 30 minutes of play a day, though not all at once. Preschoolers and older children should have at least 60 minutes of active play each day.

Cooking

Cooking activities give children firsthand experiences that involve them in the process from planning to cleanup. A sense of accomplishment, the thrill of experimentation, and

nutrition: Substances found in food that provide for growth, development, maintenance, and repair of the body.

obesity: Excess percentage of body weight as a result of fat, which puts people at risk for many health problems.

an awareness of taste, touch, and smell are all rewards of cooking experiences. Early positive encounters with food also help children gain the knowledge they will use to form lifelong eating habits. Just watch what infants and toddlers can do with a banana.

By including opportunities for children to cook, you offer additional times for them to practice math (comparing sizes, shapes, and measurements; one-to-one correspondence; fractions; and temperature), science (vegetables that are stems or roots, fruit that grows on trees, what happens to sugar on hot cereal), reading and writing (making lists and using recipes and rebus charts), social studies (learning more about their world and community resources), following directions, putting things in sequence, and learning to communicate and cooperate with each other. (See **Figure 9**-7.)

Figure 9-7   Children can learn math by measuring ingredients through cooking experiences.

“You may find that some children will need to go through a similar “messing about” stage with any significantly new type of cooking material, just as they do when they first encounter a new art material. So be prepared to allow this exploratory period before you introduce any new type of cooking experience to young children (Colker, 2005, p. 4).”

It is important that the cooking projects are appropriate for the children's ages, interests, and understanding.

When you include cooking activities in an early childhood environment, you will encourage children to:

- Feel responsible, independent, and successful.
- Learn about nutrition, the food groups, and related food skills, such as how to plan a healthy meal.
- Work independently or cooperatively in small groups (the younger the children, the smaller the group should be).
- Complete tasks from preparation to cleanup.
- Learn about new foods and become aware of recipes from cultures other than their own.
- Learn about different careers that involve foods and cooking (farmers, truckers, grocers, bakers, and chefs, for example).
- Introduce new vocabulary and concepts, such as *measure, melt, knead, shake, sift, spread, baste, peel, hull, grind, grate, chop, slice,* and *boil.*
- Develop beginning reading skills with rebus charts and simple recipe cards.
- Learn math and science concepts.

Sensory Snacks

- Dried fruits: apples, raisins, apricots, and pitted prunes. (Let the children spoon out the portions.)
- Bananas sliced in orange juice. (Let the children slice the bananas and drop them in their own bowls of orange juice.)
- Melon chunks. (Let the children feel, hold, and cut the fruit and then remove and plant the seeds.)
- Finger foods (that children can help prepare): cinnamon toast, cheese toast, popcorn, raw or cooked vegetables, hard-boiled eggs (whole, half, quarters, slices), apple slices dipped in honey, tangerine wedges, pear sections, or plum pieces.

(See **Figure 9-8**, “Butterfly Salad,” for Rebus Chart of Cooking Activity.)

BUTTERFLY SALAD

Wash hands.

Place one lettuce leaf onto a paper plate.

Slice 2 pineapple rings in 1/2 to use as an outline of

the butterfly's wings. Use one celery stick as the body.

Place a small amount of cottage cheese inside of

pineapple rings. Decorate the cottage cheese with

green and black olives.

Figure 9-8 Opportunities occur every day for children to prepare their own snacks.

When children cook in the classroom, they need equipment, supplies, and food to be available. Samples are listed in **Table 9**-2.

The following activity plan worksheet is an example of a developmentally appropriate cooking activity.

TABLE 9-2: **Cooking Equipment, Supplies, and Food**

Equipment and Supplies

Use real kitchen utensils and equipment. A list of suggested supplies follows:

- Unbreakable nesting bowls for mixing
- Individual bowls for children
- Measuring cups and spoons
- Wooden stirring spoons
- Slotted spoons
- Unbreakable pitchers
- Rubber spatula
- Vegetable peelers
- Plastic grater
- Pastry brushes
- Wire whisks
- Funnel
- Tongs
- Rolling pins
- Hand eggbeater
- Potato masher
- Colander
- Sifter
- Hand squeezing orange juicer
- Plastic serrated knives (for younger children)
- Serrated steel knives and kitchen shears (for older children)
- Plastic cutting boards or trays
- Cookie cutters and cookie sheets
- Muffin tins

- Bread loaf pans and cake pans
- Airtight containers with lids
- Hot plate or electric skillet
- Toaster oven
- Electric wok
- Electric blender or mixer
- Can opener
- Timer
- Smocks or aprons (not the ones used in the art center)
- Hot pads and mitts or holders
- Sponges used just for cooking activities
- Paper towels and paper napkins
- Waxed paper, foil, plastic wrap, and plastic bags

Basic ingredients to keep on hand

  Flour

  Milk

  Sugar

  Cornstarch

  Cornmeal

  Salt

  Baking soda

  Baking powder

  Oil

  Vinegar

  Bread

  Honey

Stone Soup

Read the Stone Soup rebus, the recipe, and visual directions for Stone Soup

Suggested books:

1. *Read Stone Soup* by M. Brown (1997), New York: Aladdin Picture.
2. Read the Stone Soup rebus.
3. Read and follow this recipe.

Stone Soup Recipe

three clean rocks
3 stalks of celery, chopped

2 large carrots, chopped
2 medium onions, chopped
2 medium potatoes, chopped
3 medium tomatoes, chopped
½ teaspoon basil
½ cup fresh parsley
1½ tablespoons salt
½ teaspoon pepper

Everyone can chop or measure something. Put all the ingredients into a big pan on the stove. (An electric crockpot will work, too.) Add water to cover. Cook using low heat for 2 to 3 hours. You can add rice (1 to 2 cups) to thicken.

STONE SOUP

Wash hands,   Wash 3 clean rocks,

Chop and measure 3 stalks of celery, 2 large carrots,

2 medium onions, 2 medium potatoes, 3 medium tomatoes,

1/2 teaspoon basil, 1/2 cup fresh parsley,

1 1/2 tablespoon salt, and 1/2 teaspoon pepper.

Put all ingredients in a big pot and place on the stove.

Add water to cover the vegetables, Cook for 2 - 3 hours.

Add 1/2 cup rice to thicken the soup. ENJOY!

Technology in Science

There are so many ways to incorporate technology into science. Record findings on a nature walk. When you get back to the classroom, play back the recording and discuss what you experienced. Create a Why? file podcast where children answer science related questions into a microphone and upload to the Internet for all to hear. Document cameras connected to a Smart Board or projector are a great way to look at the natural items enlarged as if they were under a microscope. An example of how technology can be used to teach science is a kindergarten curriculum unit that explored wild animals through photographs, video clips, and animal sounds on a computer by going online or using specific software. Field trips can also involve children with technology, such as interactive exhibits at a science museum. For example, children from a community college lab school took a bug they found on the playground over to the SEM lab to look at it under the electron microscope.

Diversity in Science

Imbedding Culture in Science

To introduce an awareness of the different environments in various parts of the world, read books to the children, display objects and artifacts from different cultures, show photographs, and explore websites of faraway places such as the rainforests in Central and South America, the deserts in the Middle East and Africa, and the rivers around the world. Keep a globe or a map of the world available for the children to find the areas discussed. Encourage them to draw or write about their world as they see it. Provide them with digital or disposable cameras to take photographs that illustrate what they see. This activity can also stimulate further investigations of the children's homes, backyards, neighborhoods, and school environments. Photographs are useful devices for developing diversity recognition and science teaching and learning. Children begin to see patterns and make connections between their own personal explorations and discoveries and what is outside in the world at large.

It is important that teachers know about all of the cultures represented in their classrooms and the customs they practice. This allows the teachers to include activities that represent all of the cultures while avoiding any activities that might be offensive.

Visit agencies and organizations in your community that offer resources and information relating to various cultures. As you gather materials and facts, ask the parents of children in your class for specific examples of what would be inappropriate to their culture. Continue to be aware of, and sensitive to, the many elements in each child's world.

Poetry, flannel-board stories, dramatic play, music, and movement offer additional opportunities for young children to become more aware of the world around them and their place in it. The poem and songs in Appendix C are creative ways for the children to share their appreciation of the world and each other. (Flannel-board characters for the poem "Seeds" can be found online at this textbook's premium website.)

Cooking experiences value cultural diversity. Foods from other cultures offer opportunities for children to taste the different ingredients and flavors. This also helps to develop their understanding that many of the foods they eat are both different *and* similar to those eaten in other countries. On an even deeper level of understanding, children can relate to the fact that many of the foods eaten in the United States are greatly influenced by all the cultures represented in the United States today.

Supporting Each and Every Child's Success

When cooking with children, watch for food allergies. Children with tactile hypersensitivity may need to be introduced to different new foods or textures slowly. They may need messy play materials to be contained to minimize the sensation. Plastic food storage bags that zip closed can serve this purpose. Rebus recipes with pictures and words and sequence charts or cards with picture icons can be a helpful cueing device to complete the steps in a science experiment and offer opportunities to practice following directions and motor planning. Children with special needs can have difficulty generalizing skills learned in one setting to another situation, so they need to practice new skills like pouring. Larger tools such as a baster instead of an eye dropper may help some children be more successful. Presenting science materials contained on trays may help some children who get overwhelmed with clutter.

Creating Partnerships with Families

Many of the activities in this chapter can be shared with parents so that science can become a family affair. Help families understand that children are natural scientists discovering their world. Send information and suggestions home. Begin with general ideas as to what parents can do with their children, and then show them specific activities that are ongoing in the classroom. For example, families also can grow a carrot-top garden or root a sweet potato at home. The following are some other specific suggestions to give families:

- Look at science experiences all around you. Observe plants, insects, animals, rocks, and sunsets with your child.
- Go for a walk in the park or in the woods and talk about the natural things you and your child see.
- Feel a tree. Talk about the parts of the tree.
- Collect all kinds of things—from shells to sticks to rocks. Talk about where they came from.
- Help your child use his or her senses—sight, smell, touch, hearing, and taste—to explore the world around him or her. Look at leaves, smell them, and run your fingers across their tops and undersides. Compare one kind of leaf with another, and look for changes over time.
- As your child begins to talk about plants in the environment, he or she can observe their growth by taking care of plants at school and at home. Together, learn the names of plants, flowers, shrubs, fruits, vegetables, and trees.
- Explain what items you recycle. Share some of these with us at school: plastic containers, egg cartons, paper towel and bathroom tissue rolls, samples and end-cuts from wallpaper, fabric, floor tile, framing materials, and newspapers.

Principles of developmentally appropriate practice can link cooking-related activities at home to school activities. You could meet with parents to discuss relationships between family and classroom goals of working together. Here are some suggestions for involving families from Marotz (2009, p. 430) and other early childhood teachers:

- Ask them to assist in planning menus.
- Place weekly menus on the parent board, as well as suggestions for foods that provide nutritional additions to each menu.
- Provide a report on the food experiences done in class and ask the families for feedback on their child's reaction to these experiences.
- Invite families to attend a potluck (food sharing) dinner and bring special ethnic or traditional foods unique to their culture.

- Help in developing guidelines for acceptable foods that families could bring to the center or school to celebrate a birthday or other holiday.
- Help families understand how they can foster positive eating habits at home. Encourage good eating behaviors, such as always sitting down for snacks and meals.
- Discuss ways to prevent obesity and why it is important to do so.
- Remind families about ways to involve their child with food in the home, such as helping prepare food with age-appropriate, safe kitchen tasks and sharing in cleanup activities.

The Teacher's Role

The teacher's role in young children's scientific learning requires just the right touch using research proven strategies. Hong and Diamond (2012) found in their study that young children learned science concepts and vocabulary better when either responsive teaching or the combination of responsive teaching and explicit instruction was used and children in the combined intervention group learned more science concepts and vocabulary and more content-specific scientific problem-solving skills.

Guidance in Science Play

The following are some suggestions for guiding children's experiences with science:

- Allow the children to control the time spent on experimenting with appropriate materials. Children need time to try out ideas, to discover, to make mistakes and learn from them, and to learn from one another.
- Explain the limits and rules to the children, such as that their hands should be washed with soap and water before and after they prepare foods or play with messy wet materials, smocks should be used for messy projects, clean smocks or aprons should be worn while cooking, and fingers and utensils should be kept out of their mouths while they are cooking or using sensory materials. Let the children help you establish other rules specific to the activity.
- Plan cooking on days when you have another adult helping you, such as an assistant, a parent, or a volunteer. Supervision is critical to ensure safety for the children.

Reflect On This

Do you believe that we, as teachers, have opportunities to instill in our children a love and respect for themselves and for all the people, animals, and plants with whom we share our world?

Case Study: Science

Emily is a second-grade teacher in Houston's NASA elementary school. Her class is studying gases. She is getting ready to demonstrate how to make a balloon blow up on top of a bottle.

Emily places the vinegar in the bottle. She then places baking soda in the balloon and places the balloon on top of the bottle. She shakes the bottle and the children continue to watch as the balloon blows up.

Her curriculum specialist had recently completed an evaluation form related to the science activity she had just completed. It included the following questions the supervisor

had asked. How would you answer the questions related to the science activity Emily had completed?

What Do You Think?

1. Were the children actively involved? Are they using the equipment?
2. Are the children making predictions? Are they getting messy?
3. What changes can the teacher make to improve this science experience?

TEACHING TIPS

Provide a variety of developmentally appropriate experiences.

- Provide hands-on experiences that make science a part of every child's day.
- Preserve and value a child's natural curiosity.
- Avoid "telling" children about a scientific activity that they themselves cannot observe or experiment with. Relying on teacher information only is not useful or appropriate for children, as we have discussed throughout this chapter.
- If you have difficulty with setting up a science environment, identify an individual interest or area of the real world you would like to know more about. Set up your early education classroom so that you can discover and learn things along with the children. Start with one of the science inquiries suggested in this chapter.
- Ask open-ended questions, and give children plenty of time to answer questions. This helps children to observe carefully and encourages them to put their ideas into words. (What does a feather look like? How does the sky look when it is going to rain?)
- Allow for across-the-curriculum integration of activities.
- Emphasize the positive aspects of healthy eating rather than the harmful effects of unhealthy eating.
- Give children many opportunities to taste foods that are low in fat, sodium, and added sugars. Taste foods high in vitamins, minerals, and fiber.
- Review the food allergies of the children. Provide alternative activities for those children who are allergic to certain foods.
- Be sensitive to the beliefs of the families in your program concerning foods. Some families may have restrictions on what foods they can eat.

- Integrate cooking opportunities into the theme and lesson plan. Cooking is a creative sensory/science activity and not necessarily a separate center. Plan appropriate transition activities into and out of each experience.
- Plan how to introduce the activities and how to plan appropriate transitions out of each activity.
- At first, and with younger children, attempt food activities that require no cooking. The children can mix ingredients together and feel successful when they taste the snack.
- Washing fruits and vegetables before they cut and eat them provides additional opportunities for beginning cooks. Remember, all cooks need practice and support to succeed.
- When interacting with the children, use correct terms for foods, measurements, equipment, and processes. Repeating and explaining terms will help extend language skills.
- Take the time to discuss foods with the children. Allow them to smell the food and ingredients, taste small portions at various stages of preparation, and experience the feel of textures.
- Take plenty of time to introduce foods to the children.
- Ample time should be available for children to complete the recipe, permitting them to learn from the process as well as the product.
- With older children, take time to explain the sequence of how things are grown, harvested, packaged, transported, placed in stores and markets, sold, transported to homes, cooked, and served. Allow time for you to answer the children's questions. Repeat this information in different ways, such as lotto games, matching games, reading books, making books, and field trips.
- Remember to have the children wash their hands before and after each activity.

⌄ **Professional Resource Download**

Summary

1. **What are the key terms related to science for children?** Process skills are the abilities to process new information through concrete experiences such as using square bubble wands to see if you can make different shaped bubbles; inquiry is a questioning process that encourages curiosity and exploration, such as asking What do you think would happen if . . . ? The opposite of rote learning, science as inquiry offers frequent opportunities to question, investigate, clarify, predict, and communicate with others like doing a study of the difference between balls, such as what they are made of, how high they will bounce, and so on. Life science is the study of living things, people, animals, and plants, such as sprouting seed in the window; physical science is the sciences (physics, chemistry, meteorology, and astronomy) that relate to nonliving materials like water; chemistry is the science dealing with the composition and transformations of substances like in cooking; Earth and space science is the study of Earth materials, objects in the sky, and changes in the Earth and sky like soil erosion;

geology is the study of the materials that make up Earth, such as rocks and shells; meteorology is the science of weather and atmosphere; astronomy is the study of the universe beyond Earth's atmosphere, such as sun, moon, planets, and stars; science in personal and social perspectives is developing understanding of personal health, changes in environments, and ways to conserve and recycle; ecology is the study of living things in relation to their environment and to each other such as animals habitats; and science and technology focus on establishing connections between natural and manmade items such as using an eggbeater to whip soap suds.

2. **How do the stages of child development relate to scientific learning?** Infants learn mostly through trial and error. Science activities for infants and toddlers focus on the senses—exploring textures, tastes, smells, and sounds and involving natural discoveries as they explore the real world. Discovery learning—Piaget's idea that children learn best through doing and actively exploring—is central to the preschool science curriculum. Good preschool science curricula use real three-dimensional materials and objects (water table, shells, etc.), observe and act on changes (size, shape, motion), notice similarities and differences (sort, measure, discuss, handle), ask open-ended questions (who, what, when, where, how), and experiment, problem solve, and use the senses. Science activities for 7- to 11-year-old children should involve children in the physical world by using equipment, getting messy, building and taking apart things, and using their hands. Children should be full participants by make decisions, helping to set up experiments, asking questions, trying new things, working together, talking about the process and their findings, evaluating results, and having fun.

3. **What are the key components of planning and preparation of environments that support scientific exploration?** The science center should include a table where children can work and a shelf to hold displays, collections, and discovery materials. Provide a variety of tools such as magnifying glasses, balance scales, sieves, funnels, magnets, thermometers, containers, tweezers, and tongs, as well as materials to explore, such as plants, seeds and bulbs, pets, rocks, soil. The center should also provide materials to investigate the physical properties of objects, such as pulleys, gears, wheels, mirrors, and flashlights. Materials should be organized on low, open shelves, labeled, and displayed so that children can use them independently.

4. **What strategies are useful to integrate and create science activities appropriate for young children?** In an appropriate science curriculum, children learn to make and test predictions, observe, make logical connections, learn by trying things in a new way, have increased knowledge of the world, use the scientific process, solve problems, and apply knowledge gained from experiences. Children need to test out their predictions and try out their ideas. The key to this step is to provide plenty of different materials and time to explore. Provide materials for free exploration in your science area so children can visit and revisit them on their own—which is how children conduct their own version of an "independent study."

5. **How can technology be used in an environment to support scientific exploration?** Record findings on a nature walk. When you get back to the classroom, play back the recording and discuss what you experienced. Create a Why? file podcast where children answer science-related questions into a microphone and upload to the Internet for all to hear. Document cameras connected to a Smart Board or projector are a great way to look at the natural items enlarged as if they were under a microscope. An example of how technology can be used to teach science is a kindergarten curriculum unit that explored wild animals through photographs, video clips, and animal sounds on a computer, either online or using specific software. Field trips can also involve children with technology.

6. **How can you incorporate diversity into science activities?** To introduce an awareness of the different environments in various parts of the world, read books to the children, display objects and artifacts from different cultures, show photographs, and explore websites of faraway places such as the rainforests in Central and South America, the deserts in the Middle East and Africa, and the rivers around the

world. Cooking experiences value cultural diversity. Foods from other cultures offer opportunities for children to taste the different ingredients and flavors. This also helps to develop their understanding that many of the foods they eat are both different *and* similar to those eaten in other countries.

7. **How can you develop partnerships with families that support children's exploration of science?** Help families understand that children are *natural* scientists discovering their world. Send information and suggestions home. Begin with general ideas as to what parents can do with their children, and then show them specific activities that are ongoing in the classroom.

8. **What is the teacher's role in promoting science in the classroom?** Teachers provide hands-on experiences that make science a part of every child's day and preserve and value a child's natural curiosity by avoiding "telling" children about a scientific activity that they themselves cannot observe or experiment with and asking open-ended questions to help children to observe carefully and to encourage them to put their ideas into words.

Reflective Review Questions

1. Reflect on your past experiences with science concepts and activities in school. Which were the most exciting or boring? Why were they exciting or boring? Based on what you now know, what did your teacher do (or not do) to help these experiences stay with you?

2. What strategies would you use to integrate other curriculum areas into science? Give examples.

3. Think about an early childhood classroom and outside area. List the materials and equipment that encourage scientific investigation. Based on information from this chapter, discuss the developmentally appropriate approach to introducing these objects to the children and how you would promote methods of exploration and discovery to take place.

Explorations

1. Select at least two early childhood classrooms. Observe for one hour in each. Describe objectively (factually) in writing how science activities were introduced to the children. Which methods of inquiry and process skills (as described in this chapter) were used? Explain by giving examples. Which science activities happened indoors and which ones occurred outdoors? Was there a science learning center as part of the room arrangement? Explain. Describe at least four activities you observed. What are your subjective (opinion) thoughts about early education science activities now that you have completed this assignment?

2. Select two of the activities suggested in this chapter, such as the carrot-top garden, rooting a sweet potato, thirsty celery, or growing grass, and experiment with them at home. Then plan how you will arrange the environment, what transitions into the activities you will use, and what materials you will supply for the scientific investigations as you set up the activities for a group of young children.

3. Based on the information from this chapter, write a letter about science activities to give to the parents of the children in your class. Be creative. Explain what science projects you and the children are doing. Give suggestions for extended activities the parents can do with their children. Describe other ways to communicate with parents.

4. Select and plan a science activity for young children. Specify which age group this activity is planned for: infants, toddlers, preschoolers, or primary-age children. In writing, list objectives, materials needed, step-by-step procedures for presenting

this activity, follow-up activities, and evaluation guidelines. (Use the activity plan worksheet in Appendix D.) Prepare this activity and demonstrate it during class or with a group of children.

5. Use the Sensory Environment Checklist in this chapter to conduct an observation of an early childhood learning environment.
   - Beside each statement, place an *X* if the classroom you observed met the statement.
   - On a separate sheet of paper, describe what you actually observed related to each statement. Place the number of the statement first and then your observation.
   - On a separate sheet of paper, for each statement that you did not check as met, describe what you would do to improve that classroom so that the statement would be met. Be sure to put the number of the statement first.
   - Submit this with the name of the location you observed and the age group.

Science Books for Children

- Aguilar, D. A. (2008). *11 planets: A new view of the solar system*. New York: National Geographic.
- Brown, P. (2009). *The curious garden*. New York: Little Brown.
- Brunelle, L. (2007). *Camp out: The ultimate kids' guide*. New York: Workman.
- Chin, J. (2009). *Redwoods*. New York: Flash Point.
- Hague, M. (2007). *Animal friends: A collection of poems for children*. New York: Henry Holt.
- Helman, A. (2008). *Hide and seek: Nature's best vanishing acts*. Photographed by G. Jecan. New York: Walker.
- Johnson, J. (2008). *Animal tracks and signs*. New York: National Geographic.
- Leslie, C. W., and Roth, C. E. (2003). *Keeping a nature journal: Discover a whole new way of seeing the world around you*. New York: Storey.
- Morgan, B. (2005). *Rock and fossil hunter*. New York: DK Publishing.
- Serafini, F. (2008). *Looking closely through the forest*. New York: Kids Can.
- Tait, N. (2008). *Insects and spiders*. New York: Simon & Schuster.
- Ward, J. (2008). *I love dirt!* New York: Trumpeter.

❯❯ Professional Resource Download

10 Math

Student Learning Outcomes

After studying this chapter, you should be able to:

- Define and give examples for key terms related to math experiences for children.

- Discuss math experiences for young children and relate stages of child development to math experiences.

- Evaluate various components of planning and preparation of environments that promote mathematical learning.

- Create math activities appropriate for young children.

- Discuss various ways to use technology to promote mathematical learning.

- Distinguish ways to incorporate diversity into math experiences.

- Describe ways to develop partnerships with families that support children's mathematical experiences.

- Analyze the teacher's role in promoting math experiences in the classroom.

Standards Covered in This Chapter

 NAEYC 5a, 5b, 5c

 DAP 2

INTASC INTASC 4, 5, 8

HS HEAD START
Domain: Mathematics Development

COMMON CORE Math Standard

Mathematics is everywhere! We are involved with math concepts from infancy onward. Much of what we do as part of our everyday lives relates to mathematics: telling time with clocks and watches, cooking and eating, getting dressed, watching a basketball game, and planning our lives by the calendar (electronic or otherwise). Daily activities involve problem solving, one-to-one correspondence, classifying, measuring, and sequencing. This is true for children, too.

As you progress through this chapter, the approach to setting up the developmentally appropriate math environment will parallel the approach to, and interconnect with, all the content areas in this book. The math-rich environment is built on basic math concepts, the children's developmental level (individually and collectively), and their interests.

In our high-tech world today, it is important that young children build their confidence in their ability to do mathematics. Cross, T., Woods, T., and Schweinguber, H. (2009) state, "Early childhood mathematics is vitally important for young children's past and future educational success. Research has demonstrated that virtually all young children have the capability to learn and become competent in mathematics." Providing hands-on, developmentally appropriate math experiences in a safe and trustworthy environment gives children opportunities to develop math awareness and understanding. Use of a math curriculum as part of an intervention significantly enhanced the mathematical knowledge of all of the children. Low-income children acquired more knowledge, relative to their starting point, than middle-income children, but the extent of mathematical knowledge at the end of the study was similar for both groups (Starkey et al., 2004). "The best way to teach children is in a purposeful manner—in a context that has a purpose to the child" (Baroody, 2000, p. 61). This is different from the rote learning, rigid rules, workbooks, and flash cards many of us grew up with. The goal for children today is to focus on conceptual math, not pencil-and-paper figuring. The new view of math is that it should be relaxed and comfortable for the teacher and the children. A study of preschool children's math-related behaviors showed that the greater gains made by children were influenced by the number of times children were observed focused on mathematics and the number of times they were observed talking about math during math activity (Hofer, Fannan, and Cummings, 2013).

Children need to acquire basic skills and concepts *first* to live in our world, which is exploding with information and continuously changing. Children build mathematical ideas based on their interactions with adults and with other children, their daily observations, and their experiences with their environment. (See **Figure 10-1**.)

It is also important to understand that the acquisition of math skills and concepts occurs in stages over time, as with all growth and development in young children. Teachers should recognize that early math instruction and experiences are not limited to a specific period or time of day. Instead, these math opportunities are a natural part of the learning environment (Texas Education Agency and University of Texas System, 2008). When a child builds with blocks, counts the number of buttons on a shirt, recognizes how many butterflies are on the page, gives each child a napkin at snack time, or claps a rhythmic pattern, he or she is learning math.

Repetition is meaningful during this process. Children need to rethink and practice what they know as they continue to add new skills and concepts. Making the environment, both indoors and outdoors, available for young children to experience the world and their place in it will encourage them to understand that mathematics is everywhere!

Child-directed play enriches math learning. Because time is a very abstract concept, especially for preschool children to understand, putting a calendar in the dramatic play center to circle and label dates of important classroom events bring context to using the calendar like families do at home. Children can decide whether

Figure 10-1 Young children continually construct mathematical ideas based on their experiences with their environment.

a date should be circled and count the days until the event occurs (Anderson, Spainhower, and Sharp, 2014).

Math Defined

> " Early childhood is a period when children actively engage in acquiring fundamental concepts and learning fundamental skills. Concepts are the building blocks of knowledge and they allow people to organize and categorize information. . . . Concepts can be applied to the solution of new problems that are met in everyday experience (Charlesworth and Lind, 2010, p. 2). "

The term **early mathematics** refers to exposure to and interaction with materials that contribute to the acquisition of knowledge about the underlying concepts of math (National Association for the Education of Young Children [NAEYC] and National Council of Teachers of Mathematics [NCTM], 2002). When child development and mathematics are mentioned together, Jean Piaget and Lev Vygotsky come to mind.

Jean Piaget pioneered the study of children's thinking (cognitive growth and development) and described how each child creates a mental image or knowledge of the world, based on encounters with the environment. Piaget called this **physical knowledge** or learning about objects in the environment and their characteristics, such as color, weight, and size. Piaget's **logico-mathematical knowledge** is the type that includes relationships each individual constructs to make sense out of the world and to organize information, such as classification, counting, and comparing (Charlesworth and Lind, 2016).

Like Piaget, Vygotsky also studied children's thinking. He contributed significant insight into the way we learn from those around us, especially those who have more skill. He believed that we develop ways of cooperating and communicating, as well as exhibiting new capacities to plan and to think ahead (Charlesworth and Lind, 2016). This resulted in his interest in what children know now but also what they are capable of learning. Refer to Chapter 1 for additional information.

Howard Gardner includes logical/mathematical thinking in his research relating to multiple intelligences, sometimes referred to as "different ways of knowing." Children strong in this form of intelligence think conceptually in logical and numerical patterns, making connections between pieces of information. Young children who excel in logico-mathematical intelligence have strong problem-solving and reasoning skills and ask questions in a logical manner. They thrive in logical and consistent sequencing of daily schedules and routines (Gardner, 1993; Nicholson-Nelson, 1998). Review Chapter 1 for information on all of Gardner's multiple intelligences.

When you observe children, you become aware of how they think (problem solve) and talk (communicate) about what they are discovering. **Concept development** is fostered by solving problems or figuring things out. Constructing knowledge by making mistakes is part of this process as well. Researchers have found that presenting children with part–whole geometric puzzles in a story context led to more improvement in the part–whole spatial thinking of kindergarten children than presenting these puzzles alone (Casey, Erkut, Ceder, and Young, 2008). In contrast, researchers found that because much learning of geometric concepts by U.S. students has been by rote, children frequently do not recognize components, properties, and relationships between properties of shapes. This study found that preschool children exhibit working knowledge of simple geometric forms, so instruction should build on this knowledge and move beyond it. The researchers recommend that teachers encourage students to describe why a figure belongs or does not belong to a shape category such as circles or squares, instead of just naming it (Clements, Swaminathan, Hannibal, and Sarama, 1999).

A curriculum that accommodates a variety of developmental levels as well as individual differences in young children sets the stage for problem-solving opportunities (Copple

early mathematics: Refers to exposure to and interaction with materials that contribute to the acquisition of knowledge about the underlying concepts of mathematics.

physical knowledge: Learning about objects in the environment and their characteristics, such as color, weight, and size.

logico-mathematical knowledge: Includes relationships constructed to make sense out of the world and to organize information, such as counting and classification.

concept development: The construction of knowledge through solving problems and experiencing the results, while being actively involved with the environment.

and Bredekamp, 2009). This, too, is a process. Beginning with the needs and interests of the children, developing themes, lesson plans, and webs and providing time, space, and materials encourages problem solving.

> "Tell me mathematics, and I will forget;
> Show me mathematics and I may remember;
> Involve me . . . and I will understand mathematics.
> (Williams quoted in Furner and Berman, 2003.)"

Developmental Stages of Math

Young children understand math in relationship to how it affects them. The infant discovers the shape of the object by putting it in his mouth and holding on to it. The toddler can let you know he or she is 2 years old by trying to show you two fingers. The 3-year-old likes to sing a number song, whereas the 4-year-old counts "one two three four five six." The 5-year-old shows you how tall his or her block building is, and the school-age child wants to win at the board game he or she is playing. All these children are using math language.

In the beginning, children can say the names of numbers in order. They remember the words, but they do not understand the meaning of what they are saying. This number sense evolves during the first eight years of a child's life. How you set up the early education environment will determine how often the child has opportunities to develop number sense and logical ways of thinking about time, space, and other mathematical ideas.

For young children, infants and toddlers especially, the schedules and routines of the day become a consistent sequence of events. This regular, predictable pattern helps put order to things, which is part of the process of math learning. When you frequently sing number songs and finger plays, read number books, share number flannel board stories, and repeat numerals, you are placing math in the environment and making it part of the day's routine.

> "All decisions regarding mathematics curriculum and teaching practices should be grounded in knowledge of children's development and learning across all interrelated areas—cognitive, linguistic, physical, and social-emotional" (NAEYC and NCTM, 2002, p. 15). With this in mind, as teachers you should plan environments that build on children's curiosity and enthusiasm and encourage them to discover math concepts in the process of play. Children have had significant mathematical experiences in their play long before they encounter school mathematics. For young children, playful activity is simply the means to learning (Eisenhauer and Feikes, 2009)."

Teachers need to find worthwhile tasks that provide a real need for young children to learn and practice mathematics; for example, incorporating mathematics into everyday situations, children's questions, games, and children's literature. (See **Figure 10-2**.) The numerical knowledge of children from low-income backgrounds trails behind that of peers from middle-income backgrounds even before the children enter school. This gap may reflect differing prior experience with informal numerical activities, such as numerical board games. The researchers found that playing numerical board games offers an inexpensive means for reducing the gap in numerical knowledge that separates less and more affluent children when they begin school (Siegler and Ramani, 2008, p. 661).

Numbers and Operations

The following discussions of math concepts, processes, and skills are based on recommendations from NCTM's *Principles and Standards for School Mathematics* (2000).

Figure 10-2 A young child needs to rethink and practice what he or she knows as he or she continues to add new skills and concepts.

Young children use numbers to solve everyday problems by constructing number meanings through real-world experiences and the use of physical materials. The following concepts, skills, and processes are fundamental to early mathematics.

Number sense is a concept and counting is a skill that children use often in their everyday activities. Number sense develops as children participate in activities that make them think about, explore, and discuss mathematical ideas. Classroom environments and teachers create experiences that are fundamental in developing children's number sense (White, 2002).

Number concepts do not occur in one lesson, one theme, or even one year. We need to understand that it is a continuous developmentally appropriate process that provides the foundation for many more math concept. The best way to work toward number sense and all the NCTM standards is to begin wherever the child is. All other strategies waste the child's time and prevent the development of the essential foundational understandings and skills needed for future success.

One-to-one correspondence is based on the premise that each object has the value of one. It is the foundation for relating one object to one counting number. This is the most fundamental component of numbers. One-to-one correspondence is also a focal point for numbers and operations at the prekindergarten level. One-to-one correspondence is established when one object is paired with one other object or a group of objects is paired with another group of equal number. The assigning of a number name (one, two, three, etc.) to each object helps children place the objects in a one-to-one correspondence. Children show an awareness of this relationship daily.

The following are examples of this awareness:

- Language is important to toddlers, so a teacher touching and counting aloud (one child, one book, one block, one doll) is expressing one-to-one correspondence. A child is learning self-help skills and one-to-one correspondence when he puts one arm into a coat sleeve.
- For preschoolers and older children, activities such as putting one peg in one hole, setting the table with one napkin for each child, or putting one sock on one foot is one-to-one correspondence. Giving a child four pennies and asking him or her to put one penny in each of four cups also demonstrates one-to-one correspondence.

Cardinality is defined as the number of elements in a given mathematical set. In other words, the total number or quantity of objects counted. Common Core State Standards for kindergarten math include standard *K.CC.4*—Understand the relationship between numbers and quantities: connect counting to cardinality, and standard *K.CC.5*—Count to answer "how many?" questions about as many as 20 things arranged in a line, a rectangular array, a circle, or as many as 10 things in a scattered configuration; given a number from 1 to 20, count out that many objects. Playing games like concentration with 10 frame grids, dot cards, or even pictures or graphing with Cuisenaire rods can help children to understand the relationship between numbers and quantities, and they can use number journals to record this information.

Rational Counting

Count anything and everything! Count real things to help children use their own experience with objects to better understand numbers. Counting is a powerful tool for extending young children's nonverbal numerical and arithmetical competencies. Teachers should provide abundant developmentally appropriate opportunities for children to learn and practice

number sense: A concept that develops over time as children think about, explore, and discuss mathematical ideas.

one-to-one correspondence: The pairing of one object to another object or one group of objects to another group of equal number.

cardinality: The number of elements in a given mathematical set. In other words, the total number or quantity of objects counted.

counting skills and should reinforce their efforts. Throughout the day sing number songs, repeat finger plays and rhymes, share number flannel-board stories, and read books that include counting. Counting with young children starts with **rote counting**, the ability to recite names of numerals in order. **Rational counting** requires children to match each numeral name, in order, to an object in a group.

A basic understanding of accurate rote counting and one-to-one correspondence is the foundation of rational counting. The ability of rational counting assists children in understanding the concept of numbers by enabling them to check their labeling of quantities as being a specific amount. It also helps them to compare equal quantities of different things and to realize that the quantity two is two, regardless of what makes up a group.

Classifying and Sorting

Children grouping objects by a common attribute or characteristic, such as size, shape, or color, are **classifying and sorting**. They are interacting with the environment, using visual discrimination, and manipulating real objects.

Figure 10-3   Classifying and sorting objects by a common characteristic.

Sorting activities allow teachers to naturally introduce the language of mathematics with words such as more, few, many, most, least, and none to describe children's collections. (See **Figure 10-3**.)

As a teacher, your role is to extend the children's concepts about the material's attributes. The following are some examples:

- Infants learn about shapes through using their hands, mouth, and eyes. They are discovering that some toys are easier to hold, whereas others roll better.
- During late infancy, babies grasp an important developmental concept—object permanence. This realization is vital for learning and is especially important for developing thinking and number skills. When toddlers understand object constancy, sorting by size and color closely follows.
- Toddlers begin noticing alike and different when they sort colored blocks into blues and reds or big and little ones. It is important to remember to keep concepts simple and consistent for toddlers. For example, have all the blue and red blocks they are sorting be the same size and shape so the children are dealing only with the concept of color. Simple puzzles also help toddlers begin to develop classification skills.
- Preschool children begin by sorting objects with one characteristic or quality. They enjoy sorting buttons, plastic animals, wooden beads, and shells. Provide a muffin tin (see **Figure 10-3**), plastic cups, or an empty, clean egg carton for the sorted objects. For older preschoolers, classifying becomes more involved by isolating a set from a collection, such as counting children and sorting them into boys and girls, and then observing which children are wearing stripes and which are not.
- Primary-grade children use more complex concepts by sorting sets into subsets and looking at what materials objects are made of (wood, plastic, metal) or what function they have (forks, knives, spoons), or which piece of string is longer (or shorter, or thicker) than the other two. Older children can explain to you their rule for making the sorting decision. This process involves comparing, beginning measurement, as well as one-to-one correspondence, counting, and classifying skills.

Patterns, Functions, and Algebra

Patterning is another way for children to see order in their world. A **pattern** is a sequence of numbers, colors, objects, sounds, shapes, or movements that repeat, in the same order or

rote counting: The ability to recite names of numerals in order.

rational counting: Requires matching each numeral name, in order, to an object in a group.

classifying and sorting: Grouping objects by a common characteristic, such as size, shape, or color.

pattern: A sequence of colors, objects, sounds, stories, or movements that repeats in the same order over and over again.

arrangement, over and over again. Patterns are the foundation of algebraic thinking. Recognizing, describing, extending, and translating patterns help children begin early math.

Mathematics is the science and language of patterns. Thinking about patterns helps children make sense of mathematics. Some examples follow:

- For infants, patterning is recognizing the human face with eyes, nose, and mouth in a specific place. For older infants, looking in a mirror helps them place their face in the same pattern.
- Toddlers asking for the same book to be read again and again soon begin to "read" the story along with the teacher. They are placing the events of the story in a sequencing pattern.
- For preschoolers and older children, stringing beads or putting pegs in a pegboard in a specific pattern, such as blue, red, green, and yellow, is visual patterning. The younger children can duplicate the pattern and the older children can duplicate and extend it.

Auditory patterning is repeating or singing sounds (such as soft, loud, soft, loud, soft) over and over again and then having the children repeat the sequence. You can do this with tactile patterning by creating a texture board with articles that are smooth, rough, smooth, rough, smooth.

- Instead of talking about a pattern, the teacher "reads" the pattern using simple vocabulary: *circle, square, circle, square, circle, square* or *a, b, a, b, a, b.* Create a pattern physically: *jump, jump, clap, clap, jump, jump, clap, clap.*
- With linking cubes the plus-one pattern can be visually shared with children.
- Not only do young children need many experiences with repeating patterns, but they also can work with growing patterns that increase (or decrease) by a constant amount. The simplest of all growing patterns increases by one and begins with a small number. For example, 1, 2, 3, 4, 5, 6 . . . is a growing pattern based on a constant change of plus one. This is best understood by young children through concrete representation.

Seriation

Teachers should provide opportunities for children to recognize, extend, and create a wide variety of patterns. **Seriation** is a concept underlying patterning. Seriation or ordering of objects is based on the ability to place them in logical sequence, such as smallest to largest. Simple seriation involves concrete objects such as arranging objects from longest to shortest or widest to narrowest. Sensory seriation can include ordering sounds from loudest to softest, tastes from sweetest to sourest, or colors from darkest to lightest. Seriation can also relate to time sequences such as what happened first, second, third, and so forth.

Comparative vocabulary develops with seriation: good, better, best; big, medium, small; lightest, light, heavy, heaviest; lightest, light, dark, darkest.

seriation: Seriation or ordering of objects is based on the ability to place them in logical sequence, such as smallest to largest or shortest to tallest.

geometry: The area of mathematics that involves shape, size, space, position, direction, and movement.

Early Geometry and Spatial Sense

Geometry

Geometry is the area of mathematics that involves shape, size, space, position, direction, and movement, and describes and classifies the physical world we live in. (See **Figure 10**-4.)

> Geometry offers students an aspect of mathematical thinking that is different from, but connected to, the world of numbers. As students become familiar with shape, structure, location, and transformations and as they develop spatial reasoning, they lay the foundation for understanding not only their spatial world but also other topics in mathematics and in art, science, and social studies (NCTM, 2000).

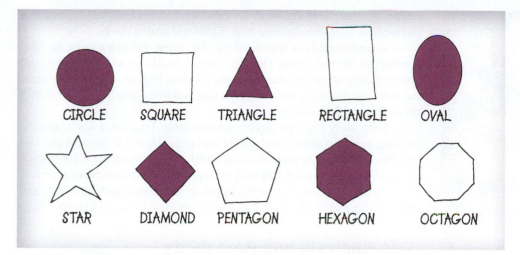

| CIRCLE | SQUARE | TRIANGLE | RECTANGLE | OVAL |
| STAR | DIAMOND | PENTAGON | HEXAGON | OCTAGON |

Figure 10-4 Real objects and abstract shapes have one-, two-, or three-dimensional features that can be examined and compared.

Spatial Sense

Spatial sense is a child's awareness of himself or herself in relation to the people and objects around him or her. Games and movement activities can be the keys to spatial relationship awareness, such as location/position (on/off, over/under), direction/movement (up/down, forward/backward, in/out, in front of/in back of, around/through), and distance (near/far, close/far from).

Manipulating shapes in space introduces children to vocabulary words. In addition, identifying differences between letters of the alphabet cause children to pay attention to shape and position. In art, geometric forms and spatial relationships are critical in both two-dimensional and three-dimensional creations. Other examples are filling and emptying, such as playing in the sandbox; fitting things together and taking them apart, such as Legos and boxes with lids; and setting things in motion, such as things that roll and spin.

Play the "hide an object" game with preschoolers. For example, hide a block or a beanbag somewhere in the room. Let the children guess if you have hidden it over, under, on top of, and so on. The child who guesses where the object is hidden becomes "it" and hides the object for the other children to guess where it is. The children are thinking in images and pictures. They are finding the object that has been placed in space and out of sight. Older children extend spatial relationships to board games, where they count squares and move forward or backward on the game board. They are exploring a new spatial layout and varying the arrangement of the game pieces in space.

Appropriate software is available for children to learn more about spatial relationships using the computer, but first it is critical that they understand the basic math concepts used in the relationships. Math language of early childhood overlaps, interconnects, and involves all the senses. No matter what terminology they use, children are counting, classifying, thinking, reasoning, comparing, measuring, problem solving, and learning about math naturally as they play.

Measurement

According to NCTM's Standards (2000), "Measurement is one of the most widely used applications of mathematics. It bridges two main areas of school mathematics—geometry and number." **Measurement** is finding the length, height, and weight of an object using units like inches, feet, and pounds. Offer children activities to identify and compare attributes of length (longer, shorter), capacity (holds more, holds less), weight (heavier, lighter), and temperature

spatial sense: Comparisons that help children develop an awareness of themselves in relation to people and objects in space, such as exploration using blocks and boxes.

measurement: Finding the length, height, and weight of an object using units like inches, feet, and pounds.

Figure 10-5 Many daily activities involve estimating, weighing, and measurement.

(colder, warmer). (See **Figure 10-5**.) Time is measured using hours, minutes, and seconds by reading time on both digital and analog clocks.

Measurement is an important way for young children to look for relationships in the real world. Through playing, imitating, and learning to use standard units of measurements, young children explore and discover measurement. By practicing measurement, they will learn how big or little things are and how to figure that out.

Many daily activities involve measurement. Here are a few examples: cooking, matching objects, comparing sizes of containers at the sand and water table, measuring the number of steps it takes to get somewhere, comparing and ordering objects according to their length using terms such as longer and shorter, estimating and measuring length to the nearest inch and foot, and linking cubes to find objects that are shorter or longer than 10 linking cubes.

Data Analysis and Probability

Data analysis is a math concept that requires strong skills in several other math-related areas. To be successful, children must first understand math concepts and be able to recognize numbers. They must then be able to count and apply one-to-one correspondence. When these have been mastered, they are ready to begin the data analysis tasks.

Questions that cannot be answered by direct observation can often be assessed by gathering data. Data can be organized, represented, and summarized in a variety of ways. Using graphs and charts, children can discover how to organize and interpret information and see relationships. Graphing and charting offer children a way to show and see information and can make it easier to make predictions about related events. The data findings can be represented through the use of a vertical or horizontal bar graph, a pie graph, a line graph, or a circle graph.

Ask the children questions that require collection and organization of data, and then display relevant data to answer the questions (NCTM, 2000). Examples of this are children asking questions about their environment and then gathering data about themselves and their surroundings, and sorting and classifying objects according to their attributes and organizing data about the objects (Charlesworth and Lind, 2010, Position Statement, p. 5).

Problem Solving

Teachers provide an environment that encourages problem solving and verbalize children's methods as they solve problems. Problem solving is critical to being able to do all other aspects of mathematics. Children learn that there are many different ways to solve a problem and that more than one answer is possible.

Many early childhood educators and researchers emphasize the importance of problem solving in helping children clarify and strengthen their math understandings (see **Figure 10-6**):

" Problem solving involves finding a solution for a problem that is not known in advance. To do this, children must use their previous knowledge to develop a new mathematical understanding. Solving problems is a goal of learning mathematics and also a major means of doing so.

The development of problem-solving skills is a long-term activity; it is not learned in one lesson. It must be focused on the process of problem-solving, not just the answer. Therefore, you must provide children with problem-solving situations and observe how they meet them. Behavior noted can be recorded with anecdotal records or checklist.

Problem solving and reasoning are the heart of mathematics. . . . While content represents the what of early childhood mathematics education, the processes—problem solving, reasoning, communication, connections, and representation—make it possible for children to acquire content knowledge. . . . Children's development and use of these processes are among the most long-lasting and important achievements of mathematics education (NAEYC and NCTM, 2002). **"**

In 2006, the NCTM introduced *Curriculum Focal Points*, an extension of its *Principles and Standards Goals* (2000): "*Focal points* present a way to bring focus to the teaching, learning, and assessing of mathematics. They provide a framework for designing and organizing curricular expectations and assessments. Collectively, they describe an approach that can be used in developing a mathematics curriculum for prekindergarten through grade 8" (NCTM Standards, 2006).

In addition, the focal points are intended as a first step toward a national discussion on how to bring consistency and coherence to the mathematics curricula used in the United States (NCTM, 2006). Integrating the NCTM standards, the Common Core State Standards provide a consistent, clear understanding of what students are expected to learn, so teachers and parents know what they need to do to help them. The standards are designed to be robust and relevant to the real world, reflecting the knowledge and skills that our young people need for success in college and careers. With U.S. students fully prepared for the future, our communities will be best positioned to compete successfully in the global economy.

The Common Core Standards for Mathematical Practice describe varieties of expertise that mathematics educators from kindergarten through high school should seek to develop in their students. These practices rest on important "processes and proficiencies" with long-standing importance in mathematics education. The first of these are the NCTM process standards of problem solving, reasoning and proof, communication, representation, and connections described in detail previously. The second are the strands of mathematical proficiency specified in the National Research Council's report *Adding It Up* include adaptive reasoning, strategic competence, conceptual understanding (comprehension of mathematical concepts, operations, and relations), procedural fluency (skill in carrying out procedures flexibly, accurately, efficiently, and appropriately), and productive disposition (habitual inclination to see mathematics as sensible, useful, and worthwhile, coupled with a belief in diligence and one's own efficacy). For more specific information on the Common Core State Standards, go to http://www.corestandards.org/the-standards.

These standards and focal points not only identify strategies that educators can use to help children clarify and strengthen their math understandings, but they also lead to the strengthening of neural pathways in the brain.

Figure 10-6   The math-rich environment is built on basic math concepts including the attributes of shape and pattern and applying them to problem solving.

Brain Research: Activity-Dependent Development

Experience can change the actual structure of the brain. Brain development is *activity-dependent*.

Knowing how children learn and understanding how the brain searches for, processes, and then organizes information is critical to providing appropriate learning experiences. Only when a concept is meaningful to a child can the symbolic language of mathematics begin to be introduced and have meaning. Active involvement in experiential learning is the cornerstone of meaning construction. Such learning is developmental and requires time. Children need time to think and extract mathematical concepts from the authentic experiences that teachers provide. Children need time to play and explore materials, independently, through free exploration

before they can attend to reflection and mathematical concepts (Ruby, 2002).

Every experience excites some neural circuits and leaves others alone. Neural circuits used over and over strengthen; those that are not used are dropped, resulting in *pruning*. The brain is undergoing explosive growth in the first years of life and needs organizing experiences to facilitate development. Learning results in more consolidation of neuronal activity—brain activity becomes more efficient.

Janice Fletcher. (2004). *Making Connections: Helping Children Build Their Brains*. Storrs, CT: National Network for Child Care at the University of Connecticut Cooperative Extension System.

Planning and Preparing the Environment

naeyc   DAP   INTASC   HS   COMMON CORE

Materials for Developing Math Concepts

As we know, young children are interested in math. Their natural curiosity is evident in their everyday play and activities. The role of teachers and parents is to provide children with the appropriate words, materials, and resources to explore their interests and scaffold new levels of understanding. Provide a variety of materials for exploring number concepts, to recognize, copy, create, and extend patterns, to explore geometric shapes and spatial relationships, to explore measurement, and to organize and represent data.

The following materials offer children many ways to develop their understanding of math concepts:

- Balances, weights, scales
- Bingo cards
- Blocks—Legos, wooden table blocks, parquetry blocks, and pattern blocks
- Board games
- Counters—unifix cubes, base-10 blocks, plastic animal shapes, popsicle sticks, straws, and beads in various colors and sizes
- Calendar
- Calculators
- Cans or egg cartons, with numbers on them to put a matching number of objects into children's socks, shoes, mittens, and gloves, to match in pairs
- Clocks with numbers (*not* digital)
- Computer software that allows children to interact with math concepts
- Geometric boards (geoboards): to manipulate rubber bands or elastic loopers to form shapes or designs
- Magnetic boards with plastic numerals
- Measuring cups, spoons, and pitchers
- Milk cartons to demonstrate liquid measures and relationships between half-pints, pints, quarts, and gallons
- Number strips and counting boards
- Objects to count, sort, and classify, such as buttons, paper clips, pennies, colored cubes, bottle caps, aluminum washers, colored plastic clothespins, empty spools, shells, popsicle or craft sticks, keys, bread tags, and nuts and bolts
- Puzzles
- Rulers, yardsticks, and measuring tapes
- Sandpaper numerals
- Self-help skill forms (buttoning, zipping, and tying)
- Shape puzzles and flannel board characters, such as circle, square, rectangle, triangle, cone, sphere, cube, cylinder, oval, diamond, star, and heart
- Stacking, nesting, and sorting boxes or blocks
- Storage containers in graduated sizes
- Table games, such as parquetry blocks, pattern blocks, card games, and dominos
- Telephones
- Thermometers (outside)
- Timer
- Unit, hollow, shape, and table blocks, which offer opportunities to learn about balance, measurement and estimation, width, height, length and dimensionality, size relationships, and how shapes fit into space
- Wooden pegboard and pegs

Math Environment Checklist

_____ 1. Is there a variety of developmental math activities for each of the math standards (number and operations, measurement, geometry, algebra and data analysis)?

_____ 2. Are there aesthetically pleasing containers that children can see into to keep all needed materials?

_____ 3. Do teachers use assessment of the children's knowledge and skills on which to select materials and activities?

_____ 4. Is there a clearly defined math area in a quiet area of the room?

_____ 5. Are there concrete materials for active manipulation?

_____ 6. Do teachers interact with children to support their understanding of number concepts?

_____ 7. Is there a clearly defined place for each math item on organized shelves?

_____ 8. Are activities based on clearly defined purposes or goals?

_____ 9. Do teachers interact with children to support their understanding of patterns?

_____ 10. Is there adequate large space for children on which they can work?

_____ 11. Are materials and activities open-ended or self-correcting?

_____ 12. Do teachers interact with children to support their understanding of geometry?

_____ 13. Is there plenty of space to display completed math-related work?

_____ 14. Are math materials and activities related to children's interests?

_____ 15. Do teachers interact with children to promote their understanding of measurement?

_____ 16. Are materials or activities in the math center?

_____ 17. Do teachers interact with children to promote their understanding of data collection, organization, and representation?

_____ 18. Are materials rotated to meet children's changing developmental needs and interests?

_____ 19. Are mathematical ideas introduced in planned, purposeful ways?

_____ 20. Are children encouraged to connect mathematical ideas to everyday experiences?

_____ 21. Are children encouraged to communicate and represent their mathematical thinking?

_____ 22. Is there a variety of materials for exploring number concepts?

_____ 23. Are materials available that allow children to recognize, copy, create, and extend patterns?

_____ 24. Is there a variety of materials for exploring geometric shapes and spatial relationships?

_____ 25. Are materials available for exploring measurement?

_____ 26. Is there a variety of materials for collecting, organizing, and representing?

⌄ Professional Resource Download

The Learning Environment

The actual physical environment plays a large role in enhancing mathematical learning. A checklist that can be used to evaluate how the environment in your own classroom or classrooms that you observe supports mathematical skill and concept development follows.

Integrating Math Activities into the Curriculum

Applications for math concepts are everywhere. Math awareness continues outdoors, too. The following examples offer a variety of ideas to help you provide these math experiences:

- Toddlers enjoy play structures that are lower and wider and allow them opportunities to climb up and down. The wheels on the tricycles are round and the sand pile is a square.
- Preschool children can look for rough and smooth objects to compare and count. They like to weave crepe paper or ribbon through a chain link fence to create a pattern and count how many times they toss a beanbag back and forth to each other.
- Older children can take chalk and make a giant hopscotch area with numerals from 0 to 20 as well as measure and record rainfall using a clear container with ¼-inch, ½-inch, and 1-inch markings.

- You can help the children collect boxes, small to large, and set up an outdoor obstacle course for them to crawl through, around, over, and under.
- Line up two rows of small, smooth stones with each row having six stones. Space the stones farther apart in one row. Ask the children if one row has more or less than the other. Most preschoolers will answer that the longer row has more rocks than the other. When children reach the developmental stage of knowing that both rows have the same amount of stones, no matter how they are spaced, they are also practicing the concept of conservation or the ability to retain the original picture in the mind when material has been changed in its arrangement in space. Ask open-ended questions to learn more about children's thinking, such as, "Which of the cups do you think will hold the most sand?"; "How many circles can you find in our room?"; "How many circles do you see outside?"; "How many steps do you think it will take to go from the tricycle to the sandbox?"; or "What can we use to measure the length of the art table?" You will get a lot of answers that will lead to more mathematical discoveries.

Math and Science

Math and science are like a two-piece puzzle. They fit together to make a whole, but each piece is important by itself. That is why these two curriculum areas are separate chapters in this book. Here are several suggestions on how to use math concepts and relate them to the science center and theme:

- Sort collections of shells, magnets, leaves, seeds, and rocks. Classify them according to size.
- Use a thermometer and ask open-ended questions, such as, "What happens when you put the thermometer into hot water?" or "What happens when you put it in cold water?" Guide the children to find the answers themselves.
- Older children can graph the daily temperature. This can extend the daily calendar activity of marking the day of the week and month of the year.
- Have children count the number of legs on insects. Use both pictures and real insects, if possible.
- Plants offer opportunities for children to keep a chart or graph of the days or times plants should be watered and how much they have grown.
- Children's literature can create strategies to integrate math and science concepts in the curriculum.
- *Planting a Rainbow* (1988) and *Growing Vegetable Soup* (1987), both by Lois Ehlert, are two books that integrate math and science in an exciting way by incorporating thinking, problem solving, and questioning.

Math and Cooking

One of the most delightful ways to invite children into the world of math is through cooking. If you ask a young child playing in the dramatic play area to explain the ingredients of the imaginary cake he is baking, the answer will probably be something like this: "I put in 20 cups of sugar, a bunch of flour, two eggs (one for each hand), and mix 'em all up and put it in the stove for 10 minutes." Even though his numbers may be inaccurate, this shows that he or she is aware of quantities in recipes.

Extend both the dramatic play and math. Let the children bake an actual cake. Just think about the ways you can help children clarify math concepts through experiences with cooking. You are involving children with counting, one-to-one correspondence, fractions, time, temperature, weight, shapes, sizes, amounts, measurements, reading a recipe, and following a sequence.

Here's an easy cake recipe, and all you do is "dump" everything together: Put one can of fruit, including juice, into a buttered cake pan. Dump one box of cake mix over the fruit.

Chop up one stick of butter or margarine. Dump these pieces on the top of the cake mix. Bake at 350 degrees for 30 to 40 minutes. Then divide into servings, one for each child, and eat! (See **Figure 10**-7.)

You can also make pretzels and cheese shapes. Children really enjoy making these. You will need:

14-ounce block of cheddar cheese
package of stick pretzels

1. Wash hands.
2. Cut cheese into various shapes.
3. Put ends of pretzels into the cheese shapes.
4. Eat and talk about the shapes the children are eating.

> "For a time, rumors circulated that Howard Gardner was going to add cooking to his list of multiple intelligences. Although I was disappointed that this addition never came to pass, I will continue always to describe cooking ability as a type of intelligence. It is an area in which children can shine and excel. It is also a domain that teachers can use to teach socioemotional, cognitive, physical, and literacy skills as well as to foster children's creativity and self-expression. My firm belief is that cooking—like block building, reading, and the arts—should be an integral part of every preschool and kindergarten program (Colker, *The Cooking book,* 2005, p. ix)."

Figure 10-7   Invite children into the world of math through cooking.

Math and Art

Children need to relate math to themselves and adding art projects to the math activities will help them do this. For example, make an "All About Me" book, poster, or chart. Include the child's weight, height, and shoe size or foot outline at the beginning of the year, at various times during the year, and at the end of the year. This offers children a concrete way to compare their stages of growth. This is also another way to do assessment.

Another art and math activity, one that has been part of the preschool curriculum for many years, is to draw an outline around a child's body on a large piece of white butcher paper or brown wrapping paper. The younger child will need you to do it, but the older child can select a partner to do it. Each child can then weigh himself or herself on a scale in the classroom, measure different parts of his or her body, and record the results on the drawing. Next, the child can add finishing art to the drawing by adding facial features, hair, clothing, and shoes.

Math and Language, Literacy, and Literature

Teachers have begun to realize that mathematics is everywhere. As we include critical thinking, problem solving, and communication as important goals within the mathematics curriculum, we have become aware that children's literature holds countless creative opportunities for working toward these goals.

For language, literacy, and literature development, select math books of all types and genres to read to the children, or have the children read and discuss during group time.

Activity Plan Worksheet

The following activity plan worksheets and songs offer opportunities for developmentally appropriate activities teachers can do along with other math projects. The songs suggest flannel-board activities, finger plays, music, and movement learning experiences.

Activity Plan Worksheet
Developmentally Appropriate and Multicultural/Anti-Biased Activity

AGES: appropriate for 2- and 3-year-olds

Name of Activity and Brief Description

The flannel board shape game is designed to help young children become aware of shapes, begin to identify them by name, and look for shapes in their environment.

Child Outcomes of Activity

- Develop shape awareness and recognition.
- Identify shapes.
- Enhance matching ability.
- Recognize equal amounts.
- Sort and classify objects by shapes and sizes.
- Develop fine motor skills.
- Offer tactile learning experience.

Space and Materials Needed

This activity can be done on the floor during circle time or at a table during small group time with a flannel board and felt pieces cut into shapes (circles, squares, triangles, and rectangles) of various colors and sizes. These shape pieces should be sizes that 2- and 3-year-olds can manipulate. Also, cut a large version of each shape from cardboard, construction paper, or felt.

Procedure

1. Introduce the activity by placing one shape at a time on the flannel board. Ask the children if they can name the shape. Discuss the properties of each shape with the children; for example, the triangle has three sides and three corners. Say, "count with me" before you point to each side.
2. Continue placing shapes on the flannel board and repeating the proceeding procedure until all the small shapes are displayed.
3. Below the flannel board, place the large shapes that you cut out.
4. Ask the children to match the shape by taking a small shape from the flannel board and placing it on the larger piece that it matches. Help the younger children take just one shape at a time from the flannel board and guide them to place it on the proper large shape.
5. Encourage them to continue matching shapes until *they* decide the activity is over, usually by wandering off to another center.

Guidance

Anticipating the sometimes-short attention span of the children in the group, the teacher should be fully prepared before beginning the activity. If the majority of the children are not interested in the activity, give them a choice of going to another center while you interact with the children who are interested. If one child takes two or three shapes at a time, give the other children two shapes as well. Then guide the children to take turns with their two shapes and make this a positive, not confrontational, time.

Assessment and Follow-Up Strategies

Were all the objectives met? Did the activity hold the children's attention? Were they able to do the activity? What will you change if you do it again?

Extend the activity by leaving the flannel board and shapes out for the children to use throughout the day. Also, take a shape walk around the room and around the center or school. Point out the shapes they see every day. See how many shapes the children recognize.

Make shape cookies with the children using shape cookie cutters. Later, the children can use the cookie cutters to make shapes with play dough. Read children's books relating to math, such as *Shapes, shapes, shapes* by Tana Hoban (1986).

Professional Resource Download

Activity Plan Worksheet
Developmentally Appropriate and Multicultural/Anti-Biased Activity

AGE: pre-kindergarten and kindergarten

Name of Activity and Brief Description

The Name Game is designed for the children to find opportunities to measure, count, and have fun with their names.

Child Outcomes of Activity

- Build math connections.
- Develop an awareness that math is everywhere.
- Develop math concepts, such as one-to-one correspondence, counting, and measuring.

Activity Plan Worksheet | Developmentally Appropriate and Multicultural/Anti-Biased Activity (continued)

- Encourage cooperative problem solving.
- Become aware of similarities and differences in names.
- Recognize the importance of names and learn names from other cultures.
- Increase listening skills and encourage language development.

Space and Materials Needed

This activity can be done in the math center, the art center, on the floor, or anywhere that the children can use rulers, measuring tape, pencils, crayons, markers, and paper.

Procedure

1. At group time introduce the activity. Briefly talk about names. Ask the children if they have ever thought about the number of letters in their names. Have they ever counted the letters? Have they ever measured their names?
2. Using your name as an example, you can demonstrate what you want them to do. Show your name printed on a piece of paper. Have the children count the number of letters in your name. Then place a ruler along the bottom of your name and measure how many inches long your name is.
3. Explain that this is what you would like for them to do with their names. They can do it now, or they can do it another time. They get to choose. Count how many want to do it now and how many want to do it later. Add the two numbers together to figure out how many children are in class today.

4. Use a transitional activity, such as the child whose first name begins with the letter closest to A goes to a center of his or her choice or begins the name activity. Continue through the alphabet until all the children have selected what they want to do.
5. You can then observe who needs assistance in getting started and who does not need any help.

Guidance

In anticipating what the children might do, remember to guide them through this activity. Let them work together to problem solve. The children will probably discover for themselves that some names are shorter than others and compare the shortest name with the longest one. You may need to facilitate, especially with the younger children.

Some children may not want to participate in this activity. That is acceptable. Guide them into another activity center.

Assessment and Follow-Up Strategies

Were all the objectives met? Did the younger children participate for a short or long period of time? How much did the children discover? Did they share and problem solve together? What would you leave the same and what would you change the next time you did this activity with the children?

Extend this activity by having children assign a color to each letter. When they use crayons and markers to "decorate" their names, they are adding another dimension to the activity. The next day at group time have the children rhyme their name with another word. Then go around the circle and have the children try to say all the rhymes together.

⌄ Professional Resource Download

Activity Plan Worksheet | Developmentally Appropriate Math Activity

AGES: Kindergarten, first, second, and third grades
Math center or small group

Name of Activity and Brief Description—Pizza Math

One way to make math fun is by using hands on materials. This pizza game is perfect for counting, adding and subtracting, or learning fractions!

Child Outcomes of Activity

- Partition objects into equal parts and name the parts, including halves, fourths, and eighths, using words.

- Explain that the more fractional parts used to make a whole, the smaller the part; and the fewer the fractional parts, the larger the part.
- Use concrete models to count fractional parts beyond one whole using words and recognize how many parts it takes to equal one whole.
- Apply mathematical process standards to develop and use strategies and methods for whole number computations in order to solve addition and subtraction problems.

Activity Plan Worksheet: Developmentally Appropriate Math Activity (continued)

Space and Materials Needed

A cardboard circle from a frozen pizza, glue gun, colored construction paper.

Using a ruler, divide the circle into eight equal parts. Next, glue on the colored paper and then cut out small toppings. Use this for a variety of math experiences. Make enough pizzas for a small group to work in pairs. Add additional props such as a cash register and play money as needed.

Procedure

1. Have children demonstrate their comprehension of beginning fractions: show ½, ¼, etc. Equivalent fractions: ½ is the same as ²⁄₄ of the pizza or ⁴⁄₈ of the pizza.

2. Have children add fractions:

   ½ + ½ = ²⁄₂ or 1 whole pizza

   ⅛ + ⅛ = ²⁄₈

   Show using pizza pie manipulative.

3. Roll a fraction: (put fractions on a cube) and race for the most slices of pizza.

4. Create story problems: Sally ate ²⁄₈ of the pizza and Bill ate ¼: How much is left? Kids can have fun creating their own problems as well!

5. Play pizza shop: Set up a small store, sell slices, and make change.

6. Describe children's actions as they play using vocabulary that they might not regularly say.

7. Ask children questions about what they are doing and what they observe.

Guidance

Encourage children to work in pairs or small groups.

Assessment and Follow-Up Strategies

Were child outcomes met? Yes___ No___
What was the children's response?
What worked well? What did not work?
How could this activity be changed to make it more effective or more appropriate?

⌄⌄ Professional Resource Download

Technology in the Mathematics Program

Technology & Teaching: Computers

Calculators and computers are part of a young child's world. They are now a given resource in learning mathematics. Kostelnik, Soderman, and Whiren (2014) suggest, "Although young children need to learn to estimate and calculate problems mentally (mental math), they must eventually learn to do paper-and-pencil math and to use a calculator. Each of them should have access to a calculator, and the calculators they are given should have easy-to-read numbers found directly on the keys, and easy-to-depress keys." Teachers must also learn to use the calculator appropriately with children.

Computers provide games and simulation that aid problem solving and skill building for young children when they practice with developmentally appropriate software.

Software for teaching math is being developed at a rapid rate. Educators should review and evaluate software carefully before using it with young children. NCTM (2000) proposed, "Technology is essential in teaching and learning mathematics; it influences the mathematics that is taught and enhances students' learning."

"Certainly the computer is not a cure-all for every problem in education, especially mathematics. It is not enough to place a few computers in a classroom and expect improvement. Improvement will not come even if every child has her or his own computer. Along with the technology must come appropriate use of the computer, effective programs that take advantage of the computers and proper training and knowledge by teachers who will use the computers in the classroom (Kennedy, Tipps, and Johnson, 2011, p. 98). ”

Technology use that is connected to what children already know and can build on leads to greater motivation and self-direction. Loss of creativity can be a problem if children use drill-and-practice software. Open-ended software—software that provides opportunities to discover, make choices, and find out the impact of decisions—encourages exploration, imagination, and problem solving. In addition, children prefer working together with a friend as they solve problems, create rules for cooperation, talk about what they are doing, and help and teach each other.

Early childhood teachers guide children's mathematical learning through the use of manipulatives—pattern blocks, Unifix cubes, Cuisenaire rods, and so on. Rosen and Hoffman (2009, p. 26) have observed, "In the past few years, online resources for virtual versions of these common manipulatives have become available."

The emergence of **virtual manipulatives**, interactive, web-based computer-generated images of objects that children can manipulate on the computer screen, can be especially beneficial to students with special needs or those who speak English as a second language. Many websites offer virtual manipulatives. One, for example, is the Utah State University National Library of Virtual Manipulatives, which is online at: http://nlvm.usu.edu. Through early exposure to computer-based math activities, young children enjoy experiences that can link successfully to their ongoing concrete experiences with math materials.

Research suggests that both digital manipulatives and traditional manipulatives can be used to teach computational skills and can assist early childhood educators in providing children with a variety of experiences (Mattoon, Bates, Shifflet, Latham, Ennis, 2015).

Diversity in Math Play

NAEYC · DAP · INTASC · HS · COMMON CORE

Children around the world play games that involve mathematical concepts, such as counting on a Chinese abacus, playing Mancala, an African count-and-capture game using stones, and shooting marble games from different countries or different versions of hopscotch.

Many different disabilities can affect children's math learning and performance, but none more than those that affect cognition—mental retardation, traumatic brain injury, attention-deficit/hyperactivity disorder, and learning disabilities, to name a few. Several specific areas of disability are clearly connected to math learning difficulties. Visual processing, visual memory, and visual-spatial relationships all impact math proficiency in that they are threads in the fabric of conceptual understanding and procedural fluency.

The National Mathematics Advisory Panel Report (2008) identified successful mathematical teaching strategies. According to this report, four methods of instruction show the most promise:

1. Systematic and explicit instruction uses a detailed approach that guides children through a defined instructional sequence.
2. Self-instruction includes children's use of prompting or solution-oriented questions and rebus charts.
3. Peer tutoring allows children of differing abilities to be paired to learn and practice particular skills.
4. Manipulatives, pictures, number lines, and graphs (visual representation) teach mathematical concepts.

Beside these teaching strategies, teachers can make simple adaptations and accommodations to support each and every child's success:

- Block distractions with partitions or place child facing the wall instead of the busy classroom.

virtual manipulatives: Refers to interactive, web-based computer-generated images of objects that children can manipulate on the computer screen.

- Make two removable partitions by cutting a three-panel science display board in half to sit on a table.
- Place the activity on a tray with a smaller container to hold the pieces alongside the tray to provide more structure and focus the child's attention.
- Tape a pegboard against the wall to strengthen arm and shoulder muscles.
- Glue knob handles on top of puzzle pieces to make them easier to grip.

Creating Partnerships with Families

naeyc   DAP   INTASC   HS   COMMON CORE

Families can do a great deal to help their children at home. These are some suggestions that can be shared with parents to assist their children in learning math:

- Your child will learn to sort and classify objects by helping you with the clean laundry. He or she could start with sorting clothes by color or could help put all the white clothes in one pile and the dark clothes in another pile. He or she can learn to sort and classify items by types, putting the shirts in one pile, the sheets in another pile, and the towels in another pile. Start simply, and then go to the complex sorting. For example, sorting socks gives practice in pairing by color, size, and design. Putting rough jeans in one pile and soft bedclothes in another pile offers sorting and classifying of items by texture.
- Your child can also learn math concepts in the kitchen. He or she can learn number concepts when helping you to set the table. How many people will be at breakfast or dinner? How many knives will you need? How many forks? How many spoons?
- Your child can also learn spatial concepts by setting the table. The fork goes next to the plate on the left. The knife goes next to the plate on the right. He or she learns about the sequence of your mealtime. First, you set the table. Next, you eat your dinner. Last, you wash the dishes. Keep the steps to three at first, and gradually add more steps. This sequencing helps your child recognize the pattern or sequence of events in the world around him.

The Teacher's Role

Guidance in Math Play

- Let the children know it is acceptable not to have an immediate answer to the math activity on which they are working. Let them know that there may be more than one way to solve a problem or complete a task.
- Break down a project into its parts when a child is overwhelmed. Describe the steps in clear terms: first we do this and then we do that. Use sequence charts to help with the explanation.
- Allow an active child to lie on the floor, stand at the table, kneel on a chair, or straddle a chair that has been turned backward.
- Hand pieces of a manipulative toy one by one to a child who is easily distracted when playing or completing a task. For example, start with objects to count or a puzzle.

Case Study: Restaurant

Jim's dramatic play center in the pre-K room at the Play and Learn children's center in Orlando, Florida, is set up as a restaurant. There are four children playing in the center.

Jim has provided the following props to support their restaurant play:

Two-column menu
Aprons
Order pad
Play food

Play cookware
Table and four chairs
Phone
Measuring cups/spoons

Empty boxes and cans of food
Tablecloths/napkins
Pencils

Stove, refrigerator, sink, shelves
Mats and utensils

What Do You Think?

1. Where is the mathematical learning in this dramatic play experience?
2. How can the teacher extend the mathematic learning?
3. What math language can he integrate into discussion with the children during their play?

TEACHING TIPS Math Activities

As you plan, facilitate, observe, and evaluate the math activities in your early education classroom, think about the following:

- Let the children make mistakes and correct them themselves.
- Encourage collective or cooperative problem solving, which builds positive self-esteem.

- Allow time for trying out new ideas and taking risks.
- Guide the children to develop math skills needed for the new, changing information age of sophisticated machines, technology, computers, and calculators.
- Allow math materials to be moved to other curriculum centers. Spontaneity and creativity are exciting and important!

Professional Resource Download

Summary

1. **What are key terms related to math experiences for children?** Physical knowledge is learning about objects in the environment and their characteristics, such as color, weight, and size. Logico-mathematical knowledge includes relationships constructed in order to make sense out of the world and to organize information, such as counting and classification. Concept development is the construction of knowledge through solving problems and experiencing the results, while being actively involved with the environment. Number sense is a concept that develops over time as children think about, explore, and discuss mathematical ideas. One-to-one correspondence is the pairing of one object to another object or one group of objects to another group of equal number. Rote counting is the ability to recite names of numerals in order. Rational counting requires matching each numeral name, in order, to an object in a group. Classifying and sorting is grouping objects by a common characteristic, such as size, shape, or color. Pattern is a sequence of colors, objects, sounds, stories, or movements that repeats in the same order over and over again. Seriation or ordering of objects is based on the ability to place them in logical sequence, such as smallest to largest or shortest to tallest. Geometry is the area of mathematics that involves shape, size, space, position, direction, and movement. Spatial sense is using comparisons that help children develop an awareness of themselves in relation to people and objects in space, such as exploration using blocks and boxes. Measurement is finding the length, height, and weight of an object using units like inches, feet, and pounds.

2. **How do the stages of child development relate to math experiences?** Young children understand math in relationship to how it affects them. Number sense evolves during the first eight years of a child's life. How you set up the early education environment will determine how often each and every child has opportunities to develop number sense and logical ways of thinking about time, space, and other mathematical ideas, so plan environments that build on children's curiosity and enthusiasm and encourage them to discover math concepts in the process of play. Young children use numbers to solve everyday problems by constructing number meanings through real-world experiences and the use of physical materials. Teachers should incorporate mathematics into everyday situations, children's questions, games, and children's literature.

3. **What are key components of environments that promote mathematical learning?** Provide a variety of materials for exploring number concepts, to recognize, copy, create, and extend patterns, to explore geometric shapes and spatial relationships, to practice measurement, and to organize and represent data.

4. **What strategies are useful to integrate and create math activities appropriate for young children?** Actively introduce mathematical ideas in planned, purposeful ways. Encourage children to connect mathematical ideas to everyday experiences. Interact with children to support their understanding of number concepts, patterns, geometry and spatial sense, and data collection and representation.

5. **How can we use technology to promote mathematical learning?** Computers provide games and simulation that aid problem solving and skill building for young children when they practice with developmentally appropriate software. Technology use that is connected to what children already know and can build on leads to greater motivation and self-direction. Loss of creativity can be a problem if children use drill-and-practice software. Select open-ended software that provides opportunities to discover, make choices, and find out the impact of decisions and encourages exploration, imagination, and problem solving. When children work at the computer together, they solve problems, talk about what they are doing, help and teach friends, and create rules for cooperation.

6. **How can you incorporate diversity into math experiences?** Use systematic and explicit instruction, self-instruction, peer tutoring, and visual representations to support children with exceptionalities. Include materials and games from different cultures to teach math concepts and skills.

7. **How can you develop partnerships with families that support child math experiences?** Provide activity ideas for families for using household items like nesting bowls and kitchen or bathroom scales as well as chores like matching socks to teach math concepts.

8. **What is the teacher's role in promoting math experiences in the classroom?** Give children plenty of time to work on math activities. Let them know that there are often several ways to solve a problem. For children having difficulty, break the problem into parts and describe the steps clearly. Allow alternative locations for the child to complete the problem rather than just at a table and in a chair. Hand pieces of a manipulative to a child one-by-one if they are one that gets easily distracted.

Reflective Review Questions

1. What is meant by the statement "*Number sense* is a concept, and *counting* is a skill"? Which of these terms is more fundamental? Does that mean the other is unimportant?

2. Describe four group activities for young children that involve *patterning*. Two should involve vigorous physical activity, and two should involve the manipulation of objects.

3. Develop criteria for the selection of developmentally appropriate math activities for a specific age group of your choice. Create a list of the materials and supplies necessary to set up these math activities, including the cost of the equipment.

Explorations

1. Interview two teachers who teach kindergarten or primary-grade children. Have them explain what math skills and concepts are important for the age of children they teach. Have them describe their math program. If possible, observe the children in the classroom doing some of the math activities. How will you use the information gained from these interviews and observations?

2. After visiting a library or a bookstore, select five children's books that relate to math concepts for young children. Discuss your selections and explain how you would use each book with the children.

3. Create a book for young children related to math. Complete an activity plan worksheet, such as the one in this chapter; then read the book to a small group of young children. Observe their responses. What age group did you select? Was your book developmentally appropriate for that age group? Explain your answers and your assessment and follow-up activities.

4. Select and plan a math activity for young children. Specify which age group this activity is planned for: infants, toddlers, preschoolers, or primary-age children. In writing, list objectives, materials needed, step-by-step procedures for presenting this activity, follow-up activities, and evaluation guidelines. (Use the activity plan worksheet in Appendix D.) Demonstrate this activity during class or with a group of children.

5. Use the Math Environment Checklist in this chapter to conduct an observation of an early childhood learning environment.
    - Beside each statement, place an *X* if the classroom you observed met the statement.
    - On a separate sheet of paper, describe what you actually observed related to each statement. Place the number of the statement first and then your observation.
    - On a separate sheet of paper, for each statement that you did not check as met, describe what you would do to improve that classroom so that the statement would be met. Be sure to put the number of the statement first.
    - Submit this with the name of the location you observed and the age group.

Math Books for Young Children

Ayers, K. (2008). *Up, down, and around*. Illustrated by N. B. Westcott. New York: Candlewick.

Diehl, D. (2007). *A circle here, a square there: My shape book*. New York: Lark Books.

Falconer, I. (2002). *Olivia counts*. New York: Atheneum.

Hoban, T. (2000). *Cubes, cones, cylinders, and spheres*. New York: Greenwillow.

Pallotta, J. (2003). *Apple fractions*. Illustrated by R. Bolster. New York: Cartwheel Books.

Tang, G. (2005). *Math for all seasons*. Illustrated by H. Briggs. New York: Scholastic.

Williams, R. L. (2001). *The coin counting book*. Watertown, MA: Charlesbridge Publishing.

Wood, A. (2004). *Ten little fish*. Illustrated by B. Wood. New York: Blue Sky Press.

⌄ Professional Resource Download

11 Fine Motor and Manipulatives

Standards Covered in This Chapter

 NAEYC 5a, 5b, 5c

DAP 2

INTASC 4, 5, 8

HEAD START
Domain: Perceptual Motor and Physical Development

Student Learning Outcomes

After studying this chapter, you should be able to:

- Define and give examples for key terms related to fine motor development and manipulative play for children.

- Discuss fine motor development and manipulative play in young children and how they relate to stages of child development.

- Evaluate various components of planning and preparation of fine motor and manipulative play environments.

- Integrate and create fine motor and manipulative play activities appropriate for young children.

- Discuss various issues in the use of technology in a fine motor and manipulative play environment.

- Distinguish ways to incorporate diversity into fine motor and manipulative play environments.

- Describe ways to develop partnerships with families that support fine motor and manipulative play.

- Analyze the teacher's role in promoting fine motor and manipulative plan in the classroom.

In an early care and education classroom, the fine motor and manipulatives area probably includes a larger variety of activities and materials than any other center. Because of this, the manipulative center might also be known as the math, table game, or puzzle area. Just about anything that uses the small movements or fine motor skills can be found as part of this learning center.

Fine Motor and Manipulative Play Defined

Fine motor skills are the small movements that occur in the hands, wrists, fingers, feet, toes, lips, and tongue. They are the smaller actions involved in picking up objects between the thumb and finger, using a pencil to write carefully, holding a fork and using it to eat, and other small muscle tasks that occur on a daily basis.

Fine motor skill is defined as the coordination of small muscle movements that occur in body parts such as the fingers, usually in coordination with the eyes. (See **Figure 11-1**.) In relation to motor skills of hands and fingers, the term **dexterity** is commonly used. Additional terms used to describe fine motor skills include the **pincer grasp**, which is using thumb and index finger to pick up an item. **Bilateral coordination** refers to using both hands together to perform a task. **Eye–hand coordination** involves focusing and coordinating eye movement and visual input to control and direct the hands. **Wrist rotation** and **wrist stability** are used to control hand movements like holding and pouring from a pitcher. **Finger dexterity** refers to the ability to move individual fingers in isolation (Gibbs, 2012, http://www.writeoutofthebox.com/).

Figure 11-1 Using the muscles in the fingers in coordination with the eyes is necessary to successfully assemble puzzles.

fine motor skill: The coordination of small muscle movements that occur in body parts such as the fingers, usually in coordination with the eyes.

dexterity: Used when referring motor skills of the hands and fingers.

pincer grasp: Using the thumb and index finger to pick up an item.

bilateral coordination: Using both hands together to perform a task.

eye–hand coordination: Focusing and coordinating eye movement and visual input to control and direct the hands.

wrist rotation: Used, with wrist stability, to control hand movements.

wrist stability: Used, with wrist rotation, to control hand movements.

finger dexterity: The ability to move individual fingers in isolation.

Developmental Stages of Fine Motor and Manipulative Play

Infant fine motor developmental sequence moves from pre-reaching as a newborn when someone can hold a rattle for the infant to reach and grasp, using a mitten or whole hand grasp at three to four months, moving objects from hand to hand at four to five months, and using a pincer or finger to thumb grasp at nine months. The pincer grasp is important to holding a pencil to write later on.

Toddler fine motor skills include filling and dumping, pushing buttons, working simple puzzles, flushing the toilet, turning knobs and switches, scribbling, and pointing.

Preschool children show their development of fine motor abilities by their increasing skill in dressing themselves. Two- to 3-year-old children can put on and remove their clothes including zipping jackets, if the zipper is started for them. Three- to 4-year olds can button clothes and 4- to 5-year olds dress by themselves. More than just dressing skills, as children learn to lace, buckle, zip, button, snap, and tie, they develop problem-solving and memory skills.

You can add dress up clothes that have zippers, buttons, and snaps and an old shoe that ties to the manipulative area for practice. You can also make dressing boards yourself using picture frames, old clothes, and a staple gun or hot glue.

Preschool children become increasing adept at using fine motor skills in feeding themselves.

- Two- to 3-year-olds can use a spoon and serve themselves items such as bread.
- Three- to 4-year-olds serve themselves, pour milk, and set the table.
- Four- to 5-year-olds use a fork.
- Five- to 6-year-olds use a knife on soft food.

Family style dining encourages children to develop these skills.

Preschool children develop other fine motor skills.

- At 2 to 3 years old, open doors and string beads.
- At 3 to 4 years old, use scissors and copy line and circle.
- At 4 to 5 years old, cut on a line, copy triangle, a cross, and some letters.
- At 5 to 6 years old, tie shoes and draw a six-part person.
- As children develop these skills they are preparing to write.

Primary-aged children show dramatic improvements with regard to their printed handwriting and ability to write in cursive letters. They also develop the ability to draw complex and detailed pictures that for the first time begin to incorporate depth cues (such as drawing farther away objects smaller) and three-dimensional elements. Often, children's artistic ability can truly begin to shine during this stage as improved fine motor skills and imagination combine.

During this stage, children also learn how to use their hands to successfully accomplish manual activities other than drawing or writing. For instance, they become capable of executing complex detail-oriented craft projects involving beading, sewing, scrap booking, and building models and are good at using simple tools such a hammer or a hand mixer (both under adult supervision). Children also commonly become quite skillful at playing complicated games involving eye–hand coordination, including video and computer games. (Oswalt and Dombeck, 2013, http://www.sevencounties.org/poc/view_doc.php?type =doc&id=37676&cn=1272.)

Brain Research: Math, Science, and Reading

Hand movements are initiated by commands originating from a region of the primary motor cortex that contains a high number of specialized corticospinal (CST) neurons, termed *corticomotoneuronal (CM) cells*. CM cells descend into the spinal cord to form monosynaptic connections with motor neurons in the anterior horn. Research has shown that these monosynaptic connections may account for the high amount of manual dexterity observed in humans.

Recent research has demonstrated a clear connection between the development of fine motor skills in early life and later success in math, science, and reading. According to researchers, "There are few interventions directly testing whether strengthening early attention, fine motor skills, or knowledge of the world would improve later math and reading achievement."

Grissmer, David, Grimm, Kevin J., Aiyer, Sophie M., Murrah, William M., and Steele, Joel S. Fine motor skills and early comprehension of the
world: Two new school readiness indicators. *Developmental Psychology*, 46(5) (September 2010), pp. 1008–1017.

That said, some facts are quite clear:

- There is a clear connection in the circuitry of the brain between areas controlling fine motor skills and areas controlling cognition.
- These areas are developing simultaneously, with exceptional speed during early brain development.
- Motor skills are a proven indicator of future math and reading success.

Grissmer, David, Grimm, Kevin J., Aiyer, Sophie M., Murrah, William M., and Steele, Joel S. Fine motor skills and early comprehension of the world: Two new school readiness indicators. *Developmental Psychology*, 46(5) (September 2010), pp. 1008–1017.

Planning and Preparing the Environment

Although fine motor skills are developed in many learning centers of the early childhood classroom, the manipulative center, sometimes called the table toy area, provides rich experiences in developing fine motor skills.

The manipulative center should be planned as a quiet area for children to work and is well lighted and contains low open shelves for materials. (See **Figure 11-2**.) The center should include labeled tubs, trays, or baskets to hold all the materials needed for each activity. A good variety of materials should be displayed attractively and there should be enough materials for four to six children to have several choices each (Bullard, 2010).

These fine motor materials include items such as play dough with a pizza cutter or mini rolling pin, squeeze squirters, spin tops, puzzles, locks and keys, hole punches, wind-up toys, peg boards, tweezers, tongs, squeeze balls, lacing cards, Legos®, colored cubes, interlocking links, parquetry blocks, Cuisenaire rods, Lotto, eye dropper, alphabet bingo, card games, board games, Slinkys®, Chinese yo-yos, silly putty with beads and buttons, and building sets that fit together. Minimize passive entertainment usage such as Game Boy®, PlayStation®, and Xbox® because these do not build efficient pencil grasp patterns (Gibbs, 2012).

Both horizontal and vertical work surfaces should be provided. Use of a vertical surface such as a chalkboard, easel, or wall when prewriting, painting, or coloring enhances successful positioning of the hand and arm. Also, providing foot support when seated at a table improves hand use and control when performing fine motor activities (Gibbs, 2012). (See **Figure 11-3** here.)

The physical environment plays a large role in enhancing fine motor and manipulative experiences. A checklist that can be used to evaluate the fine motor and manipulative play environment in your own classroom or classrooms that you observe follows:

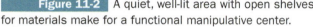

Figure 11-2 A quiet, well-lit area with open shelves for materials make for a functional manipulative center.

Figure 11-3 A light table and pipettes can provide fine motor experiences.

Fine Motor and Manipulative Environment Checklist

_____ 1. Are there trays or baskets to hold all the materials needed for each activity?

_____ 2. Is there a quiet, uninterrupted area to work?

_____ 3. Are there low, open, labeled shelves to hold materials?

_____ 4. Is the manipulative area well lighted, preferably with natural light?

_____ 5. Are there enough materials to provide four to six children with several choices each?

_____ 6. Is there storage for additional materials?

_____ 7. Are there adequate horizontal surfaces such as tables, chairs, and floor space?

_____ 8. Do the materials meet the children's developmental needs?

_____ 9. Are there vertical surfaces?

_____ 10. Is the manipulative center available as a choice activity on a daily basis?

_____ 11. Are there aesthetically pleasing materials?

_____ 12. Is there a variety of self-correcting toys such as puzzles, stacking rings, and nesting boxes?

_____ 13. Are the materials provided of high interest to the children?

_____ 14. Is there a variety of open-ended toys such as Lego®, colored cubes, parquetry blocks, pegboards and pegs, and interlocking links?

_____ 15. Are tools, such as scissors, of high quality?

_____ 16. Is there a variety of collectibles such as keys buttons and bottle caps?

_____ 17. Does the area allow children to find what they need and return it when finished such as short stacks of game boxes and picture or word labels?

_____ 18. Are there a variety of materials from simple to complex to meet varying ability levels?

⌄⌄ Professional Resource Download

Integrating Fine Motor and Manipulative Play into the Curriculum

According to the American Academy of Pediatrics, young infants typically only have the ability to rake objects with all five fingers, using what is called the palmer grasp; older babies can use a true pincer grasp; and toddlers can manipulate items such as toys easily.

Fine Motor Play for Infants

You can help to build an infant's fine motor skills with simple activities that help to increase typical hand and finger movements of this stage, such as using a pincer grasp to take objects out and put them in a container or to poke an object, such as a button that causes something to pop-up or spin, with the index finger. An easy activity is filling a bucket with baby toys or soft blocks for the infant to reach in and take out the objects, and then place them back into the bucket. This type of fill-and-dump activity is a favorite of infants and toddlers. Shape sorters and toys made from recycled containers with plastic lids where holes or slots are cut in the lid so clothespins or jar lids can be dropped in are other examples of drop-in toys. To increase finger control and coordination, fill a recycled plastic diaper wipe container with scarves to pull out one by one, give older infants a thick crayon to hold onto and scribble with, finger paint, or a stubby brush to paint with. These activities will require your supervision to make sure items do not end up in the mouth and that objects used are too large to be choke hazards.

Fine Motor Play for Toddlers

As children move into the toddler years, you can help to build up fine motor skills with more complex manipulative activities. Toddlers can build a tower with up to six blocks, press together manipulative pieces such as pop beads or Starbuilders to create, and string big beads on a thick shoelace. Thick board books are ideal for practicing skills such as lifting and turning pages. Like older infants, toddlers enjoy using crayons to color and draw with as well as finger-painting, painting with nontoxic shaving cream, and painting with brushes. Now is the time to introduce low easels to provide a vertical surface for making marks. Although toddlers will still scribble, they may make more purposeful marks and may have the ability to draw lines in different directions on their own as well as make simple shapes such as a circle or cross.

Fine Motor Play for Preschoolers

Preschool aged children benefit from experiences that support the development of fine motor skills in the hands and fingers. Children should have strength and dexterity in their hands and fingers before being asked to manipulate a pencil on paper. Working on dexterity and strength first can eliminate the development of an inappropriate pencil grasp, which is becoming more commonplace as young children are engaged in writing experiences before their hands are ready. The following activities involve the use of manipulatives, implements, and tools found in various learning centers that will support young children's fine motor development and will help to build the strength and dexterity necessary to hold a pencil appropriately.

Sensory Play

- Molding and rolling play dough into balls, using the palms of the hands facing each other and with fingers curled slightly toward the palm.
- Rolling play dough into tiny balls (peas), using only the finger tips.
- Using pegs or toothpicks to make designs in play dough.
- Cutting play dough with a plastic knife or with a pizza wheel by holding the implement in a diagonal grasp.
- Scrunching up one sheet of newspaper in one hand. This is a super strength builder.
- Using a plant sprayer to spray plants (indoors, outdoors), to spray snow (mix food coloring with water so that the snow can be painted), or melt "monsters." (Draw monster pictures with markers and the colors will run when sprayed.)
- Catching (clapping) bubbles between hands.
- Drawing in a tactile medium such as wet sand, salt, rice, or "goop."
- Making goop by adding water to cornstarch until you have a mixture similar in consistency to toothpaste. The "drag" of this mixture provides feedback to the muscle and joint receptors, thus facilitating visual motor control.
- Reaching for objects under water.
- Pouring water or sand from one container to another.
- Using a turkey baster in water play.

Art

- Tearing newspaper into strips and then crumpling them into balls. Use to stuff scarecrow or other art creation.
- Using eye droppers to "pick up" colored water for color mixing or to make artistic designs on paper or coffee filters.
- Spraying paintings with water in a small spray bottle to create a "rained on" effect.
- Painting at an easel. Children will develop prewriting skills best when they work on a vertical surface as much as possible. In particular, the wrist must be in extension (i.e., bent back in the direction of the hand).
- Using spray bottles to paint a mural on butcher paper attached to the wall outside.
- Rolling small balls out of tissue paper and then gluing the balls onto construction paper to form pictures or designs.
- Tearing colored tissue to create a "stained glass window" on waxed paper when covered with a mixture of water and glue applied with a brush and allowed to dry.
- Making pictures using stickers or self-sticking paper reinforcements.

Dramatic Play

- Playing games with the "puppet fingers" (i.e., the thumb, index, and middle fingers). At circle time, have each child's puppet fingers tell about what happened over the weekend or use them in songs and finger plays.
- Putting on dress-up clothes using buttons, zippers, and snaps.
- Using puppets to act out stories.
- Stirring pretend food while cooking.
- Picking up and holding pots and pans to "cook."

Music and Movement

- Holding and shaking instruments.
- Clapping to the beat.
- Throwing beanbags into a hula hoop placed flat on the floor, gradually increasing the distance.
- Playing throw and catch with a ball. Start with a large ball and work toward a smaller ball. (Koosh balls are easier to catch than a tennis ball.)
- Hitting bowling pins with a ball. (You can make your own bowling game with soda bottles and a small ball.)
- Playing "Hit the Balloon" with a medium-sized balloon (for children older than age 3).

Manipulatives

- Lacing and sewing activities such as stringing beads. (See **Figure 11-4**.)
- Turning over cards, coins, checkers, or buttons, without bringing them to the edge of the table.
- Picking out small objects such as pegs, beads, or coins from a tray of salt, sand, rice, or putty. Try it with eyes closed to develop sensory awareness in the hands.
- Playing connect the dots. Encourage the child to connect dots from left to right and from top to bottom.
- Tracing around stencils; the nondominant hand should hold the stencil flat and stable against the paper, and the dominant hand pushes the pencil firmly against the edge of the stencil. The stencil must be held firmly.
- Attach a large piece of felt to the wall, or use a felt board. The child can use felt shapes to make pictures. Magnetic boards can be used the same way.
- Using small-sized screwdrivers like those found in an erector set.
- Tying knots in string is a great fine motor activity for younger preschool children. The repetitive motion helps prevent fatigue in the fingers and wrists, which will aid in more difficult activities. Teachers can tape the string to either the wall or table depending on level of development.
- Set out objects on the table that can be picked up with clothespins. Some examples of these objects are: cotton balls, cotton swabs, or small pieces of fabric.

Figure 11-4   Stringing beads helps strengthen finger dexterity.

Midline Crossing

Establishment of hand dominance is still developing in preschool children. The following activities will facilitate midline crossing:

- Encourage reaching across the body for materials with each hand. It may be necessary to engage the other hand in an activity to prevent switching hands at midline.
- Refrain specifically from discouraging a child from using the left hand for any activity. Allow for the natural development of hand dominance by presenting activities at midline and allowing the child to choose freely.

- Start making the child aware of the left and right sides of his or her body through spontaneous comments such as, "kick the ball with your right leg." Play imitation posture games such as "Simon Says" with across the body movements.
- When painting at easel, encourage the child to paint a continuous line across the entire paper and also from diagonal to diagonal.

Scissor Activities

When scissors are held correctly, and when they fit a child's hand well, cutting activities will exercise the same muscles that are needed to manipulate a pencil in a mature tripod grasp. The correct scissor position is with the thumb and middle finger in the handles of the scissors, the index finger on the outside of the handle to stabilize, with fingers four and five curled into the palm. (See **Figure 11-5.**)

- Children can cut junk mail or cards found in magazines.
- Fringe a piece of construction paper.
- Cut play dough with scissors.
- Cut straws into sections.

(These are adopted from www.shrewsbury-ma.gov/schools/beal/readiness/finemotoractivities/.)

Here are some fun prehandwriting exercises that can be done as part of finger plays during circle time:

- Finger Opposition: Have the children put their open hands next to their ears and have their thumb touch each of their fingers one at a time. Repeat in reverse order. Repeat several times.
- Bunny Ears: Have the children place their fists next to their ears, squeeze, open their fingers, wiggle the fingers like a bunny's ears and then close the fingers. Repeat two to three times.
- Door Knob Turns: Have the children extend their arms in front of them with their elbows slightly bent. Have them move their wrists from side to side as if you are opening a doorknob. Move wrists to the right and then to the left. Repeat several times.

The National Council for Teachers of Mathematics (NCTM) recognizes the link between the manipulation of materials and understanding concepts, so it calls for manipulatives to be used in teaching a wide variety of topics in mathematics.

- Sorting—a premathematical skill that aids in comprehension of patterns and functions
- Ordering—a premathematical skill that enhances number sense and other math-related abilities
- Distinguishing patterns—the foundation for making mathematical generalizations
- Recognizing geometric shapes and understanding relationships among them
- Making measurements, using both nonstandard and standard units with application to both two- and three-dimensional objects
- Understanding the base-10 system of numbers
- Comprehending mathematical operations—addition, subtraction, multiplication, and division
- Recognizing relationships among mathematical operations
- Exploring and describing spatial relationships
- Identifying and describing different types of symmetry
- Developing and using spatial memory
- Learning about and experimenting with transformations
- Engaging in problem solving
- Representing mathematical ideas in a variety of ways
- Connecting different concepts in mathematics
- Communicating mathematical ideas effectively

Figure 11-5 Fine motor skills are being mastered as children use scissors.

Fine Motor Play for Primary-Age Children

Primary-age children often have trouble with fine motor tasks that require control and precise movement of small muscles. It is important for children to develop fine motor control in order to master writing. Here are some fun activities to continue to refine fine motor skills:

- Tear tissue paper into strips, by placing both hands on the top of each sheet and pulling in opposite directions. Once the sheet of tissue is in strips, have the child try to crumple it into a ball using just the fingers of one hand.
- Have the children practice drawing a line from the top to the bottom of a large piece of paper taped to a vertical surface, such as an easel or wall.
- Move small items from one container to another using tweezers or a clothespin.
- Include materials such as peg boards, lacing cards, and Lego® in your manipulative center.
- Have the children use their fingers to make their artistic creations in finger paint. After finishing, place a piece of construction paper of a different color than the paint over the child's work. Have children press the paper down and pull up a print of the painting. Then give them a sponge to wipe away the paint left on the table in a side-to-side motion, encouraging them to use their arms and wrists while keeping their shoulder still.
- In your writing center, provide the children with a variety of stencils to trace and implements of various sizes.

Reflect On This

Do you think tracing letters on paper is the best fine motor activity to use to teach writing to 3-year-olds?

Activity Plan Worksheet

Developmentally Appropriate Fine Motor Activity

AGE: infants, toddlers, and preschool children

Name of Activity and Brief Description
The Object Transfer activity is designed for children to develop their hand grasp to pick up objects and transfer them to another container, with older children sorting the objects according to category.

Child Outcomes of Activity
- Encourage problem solving.
- Use tools such as: fingers, tongs, tweezers, strawberry hullers, eye droppers, and tea strainers.
- Strengthen eye–hand coordination and wrist stabilization.
- Develop small muscles, pincher grasp, and wrist rotation.

Space and Materials Needed
This can be done at the manipulative center table or in the sensory table.

For infants, small food items such as Cheerios® in a cup or on a tray to pick up with fingers and put in their mouth.

For other children, the size of the objects and the tools used to pick them up decreases as the child gets older. For example, provide tongs, large pompoms, an ice tray, and a bowl for toddlers, whereas 4-year-olds can do the same activity with tweezers, small pompoms, mini ice cube trays, and cups to sort the different colored pompoms.

- Suggested materials include: trays, muffin tins, bowls, cups, ice trays, egg cartons, candy boxes with dividers, tongs, tweezers, strawberry hullers, tea strainers, pompoms, ping-pong balls, golf balls, spoons, natural items such as small stones and whole tree nuts as well as small plastic frogs, bugs, cars, trucks, or toys.

Procedure
- Set up items to be used together for the activity on a tray.
- Include a container to hold items before transfer, such as a bowl or basket, items to be transferred, tool used to transfer items, such as small tongs, tweezers, or a strawberry huller and container to receive transferred items like an egg carton.
- Encourage children to transfer items using the tools provided.

Guidance
This is a one- or two-person activity, so you may want to provide multiple sets with different tools and items to transfer. Act as a resource to discuss possible solutions as needed. Be sure to allow the children to guide the direction and flow of the play.

Assessment and Follow-Up Strategies
Take photographs of the children as they transfer and sort the items. Once children have mastered a particular tool or size of items to sort, increase the difficulty by providing different, smaller, or harder-to-use tools.

Activity Plan Worksheet   Developmentally Appropriate Motor Activity

AGES: primary-age children

Name Of Activity and Brief Description

The Electric Matching Game activity is designed for children to make and use a matching game to learn about circuits and energy conversions while developing small muscles and eye–hand coordination.

Child Outcome of Activity

- Encourage problem solving.
- Apply scientific concept to make an electrical circuit.
- Strengthen eye–hand coordination and wrist stabilization.
- Develop small muscles, pincher grasp, and wrist rotation.

Space and Materials Needed

This can be done at the manipulative center table.

Materials (per person):

file folder (colored is best)
10 brass-colored brads
aluminum foil (about six inches long and as wide as the roll)
masking tape

Equipment to share:

two lights (small flashlight size)
two pieces of wire (insulated, approximately 1.5 feet long)
two D batteries
markers
hole punch (single)
scissors
glue (white glue or glue stick)
wire strippers (the wires can be stripped ahead of time)
Scotch tape or stapler

Procedure

Discuss the concept of an electrical circuit and demonstrate how it works.

To make the game board:

1. Use the hole punch to punch 10 holes, 5 on each side of the outside edge of the front of the file folder. (Do not punch all the way through the folder.)
2. Draw or cut out the five pairs of choices to match such as capitals and states, sports team and mascots, or TV stars and shows and glue each one next to a hole.

3. Cut and fold aluminum foil strips and use to connect the matching holes from the inside of the folder. Insert one brad per hole from the front of the folder and use to fasten the ends of the foil strips between the matches. Use masking tape to secure the foil to the brad and separate anywhere that the aluminum foil strips touch each other. (If two strips touch each other without masking tape in between them, all of the holes will be on the same circuit and light up instead of just the two that match.)

To make the testing light apparatus:

1. Strip both ends of the insulated wire about 1.5 inches. Bend the wire ends into a circle.
2. Use masking tape to connect one end of the wire to the top of the battery.
3. Connect the other wire end to the light by placing the light bulb in the circle of wire.
4. Test by placing the battery on top of the brad for one answer and the light on top of the matching answer; the light should come on. Because the wire on top of the battery is covered with masking tape, you should not feel an electrical shock when holding the light bulb.
5. You can try using a holiday light and a double-A battery.

The testing apparatus may be used with different game boards.

Guidance

Limit the group to four to five children working at one time on this project as they make the game board. Provide support as children make the game boards and light-testing apparatus. Store folder games and light testing apparatus together in a big Ziploc bag or box. Encourage children to make more game boards to create collection to be kept in the manipulative or gaming center for independent use.

Assessment and Follow-Up Strategies

Take photos or a video of the children making the boards. Create a documentation board with sample game boards, photos, and comments from the children to show parents what the children have accomplished.

⌄⌄ Professional Resource Download

Technology in Fine Motor and Manipulative Play

Study after study suggests that handwriting is important for brain development and cognition—helping children hone fine motor skills and learn to express and generate ideas. Yet the time devoted to teaching penmanship in most grade schools has shrunk to just one hour a week. University of Wisconsin psychologist Virginia Berninger tested students in grades 2, 4, and 6 and found that they not only wrote faster by hand than by keyboard, but they also generated more ideas when composing essays in longhand. In other research, Berninger shows that the sequential finger movements required to write by hand activate brain regions involved with thought, language, and short-term memory.

Touch-screen phones and tablets, such as the iPhone and iPad, are providing new opportunities by translating handwriting into digital letter forms and making writing practice fun. Apps such as Dexteria, Chalk Walk, and Ready to Print are designed to provide fine motor practice for holding a pencil (Richards, Berninger, and Chanquoy, 2009).

Diversity in Fine Motor and Manipulative Play

Diversity can be added to manipulative play through adding materials from other countries to the classroom, such as nesting dolls from Russia, worry dolls from Guatemala, fans and chopsticks from Japan, a *molcajete* from Mexico, an abacus from China, and a mancala game from Africa.

Fine motor activities can be planned to explore customs from other countries, such as making stamped cookies from Sweden or Belgium, creating a Southeast Asian name chop out of clay, making *cascarones* out of egg shells and confetti to break on people's heads at carnival time, and making origami sculptures.

The following strategies help children to be successful in developing fine motor skills (Gould and Sullivan, 1999):

- Encourage children to attempt buttons, zippers, and snaps, giving them only as much assistance as needed.
- Many children are easily distracted, so block distractions by placing the manipulative table facing a shelf or make partitions out of laminated file folders or three-section display boards cut in half to make them shorter.
- Define play spaces by putting materials on individual trays, cookie sheets, or small throw rugs on the floor.
- Create a nonslip workspace by putting down rubbery shelf liner material.
- Provide a small container to put manipulative pieces in next to the puzzle or game while working to decrease clutter.
- Use manipulatives on the floor as well as the table.
- Tape the base of a manipulative toy to the table to stabilize it.
- Use the easel to create a vertical work space for manipulatives.

Creating Partnerships with Families

Parents want to help their child succeed but often do not realize the impact of fine motor development on school success. Teachers can help parents recognize how they can have an impact by helping their children improve their fine motor skills. There are lots of activities parents can do at home to develop their child's fine motor skills using common household items that most families have on hand. Share these ideas with your children's families, from Kennett Square Preschool (www.kennettsquarepreschool.com):

Sorting socks: Have children help you match and sorts clean socks from the laundry. Not only does this activity improve eye–hand coordination and wrist dexterity, it teaches the math concept of one-to-one correspondence.

Tearing paper: Create art projects by tearing paper into small pieces instead of using scissors.

Cutting with scissors: Cut play dough or paper with scissors. Start with play dough and then move to paper, first using basic lines and then cutting more complex shapes.

Tracing: Use stencils to trace objects, shapes, or letters.

Making letters: Make letters using yarn, shoestrings, or wax-coated string.

Stapling paper: Staple papers together while making books or packets to encourage the use of both hands.

Punching holes: Use single-hole punchers to make designs on paper.

Wringing out sponges: Wring out sponges to increase hand and wrist muscle development.

Sewing and lacing: Use string or yarn to lace index cards with holes punched in them.

Stringing beads: Make necklaces by stringing colored beads in a pattern onto household string.

Performing finger plays: Sing songs that require the use of both hands such as "Where is Thumbkin?"

Clapping: Use both hands to clap syllables in words or to clap to the beat of a song.

The Teacher's Role

It should not be surprising that research has established a substantial relationship between the use of manipulative materials and students' achievement in mathematics. Learning theorists have suggested for some time that children's concepts evolve through direct interaction with the environment. The development of fine motor skills is critical to the child's ability to write through the building of the small muscles located in the fingers (index, middle, and thumb) and wrists. Without the correct development of these hand skills, children can find everyday tasks to be difficult, resulting in frustration and low self-esteem. Early childhood teachers build the foundation required to help children become proficient in fine motor skills, which are needed for proper growth. It is important for teachers to create activities that captivate children's interest and keep them engaged in learning.

Case Study: Toddler Fine Motor Materials

The director of the Babies to School Child Development Center in Boulder, Colorado, has given the toddler teacher, Carlos, a budget of $100.00 to purchase materials to support toddler fine motor development. Carlos wants to make sure he has a variety of activities for his toddlers, and he isn't sure $100.00 will be enough to cover all he wants.

He is considering making some materials himself, but wants to think more about it.

What Do You Think?

1. What types of materials would you suggest Carlos purchase with the money he has been given?
2. What activities could Carlos make to supplement the materials he could purchase?
3. Which of these materials would Carlos want in duplicates to avoid having to share?

Guidance in Fine Motor and Manipulative Play

Children need to start with simpler fine motor activities to build strength in the fingers and wrists while developing eye–hand coordination. It is important for teachers to remember that development takes place at different times in children. Patience, understanding, and positive reinforcement help when developing fine motor skills. Allowing children access to manipulative materials at all times during child initiated play encourages them to be creative. They will be able to practice fine motor skill development without having to follow a guided activity.

TEACHING TIPS Fine Motor Development

Activities should:

- Allow each and every child to succeed.
- Offer a range of opportunities to practice developing fine motor skills.
- Use various materials for drawing, painting, and writing.
- Break fine motor skills into sequenced steps.
- Explicitly teach a new skill.
- Build skills on the previously mastered skills.

Model appropriate language by:

- Talking about what you are doing as you demonstrate new skills.

- Positively recognize effort, such as, "You were very careful when you cut around the circle."
- Discussing how to do tasks, such as, "Put the scissors on the edge of the paper."
- Sequencing the action through descriptive language, such as, "Hold the scissors in your cutting hand, open them, put them on top of the cutting line, close them."

(This is adapted from www.education.nt.gov/.)

⌄⌄ **Professional Resource Download**

Summary

1. **What are some examples of key terms related to fine motor development and manipulative play for children?** Fine motor skill is the coordination of small muscle movements such as the fingers, usually in coordination with the eyes. The pincer grasp is using thumb and index finger to pick up an item. Bilateral coordination refers to using both hands together to perform a task. Eye–hand coordination involves focusing and coordinating eye movement and visual input to control and direct the hands. Wrist rotation and wrist stability are used to control hand movements, such as holding and pouring from a pitcher. Finger dexterity refers to the ability to move individual fingers in isolation.

2. **How does fine motor development and manipulative play relate to stages of child development?** Infant fine motor developmental sequence moves from pre-reaching as a newborn, using a mitten or whole hand grasp at 3 to 4 months, moving objects from hand to hand at 4 to 5 months, and using a pincer or finger to thumb grasp at nine months. Toddler fine motor skills include filling and dumping, pushing buttons, working simple puzzles, flushing the toilet, turning knobs and switches, scribbling, and pointing.

   Preschool children show their development of fine motor abilities by their increasing skill in dressing themselves. Preschool children become increasing adept at using fine motor skills in feeding themselves.

   Primary-age children show dramatic improvements with regard to their printed handwriting and ability to write in cursive letters. They also develop the ability to draw complex and detailed pictures.

3. **What should be considered in the planning and preparation of fine motor and manipulative play environments?** The manipulative center should be planned as a quiet area for children to work that is well lighted and contains low, open shelves for materials. The center should include labeled tubs, trays, or baskets to hold all the materials needed for each activity. A good variety of materials should be displayed attractively and there should be enough materials for four to six children to have several choices each. Both horizontal and vertical work surfaces should be provided.

4. **What are some ways to integrate and create fine motor and manipulative play activities appropriate for young children?** You can help to build an infant's fine motor skills with simple activities that help to increase typical hand and finger movements of this stage, such as using a pincer grasp to take objects out and put them in a container or to poke an object. Toddlers can build a tower with up to six blocks, press together manipulative pieces such as pop beads, and string big beads on a thick shoelace. Thick board books allow for practicing lifting and turning pages. Toddlers enjoy using crayons to color and draw with as well as painting with brushes. Introduce low easels to provide a vertical surface for making marks.

   Preschool-age children benefit from experiences that support the development of fine motor skills in the hands and fingers. The use of manipulatives, implements, and tools found in various learning centers help to build the hand and wrist strength and dexterity necessary to hold a pencil appropriately.

   Even when children are already in school, tasks requiring fine motor skills can often present difficulties. Although many children do not have trouble with gross motor skills—such as running or jumping—fine motor skills require more control and more precise movements of smaller muscles. As fine motor control is an important skill to master for writing, it is important to make sure children are continually improving those skills.

5. **How can technology be used in a fine motor and manipulative play environment?** Touch-screen phones and tablets, such as the iPhone and iPad, are providing new opportunities by translating handwriting into digital letter forms and making writing practice fun. Apps such as Dexteria, Chalk Walk, and Ready to Print are designed to provide fine motor practice for holding a pencil.

6. **How can you incorporate diversity into fine motor and manipulative play environments?** Diversity can be added to manipulative play through adding materials from other countries to the classroom. Fine motor activities can be planned to explore customs from other countries. Strategies to help each and every child be successful include: encouraging children's self-help skills, reducing distractions, organizing materials, and defining play spaces.

7. **What are some ways to develop partnerships with families that support fine motor and manipulative play?** There are lots of activities parents can do at home to develop their child's fine motor skills using common household items that most families have on hand. Teachers can provide information to parents about how to implement these easy activities.

8. **What is the role of the teacher in developing fine motor and manipulative skills in the classroom?** Research has established a relationship between the use of manipulative materials and students' achievement in mathematics. Learning theorists have suggested that children's concepts evolve through direct interaction with the environment. The development of fine motor skills is critical to the child's ability to write through the building of the small muscles located in the fingers (index, middle, and thumb) and wrists. Without the correct development of these hand skills, children can find everyday tasks to be difficult, resulting in frustration and low self-esteem. Early childhood teachers build the foundation required to help children become proficient in fine motor skills, which are needed for proper growth. It is important for teachers to create activities that captivate children's interest and keep them engaged in learning.

Reflective Review Questions

1. A great deal of emphasis is being placed on having children able to count and do math when they enter kindergarten. How can teachers help in an appropriate way to build the foundations required for children to be successful in math in school?
2. How can pushing children to write too early hinder their fine motor development? What problems can these children have once they enter public school?
3. What is the connection between handwriting and brain development?

Explorations

1. Select at least two early childhood classrooms. Observe for one hour in each. Describe objectively (factually) in writing how fine motor activities were introduced to the children. Which fine motor activities happened indoors and which ones occurred outdoors? Was there a manipulative learning center as part of the room arrangement? Explain. Describe at least four activities you observed. What are your subjective (opinion) thoughts about early education fine motor activities now that you have completed this assignment?
2. Based on the information from this chapter, write a letter about fine motor activities to give to the parents of the children in your class. Be creative. Explain what fine motor projects you and the children are doing. Give suggestions for extended activities the parents can do with their children. Describe other ways to communicate with parents.
3. Select and plan a fine motor activity for young children. Specify which age group this activity is planned for: infants, toddlers, preschoolers, or primary-age children. In writing, list objectives, materials needed, step-by-step procedures for presenting this activity, follow-up activities, and evaluation guidelines. (Use the activity plan worksheet in Appendix D.) Prepare this activity and demonstrate it during class or with a group of children.
4. Use the Fine Motor and Manipulative Environment Checklist in this chapter to conduct an observation of an early childhood learning environment.
   - Beside each statement, place an *X* if the classroom you observed met the statement.
   - On a separate sheet of paper, describe what you actually observed related to each statement. Place the number of the statement first and then your observation.
   - On a separate sheet of paper, for each statement that you did not check as met, describe what you would do to improve that classroom so that the statement would be met. Be sure to put the number of the statement first.
   - Submit this with the name of the location you observed and the age group.

Fine Motor and Manipulative Play Books for Young Children

Van Der Put, K., and Bennett, M. (2007). *Little Puppy: Finger Puppet Board Book*. Chronicle Books.

Van Der Put, K., and Bennett, M. (2007). *Little Mouse: Finger Puppet Board Book*. Chronicle Books.

Kubler, A. (2003). *Ten Little Fingers/Tengo Diez Deditos*. Child's Play International.

Gillingham, S., and Siminovich, L. (2009). *In My Nest*. Chronicle Books.

Lalgudi, S., (2013). *Finger Counting Fun, A Number Counting Picture Book for Children*.

Beall, P. C., and Nipp, S. H. (2005). *Wee Sing Children's Songs and Fingerplays*.

Feierabend, J. M., (2003). *The Book of Finger Plays and Action Songs*. Gia Publications.

Gillingham, S., and Siminovich, L. (2009). *In My Pond*.

Large Motor and Outdoor Play

12

Student Learning Outcomes

After studying this chapter, you should be able to:

- Define and give examples for key terms related to large motor development and outdoor play for children.

- Discuss large motor development and outdoor play in young children and how they relate to stages of child development.

- Evaluate various components of planning and preparation of large motor and outdoor play environments.

- Integrate and create large motor and outdoor play activities appropriate for young children.

- Discuss various issues in the use of technology in a large motor and outdoor play environment.

Standards Covered in This Chapter

 NAEYC 5a, 5b, 5c

DAP 2

 INTASC 4, 5, 8,

 HEAD START
Domain: Perceptual Motor and Physical Development

NAEYC, DAP, and INTASC standards described on Part II introduction page

Figure 12-1 Children being active when they are young can influence them for a lifetime.

- Distinguish ways to incorporate diversity into large motor and outdoor play environments.

- Describe ways to develop partnerships with families that support large motor and outdoor play.

- Analyze the teacher's role in promoting large motor and outdoor play in the classroom.

As Michelle Obama's Let's Move Campaign (http://www.letsmove.gov) tells us:

"Physical activity is an essential component of a healthy lifestyle [see **Figure 12-1**]. In combination with healthy eating, it can help prevent a range of chronic diseases, including heart disease, cancer, and stroke, which are the three leading causes of death. Physical activity helps control weight, builds lean muscle, reduces fat, promotes strong bone, muscle and joint development, and decreases the risk of obesity. Children need 60 minutes of play with moderate to vigorous activity every day to grow up to a healthy weight. In addition to keeping kids healthy and strong, being active for 60 minutes each day has been shown to:

- Increase concentration and focus.
- Improve classroom attendance and behavior.
- Boost academic performance."

Large motor activities develop skill and strength in arms, legs, and torso, help release tension, and promote relaxation.

What are your favorite memories of play as a child? When I ask this question of my students and other early childhood professionals, most remember a place outdoors where they felt a sense of privacy and independence, and where they could arrange the environment as they wished. Often times, their memories are of natural outdoor areas where they used leaves to be pretend food or raced through tall grass. Do these places still exist for children, or are these vanishing habitats? Traffic, more people, family and school schedules that limit play, and security issues have all taken their toll on children's time for vigorous play and exploration outdoors. As a result, children know less about nature.

Through outdoor play children develop their small muscles, eye–hand coordination, balance and coordination, large muscles, general health, a sense of freedom, an understanding of nature, creativity, social play skills, multisensory integration and learning, ability to explore and solve problems, and their imaginations. Health benefits to playing outdoors include opportunities to exercise and improve physical fitness, exposure to sunlight needed to produce vitamin D, and an environment with less-concentrated disease organisms. (See **Figure 12-2**.)

Large Motor and Outdoor Play Defined

Figure 12-2 Children develop balance, coordination, and large muscles in outdoor play.

Basic types of movement in young children, identified by Greenberg (1979) and expanded by Pica (2010), are locomotor, nonlocomotor, combination, and manipulative. All these actions need practice, encouragement, and an adult's understanding of individual growth patterns.

Locomotor movement (fundamental movement) is the ability to move the whole body from one place to another. This is demonstrated by crawling, creeping, walking, running, jumping, hopping, skipping, and climbing. Children vary greatly in the progression from crawling to creeping, and any two children may look quite different as they crawl and creep. When children begin running, they have become toddlers. Closely following in development are the rest of the locomotor skills mentioned previously with a reminder that hopping on one foot is a difficult skill for young children to control. As with all motor skills, children need opportunities to practice developing their physical abilities. (See **Figure 12-3.**)

Nonlocomotor movement (axial or body movement) occurs when the feet remain stationary (as in standing, kneeling, sitting, or lying) while other parts of the body move. Examples are stretching, reaching, bending, twisting, bouncing, shaking, and clapping.

A combination of the previous two types of movement involves various motions that enhance coordination while giving children movement and rhythm combinations that occur simultaneously. An example of this is walking and clapping at the same time or hopping and shaking (Greenberg, 1979).

Manipulative movement skills in the physical education field are described by Pica (2010, p. 94) as "gross motor movements involving force imparted to or received from objects . . . [or] any gross motor skill in which an object is usually involved (manipulated)." This is demonstrated by pulling, pushing, lifting, striking, throwing, kicking, and ball catching. Catching is harder to master than throwing. When first attempting to do this, young children often stand with their eyes closed and their arms rigidly outstretched. This is part of the developing stage that children go through. As teachers, we should continue to offer encouragement.

Isbell and Raines (2013) add another important factor: **kinesthetics**, which is the use of the body to learn about physical capabilities, develop body awareness, and gain understanding of the world. Howard Gardner's (1983) theories of multiple intelligences describe bodily-kinesthetic intelligence as the ability to unite the body and mind in physical performance.

Children love swinging, playing Ring around the Rosie, and otherwise getting dizzy because it feels great to their vestibular system! The vestibular system processes the body's relationship to the earth; it tells us if we're falling, leaning forward, or standing perfectly still. The development of this sense results in balanced and coordinated movement through space. Children develop their vestibular senses by swinging, spinning, twirling, and rolling around on the ground. Children gravitate toward these movements naturally.

These key terms are used to describe large motor development:

- **Strength** is physical energy available for movement or resistance.
- **Stamina/endurance** is capacity for sustained use of strength or physical energy.
- **Flexibility** is ease and range of movement.
- **Agility** is ability to move with speed, grace, and precision.

Movement activities should be provided every day, planned by teacher for both indoor and outdoor play including balancing, spinning, rocking, running, jumping, and other vigorous movement. (See **Figure 12-4.**)

Recess

"Recess is at the heart of a vigorous debate over the role of schools in promoting the optimal development of the whole child. A growing trend toward reallocating time in school to accentuate the more academic subjects has put this important facet of a child's school day at risk. Recess serves as a necessary break from the rigors of concentrated, academic challenges in the classroom. But equally important is the fact that safe and well-supervised recess offers cognitive, social, emotional, and physical benefits that may not be fully appreciated when a decision is made to diminish it. Recess is unique from, and a complement to, physical education—not a substitute for it. The American Academy of Pediatrics believes that recess is a crucial and necessary component of a child's development and, as such, it should not be withheld for punitive or academic reasons (Murray and Ramstetter 2013)."

Figure 12-3

Manipulative movement, a gross motor skill, is seen when a young child attempts to catch a ball. The child often stands with eyes closed and arms rigidly outstretched.

locomotor movement: The ability to move the whole body from one place to another.

nonlocomotor movement: Axle or body movement that occurs when the feel remain stationary while other parts of the body move.

manipulative movement: Gross motor movements involving force imparted to or received from objects or any gross motor skill in which an object is usually involved.

kinesthetics: The use of the body to learn about physical capabilities, develop body awareness, and gain.

strength: Physical energy available for movement or resistance.

stamina/endurance: Capacity for sustained use of strength or physical energy.

flexibility: Ease and range of movement.

agility: Ability to move with speed, grace, and precision.

Reflect On This

Many schools are reducing or eliminating outdoor time to give more time to academics. What do you think of this practice?

Figure 12-4   Permanent climbers can meet many of the requirements for quality outdoor play experiences.

Developmental Stages of Large Motor and Outdoor Play

Large motor skills development occurs in stages, with each building on the previous ones that can vary in their timing. Young infants can reach, play with their hands and feet, lift their heads, and put things in their mouths. Older babies go from rolling over and sitting, to scooting, bouncing, creeping, pulling themselves up, and standing. One-year olds can walk steadily and climb stairs. Toddlers test their physical skills by jumping from heights, climbing, hanging by their arms, rolling, and rough-and-tumble play. Preschool children like to experiment with their physical skills such as kicking, throwing, catching, running, jumping, galloping, hopping on one foot, and finally skipping. During the primary years, children increase agility, strength, and endurance as they take on the challenges of organized sports.

Brain Research: Physical Activity

Research suggests that physical activity is a strong determinant in the early development of the brain, not just motor control. This information has strong implications for developing the primary circuits needed for learning skills that require a high degree of manual dexterity, such as playing a musical instrument or performing precise manual operations. There is also speculation that the general window of opportunity for most behavioral functions narrows considerably around age 10.

When they analyzed the MRI data, researchers found that physically fit 9- and 10- year-old children tended to have bigger hippocampal volume—about 12 percent bigger relative to total brain size—than their out-of-shape peers. Children with larger hippocampal volumes generally had better relational memory (Chugani, 1998).

Children's mental spatial transformation abilities benefit from active movement, by allowing them to tap into well-established and fine-tuned links between action and cognition that are primarily used for keeping track of the environment during movement and for tracking objects such as blocks during manipulation of them.

Gabbard, C., and Rodrigues, L. (2013). Optimizing early brain and motor development through movement. *Early Childhood News*. Retrieved October 16, 2013, from http://www.earlychildhoodnews.com /earlychildhood/ article_view.aspx?ArticleID=360.

Chugani, H. T. (1998). A critical period of brain development: Studies of cerebral glucose utilization with PET. *Preventive Medicine*, 27, 184–188.

Planning and Preparing the Environment

An effective outdoor playground has adequate space that is divided into play zones such as active play, sand and water, gardening, dramatic play, trike and wheel toy area, and shaded area for relaxing, circulation paths to get from place to place, an exciting entry, shade and protection from the elements, sufficient storage areas located throughout the playground near the location where materials will be used and access to toileting, hand washing, and drinking water.

The selection of outdoor equipment and materials emphasizes safety, durability, and age appropriateness for all children. The outdoor space should contribute to physical, intellectual, creative, emotional, and social development and offer a variety of stimulation for play and exploration. The design should also offer ramps and tracks that accommodate wheelchairs and adapted vehicles, giving proper attention to slope, width, types of surface, and direct and safe accessibility to play and structures (Frost, 1992). The surfaces should offer various textures and colors, such as a hard-surfaced area for games and wheeled toys, a large, soft grassy area with trees, a garden area, organic loose material such as play bark/wood chips and pine bark mulch, inorganic loose material such as sand and pea gravel, and rubber or foam mats.

The following are suggestions for equipment selection:

- Permanent climbers
- Take-apart climbers for older children to rearrange
- Sturdy wooden crates and barrels
- Tire swings with holes punched in several places for drainage (steel-belted tires are not appropriate)
- Slides
- Balance beam
- Tricycles, wagons, and other wheeled toys
- Plastic hoops
- Balls of various sizes
- Mounted steering wheel
- Sturdy cardboard boxes
- Equipment and materials that eliminate head entrapment points

The outdoor environment should invite you to "come on out." Open the door to outside play and learning. Planning includes a process for developing curriculum for the outdoors in a way that parallels what teachers do indoors.

With the decrease of our natural environments and many schools limiting the amount of time allowed in the child's day for outdoor experiences, teachers are faced with the dilemma of trying to provide lifelong attitudes about nature that are necessary for the preservation of these natural environments.

Planning a balanced and varied outdoor environment is much like planning for an indoor environment. Teachers must understand perception and large motor development of each and every child in their classroom. Then they should know how to incorporate developmentally appropriate activities into the lesson plan. Teachers must also be able to alternate the outdoor environment regularly so that children have a variety of experiences to enhance their skills. Many outdoor activities can also encourage independence and socialization. (See **Figure 12-5**.)

Simple experiences with nature can be powerful opportunities for teaching and learning with young children. Observing and talking about the many sensory aspects of nature—the sounds and smells of wind and rain, changing colors of the seasons, the tastes of fruits, vegetables, and herbs—inspire interest and appreciation of the beauty of nature (Torquati and Barber, 2005).

Nature Explore, a collaborative project of the Arbor Day Foundation and Dimensions Educational Research Foundation, has developed a certification for Outdoor Classrooms. Certification requirements include a well-designed outdoor space using principles from the *Learning with Nature Idea Book*, staff development including attendance at a full-length Nature Explore Workshop, and family involvement to increase family awareness and involvement in nature education. (See **Figure 12-6**.)

Reflect On This

Do you think slides are a safe piece of equipment for an outdoor play space? Why or why not?

Figure 12-5   Taking dramatic play outside into a playhouse.

An outdoor space for infants can be as simple as placing a blanket or mat down on an unused section of a larger playground, or it can be an area with appropriate infant-sized equipment. It is important that infants have access to the outdoors where they can experience the change in temperature, color, smell, sounds, and textures (Reynolds, 2002).

Outdoor play is an essential part of the overall primary grade curriculum. Play reflects and enhances all areas of children's development, yet today outdoor recess is in jeopardy in

Figure 12-6   Integrating natural materials and gardening experiences creates a nature classroom.

many schools. Recess is increasingly viewed as the most useless of activities. Nonetheless, the available research suggests that recess can play an essential role in the learning, social development, and health of elementary school children. Recess may be the only opportunity for some children to engage in social interactions with other children. According to Louv (2008):

> "One U.S. researcher suggests a generation of children is not only being raised indoors, but is being confined to even smaller spaces. . . . [T]hey spend more and more time in car seats, high chairs, and even baby seats for watching TV. When small children do go outside, they're often placed in containers—strollers—and pushed by walking or jogging parents."

As you continue to plan outdoor spaces for play and learning, think back to when you were a child. What were your favorite outdoor play settings? They probably included dirt, water, flowers, trees, places to be alone, places to climb, places to hide, places to build, and plenty of unstructured playing time with your friends. As teachers, we have the opportunity to give the children in our care these same activities in safe, creative, stimulating, and developmentally appropriate play environments. Chapter 9 also suggests other nature and science activities for outdoors.

To promote large motor development indoors, equip a large motor room or a center in the classroom with beanbags, parachutes, hoops, large and small balls to grasp, kick and throw, hippity-hop balls, push-and-pull toys, low, soft things for infants to crawl over, ride-on toys without pedals for toddlers, a sit and spin, rocking boat, tunnels, low climbers with soft material underneath, and pounding and hammering toys, plastic bats and balls, scarves, plastic bowling pins, targets and things to throw at them, and a workbench with a vise, hammer, nails, and saw for children 4- to 9-year-olds.

The physical environment plays a large role in enhancing large motor and outdoor play experiences. A checklist can be used to evaluate the large motor and outdoor play environment in your own classroom/outdoor area or classrooms/outdoor areas that you observe.

Large Motor and Outdoor Environment Checklist

_____ 1. Is the outdoor play space zoned?

_____ 2. Are the zones visibly separated by dividers or different ground surfaces?

_____ 3. Does the outdoor area have tools (child-sized rakes, shovels, magnifying glasses for child-initiated nature exploration)?

_____ 4. Is the outdoor play space S.A.F.E (appropriate supervision, developmentally appropriate equipment, appropriate fall zones and surfaces, well-maintained equipment)?

_____ 5. Are nonmobile children protected from mobile children?

_____ 6. Is there shade and protection from the elements?

_____ 7. Are there areas to climb, crawl, balance, and jump?

_____ 8. Is there sufficient storage space?

_____ 9. Are there areas to swing?

_____ 10. Is the storage space located near where the materials will be used?

_____ 11. Are there water areas?

_____ 12. Is there an area for riding tricycles, scooters, and bikes?

_____ 13. Are there areas for plants and gardens?

_____ 14. Does the outdoor play space provide access to toileting, hand washing, and drinking water?

_____ 15. Are there places to slide?

_____ 16. Is there a place to seek refuge?

_____ 17. Are there messy areas (mud, sand)?

_____ 18. Is there an outdoor block and building center?

_____ 19. Are there many different places to sit?

_____ 20. Is there an outdoor art center?

_____ 21. Are there places to observe and interact with insects, animals, and birds?

_____ 22. Is there an outdoor music center?

_____ 23. Are there large areas for gathering and for large motor play?

_____ 24. Is there an outdoor dramatic play center?

_____ 25. Are there outdoor science and math centers?

_____ 26. Is there an outdoor literacy center?

_____ 27. Are there loose parts available to enhance possibilities?

_____ 28. Does the outdoor play space provide "a sense of place" (reflects local materials, local plants, location, values and culture)?

_____ 29. Are adults scaffolding children's learning?

Large Motor and Outdoor Environment Checklist (continued)

_____ **30.** Does the outdoor area have places to be alone or with one or two friends?

_____ **31.** Is the outdoor aesthetically pleasing (clean, curved lines, designed for rich sensory experiences, materials and colors from nature, attention to detail, personalized with children's ideas and art, created with beauty in mind)?

_____ **32.** Are there ways children can feel powerful (ringing a bell when they reach the top of a climbing structure)?

_____ **33.** Does the outdoor play space have the right amount of challenge?

_____ **34.** Is there a range of activities to meet the needs of different skill levels (different types of swings, different ways to climb a structure, balance beams at different widths)?

_____ **35.** Is the outdoor play available on a daily basis?

_____ **36.** Are all children able to use the playground successfully (equipment accessible to all)?

_____ **37.** Does the outdoor area have paved or hard surfaces large enough for riding wheeled toys safely?

_____ **38.** Is there sufficient space to accommodate all the children using the outdoor area at one time (approximately 80 to 100 square feet per child)?

_____ **39.** Are adults interacting with the children (playing, reading a book, conversing, or disciplining)?

_____ **40.** Does the outdoor area have open spaces for large motor skills?

_____ **41.** Is the outdoor area a safe place for outdoor play (protected from traffic, free from debris, cushioning materials under the equipment, and no sharp edges)?

_____ **42.** Does the outdoor area have varied spaces that include sort materials (sawdust, sand, or bark under equipment)?

❯❯ Professional Resource Download

Integrating Large Muscle and Outdoor Play into the Curriculum

Motor Development and Physical Fitness

❝Developing physical skills can be compared to learning to read and write, or understanding principles of math and science. Each requires a manipulative of some type to best develop skills and knowledge. Developing skill in physical activity requires the manipulation of balls, bean bags, paddles, scarves, hoops, ropes, and other objects. Children cannot learn to write without a pencil; they cannot learn to throw without a ball (Sanders, 2006, p. 6).❞

Music and movement early education curriculum should include well-defined opportunities, both indoor and outdoor, for young children to develop motor skills. As discussed in previous chapters, setting up the environment and planning appropriate activities depends on the developmental skills, interests, and needs of the children.

Large muscle (gross motor) development usually precedes small muscle (fine motor) development. For this chapter, we will focus on motor development that includes locomotor skills, large muscle activities, and physical fitness. Underlying all of this is the understanding that possibilities for exploration, creativity, and self-expression are included as part of the motor skill planning process.

For you, as a teacher of young children, this means planning and providing daily developmentally appropriate movement and exercise activities for the children in your care. This specifies allowing time for movement exploration. Start with slow stretches to get their bodies "warmed up." For example, the children can touch their toes, then make circles with their arms, and finally, stretch their arms way above their heads. You should demonstrate the importance of health and fitness by encouraging and participating with your actions as well as your words. Gagen, Getchell, and Payne, cited in Essa and Burnham (2009) offer the following insight, "[C]hildren who become proficient movers are more likely to use those movement skills in activities that will enhance the state of their health and well-being over their entire lifespan." (See **Figure 12-7.**)

Locomotor, large muscle, and fitness activities can easily be combined with creative movement and music activities. There are no limits on how to accomplish this. You and

Figure 12-7   Plan and provide daily developmentally appropriate movement and exercise activities for the children.

the children together can discover wonderful things through outdoor play, movement, and music! Other large muscle and outdoor activities include the following.

Outdoor Art

Take it all outdoors! Children enjoy the space and freedom offered by outdoor art activities. Take the easels, a table, long sheets of butcher paper, paints, and cleanup buckets outdoors. Plan big messy art projects such as using brooms to paint on butcher paper or bouncing balls that are dipped in paint on paper placed in a plastic pool. Let the children use chalk on the sidewalk; paint outdoor surfaces with water using large house-painting brushes or rollers; explore rocks, shells, flowers, trees, birds, and butterflies; go for walks and look for colors, textures, and shapes; and gather leaves for making rubbings or prints or for using as materials on paintings and collages.

> "Nature excursions also can inspire creativity in artwork. Children can draw or paint pictures about their experiences. Collections of natural materials (berries for dyes; dried weed stalks for tracing or relief rubbings; acorns, seeds, sticks, and pebbles for collages) can be used to create artistic masterpieces. You may even find real clay to dig up and sculpt (Humphryes, 2000, p. 19). "

If your playground has a chain link fence, it can be used as a drying area. Clothespins easily attach the paintings or murals to the fence. A safe drying area can also be arranged inside a large cardboard box. Plan for cleanup with buckets, hoses, and lots of paper towels. Chapters 8 and 13 offer additional ideas for outdoor activities with sand, water, and woodworking.

Beanbag Activity

Use beanbags for many lively activities. They are easier for some children to catch than a ball. Ask the older children to experiment with how many different ways they can catch a beanbag, such as with one hand, two hands, their feet, or their head.

Set up several baskets into which children can practice throwing beanbags. Mark a tossing line on the floor with masking tape (or a wide chalk line, if the activity is played outdoors).

The children can take turns tossing beanbags into the basket. A variation of this game can be two teams tossing beanbags at the same time or moving the toss line up closer or farther back to make the activity easier or more difficult.

Make beanbags from colorful fabric or felt. The children can help you by deciding if they want them to be circles, squares, rectangles, triangles, or ovals. Fill the beanbags with bird seed, Styrofoam "peanuts," or dried beans.

"Simon Says Move" Activity

Start this activity by explaining to the children that they will play a game by moving a part of their body without music, such as their fingers, hands, or arms. Later, add music. This can be played as a "Simon Says" type of game. Introduce the movements first, a few at a time, suggesting only the movement exercises that are applicable to the age and stage of development of the children in your classroom. Remind the children to stay in their "own space." Let one of the children take your place, inserting the child's name to replace "Simon" or "Teacher Says." Accept whatever movement each individual child makes, unless it is inappropriate. The following are some examples:

- Moving fingers and hands: bending, separating, stretching, curling, and making fists
- Moving arms: pushing, pulling, stretching, and swinging
- Moving feet and legs: stomping, kicking, crossing, and uncrossing
- Moving elbows: touching and making circles
- Moving head: bending, shaking, rolling, and nodding
- Moving eyes: opening; shutting; looking up, down, side to side, and around
- Nose: wiggling and breathing in and out
- Mouth: opening wide, making shapes, and shutting tight

Friends Go Marching Activity

This is a variation of the traditional activity "The Ants Go Marching." It can be both a movement/music and a transition activity.

> The friends go marching two by two,
> Hurrah, hurrah.
> The friends go marching two by two,
> Hurrah, hurrah.
> The friends go marching two by two,
> It is the greatest thing to do.
> As we all go marching,
> Marching around the room,
> In a line, like ants.

Expand this activity by adding extra verses, such as: friends go jumping, stomping, skipping, tiptoeing, and walking. Add musical instruments to emphasize the beat.

Poem, Music, and Movement Activity

The following are several verses of a poem a kindergarten class helped me create. We tried to move like many animals and fly like a lot of birds before we decided on the ones included in the poem. The next day we tried to put the poem to music. Each child selected a part of the poem to sing and made up his or her own tune. This activity continued for several days as the children proceeded to think up new words and melodies. I recorded their wonderful songs and put the CD in the music center for them to listen to whenever they chose to do so. We also made a book of the poem, with the children drawing the illustrations. This went into the book center.

Here is the poem:

> I can hop like a bunny.
> I can spin like a top.
> Hop, spin, hop, hop, hop!
> I can gallop like a horse.
> I can jump like a clown.
> Gallop, jump, up and down!

Here is another verse the children created later:
I can bark like a dog. Arf! Arf!
I can moo like a cow. Moo! Moo!
I can sound like a cat. Mee-ow!
I can hoot like an owl. Whoo! Whoo!

Activity Plan Worksheet	Developmentally Appropriate Large Motor Activity

AGES: toddlers, preschool, kindergarten, and primary age children

Name of Activity and Brief Description

The Obstacle Course activity is designed for children to follow a sequence of different large motor activities while practicing gross motor skills, balance, and coordination. The length and complexity of the course can be adapted to fit the age and ability of the children participating.

Child Outcomes of Activity

- Encourage problem solving.
- Describe actions using positional words such as over, under, and through.
- Remember and follow a sequence of actions.
- Strengthen physical coordination and balance.
- Develop flexibility, range of motion, and strength.
- Develop large muscles.

Space and Materials Needed

Design an obstacle course (an arrangement of physical challenges or tasks) for older children by setting up a path that leads around chairs and boxes, over piles of pillows, and through tunnels made of tables covered with blankets (or commercially made tunnels of varying lengths). An obstacle course can be set up with items you may already have. Usually an obstacle course is set up outdoors, but it can be a great indoor activity when the weather is bad. To set up an obstacle course, think of terms such as jump, hop, crawl under, climb over, walk along, go right, or go left. Plan out the course by listing the skills you want the children to practice. For the younger children, set up an obstacle course with fewer parts and hand or feet prints for the children to follow.

Two to 3 stations will work for toddlers, whereas 8 to 10 stations are a good number for primary-age children.

Some suggested materials include tables, chairs, blankets, fabric tunnels, hula hoops, yardstick, ball, wastebasket, jump rope, beanbag, laundry basket, or tricycle.

Procedure

Set up stations a label them with the action needed. Mark the direction that children should follow with masking tape or chalk. Adapt and change the course to fit your location and abilities of the children. This activity can be set up indoors or outdoors.

Some ideas of stations include:

- Crawl under a table.
- Hop through hula hoops set on the ground.
- Step over an obstacle such as yardstick between two chairs at knee height.
- Walk across balance beam (four-by-four-inch board) or on a piece of masking tape on the floor.
- Squeeze through two objects placed close so child walks sideways.
- Throw ball into wastebasket.
- Carry an object on a spoon (water balloon outdoors, small ball indoors).
- Jump or skip five times with jump rope.
- Bounce or dribble ball to next station (at least five times).
- Crawl under or over a row of chairs.
- Throw a beanbag into a laundry basket.
- Walk or run while balancing a beanbag on your head.
- Ride a tricycle along a predetermined route.

Help children remember the sequence of actions and encourage them as they do the action at each station.

Guidance

Limit the number of children so they do not have to wait too long for a turn. Encourage children waiting or who have finished to cheer others on. Monitor the activity and modify the course if it seems too long or too short or activities seem too easy or difficult. Emphasize that the obstacle course is not a race, and they should not speed through the activities. Stress to the children that they should keep some space between them. If a "traffic jam" does occur, help the children wait until it is their turn (Krull, 2009).

Assessment and Follow-Up Strategies

Take photographs of the children as they complete each station. Work with the children to create a map of the course or class book using the photos to develop a timeline and have the children describe what they were doing in the pictures. Children can vote for their favorite activity station.

⌄⌄ **Professional Resource Download**

Activity Plan Worksheet — Developmentally Appropriate Large Motor Activity

AGES: toddlers, preschool, kindergarten, and primary-age children

Name of Activity and Brief Description
Foil River: Children will experience the effects of water flow, gravity, sink and float by experimenting with a stream of water.

Child Outcomes of Activity
- Observe, describe, and demonstrate the various way objects can move.
- Discover the properties of water.
- Observe, describe, and demonstrate the effect of slope, distance, weight, gravity, and speed on the flow of water.

Space and Materials Needed
An open area outside where the ground gently slopes, a long piece of heavy-duty foil with the long edges folded up to create a channel for water, water, hose, buckets, items to flow on the water such as jar-cap boats (made with a juice lid, a small ball of clay, a toothpick, and a paper sail) or other small boats, twigs, leaves, etc.

Procedure
1. Set up the activity in an area outside where the ground gently slopes.
2. Fold up the long edges of a length of heavy-duty aluminium foil.
3. Place your garden hose nozzle on the higher end, and turn on a small stream of water.
4. Float boats, twigs, leaves, etc. down the river.
5. Describe children's actions as they play using vocabulary that they may not regularly say.
6. Ask children questions about what they are doing and what they observe.

Guidance
Have plenty of supplies so children do not have to share materials. Dress children in swimsuits or smocks over play clothes. Have towels handy for drying off after the fun.

Assessment and Follow-Up Strategies
1. Were child outcomes met? Yes_____ No_____
2. What was the children's response?
3. What worked well? What did not work?
4. How could this activity be changed to make it more effective or more appropriate?

⌄⌄ Professional Resource Download

Technology in Large Motor and Outdoor Play

Technology & Teaching: Issues Relating to Large Motor and Outdoor Play

Noninteractive media, such as most television shows and children's videos, can lead to passive viewing and overexposure to screen time for young children and are not substitutes for interactive and engaging uses of digital media or for face-to-face interactions with other children and adults. In fact, the American Academy of Pediatrics (AAP) recommends that children 2-years old and younger should not be exposed to television, and children older than age 2 should limit daily media exposure to only 1 to 2 hours of quality programming.

Yet, one study found that 43 percent of children younger than age 2 watch television daily, and 26 percent have a television in their room. Ninety percent of 4- to 6-year-old children use some sort of screen media for an average of two hours per day. More than 40 percent of children in this age group have a television in their bedroom, a third have a portable DVD player, and a third have a portable handheld video game player. Children from lower-income families and children of color spend more time watching television and are more likely to live in a home where the TV is left on most of the time.

Studies show a relationship between television viewing and the risk of being overweight in preschool children, independent of sociodemographic factors. For each additional hour of television viewing, the odds ratio of children having a BMI greater than the eighty-fifth percentile was 106. Having a television in the bedroom had a stronger association, with an odds ratio of 131. One study noted that preschool children who watched television for more than two hours a day

Technology & Teaching: Issues Relating to Large Motor and Outdoor Play (continued)

were more likely to be overweight than children who watched television two hours or less daily. Another study found that television exposure was correlated with fast-food consumption in preschool children, even after adjusting for a variety of sociodemographic and socioenvironmental factors.

The White House Task Force on Childhood Obesity Report to the President in May 2010 recommends that early childhood programs adopt standards consistent with AAP recommendations not to expose children 2 years of age and younger to television, as well as to limit media exposure for older children by treating it as a special occasion activity rather than a daily event.

American Academy of Pediatrics Committee on Public Education (2001). *Children, Adolescents, and Television*. Retrieved from: pediatrics.aapublications. org/content/107/2/423.

Rideout, V., Vandewater, E., and Wartella, E. (2003). *Zero to Six: Electronic Media in the Lives of Infants, Toddlers and Preschoolers*. Menlo Park, CA: Henry J Kaiser Foundation.

Rideout, V., and Hame, E. (2006). *The Media Family: Electronic Media in the Lives of Infants, Toddlers, Preschoolers, and Their Parents*. Menlo Park, CA: Henry J Kaiser Family Foundation. Retrieved from: http://www.kff.org/tbs_media_family_electronic_media_in_the/.

Dennison, B. A., Erb, T. A., and Jenkins, P. L. (2002). Television viewing and television in bedroom associated with overweight risk among low-income preschool children. *Pediatrics*, 109, 1028–1035.

Mendoza, J. A., Zimmerman, F. J., and Christakis, D. A. (2007). Television viewing and obesity in US preschool children. *International Journal of Behavioral Nutrition and Physical Activity*, 4(1), 44.

Taveras, E. M., Sandora, T. J., Shihm, M. C., Ross-Degnan, D., Goldmann, D. A., and Gillman, M. W. (2006). The association of television and video viewing with fast food intake by preschool-age children. *Obesity (Silver Spring)*, 14(11), 2034–2041.

Diversity in Large Motor and Outdoor Play

Including traditional children's games such as Ring around the Rosie, London Bridge, and Miss Mary Mack is a great way to bring in diversity as well as help carry on the culture of childhood. Introduce primary-age children to games from other countries, including jump rope games, hopscotch games, tag and chase games, and games with balls. One Hide and Seek game from Germany called Sardines is played the opposite to U.S. Hide and Seek. In this game, the child who is "it" hides and others seek his or her hiding place to join him or her and pack in close together, so others cannot find them. The game ends when all players are packed together like a can of sardines.

To include each and every child successfully in large motor activities, design activities at the child's current level of skill, and adapt activities as needed. Start with one-step directions, teach skills in slow motion, demonstrate and use pictures when explaining movement activities, use hula hoops or carpet squares to define personal space during activities, provide adaptive equipment as needed, and invite children to partner and teach each other the activity. Provide activities that stimulate the vestibular system such as rocking, spinning, and swinging. These can have a calming effect. Also, use heavy work such as hauling buckets of water or moving heavy wooden blocks to calm children.

Creating Partnerships with Families

Engaging in physical activity as a family can be fun. Studies show that children who believe they are competent and have the skills to be physically active are more likely to be active. And those who feel supported by friends and families to become active, or are surrounded by others interested in physical activity, are more likely to participate.

Children need at least 60 minutes of play with moderate to vigorous activity every day, but it does not have to occur at once. Sleep is just as important and is an essential part of living an active life. A recent study found that with each extra hour of sleep, the risk of a child being overweight or obese dropped by 9 percent (www.letsmove.gov).

The Let's Move Campaign website, www.letsmove.gov, suggests the following activities and steps that families can consider to get started on a path to a healthier lifestyle:

- Give children toys that encourage physical activity like balls, kites, and jump ropes.
- Encourage children to join a sports team or try a new physical activity.
- Limit TV time and keep the TV out of a child's bedroom.
- Organize a family walk a few times a week.
- Walk around the block after a meal.
- Make a new house rule: no sitting still during television commercials.
- Find time to spend together doing a fun activity: family park day, swim day, or bike day.
- Issue a family challenge to see who can be the first to achieve a Presidential Active Lifestyle Award by committing to physical activity five days a week, for six weeks. Adults and children can both receive the award!
- Be sure that children get the sleep they need. Most children younger than age 5 need to sleep for 11 hours or more per day, children age 5 to 10 need 10 hours of sleep or more per day, and children older than age 10 need at least 9 hours per day.
- Learn how engaging in outside activities can be fun and affordable for families through *Let's Move Outside*, which promotes a range of healthy outdoor activities for children and families across the country.

The Nature Explore Families' Club Kit includes research-based, field-tested resources designed to help you organize a Families' Club at your school, organization, or in your neighborhood (www.natureexplore.org).

The Teacher's Role

Guidance in Large Motor and Outdoor Play

As a part of learning, children explore and test the environments, and so the playground, like the indoor classroom, must have limits. Fences, mandated by licensing requirements, set the parameters, and the teacher sets reasonable and appropriate rules that are consistently enforced. For example, "We sit on the slides and come down feet first."

Most injuries occurring on playgrounds are the result of falls, with more injuries on climbers than other playground equipment. Supervision is also key to safe outdoor play, so teachers should stay involved, have specific duties, and be sure to check hiding places such as under the climber.

Safety is the first priority. At least two adults should be supervising the playground at all times. McCracken (2000, *Playgrounds: Safe and Sound Brochure*, NAEYC) advises, "Outdoor time requires adults who are playful, have sharp senses and quick reactions, and who will closely observe children. Save reading, resting, parent conferences, team meetings, and even casual conversations with other adults for more appropriate occasions. Your attentive eyes can prevent an injury."

Case Study: Gross Motor for Infants

The infant teachers at the Little Miracles Early Learning Center in Cleveland, Ohio, decide to take the infants outside in a buggy ride instead of the regularly scheduled playtime. The day is over 60 degrees and calm. As they push the buggies, the teachers focus on sights, sounds, and natural items such as trees and clouds.

What Do You Think?

1. What domains of development is this experience targeting and what domains are not being addressed?
2. What types of outdoor play would address the domains that are being missed by the buggy ride?
3. What could the teachers plan to provide rich outdoor experiences with infants?

To teach safety rules be sure to show as well as tell; remind children of the rules often and remove temptations such as the barrel that has rolled over by the fence making it easy to climb. Take child development into account. Remember that young children are usually egocentric, so they cannot understand other children's wants and needs, and children want autonomy so they need to do things for themselves, and operate in the here and now so they do not remember what you told them five minutes ago.

Some common safety rules for outdoor play include:

- Wear shoes when outside.
- Make room for others.
- Hold on to grips and rails.
- Stay away from swings.
- Keep fingers away from moving parts.
- Always climb up and slide to go down.

Indirect causes of conflict can be:

- Space: either not enough space, too much open space that promotes rough-and-tumble play, or overlapping use zones for play equipment causing children to run into each other.
- Group size or ratio: Include too many children on the playground at once, the age range playing together is too broad, or not enough staff.
- Equipment: not enough play spaces so children are crowded, lack of loose parts such as balls and sand buckets, or equipment that is not age appropriate.

TEACHING TIPS Outdoor Play

Include large motor activities and outdoor play as part of the curriculum each day:

- Follow large motor and outdoor activities with quiet activities.
- Model active and enthusiastic participation in large motor and outdoor activities.
- Demonstrate the movement or skill you want children to learn.
- Encourage experimentation through open-ended questions.
- Individualize your teaching to meet differing needs.
- Encourage and reinforce each child's efforts.
- Practice the movement in fun and unique ways to build the skill over time (see **Figure 12-8**).
- Recognize the importance and possibilities of outdoor play.
- Create rich, challenging outdoor environments.
- Plan special activities for outdoor time.
- Provide props and loose parts to extend children's play.
- Observe and document children's learning.

When exploring the outdoors with children, share their enthusiasm and wonder, notice what is on their eye level, teach less and share more, take cues from children about they find interesting, encourage hands-on, multisensory, active exploration of the environment, and help children notice small things.

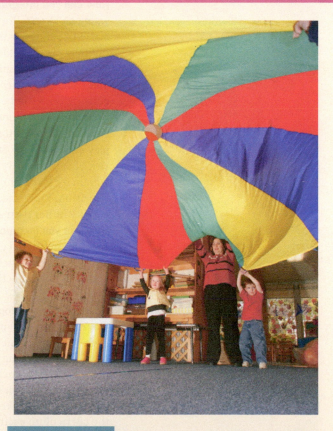

Figure 12-8 Indoors or outdoors, a parachute offers young children a unique experience in active body movement.

Summary

1. **What are key terms related to large motor development and outdoor play for children?** Locomotor movement (fundamental movement) is the ability to move the whole body from one place to another; nonlocomotor movement occurs when the feet remain stationary (as in standing, kneeling, sitting, or lying) while other parts of the body move; manipulative movement skills are gross motor movements involving force imparted to or received from objects; strength is physical energy available for movement or resistance; stamina or endurance is the capacity for sustained use of strength or physical energy; flexibility is the ease and range of movement; and agility is the ability to move with speed, grace, and precision.

2. **How do large motor development and outdoor play relate to stages of child development?** Large motor skills development occurs in stages with each building on the previous ones that can vary in their timing. Young infants develop hand and grasping skills, whereas mobile infants progress in locomotor movements resulting in walking and climbing. Toddlers increase coordination of large motor skills and preschool children greatly expand the types of movements they are able to perform. During the primary years, children increase agility, strength, and endurance.

3. **How can you prepare large motor and outdoor play environments?** The selection of large muscle and outdoor equipment and materials emphasizes safety, durability, and age appropriateness for all children and should contribute to the development of agility, coordination, and strength as well as locomotor, nonlocomotor, and manipulative skill development and offer a variety of stimulation for play and exploration.

4. **How can you integrate large motor and outdoor play into activities appropriate for young children?** Provide daily developmentally appropriate movement and exercise activities, allowing time for movement exploration both indoors and out. Provide outdoor play for at least an hour per day. Demonstrate the importance of health and fitness by encouraging and participating with your actions. Locomotor, large muscle, and fitness activities can easily be combined with creative movement and music activities and can be integrated into other learning centers such as sand and water play, blocks and construction, and dramatic play.

5. **What are some of the issues in the use of technology in a large motor and outdoor play environment?** Studies show a relationship between television viewing and the risk of being overweight in preschool children, so programs should limit screen time whether TV or computers use. Do not expose children 2 years of age and younger to television. Limit media exposure for older children by treating it as a special occasion activity rather than a daily event.

6. **How can you incorporate diversity into large motor and outdoor play environments?** Include traditional childhood games such as Ring around the Rosie, London Bridge, and Miss Mary Mack. To include each and every child successfully in large motor activities, design activities at the child's current level of skill, and adapt activities as needed.

7. **How can you develop partnerships with families that support large motor and outdoor play?** Suggest activities that families can do together that promote a healthier lifestyle, such as finding time to spend together doing a fun activity: family park day, swim day, or bike day, limiting screen time for everyone, and giving children toys that encourage physical activity such as balls, kites, and jump ropes.

8. **What is the teacher's role in promoting large motor and outdoor play in the classroom?** Teachers should include large motor activities and outdoor play as part of the curriculum each day. Model active and enthusiastic participation in large motor and outdoor activities. Demonstrate the movement or skill you want children to learn. Encourage safe experimentation. Individualize your teaching to meet differing needs and reinforce each child's efforts.

Reflective Review Questions

1. What is the difference between locomotor movement, nonlocomotor movement, and manipulative movement? Identify four examples of each.
2. Why is it important that children have daily outdoor time?
3. Reflect on your past experiences outdoors as a child. Which were the most exciting or boring? Why were they exciting or boring? Based on what you now know, what did your teacher do (or not do) to help these experiences stay with you?

Explorations

1. Select an early education outdoor play environment and observe for at least one hour. Describe, in writing, several outdoor activities the children were involved with at the time of your observation. Describe the activities, which learning centers were part of the activities, how props were used, who initiated the play, and how many joined it.
2. Discuss children's play on the playground. What are some of the activities that take place? What limits does the teacher place on outdoor activities? Are they different from indoor play activities? Explain.
3. Select and plan an outdoor play activity for young children. Specify which age group this activity is planned for: infants, toddlers, preschoolers, kindergarteners, or primary-age children. In writing, list objectives, materials needed, step-by-step procedures for presenting this activity, follow-up activities, and evaluation guidelines. (Use the activity plan worksheet in Appendix D.) Prepare this activity and demonstrate it during class or with a group of children.
4. Use the Large Motor Outdoor Environment Checklist in this chapter to conduct an observation of an early childhood learning environment.
   - Beside each statement, place an *X* if the classroom you observed met the statement.
   - On a separate sheet of paper, describe what you actually observed related to each statement. Place the number of the statement first and then your observation.
   - On a separate sheet of paper, for each statement that you did not check as met, describe what you would do to improve that classroom so that the statement would be met. Be sure to put the number of the statement first.
   - Submit this with the name of the location you observed and the age group.
5. Based on the information in this chapter and on your observations of early education environments, design a pre-K outdoor environment. Using paper and colored pens, pencils, or markers, design the learning environment showing where materials, supplies, and equipment are placed. What criteria will you use?

Large Motor and Outdoor Play Books for Young Children

- Bassett, C. (2003). *Walk like a bear, stand like a tree, run like the wind: Cool yoga stretching and aerobic activities.* New York: Nubod Concepts.
- Kubler, A. (2002). *Head, shoulders, knees, and toes.* Auburn, ME: Child's Play International.
- Pham, L. (2012). *A Stick Is an Excellent Thing.* New York: Houghton-Mifflin Harcourt.
- Willems, M. (2008). *Are You Ready to Play Outside?* New York: Disney-Hyperion.

⌄ Professional Resource Download

13

Construction: Blocks and Woodworking

Standards Covered in This Chapter

 NAEYC 5a, 5b, and 5c

DAP DAP 2

INTASC INTASC 4, 5, and 8

HS HEAD START
Domain: Perceptual Motor and Physical Development; Domain: Mathematics

Student Learning Outcomes

After studying this chapter, you should be able to:

- Define and give examples for key terms related to block play and woodworking for children.

- Discuss block play and woodworking in young children and relate stages of child development to construction play.

- Evaluate various components of planning and preparation of construction environments.

- Integrate and create construction activities appropriate for young children.

- Discuss various ways to use technology in a construction environment.

- Distinguish ways to incorporate diversity into construction play.

- Describe ways to develop partnerships with families that support child construction play.

- Analyze the teacher's role in promoting construction play in the classroom.

"Current interest in problem solving and brain research provides new support for integrating curriculum using blocks in both preschool and primary grades" (Starns, 2002, p. 3). When children are exposed to well-planned block play and wood working experiences, they create, they build, they construct, and they stay engaged. Bringing block play and woodworking to your program will help you facilitate children's development across domains in an engaging context. Blocks, especially hardwood unit blocks, are a key element in the preschool classroom. Wooden blocks naturally appeal to young children because they feel good to the touch, are symmetrical, and encourage open-ended explorations. Blocks have the potential for stimulating a broad range of creative, imaginative, and constructive play. Children represent their view of the world from simple to complex structures as they build roads, bridges, tall buildings, and whole neighborhoods.

Children love woodworking, but it can strike fear in the heart of the most capable of teachers and conjures up images of a child hitting another in the head with a hammer or smashing their own finger. Children need to be taught to use the woodworking area appropriately and learn to respect tools, just as in any other center in the classroom. Children need to feel in control of what they do and learn, within the framework chosen by the adults. Teachers have a responsibility to be active in creating the conditions that make children feel that almost anything is possible and achievable. Woodworking fosters that sense of control and empowerment within an environment where risk and safety are carefully balanced. If implemented and supervised correctly, the benefits and the learning associated with this activity for children ages 4 years and older, far outweigh the potential for problems.

Block Play and Woodworking Defined

Block building provides a natural context for development of early math concepts, such as number, quantity, measuring, symmetry, and pattern as well as comparisons such as more or less. In fact, research shows that early block play is related to later math competence. Early block play and later math performance were related in junior high and high school, when youth were grappling with more advanced math concepts. The researchers found a significant relationship between preschool block performance and number of math courses taken, number of honors courses, mathematics grades achieved, and math test scores. Even when controlling for IQ and gender, preschool block performance still showed a relationship to later math performance (Wolfgang, Stannard, and Jones, 2001).

When they build with blocks or work with wood, children learn geometry as they name and describe shapes, transform shapes, and describe **spatial relationships**. Although there are many types of blocks, unit blocks offer the most learning value. What is it about unit blocks that make them such an important part of any early childhood classroom? To begin with, unit blocks are proportional in size to develop mathematical concepts. Children learn about measurement while building as they explore which block is the right length to balance on top of two other blocks to make a bridge or use a tape measure to mark a piece of wood before cutting it, thus developing concepts of shorter, longer, and equal length. Children strengthen such perceptions of space as under, below, in front of, behind, above, inside, and outside, develop concepts of big/little, more than/less than, equal to, and taller/shorter, develop concepts of shape, depth, width, height, length, fractions, and multiples, become aware of whole-part relationships. Children learn algebra as they sort blocks into groups by size and shape or make patterns as they build with blocks or wood. Children gain number sense as they use one-to-one correspondence or matching to make sure each side of their structure is balanced so it will not fall and discover that one large unit block is equal to two smaller unit blocks when they run out of the larger blocks before finishing their building. Children experiment and problem solve through trial and error, create architectural forms by bridging and making tunnels, ramps, and grids, and develop awareness of scientific principles such as gravity, levers, pulleys, and rollers.

spatial relationships: The relationship in space between two objects such as blocks.

Children learn math vocabulary and other descriptive language as they discuss their creations and how they solved problems they encountered while building. They improve inquiry skills by asking questions and discovering answers and make use of imagery and recall by reproducing and recreating forms from past experiences. Writing experiences can be introduced into this work by having children draw up and label construction plans of what they are going to build.

Play with blocks provides an excellent opportunity for social and physical development. Although twos and young threes build towers and roads by themselves or right next to another child, block play for preschool and primary children is a big social event that fosters lots of negotiation, problem solving, discussion, and cooperation. Children participate in cooperative block play with peers while combining ideas and solving problems, and release emotions in an acceptable way. This center is such a popular socializing spot that many children go there day after day. Children develop large muscles when they bend, lift, and carry large **unit blocks** and **hollow blocks** from the shelf to where they are building. Finer motor skills are developed as children manipulate the smaller blocks including grasping and squeezing, eye-hand coordination, as well as wrist rotation and stability. These are all skills used in writing.

Constructing with blocks and wood fosters creativity. Children are really creating artistic three-dimensional sculptures as they build. They often want to preserve their work through drawings, photos, and stories that tell the tale behind the creation.

When you provide time, space, materials, and freedom for children to gain sensory and creative experiences with blocks, you will encourage children to practice balancing stabilizing, and matching skills; classify according to shapes, sizes, colors, textures, and types; develop symbolic representations as the blocks become whatever the children want them to be; and strengthen large and small muscle skills and eye–hand coordination.

Children use wood as a medium of creative expression; they communicate, plan, and work cooperatively with others; they use woodworking as an emotional release and means of nonverbal expression; they focus on the process while mastering the skills of sanding, gluing, hammering, nailing, sawing, and drilling to gain a sense of self-esteem, and they sharpen their senses through the smells, textures, and sounds of woodworking, They learn to sustain interest and overcome frustration successfully, and extend concepts of experimenting, creating, investigating, and problem solving into other areas of the curriculum.

> "Woodworking provides children with opportunities to become aware of textures and forms. Senses are sharpened as children explore the field of construction. Fingers explore many textures, ears pick out the sounds of different tools, noses test the different smells of various woods, and eyes see the many hues of wood (Mayesky, 2006, p. 331)."

unit blocks: Hardwood blocks sized in standard mathematical units and used in early education environments, especially in block center play.

hollow blocks: Wooden blocks larger than unit blocks and open on the sides.

Developmental Stages of Block Building

There are developmental stages in the way children use and play with blocks: First, infants and toddlers carry blocks from place to place. They are learning about how the blocks feel, how heavy they are, and how many they can carry at once. This may not look much like block building, but it is a necessary stage.

Next, the children pile blocks one on top of another. In the beginning, there is an irregular pattern to the stacking, and then the blocks begin to form a tower, which often falls when additional blocks are added. Repetition of this activity will help children know how many blocks they can add before the tower will fall (toddlers).

At the same time children are making block towers, they are also trying to make block rows. They lay blocks close together, side-by-side, or edge-to-edge (flat rows suggest roads, so adding small trucks and cars is appropriate). The children may also space the blocks, alternating the sizes as they place them in rows (toddlers and 3-year-olds).

Each of these steps in developmental block building includes repetition. (See **Figure 13-1**.) Practicing their accomplishments over and over is important to young children as they get more comfortable with using blocks. The next stage for children is **bridging**. This is observable by watching children set up two blocks, leaving space between them, and roofing that space with another block. Through repetition, the structures increase in complexity and difficulty (3- and 4-year-olds).

Enclosures made by children, sometimes done simultaneously with bridging, involve putting blocks together to enclose a space. Placing four blocks together so that a space is completely enclosed is not a simple task (2-, 3-, and 4-year-olds). Patterns and designs begin to appear when children feel comfortable enough with blocks to build balanced and decorative patterns (4-year-olds). Finally, **representation** occurs with the naming of block constructions and the combination of all elements of block building. Children (4-year-olds and older) demonstrate that they are aware of their world and their place in it with these structures (Hirsch, 1993).

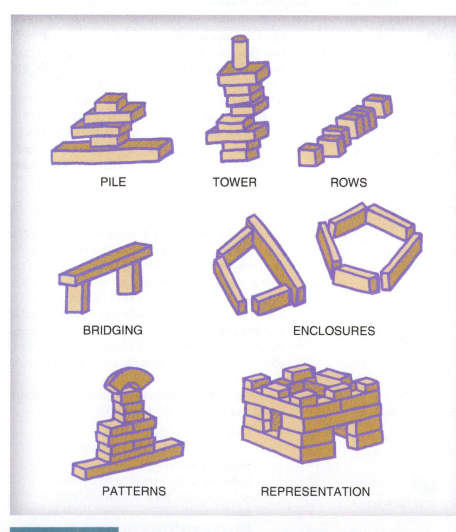

PILE TOWER ROWS

BRIDGING ENCLOSURES

PATTERNS REPRESENTATION

Figure 13-1 Examples of the developmental stages of block building.

bridging: Setting up two blocks, leaving space between them, and roofing that space with another block.

representation: Occurs in block building with the naming of block constructions and the combination of all elements of block building.

Brain Research: Spatial Reasoning

Spatial reasoning, which is the ability to mentally visualize and manipulate two- and three-dimensional objects, is a great predictor of talent in science, technology, engineering, and math, collectively known as STEM. Construction with blocks and woodworking, along with working puzzles, develop these skills in young children.

Spatial reasoning skills are present in toddlers and preschool children, but they undergo considerable development during this time and into middle childhood. Mental rotation and perspective taking are affected by different performance factors and involve different neural processes. However, the two abilities have in common that their developmental progress is closely linked to motor development.

Newcombe, N. S., and Frick, A. (2010). "Early Education for Spatial Intelligence: Why, What, and How," *Mind, Brain and Education*, 4 (3): 106.

The Society for Research in Child Development reports that playing with blocks may help preschoolers develop the kinds of skills that support later learning in science, technology, engineering, and math, according to a new study that examined over a hundred 3-year-olds of various socioeconomic levels. Researchers emphasized the importance of the study's implications because block building and puzzle play can improve children's spatial skills that, in turn, support complex mathematical problem solving in middle and high school (Verdine, et al., 2013).

Planning and Preparing the Environment

When you are setting up an early childhood environment, one of the first items you should purchase is blocks. Many teachers consider blocks to be the most used and the most useful materials in a program for young children. They are a valuable open-ended, nonconsumable material that can provide many hours of play-based learning experiences. Along with selecting blocks, you should plan carefully what type and quantity you choose, the way in which the blocks will be organized, and how you will arrange the physical environment to ensure developmentally appropriate activities with blocks. Placing the block center next to the dramatic play center stimulates shared use of the materials in each center to create more complex play scenarios.

Equipment and Materials

Unit blocks are the most popular variety used in early education environments. Children continue to use them as they grow from infancy to primary age. Blocks were first introduced in an educational setting by Friedrich Froebel in 1837 (Tunks, 2009). The sturdy hardwood blocks used today were designed by Carolyn Pratt in the early 1890s. The individual unit block is 1.375 inches by 2.75 inches by 5.5 inches, and all other blocks are multiples or divisions of this basic size. (See **Figure 13-2**.)

The cylinders and curved blocks are of similar width and thickness. Pratt's blocks were of

> smooth, natural-finish hardwood—free from details or color. In addition, she designed unpainted wooden people, 6 inches tall, in the form of family members and community workers, to be used with the unit blocks. She omitted painted details on any of her toys because she wanted children to apply their own imagination in their use of the materials (Beaty, 2013 p. 49).

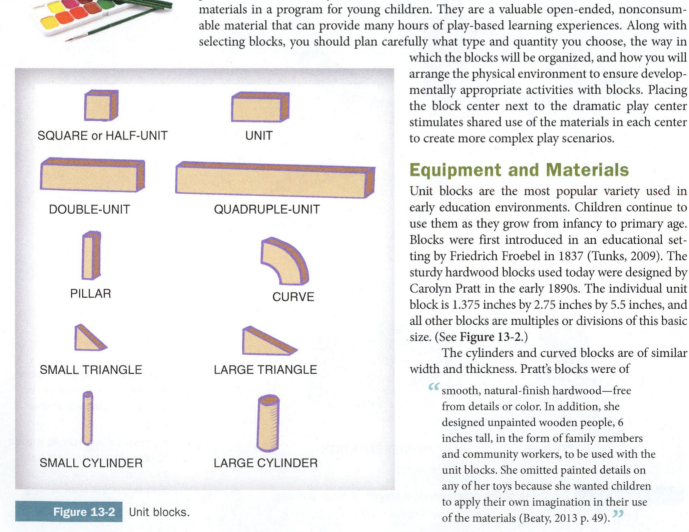

Figure 13-2   Unit blocks.

Hollow blocks are also made of wood and are larger than unit blocks. "The basic square is 5½ inches by 11 inches by 11 inches. There are five other pieces in a set: a half-square, a double square, two lengths of flat board, and a ramp. Hollow blocks are open on the sides so they can be carried more easily" (Dodge, Colker, and Heroman, 2008, p. 249). Hollow blocks require additional space both indoors and outdoors for optimal use by the children. (See **Figure 13-3**.)

Other types of blocks appropriate for young children's play are: shoe-box-size cardboard blocks, some of which are designed to look like bricks; small, wooden, colored ones that can be used as table blocks; log-type building blocks; interlocking blocks, such as Lego® or Bristle Blocks®; and foam blocks and large, brightly colored lightweight blocks for infants' and toddlers' first experiences with block play.

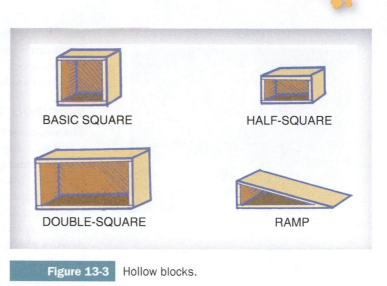

BASIC SQUARE   HALF-SQUARE

DOUBLE-SQUARE   RAMP

Figure 13-3   Hollow blocks.

The unit blocks should be placed on low shelves with the long side showing according to shape and size for organization and storage. Label the shelves with the outlines of the shapes and sizes of the different types of blocks. This assists children with cleanup and emphasizes **classification**. Place blocks other than the unit or hollow blocks in plastic containers or boxes clearly labeled for identification. (See **Figure 13-4**.)

Block play is noisy, so the center should be placed next to other active areas, such as dramatic play. The block area should be clearly defined on three sides and be shielded from traffic. Children should be discouraged from building too close to the block shelves so that others can easily reach in to get their block materials without interfering with others block structures and play. This offers protection and security for the children's activities. An area rug or carpeting should be on the floor to absorb some of the noise as well as to offer comfort to the children playing (Dodge, Colker, and Heroman, 2008).

To maximize the value of block play, accessories are important to expand children's experiences. Samples of appropriate accessories are rubber, plastic, or wooden animals, traffic signs, cars, trucks and airplanes, rubber, plastic or wooden people, colored cubes, popsicles sticks, Easter grass, chenille strips, wooden beads, and dollhouse furniture. Some more nontraditional

Reflect On This

Do you think real tools or plastic tools should be used in woodworking? Why?

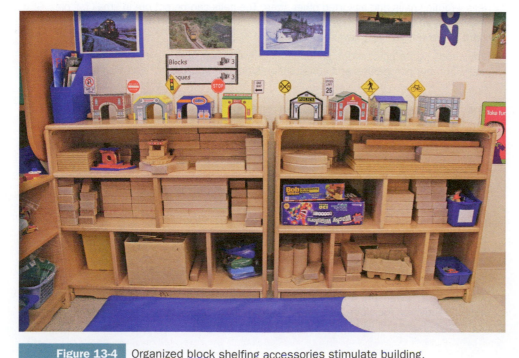

Figure 13-4   Organized block shelfing accessories stimulate building.

classification: Grouping of blocks or other objects together based on common characteristics.

Figure 13-5   Tool board.

construction materials include bamboo sticks, tree cookies, cardboard or Styrofoam pieces, boxes, mailing tubes, carpet squares, tile or vinyl flooring samples, spools, vinyl guttering, yarn or string, cans, wallpaper samples, paper towel or toilet paper tubes, plastic lids and butter tubs, foil, or cellophane.

Woodworking

The **woodworking center** in an early childhood environment has been a part of many early education classrooms for a number of years. This activity center provides young children with many different sensory and three-dimensional experiences.

Unfortunately, in some settings the woodworking center is often nonexistent or underused. Think about how and when you can successfully incorporate carpentry into your curriculum. Boys and girls alike can develop physical, cognitive, social, and language skills through woodworking activities.

Equipment and Materials

Use real tools. They are much safer than toy ones, which do not work effectively, causing children to misuse them. Some real tools are especially designed for woodworking centers, like the square-end saw. You might have to remind children to put on safety goggles before they start working with wood. You might also want to install a pegboard near the woodworking table on which to hang the tools. (See **Figure 13-5**.) A list of suggested equipment and materials is shown in **Table 13-1**.

The actual physical environment plays a large role in enhancing block building and woodworking. A checklist can be used to evaluate the block and woodworking environment in your own classroom or classrooms that you observe.

TABLE 13-1:   Woodworking Equipment and Materials
Workbench—sturdy in construction, with vise or C-clamps attached, approximately 24 inches high or as high as the children's waists; a sturdy table can also be used.
Hammers—small claw hammers weighing 8 to 12 ounces.
Nails—roofing nails and assorted other sizes. The nails can be set out in small foil pie plates to keep the sizes from getting mixed up. The pie plates can be nailed to a long board to prevent spilling (Mayesky, 2015).
Soft wood—white pine, cedar, spruce, and redwood are light in weight and take nails easily. Lumber companies and construction sites are sources for soft wood scraps.
Glue
Cross-cut saw—approximately 18 inches long
C-clamps or vise
Braces and bits
Sandpaper or sanding sponges
Ruler or square
Tape measures
Pencils and paper
Toolbox
Pegboard tool rack or tool cabinet to store items
Markers, crayons, and thinned tempera paint
Screws and screwdrivers are difficult for young children to use. Perhaps you can add these to activities for older children along with wood files, planes, levels, and an egg-beater-style hand drill with two or three different size bits.

woodworking center: An activity center containing tools and wood that provides sensory and three-dimensional experiences.

Construction Environment Checklist

_____ 1. Is there an area specifically designated for blocks?

_____ 2. Are a variety of different cultures represented in the block center pictures and accessories?

_____ 3. Does the block area contain enough unit blocks to create the structures that children wish to make (586 blocks for 3-year-olds, 748 for 4-year-olds, 908 blocks for 5-year-olds and older)?

_____ 4. Are writing materials available for preschool- and early elementary-age children?

_____ 5. Is there a carpentry area available?

_____ 6. Does the carpentry area contain real tools and items to build with?

_____ 7. Are pictures and accessories anti-biased?

_____ 8. Does the carpentry area contain protective devices such as goggles?

_____ 9. Is the block area on a surface appropriate for block building?

_____ 10. Are the stage of development and children's interests supported through the accessories?

_____ 11. Can children create their own accessories through open-ended materials?

_____ 12. Are motivational materials (such as books, pictures, and photos) available to provide ideas and information about structures?

_____ 13. Are the blocks arranged mathematically on open shelves?

_____ 14. Is enough time allowed in the schedule for children to engage in in-depth building?

_____ 15. Are block outlines used to label shelves?

_____ 16. Is the block area on a low-pile carpet to reduce noise?

_____ 17. Are the accessories effectively grouped and organized?

_____ 18. Is the block center enclosed on three sides to decrease traffic and protect children's constructions?

_____ 19. Are there at least four to six props such as animals, people, road signs, and small vehicles in labeled containers or on labeled shelves?

_____ 20. Are all children involved in the block area over time?

_____ 21. Is the block area large enough for three to four children to play at one time?

_____ 22. Are blocks arranged by size and shape on open shelves?

_____ 23. Is the block center available as a choice activity daily?

_____ 24. Are there several types of blocks provided in addition to unit blocks such as hollow, foam, cardboard, and Lego®?

❯❯ Professional Resource Download

Integrating Construction Play into the Curriculum

Construction play is a form of symbolic play that helps children understand the world by transforming an experience or object into a concrete representation of the event or object (Kostelnik, Soderman, and Whiren, 2014). They are recreating the world on a smaller scale as they build and create play scenarios involving what they have built. Children need to have many opportunities to explore the construction materials naturally as they discover the properties of various types of blocks and wood, as well as other construction materials while they construct. As children become more skilled builders, teachers can suggest construction projects that go along with the curriculum theme or project and scaffold their learning by adding reference books and props and taking field trips to research structures, construction materials, and methods. The play shifts between construction and dramatic play in these complex play episodes in which children construct props and settings to support their pretend play themes. (See **Figure 13-6.**)

Blocks

Blocks stimulate children to build and encourage them to engage in dramatic play using the building process and the structure they build to represent what they know and feel about

Figure 13-6   The teacher in this classroom has provided time, space, materials, and freedom for children to develop creative experiences with blocks.

the world (Butler, 2004). The block center should be available for the children to use daily throughout the year. Inspire children to think and create in different ways by adding new and unique building materials periodically. Children use problem solving, negotiation skills, and cooperative learning as they make decisions about what to construct and the methods to use in construction. (See **Figure 13-7**.) Adding small dollhouses, barns, animals, cars, trucks,

Figure 13-7   Young children participate in cooperative block play with peers while combining ideas and solving problems.

boats, and people to construction materials encourage pretend play as children manipulate the figures to create a story. Using large blocks and construction materials such as cardboard boxes to create allows children to be the characters in the story and explore spatial relationships with their own bodies.

Woodworking

Woodworking is of great interest to both boys and girls. Woodworking offers unique possibilities for children to experiment and investigate with real tools. Construction activities allow children to plan and execute ideas, resulting in a concrete product that children can evaluate and improve (Bacon, 2004). Children gain math, science, and physical skills as they measure, hammer nails, sand and saw wood, drill holes, and use glue. Safety rules and supervision are critical to successful woodworking experiences. To protect the children's safety, you must set specific limits and reinforce them. (See Figure 13-8.)

Figure 13-8 The woodworking center provides sensory experiences for young children.

Activity Plan Worksheet | **Construction Zone**

AGES: appropriate for 3- through 5-year-olds

Name of Activity and Brief Description
Construction Zone is designed to help children role play and practice the steps and processes of constructing a building.

Child Outcomes of Activity
- Develop spatial awareness and balance.
- Identify shapes.
- Sort and classify objects by shape and sizes.
- Develop fine motor skills.
- Identify different types of machinery used in construction.
- Apply construction strategies discussed in a book to create a structure.

Space and Materials Needed
This activity can be done in the block center during learning center time or on the playground during outdoor play, if construction materials are available outside. Children will need a large space to build and move the equipment around as they load and unload materials. Materials needed include unit blocks, people figures, plastic hard hats, graph paper and pencils, carpenters belts with plastic or wooden tools, small dump trucks, backhoes and other construction

machinery, blueprints or construction plans, rulers, construction measuring tape, and a book about construction. Posting pictures of construction sites can set the stage for building. Adding surveyors tape, a pulley, lever, level and other simple machines, and cellophane to make windows can enhance the play.

Procedure
1. Read the book *Construction Zone* and examine the pictures of construction sites.
2. Discuss the stages in construction using the book and pictures.
3. Allow the children to explore new props.
4. Suggest that the blocks be used to build a big building.
5. Suggest that the children draw a blueprint of what they want to build.
6. Ask open-ended questions to stimulate problem solving and help children focus on the task.
7. Encourage use of math skills and math language such as using a level, measuring, comparing, and estimating.

Guidance
Anticipating the active nature of block play, provide plenty for space for children to construct. Limit the number of builders

to fit the space you have, but if possible, allow four to five children to play so that they can take on different roles. You can use the number of hard hats available as a way to set the limit. Discuss the different roles they can play with the children so everyone can have a part: truck driver, architect/engineer, or construction crew. Be ready to add more props, such as Post-it notes to make signs, as you see they would expand the play. Clean up is always part of the process, so give plenty of warning to finish building and clean up. Make clean up part of the play by having children scoop blocks toward the shelf like a steam shovel.

Assessment and Follow-Up Strategies

Take photos of the construction process and ask children to put them in sequence and add written captions to the photos. Take a tour of the construction site and have children tell you about their building. Ask questions about how they constructed different parts of the structure and record their descriptive language.

⌄ Professional Resource Download

AGES: Primary Grades 1 and 2

Name of Activity and Brief Description—Can Birdhouses

Children will follow a pattern and written instructions to build birdhouses.

Child Outcomes of Activity

- Analyze and interpret written directions for building a birdhouse.
- Recognize the importance of safe practices to keep self and others safe.
- Measure for placement of holes and entrance opening.
- Utilize tools safely to build a birdhouse.

Space and Materials Needed

This can be done on a woodworking table inside or picnic table outside. A large metal or plastic can, hammer and nails, and heavy scissors are needed. Houses may be painted.

Procedure

1. Discuss safety procedures and how to use tools.
2. Rinse the can in a weak bleach solution.
3. Use a nail to puncture five or six drainage holes in the bottom of the house, staggering placement so they will not all be covered with nesting material by the resident birds.
4. Flatten out rough edges caused by puncturing the holes so birds will not be injured.
5. Add several holes in the top third of the can for additional ventilation,
6. Use heavy scissors to cut a 1- to 1.5-inch hole in the can's plastic lid. The entrance hole can be centered or slightly above center, but should not be low on the lid to minimize the risk of hatchlings accidentally falling out.
7. Fit the lid snugly back onto the can, and the house is ready to use.
8. Mount under an eave or under branches that will provide some additional shade and shelter by nailing it to a branch or fence.
9. Ask children questions about what they are doing and what they observe.

Guidance

Limit the number of children to three or four at a time. Supervise for safe use of tools.

Assessment and Follow-Up Strategies

Were child outcomes met? Yes___ No___
What was the children's response?
What worked well? What did not work?

Technology in Blocks and Woodworking

Technology & Teaching: Construction Play

Block play is an excellent way in which technological processes are demonstrated and the block itself becomes a technological tool because it is an open-ended resource that offers endless possibilities in design, problem solving, and logical thinking (Rogers and Russo, 2003). Children who repeatedly play with blocks over extended periods of time gain knowledge about the properties of blocks and develop skills in balance, manipulation, and design, combining this newfound knowledge and skills to develop more intricate and elaborate designs. Children who work with blocks use materials, design, propose alternatives, modify, and appraise. These are all characteristics of technological processes.

Play with traditional building blocks promotes language, cognitive schema, and impulse control (Christakis, Zimmerman, and Garrison, 2007, pp. 967–971).

Manipulating blocks on a computer screen, as in Tetris, may promote the same abilities. Use a digital camera to document the sequence of children's work in progress. Upload the pictures onto the computer and add captions to let the children review it as a slide.

Rogers, A. and Russo, S. (2003). Blocks: A commonly encountered play activity in the early years, or a key to facilitating skills in science, math and technology. *Investigating*, 19 (1), 17–21.

Christakis, D. A., F. J. Zimmerman, and M. Garrison. (2007). Effect of block play on language acquisition and attention in toddlers a pilot randomized controlled trial. *Archives of Pediatric and Adolescent Medicine*, 161 (10), 967–971.

Diversity in Construction Play

The addition of miniature people representing various cultures, doll furniture, small animals, cars, trucks, boats, barges, canoes, sleds, airplanes, trains, and buses extends children's block play. Offer photographs showing buildings from each child's native culture, such as the Eiffel Tower; Aztec, Mayan, or Egyptian pyramids; or the Burj Khalifa in Dubai, so children can refer to them while building acknowledges the diversity of cultures in the classroom. For self-selection by the children, put each group of small items in clearly labeled (with pictures and words) plastic tubs or boxes near the unit blocks. This will also help with cleanup.

Books and pictures of different buildings from all around the world can stimulate children to build all kinds of structures. Older children create elaborate highways, bridges, and ramps. They add traffic signs, "Do Not Touch!" signs, and other kinds of labels.

Gould and Sullivan (1999) identify the following strategies to support each and every child in the block center: Place a basket of blocks next to each child or pair of children, use mats or tape to define children's building spaces, let a child lie on a wedge while building on the floor, and allow children to build inside a large, empty appliance box.

Creating Partnerships with Families

Let the parents know what the children are accomplishing through their block play. Invite the parents to participate in the block center when they drop off or pick up their children. Post or email pictures of children building where parents can see them, and share dictated or written stories about the structures. Have children show their parents the block area when new cars or trucks and other new accessories are added. Develop an information sheet for parents including items such as the rules for the working area, how tall the children can build with blocks, what children are learning in the block or woodworking areas, and what parents could talk about with their children in that activity area. Provide opportunities for a family member who is in construction or architectural work to share his or her time and talent with the children.

The Teacher's Role

Observe developmental levels of the children. This knowledge will enable you to know when to introduce hollow blocks, other blocks, or accessories to the block center. Keep in mind the natural stages of block building as you support the children's efforts to gain confidence and to feel comfortable with blocks. Take photographs often of the block constructions. This offers an alternative to leaving the structures up for extra long periods of time if you do not have the space to do so. The children can have photos to remember their special buildings. This will also help the children understand that you value their efforts. The photos can lead to children dictating stories about their creations. Perhaps they will recreate them in the art center as well.

Guidance Guidelines

DAP

The use of developmentally appropriate guidance is critical in the block center and woodworking. It is difficult for young children to take turns or clean up blocks when they are absorbed in their vision for a specific block structure. This sensory experience involves the total child:

> We give subtle messages to children about how we expect them to behave by the surroundings we plan for them. We can prevent many behavior problems before they ever begin by careful planning, by understanding children's developmental needs, and by creating a perfect match between their needs and the settings around them (Miller, 2016, p. 167).

For the block building center, see **Table 13-2**.

Case Study: Block Building

Shenequa Richards is a teacher of a group of 4-year-olds in Amelia Earhart Elementary School. Her children represent a variety of cultures, including Mexican, Native American, Anglo, African American, Syrian, Vietnamese, and Indian.

A group of four children is playing in the block area during learning center time. Darius said, "Ooh! Let's build something."

"Yes, tall," replied Hon.

The teacher asked, "What tall building will you build?"

"I live in a partment," Caitlyn replied. "Me, too. Partment!" shouted Maricella.

"What kind of blocks would we need for a tall apartment?" asked Ms. Richards.

"Lots blocks," said Hon.

The children then started gathering blocks to build their apartment.

What Do You Think?

1. What props could the teacher add to this play?
2. What additional resources should the teacher provide the children?
3. What open-ended questions should the teacher ask to support dual-language learners and math learning?
4. What teaching strategies can the teacher incorporate?

TABLE 13-2: Suggested Guidance Techniques

- Supply an adequate number and enough different shapes of blocks and a variety of materials for the number of children using them.

- Provide ample space. Help prevent children from knocking over constructions made by other children. Mark off one to two feet of space away from the perimeter of the block shelves with colored masking tape. Explain that structures cannot be built between the shelves and the tape. This will help prevent conflicts.

- Use open shelves, not baskets or bins, for easy access to the blocks. This helps to show the children that the block center is a place with purpose and a sense of order.

- Guide children to match the blocks to the shapes on the shelves to put them away.

- Help children understand that they should take down their *own* buildings using only their hands.

- Have children put blocks away before leaving the block center. Children need guidance and sometimes teacher's physical assistance in putting blocks and other classroom materials away.

- Preserve structures, if possible, from day to day if the children make a request to do so. This shows respect for their buildings and roadways.

- Have a camera available for photographs. Taking photographs and making sketches are important to preserve the children's block designs.

- Encourage the children to make signs for their structures.

- Approach each difficulty in the block area with a developmentally appropriate response.

For Woodworking

Practice using all the tools yourself until you are comfortable with them. If you are a female teacher competently using tools, you become a role model, especially for girls.

When starting, be sure you (or another teacher) are available the entire time to closely supervise and observe the children. Limit the center to one child at a time. Add a second child later, when all children are comfortable with the tools.

The woodworking center requires specific rules that are consistently reinforced: Goggles must be worn at all times.

Tools must be kept at the workbench, and they are to be used only for the purpose for which they are designed. (Help the children learn to use tools properly.) Return the tools to the tool kit or rack when finished. Use only one tool at a time.

When two children are working at the workbench, let one stand on each side with plenty of space between them. Safety is always the first consideration when children are using tools. They must learn where to put their hands when hammering and sawing.

Place your workbench in a highly visible area, but away from traffic paths. You may also want to locate the workbench away from the block area so that wooden blocks are not used as wood scraps.

Expect and model respect for the tools and the woodworking area. Learn and teach the children the correct names of all of the tools. Trace the outline of the tools on the pegboard for children to put the tools back when they are finished with them. Goggles should always be worn. (Hard hats and construction aprons can also be used.)

TEACHING TIPS   Blocks and Woodworking

- Remember blocks are for all ages. The primary-grade children will often surprise you with their exploration of structural engineering by testing the stability of their buildings.

- Watch for teachable moments that provide an opportunity for scaffolding. Help the children develop new skills in block construction by building on their existing skills.

  " During the years children are in the primary grades, their thinking abilities change considerably. . . . [D]evelopmental changes are reflected in primary age children's approach to constructive play and block-building activities. . . . Negotiation, problem-solving, and collaboration are characteristic of the social constructive play of primary-age children (Wellhousen and Kieff, 2001, p. 118). "

- Provide big pieces of paper and blue markers for children to make blueprints, both before or after building.

- Before beginning carpentry with real tools, plan for the children to have many spontaneous play experiences with bits of wood used as building blocks, match tools to shapes in puzzles, and (in the math center) pair up photos of tools and supplies, such as hammer and nails and screwdriver and screws.

- Be sure to allow plenty of time to explore.

- If you have not worked with tools or wood before, practice before you supervise the children. Ask a colleague or parent to share knowledge with you and the children.

- Place this center away from quiet centers. Many teachers like to take woodworking outdoors or into the hallway right outside the classroom door.

- Allow enough time for the children to explore the materials at their own pace.

- Remember, it is the process that is important, not the result.

- To ensure success for children from the beginning, start with white glue and wood. Then gradually add hammers, roofing nails, soft wood, and a saw.

- If a child is using a hammer for the first time, you can pound several nails halfway into the wood to get him or her started. Roofing nails with large heads are the easiest for young children to use.

- The best types of wood to use are soft woods: white pine, cedar, fir, and redwood. Lumber companies, cabinetmakers, karate schools, and hardware stores, if asked, often will donate scraps of wood.

- Do not have nails that are longer than the wood, to prevent a nail sticking out of the bottom of a "creation."

- Place construction pictures and related magazines in this area to foster ideas, creativity, and language development.

- Children may want to paint the projects they have made. Allow time for completion of this activity, too.

- Evaluate throughout each step of the process. Planning, initiating, and evaluating will help you and the children be successful in the woodworking center.

  " For very young children, wood can be replaced by thick Styrofoam packing material, which is much softer and easier to saw. . . . Older preschoolers who have gained proficiency in using the tools and purposefully made objects in wood will be interested in adding props. These should include round objects that suggest wheels, such as wooden spools, slices of large dowels, bottle caps, the metal ends from 6-ounce frozen juice containers, and a variety of other items (Essa, 2012). "

A child should have plenty of time in the woodworking center to explore the materials at his or her own pace.

Summary

1. **What are examples of key terms related to blocks and woodworking for children?** Spatial relationships is how objects are located in space in relation to other objects; unit blocks are a type of standardized wooden toy block based on mathematical units; hollow blocks are large, heavy wooden blocks that are hollow to decrease the weight and allow children to hold the block more easily; eye–hand coordination is focusing and coordinating eye movement and visual input to control and direct the hands; classification is the process of sorting items into groups according to one or more attribute or characteristic; bridging is balancing a block across the top of the open space between two blocks; enclosure is building a circle of blocks that is used to contain objects such as small animal or people figures; and representation is when children develop the ability to form mental representations of objects and events which they reproduce in their block play.

2. **How do block play and woodworking relate stages of child development in construction play?** Children learn many concepts, especially math concepts, through block play and woodworking. There are several stages in the development of construction play:
   - Stage 1: Toting, carrying, dumping, and dropping blocks
   - Stage 2: Building towers and rows
   - Stage 3: Building bridges
   - Stage 4: Building enclosures
   - Stage 5: Adding patterns and elaboration to basic structures

3. **What should be considered in the planning and preparation of construction environments?** Plan carefully what type and quantity of blocks you choose, the way in which the blocks will be organized, and how you will arrange the physical environment to ensure developmentally appropriate activities with blocks. Block play and woodworking are noisy, so these centers should be placed next to other active areas, such as dramatic play. Woodworking can also be placed outside or in a hallway adjacent to the classroom. The block area should be clearly defined on three sides. This offers protection and security for the children's activities. An area rug or carpeting should be on the floor to absorb some of the noise as well as to offer comfort to the children playing. Before beginning carpentry with real tools, plan for the children to have many spontaneous play experiences with bits of wood used as building blocks, match tools to shapes in puzzles, and (in the math center) pair up photos of tools and supplies, such as hammer and nails and screwdriver and screws. Place your workbench in a highly visible area, but away from traffic paths. You may also want to locate the workbench away from the block area so that wooden blocks are not used as wood scraps.

4. **How can you integrate and create construction activities appropriate for young children?** Think about how and when you can successfully incorporate carpentry into your curriculum beginning with gluing wood pieces together, then hammering golf tees into cardboard or Styrofoam, moving on to soft wood and large nails and finally adding saws and cardboard boxes. Add props to the block center that stimulate building new things. Plan to incorporate the building experiences around the theme you are studying, such as building an airport or plane. Books and pictures of different buildings from all around the world can stimulate children to build all kinds of structures.

5. **What are some ways to use technology in a construction environment?** Block play is an excellent way in which technological processes are demonstrated, and the block itself becomes a technological tool because it is an open-ended resource that offers endless possibilities in design, problem solving, and logical thinking. Use a digital camera to document the sequence of children's work in progress. Upload the pictures onto the computer to let them review it as a slide show and add captions.

6. **How can you incorporate diversity into construction play?** Add props such as miniature people representing various cultures and books and pictures of different buildings from all around the world. Use teaching strategies that support children with differing abilities and needs to be able to build successfully.

7. **How can you develop partnerships with families that support child construction play?** Allow family members to join their children in block play and provide information for families about the benefits of block play. Post pictures of children building and stories about their structures. Ask parents who work in construction to come talk with children.

8. **What is the teacher's role in promoting construction play in the classroom?** Organize the block and woodworking centers to stimulate interest in building. Watch for teachable moments that provide an opportunity for scaffolding. Help the children develop new skills in block construction and woodworking by building on their existing skills. Before beginning carpentry with real tools, plan for the children to have many spontaneous play experiences with bits of wood used as building blocks, match tools to shapes in puzzles, and (in the math center) pair up photos of tools and supplies, such as hammer and nails and screwdriver and screws. Supervise the woodworking area carefully. Teach and stress safety precautions.

Reflective Review Questions

1. What is the role of the teacher as young children engage in block play?
2. Why does an early childhood classroom need so many blocks?
3. How could you offer the woodworking experience in a classroom that does not have a carpentry table and tools?
4. How would you answer a parent of a 4-year-old who says, "Why are you letting my child play with saws and hammers? They are dangerous!"

Explorations

1. Select an early childhood education classroom and observe for one hour. Describe, in writing, what happened in the block center during your observation. How many children were in the center at one time? Were these the same children for the entire hour you observed? How many boys? How many girls? What were they building? Describe the developmental stages you saw. What did you learn from this observation? Explain. Were any props or additional materials added to the block activities? Did the nature of the activities change? Describe how the children used the added props and materials.

2. As a teacher in a preschool classroom, discuss how and when you can successfully incorporate woodworking into your classroom. What skills will this activity area develop in young children? Create a list of essential equipment for a woodworking center, as well as a budget for the equipment.

3. Create a book on construction for young children. Complete an activity plan worksheet, such as the one in this chapter; then read the book to a small group of young children. Observe their responses. What age group did you select? Was your book developmentally appropriate for that age group? Explain your answers and your assessment and follow-up activities.

4. Based on the information in this chapter and on your observations of early education environments, design a pre-K block center and a pre-K woodworking center. Using paper and colored pens, pencils, or markers, design the learning center showing where materials, supplies, and equipment are placed. What criteria will you use?

Think about how this center will relate to the other learning centers in the classroom. How do the block and woodworking centers support the creativity of the children?

5. Use the Block and Woodworking Environment Checklist in this chapter to conduct an observation of an early childhood learning environment.
   - Beside each statement, place an *X* if the classroom you observed met the statement.
   - On a separate sheet of paper, describe what you actually observed related to each statement. Place the number of the statement first and then your observation.
   - On a separate sheet of paper, for each statement that you did not check as met, describe what you would do to improve that classroom so that the statement would be met. Be sure to put the number of the statement first.
   - Submit this with the name of the location you observed and the age group.

Construction Books for Children

- Barton, B. (1981). *Building a House*. New York: Greenwillow Books.
- Beaty, A. (2007). *Iggy Peck, Architect*. Harry N. Abrams, Inc.
- Dahl, M. (2006). *One Big Building: A Counting Book About Construction (Know Your Numbers)*. Picture Window Books.
- Gibbons, G. (1990). *How a House is Built*. Holiday House.
- Hoban, T. (1992). *Construction Zone*. New York: Greenwillow Books.
- Hutchins, P. (1987). *Changes, Changes*. New York: McMillan Children's Book Group.
- McLerran, A. (2004). *Roxaboxen*. New York: Harper Collins.
- Morris, A. (1995). *Houses and Homes (Around the World Series)*. New York: Harper Collins.
- Stephenson, R. L. (2005). *Block City*. New York: Simon & Schuster Books for Young Readers.

⌄ **Professional Resource Download**

14

Putting It All Together: Evaluation and Documentation

Standards Covered in This Chapter

 NAEYC Early Childhood Associate Degree Accreditation 4d, 5c, 6d

 NAEYC Early Childhood Program Accreditation 10

DAP DAP 3

Student Learning Outcomes

After studying this chapter, you should be able to:

- Define and give examples for key terms related to evaluation and documentation.

- Describe the process of evaluation, including identifying standards for evaluation, ethical issues, and methods used for evaluation.

- Compare methods for interpreting and using evaluation results.

- Analyze the process for creating a documentation plan.

Evaluation is the process of determining whether the philosophy, goals, and objectives of the program have been met. Interpretations and decisions are made based on the collected information. Assessment and evaluation are closely related and can happen simultaneously. Gordon and Browne (2016, p. 206) explain further: "Evaluation is a continuous process. It is at once a definition, an assessment, and a plan. . . . In its simplest form, evaluation is a process of appraisal." Informal and formal evaluation of a program should include the indoor and outdoor environments, schedule, routines, the curriculum as a whole, themes, lesson plans, activities, performances of the children, and the teacher's role. Ongoing evaluation is part of the curriculum process. Evaluation provides feedback concerning the effectiveness of the program, the goals and objectives, the teaching approach, the observation cycle, and once again the evaluation process.

Evaluation Defined

Early childhood educators use two distinct processes to help children build lifelong learning skills: assessment and evaluation. Assessment provides feedback on knowledge, skills, attitudes, and work products for the purpose of improving future performances and learning outcomes. Child assessment was discussed in Chapter 2. Evaluation determines the level of quality of a performance or outcome and enables decision making based on the level of quality demonstrated. These two processes are complementary and necessary in education.

Evaluation examines a program or process to determine what's working, what's not, and why. Evaluation determines the value of programs and acts as a blueprint for judgment and improvement (Rossett and Sheldon, 2001). Often, programs know the reason that they are conducting an evaluation, such as to seek national accreditation or compare their program to standards in their state's quality rating and improvement system (QRIS). No matter the reason for the evaluation, before you begin the evaluation process, it is important to ask questions to determine the focus and scope of your evaluation. Ask yourself:

1. What is the purpose of the evaluation? Why is this evaluation being undertaken? What is it expected to achieve or to provide insight about?
2. Who will use the information? Is this evaluation only for your own use? Are there others who are asking for this evaluation? What are their expectations and agendas? Who else might be interested in the process and results of the evaluation?
3. How will they use the information? What will the different users do with the evaluation results? What decisions or actions are likely to be influenced by the results?
4. What questions will the evaluation seek to answer? What specifically do you and others want to know?
5. When are the evaluation results needed? What's your timeline?
6. What are your own abilities and skills? Are there others who can help?
7. What resources do you have or can you access, including time, money, and people?

Once you have answered these questions, you can develop your plan.

Program evaluations describe and measure both the quantity and the quality of services provided to young children and families. Quantity measures include factors such as education and training of personnel, amount of space, schedule of operations, and components of service. Quality measures tend to focus on the results of services for children and families, such as developmental and early learning outcomes, family involvement, ratings of the physical environment, and satisfaction with services. A variety of qualitative and quantitative methods are used to evaluate programs: focus groups, interviews, surveys, review of records, observations, and direct testing (Washington State Office of Superintendent of Public Instruction, 2008).

Quantitative evaluation is defined as an evaluation approach involving the use and analysis of numerical data and measurement. **Qualitative evaluation** is typically conducted through interviews, observation, focus groups, portfolios, and journals to determine the

evaluation: The process of determining whether the philosophy, goals, and objectives of the program have been met.

quantitative evaluation: An evaluation approach involving the use and analysis of numerical data and measurement.

qualitative evaluation: An evaluation typically conducted through interviews, observation, focus groups, portfolios, and journals to determine the quality of the program.

quality of the program. Determine what data you want to collect: Do you want to know how many children participated in the activity (quantitative), or do you want to know that each and every child was successful in completing the activity to the standard you had established for the activity (qualitative)?

Whether quantitative or qualitative in nature, evaluations are normally divided into two broad categories: formative and summative. **Formative evaluation** is a method for judging the worth of a program or project while the program activities are forming or in progress. This part of the evaluation focuses on the **process**. In other words, how are we doing?

Thus, formative evaluations are done regularly, at least annually. They permit the teachers and faculty, administrators, and parents to monitor how well the program goals and objectives are being met. Its main purpose is to catch deficiencies so that the proper interventions can take place that improve program outcomes. Formative evaluation is also useful in analyzing learning materials, curriculum, and teacher effectiveness. Formative evaluation is primarily a building process of collecting information over time to help you improve your program. Children's developmental portfolios are an example of a child assessment that can also serve as a formative evaluation of curriculum effectiveness that allows you to look at a group of children's current level of development, so you can identify areas of the curriculum implementation that need strengthening.

Summative evaluation is a method of judging the worth of a program at the end of the program activities (summation) or end of a specific time period, such as a program year. This type of evaluation is used in accreditation studies to see how your program measures up every 3, 5, or 10 years using the accreditation standards and criteria. Summative evaluation might also be used to determine how well the children in your program did in meeting the learning goals you set out for them before moving on to kindergarten. The focus is on the outcome.

Formative evaluation is intended to foster development and improvement within an ongoing activity or program. Summative evaluation, in contrast, is used to assess whether the results of the program, project, intervention, or person being evaluated met the stated goals.

formative evaluation: A method for judging the worth of a program or project while the program activities are forming or in progress.

process: A natural continuing action or series of actions or changes.

summative evaluation: A method of judging the worth of a program at the end of the program activities or end of a specific time period.

Process of Evaluation

After you have developed your plan and determined what evaluation processes and tools you will use, you then need to designate who will organize the data, calculate the results, and compare what you found to the standards you had set. After you have the results, you need to ask yourself, "What does it all mean?" If the children were not successful at completing the activity, it might mean that your objective for the children was unrealistic or that you didn't have a clear child-learning outcome stated when you developed the activity. It could mean that the children had been inside all day and were too hyperactive to be successful on that day. Each activity, day, child, setting, or many other variables will have its own set of questions when asking, "What does it all mean?"

Standards

Early childhood programs and teachers are evaluated using many different standards and criteria for different purposes. We have referred to many of these standards throughout the book. Let's take a minute to look at some nationally recognized standards that are commonly used in evaluation of early childhood programs.

Developmentally Appropriate Practice in Early Childhood Programs, 3rd Edition

Professional standards of practice are developed as a position statement and detailed in a book by the National Association for the Education of Young Children (NAEYC). These are voluntary standards used to provide specific guidance for teachers with clear interpretation of elements of quality in early childhood programs.

Reflect On This

Why do you think the use of standards has become so important?

NAEYC Early Childhood Program Standards and Accreditation Criteria NAEYC's national accreditation system for children's programs has a set of 10 professional standards, including numerous criteria for early childhood education programs, allowing families to find high-quality programs for their children. There are four steps to the evaluation process to achieve NAEYC accreditation of programs for young children that ensure that the crucial components of program quality are in place.

Advancing the Early Childhood Profession: NAEYC Standards and Guidelines for Professional Development Designed as a resource for the entire early childhood field, across all roles and settings.

DEC Recommended Practices: A Comprehensive Guide for Practical Application in Early Intervention/Early Childhood Special Education Designed as a guide to identify practices that lead to better outcomes for young children with disabilities, their families, and the personnel who serve them.

QRIS State quality rating and improvement systems are used for (1) increasing the supply of and access to higher quality early childhood programs, (2) creating systemwide improvements in the quality of all programs, including all settings, auspices, and ages of children served, (3) providing resources to help programs improve and sustain higher quality, and (4) creating greater consumer awareness of the importance of program quality indicators and the supply of high-quality early childhood programs.

Caring for Our Children: National Health and Safety Performance Standards; Guidelines for Early Care and Education Programs, 3rd Edition National health and safety recommendations and guidelines for children in family- and center-based child-care programs published by the American Academy of Pediatrics along with the American Public Health Association and National Resource Center for Health and Safety.

Common Core State Standards in Child Care As of spring 2016, 41 states are still participating in the Common Core State Standards Initiative for English language, arts, and mathematics designed to provide teachers and parents with a common understanding of what students are expected to learn in K–12 education.

InTASC Model Core Teaching Standards A set of model core teaching standards that outline what teachers should know and be able to do to ensure every K–12 student reaches the goal of being ready to enter college or the workforce in today's world. These standards outline the common principles and foundations of teaching practice that cut across all subject areas and grade levels as developed by the Council of Chief State School Officers (CCSSO), through its Interstate Teacher Assessment and Support Consortium (InTASC).

State Pre-Kindergarten through Grade 3 Curriculum Guidelines Most states have developed curriculum standards to strengthen instruction in pre-K through grade 3 classrooms in all settings, as well as help administrators and educators align pre-K standards with the K–12 system.

Professional Educator Curriculum Standards National professional teacher organizations representing different curriculum content areas have developed standards that outline the understanding, knowledge, and skills that students should acquire from pre-K through grade 12. These groups include: International Literacy Association (ILA), National Coalition for Core Arts Standards (NCCAS), National Society of Music Educators (NSME), National Council for the Social Studies (NCSS), National Science Education Standards (NSES), and National Council of Teachers of Mathematics (NCTM).

Head Start/Early Head Start Performance Standards These standards are set by the office of Head Start as performance standards and minimum requirements for grantees to use with respect to health, education, parent involvement, nutrition, social, transition, and other Head Start services as well as administrative and financial management, facilities, and other appropriate program areas.

Using Scientific Research-Based Interventions: Improving Education for All Students (SRBI) Early childhood SRBI offers a system to determine whether the current curriculum and instruction are effective by examining data about whether children are making appropriate progress toward learning goals. It also provides a system for determining who is not making progress and might need additional support. Finally, early childhood SRBI includes a system for monitoring the effectiveness of the supports that are put in place.

However, several subtle differences exist in the implementation of SRBI in early childhood settings. Some adjustments are necessary due to variations in the delivery systems for preschool education, while other adjustments are necessary due to the nature of young children's development.

Ethical Issues

Good evaluation tools and techniques are objective, reliable, and valid. **Objectivity** refers to obtaining and using facts, information, or data without distortion by personal feelings, beliefs, or prejudgment. When our personal beliefs strongly influence our perception of facts or behaviors, we are expressing our opinion, which is subjective, instead of objectively stating the facts of what we observe. **Reliability** refers to the extent to which any evaluation technique yields results that are accurate and consistent over time. Inter-rater reliability refers to when different people use the same evaluation tool or technique and get the same results with few exceptions. **Validity** is the extent to which any evaluation technique fulfills the purpose for which it is intended.

The evaluation process should also be conducted fairly without bias. **Bias** in evaluation refers to a test, process, procedure, or use of the results that unfairly discriminates against one individual or group in favor of another (McAfee and Leong, 2011). For example, evaluation instruments and procedures must be culturally and linguistically relevant. The NAEYC developmentally appropriate practices (DAP) expanded the original definition that DAP should be age appropriate and individually appropriate and that these practices also should happen within a cultural context to avoid any bias in interpretation. Results of an evaluation should only be used for the purpose it was intended and details should be kept confidential.

Methods of Evaluation

The evaluation plan or methodology used to gather the information or data should be a specified step-by-step procedure. It should be carefully designed and executed to ensure the data is accurate and valid. Evaluation instruments are intended as tools for gathering information, not as meaningful stand-alone products. Think of the actual evaluation tools such as Internet browsers used to find information on the computer. An evaluation instrument, like a browser, is only as good as the information it yields.

Evaluation tools provide a structure for accessing and organizing information. The various instruments used to collect the data include questionnaires, surveys, interviews, observations, portfolios, and checklists. (See **Figure 14-1**.) Qualitative methods such as focus groups, observations, and interviews are typically used to gather information about the processes of program operations, such as identification of services offered and the process of program intake and referral for special services, assessment system, curriculum design, professional development, parent support, and community collaboration. Two common tools used are questionnaires and surveys.

A **survey** is a way to collect information directly from people in a systematic, standardized way. Surveys use questionnaires that ask the same question in the same way to all respondents. Data collected this way can then be used to make inferences about the population of interest (e.g., parents who attend a parenting workshop, etc.). Information can be collected about people's opinions, knowledge, attitudes, beliefs, behaviors, plans, and backgrounds. Electronic survey services, such as Survey Monkey, have simplified the collection of this kind of data.

Figure 14-1 Child being interviewed by his teacher for description of a portfolio entry.

objectivity: Obtaining and using facts, information, or data without distortion by personal feelings, beliefs, or prejudgment.

reliability: The extent to which any evaluation technique yields results that are accurate and consistent over time.

validity: The extent to which any evaluation technique fulfills the purpose for which it is intended.

bias: A test, process, procedure, or use of the results that unfairly discriminates against one individual or group in favor of another.

survey: A way to collect information directly from people in a systematic, standardized way.

Questionnaires are the least expensive procedure for external evaluations and can be used to collect large samples of aggregate information. The questionnaires should be tested before using to ensure the recipients understand their operation the way the evaluator intended. When designing questionnaires, keep in mind that the most important feature is the guidance given for its completion. All instructions should be clearly stated; nothing should be taken for granted.

A **checklist** is a record of direct observation that involves selecting from a previously prepared list the statement that best describes the behavior observed, the conditions present. (For more information about checklists and several of the tools listed here, refer back to Chapter 2.)

A **rating scale** is also a record of direct observation that involves selecting from a previously prepared list the statement that best describes the behavior observed or conditions present. It differs from a checklist, which allows respondents to answer yes or no, in that the person answering is asked to rate the quality of the behavior or condition. Rating scales are often used in job performance evaluations and training evaluations. For example, "How well did this training meet your needs?"

An **anecdotal record** is a type of document that is used by teachers for keeping track of observations about their students. This brief narrative documents observations of what a child or children did, what they said while they were working, and the materials the child or children were working with. A common use of this type of documentation is an accident or incident report. An analysis of collected reports can be used to determine possible safety hazards or needed safety training.

An **event sampling or frequency count** measures the number of times an event is observed. This method is often used to track a specific child behavior such as hitting or teacher behavior like saying *no* or *don't*, the use of different learning centers in a classroom, or classroom visits by parents. This is usually documented in a chart or table. To give a more qualitative view of the event, some basic information can be added to the chart, such as time, location, and who was involved. An event sampling form that is recommended is the ABC form, which records the *a*ntecedent or trigger (what happened before the behavior or event), *b*ehavior (what happened), and *c*onsequence (what happened as a result of the behavior or event). By documenting this type of information over time, trends and patterns emerge that can be helpful in evaluation. (See **Figure 14-2**.)

A **time sample** records what is happening at different time intervals, such as every 10 minutes. This type of observation tool allows the evaluator to observe the natural behavior of children and teachers because it does not disturb the flow of the day. A time sample can give a picture of children's choices of and engagement in activities. Analysis of this data can determine the popularity of different learning centers and which activities held children's interest over time. Further analysis can lead to making changes in the environment or curriculum to enhance learning. (See **Figure 14-3**.)

Portfolio assessment is based on a systematic collection of information gathered over time from all available sources. It can be about a child's ongoing development and the child's work gathered by both the child and teacher or a classroom or program. A classroom portfolio is a collection of child- and teacher-produced material and product samples showing a program's strengths related to a set of criteria such as the NAEYC Children's Program Accreditation Standards, such as samples of a child's self-initiated "work" in art or other curriculum area; photographs, audio and video tapes; program objectives, observations and anecdotal records, programmatic and environmental checklists; and family surveys and comments.

Portfolios are a creative means of organizing, summarizing, and sharing artifacts, information, and ideas about teaching or learning, along with personal and professional growth. The reflective process of portfolio development can be as important as the final product. A portfolio is a sampling of the breadth and depth of a child's, classroom teacher's, or program's work conveying the range of abilities, attitudes, experiences, and achievements. Traditionally, portfolios have been stored in boxes and three-ring binders. Although this format works fine for paper and other print-based materials, it misses many other ways of communicating ideas. Over the past decade, many people have found electronic portfolios an effective way to

questionnaires: The least expensive procedure for external evaluations and can be used to collect large samples of information.

checklist: A record of direct observation that involves selecting from a previously prepared list the statement that best describes the behavior observed and the conditions present.

rating scale: A record of direct observation that involves selecting from a previously prepared list the statement that best describes the behavior observed or conditions present. It differs from a checklist, which allows respondents to answer yes or no, in that the person answering is asked to rate the quality of the behavior or condition.

anecdotal record: A type of document that is used by teachers for keeping track of observations about their students.

event sampling or frequency count: Measures the number of times an event is observed.

time sample: Records what is happening at different time intervals.

portfolio assessment: Based on a systematic collection of information gathered over time from all available sources.

FREQUENCY COUNT

Date <u>March 01 Year</u> Recorder <u>BAN</u>

Make a tally mark in the column next to the child's name each time you observe a behavior that you would classify as prosocial or antisocial.

CHILD'S NAME	PROSOCIAL Helping, sharing, hugging, calling another child by a kind name	ANTISOCIAL Hurting, hoarding, bad name calling, rejecting another child
Alina	✓ ✓	
Bajik	✓ ✓ ✓	✓ ✓ ✓ ✓
Chris	✓ ✓ ✓ ✓ ✓	✓ ✓ ✓ ✓ ✓ ✓
David	✓	✓ ✓
Ethan		✓ ✓ ✓ ✓ ✓ ✓ ✓
Fatima	✓	
Gabriela	✓ ✓ ✓	
Huy		
Irma	✓ ✓	✓
Juan	✓ ✓	✓ ✓
Karly	✓ ✓ ✓ ✓	
Totals	24	22

Figure 14-2 Frequency chart.

more clearly present information not only through text but also through visuals, audio, and video formats. Documents can be stored on hard drives, flash drives, or CD-ROM in many digital formats such as text documents, picture files, web pages, digital video, and presentation files (Johnson and Lamb, 2007).

There are many existing instruments to use in designing an approach that will work best for any given program. The instruments listed here are useful measures of specific interactional and environmental components that might be included in comprehensive program evaluations. Some instruments specifically designed and frequently used to evaluate components of early childhood programs are:

- Classroom Assessment Scoring System (CLASS), University of Virginia Press.
- Early Childhood Environmental Rating Scale Revised Edition (ECERS-R), Teachers College Press.
- Early Childhood Classroom Observation Measure (ECCOM), D. Stipek and P. Byler, Stanford University School of Education.
- Early Language and Literacy Classroom Observation Tool (ELLCO), Brookes Publishing.

TIME SAMPLE

Red Class
Class a.m. (fours) _____   Date 9/3/20_   Recorder B. Smith _____

	TIMES (at 5-minute intervals)					
	9:20	9:25	9:30	9:35	9:40	9:45
Dramatic play	Alina Carter Howard → ⟨Jenny⟩	Alina → → → TA Ole	→ → → → TA	Marvin Karly	Juan	Bajik
Art	Ole Irma Patty TA	Juan	Alina → (Jenny)	Carter → Ned → FV Bajik →	→ → FV →	→ → FV
Music	Karly	Irma/Patty	Irma	Howard		Gabriela/Juan
Library	(Edward Fatima)	Gabriela	Juan	Irma (Jenny)	Gabriela Karly Ole TA	Irma (Patty)
Sensory play	Gabriela Marvin	(Edward Fatima) →	→ ( ) → Gabriela →	→ ( ) → →	(Irma Patty)	Karly Marvin
Manipulative play	Juan	Karly ⟨Jenny⟩ Marvin →	Ole → TA	Ole Fatima Patty TA	Alina → (Edward) →	→ → Ole TA
Science		Alina		Juan	Marvin	
Blocks	David → Ned → FV →	→ Bajik → →	Patty → → →		Jenny TA	Irma → TA
Watching	Bajik					

◯ denotes cooperative play   → denotes continued play   ✷ denotes play difficulty
FV family volunteer   TA teacher assistant

Figure 14-3   Time sample.

- Infant Toddler Environment Rating Scale Revised Edition (ITERS-R), Teachers College Press.
- School Age Care Environment Rating Scale (SACERS), Teachers College Press.
- Supports for Early Literacy Assessment (SELA), National Institute for Early Education Research (NIEER).

Drawing conclusions and making decisions comes after the collection of data. Analysis of the documents you have collected will help you make the important connections between your teaching and the children's learning.

Program evaluation is complex and ideally conducted by objective third parties with no investment in the results. In reality, early childhood professionals are often responsible for collecting program evaluation and accountability data on their own programs. It is difficult (and probably undesirable) to be objective and neutral about your life's work, and usually classroom personnel and family child-care providers would rather be interacting with, teaching, and otherwise supporting the development of young children.

A Guide to Assessment in Early Childhood: Infancy to Age Eight by the Washington State Office of Superintendent of Public Instruction (2008, p. 59), recommends three practices in program evaluation:

Reflect On This

Why is it hard to interpret what you have observed?

1. Program goals provide the best starting point. The goals a program is seeking to achieve will determine what the desired outcomes are, which will then guide selection of evaluation and accountability measures.
2. Collecting objective input from multiple perspectives including parents, providers, administrators, community partners, and children themselves (when appropriate) will ensure that program evaluation data are objective and representative.
3. The best results of program evaluation, either negative or positive, are those that are used to maintain and improve effective service delivery (Washington State Office of Superintendent of Public Instruction, 2008).

Interpreting and Using Evaluation Results

You can use all of the available tools to evaluate data. You can address all of the applicable ethical issues related to evaluation. You can use the appropriate evaluation methods. These won't make any difference unless you know what the data mean and how to use the data for growth, improvement, and learning.

Interpretation of Information

Before information can be interpreted, it is important to ask yourself five questions:

1. Are there enough samples?
2. Has a large enough sample been used to compare whether a group of children is growing at a normal rate of growth? If so, this type of research has already been conducted, and there are published growth charts available you can use as comparisons for the growth of a smaller group.
3. Have you collected enough information over time to see change or is this a one-time observation?
4. Has something occurred at the time of the assessment that could affect the results?
5. Are the assessment tools you used valid instruments?

The first step in interpreting the information gathered is to identify as many explanations as possible for what was learned. When interpreting information about a child's development based on multiple assessment tools, it helps to consider that the children might not respond because they don't understand the instructions and not because they don't know the answer. This can be as a result of them possessing limited ability to speak English, or they might have a language disability. Outside influences can also affect child behavior and

| **Figure 14-4** | Classroom environments can affect a child's behavior. |

performance such as home issues, hunger, or illness. Not identifying these issues in each child can result in incorrect conclusions.

Children cannot be assessed apart from also being aware of the effect the sociocultural context has on them. For example, how does the classroom affect the child's behavior? Has the teacher arranged the environment to foster the child or hinder the child's development? (See **Figure 14-4**.)

When outside assessors attempt to interpret their results from a particular day's observations of a classroom and teacher behaviors, their interpretation results might be different if they had been made aware that the teacher observed was a substitute who had only been working a week, a major piece of classroom equipment that the children loved had broken the previous day and had not yet been replaced, and there were three new children in the room that day.

When interpreting data collected on children's development, it's helpful to examine expected outcomes from standard growth tables that have been developed on statistical analysis from large groups of children. Samples of charts for children on height and weight can be found in **Figure 14-5**. The information can alert observers of possible significant variations that might need further investigation (Nilsen, 2013). Make sure to compare the outcomes of assessment with your goals, objectives, and standards.

In the activities that are developed for a classroom of children, it is important that the child objectives be stated is such a way that they can be measured to determine the child's ability to accomplish that objective. If done correctly, it is an excellent way to assess that child's mastery of the particular objective. When interpreting the results, it is found that the objective was not written to be measurable or the expectations were not realistic for children in the particular stage of development for which the activity was developed.

Often, it is difficult to interpret evidence so educators have found it useful to use **rubrics** to assess children's level of functioning, staff performance, curriculum, or program standards. Rubrics are charts that identify different levels and qualities of attainment of each benchmark or standard. It presents rules or guidelines by which a complex performance can be judged (McAfee and Leong, 2011). An example of part of a rubric that can be used to assess a student's performance based on an NAEYC associate degree standard can be found in **Table 14-1**. The interpretation of this example could be that the student didn't understand the instructions and completed that section incorrectly or that he or she didn't understand how to assess his or her performance on a rubric. The interpretation could also be that the program

rubric: Chart that identifies different levels and qualities of attainment of each benchmark or standard.

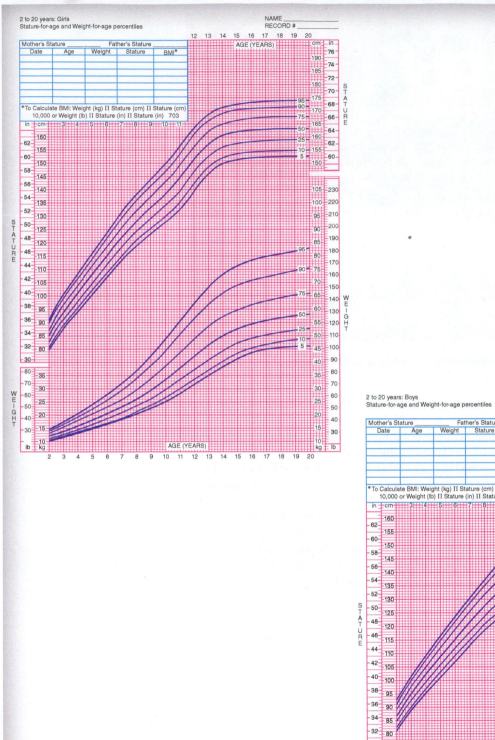

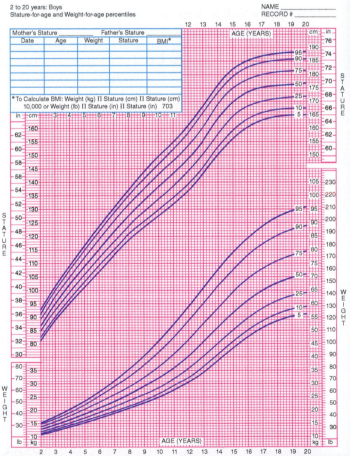

Figure 14-5   Height and weight charts.

	TABLE 14-1: **Case Study Rubric**				

Standards	Exceeds Expectations 7–9 pts.	Meets Expectations 4–6 pts.	Below Expectations 1–3 pts.	POINTS Student	POINTS Faculty
Standard 1 - PROMOTING CHILD DEVELOPMENT AND LEARNING 1a. Knowing and understanding young children's characteristics and needs	Student provided appropriate characteristics for each developmental domain.	Student provided appropriate characteristics for most developmental domains.	Student provided appropriate characteristics for few or no developmental domains.	9	7
	Student provided examples or explanation of appropriate characteristics for each developmental domain.	Student provided examples or explanation of appropriate characteristics for most developmental domains.	Student provided examples of explanation of appropriate characteristics for few or no developmental domains.	9	6
	Student gave only facts when describing the child and saved opinions for the summary.	Student gave facts most of the time when describing the child and saved opinions for the summary.	Student gave facts part or none of the time when describing the child and gave opinions.	9	5
1b. Knowing and understanding the multiple influences on development and learning	Student's introduction provided a clear, complete picture of the child.	Student's introduction provided a picture of the child but information was missing.	Student's introduction provided a picture of the child but a great deal of information was missing.		6
	Student provided comprehensive information pertaining to family and home and how it influenced the child's development.	Student provided some information pertaining to family and home and how it influenced the child's development.	Student provided little or no information pertaining to family and home and how it influenced the child's development.	1	7

had not provided enough learning opportunities so the student could be successful. Another interpretation might be that the student didn't complete that portion of the assessment and therefore left it blank. All of these would have to be explored before the true reason can be determined and improved.

Interpretation isn't easy. It calls on the person responsible for the interpretation to be creative, open-minded, and resourceful. Every possibility has to be identified and examined. Those possibilities that can't be validated should be eliminated leaving the most probable one to be acted on as the reason for what was observed and assessed.

Using Assessment Information

Use of data is simple, change. No matter what we are assessing, the intent is to determine how we can improve or change it. To provide a strong foundation, we want to use what we know to enhance each and every child's growth and development. As we interpret what we have learned, we can find areas that have been missed or need to be strengthened. These may be related to

Figure 14-6 Classroom materials need to be evaluated on a regular basis.

quality of the curriculum created, the appropriateness of the environments in which the children will grow, and the knowledge and skills of the teachers selected to foster optimum learning experiences. (See **Figure 14-6**.) Chapters 5 to 13 can be beneficial in helping teachers and programs to provide the highest quality in skills, environments, and curriculum to best teach children.

Interpretation of data can be beneficial in examining the educational programs and field experiences in which the classroom teachers gain their abilities to support and teach each child.

Determining how to use assessment information does take time and isn't a one-time process. You can start by reflecting on what do to with the evaluation results. Then make a plan for continued data collection, interpretation, and change. Make sure to balance what you might like to change with what is possible. Then implement your plans for change. Your plan will be individualized because each child and program is unique. Assessing and interpreting evaluation information is an ongoing process and determining uses for the information should also be ongoing. (See **Figure 14-7**.)

Figure 14-7 Teachers using evaluation information to plan curriculum changes.

Documentation

Collecting and recording information are often thought of as the same thing. However, the information that is collected by observation or interview may be recorded or documented on a rating scale or anecdotal record.

> " An effective piece of documentation tells the story and the purpose of an event, experience, or development. It is a product that draws others into the experience—evidence or artifacts that describe a situation, tell a story, and help the viewer to understand the purpose of the action (Seitz, 2008, p. 88). "

Method of Documentation

As with anything you do that might require time and planning, it is best to have steps to make the job easier and more organized. An easy method is the *why, who, what, where, when,* and *how* method. With this method, you look at each of these words separately and apply it to the task.

Why are You Wanting to Collect Information on Child Success in Your Class?

For example, you may be

- Seeking national accreditation,
- Measuring child outcomes to share with parents (see **Figure 14-8**),
- Planning program improvement, or
- Compiling information for a funder's report.

Who to Target

Who are you documenting information for?

- The children so they can see what they learned.
- Families so they can track their child's progress.
- Accrediting body to document your program's quality.
- State education or licensing agency to confirm compliance with standards.
- The community to inform them of program accomplishments.
- Your governing board to report progress towards goals.
- Funders to confirm their investment was sound.

What to Document

What you document depends on your purpose:

- Child outcomes for planning and evaluating curriculum and teaching methods
- Program outcomes for program evaluation
- Program improvement for comparison and planning (See **Figure 14-9**.)
- Learning to share with children and parents
- Room arrangement and function to plan improvements
- Outdoor environment to plan improvements
- Health and safety to confirm compliance with regulations and improve practices

Figure 14-8 Sharing child outcomes with a parent.

Figure 14-9 The director spends a great deal of time documenting program outcomes and planning.

- Parent involvement to assess and improve practices
- Meal service to improve quality and cost efficiency
- Community involvement to plan marketing
- Services for culturally, linguistically, and ability-diverse children to improve practices

Where to Document

Where to document includes places such as

- In classrooms to evaluate teaching practices and curriculum implementation
- Learning centers to determine their effectiveness
- The entire program to evaluate all the components that determine program effectiveness
- Outdoors to evaluate equipment maintenance and appropriateness and nature experiences

When to Document

The when of documentation depends on what is being documented:

- Document all the time to provide continuous feedback.
- Conduct child assessments two to three times annually.
- Evaluate programs annually.
- Record project results at the end of a project.
- Document curriculum implementation and children's learning ongoing to inform continuous improvement and plan learning experiences and interventions.

How to Document

There are several methods for documentation:

- Create portfolios to track progress over time.
- Use technology to conduct surveys, evaluate child outcomes, plan interventions, and document compliance with standards.
- Develop documentation boards and books to share children's learning. (See **Figure 14-10**.)

Documentation boards and books are used to make learning visible and teaching intentional. Katz and Chard (1996 as cited by Seitz, 2008, p. 88) offer this explanation:

> Documentation typically includes samples of a child's work at several different stages of completion: photographs showing work in progress; comments written by the teacher or other adults working with the children; transcriptions of children's discussions, comments, and explanations of intentions about the activity; and comments made by parents.

They can also contain photographs of children participating in a particular activity. Everything that is included in a documentation board is done so for a reason. They can be used by teachers to scaffold learning opportunities for the children so they can progress smoothly to the next stage in their development. Teachers can also use them to evaluate their own teaching practices. These boards, when shared with parents, can help them to feel more of a connection with their child's development.

Remember these objective recording guidelines when you are documenting observations:

- Record only the facts.
- Record every detail.
- Do not interpret while you observe.
- Do not record what you do not see.
- Use objective words.
- Record the facts in order.
- Date your entries or work samples.
- Keep your entries short.

Figure 14-10   "What Will Kindergarten Be Like" documentation.

Keeping up with documentation can be a challenge for busy teachers and administrators. Authentic documentation of learning takes:

- Practice to remember to take photos of children's engagements and work
- Organization of ways to save authentic work and representations
- Finding time to record conversations or anecdotal notes
- Commitment to keep documentation current and relevant to recent interests and investigations

Documentation can come in many forms. The more technology that becomes available to us at more and more affordable rates, the easier it becomes to create more realistic portrayals of our work. For example, a digital video recorder combined with a PowerPoint presentation with the actual video clips of children's accomplishments can clearly demonstrate DAPs for accrediting bodies, governing boards, and families. Also as educators, using this form of documentation can reduce the amount of space taken up previously by traditional handwritten documentation.

Final Thoughts

This book is now complete except for a few final thoughts. We've examined the history and theories related to early childhood curriculum and the role of observation and assessment in planning quality curriculum. Curriculum development has been explored and the use of environment has been discussed. Chapters 5 to 13 examined the learning centers of a classroom

and all of the components of those areas as they are used to enhance children's growth and development. The development of the child, the actual contents of the room, diversity, technology and the teacher all played a role in learning. Finally, how evaluation is interpreted and used to improve many aspects toward learning was reflected upon.

We hope that you have learned that early childhood curriculum is not just a set of activities. It encompasses every experience that a child has. Therefore, it is important that each teacher realize that everything they do and provide is intentional in fostering each and every child's success. You prepare, you teach, you evaluate, you interpret data, you improve, and you start all over again. It's an ongoing process for every child.

We hope that you have gained some skills from our book to help you in this process.

Summary

1. **What are some examples of key terms related to evaluation and documentation?** Evaluation is the process of determining whether the philosophy, goals, and objectives of the program have been met. Quantitative evaluation is defined as an evaluation approach involving the use and analysis of numerical data and measurement. Qualitative evaluation is typically conducted through interviews, observation, focus groups, portfolios, and journals to determine the quality of the program. Formative evaluation is a method for judging the worth of a program or project while the program activities are forming or in progress. Summative evaluation is a method of judging the worth of a program at the end of the program activities (summation) or end of a specific time period, such as a program year.

2. **What are key standards, ethical issues, and methods used for evaluation?**

   - *Developmentally Appropriate Practice in Early Childhood Programs,* 3rd Edition; *NAEYC Early Childhood Program Standards and Accreditation Criteria*
   - *Advancing the Early Childhood Profession: NAEYC Standards and Guidelines for Professional Development*
   - *DEC Recommended Practices: A Comprehensive Guide for Practical Application in Early Intervention/Early Childhood Special Education*
   - Common Core State Standards
   - InTASC Model Core Teaching Standards
   - Head Start/Early Head Start Performance Standards

   Ethical issues include: Objectivity refers to obtaining and using facts, information, or data without distortion by personal feelings, beliefs, or prejudgment. Reliability refers to the extent to which any evaluation technique yields results that are accurate and consistent over time. Validity is the extent to which any evaluation technique fulfills the purpose for which it is intended. Bias in evaluation refers to a test, process, procedure, or use of the results that unfairly discriminates against one individual or group in favor of another. Results of an evaluation should only be used for the purpose it was intended and details should be kept confidential.

   Evaluation methods for collecting data include questionnaires, surveys, interviews, observations, portfolios, and checklists. Qualitative methods such as focus groups, observations, and interviews are typically used to gather information about the processes of program operations, such as identification of services offered, and the process of program intake and referral for special services, assessment system, curriculum design, professional development, parent support, and community collaboration.

3. **What are some methods for interpreting and using evaluation results?** Methods to use for interpreting evaluation results include identifying all possible explanations, examining the child's sociocultural context, comparing data with standardized data, and comparing outcomes with goals, objectives, and standards.

Methods used for using evaluation results include reflection on what to do with the evaluation results, making a plan for continued data collection, interpretation and change, balance what you might like to change with what is possible and implement your plans for change.

4. **How can you create a documentation plan for a specific early childhood situation?** Follow the *who, what, when, why,* and *how plan* and apply it to the situation. The plan asks the following questions:

- *Who* is the documenting information for?
- *What* are you documenting?
- *Where* are you collecting the documentation?
- *When* will you collect the documentation?
- *Why* do you want to collect information in this situation?
- *How* will you conduct the documentation?

Reflective Review Questions

1. Many programs purchase a complete curriculum package or a book of activities and teach from that. Why might this not be an effective way to teach children?
2. Why do you think public schools that use "teach to the test" and standardized testing aren't getting the results they hope for? What could they do to improve test scores based on what you have learned in this chapter and developmentally appropriate practices?

Explorations

1. Develop an evaluation plan for the center or school where you work or have observed using the information in the Methods of Evaluation section.
2. Observe 30 minutes in a center or school classroom. Describe in detail what you observed. Interpret what you saw. What are your suggestions for improvement?
3. You have been asked to give some suggestions on a situation that is occurring quite frequently in the 4-year-old classroom. The children in the block center are having problems with their tempers and fights are occurring. Make a total plan for observation, assessment, evaluation, and documentation using the plan for documentation to describe what you would suggest. Describe in depth each of the steps you would use, tools, and documentation methods.

My Self Integrated Curriculum Theme with Activities

MY SELF

FEELINGS

Loving
Happy   Sad
Afraid
Surprised
Angry   Lonely
Friendly
Excited
Verbal   Nonverbal

SELF ESTEEM

Being special
Having ideas and thoughts
Being creative
Doing some things well
Having a special body
Having a family
and friends

SELF-CONTROL

Learning appropriate ways
to show and say
how I feel
Listening to others
Saying "no" to things
that will hurt me
or others

SELF-MOTIVATION

Learning how to
do new things
Learning by using my mind
and all my senses
Playing and doing things
by myself
or with friends

Theme Goals

To provide opportunities for children to learn the following:

- I am special because I am me. There is no one else just like me.
- I am still discovering how to do new things.
- I can use my mind and my senses to accomplish many things.
- I can play and do things by myself or with friends and family.
- I can show my emotions and say how I feel without hurting others.
- I can say *no* to things that will hurt me or others.

Integrated Curriculum Theme with Activities

Children-Created Bulletin Board

This bulletin board gives children an opportunity to express how they feel about themselves. Throughout the theme, the bulletin board changes as the children learn more about feelings, self-esteem, self-motivation, and self-control.

> Cut poster board cards in various shapes, such as circles, squares, rectangles, and triangles.
> Have each child select one card in his favorite shape.
> Write or have the child write anything about himself or herself on the card, including the suggestions that follow in the "Special Recipe."

"Special Recipe for (Child's Name)"

> Two big (color) eyes,
> One great smile,
> (Long, short—color) hair,
> Smooth (color) skin,
> One cup of niceness,
> Two cups of laughter.

- Children add anything they want about themselves. Give a few examples to get them started: "Add one cup of books. Stir in puzzles. Mix together and discover (child's name)."
- You may find it easier to do this with each child individually.
- Put the finished recipes on the bulletin board.

- Have the children add photos of themselves or pictures they draw of themselves.
- As they learn to do more things during this theme, children can add to the original recipe.
- Drawings that express feelings also can be added.
- Adding new items will make this an interactive bulletin board.

Vocabulary Starters

Let the children add words.

creative: discovering new ways of doing things.

feelings: what you mean when you talk about or show being happy, sad, afraid, angry, or surprised.

learn: to know and understand something you did not know or understand before.

self: whatever is just about you and nobody else.

thoughts: what happens when you get ideas and decide to do things?

Language Experiences

Ball Name Game

All you need for this activity are the children and a large ball. This is a good transition activity. When a child's name is called, he or she can choose a learning center and go to it.

- Everyone sits on the floor in a circle.
- Talk about how special everyone's name is.
- Roll the ball to a child. Everyone says the child's first name.
- Ask the toddler to roll or bring the ball back to you. Continue rolling the ball and saying each child's name.
- The preschooler can roll the ball to someone else. Everyone says that child's name. The ball passes from one child to another until each child's name is called and repeated.
- Extend this activity by rolling the ball to a child and saying the child's last name.
- Continue until each child's last name has been called.

Whose Voice Is This?

Use a recorder to record each child's conversational voice, giggling, laughing, or singing.

- Record each child privately, away from the other children. If children do not know what to say, help them say something with you. This way you are recording your voice, too.
- Next, play back what each child recorded and have the other children guess whose voice they hear.
- Talk about how each person's voice is unique.
- Place the recorder in the music center. The children can listen to the voices whenever they wish.

Let's Share

- Read Hutchins's *The Doorbell Rang*, listed in the Children's Books section in this appendix.
- Discuss the concept of sharing as a way of showing someone you care about him or her.
- Ask open-ended questions such as: "What have you shared?" "With whom did you share it?" "Why do you need to share?" "How do you feel when someone shares with you?" "What are some things we could share in the classroom?"
- *The Doorbell Rang* is about sharing cookies. Buy or bake a giant cookie, and let the children find ways to share.

Dramatic Play

I Am Happy

This activity can be done indoors or outdoors.

- Give the children opportunities to show emotions (happy, sad, angry, afraid, and surprised) by the way they run, walk, hop, throw a ball, or move their bodies.
- Role-play appropriate ways to handle situations.
- Ask children to share what makes them feel happy, sad, and so on.
- This could be repeated throughout the year to help children deal with their feelings.
- Puppets can also help children talk about how they feel.

Pantomime Time

Read Carle's *The Mixed-Up Chameleon*. See the Children's Books section in this appendix.

- Ask open-ended questions, such as: "Why do you think the chameleon was feeling unhappy?" "What feelings do you have about the chameleon?"
- Help the children decide which "chameleon character" they want to pantomime. Act without using words. One child can even be the sun and another, the fly.
- Read the story again.
- The children pantomime their roles as the story unfolds.
- To extend this activity, have the children create paper costumes of the different "chameleon characters."
- The children also can draw their own chameleons.

Puppet Play

Tennis Ball Puppet Friend

Let the children name this puppet. For the purpose of describing this activity, we will call the tennis ball puppet

"Happy." This activity promotes positive self-esteem, self-motivation, and self-control.

- To make Happy, an adult should cut a slit in the middle of a tennis ball, across from one seam to the next. (See the illustration for clarification.) **Caution:** Be careful when cutting. A tennis ball is difficult to cut. It is hard to hold without slipping.
- Use markers or "puff paint" to make eyes, eyebrows, nose, and mouth.
- To make Happy "talk," press the sides of the ball.
- Use a box to make a special home for the puppet.
- Let a different child take Happy home each day after school and bring it back the next day.
- Happy reports on overnight (or weekend) adventures at the child's home.
- This gives the child an opportunity to develop a voice for the puppet and tell what happened.

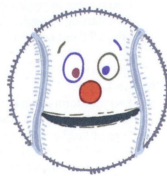

- You and the children can write in a special book what happens to Happy. Where did it go? What did it eat? Whom did it see? Where did it sleep?
- The children also can illustrate their books.
- Children vote on who gets to take Happy home.
- Next, you and the children can make a calendar and count the days until Happy goes home with the next child.

Feelings Puppet

Children of all ages enjoy this activity.

- Put tongue depressors, crayons, and markers out for the children to use.
- Encourage the children to make a set of "feelings" puppets.
- Children can draw faces on the tongue depressors that show happy, sad, fearful, angry, and surprised expressions.

- Give the children envelopes in which to put their "feelings." They place the envelopes in their individual cubbies. When the children want to express how they feel, they can pull out their "feelings" puppet.

Music

Song: "Hello, Hello"

The following song is a *musical beat* activity. It also can be chanted.

> *Hello, hello,*
> *We sing in many ways.*
> *Hello, hello,*
> *Let's sing them now today.*

In the following verses of this "Hello" chant, a simple method of indicating the beat is used. Though the chant is original, the system of indicating the beat is adapted from Sally Moomaw's *More Than Singing* (1997).

Use a drum or other musical instrument to reinforce the beat. A vertical line (|) above a syllable means that it is accented. An asterisk (*) indicates a pause (or "rest," as in music) in the phrasing. In addition, phonetic pronunciations are provided under the foreign words.

English

> *Hel-lo* hel-lo **
> *We sing in ma-ny ways **
> *Hel-lo * hel-lo **
> *Let's sing them now to-day **

Spanish

> *Ho-la * ho-la **
> *(oh-la oh-la)*
> *We sing in ma-ny ways **
> *Ho-la * ho-la **
> *Let's sing them now to-day **

French

> *Bon-jour * bon-jour **
> *(bone-zhoor bone-zhoor)*
> *We sing in ma-ny ways **
> *Bon-jour * bon-jour **
> *Let's sing them now to-day **

German

> *Gu-ten tag * gu-ten tag **
> *(goo-ten tog goo-ten tog)*

Italian

> *Ci-a-o * ci-a-o **
> *(chee-ah-oh chee-ah-oh)*

Japanese

*Kon-ni-chi- wa * kon-ni-chi- wa **
(koh-nee-chee-wah koh-nee-chee-wah)

Chinese

*Ni-hao * ni-hao **
(nee-how nee-how)

Korean

*An nung * an nung **
(ahn nyong ahn nyong)

Vietnamese

*Chao * chao **
(chow chow)

Hebrew

*Sha-lom * sha-lom **
(sha-lome sha-lome)

Arabic

*Mar-h-ba * mar-h -ba**
(mar-hah-bah mar-hah-bah)

Movement

Exercises for Older Infants and Toddlers

- **Push the chair,** to practice walking. Have the infant on his or her feet holding onto the back of a low, sturdy child's chair. Help him or her push the chair while practicing walking.
- **In and out of the box,** for coordination. Use a heavy cardboard box or tub, and place the baby inside. Encourage him or her to climb in and out.
- **The rocking chair,** for fun and to strengthen muscles. Have the infant sit on the floor next to you. Bring your knees up, and rock back and forth. Encourage the child to do the same.
- **Pop-up,** for upper body and stomach strength. Do this exercise together. Have the baby sit on the floor and bend over. Quickly have him or her straighten his legs while sitting upright and stretching his or her arms up high. Hold for two seconds and then quickly return to bent-over position. Repeat.

Let's Wave, Wobble, and Wiggle

Do this activity with or without recorded music, or try it using the traditional tune "The Bear Went over the Mountain."

My thumbs, my thumbs want to pop up.
My thumbs, my thumbs want to pop up.
My thumbs, my thumbs want to pop up.
That's what they like to do.
Continue the pattern with the following changes:
My hands, my hands want to shake . . .
My arms, my arms want to wave . . .
My head, my head wants to wobble . . .
(That's what *it* likes to do.)
My legs, my legs want to wiggle . . .
My feet, my feet want to dance . . .
Now all of me wants to jump . . .
(That's what *I* like to do.)
End with:
Oh, I am starting to giggle,
I am starting to giggle,
I am starting to giggle,
I think I'll just sit down!

I'm the Leader

- Everyone forms a big circle. Select one of the children to be the leader.
- Suggest that he or she hop, jump, or crawl, and say, "Do it just like me."
- The other children then try to do what the leader does.
- Continue with the children taking turns.
- This is one of those quick activities that can be used anytime.

Right, Left, Right, Stop!

This movement activity helps with recognition of left and right.

- Let the children help you come up with other ideas.
- Older children like to combine several body movements at one time.
- Children like to do this at home with family members too.

March with feet	Sway with upper body
Left, right,	Right, left,
Left, right,	Right, left
Left, right,	Right, left,
Stop!	Stop!
Raise arms	Move head
Left, right,	Right, left,
Left, right,	Right, left,
Left, right,	Right, left,
Stop!	Stop!

- Have each child decorate the "I'm Special" vest with crayons, markers, felt and fabric scraps, construction paper, feathers, cotton balls, and all kinds of shapes, stickers, and buttons.
- Put magazines and catalogs out as well, and suggest that children cut out pictures of what they like and glue these to the vest.

Two-Dimensional Art Gallery

In a school hallway, walkway, or entrance area, display some of the children's art along with posters or pictures of famous paintings.

- Mat and attractively exhibit all of the art, so that the children's creativity is treated the same as that of well-known artists.
- Let the children help you mount the exhibition.
- This is a good way to introduce the children to great works of art and the painters who created the works.
- Many children's books on art are available to share with the children, for example, *Getting to Know the World's Greatest Artists Series* and *New York's Metropolitan Museum of Art Series.*

Sensory Art

Expressing Feelings

To ease the times a child may feel frustrated, angry, or full of energy (and "using words" won't help), bring out the clay or play dough. Many types and textures are available. A recipe for play dough is provided in Chapter 8.

- Set up a special space for the child to have some alone time with the clay or play dough.
- For a toddler, a special place to pound, such as on a plastic pounding bench, can help defuse feelings.

Make an "I'm Special" Vest

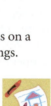

Do this project with each child individually, if possible.

- Take a large paper grocery sack and invert it.
- Cut straight up the center of one of the wide sides to where the bottom creases.
- Here, cut a large round circle out of the bottom of the sack.
- On each narrow side of the sack, cut a vertical oval that starts at the bottom crease and extends about 8 inches.
- The child puts the vest on by placing his or her head through the large, round opening, with the long vertical slit to the front and arms through the two side ovals.

Creative Food Experiences

Happy Faces

You will need the following:

a loaf of bread
cream cheese

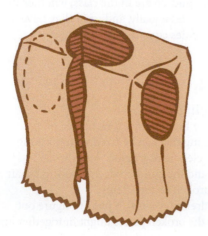

HAPPY FACES!

Wash hands.

Cut circles from bread with a round cookie cutter.

Spread bread with cream cheese, peanut butter,

or apple jelly. Use raisins and nuts to make

eyes, nose, and mouth.

ENJOY!

peanut butter
apple jelly
raisins
nuts

1. Let the children cut circles from bread with a round cookie cutter.
2. Spread bread with cream cheese, peanut butter, or apple jelly. Children sometimes use all three.
3. Use raisins and nuts to make eyes, nose, and mouth. Enjoy!

Note: Omit peanut butter and nuts if your group includes children who are allergic.

Let's Make a Cake

This recipe is easy for the children to do and can give them a sense of accomplishment. It also is a fun one to pass on to families.

1. Wash hands.
2. Put one can of fruit, with the juice, into a buttered 9-inch × 13-inch metal or glass pan.
3. Dump one box of white or yellow cake mix over the fruit.
4. Cut one stick of butter or margarine into small-pieces.
5. Dump butter or margarine pieces on top of the cake mix.
6. Bake at 350 degrees for 30 to 40 minutes.
7. Eat!

Math

The Languages of Math

This activity encourages learning to count from one to five in many languages. It also helps build self-esteem for children of other cultures.

English	Spanish	French	German	Italian
One	Uno (oo'-no)	un (oon)	eins (ines)	Uno (oo' –no)
Two	Dos (dose)	deux (doo)	zwei ([ts]vye)	Due (doo'-eh)
Three	Tres (trais)	trois (t(r)wah)	drei (dry)	Tre (treh)
Four	Cuatro (kwáh-tro)	quatre (ká-tra)	vier (fear)	Quattro (kwáh-tro)
Five	Cinco (seén-ko)	cinq (sank)	funf (foonf)	Cinque (cheén-kay)

English	Chinese	Japanese	Hebrew	Arabic
One	Yi (yee)	ichi (ée-chee)	achat (a-(h)áht)	Wahid (wáh-hid)
Two	Er (uhr)	ni (nee)	shta'yim (shtah-yéem)	Ithinin (ith-nín)
Three	San (sahn)	san (sahn)	shalosh (shah-lōśh)	Thalatha (ta-lá-ta)
Four	Si (suh)	shi (shee)	(ar-báh)	arba'a (ar-báh)
Five	Wu (woo)	go (go)	hamesh ([h]ah-meśh)	Kamisa (k(h)ah´ m-sa)

Math Cookies

Relate this activity to Hutchins's book *The Doorbell Rang*. See the language experience activity in this theme. This activity promotes problem solving, one-to-one correspondence, and cooperation.

- You and the children make three dozen "cardboard cookies." These can be made easily out of heavy cardboard or poster board cut into circles.
- Decorate the cookies with markers and crayons.
- Some of the cookies should be alike.
- Make up math games that can be played with the cardboard cookies.
- Younger children can sort the cookie circles by color or by the number of "chocolate chip" dots on the cookies. They also can practice making a straight line with the cookies.
- Older children can practice counting and sorting the cookies into pairs, as well as figuring out how many children are in the class, whether they can share the cookies equally, and what they have to do to share the cookies equally.

Science

Fixing Things

- Collect broken toys, torn books, or anything that can be fixed with masking tape, clear tape, or glue.
- You and the children decide how to repair the broken or torn items.
- Children may work in pairs to figure out how the broken pieces might fit together again.

My Body Is Made of Hinges

This project has many levels. The beginning levels are appropriate and interesting for preschoolers. The entire procedure is fascinating for older children. To introduce this activity, have a variety of hinges in a box.

- Demonstrate how the hinges work, and allow the children to experiment with them for several days.
- Next, talk about hinges in the room, and then show how children's bodies have "hinges."
- Let children bend their fingers, wrists, knees, and so on to music.
- Introduce silhouette pieces, such as head, neck, trunk, arms, hands, legs, and feet. These can be made from black construction paper or shiny, lightweight black art paper.
- Have a prepared figure put together with brads to show how the body moves.
- Prepare the silhouette body parts for each child, and place the pieces in individual envelopes.
- Go through magazines and catalogs for action poses.
- Encourage each child to select one picture. Using glue sticks, glue it on half of an 8½-inch × 11-inch piece of white paper.
- On the side of the page opposite the picture, have the child position the silhouette body parts in the same position. Children may need guidance to do this.
- When each child is satisfied with the pose, he or she glues the parts, one at a time, onto the paper.
- Place all of the finished silhouette pictures on the bulletin board.

Social Studies

Celebrating Birthdays and Special Months

Birthdays are special days for children. Help them celebrate by setting up a big classroom calendar that you and the children design.

- Have each child write his or her name and birth date on the calendar.

- Because some cultures and religions do not emphasize birthdays, also include on the calendar special events that happen each month in your community or nationally.
- You can celebrate birthdays and other special days at the same time.
- Play special recorded music, eat a new snack, or read a new book to celebrate each child's birthday.

Here are some suggestions for special events to celebrate. You and the children can decide how you will observe the day.

September	Monarch Butterfly Migration Month Good Neighbor Day (fourth week)
October	Popcorn Month Apple Month Teddy Bear Day (Oct. 27)
November	National Children's Book Week (third week) Homemade Bread Day (Nov. 17)
December	Birds in the Snow Week (fourth week) Poinsettia Day (Dec. 12)
January	National Soup Month New Year's Day in 123 nations (Jan. 1)
February	Black History Month Presidents' Day (second week)
March	National Nutrition Month Children's Poetry Day (March 21)
April	Week of the Young Child (Consult the National Association for the Education of Young Children for specific dates: 1-800-424-2460.) Earth Day (April 22)
May	Be Kind to Animals Month National Safe Kids Week (second week)
June	Children's Day (second week) Flag Day (June 14)
July	Blueberry Month National Ice Cream Day (third week)
August	National Clown Week (first week) Family Day (second week)

Children's Books

Anderson, Peggy P. (2002). *Let's Clean Up!* Boston: Houghton Mifflin.

Carle, Eric. (1984). *The Mixed-Up Chameleon.* New York: HarperTrophy.

Carle, Eric. (1996). *The Grouchy Ladybug.* New York: Harper-Collins.

Catalanotto, Peter. (2002). *Matthew ABC. . . .* New York: Atheneum.

Cowell, Cressida. (2003). *Super Sue*. Illustrated by Russell Ayto. Cambridge, MA: Candlewick Press.

French, Simon. (2002). *Guess the Baby*. Illustrated by Donna Rawlins. New York: Clarion.

Getting to Know the World's Greatest Artist Series. (1990). Chicago: Children's Press.

Got, Yves. (2003). *Sam's Busy Day*. San Francisco: Chronicle.

Hill, Elizabeth S. (2002). *Chang and the Bamboo Flute*. Illustrated by Lesley Liu. New York: Farrar, Straus & Giroux.

Hoffman, Mary. (2002). *The Color of Home*. Illustrated by Karin Littlewood. New York: Putnam.

Hutchins, Pat. (1989). *The Doorbell Rang*. New York: Mulberry Books.

Isadora, Rachel. (2003). *On Your Toes: A Ballet ABC*. New York: Greenwillow.

Lebrun, Claude. (1997). *Little Brown Bear Is Growing Up*. New York: Children's Press.

Lee, Suzy. (2009). *Wave*. New York: Chronicle.

MacCarone, Grace. (1995). *The Lunch Box Surprise*. New York: Cartwheel Books.

Mayer, Mercer. (1995). *I Am Sharing*. New York: Random House.

McGee, Marni. (2002). *Wake Up, Me!* Illustrated by Sam Williams. New York: Simon & Schuster.

McGhee, Alison. (2009). *Little Boy*. Illustrated by Peter H. Reynolds. New York: Atheneum.

New York's Metropolitan Museum of Art's Series. (1993). *What Makes. . . a. . . ?* New York: Author and Viking.

Raposo, Joe. (2001). *Imagination Song*. Illustrated by Laurent Linn. New York: Random House.

Reiser, Lynn, Rebecca Hart, and Corazones Valientes. (1998). *Tortillas and Lullabies/Tortillas y cancioncitas*. New York: Greenwillow.

Singer, Marilyn. (2003). *Boo Hoo Boo-Boo*. Illustrated by Elivia Savadier. New York: HarperCollins.

Stuve-Bodeen, Stephanie. (2002). *Elizabeti's School*. Illustrated by Christy Hale. New York: Lee & Low.

Waber, Bernard. (2002). *Courage*. Boston: Houghton Mifflin.

Walsh, Melanie. (2009). *10 Things I Can Do to Help My World: Fun and Easy Eco-Tips*. Cambridge, MA: Candlewick.

Wollman, Jessica. (2002). *Andrew's Bright Blue T-Shirt*. Illustrated by Anna L. Escriva. New York: Doubleday.

Zemach, Kaethe. (2003). *Just Enough and Not Too Much*. New York: Arthur A. Levine/Scholastic.

Zolotow, Charlotte. (1985). *William's Doll*. Illustrated by William Pene DeBois. New York: HarperTrophy.

Family Letter (Preschool)

Dear Family,
We are starting another theme this week, "My Self." We will provide opportunities for the children to learn the following:

- I am special because I am me. There is no one else like me.
- I am still discovering how to do new things.
- I can use my mind and my senses to accomplish many things.
- I can play and do things by myself or with friends and family.
- I can show emotions and say how I feel without hurting others.
- I can say no to things that will hurt me or others.

We will be talking about the following:

- feelings
- verbal expression
- nonverbal expression
- self-esteem
- self-motivation
- self-control

Things you can do at home with your preschool child include:

- Welcome "Happy" (the tennis ball puppet) when it comes home with your child. It will be in the box it "lives in," but Happy enjoys getting out sometimes. Happy should be included in family activities, such as going where your child goes and sleeping in the room with your child.
- Sing songs with your child, and record these on a tape recorder or video camera. This will give your family a special musical cassette or videotape.
- Make cookies or a cake with your child.
- Let your child help you repair things around the house.

Family participation opportunities at school will include:

- Help us make "I'm Special" vests.

    Date _____ Time _____

- Come visit the children's art gallery.
- Help us make silhouettes.

    Date _____ Time _____

Our wish list for this theme includes:

magazines and catalogs

posters of famous paintings

tennis balls

large paper sacks

heavy cardboard

Thanks!

Hip-Hop! (Finger Play Activity with Song)

(*Suitable for Ages Toddler to Three*)

Teacher: Let's tell a story together. Our hands can help.

First, make a fist, like this:

(*Teacher makes a fist and continues to model for the children all the actions that follow.*)

Now, hold up two fingers (*index and middle fingers*).

See, we have a bunny! These are his ears. (*Wiggle fingers.*)

Wiggle, wiggle, wiggle, it's Robby Rabbit! Can he hop? (*Make hopping motions.*)

Up and down, up and down—good!

Now, make another bunny with your other hand.

This is Reba Rabbit. Wiggle her ears—wiggle, wiggle, wiggle.

Now we have two bunnies. Can they both hop? Good!

Let them hop behind your back and hide.

Now we can begin our story.

Everyone sing softly: "Ta-dah!"

Children: Ta-dah!

Teacher: (*Bringing one hand forward with hopping motion.*)

Here comes Robby Rabbit—wiggle, wiggle, wiggle!

And here comes Reba Rabbit! (*Other hand*) Wiggle, wiggle, wiggle!

(*Bunnies face one another. When they speak, their ears wiggle. Reba's voice should be pitched higher than Robby's.*)

Teacher: Robby Rabbit says, "Hello!"

Reba: Hello Robby! How are you?

Robby: I'm fine.

(*Both bunnies gasp and begin to tremble.*)

Teacher: Now they're both so scared that they hop behind you and hide.

Do you want to see them again? Sing, "Ta-dah!"

(*Repeat the whole procedure through Robby's line, "I'm fine!" This time, only Reba begins to tremble.*)

Teacher: Reba is so scared, she hops behind you to hide again. But

Robby Rabbit is not scared. He sings this song:

(*Robby hops and sings.*)

Reproduced by permission of B. Wolf.

Song to Accompany HOP-HOP!*

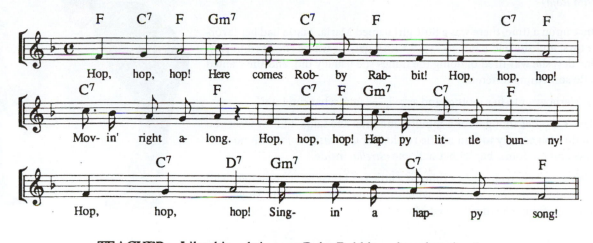

TEACHER: Like this -- bring out Reba Rabbit --- hop, hop, hop!

Now we have two bunnies again. Let them hop and sing together:

*Reproduced by permission of B. Wolf
Copyright B. Wolf - 1993

A Little Red House
(*Una Casita Roja*)

Once upon a time, there was a little girl named Maria. Maria had her favorite toys, and she had a big backyard with a garden where she liked to play. One day, she was tired of doing the things she usually did, and she wanted to do something different.

So, Maria went to her mother and asked, "Mamá, what can I do?"

Maria's mother thought for a minute, and then she said, "I know what you can do. You can try to find a little red house, *una casita roja*, with no windows and no doors, but with a star, *una estrella*, inside."

"Mamá, is there really such a thing as a little red house, *una casita roja*, with no windows and no doors, but with a star, *una estrella*, inside? How can I find something like that?" asked Maria.

"Yes, sí, Maria, there is," answered her mother, "and I know that you can find it, if you look."

Maria thought and thought about what her mother had said, but she didn't know where to find a house like that. So, she went to her big brother, Paco, and asked him, "Paco, do you know where I can find a little red house, *una casita roja*, with no windows and no doors, but with a star, *una estrella*, inside?"

"Maria," Paco said, "I have never heard of a little red house, *una casita roja*, with no windows and no doors, but with a star, *una estrella*, inside. I cannot help you. Why don't you go and ask Papá?"

So, she went to the back yard, where her father was working in the garden, and asked him, "Papá, do you know where I can find a little red house, *una casita roja*, with no windows and no doors, but with a star, *una estrella*, inside?"

Papá looked at Maria, and smiled, and said, "Our house is red, *roja*, but it has doors and windows, and I don't think there is a star, *una estrella*, inside. I'm afraid I can't help you, Maria."

Maria was getting a little tired of looking by now, so she sat down in her favorite back yard spot, under the apple tree, to rest and to think. Her cat, Chica, came and sat in her lap. Maria stroked Chica's soft fur and asked, "Chica, do you know where I can find a little red house, *una casita roja*, with no windows and no doors, but with a star, *una estrella*, inside?" Chica didn't answer. She just went on purring her soft purr.

Maria thought to herself, "I'm not having much luck. I might as well ask the wind." So she did. "Señor Wind, can you help me? I am looking for a little red house, *una casita roja*, with no windows and no doors, but with a star, *una estrella*, inside." Just then, the wind began to blow gently, and down from the tree fell a bright, shiny

red apple. Maria picked up the apple, and went to find her mother to tell her that she just could not find the little red house, *una casita roja*.

When Maria's mother saw her walking in the door with the apple, she said, "Maria, I see you found the little red house, *una casita roja*, with no windows and no doors, but with a star, *una estrella*, inside." Maria was puzzled, but followed her mother into the kitchen, where she took out a knife, and cut the apple in half, and . . .

There Was the Star! (*Una Estrella!*)*

(Cut the apple through the center perpendicular to the core.)

una—oo' na	casita—cas ee' ta	roja—ro' ha
estrella—ess tray' ya	señor—seen yore'	Sí—see

By Janet Galantay
Reprinted with permission

CRUNCHY SALAD

Wash hands.

Wash 2 carrots, 1 stalk celery, and 2 apples.

Cut off ends of carrots, peel, then grate.

Put in large mixing bowl. Cut out apple cores.

Cut the apples and celery into small bite-size pieces

and add to the mixing bowl. Add 1/2 cup raisins.

Sprinkle with lemon juice and salt.

Stir in 1/2 cup yogurt or sour cream. Mix and eat!

Puppy Dog Story

Once there was a puppy dog, as nice as he could be.

He thought he'd like a little playmate, just for company.

One day he saw a kitty who was playing in a tree.

He called to her, "Sweet kitty cat! Will you come play with me?"

And the puppy dog said, "Bow-wow!"

And the kitty cat said, "Meow!"

Then the puppy dog said, "Let's play!"

But the kitty cat said, "Go 'way!"

Then the puppy saw the kitty was afraid of him.

She thought that he would bite her,

So she climbed out on a limb!

But then the puppy told her he was gentle, good and kind;

He'd be the nicest playmate anyone could ever find.

And the puppy dog said, "Bow-wow!"

And the kitty cat said, "Meow!"

Then the puppy dot said, "Let's play"

And the kitty cat said, "Okay!"

The pup was very gentle, and the kitty wasn't rough'

And all the time they played

They never got into a huff!

Now the puppy and the kitty are the best of friends.

They play together every day,

And so our story ends.

With the puppy who says, "Bow-wow!"

And the kitty who says, "Meow!"

When the puppy dog says, "Let's play!"

Then the kitty cat says, "Okay!

Song to Accompany Puppy Dog Story*

Windshield Wipers

(Activity Song)

(Suitable for Two- to- Five-Year Olds Entertainingly Presents Concepts of Big/Little, Loud/Soft)

If children are old enough to understand, lead a short discussion about windshield wipers—when they are used and why. Then introduce the song and proceed to the following three activities:

Part 1: With children seated, explain that first we are going to be the windshield wipers on a small car: therefore, we will use our small, soft voices to sing. As the song is sung, children use up-raised index fingers and move hands in rhythm to simulate small windshield wipers.

Part 2: Explain that next we will be windshield wipers on a larger vehicle, such as a big car or perhaps even a pickup truck. We will use medium voices for this, and we will make the windshield wipers by extending arms in front of us, bent at the elbows, with hands and fingers stretching up. Forearms, hands and fingers then act as a unit to imitate wiper motions as song is sung. Children may perform this part of the activity either seated or standing.

Part 3: Now we are going to be windshield wipers on a *really* big vehicle, such as a bus. Children may wish to contribute their own examples of huge vehicles—fire trucks, eighteen wheelers, etc. We will become the largest windshield wipers we can be by standing, extending arms up as high as we can, and using our bodies from the waist up to simulate the wipers in motion. We will sing the song with our *very* loud voices.

Song to Accompany Windshield Wipers*

Wind- shield wi- pers, wind-shield wi- pers, in! Out! In! Out!

Wind-shield wi- pers, wind- shield wi- pers, wi- ping off the rain.

Rain- drops fall- ing, rain- drops fall- ing down!

Humpty Dumpty

(*Finger Play Activity with Song*)

(Suitable for Toddlers and Three-Year Olds)

Before attempting this activity, read or recite the rhyme to the children on several occasions so they become thoroughly familiar with it. If possible, find a colorful illustration to stimulate their interest. The teacher asks the children questions while pointing to various features of the illustration:

Teacher: Who is this?

Children: Humpty Dumpty!

Teacher: What is Humpty Dumpty sitting on?

Children: The wall!

(If children are too young to answer, teacher supplies the answers.)

Teacher guides the children in identifying articles of clothing worn by Humpty Dumpty, points out the horses and soldiers and anything else of visual interest. If children are old enough to understand, some discussion may take place about the fact that Humpty Dumpty is an egg and eggs can break. Children are prepared for the activity when they appear well acquainted with the rhyme.

Teacher: Now we're going to tell the story of Humpty Dumpty with our hands.

First, make a wall, like this: *(Teacher holds forearm as though looking at a Wristwatch.)*

Now, make a fist with your other hand. This is Humpty Dumpty! Set him down on the wall. Is he happy there? Let him sway back and forth.

(Sway fist as though rocking back and forth on forearm.)

Teacher: Now everyone sing (or say):

Humpty Dumpty sat on a wall

Humpty Dumpty had a great fall—Boom!

(Bend wrist down so that Humpty Dumpty drops off wall. Establish a rhythm by beating hands on thighs to simulate horses galloping. Sing or chant the next lines to this rhythm:)

All the king's horses and all the king's men

Couldn't put Humpty together again—

Couldn't put Humpty together again!

Why? *(Extend hands outward in a large shrug.)*

(During the next phrase extended hands slowly rise to meet over head, simulating an egg shape. Fingers meet on the word egg.)

Because he was an egg!

(This activity provides a good opportunity to point out that an egg is oval shaped and to practice shaping ovals using fingers, hands, and arms.)

Review the nursery rhyme. Conduct a group discussion based on the fact that, once broken, an egg can never be put together again. Many children will have their own experiences to relate regarding this subject.

Announce that we are about to dramatize Humpty Dumpty. Explain that the word *dramatize* means to act out.

Guide the children in "falling" safely from a seated position to a lying down position on the floor. For this practice, children should already be seated on the floor so there is little distance to fall. Explain that this is a fake fall, that we are acting, and that everyone must fall softly so as not to be hurt. Allow a short time for fake fall practice (two or three falls should do it). Then guide children in pretending to be soldiers or king's men on horseback. Let them pretend to hold reins and gallop about for a short time then announce that everyone seems ready to dramatize the story.

Divide the class into two groups. Group 1 consists of Humpty Dumptys, and group 2 of king's men. Instruct the king's men to wait quietly in a designated area until they hear their cue, which is the galloping rhythm the teacher will clap at the appropriate time. Instruct the Humpty Dumptys to sit on their wall, which can be a line on the floor. When everyone is ready, start the Humpty Dumptys swaying back and forth as all sing or say the first two lines of the rhyme. On "had a great fall," all Humpty Dumptys fake fall on the floor And lie still. The teacher then claps the gallop rhythm. All the king's men then gallop over to the fallen Humpty Dumptys, dismount, and pat them gently, trying to put them together. On "Why?" the Humpty Dumptys sit up and all the children shrug with hands out. On "Because he was an egg," all slowly form an oval shape with arms above heads, fingers meeting on the word egg.

Repeat the dramatization, with group 1 switching roles with group 2.

Humpty Dumpty Song*

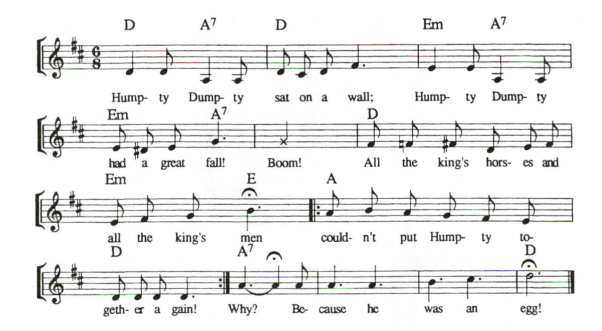

The Doughnut Shop

(Dramatic Play for Four- and Five-Year Olds): Entertainingly Illustrates the Concept of Subtraction)

This activity requires the following cast:

1. A group of children who act as doughnuts.
2. A group of children who each purchase a doughnut.
3. A cashier or shopkeeper.

Begin by selecting the shopkeeper. The teacher can fill that role herself, delegate the role to a child or select the shopkeeper in some impartial way.

The children who act as doughnuts are seated in a row, on chairs or on the floor in a designated area. The purchasers, each equipped with an imaginary or simulated coin, sit or stand on a different area. The shopkeeper sits near the doughnuts and operates an imaginary cash register.

The song is sung as many times as there are doughnuts lined up. Each time it is sung, a different child is named from the group of purchasers. That child walks over to the "shop," pays the shopkeeper, and selects a doughnut to take "home" (back to the purchaser area). Between each repetition of the song the teacher asks, "Now, how many doughnuts are left in the shop?"

After the last doughnut has been purchased, children usually wish to repeat the activity, with the groups switching roles.

Reproduced by permission of B. Wolf

The Doughnut Song*

Ten do- nuts in the Do- nut Shop, big and round, with

sug-ar on the top! A- long came Mike with a quart- er one day, (Bet-ty)

bought a do- nut and took it a- way. Do- nuts! ———

Do- nuts! ——— Do- nuts ——— for sale to- day!

Spring Showers

The sunlight is shining down through the trees.

The flowers stir and sway in the breeze.

Then here come the clouds—crowds of clouds—
Hurrying, scurrying, covering the sun.

The lightening flashed!

The thunder crashes!!

The flowers are happy, for now the rain has begun.

Listen!

Raindrops falling, Raindrops falling,

Rain falls with a lovely sound.

Rain is very fine, I think!

Rain falls on the thirsty ground, giving all the plants
a drink.

Raindrops falling, Raindrops falling, down

And now the clouds all blow away—

Leaving a bright, sunshiny day.

And all the flowers faces glow;

And all the plants begin to grow,

s-t-r-e-t-c-h-i-n-g...r-e-a-c-h-i-n-g...

up...so...high...

to...touch...the...sky!

t-r-y-i-n-g,...t-r-y-i-n-g...

Now rainbows are sparkling over the trees

The flowers stir and sway in the breeze.

"What a Splash!"

If all the lakes were one lake,

What a great lake that would be!

And if all the oceans were one ocean,

What a great sea that would be!

And if all the people were one person,
What a great person that would be!
And if the great person took a great jump
And jumped as high as could be,
And jumped into the great ocean
What a great splash that would be!

Looking at the World

When I wake up
What do I do?
I open my eyes
Just like you.

When I get up
What do I see?
I see my bedroom.
It's all around me.

I go to the window
And look outside.
I see the world
So big and wide.

It's filled with wonderful
Things to see.
Like the sun and flowers,
Like grass and trees.

Like cars on the street,
Like clouds in the sky.
I love to watch

The world with my eyes.

One (one) one two (one two) one two three (one two three)

one two three four (one two three four) one two three four five

(one two three four five) It's good to be a - live! Six (six)

six se-ven (six se-ven) six se-ven eight (six se-ven eight) six se-ven eight nine

(six se-ven eight nine) six se-ven eight nine ten (six se-ven eight nine

ten Let's do it a - again We did it a - gain.

Counting Is Fun

Words and Music by Jo Eklof

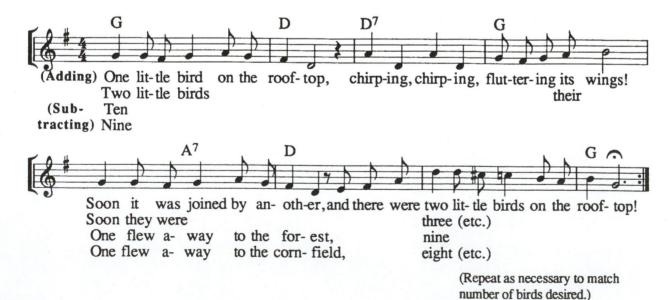

(Adding) One lit-tle bird on the roof-top, chirp-ing, chirp-ing, flut-ter-ing its wings!
Two lit-tle birds their
(Sub- Ten
tracting) Nine

Soon it was joined by an - oth-er, and there were two lit-tle birds on the roof-top!
Soon they were three (etc.)
One flew a- way to the for-est, nine
One flew a- way to the corn-field, eight (etc.)

(Repeat as necessary to match
number of birds desired.)

Birds on the Rooftop
Words and Music by B. Wolf

Seeds

The little seeds are sleeping under their blanket made of earth.

They dream until the rainclouds cover the sky;

then all the little seeds begin to sigh,

"We are thirsty! We're thirsty!

We need some rain to drink!"

And now there are raindrops falling, raindrops falling,

And all the little seeds are busy drinking up all the

raindrops falling, raindrops falling, and soon——

the little seeds begin to grow——

slowly...slowly–.–.–.

and some turn into flowers–.–.–.–.

and others turn into trees,

and many turn into good things to eat!

And all of them are beautiful;

They're very beautiful, reaching up so high

As they try to touch the sky!

Let's Handle Our World with Care
Words and Music by Jo Eklof

Let's han-dle our world with care. Our world is meant to
share. It's home to me. It's home to you. It's home to ev - 'ry -
bo-dy, too. What do we need to do? Let's han-dle our world with care.

I'm So Glad That You Live in the World with Me

Words and Music by Jo Eklof

What a Lucky Day
Words and Music by Jo Eklof

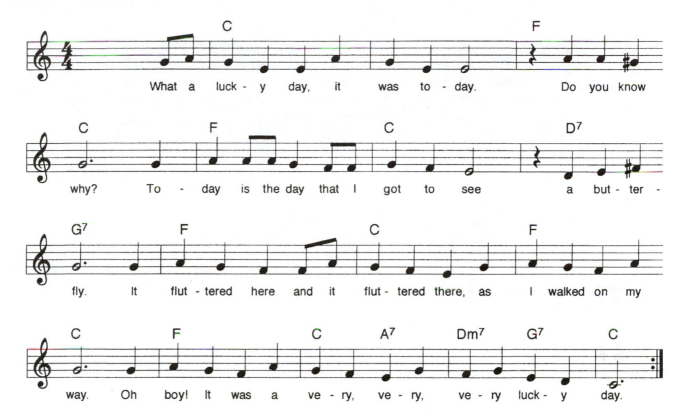

Additional verses

What a lucky day it was for me. Do you know that? Today is the day that I got to see a cat.
It meow-meowed here and it meow-meowed there as I went on my way.
Oh boy, it was a very very very lucky day.

What a lucky day it was for me.   Please take my word. Today is the day that I got to see a bird.
It flapp-flapped here and it flap-flapped there as I went on my way.
Oh boy, it was a very very very lucky day.

What a lucky day it was for me. Make no mistake. Today is the day that I got to see a snake.
It wiggled here and it wiggled there as I went on my way.
Oh boy, it was a very very very lucky day.

Everyday is lucky. The world is a beautiful place. It's full of wonderful things that put smiles on my face.
I look and learn and listen and then go on my way.
Everyday is a very very very lucky day.

Smiles and Hugs and I Love You's
Words and Music by Jo Eklof

Smiles and hugs and I love you's, we need them eve-ry day. And the won-der-ful thing a-bout life is, we get back what we give a-way. Yes, we get back what we give a-way.

I'm a Special Person and So Are You
Words and Music by Jo Eklof

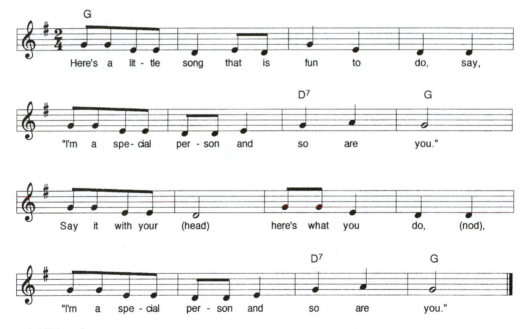

Here's a lit-tle song that is fun to do, say, "I'm a spe-cial per-son and so are you." Say it with your (head) here's what you do, (nod), "I'm a spe-cial per-son and so are you."

Additional verses:

Eyes - blink..........
Tongue - click..........
Shoulders - hunch..........
Arms - flap..........
Hips - sway..........
Feet - jump..........
Now sit down - bump..........
Hands - clap..........
Now let's whisper - say (whisper)..........

Walking Trip Permission Form

I give my permission for my child _____ (child's name) to take part in any walking field trip around the neighborhood immediately surrounding _____ (center or school name). This permission is valid for the entire year_____ (year date).

(Signature of parent or guardian)

(Date)

❯❯ Professional Resource Download

Field Trip Permission Form

Dear Parent,

We will be going on a field trip to _____ (name of site) on _____ (day-date-time-return time). We will travel by _____ (mode of transportation).

If you give permission for your child to go on this field trip, please sign this form in the space provided below.

(Child's name)

(Signature of parent or guardian)

(Date)

Cost (if any) to be paid to the center (or school) by (date) in the amount of (amount).

❯❯ Professional Resource Download

Name of Possible Site/Location

Address: _____

Phone: _____

Contact: _____

Days and hours open: _____

Length of tour or presentation: _____

What the tour or presentation consists of: _____

_____

Size of group permitted: _____

Ages of children: _____

Adult/child ratio required: _____

How early do reservations need to be made: _____

Special notes: _____

❯❯ **Professional Resource Download**

Teacher Checklist for Field Trip

1. Notification of field trip was posted in a prominent place for the parents to see at least 48 hours before the planned trip. Name, address, and phone number of where we are going was clearly stated. Name of contact person was listed. Times of departure and return were clearly stated.

   Yes ___ No ___

2. Field trip permission forms, specifically for this trip, have been signed by each child's parent or guardian. These permission forms are on file in the director's or administrator's office.

   Yes ___ No ___

3. Only adults, 18 years of age or older, are counted as part of the child-adult ratio. Requirements have been met for the number of adults to accompany the children, including the teachers.

   Yes ___ No ___

4. The medical emergency consent form signed by the parent or guardian for each child is being taken on the field trip, as well as the emergency phone numbers for each child's family and a written list of children in the group taking the field trip. This information should be put in the vehicle transporting the child.

   Yes ___ No ___

5. An emergency first-aid kit is in each vehicle going on the trip.

   Yes ___ No ___

Teacher Checklist for Field Trip (continued)

6. There is an adult trained in first aid and another adult trained in CPR going on the field trip.

Yes ___ No ___

7. Arrangements for lunch or snack have been made. They are the following:

8. The driver(s) of the bus (van or cars) is/are:

_____

The driver's license number of each is: _____

The license plate number of each vehicle is: _____

9. Names of adults going on trip:

10. Names of children going on trip:

11. Departure time: _____ Return time: _____

12. Additional information:

❯❯ **Professional Resource Download**

Activity Plan Worksheet Template

Date of activity: _____

Children's age group: _____

Number of children in this group: _____ large group _____ small group

or individual activity: _____

Learning center to be used: _____

NAME OF ACTIVITY AND BRIEF DESCRIPTION

PURPOSE/OBJECTIVES OF ACTIVITY

CHILD OUTCOMES FOR ACTIVITY
(Concepts, skills, awareness, or attitudes you have designed the activity to teach or develop. Describe in measurable objectives. These should align with your state curriculum standards.)

(continued)

Activity Plan Worksheet Template (continued)

SPACE AND MATERIALS NEEDED

PROCEDURE
(Step-by-step description of the activity. Tips for getting started: describe what you will say or do to get the children interested in the activity, and let them know what they will be doing. Describe the activity in the sequential order you will use with the children. Where will this activity take place? Plan for ending the activity. How will you help the children make a smooth transition to the next activity?)

GUIDANCE
Establish necessary limits for behavior and boundaries of activity. Anticipate problems that may develop during this activity and consider ways to handle them.

ASSESSMENT AND FOLLOW-UP
Were child outcomes met? _____Yes _____ No

What was the children's response? What worked well? What didn't work? How could this activity be changed to make it more effective or more appropriate? List possible activities that would extend or give practice to the objectives of this activity.

❯❯ **Professional Resource Download**

The following online resources offer publications, educational and interactive materials, services, and other resources for teachers. They are listed in association with chapter content.

Internet Disclaimer

The author and Cengage Learning make every effort to ensure that all resources are accurate at the time of printing. However, because the fluid, time-sensitive nature of the Internet, Cengage Learning cannot guarantee that all URLs and website addresses will remain current for the duration of this edition.

- Activities Integrating Mathematics and Science (AIMS) Education Foundation
  http://www.aimsedu.org

- Aline D. Wolf's "Mommy, It's a Renoir" and four volumes of accompanying art postcards titled "Child-Size Masterpieces" at Parent Child Press (Click on Art Education)
  http://www.Montessoriservices.com

- American Academy of Pediatrics Committed to the attainment of optimal physical, mental, and social health and well-being for all infants, children, adolescents, and young adults; this website has current and helpful information for teachers and parents.
  http://www.aap.org

- American Dental Association Provides information on good dental health for children, parents, and teachers.
  ada.org

- American Foundation for the Blind
  http://www.afb.org

- American Montessori Society
  http://www.amshq.org

- Anti-Defamation League ADL Resources for Classroom and Community Search "Resources" in the website for anti-bias/multicultural curriculum materials for teacher resources and audiovisual materials. Many cities have a local office that also has these materials.
  http://www.adl.org

- Arbor Day and Earth Day—Arbor Day (Foundation's Nature Explore Program for teachers and children)
  natureexplore.org

- ArtsEdge (Supports the place of arts education at the center of the curriculum through the creative and appropriate uses of technology as part of The John F. Kennedy Center for the Performing Arts)
  http://www.artsedge.kennedy-center.org

- Association Montessori Internationale/USA
  http://www.montessori-ami.org

- Association of Children's Museums
  http://childrensmuseums.org

- Audubon Magazine National Audubon Society (Click on Education)
  http://www.audubon.org

- Bank Street Children's Book Committee (Founded more than 100 years ago to guide librarians, educators, and parents to the best books for children published each year; also publishes the best children's books of the year and books to read aloud for children of all ages)
  http://www.bankstreet.edu/bookcom

- Bank Street College of Education
  http://www.bankstreet.edu

- Center for Puppetry Arts (Information about the Center for Puppetry Arts Museum, featuring puppets from all over the world and their special "Create a Puppet" workshops)
  http://www.puppet.org

- Centers for Disease Control and Prevention—Childhood Obesity (Offers information for parents and teachers on obesity and multiple children's health issues)
  http://www.cdc.gov

- ChildCare Information Exchange (Professional magazine for early childhood administrators and teachers)
  http://www.ccie.com

- Children and Computers
  http://www.childrenandcomputers.com

- The Children's Book Council (CBC) (A nonprofit trade organization dedicated to encouraging literacy and the use and enjoyment of books; CBC is the official sponsor of *Young People's Poetry Week* and *Children's Book Week*)
  http://www.cbcbooks.org

- Children's Music Network (Connecting people who celebrate the positive power of music in children's lives by exchanging ideas, visions, and music)
http://www.cmnonline.org

- Children's Music Network
http://www.childrensmusic.org

- Common Sense Media
http://www.commonsensemedia.org

- Cooking with Kids (Hands-on nutrition and food education curriculum guide)
http://www.cookingwithkids.net

- Council for Exceptional Children (Offers comprehensive information and publications)
http://www.cec.sped.org

- Council for Professional Recognition, Child Development Associate (CDA)
http://www.cdacouncil.org

- Crayola (Explore this site—it's full of ideas and information for stimulating creativity)
http://www.crayola.com

- Cricket Magazine Group: *Babybug* for infants and toddlers; *Ladybug* for young children; *Spider* for beginning readers; *Cricket* for young people; *Ask* for young people
http://www.cricketmag.com

- Culturally and Linguistically Appropriate Services
http://www.clas.uiuc.edu

- Early Childhood Music and Movement Association
http://www.ecmma.org

- EPA—U.S. Environmental Protection Agency (Provides information and services on teaching about the environment, especially designed for classroom use)
http://epa.gov

- The Eric Carle Museum of Picture Book Art
http://www.picturebookart.org

- Especially for Parents
www2.ed.gov/parents

- Folkmanis Puppets (Offers many play and creative activities plus a wonderful collection of puppets to see or buy)
http://www.folkmanis.com

- Friends of the Environment Foundation—Earth Day Canada
http://www.ecokidsonline.com

- Get Ready to Read
http://www.getreadytoread.org

- Green Teacher
http://www.greenteacher.com

- Gryphon House Inc.
https://www.gryphonhouse.com

- Office of Head Start
www.acf.hhs.gov/programs/ohs

- Helping Your Child Learn Math (Site for parents—what to do to help your child achieve in math)
http://www.ed.gov/pubs/parents/Math/index.html

- HighScope
http://www.highscope.org

- Highlights for Children Magazine
http://www.highlights.com

- Individuals with Disabilities Education Act
idea.ed.gov

- Internet Public Library (Offers references, reading zone, books and authors, teacher and parent information, and activities on art, music, science, math, etc.; click on For Kids)
http://www.ipl.org

- Kathy Burks Theatre of Puppetry Art (Artist in residence at Dallas Children's Theater)
http://www.kathyburkspuppets.com

- The Kennedy Center Alliance for Art Education Network (Includes 46 state alliance organizations operating in partnership with the Kennedy Center. (Search "state alliance organizations" at the website.)
http://www.kennedy-center.org

- The Math Forum @ Drexel University (Provides resources, materials, activities, person-to-person interactions, and educational products and services that enrich and support teaching and learning)
http://mathforum.org

- M.U.S.I.C.
http://learningfromlyrics.org

- Music Together (Program for children, infant to kindergarten, and their adult primary caregivers)
http://www.musictogether.com
(Click on the videos; for example, preschool classes)

- Mister Rogers' Neighborhood (Information on training and curriculum materials)
http://pbs.org/Rogers

- National Association for Bilingual Education
http://www.nabe.org

- National Association for Family Child Care (NAFCC)
http://www.nafcc.org

- National Association for Gifted Children
http://www.nagc.org

- National Association of Music Education (MENC)
http://www.menc.org

- National Association for the Education of Young Children (NAEYC)
http://www.naeyc.org

- National Center for Families Learning
http://www.famlit.org

- National Child Care Information Center, U.S. Department of Health & Human Services Administration for Children & Families (A national resource information link to ensure that all children and families have access to high-quality comprehensive services)
http://icfi.com

- National Children's Literacy (Part of The Soho Center's National Children's Literacy Information Project)
http://www.child2000.org
(Click on "Yes," then click on "National Children's Literacy Website")

- National Council of Teachers of English (NCTE) (Click on ECE Assembly of NCTE)
http://www.ncte.org

- National Council of Teachers of Mathematics
http://www.nctm.org

- National Council for the Social Studies
http://www.socialstudies.org

- National Geographic Society (Source for materials about geography, environmental science, and global studies; in the Search box, type "for teachers")
http://www.nationalgeographic.com

- National Institute for Play (Emphasizes the importance of play)
http:/www.nifplay.org

- National Institute on Early Child Development and Education U.S. Department of Education
http://www.ed.gov

- National Library of Virtual Manipulatives
http://nlvm.usu.edu/en/nav/vlibrary.html

- National Program for Playground Safety (NPPS) University of Northern Iowa School for Health, Physical Education, and Leisure Services
http://www.playgroundsafety.org

- National Science Teachers Association (Information focused on you and your teaching environment)
http://www.nsta.org

- National Wildlife Federation (Offers several magazines and programs especially for young children) Some of these are:
  1. *Wild Animal Baby*—12 months to 3 years
  2. *Your Big Backyard*—ages 3 to 6
  3. *Ranger Rick Magazine*—ages 7 to 12
  (Explore schoolyard habitat, backyard wildlife habitat, and National Wildlife Week online)
  http://www.nwf.org

- Nature's Classroom (Environmental education programs)
http://www.naturesclassroom.org

- The Natural Child Project (Click on Global Children's Art Gallery under Art and view more than 1,000 works of children's art from more than 69 countries)
http://www.naturalchild.com

- Nutrition Explorations (This website is an excellent resource for children, educators, parents, and school food service personnel)
http://www.nutritionexplorations.com

- PBS Teachers (Classroom resources for all ages and professional development online)
http://www.pbs.org/teachers

- PE Central (Website for health and physical education teachers, parents, and students—their goal is to provide the latest information about developmentally appropriate physical education programs for children and youth; click on Preschool Physical Education)
http://www.pecentral.org

- Project Approach (Katz & Chard) (Provides resources for project-based learning with young children)
http://www.projectapproach.org

- The Puppet Museum (The Olde World Puppet Theatre, Ping Pong's Puppet Workshop, and puppet website provide links around the world, and many other places.)
http://www.puppetmuseum.com

- The Puppeteers of America, Inc.
http://www.puppeteers.org

- The Puppetry Home Page (A free resource for the puppetry community and dedicated to helping people connect to the world of puppetry)
http://www.sagecraft.com/puppetry

- Reading Is Fundamental
http://www.rif.org

- Reading Rockets
http://www.readingrockets.org

- Redleaf Press (Resources for early childhood professionals)
http://www.redleafpress.org

- North American Reggio Emilia Alliance (NAREA) provides information for educators.
http://www.reggioalliance.org

- Official website for Reggio Children with information in both English and Italian
http://www.reggiochildren.it

- Scholastic Early Childhood Today (Professional magazine for early childhood teachers at Scholastic Inc.)
http://www.scholastic.com

- School-Age Notes (National resource organization for school-age care)
http://www.extendednotes.com

- Sesame Street Workshop
http://www.ctw.org

- Smithsonian Institution
http://www.si.edu

  http://nationalzoo.si.edu (National Zoo from the Smithsonian)

- Society of Children's Book Writers and Illustrators (Helpful research links that offer literacy and literature websites for teachers and parents)
http://www.scbwi.org/links/research.htm

- Society for Research in Child Development
http://www.srcd.org

- Space Day (Generally held in May and designed to advance science, mathematics, and technology education)
http://www.nationaldaycalendar.com/national -space-day-first-friday-in-may/
(Try the Space Puzzlers. Click on Games. The children will enjoy this site.)

- Stone Soup
http://www.stonesoup.com

- Teaching Tolerance (Project of the Southern Poverty Law Center) (A principal online destination for people interested in dismantling bigotry and creating communities that value diversity; helpful site for teachers who want to implement anti-bias practices in their classrooms)
http://www.tolerance.org

- U.S. Committee for UNICEF (United Nations Children's Fund to receive their catalog of cards and gifts, type "catalog of cards and gifts" in the Search box, then click on the "Order a Catalog" link, and then enter your information)
http://www.unicefusa.org

- USDA Forest Service (Under Forest Service Home, click on Just for Kids)
http://www.fs.fed.us

- WebMATH (Resource site for children, teachers, and parents—helps children with math problems they are working on right now; teachers can create a math test online)
http://www.webmath.com

- Weekly Reader
http://www.weeklyreader.com

- West Music
http://www.westmusic.com

- Wolf Trap Institute for Early Learning Through the Arts (Offers workshops for teachers, parents, and administrators to introduce performing arts activities that will help early childhood educators teach a variety of physical, cognitive, social, and emotional skills to preschool children; these staff development workshops stress the importance of children creating their own stories, songs, and dances, and include material that is appropriate for children with special needs)
http://www.wolf-trap.org

- Zero to Three
http://www.zerotothree.org

Standards for NAEYC, DAP, InTASC, and Head Start are found inside the front and back covers. Standards listed in Appendix F are other standards that are less commonly used throughout the book.

Chapter 1 Starting the Process

DEC CEC DEC

C12 Practices are individualized for each child based on: (a) the child's current behavior and abilities across relevant domains instead of the child's diagnostic classification; (b) the family's views of what the child needs to learn, (c) interventionists' and specialists' views of what the child needs to learn; and (d) the demands, expectations, and requirements of the child's current environments. The practices as well as goals are individualized.

C14 Data-based decisions are used to make modifications in the practices. Child performance is monitored and data collected to determine the impact of the practices on the child's progress, and monitoring must be useful within the child's environments.

C15 Recommended practices are used to teach/promote whatever skills are necessary for children to function more completely, competently, adaptively, and independently in the child's natural environment. These skills should include teaching those that maximize participation and membership in home, school, and community environments—including those that are typical or similar to other persons' in the environment.

Chapter 2 Observation and Assessment

DEC CEC DEC

C12 Practices are individualized for each child based on: (a) the child's current behavior and abilities across relevant domains instead of the child's diagnostic classification; (b) the family's views of what the child needs to learn; (c) interventionists' and specialists' views of what the child needs to learn; and (d) the demands, expectations, and requirements of the child's current environments. The practices as well as goals are individualized.

C14 Data-based decisions are used to make modifications in the practices. Child performance is monitored and data collected to determine the impact of the practices on the child's progress, and monitoring must be useful within the child's environments.

C19 Planning occurs prior to implementation and that planning considers the situation to which the interventions will be applied.

Chapter 3 Creating Curriculum

DEC CEC DEC

C15 Recommended practices are used to teach/promote whatever skills are necessary for children to function more completely, competently, adaptively, and independently in the child's natural environment. These skills should include teaching those that maximize participation and membership in home, school, and community environments—including those that are typical or similar to other persons in the environment.

C22 Systematic naturalistic teaching procedures such as models, expansions, incidental teaching, mand-modeling procedure, and naturalistic time delay are used to promote acquisition and use of communication and social skills.

Chapter 4 The Learning Environment

DEC CEC DEC

C1 Physical space and materials are structured and adapted to promote engagement, play, interaction, and learning by attending to children's preferences and interests, using novelty, using responsive toys, providing adequate amounts of materials, and using defined spaces.

C5 Environments are designed and activities are conducted so that children learn or are exposed to multiple cultures and languages by, among other practices, allowing children and families to share their cultures and languages with others, to the extent that they desire.

C6 Learning environments meet accepted standards of quality, including curriculum, child-staff ratios, group size, and physical design of classroom.

C8 A variety of appropriate settings and naturally occurring activities are used to facilitate children's learning and development.

Chapter 5 Language and Literacy

ILA

1. Students read a wide range of print and nonprint texts to build an understanding of texts, of themselves, and of the cultures of the United States and the world; to acquire new information; to respond to the needs and demands of society and the workplace; and for personal fulfillment.
2. Students read a wide range of literature from many periods in many genres to build an understanding of the many dimensions (e.g., philosophical, ethical, aesthetic) of human experience.
3. Students apply a wide range of strategies to comprehend, interpret, evaluate, and appreciate texts.
4. Students adjust their use of spoken, written, and visual language (e.g., conventions, style). Students employ a wide range of strategies as they write and use different writing process elements appropriately to communicate with different audiences for a variety of purposes.
5. Students apply knowledge of language structure, language conventions (e.g., spelling and punctuation), media techniques, figurative language, and genre to create, critique, and discuss print and nonprint texts.
6. Students use spoken, written, and visual language to accomplish their own purposes (e.g., for learning, enjoyment, persuasion, and the exchange of information).

CC English Language Arts Standards CCSS

Reading: Key Ideas and Details, Craft and Structure, Integration of Knowledge and Ideas, Range of Reading and Level of Text Complexity, Print Concepts. Phonological Awareness, Phonics and Word Recognition, Fluency

Writing: Text Types and Purposes, Production and Distribution of Writing, Research to Build and Present Knowledge Listening/Speaking: Comprehension and Collaboration

Language: Conventions of Standard English, Knowledge of Language, Vocabulary Acquisition and Use

Chapter 6 Creativity: Art and Music

NVAS

1. Content Standard: Understanding and applying media, techniques, and processes.
2. Content Standard: Using knowledge of structures and functions.

3. Content Standard: Choosing and evaluating a range of subject matter, symbols, and ideas.
4. Content Standard: Making connections between visual arts and other disciplines.

NSME

1. Singing, alone and with others, a varied repertoire of music.
2. Performing on instruments, alone and with others, a varied repertoire of music.
3. Improvising melodies, variations, and accompaniments.
4. Listening to, analyzing, and describing music.
5. Evaluating music and music performances.
6. Understanding relationships between music, the other arts, and disciplines outside the arts.

Chapter 7 The Child's World: Social Studies and Dramatic Play

NCSS

Social Studies Standards Themes

1. Culture
2. Time, Continuity, and Change
3. People, Places, and Environments
4. Individual Development and Identity

DEC

C4 Play routines are structured to promote interaction, communication, and learning by defining roles for dramatic play, prompting engagement, prompting group friendship activities and using specialized props.

C5 Environments are designed and activities are conducted so that children learn or are exposed to multiple cultures and languages by, among other practices, allowing children and families to share their cultures and languages with others, to the extent that they desire.

Chapter 8 Sensory Play

No additional standards.

Chapter 9 Science

NSES

Standards will be added when updated.

Chapter 10 Math

No additional standards.

Chapter 11 Fine Motor and Manipulatives

NCTM

Number and Operations

Algebra
Geometry
Measurement
Data Analysis and Probability
Problem Solving
Reasoning and Proof
Communications
CC Standards for Mathematical Practice
Counting & Cardinality
Operations & Algebraic Thinking
Number & Operations in Base Ten
Measurement & Data
Geometry

Chapter 12 Large Motor and Outdoor Play

No additional standards.

Chapter 13 Construction: Blocks and Woodworking

No additional standards.

Chapter 14 Putting It All Together: Evaluation and Documentation

No additional standards.

Common Core State Standards Initiative

www.corestandards.org

States that have not adopted or have dropped the Common Core State Standards Initiatives:

Alaska - www.asdk12.org/commoncore/
Indiana –https://learningconnection.doe.in.gov
      /Standards/About.aspx?art=/11
Minnesota –http://education.state.mn.us/MDE
      /EdExc/StanCurri/K-12AcademicStandards/
Nebraska –https://www.education.ne.gov
      /academicstandards/SIT_Intro.html
Oklahoma – sde.ok.gov/sde
      /Oklahoma-academic-standards
Puerto Rico – www.de.gobierno.pr/files/estandares
      /Estandares_de_ingles_2014.pdf
South Carolina – ed.sc.gov/instruction
      /standards-learning/
Texas – tea.texas.gov/index2.aspx?id=6148
Virginia – www.doe.virginia.gov/testing
      /common_core/

A

Associate Degree Early Childhood Teacher Educators (ACCESS), membership association to share knowledge and practice for early childhood educators
http://www.accessece.org

Alliance for Childhood, publishes multiple reports and policy briefs
PO Box 20973
Park West P.O.
New York, NY 10025
http://www.allianceforchildhood.org

National Association for Early Childhood Teacher Educators (NAECTE), publishes *Journal of Early Childhood Teacher Education*
http://www.naecte.org

American Academy of Pediatrics, publishes information for parents and teachers on children's health issues
141 Northwest Point Blvd.
Elk Grove Village, IL 60007

American Library Association (ALA), publishes American Libraries Booklist
50 E. Huron Street
Chicago, IL 60611
http://www.ala.org

American Speech-Language-Hearing Association, offers online ASHA Leader newspaper
2200 Research Blvd.
Rockville, MD 20850
http://www.asha.org

Association for Childhood Education International (ACEI), publishes *Childhood Education* and *Journal of Research in Childhood Education*
1200 18th Street NW, Suite 700
Washington, DC 20036
http://www.acei.org

Association for Supervision and Curriculum Development (ASCD), publishes *Educational Leadership* and *Journal of Curriculum and Supervision*
1703 N. Beauregard Street
Alexandria, VA 22311
http://www.ascd.org

C

Canadian Association for Young Children (CAYC), publishes *Canadian Children*
http://www.cayc.ca

Children's Defense Fund, publishes *The State of America's Children*
25 E Street NW
Washington, DC 20001
http://www.childrensdefense.org

Council for Professional Recognition (CDA), publishes Council Newsletter and CDA Assessment and materials, training materials, and general early childhood resources
2460 16th Street NW
Washington, DC 20009
http://www.cdacouncil.org

Council for Environmental Education (CEE), publishes materials and provides programs, services, and training for conservation and environmental issues
5555 Morningside, Suite 212
Houston, TX 77005
http://www.councilforee.org

Council for Exceptional Children (CEC), publishes *Exceptional Children's Journal* and *Teaching Children*
2900 Crystal Drive, Suite 1000
Arlington, VA 22202
http://www.cec.sped.org

E

Early Childhood Music and Movement Association (ECMMA), publishes the journal *Perspectives*
805 Mill Avenue
Snohomish, WA 98290
http://www.ecmma.org

F

Families and Work Institute, publishes research and other materials

245 Fifth Avenue, Suite 1002
New York, NY 10016
http://www.familiesandwork.org

I

International Literacy Association, publishes
Reading Today, The Reading Teacher, and *Reading
Research Quarterly* online
800 Barksdale Road
Box 8139
Newark, DE 19714
http://www.reading.org

L

Learning Disabilities Association of America, publishes
Learning Disabilities Journal
4156 Library Road
Pittsburgh, PA 15234
http://www.ldanatl.org

N

National Art Education Association (NAEA),
publishes NAEA Newsletter and *Art Education*,
a quarterly journal
901 Prince Street
Alexandria, VA 22314
https://www.arteducators.org
National Association for Bilingual Education (NABE),
publishes *NABE News Magazine* and *Bilingual
Research Journal*
11006 Veirs Mills Road, L-1
Wheaton, MD 20902
http://www.nabe.org
National Association of Early Childhood Teacher Educators,
publishes *Journal of Early Childhood Teacher Education*
http://www.naecte.org
National Association for the Education of Young
Children (NAEYC), publishes *Young Children*
and *Teaching Young Children*
1313 L Street NW, Suite 500
Washington, DC 20005
http://www.naeyc.org
National Association for Family Child Care (NAFCC),
publishes NAFCC accreditation materials
1743 W. Alexander Street
Salt Lake City, UT 84119
https://www.nafcc.org
National Association for Gifted Children (NAGC),
publishes *Gifted Children Quarterly*
1331 H Street, Suite 1001

Washington, DC 20005
http://www.nagc.org
National Association of Community College Teacher
Education Programs (NACCTEP), supports
community colleges in their efforts to provide quality
teacher education programs
2323 W. 14th Street
Tempe, AZ 85281
http://nacctep.riosalado.edu/new/home.html
National Association of Music Education, publishes
Music Educators Journal, Teaching Music,
and *General Music Today* online
1806 Robert Fulton Drive
Reston, VA 20191
http://www.nafme.org
National Black Child Development Institute (NBCDI),
publishes Child Health Talk
1313 L Street NW, Suite 110
Washington, DC 20005
http://www.nbcdi.org
National Coalition for Campus Children's Centers
(NCCCC), educational membership organization
for campus child-care centers
2036 Larkhall Circle
Folsom, CA 95630
http://www.campuschildren.org
National Council for the Social Studies, publishes *Special
Education and the Young Learner*
8555 16th Street, Suite 500
Silver Spring, MD 20910
http://www.socialstudies.org
National Council of Teachers of Mathematics (NCTM),
publishes *Teaching Children Mathematics*
1906 Association Drive
Reston, VA 20191
http://www.nctm.org
National Head Start Association
1651 Prince Street
Alexandria, VA 22314
http://www.nhsa.org
National Institute for Literacy, publishes
resources on literacy
1775 1 Street NW, Suite 730
Washington, DC 20006
**https://www.federalregister.gov/agencies
/national-institute-for-literacy**
National Science Teachers Association (NSTA),
publishes science and children and e-newsletters
1840 Wilson Blvd.
Arlington, VA 22201
http://www.nsta.org

S

Save the Children
501 Kings Highway East, Suite 400
Fairfield, CT 06825
http://www.savethechildren.org

Southern Early Childhood Association (SECA),
publishes *Dimensions of Early Childhood*
1123 S. University Ave., Suite 255
Little Rock, AR 72204
http://www.SouthernEarlyChildhood.org

Stand for Children, publishes an e-newsletter, *Stand Update*
2121 SW Broadway #111
Portland, OR 97201
http://www.stand.org

Z

Zero to Three—National Center for Infants, Toddlers,
and Families, publishes *The Zero to Three Journal*
1255 23rd Street NW, Suite 350
Washington, DC 20037
http://www.zerotothree.org

A

accommodation: Piaget's theory of modification of existing cognitive information. Cognitive schemes are changed to accommodate new experiences or information.

aesthetic environment: An environment that cultivates an appreciation for beauty and a feeling of wonder and excitement of the world in which we live.

agility: Ability to move with speed, grace, and precision.

alphabet books: Simple stories based on the alphabet that present letter identification and one-object picture association.

anecdotal record: A brief, informal narrative account describing an incident of a child's behavior that is important to the observer. Also, a type of document that is used by teachers for keeping track of observation about their students.

anthropology: The study of the way people live, such as their beliefs and customs.

anti-bias: An attitude that actively challenges prejudice, stereotyping, and unfair treatment of an individual or group of individuals.

assessment: Refers to the collection of information for the purpose of making educational decisions about children or a groups of children or to evaluate a program's effectiveness.

assimilation: Piaget's process of cognitive development, which occurs when a child handles, sees, or otherwise experiences something.

associative play: An activity of a 3- or 4-year-old child playing with other children in a group; the child drops in and out of play with minimal organization of activity.

astronomy: The study of the universe beyond the Earth's atmosphere, such as sun, moon, planets, and stars.

B

beginning-to-read books: Predictable books that are easy to read and present words that are simple and repetitive.

bias: Any attitude, belief, or feeling that results in unfair treatment of an individual or group of individuals. Also a test, process, procedure, or use of the results that unfairly discriminates against one individual or group in favor or another.

big books: Oversized books that present extra-large text and illustrations.

bilateral coordination: Using both hands together to perform a task.

board books: First books for infants and toddlers made of laminated heavy cardboard.

bridging: Setting up two blocks, leaving space between them, and roofing that space with another block.

C

cardinality: The number of elements in a given mathematical set. In other words, the total number or quantity of objects counted.

case study: A way of collecting and organizing all of the information gathered from various sources to provide insights into the behavior of the child studied.

checklist: A record of direct observation that involves selecting from a previously prepared list the statement that best describes the behavior observed, the conditions present, or the equipment, supplies, and materials available.

chemistry: The science dealing with the composition and transformations of substances.

child outcomes: What happens as a result of services provided to children and that are measured by the attainment of different child development milestones or skills.

classification: Grouping of blocks or other objects together based on common characteristics.

classifying and sorting: Grouping objects by a common characteristic, such as size, shape, or color.

cognitive development: The mental process that focuses on how children's intelligence, thinking abilities, and language acquisition emerge through distinct ages; Piaget's study of children's thinking, involving creating their own mental images of the world, based on encounters with the environment.

collage: An art activity that involves making a picture containing glued-on objects on paper.

concept books: Books that present themes, ideas, or concepts with specific examples. They also identify and clarify abstractions, such as color or shape, and help with vocabulary development.

concept development: The construction of knowledge through solving problems and experiencing the results, while being actively involved with the environment.

constructive play: Play that helps children understand their experiences. Involves planning or manipulation of objects or people to create a specific experience.

cooperative play: A type of play organized for some purpose by the 4-year-old and older child. It requires group membership and reflects a child's growing capacity to accept and respond to ideas and actions not originally his own.

counting books: Books that describe simple numeral and picture associations, and often tell a story. They show representations of numbers in more than one format and vary from simple to complex.

crayon resist: A type of art for older children that involves drawing a picture in light-colored crayons then covering the picture with watercolors or thin tempera paint. The paint will cover all but the crayon drawing.

crayon rubbings: Duplicating an object of texture by placing it under paper and rubbing over it with a crayon.

creativity: The process of doing, of bringing something new and imaginative into being.

culture: The sum total of a child's or family's ways of living: their values or beliefs, language, patterns of thinking, appearance, and behavior. These are passed or learned from one generation to the next.

curriculum: A multileveled process that encompasses what happens in an early education classroom each day, reflecting the philosophy, goals, and objectives of the early childhood program. Also, the planned interaction of children with instructional content, material, resources and processes for evaluating the attainment of educational objectives.

curriculum planning cycle: An ongoing process that links with child assessment.

curriculum web: A visual illustration or process that integrates various learning activities and curriculum areas.

D

development: Systematic and adaptive changes in the body and mind.

developmentally appropriate practice (DAP): The curriculum planning philosophy expressed by NAEYC defines and describes what is developmentally appropriate for young children in childhood programs serving children and families, birth through age eight.

dexterity: Used when referring motor skills of the hands and fingers.

dramatic play: A type of creative, spontaneous play in which children use their imaginations to create and dramatize pretend characters, actions, or events. (Also known as symbolic play.)

E

early mathematics: Refers to exposure to and interaction with materials that contribute to the acquisition of knowledge about the underlying concepts of mathematics.

Earth and space science: The study of Earth materials, objects in the sky, and changes in the Earth and sky.

ecology: The study of living things in relation to their environment and to each other.

economics: The study of the production, distribution, and consumption of goods and services.

egocentric: A stage when individuals think about the world only in relation to themselves.

emergent curriculum: A curriculum that emerges out of the interests and experiences of the children.

emergent literacy: A process of developing awareness about reading and writing before young children can read or write.

environment: All of the conditions and surroundings affecting the children and adults in an early childhood setting.

equilibrium: A balance of one's cognitive schemes and information gathered from the environment; assimilation and accommodation.

evaluation: The process of determining whether the philosophy, goals, and objectives of the early childhood program have been met.

event sampling or frequency count: Measures the number of times an event is observed.

eye–hand coordination: Focusing and coordinating eye movement and visual input to control and direct the hands. Also, the ability of vision to coordinate the information received through the eyes.

expressive language: Speaking.

F

fine motor skills: The coordination of small muscle movements that occur in body parts such as the fingers, usually in coordination with the eyes.

finger dexterity: The ability to move individual fingers in isolation.

flannel board: Used as a prop to tell or extend a story effectively.

flexibility: Ease and range of movement.

folk literature: Tales that come from the oral tradition of storytelling that appeal to the child's sense of fantasy.

format: The overall arrangement of the way a book is put together, such as size, shape, paper quality, colors, and content of each page.

formative evaluation: A method for judging the worth of a program or project while the program activities are forming or in progress.

functional play: Play that occurs when a child takes on a role and pretends to be someone else.

G

games with rules: Children's spontaneous physical and cognitive play that occurs during Piaget's concrete operations stage of development (7 years and older).

genre: Category used to classify literary works, usually by form, technique, or content.

geography: The study of the Earth's surface, resources, and the concepts of direction, location, and distance.

geology: The study of the Earth, such as rocks and shells.

geometry: The area of mathematics that involves shape, size, space, position, direction, and movement.

goals: The general overall aims or overview of an early childhood program that consider what children should know and be able to do developmentally across the disciplines.

H

hand puppets: Puppets that are put on the hand; come in many types and varieties and are easy for young children to make and manipulate.

history: The study of what has happened in the life of a country or people.

hollow blocks: Wooden blocks larger than unit blocks and opened on the sides.

I

inclusive curriculum: Underscores the importance of individual differences, special needs, and cultural and linguistic diversity among young children.

informational books: Books that offer nonfiction for emergent readers by providing accurate facts about people and subject matter.

inquiry: A questioning process that encourages curiosity and exploration. The opposite of rote learning.

integrated curriculum: Encourages young children to transfer knowledge and skills from one subject to another while using all aspects of their development.

intentional curriculum: Curriculum that incorporates explicit learning outcomes, strategic learning design, and meaningful assessment.

interaction books: Books used to stimulate imagination by using some device for involving young readers, such as pop-ups, fold-outs, scratch and sniff, pasting, puzzle pictures, humor, and riddles.

K

kinesthetics: The use of the body to learn about physical capabilities and to develop body awareness, and gain understanding of the world.

L

language: Human speech, the written symbols for speech, or any means of communicating.

language development: Developmental process of a predictable sequence that includes both sending and receiving information. It is related, but not tied, to chronological age.

learning: Change in behavior or cognition that occurs as children construct knowledge through active exploration and discovery in their physical social environments.

learning centers: Curriculum centers (sometimes called interest centers, zones, clusters, or activity centers) where materials and supplies are combined around special groupings and common activities.

lesson plan: An outgrowth of theme selection, brainstorming/webbing, and selection of projects and activities. Involves making a series of choices based on the developmental stages, learning styles, and interests of the children; the goals and objectives of the program; and the availability of materials, supplies, and resources.

life science: The study of living things, people, plants, and animals.

literacy: The ability to read and write, which gives one the command of a native language for the purpose of communicating.

literature: All the writings (prose and verse) of a people, country, or period, including those written especially for children.

locomotor movement: The ability to move the whole body from one place to another.

logico-mathematical knowledge: Includes relationships constructed in order to make sense out of the world and to organize information, such as counting and classification.

M

manipulative movement: Large (gross) motor movements demonstrated by pulling, lifting, throwing, or kicking an object.

marionettes: Puppets controlled by strings that offer an extra range of expression and full body movement.

measurement: Finding the length, height, and weight of an object using units like inches, feet, and pounds.

meteorology: The science of weather and atmosphere.

Mother Goose and nursery rhyme books: Books passed from generation to generation and known by children all over the world. These are often a child's first introduction to literature.

multicultural books: Books that develop awareness of and sensitivity to other cultures. They also help to increase positive attitudes toward similarities and differences in people.

multiple intelligences: Gardner's theory, which proposes that one form of intelligence is not better than another; all eight are equally valuable and viable.

N

nonlocomotor movement: Axle or body movement that occurs when the feet remain stationary (as in standing, kneeling, or sitting), while other parts of the body move.

number sense: A concept that develops over time as children think about, explore, and discuss mathematical ideas.

nutrition: Substances found in foods that provide for the growth, development, maintenance, and repair of the body.

O

obesity: An excess percentage of bodyweight due to fat, which puts people at risk for health problems.

objectives: The specific purposes or teaching techniques that interpret the goals of planning, schedules, and routines, as well as meaningful descriptions of what children are expected to learn. These objectives are designed to meet the physical, intellectual, social, emotional, and creative development of young children.

object permanence: A mature state of perceptual development. According to Piaget's theory, a baby thinks that objects, including people, cease to exist the moment he stops seeing them. An older child starts to search for the missing object or person.

objectivity: Obtaining and using facts, information or data without distortion by personal feelings, beliefs, or prejudgment.

observation: The process of observation is taking in information and objectively interpreting it for meaning.

one-to-one correspondence: The pairing of one object to another object or one group of objects to another group of equal number.

onlooker play: The play of young children introduced to new situations that focuses on an activity rather than the environment.

P

parallel play: Observable play in the older toddler and young 3-year-old that emphasizes being near another child while playing with an object rather than playing with a child.

pattern: A sequence of colors, objects, sounds, stories, or movements that repeats in the same order over and over again.

perceptual development: Type of development in which children use their senses to learn about the nature of objects, actions, and events.

phonemes: The smallest units of speech.

phonics: The relationship between the letters of the written language and the sounds of spoken language.

phonological or phonemic awareness: The ability to hear and identify individual sounds and spoken words.

physical development: Type of development involving children using large muscles, manipulating small muscles, developing eye–hand coordination, and acquiring self-help skills.

physical knowledge: Learning about objects in the environment and their characteristics, such as color, weight, and size.

physical sciences: The sciences (physics, chemistry, meteorology, and astronomy) that relate to nonliving materials.

picture books: Books written in a direct style that tell a simple story with illustrations complementing the text.

pincer grasp: Using the thumb and index finger to pick up an item.

play: A behavior that is self-motivated, freely chosen, process-oriented, and enjoyable.

poetry: A form of literature that contributes imaginative rhyme, rhythm, and sound.

portfolio: A collection of a child's work over time and a record of the child's process of learning.

portfolio assessment: A systematic collection of information about a child's ongoing development and the child's work, gathered by both the child and teacher over time from all available sources.

practice play or sensorimotor play: The stage in cognitive development during which the young child learns through repetitive sensory and motor play activities. During Piaget's sensorimotor stage (infancy to toddlers), infants explore the sensory qualities of objects and practice motor skills.

predictable books: Books that contain familiar and repetitive sequences.

prejudice: An attitude, opinion, or idea that is preconceived or decided, usually unfavorably.

process: A natural continuing action or series of actions or changes.

process skills: The abilities to process new information through concrete experiences.

project: An in-depth investigation of a topic.

prop box: A collection of actual items related to dramatic play activities that focuses on a specific theme or lesson plan.

psychology: The study of the mind, emotions, and behavioral processes.

psychosocial: Erikson's eight stages that describe the interaction between an individual's social-emotional condition and the interpersonal environment.

puppetry: The art of making or operating puppets or producing puppet shows.

Q

quantitative evaluation: An evaluation approach involving the use and analysis of numerical data and measurement.

qualitative evaluation: An evaluation typically conducted through interviews, observation, focus groups, portfolios, and journals to determine the quality of the program.

questionnaire: The least expensive procedure for external evaluations and can be used to collect large samples of information.

R

rating scale: A record of direct observation that involves selecting from a previously prepared list the statement that best describes the behavior observed and the conditions present.

rational counting: Requires matching each numeral name, in order, to an object in a group.

realistic literature: A form of literature that helps children cope with common, actual experiences by offering positive solutions and insights.

rebus chart: Visual pictures, such as signs, illustrations, and directions, to help children make sense of any activity.

receptive language: Listening and understanding.

reference books: Books that emphasize individualized learning through special topic books, picture dictionaries, and encyclopedias.

reflective log or diary: A teacher or administrator's record of the most significant happenings, usually made at the end of the day or during an uninterrupted block of time.

reliability: The extent to which an evaluation technique yields results that are accurate and consistent over time.

representation: Occurs in block building with the naming of block constructions and the combination of all elements of block building.

rhyming: The ability to auditorily distinguish two words that end the same way.

rote counting: The ability to recite names of numerals in order.

routines: The events that fit into the daily time frame of an early childhood program.

rubric: Chart that identifies different levels and qualities of attainment of each benchmark or standard.

S

scaffolding: The adjustable support the teacher offers in response to the child's level of performance.

schedule: The basic daily timeline of an early childhood program.

schema: An integrated way of thinking or of forming mental images.

science as inquiry: Offers frequent opportunities to question, investigate, clarify, predict, and communicate with others.

science in personal and social perspectives: A developing understanding of personal health, changes in environments, and ways to conserve and recycle.

science and technology: The focus on establishing connections between natural and manmade items.

self-help skills: In early childhood, a child's ability to care for himself, such as dressing, feeding, and toileting.

self-regulation: A child's natural ability to exercise control over physical and emotional behavior in the face of changing circumstances.

sensory awareness: The use of the senses.

sensory experiences: Experiences that use the senses and offer opportunities for free exploration in a variety of curriculum areas.

sensory processing: The way the nervous system receives messages from the senses and turns them into appropriate motor and behavioral responses.

sensory processing disorder: Condition that exists when sensory signals don't get organized into appropriate responses.

seriation: Seriation or ordering of objects is based on the ability to place them in logical sequence, such as smallest to largest or shortest to tallest.

series books: Books written for primary-grade children and built around a single character or group of characters.

shadow puppets: Puppets held from rods against a translucent screen lit from behind. These puppets offer a visual dimension that other types do not.

social and emotional development: Type of development consisting of children developing positive images of themselves, expressing personality and individualism, representing imagination and fantasy, establishing enjoyable relationships with others, and expressing feelings.

social sciences: The core of social studies: anthropology, sociology, history, geography, economics, and psychology.

sociodramatic play: The highest level of symbolic play in which young children create their own happenings based on their experiences.

sociology: The study of group living, cooperation, and responsibilities.

solitary play: Independent play behavior of a child without regard to what other children or adults are doing.

spatial relationships: The relationship in space between two objects such as blocks.

spatial sense: Comparisons that help children develop an awareness of themselves in relation to people and objects in space, such as exploration using blocks and boxes.

stamina/endurance: Capacity for sustained use of strength or physical energy.

stereotype: An oversimplified generalization about a particular group, race, or sex, often with negative implications.

stick or rod puppets: Puppets controlled by a single stick, such as a tongue depressor, dowel rod, paper towel roll, craft stick, or ice cream stick.

strength: Physical energy available for movement or resistance.

string painting: A type of painting that involves moving string dipped in paint around on paper to make a design.

summative evaluation: A method of judging the worth of a program at the end of the program activities or end of a specific time period.

survey: A way to collect information directly from people in systematic, standardized way.

symbolic or dramatic play: A type of play that allows the child to transfer objects into symbols (things that represent something else) and images into people, places, and events within his experiences. Symbolic play occurs during Piaget's preoperational stage (2 to 7 years). Superhero fantasy play is considered a type of symbolic play for a young child.

symbolic thinking: The formation of symbols or mental representations, allowing children to solve problems by thinking before acting.

T

teacher- and child-made books: Books made by the teacher and child that encourage self-esteem, creativity, and the sharing of ideas. They also encourage children to articulate experiences.

theme: A broad concept or topic that enables the development of a lesson plan and the activities that fit within this curriculum plan.

time sample: Records what is happening at different time intervals.

transitions: Activities or learning experiences that move children from one activity to another.

three-dimensional art: Any art form that has three sides. Play dough and clay are examples of three-dimensional materials.

U

unit: A section of the curriculum based on the unifying theme around which activities are planned.

unit blocks: Hardwood blocks used in early education environments, especially in block center play.

unoccupied behavior: Refers to a child (infant or toddler) who occupies himself/herself by watching anything of momentary interest.

V

validity: The extent to which an evaluation technique fulfills the purpose for which it is intended.

virtual manipulatives: Refers to interactive, web-based computer-generated images of objects that children can manipulate on the computer screen.

vocabulary: This refers to the words we must know to communicate.

W

woodworking center: An activity center containing tools and wood that provides many different sensory and three-dimensional experiences.

wordless picture books: Books that tell a story with visually appealing illustrations. These books promote creativity by encouraging a child to talk about experiences and use his or her imagination.

word wall: An alphabetically arranged display or chart of words that children have experienced throughout the school year.

wrist rotation: Used, with wrist stability, to control hand movements.

wrist stability: Used with wrist rotation, to control hand movements.

Z

zone of proximal development: The range of potential each child has for learning, with that learning being shaped by the social environment in which it takes place.

A

Ahola, D., and Kovacik, A. (2007). *Observing and understanding child development: A child study manual*. Clifton Park, NY: Delmar Cengage Learning.

Alaby, R. G., Roedell, W. C., Arezzo, D., and Hendrix, K. (1995). *Early violence prevention*. Washington, DC: National Association for the Education of Young Children.

Albrecht, K. (1996, fall). Reggio Emilia: Four key ideas. *Texas Child Care, 20*(2), 2–8.

Alexander, N. P. (2008). All about unit block play. *Early Childhood News*. Retrieved November 30, 2013, from http://www.earlychildhoodnews.com/earlychildhood/article_view.aspx?ArticleID=397.

Allen, J., McNeill, E., and Schmidt, V. (1992). *Cultural awareness for children*. Menlo Park, CA: Addison-Wesley.

Allen, K. E., and Marotz, L. R. (2010). *Developmental profiles: Pre-birth through twelve* (6th ed.). Clifton Park, NY: Wadsworth Cengage Learning.

Allen, M. (2007). *Look, think, discover: Adding the wonder of science to the early childhood classroom*. Retrieved November 30, 2013, from http://www.earlychildhoodnews.com/earlychildhood/article_view.aspx?ArticleID=192.

American Academy of Pediatrics. (2001). Children, adolescents, and television. *Pediatrics 107*(2), 423–426. Retrieved December 1, 2013, from http://pediatrics.aappublications.org/content/107/2/423.full.pdf.

Arzubiaga, A., Ceja, M., and Artiles, A. J. (2000). Transcending deficit thinking about Latinos' parenting styles: Toward an ecocultural view of family life. In C. Tejeda, C. Martinez, Z. Leonardo, and P. McLaren (Eds.), *Charting new terrains of Chicana(o)/Latina(o) education* (pp. 93–106). Cresskill, NY: Hampton Press.

Association for Childhood Education International's (ACEI), "Play: Essential for All Children." (2002).

Aulthouse, R., Johnson, M. H., and Mitchell, S. T. (2003). *The colors of learning: Integrating the visual arts into the early childhood curriculum*. New York: Teachers College Press.

B

Bacon, G. (2004). *Room to Grow*. Austin, TX: Gryphon House.

Baghban, M. (2007, January). Scribbles, labels, and stories: The role of drawing in the development of writing. *Young Children, 62*(1), 20–26.

Bank Street College of Education. (1992). *Exploration with young children*. Mt. Rainier, MD: Gryphon House.

Bank Street School for Children. (2002). *Bank Street School for Children's Parent Handbook*. New York: Author.

Baroody, A. J. (2000, July). Does mathematics instruction for three- to five-year-olds really make sense? Research in review. *Young Children, 55*(4), 61–67.

Batzle, J. (1992). *Portfolio assessment and evaluation*. Cypress, CA: Creative Teaching Press.

Beaver, N. (2002). Sand and water play. *Room to Grow*. (2nd ed.). Austin: Texas Association for the Education of Young Children.

Ben-Sasson, A., Carter, A. S., Briggs-Gowan, M. J. (2010). *Early screening for autism spectrum disorder in day care*. SPD Foundation. www.spdfoundation.net/research/collaboration/ben-sasson. Retrieved June 13, 2016

Bentzen, W. R. (2009). *Seeing young children* (6th ed.). Clifton Park, NY: Wadsworth Cengage Learning.

Bergen, D. (2012). The role of pretend play in children's cognitive development. *Early Childhood Research and Practice*. V1, N 4. Retrieved November 30, 2013, from http://ecrp.uiuc.edu/v4n1/bergen.html.

Berk, L. E. (2013). *Child Development* (9th ed.). Upper Saddle River, NJ. Pearson Education.

Berk, L. E., and Winsler, A. (1995). *Scaffolding children's learning: Vygotsky and early childhood education*. Washington, DC: National Association for the Education of Young Children.

Berninger, V., and Chanquoy, L. (2012). What writing is and how it changes across early and middle childhood development: A multidisciplinary perspective. In E. Grigorenko, E. Manbrino and D. Preiss (Eds.) *Writing: A mosaic of perspective and views* (65–83). New York: Psychology Press.

Blackwell, C. K., Wartella, E., Lauricella, A., & Robb, M. B. Technology in the Lives of Educators and Early Childhood Programs: Trends in Access, Use, and Professional Development from 2012 to 2014. Latrobe, PA: The Fred Rogers Center for Early Learning and Media at Saint Vincent College. http://www.fredrogerscenter.org/wp-content/uploads/2015/07/Blackwell-Wartella-Lauricella-Robb-Tech-in-the-Lives-of-Educators-and-Early-Childhood-Programs.pdf retrieved July, 16, 2016.

Bobys, A. R. (2000, July). What does emerging literacy look like? *Young Children, 55*(4), 20–22.

Bosse, S., Jacobs, G., and Anderson, T. L. (2009, November). Science in the air. *Young Children, 64*(6), 10–15.

Bowman, B. (1994). The challenge of diversity. *Phi Delta Kappan, 76*(3), 218–225.

Bowman, B., Donovan, M. S., and Burns, M. S. (Eds.). (2000). *Eager to learn: Educating our preschoolers.* Washington, DC: National Academy Press.

Bredekamp, S. (1993, November). Reflections on Reggio Emilia. *Young Children, 49*(1), 13–17.

Bredekemp, S. (2013). *Effective Practices in Early Childhood Education: Building a Foundation* (2nd ed.). Upper Saddle River, NJ: Pearson Education, Inc.

Brinson, S. A. (2009, January). Behold the power of African American female characters! *Young Children, 64*(1), 26–31.

Brophy, J., and Alleman, J. (2013). *Powerful social studies for elementary students* (3rd ed.). Clifton Park, NY: Wadsworth Cengage Learning.

Brown, E. D., Benedett, B., and Armisteas, M. E. (2010). Arts enrichment and school readiness for children at risk. *Early Childhood Research Quarterly, 25*(1), 112–124.

Brown, S. (2009). *Play: How it shapes the brain, opens the imagination, and invigorates the soul.* New York: Penguin.

Buchanan, B. L., and Rios, J. M. (2004, May). Teaching science to kindergartners. *Young Children, 59*(3), 82–87.

Buckleitner, W. (2009, April). What should a preschooler know about technology? *Early Childhood Today.* Retrieved November 30, 2013, from www2.scholastic .com/browse/article.jsp?id=3751484

Buell, M. J., and Sutton, T. M. (2008, July). Weaving a web with children at the center. *Young Children, 63*(4), 100–105.

Bullard, J. (2014). *Creating environments for learning* (2nd ed.). Upper Saddle River, NJ: Pearson Education, Inc.

C

Care Research Network. (2004). Multiple pathways to early academic achievement. *Harvard Educational Review, 74*(1), 1–28.

Casey, M. B., Erkut, S., Ceder, I., and Young, J. M. (2008). Use of a storytelling context to improve girls' and boys' geometry skills in kindergarten. *Journal of Applied Developmental Psychology, 29,* 29–48.

Center on the Developing Child at Harvard University. (2011). *Building the brain's "air traffic control" system: How early experiences shape the development of executive function* (Working paper #11). Retrieved December 1, 2013, from http://developingchild.harvard.edu/resources/reports _and_working_papers/working_papers/wp11/.

Chalufour, I., and Worth, K. (2004). *Building structures with young children: The young scientist series.* St. Paul, MN: Redleaf Press and Washington, DC: National Association for the Education of Young Children.

Chard, S. (2001). *Project approach: Learning and teaching.* Retrieved November 29, 2013, from http://www .projectapproach.org/learning_and_teaching.php.

Charlesworth, R. (2011). *Understanding child development* (8th ed.). Clifton Park, NY: Wadsworth Cengage Learning.

Charlesworth, R., and Lind, K. K. (2016). *Math and science for young children* (6th ed.). Clifton Park, NY: Wadsworth Cengage Learning.

Christakis, D. A., Zimmerman, F. J., and Garrison, M. (2007). Effect of block play on language acquisition and attention in toddlers a pilot randomized controlled trial. *Archives of Pediatric and Adolescent Medicine, 161*(10), 967–971.

Christie, Scott, B. (2010, Oct 15). The brain: Utilizing multi-sensory approaches for individual learning styles. Retrieved October 29, 2013, from http://www.questia .com/library/journal/1G1-70450750/the-brain -utilizing-multi-sensory-approaches-for.

Chugani, H. T. (1998). A critical period of brain development: Studies of cerebral glucose utilization with PET. *Preventive Medicine, 27*(2), 184–188.

Church, E. B. (2006). *Scientific thinking: Step by step.* Retrieved November 30, 2013, from http://www.scholastic.com /teachers/article/scientific-thinking-step-step.

Clements, D. H., Swaminathan, S., Hannibal, M. A. Z., and Sarama, J. (1999). Young children's concepts of shape. *Journal for Research in Mathematics Education, 30*(2), 192–212.

Click, P. M., and Parker, J. (2009). *Caring for school-age children* (5th ed.). Clifton Park, NY: Wadsworth Cengage Learning.

Coates, E. (2002). I forgot the sky: Children's stories contained within their drawings. *International Journal of Early Years Education 10*(1), 21–35.

Cohen, L. (1999, February). The power of portfolios. *Early Childhood Today, I*(5), 31–33.

Colbert, J. (2007). *Bridging differences with understanding: Helping immigrant children be more ready to learn.* Retrieved November 30, 2013, from http://www .earlychildhoodnews.com/earlychildhood/article _view.aspx?ArticleId=475.

Colker, L. J. (2005). *The cooking book: Fostering young children's learning and delight.* Washington, DC: National Association for the Education of Young Children.

Connell, C. M., and Prinz, R. J. (2002). The impact of childcare and parent–child interactions on school readiness and social skills development for low-income African American children. *Journal of School Psychology, 40*(2), 177–193.

Copley, J. V. (2000). *The young child and mathematics.* Washington, DC: National Association for the Education of Young Children and Reston, VA: National Council of Teachers of Mathematics.

Copple, C., and Bredekamp, S. (Eds.). (2009). *Developmentally appropriate practice* (3rd ed.). Washington, DC: National Association for the Education of Young Children.

Council of Chief State School Officers (CCSSO), Early Childhood Education Assessment Consortium. (2008). Glossary. Washington, DC: Author.

Cross, C. T., Woods, T. A., and Schweingruber, H. (2009). *Mathematics learning in early childhood: Paths toward excellence and equity.* Washington, DC: The National Academies Press. Retrieved December 1, 2013, from http://www.nap.edu/openbook.php?record_id=12519.

Crosser, S. (2005). *What do we know about early childhood education? Research-based practice.* Clifton Park, NY: Delmar Cengage Learning.

Cummons, J. (2010). "Brain Education Through Sensory Integration" *Ominbus Writing.* (www.omnibuswritings .com/braineducationthroughsensoryintegration.html).

D

de Melendez, W., Beck, V., and Fletcher, M. (2000). *Teaching social studies in early education.* Clifton Park, NY: Delmar Cengage Learning.

de Melendez, W. R., and Beck, V. (2010). *Teaching young children in multicultural classrooms.* Clifton Park, NY: Wadsworth Cengage Learning.

Deiner, P. L. (2012). *Inclusive early childhood education* (6th ed.). Clifton Park, NY: Wadsworth Cengage Learning.

Dennison, B. A., Erb, T. A., and Jenkins, P. L. (2002). Television viewing and television in bedroom associated with overweight risk among low-income preschool children. *Pediatrics, 109*(6), 1028–1035.

Derman-Sparks and the A.B.C. Task Force. (1989).

Derman-Sparks and the A.B.C. Task Force. (2012).

Derman-Sparks and the A.B.C. Task Force. (2010).

Derman-Sparks, L., and Edwards, J. O. (2010). *Anti-bias education for young children and ourselves.* Washington, DC: National Association for the Education of Young Children.

Dodge, D. T. and Bickhart, T. *Children and Families*, Vol. XVII. No. 1. Winter 2003. (P. 28–32).

Dodge, D. T., Colker, L. J., and Heroman, C. (2000). *Creative curriculum for early childhood: Connecting content, teaching, and learning* (3rd ed.). Washington, DC: Teaching Strategies.

Dodge, D. T., Colker, L. J., and Heroman, C. (2008). *The creative curriculum for preschool* (College Edition). Washington DC: Teaching Strategies.

Dodge, D. T., Heroman, C., Charles, J., and Maiorca, J. (2004, January). Beyond outcomes: How ongoing assessment supports children's learning, and leads to meaningful curriculum. *Young Children, 59*(1), 21–28.

Dodge, D. T., Rudick, S., and Berke, K. L. (2006). *The creative curriculum for infants, toddlers and twos.* Washington DC: Teaching Strategies.

Dow, C. B. (2010, March). Young children and movement: The power of creative dance. *Young Children, 65*(2), 30–35.

Duncan, S., and Salcedo, M. (2015). *Learning Environment for Young Children. Child Care Information Exchange,* January/February 2015.Eisenhauer, M. J., and Feikes, D. (2009, May). Dolls, blocks, and puzzles: Playing with mathematical understandings. *Young Children, 64*(3), 18–24.

E

Eklof, J. (2003). *Animals in the classroom.* Dallas: Miss Jo Publications.

Elkind, D. (2001, summer). A place for us: Children's museums in a child unfriendly world. *Hand to Hand: Newsletter of the Association of Children's Museums, 15*(2), 1–2, 6.

Elkind, D. (2002, November–December). The connection between play and character. *Child Care Information Exchange, 148,* 41–42.

Elkind, D. (2009). *The Hurried Child.* Massachusetts: Persews Publishing.

Engel, S. (1996/1997). The guy who went up the steep nicken: The emergence of storytelling during the first three years. *Zero to Three, 17*(3), 1, 3–9. Retrieved October 29, 2013, from http://www.zerotothree.org /child-development/early-language-literacy/the -emergence-of-storytelling.html.

Epstein, A. S. (2001, May). Thinking about art: Encouraging art appreciation in early childhood settings. *Young Children, 56*(3), 38–43.

Epstein, A. S. (2003, summer). Early math: The next big thing. *High/Scope Resource. A Magazine for Educators,* 5–10.

Epstein, A. S. (2007). *The intentional teacher: Choosing the best strategies for young children's learning.* Washington, DC: National Association for the Education of Young Children.

Erikson, E. (1963). *Childhood and society* (2nd ed.). New York: Norton.

Esch, G., and Long, E. (2002, January). The fabulously fun finger puppet workshop. *Young Children, 57*(1), 90–91.

Espiritu, E., Meier, D., Villazana-Price, N., and Wong, M. K. (2002, September). A collaborative project on language and literacy learning. *Young Children, 57*(5), 71–78.

Essa, E. (2014). *Introduction to early childhood education* (7th ed.). Clifton Park, NY: Wadsworth Cengage Learning.

Essa, E. L., and Burnham, M. M. (Eds.). (2009). *Informing our practice: Useful research on young children's development.* Washington, DC: National Association for the Education of Young Children.

F

Family Child Care Academy (2014) "Sensory Development" Retrieved December 27, 2015 from http://familychildcareacademy.com/sensory -development/.

Feeney, S., Moravcik, E., Nolte, S., and Christensen, D. (2015). *Who am I in the lives of children?* (8th ed.). Upper Saddle River, NJ: Merrill.

Feldman, J. (2002, spring). Keep a song in your heart! *Early Years, 24*(1), 6–7.

Fields, M. V., and Spangler, K. L. (2000). *Let's begin reading right: Developmentally appropriate literacy* (4th ed.). Upper Saddle River, NJ: Merrill.

Fleming, B. (2002). Brain keys language development. Retrieved October 29, 2013, from http://www.nncc .org/release/brain.language.html.

Fletcher, J. (2004). Making connection: Helping children build their brains. *Connections.* Retrieved December 1, 2013 from http://www.canr.uconn.edu/ces/child /newsarticles./CCC712.html.

Flohr, J. W., Miller, D. C., and deBeus, R. (2000). EEG studies with young children. *Music Educators Journal, 87*(2), 28–32, 54. Retrieved June 13, 2007, from JSTOR.

Fox, J. E, and Schirrmacher, R. (2015). Art and creative development for young children (8th ed.). Clifton Park, NY: Wadsworth Cengage Learning.

Fox, J. E., and Diffily, D. (2001, winter). Integrating the visual arts: Building young children's knowledge, skills, and confidence. *Dimensions of Early Childhood, 29*(1), 3–10.

Freeman, N. K., and Feeney, S. (2006, September). The new face of early care and education. *Young Children, 61*(5), 10–16.

Furner, J. M., and Berman, B. T. (2003, spring). Math anxiety: Overcoming a major obstacle to the improvement of student math performance. *Childhood Education, 79*(3), 170–174.

G

Gabbard, C., and Rodrigues, L. (2002, May/June). Optimizing early brain and motor development through movement. *Early Childhood News, 14*(3), 32–38.

Gallagher, K. C. (2005, July). Brain research and early childhood development: A primer for developmentally appropriate practice. *Young Children, 60*(4), 12–20.

Gandini, L. (1993, November). Fundamentals of the Reggio Emilia approach to early childhood education. *Young Children, 49*(1), 4–8.

Gardner, H. (1983). *Frames of mind: The theory of multiple intelligences.* New York: Basic Books.

Gardner, H. (1993). *Multiple intelligences: The theory in practice.* New York: Basic Books.

Gardner, H. (1997). Teaching for multiple intelligences. *Educational Leadership, 55*(1), 9–12.

Genishi, C. (2002, July). Young English language learners— Resourceful in the classroom. *Young Children, 57*(4), 66–72.

Genishi, C., and Dyson, A. H. (2009). *Children, language, and literacy: Diverse learners in diverse times.* New York: Teachers College Press and Washington, DC: National Association for the Education of Young Children.

Gestwicki, C. (2013). *Home, school, & community relations* (8th ed.). Clifton Park, NY: Wadsworth Cengage Learning.

Gestwicki, C. (2014). *Developmentally appropriate practice: Curriculum and development in early education* (5th ed.). Clifton Park, NY: Wadsworth Cengage Learning.

Gibbs, M. (2012). *Fine motor skills write out of the box: Fine motor development information to assist parents of young children* [Brochure]. Katy, TX: Gibbs Consulting, Inc.

Glazer, J. I. (2000). *Literature for young children* (4th ed.). Upper Saddle River, NJ: Merrill.

Gober, S. Y. (2002). *Six simple ways to assess young children.* Clifton Park, NY: Delmar Cengage Learning.

Goffin, S. G. (2001). *Curriculum models and early childhood education* (2nd ed.). Upper Saddle River, NJ: Merrill.

Gonzalez-Mena, J. (2001). *Multicultural issues in child care* (3rd ed.). New York: McGraw Hill.

Gonzalez-Mena, J., and Shareef, I. (2005, November). Discussing diverse perspectives on guidance. *Young Children, 60*(6), 34–38.

Gordon, A. M., and Browne, K. W. (2013). *Beginning essentials in early childhood education.* Clifton Park, NY: Delmar Cengage Learning.

Gordon, A. M., and Browne, K. W. (2016). *Beginnings & beyond: Foundations in early childhood education* (8th ed.). Clifton Park, NY: Wadsworth Cengage Learning.

Gould, P., and Sullivan, J. (1999). *The inclusive early childhood classroom: Easy ways to adapt learning centers for all children.* Lewisville, NC: Gryphon House.

Graham, J. (2000, July). Creativity and picture books. *Reading, 34*, 61–69.

Greenberg, P. (2000, January). What wisdom should we take with us as we enter the new century?—An interview with Millie Almy. *Young Children, 55*(1), 6–10.

Greenman, J. (1987, November). Thinking about the aesthetics of children's environments. *Child Care Information Exchange, 58*, 9–12.

Grieshaber, S., and Diezmann, C. (2000). The challenge of teaching and learning science with young children. In N.J. Yelland (Ed.), *Promoting meaningful learning: Innovations in educating early childhood professionals* (pp. 87–94). Washington: National Association for the Education of Young Children (NAEYC).

Griss, S. (1994, February). Creative movement: A language for learning. *Educational Leadership, 51*(5), 78–80.

Gullo, D. F. (Ed.). (2006). *K today: Teaching and learning in the kindergarten year.* Washington, DC: National Association for the Education of Young Children.

H

Hachey, A. C., and Butler, D. L. (2009, November). Science education through gardening and nature-based play. *Young Children, 64*(6), 42–28.

Haney, M. H., and Hill, J. (2004). Relationships between parent-teaching activities and emergent literacy in preschool children. *Early Child Development and Care, 17*(3), 215–228.

Hanvey, C. E. (2010, January). Experiences with an outdoor prop box. *Young Children, 65*(10), 30–33.

Harman, M. (2007). Music and movement: Instrumental in language development. *Early Childhood News.* Retrieved November 30, 2013, from http://www .earlychildhoodnews.com/earlychildhood/article _view.aspx?ArticleID=601.

Harris, M. E. (2009, May). Implementing portfolio assessment. *Young Children, 64*(3), 82–85.

Harris, P. (2002). Imagination is important for children's cognitive development. Retrieved October 29, 2013, from http://news.harvard.edu/gazette/story/2002/03 /imagination-important-for-childrens-cognitive -development/.

Hart, B., and Risley, T. (1995). *Meaningful differences in the everyday experiences of young American children.* Baltimore, MD: Brookes.

Haugen, I. (2002, November-December). Time, trust, and tools: Opening doors to imagination for all children. *Child Care Information Exchange* (148), 36–40.

Head Start. (2003). *Head Start: A child development program* [Brochure]. Washington, DC: U.S. Department of Health and Human Services.

Head Start Bureau. (2014). *Head Start Program Information Report.* U.S. Department of Health and Human Services.

Head Start Bureau. (2005). *Head Start Facts.* Washington, DC: U. S. Department of Health and Human Services.

Helm, J., Beneke, S., and Steinheimer, K. (2007). *Windows on learning: Documenting young children's work* (2nd ed.). New York: Teachers College Press.

Helm, J., Huebner, A., and Long, B. (2000, May). Quiltmaking: A perfect project for preschool and primary. *Young Children, 55*(3), 44–49.

Helm, J. H., and Katz, L. (2010). *Young investigators: The project approach in the early years.* New York: Teachers College Press and Washington, DC: National Association for the Education of Young Children.

Hemmeter, M. L., Ostrosky, M. M., Artman, K. M., and Kinder, K. A. (2009, May). Planning transitions to prevent challenging behavior. *Young Children, 63*(3), 18–25.

Hendrick, J. (2003). *Total learning—Developmental curriculum for the young child* (6th ed.). Upper Saddle River, NJ: Merrill.

Hendrick, J., Weissman, P. (2010). *The Whole Child.* Upper Saddle, NJ: Pearson.

Hernandez, A. (1995, July–August). Language acquisition: What to expect. *Instructor, 105*(1), 56–57.

Hickman-Davis, P. (2002, spring). "Cuando no hablan Inglés": Helping young children learn English as a second language. *Dimensions of Early Childhood, 30*(2), 3–10.

High/Scope Educational Research Foundation. (2003). *Professional development programs.* Ypsilanti, MI: Author.

Hill, D. M. (1977). *Mud, sand, and water.* Washington, DC: National Association for the Education of Young Children.

Hine, C. (1996, November–December). Developing multiple intelligences in young children. *Early Childhood News, 8*(6), 23–29.

Hirsch, E. S. (Ed.). (1993). *The block book* (Rev. ed.). Washington, DC: National Association for the Education of Young Children.

Hofer, K. G., Farran, S. C., Cummings, T. P. (2013). Preschool children's math-related behaviors mediate curriculum effects on math achievement gains. *Early Childhood Research Quarterly, 28*(3), 487–495.

Hohmann, M., Banet, B., and Weikert, D. P. (1995). *Young children in action: A manual for preschool educators* (2nd ed.). Ypsilanti, MI: The High/Scope Press.

Hoisington, C. (2002, September). Using photographs to support children's science inquiry. *Young Children, 57*(5), 26–32.

Hong, S. Y., and Diamond, K. E. (2012). Two approaches to teaching young children science concepts, vocabulary, and scientific problem-solving skills. *Early Childhood Research Quarterly, 27* (2), 295–305.

Honig, A. S. (2002). *Secure relationships: Nurturing infant/ toddler attachment in early care settings.* Washington, DC: National Association for the Education of Young Children.

Houle, A., and Krogness, A. (2001, September). The wonder of word walls. *Young Children, 56*(5), 92–93.

Humphryes, J. (2000, March). Exploring nature with children. *Young Children, 55*(2), 16–20.

Hunt, T., and Renfro, N. (1982). *Puppetry in early childhood education.* Austin: Nancy Renfro Studios.

Hunter, D. (2008, November). What happens when a child plays at a sensory table? *Young Children, 63*(6), 77–79.

Huntsinger, C. S., Jose, P. E., Krieg, D. B., and Luo, Z. (2011). Cultural differences in Chinese American and European American children's drawing skills over time. *Early Childhood Research Quarterly, 26*(1), 134–145.

I

Im, J., Parlakian, R., and Osborn, C. A. (2007, January). Stories: Their powerful role in early language and literacy. *Young Children, 61*(1), 52–53.

International Reading Association (IRA) and National Association for the Education of Young Children (NAEYC). (1999). *A joint position paper: Learning to read and write, developmentally appropriate practice for young children.* [Booklet]. Washington, DC: National Association for the Education of Young Children.

Irvine, J. J. (2009, fall). Relevant beyond the basics. Retrieved December 11, 2015, from http://www.tolerance.org /magazine/number-36-fall-2009/feature/relevant -beyond-basics.

Isbell, R. (2007). *An environment that positively impacts young children.* Retrieved December 11, 2015, from http://www.earlychildhoodnews.com/earlychildhood/article_view.aspx?ArticleID=334.

Isbell, R. T., and Raines, S. (2013). *Creativity and the arts with young children* (3rd ed.). Clifton Park, NY: Delmar Cengage Learning.

J

Jackman, H. L. (2005). *Sing me a story! Tell me a song!* Clifton Park, NY: Delmar Cengage Learning.

Jacobs, G., and Crowley, K. (2010). *Reaching standards & beyond in kindergarten.* Thousand Oaks, CA: Corwin Press, and Washington, DC: National Association for the Education of Young Children.

Jalongo, M. R. (2004). *Young children and picture books* (2nd ed.). Washington, DC: National Association for the Education of Young Children.

Jambor, T. (2000, fall). Informal, real-life play: Building children's brain connections. *Dimensions of Early Childhood, 28*(4), 3–8.

Jensen, B. J., and Bullard, J. A. (2002, May). The mud center: Recapturing childhood. *Young Children, 57*(3), 16–19.

Johnson, L., and Lamb, A. (2007). *Electronic portfolios: Students, teachers, and life long learners, teacher tap.* Retrieved October 29, 2013, from http://eduscapes.com/tap/topic82.htm.

Jones, E., and Nimmo, J. (2012). *The emergence of emergent curriculum.* Retrieved December 11, 2015 from http://www.naeyc.org/YC/article/The-emergence-of-emergent-curriculum

K

Kellogg, R. (1959). *What children scribble and why.* Palo Alto, CA: National Press Books.

Kellogg, R., and O'Dell, S. (1967). *The psychology of children's art.* New York: Random House.

Kennedy, L. M., Tipps, S., and Johnson, A. (2011). *Guiding children's learning of mathematics.* Clifton Park, NY: Wadsworth Cengage Learning.

Kim, J., and Robinson, H. M. (2010, March). Four steps for becoming familiar with early music standards. *Young Children, 65*(2), 42–47.

Klein, A. S. (2002, spring). Infant & toddler care that recognized their competence. *Dimensions of Early Childhood, 30*(2), 11–17.

Klein, A. S. (2007). *Creating peaceful environmental designs for the classroom.* Retrieved November 30, 2013, from http://www.earlychildhoodnews.com/earlychildhood/article_view.aspx?ArticleId=390.

Koralek, D. (Ed.). (2004). *Spotlight on young children and play.* Washington, DC: National Association for the Education of Young Children.

Kostelnik, M., Soderman, A., and Whiren, A. P. (1999). *Developmentally appropriate programs in early childhood education* (2nd ed.). Upper Saddle River, NJ: Merrill.

Kostelnik, M. J., Soderman, A. K., and Whiren, A. P. (2014). *Developmentally appropriate curriculum: Best practices in early childhood education* (5th ed.). Upper Saddle River, NJ: Prentice Hall.

Koster, J. (2015). *Growing artists: Teaching art to young children* (6th ed.). Clifton Park, NY: Wadsworth Cengage Learning.

Krashen, S. D. (2003). *Principles and Practice in Second Language Acquisition.* Portsmouth, NH: Heinemann.

Krissansen, D. (2002, November–December). Getting along with imaginary friends. *Child Care Information Exchange, 148,* 51–53.

Krull, S. (2013). *Celebrate children: Rediscover the child in you.* Retrieved November 29, 2013, from http://sharronkrull.com/workshops/CelebrateChildrenho2.pdf, www.earlychildhoodnews.com.

Kupetz, B. (2008). Do You See What I See? Appreciating Diversity in Early Childhood Settings. *Early Childhood News.* Retrieved November 30, 2013, from http://www.earlychildhoodnews.com/earlychildhood/article_view.aspx?ArticleID=147.

L

Lamme, L. L. (2002, fall). Reading good books: Priming the pump for literacy development. *Dimensions of Early Childhood, 30*(4), 17–21.

Leipzig, J. (1993, May–June). Community field trips. *Pre-K Today, 78*(8), 44–51.

Let's Move. (n.d.) *Active schools.* Retrieved December 1, 2013, from http://www.letsmove.gov/active-schools.

Let's Move. (n.d.) *Get active.* Retrieved December 1, 2013, from http://www.letsmove.gov/ get-active.

Libby, W. M. L. (2000). *Using art to make art: Creative activities using masterpieces.* Clifton Park, NY: Delmar Cengage Learning.

Lindman, C. A. (2011). *Musical Children.* New York: Routledge.

Louv, R. (2008). *Last child in the woods: Saving our children from nature-deficit disorder.* Chapel Hill, NC: Algonquin Books.

M

Machado, J. M. (2010). *Early childhood experiences in language arts* (10th ed.). Clifton Park, NY: Delmar Cengage Learning.

Magruder, E. S., Hayslip, W. W., Espinosa, L. M., and Matera, C. (2013).

Marcon, R. A. (2003, January). The physical side of development. *Young Children, 58*(1), 80–87.

Marotz, L. R. (2009). *Health, safety, and nutrition for the young child* (7th ed.). Clifton Park, NY: Wadsworth Cengage Learning.

Marshall, H. H. (2001, November). Cultural influences on the development of self-concept. *Young Children, 56*(6), 19–25.

Martin, K. (2008). What's in a name? Letter identification in authentic contexts. *ACEI Focus on Pre-K & K, 20*(3), 13, 6.

Mayer, K. (2007). Emerging knowledge about emerging writing. *Young Children, 62*, 34–40.

Mayesky, M. (2011). *Creative activities for young children* (10th ed.). Clifton Park, NY: Wadsworth Cengage Learning.

McAfee, O., and Leong, D. (2011). *Assessing and guiding young children's development and learning* (5th ed.). Upper Saddle River, NJ: Pearson.

McCaslin, N. (1990). *Creative dramatics in the classroom* (5th ed.). New York: Longman.

McCracken, J. B. (2000). *Playgrounds safe and sound* [Brochure]. Washington, DC: National Association for the Education of Young Children.

McGraw, G. (2002, winter). Songs of childhood. *Early Childhood Connections*, Leadership Bulletin, *Vol. 8*, No. 1. Greensboro, NC: Foundation for Music-Based Learning.

McLeod, S. A. (2009). *Jean Piaget | cognitive theory— Simply psychology*. Retrieved October 29, 2013, from http://www.simplypsychology.org/piaget.html.

McWayne, C., Hampton, V., Fantuzzo, J., Cohen, H. L., and Sekino, Y. (2004). A multivariate examination of parent involvement and the social and academic competencies of urban kindergarten children. *Psychology in the Schools, 41*(3), 363–377.

Mendoza, J. A., Zimmerman, F. J., and Christakis, D. A. (2007). Television viewing and obesity in US preschool children. *International Journal of Behavioral Nutrition and Physical Activity, 4*(1), 44–53.

Miche, M. (2002). *Weaving music into young minds*. Clifton Park, NY: Delmar Cengage Learning.

Miller, D. F. (2016). *Positive Child Guidance*. (8th ed.) Clifton Park, NY: Cengage.

Miller, D. F. (2010). *Positive child guidance* (6th ed.). Clifton Park, NY: Wadsworth Cengage Learning.

Miller, E. and Almon, J. (2009). *Crisis in the kindergarten: Why children need to play in school*. College Park: MD. Alliance for Childhood.

Miller, K. (2002, November–December). The seeds of dramatic play: Enhanced by adults. *Child Care Information Exchange* (148), 25–26.

Miller, S. A. (1994, March). Sand and water around the room. *Early Childhood Today, 8*(6), 37–45.

Mindes, G. (2005, September). Social studies in today's early childhood curricula. *Young Children, 60*(5), 12–18.

Mitchell, A. (2006, November). From our president. *Young Children, 61*(6), 6.

Moore, T. (2002, July). If you teach children, you can sing! *Young Children, 57*(4), 84–85.

Moravcik, E. (2000, July). Music all the livelong day. *Young Children, 55*(4), 27–29.

Morrison, G. (2014). *Early Childhood Education Today*. Boston, MA: Cengage.

Morrow, L. M. (1989). *Literacy development in the early years*. Upper Saddle River, NJ: Prentice Hall.

Mulcahey, C. (2009, July). Providing rich art activities for young children. *Young Children, 64*(4), 107–112.

Music Educators National Conference (MENC). *The school music program? A new vision* (pp. 9-10) by MENC, Reston, VA: Author. Copyright 1994.

N

National Association for the Education of Young Children (NAEYC) and the Fred Rogers Center for Early Learning and Children's Media at Saint Vincent College. (2012). *Technology and interactive media as tools in early childhood programs serving children from birth through age 8*. Retrieved November 29, 2013, from http://www.naeyc.org/files/naeyc/PS_technology_WEB.pdf.

National Association for the Education of Young Children and NAECS/SDE (National Association of Early Childhood Specialists in State Departments of Education). (2002). Early learning standards: Creating the conditions for success. Joint position statement. Retrieved November 30, 2013, from http://www.naeyc.org/files/naeyc/file/positions/position_statement.pdf.

National Association for the Education of Young Children (NAEYC) and National Association of Early Childhood Specialists in State Departments of Education (NAECS/SDE). (2003). *Joint Position Statement. Early childhood curriculum, assessment, and program evaluation: Building an effective, accountable system in programs for children birth through age 8*. Retrieved October 29, 2013, from http://www.naeyc.org/files/naeyc/file/positions/pscape.pdf.

National Association for the Education of Young Children (NAEYC) and National Council of Teachers of Mathematics (NCTM). (2002). *Joint position paper— Early childhood mathematics: Promoting good beginnings*. Washington, DC: National Association for the Education of Young Children and Reston, VA: NCTM.

National Association for the Education of Young Children (NAEYC). (2000). *Helping children learn self-control* [Brochure]. Washington, DC: National Association for the Education of Young Children.

National Association for the Education of Young Children (NAEYC). (2001). *NAEYC at 75, 1926–2001*. Washington, DC.

National Association for the Education of Young Children (NAEYC). (2002, January). Our promise for children. *Young Children, 57*(1), 56.

National Association for the Education of Young Children (NAEYC). (2005). *Code of ethical conduct and statement of commitment*. Retrieved November 30, 2013, from http://www.naeyc.org/positionstatements /ethical_conduct.

National Association for the Education of Young Children (NAEYC). (2005). NAEYC position statement responding to linguistic and cultural diversity. Retrieved October 29, 2013, from http://www.naeyc .org/files/naeyc/file/positions/PSDIV98.PDF.

National Association for the Education of Young Children (NAEYC). (2007). *Where we stand on responding to cultural and linguistic diversity*. Retrieved November 29, 2013, from http://www.naeyc.org/files/naeyc/file /positions/diversity.pdf.

National Association for Music Education (http://www .nafme.org/about/position-statements/early -childhood-education-position-statement/early -childhood-education/_.

National Council for the Social Studies. (1994). *Expectations for excellence: Social studies* (Bulletin 89). Washington, DC: Author.

National Council for the Social Studies. (2008, May/June). *Curriculum guidelines for social studies teaching and learning* (Position Statement). Washington, DC: Author. Retrieved November 30, 2013, from http://www.socialstudies.org/positions /curriculumguidelines.

National Council of Teachers of Mathematics (NCTM). (2000). *Principles and standards for school mathematics: Executive summary* Reston, VA: Author. Retrieved November 30, 2013, from http://www.nctm.org /uploadedFiles/Math_Standards/12752_exec_pssm.pdf.

National Council of Teachers of Mathematics. (2006). *Curriculum focal points for prekindergarten through 8th grade*. Retrieved November 30, 2013, from https://www2.bc.edu/solomon-friedberg/mt190/nctm -focal-points.pdf.

National Institute of Child Health and Human Development, Early Child Care Research Network. (1998). Early child care and self-control, compliance and problem behavior at twenty-four and thirty-six months. *Child Development*, 69(4), 1145–1170.

National Institute of Child Health and Human Development, Early Child Care Research Network. (2004). Multiple pathways to early academic achievement. *Harvard Educational Review*, 74(1), 1–28.

National Institute for Early Education Research (NIEER). (2015). *State standards database*. http://nieer.org /standards/statelist.php.

National Institute for Early Education Research (NIEER). (2016). *Quality and Curriculum*. http://nieer.org /research/quality-and-curriculum. Retrieved June 8, 2016.

National Institute for Early Education Research (NIEER). (2009). *The state of preschool 2009: State preschool yearbook*. Retrieved November 29, 2013, from http://nieer.org/sites/nieer/files/2009%20yearbook.pdf.

National Institute for Literacy. (2009). Online at http://www .nifl.gov.

National Mathematics Advisory Panel. (2008). *Foundations for success: The final report of the National Mathematics Advisory Panel*. Retrieved December 1, 2013, from http://www2.ed.gov/about/bdscomm/list/mathpanel /report/final-report.pdf.

National Research Council. (1996). *National Science Education Standards (NSES)*. Washington, DC: The National Academies Press.

National Research Council. (2001). *Adding it up: Helping children learn mathematics*. Washington, DC: The National Academies Press.

Nelsen, M., and Nelsen-Parish, J. (2002). *Peak with books: An early childhood resource for balanced literacy* (3rd ed.). Clifton Park, NY: Delmar Cengage Learning.

Nemeth, K. (2009, March). Meeting the home language mandate. *Young Children*, 64(2), 36–42.

Neuman, S. B., Copple, C., and Bredekamp, S. (2000). *Learning to read and write: Developmentally appropriate practices for young children*. Washington, DC: National Association for the Education of Young Children.

Nevills, P., and Wolfe, P. (2009). *Building the reading brain* (2nd ed.). Thousand Oaks, CA: Corwin Press.

New, R., Palsha, S., and Ritchie, S. (2009). *Issues in preK–3rd education: A FirstSchool framework for curriculum and instruction*. (#7). Chapel Hill, NC: The University of North Carolina at Chapel Hill, FPG Child Development Institute, FirstSchool.

New, R. S. (2000). Reggio Emilia: Catalyst for change and conversation (Report No. EDO-PS-00-15). *ERIC Digest*. Urbana, IL: ERIC Clearinghouse on Elementary and Early Childhood Education.

Newcombe, N. S., and Frick, A. (2010). Early education for spatial intelligence: Why, what, and how. *Mind, Brain and Education*, 4(3), 102–111.

Nicholson-Nelson, K. (1998). *Developing students' multiple intelligences*. New York: Scholastic Professional Books.

Nielsen, D. M. (2006). *Teaching young children: Preschool–K* (2nd ed.). Thousand Oaks, CA: Corwin Press.

Nilson, B. (2011). *Week by Week* (5th ed.). Clifton Park, NY: Wadsworth Cengage Learning.

Nimmo, J., and Halett, B. (2008, January). Childhood in the garden: A place to encounter natural and social diversity. *Young Children*, 63(1), 32–38.

Nord, C. W., Lennon, J., Liu, B., and Chandler, K. (1999). *Home literacy activities and signs of children's emerging literacy, 1993 and 1999*. Retrieved November 29, 2013, from http://nces.ed.gov/pubs2000/2000026.pdf.

Northwest Regional Educational Laboratory. (2001, June). Technology in Early Childhood Education. Retrieved October 29, 2013, from http://educationnorthwest.org /webfm_send/458.

O

Ogu, U., and Schmidt, S. R. (2009, March). Investigating rocks and sand. *Young Children, 64*(2), 12–18.

Okolo, C., and Hayes, R. (1996). *The impact of animation in CD-ROM books on students' reading behaviors and comprehension.* Paper presented at the Annual International Convention of the Council for Exceptional Children, Orlando, FL.

Oswalt, A., and Dombeck, M. (Ed.) (2013). *Physical development: Motor development.* Retrieved December 1, 2013, from http://www.sevencounties.org/poc/view_doc.php?type=doc&id=37676&cn=1272.

P

Palmer, H. (2001, September). The mu, music, movement, and learning connection. *Young Children, 56*(5), 13–17.

Papic, M., Mulligan, J. T., and Mitchelmore, M. C. (2011). Assessing the development of preschoolers' mathematical patterning. *Journal for Research in Mathematics Education, 42*(3), 237–268.

Parette, H. P., Hourcade, J. J., Boeckmann, N. M., and Blum, C. (2008). Using Microsoft Powerpoint™ to support emergent literacy skill development for young children at-risk or who have disabilities. *Early Childhood Education Journal, 36*(3), 233–240.

Parks, L. (1994, Fall). Make it with a box. *Texas Child Care, 18*(2), 22–28.

Parks, L. (Ed.). (1994, spring). Make a friendship quilt. *Texas Child Care, 17*(4), 22–28.

Parlakin, R., and Lerner, C. (2010, March). Beyond twinkle, twinkle: Using music with infants and toddlers. *Young Children, 65*(2), 14–19.

Parten, M. B. (1932). Social participation among preschool children. *Journal of Abnormal and Social Psychology, 27*, 243–269.

Perry, B. D. (2002, November–December). A different world. *Parent and Child, 10*(3), 47–49.

Petersen, E. A. (2003). *Early childhood planning, methods, and materials* (2nd ed.). Boston: Allyn & Bacon.

Peyton, J. (2009). *Riding the Big Bang of Play into 21st Century Education* (p. 7). Retrieved November 30, 2013, from www.puppetools.com/ebook.pdf.

Piaget, J. (1926). *The language and thought of the child.* New York: Harcourt Brace.

Pica, R. (2003, March–April). But we don't have room. *Early Childhood News, 15*(2), 24–26.

Pica, R. (2007). *Moving and learning across the curriculum* (2nd ed.). Clifton Park, NY: Wadsworth Cengage Learning.

Pica, R. (2010). *Experiences in movement and music: Birth to age 8* (4th ed.). Clifton Park, NY: Wadsworth Cengage Learning.

Pine, C., and Matthews, J. (2006). *Assessment of student competencies: Teacher handbook programming resource.*

Retrieved October 29, 2013, from http://www.education.nt.gov.au/__data/assets/pdf_file/0019/991/TeacherHandbook.pdf.

Puranik, C. S., Lonigan, C. J., and Kim, Y. S. (2011). Contributions of Emergent Literacy Skills to Name Writing, Letter Writing, and Spelling in Preschool Children. *Early Child Research Quarterly, 26*(4): 465–474.

R

Raines, S., and Isbell, R. (1994). *Stories: Children's literature in early education.* Clifton Park, NY: Delmar Cengage Learning.

Rauscher, F. H., Shaw, G. L., and Ky, C. N. (1993). Music and spatial task performance. *Nature 365*(6447), 611.

Rauscher, F. H., and Zupan, M. A. (2000). Classroom keyboard instruction improves kindergarten children's spatial-temporal performance: A field experiment. *Early Childhood Research Quarterly, 15*(2), 215–227.

Ray, J. A., Pewitt-Kinder, J., and George, S. (2009, September). Partnering with families of children with special needs. *Young Children, 64*(5), 16–22.

Read, K., Gardner, P., and Mahler, B. (1993). *Early childhood programs: Human relationships and learning* (9th ed.). New York: *Harcourt.*

Reading Is Fundamental (RIF). (2009). *Choosing good books.* Retrieved November 29, 2013, from http://www.rif.org/us/literacy-resources/articles/choosing-good-books.htm.

Richards, T. Berninger, V., Stock, P., Altemeier, L., Trivedi P., and Maravilla, K. (2009). fMRI sequential-finger movement activation differentiating good and poor writers. *Journal of Clinical and Experimental Neuropsychology, 31*(8), 967–983.

Richardson, K. (2000). Mathematics standards for pre-kindergarten through grade 2. (Report EDO-PS-00-11) *Eric Digest.* Urbana, IL: ERIC Clearinghouse on Elementary and Early Childhood Education.

Rideout, V., and Hame, E. (2006). The media family: Electronic media in the lives of infants, toddlers, preschoolers and their parents. Menlo Park, CA: Henry J Kaiser Family Foundation. Retrieved December 1, 2013, from http://kff.org/other/the-media-family-electronic-media-in-the/.

Rideout, V., Vandewater, E., and Wartella, E. (2003). *Zero to six: Electronic media in the lives of infants, toddlers and preschoolers.* Menlo Park, CA: Henry J Kaiser Foundation.

Riley, J. G., and Boyce, J. S. (2007, winter). Buddying or bullying? A school-wide decision. *Dimensions of Early Childhood, 35*(1), 3–11.

Robertson, C. (2010). *Safety, nutrition, & health in education* (4th ed.). Clifton Park, NY: Wadsworth Cengage Learning.

Rockwell, R. E., Andre, L. C., and Hawley, M. K. (2010). *Families and educators as partners* (2nd ed.). Clifton Park, NY: Wadsworth Cengage Learning.

Rogers, F. (2003). *The world according to Mister Rogers: Important things to remember*. New York: Hyperion, www.fredrogers.org/pro-dev/may-2012.html.

Rogers, A., and Russo, S. (2003). Blocks: A commonly encountered play activity in the early years, or a key to facilitating skills in science, math and technology. *Investigating, 19*(1), 17–21.

Roley, S. S., Bissell, J., and Clark, G. F. (2009). Commission on Practice. Providing occupational therapy using sensory integration theory and methods in school-based practice. *American Journal of Occupational Therapy, 63*(6), 823–842.

Rosen, D., and Hoffman, J. (2009, May). Integrating concrete and virtual manipulatives in early childhood mathematics. *Young Children, 64*(3), 26–33.

Rossett, A., and Sheldon, K. (2001). *Beyond the podium: Delivering training and performance to a digital world*. San Francisco: Jossey-Bass/Pfeiffer.

S

Sanders, S. W. (2006, winter). Physically active for life. *Dimensions of Early Childhood, 34*(1), 3–10.

Santos, R. M. (2004, January). Ensuring culturally and linguistically appropriate assessment of young children. *Young Children, 59*(1), 48–50.

Sawyer, W. E. (2009). *Growing up with literature* (5th ed.). Clifton Park, NY: Delmar Cengage Learning.

Schiller, P., and Willis, C. A. (2008). Using brain-based teaching strategies to create supportive early childhood environments that address learning standards. Retrieved November 30, 2013, from http://www.naeyc.org/files/yc/file/200807/BTJPrimaryInterest.pdf.

Schilling, T., and McOmber, K. A. (2006, May). Tots in action on and beyond the playground. *Young Children, 61*(3), 34–36.

Schirrmacher, R., and Fox, J. E. (2009). *Art and creative development for young children* (6th ed.). Clifton Park, NY: Wadsworth Cengage Learning.

"The Beat Goes On," Scholastic Magazines. (2016, May 4). (www.scholastic.com/teachers/article/beat-goes).

Seefeldt, C., Castle, S. P., and Falconer, R. (2010). *Social studies for the preschool–primary child* (8th ed.). Upper Saddle River, NJ: Merrill.

Seekonk Public Schools, *Curriculum Review Cycle.* (2009).

Seitz, H. (2008, March). The power of documentation in the early childhood classroom. *Young Children, 63*(2), 88–93. Retrieved November 30, 2013, from https://www.naeyc.org/files/tyc/file/Seitz.pdf.

Seto, K. (1999). *Getting ready to teach second grade*. Torrance, CA: Frank Schaffer.

Shidler, L. (2009, September). Teaching children what we want them to learn. *Young Children, 64*(5), 88–91.

Shiver, E. (2001). Brain Development and Mastery of Language in the Early Childhood Years *Intercultural Development Research Association Newsletter*, IDRA. http://www.idra.org/IDRA_Newsletter/April_2001_Self_Renewing_Schools_Early_Childhood/Brain_Development_and_Mastery_of_Language_in_the_Early_Childhood_Years/.

Shore, R., and Strasser, J. (2006, March). Music for their minds. *Young Children, 61*(2), 62–67.

Siegler, R. S., and Ramani, G. B. (2008). Playing board games promotes low-income children's numerical development. *Developmental Science, 11*(5), 655–661.

Sinker, M., and Russell, I. (2000, summer). Describing for play. *Hand to Hand: Newsletter of the Association of Children's Museums, 14*(2), 3–4, 10.

Sluss, D. J. (2005). *Supporting play: Birth through age eight*. Clifton Park, NY: Delmar Cengage Learning.

Smilansky, S. (1968). *The effects of sociodramatic play on disadvantaged children*. New York: John Wiley & Sons.

Smith, K. L. (2002, March). Dancing in the forest. *Young Children, 57*(2), 90–94.

Southern Early Childhood Association. SECA position statement on *Valuing Diversity for Young Children*. Retrieved November 30, 2013, from http://www.southernearlychildhood.org/policy_position.php.

Starkey, P., Klein, A., and Wakeley, A. (2004). Enhancing children's mathematical knowledge through a pre-kindergarten mathematics intervention. *Early Childhood Research Quarterly, 19*(1), 99–120.

Starns, L. (2002, summer). Don't take the blocks away!— Block centers in preschool and primary classrooms. *The Early Years, 24*(2), 2–3.

Stephenson, A. (2001, May). What George taught me about toddlers and water. *Young Children, 57*(3), 10–14.

Stott, F. (1994, September). In memoriam: Erik H. Erikson. *Young Children, 49*(6), 43.

Strickland, D. S. (2002). Bridging the gap for African American children. In B. Bowman (Ed.), *Love to read: Essays in developing and enhancing early literacy skills of African American children*. Washington, DC: National Black Child Development Institute, Inc.

Stuber, G. M. (2007, July). Centering Your Classroom Setting the Stage for Engaged Learners. *Young Children* 62(4), 58–59.

Swim, T. J., and Watson, L. (2011). *Infants and toddlers* (7th ed.). Clifton Park, NY: Wadsworth Cengage Learning.

Swim, T. J., and Watson, L. (2014). *Infants and Toddlers*. Belmont, CA: Cengage.

T

Taunton, N., and Colbert, C. (2000). Art in the early childhood classroom. In N. J. Yelland (Ed.). *Promoting meaningful learning* (67–76). Washington, DC: National Association for the Education of Young Children.

Taveras, E. M., Sandora, T. J., Shihm, M. C., Ross-Degnan, D., Goldmann, D. A., and Gillman, M. W. (2006). The association of television and video viewing with fast food intake by preschool-age children. *Obesity (Silver Spring), 14*(11), 2034–2041.

Taylor, B. J. (2004). *A child goes forth* (10th ed.). Upper Saddle River, NJ: Merrill.

Taylor-Cox, J. (2003, January). Algebra in the early years? Yes! *Young Children, 58*(1), 14–21.

Texas Education Agency. (2008). *Revised Texas Prekindergarten Guidelines.* tea.texas.gov/index2.aspx?id=2147495508. Retrieved June 15, 2016.

The Metropolitan Museum of Art. (1959). *How to look at paintings: A guide for children.* New York.

Thomson, B. J. (1993). *Words can hurt you: The beginning of anti-bias education.* Menlo Park, CA: Addison Wesley.

Torquati, J., and Barber. J. (2005, May). Dancing with trees: Infants and toddlers in the garden. *Young Children, 60*(3), 40–46.

Tsao, L. L. (2002, summer). How much do we know about the importance of play in child development? *Childhood Education, 78*(4), 230–233.

Tunks, K. W. (2009). Block play: Practical suggestions for common dilemmas. *Dimensions of Early Childhood, 37*(1), 3–8.

Tunks, K. W., and Giles, R. M. (2009). Writing their words: Strategies for supporting young authors. *Young Children, 64*(1), 22–25.

U

US Department of Education. (2001). *No Child Left Behind Act of 2001.* Retrieved November 30, 2013, from http://www2.ed.gov/policy/elsec/leg/esea02/107-110.pdf.

US Department of Education. (2009). *Helping your child become a reader: No child left behind.* Washington, DC: Author.

US Department of Education, Office of Educational Research and Improvement. The Condition of Education 2001 (NCES Publication No. 2000-026). Washington, DC: National Center for Education Statistics.

US Department of Health and Human Services, Office of Head Start. (2005). *Head Start program performance standards.* Retrieved December 11, 2015 at http://eclke.ohs.acf.hhs.gov/hslc

University of Texas System and Texas Education Agency. (2008). *Texas pre-k guidelines* (Rev. ed.). Austin, TX: Author.

V

Vail, P. L. (1999). January. Observing learning styles in the classroom. *Early Childhood Today, 13*(4), 20–22.

Vygotsky, L. S. (1986). *Thought and language.* Cambridge, MA: MIT Press.

W

Wall, K. (2011). *Special needs and early years: A practitioner's guide* (3rd ed.) Thousand Oaks, CA: SAGE Publications. Retrieved November 29, 2013, from http://www.sagepub.com/upm-data/9656_022816Ch5.pdf.

Wardle, F. (2007). The role of technology in early childhood programs. *Early Childhood News.* Retrieved November 30, 2013, from http://www.earlychildhoodnews.com/earlychildhood/article_view.aspx?ArticleId=302.

Washington State Office of Superintendent of Public Instruction. (2008). *A guide to assessment in early childhood: Infancy to age eight.* Retrieved November 30, 2013, from http://www.k12.wa.us/earlylearning/pubdocs/assessment_print.pdf.

Watson, A., and McCathren, L. (2009, March). Including children with special needs. *Young Children, 64*(2), 20–26.

Weikart, D. P., and Schweinhart, L. J. (2007). *Perry preschool project through age 40.* Retrieved November 30, 2013, from http://www.highscope.org/file/Research/PerryProject/3_specialsummary%20col%2006%2007.pdf.

Wellhousen, K. (2002). *Outdoor play every day: Innovative play concepts for early childhood.* Clifton Park, NY: Delmar Cengage Learning.

Wellhousen, K., and Kieff, J. (2001). *A constructivist approach to block play in early childhood.* Clifton Park, NY: Delmar Cengage Learning.

Wertsch, J. V. (1991). *Voices of the mind.* Cambridge, MA: Harvard University Press.

West, M. M. (2001, November). Teaching the third culture child. *Young Children, 56*(6), 27–32.

White, D. Y. (2002, Summer). Developing number sense in prekindergarten and kindergarten children. *ACEI Focus on PreK and K Newsletter, 14*(4), 1–5.

Whitebread, D. *The importance of play.* Belgium. University of Cambridge for toy industries of Europe. April 2012.

Williams, D. (1995). *Teaching mathematics through children's art.* Portsmouth, NH: Heinemann.

Willis, C. (2009). *Creating inclusive learning environments for young children.* Thousand Oaks, CA: Corwin Press.

Wilson, K. T. (2007). *Music and arts education: Its effect on brain development and academic achievement.* Retrieved November 29, 2013, from http://classroom.jc-schools.net/wilsont /Litreviewfinaldraft.pdf.

Wolfgang, C., Stannard, L., and Jones, I. (2001). Block play performance among preschoolers as a predictor of later school achievement in mathematics. *Journal of Research in Childhood Education, 15*(2), 173–181.

Wortham, S. C. (2010). *Early childhood curriculum: Development bases for learning and teaching* (5th ed.). Upper Saddle River, NJ; Pearson Prentice Hall.

Y

York, S. (2003). *Roots and wings.* (Rev. ed.). St. Paul, MN: Redleaf Press.

Z

Zachopoulou, E., Tsapakidou, A., and Derri, V. (2004). The effects of a developmentally appropriate music and movement program on motor performance. *Early Childhood Research Quarterly, 19*(4), 631–642.

Ziemer, M. (1987, September). Science and the early childhood curriculum. *Young Children, 42*(6), 44–51.

Index

STANDARDS CORRELATION CHART

New to this edition is a greater focus on the major standards of the field. These are shown throughout the text with icons that highlight professionally recognized standards and practices from NAEYC's Professional Preparation Standards (2010), NAEYC's Developmentally Appropriate Practice (DAP) Guidelines, Interstate Teacher Assessment and Support Consortium (InTASC), and Head Start Early Learning Outcomes Framework (HS) 2015. This handy chart provides a chapter-by-chapter summary of where these standards are covered in each chapter.

Chapter	**naeyc** NAEYC's Professional Preparation Standards	**DAP** Developmentally Appropriate Practice (DAP) Guidelines	**INTASC** Interstate Teacher Assessment and Support Consortium (InTASC)	**HS** Head Start Early Learning Outcomes Framework (HS)
Chapter 1: Starting the Process Starting the Process	1a. Knowing and understanding young children's characteristics and needs 1b. Knowing and understanding the multiple influences on development and learning 1c. Using developmental knowledge to create healthy, respectful, supportive and challenging learning environments 2b. Supporting and engaging families and communities through respectful, reciprocal relationships 2c. Involving families and communities in their children's development and learning 4b. Knowing and understanding effective strategies and tools for early education 4c. Using a broad repertoire of developmentally appropriate teaching/learning approaches 5c. Using their own knowledge, appropriate early learning standards, and other resources to design, implement, and evaluate meaningful, challenging curricula for each child 6b. Knowing about and upholding ethical standards and other professional guidelines 6d. Integrating knowledgeable, reflective and critical perspectives on early education	2. Teaching to Enhance Development and Learning 3. Planning curriculum to achieve important goals 4. Assessing children's development and learning	**Standard #1:** Learner Development. The teacher understands how learners grow and develop, recognizing that patterns of learning and development vary individually within and across the cognitive, linguistic, social, emotional, and physical areas, and designs and implements developmentally appropriate and challenging learning experiences **Standard #2:** Learning Differences. The teacher uses understanding of individual differences and diverse cultures and communities to ensure inclusive learning environments that enable each learner to meet high standards **Standard #7:** Planning for instruction. The teacher plans instruction that supports every student in meeting rigorous learning goals by drawing upon knowledge of content areas, curriculum, cross-disciplinary skills, and pedagogy, as well as knowledge of learners and the community context **Standard #8:** Instructional Strategies The teacher understands and uses a variety of instructional strategies to encourage learners to develop deep understanding of content areas and their connections, and to build skills to apply knowledge in meaningful ways	**Domain:** Approaches to Learning **Domain:** Perceptual, Motor, and Physical Development

Chapter	NAEYC's Professional Preparation Standards	Developmentally Appropriate Practice (DAP) Guidelines	INTASC Interstate Teacher Assessment and Support Consortium (InTASC)	Head Start Early Learning Outcomes Framework (HS)
Chapter 2: Observation and assessment	3a. Understanding the goals, benefits, and uses of assessment 3b. Knowing about and using observation, documentation, and other appropriate assessment tools and approaches 3c. Understanding and practicing responsible assessment to promote positive outcomes for each child 3d. Knowing about assessment partnerships with families and with professional colleagues to build effective learning environments	4. Assessing children's development and learning	**Standard #6:** Assessment. The teacher understands and uses multiple methods of assessment to engage learners in their own growth, to monitor learning progress, and to guide the teacher's and learner's decision making **Standard #7:** Planning for Instruction. The teacher plans instruction that supports every student in meeting rigorous learning goals by drawing upon knowledge of content areas, curriculum, cross-disciplinary skills, and pedagogy, as well as knowledge of learners and the community context	NONE
Chapter 3: Creating Curriculum	4b. Knowing and understanding effective strategies and tools for early education, including appropriate uses of technology 4c. Using a broad repertoire of developmentally appropriate teaching/ learning approaches 5a. Understanding content knowledge and resources in academic disciplines 5b. Knowing and using the central concepts, inquiry tools, and structures of content areas or academic disciplines 5c. Using own knowledge, appropriate early learning standards, and other resources to design, implement, and evaluate developmentally meaningful and challenging curriculum for each child	3. Planning curriculum to achieve important goals	**Standard #1:** Learner Development. The teacher understands how learners grow and develop, recognizing that patterns of learning and development vary individually within and across the cognitive, linguistic, social, emotional, and physical areas, and designs and implements developmentally appropriate and challenging learning experiences **Standard #2:** Learning Differences. The teacher uses understanding of individual differences and diverse cultures and communities to ensure inclusive learning environments that enable each learner to meet high standards **Standard #7:** Planning for instruction. The teacher plans instruction that supports every student in meeting rigorous learning goals by drawing upon knowledge of content areas, curriculum, cross-disciplinary skills, and pedagogy, as well as knowledge of learners and the community context	**Domain:** Approaches to Learning

Chapter	NAEYC's Professional Preparation Standards	Developmentally Appropriate Practice (DAP) Guidelines	Interstate Teacher Assessment and Support Consortium (InTASC)	Head Start Early Learning Outcomes Framework (HS)
Chapter 4: The Learning Environment	1c. Using developmental knowledge to create healthy, respectful, supportive, and challenging learning environments for young children	2. Teaching to Enhance Development and Learning	Standard #3: Learning Environments. The teacher works with others to create environments that support individual and collaborative learning, and that encourage positive social interaction, active engagement in learning, and self-motivation	Domain: Approaches to Learning
Chapter 5: Language and Literacy	5a. Understanding content knowledge and resources in academic disciplines 5b. Knowing and using the central concepts, inquiry tools, and structures of content areas or academic disciplines 5c. Using own knowledge, appropriate early learning standards, and other resources to design, implement, and evaluate developmentally meaningful and challenging curriculum for each child	2. Teaching to Enhance development and learning	Standard #4: Content Knowledge. The teacher understands the central concepts, tools of inquiry, and structures of the discipline(s) he or she teaches and creates learning experiences that make the discipline accessible and meaningful for learners to assure mastery of the content Standard #5: Application of Content. The teacher understands how to connect concepts and use differing perspectives to engage learners in critical thinking, creativity, and collaborative problem solving related to authentic local and global issues Standard #8: Instructional Strategies. The teacher understands and uses a variety of instructional strategies to encourage learners to develop deep understanding of content areas and their connections, and to build skills to apply knowledge in meaningful ways	Domain: Literacy Domain: Language Development
Chapter 6: Creativity - Art & Music	5a. Understanding content knowledge and resources in academic disciplines 5b. Knowing and using the central concepts, inquiry tools, and structures of content areas or academic disciplines	2. Teaching to Enhance development and learning	Standard #4: Content Knowledge. The teacher understands the central concepts, tools of inquiry, and structures of the discipline(s) he or she teaches and creates learning experiences that make the discipline accessible and meaningful for learners to assure mastery of the content	Subdomain: Creativity

Chapter	**naeyc** NAEYC's Professional Preparation Standards	**DAP** Developmentally Appropriate Practice (DAP) Guidelines	**InTASC** Interstate Teacher Assessment and Support Consortium (InTASC)	**HS** Head Start Early Learning Outcomes Framework (HS)
	5c. Using own knowledge, appropriate early learning standards, and other resources to design, implement, and evaluate developmentally meaningful and challenging curriculum for each child		**Standard #5:** <u>Application of Content</u>. The teacher understands how to connect concepts and use differing prospecivies to engage learners in critical thinking, creativity, and collaborative problem solving related to authentic local and global issues **Standard #8:** Instructional Strategies. The teacher understands and uses a variety of instructional strategies to encourage learners to develop deep understanding of content areas and their connections, and to build skills to apply knowledge in meaningful ways	
Chapter 7: Social Studies and Dramatic Play	5a. Understanding content knowledge and resources in academic disciplines 5b. Knowing and using the central concepts, inquiry tools, and structures of content areas or academic disciplines 5c. Using own knowledge, appropriate early learning standards, and other resources to design, implement, and evaluate developmentally meaningful and challenging curriculum for each child	2. Teaching to Enhance development and learning	**Standard #4:** <u>Content Knowledge</u>. The teacher understands the central concepts, tools of inquiry, and structures of the discipline(s) he or she teaches and creates learning experiences that make the discipline accessible and meaningful for learners to assure mastery of the content **Standard #5:** <u>Application of Content</u>. The teacher understands how to connect concepts and use differing perspectives to engage learners in critical thinking, creativity, and collaborative problem solving related to authentic local and global issues **Standard #8:** <u>Instructional Strategies</u>. The teacher understands and uses a variety of instructional strategies to encourage learners to develop deep understanding of content areas and their connections, and to build skills to apply knowledge in meaningful ways	**Subdomain:** Creativity

STANDARDS CORRELATION CHART

Chapter	NAEYC's Professional Preparation Standards	Developmentally Appropriate Practice (DAP) Guidelines	INTASC Interstate Teacher Assessment and Support Consortium (InTASC)	Head Start Early Learning Outcomes Framework (HS)
Chapter 8: Sensory Play	5a. Understanding content knowledge and resources in academic disciplines 5b. Knowing and using the central concepts, inquiry tools, and structures of content areas or academic disciplines 5c. Using own knowledge, appropriate early learning standards, and other resources to design, implement, and evaluate developmentally meaningful and challenging curriculum for each child	2. Teaching to Enhance development and learning	**Standard #4:** Content Knowledge. The teacher understands the central concepts, tools of inquiry, and structures of the discipline(s) he or she teaches and creates learning experiences that make the discipline accessible and meaningful for learners to assure mastery of the content **Standard #5:** Application of Content. The teacher understands how to connect concepts and use differing perspectives to engage learners in critical thinking, creativity, and collaborative problem solving related to authentic local and global issues **Standard #8:** Instructional Strategies. The teacher understands and uses a variety of instructional strategies to encourage learners to develop deep understanding of content areas and their connections, and to build skills to apply knowledge in meaningful ways	**Domain:** Scientific Reasoning
Chapter 9: Science	5a. Understanding content knowledge and resources in academic disciplines 5b. Knowing and using the central concepts, inquiry tools, and structures of content areas or academic disciplines 5c. Using own knowledge, appropriate early learning standards, and other resources to design, implement, and evaluate developmentally meaningful and challenging curriculum for each child	2. Teaching to Enhance development and learning	**Standard #4:** Content Knowledge. The teacher understands the central concepts, tools of inquiry, and structures of the discipline(s) he or she teaches and creates learning experiences that make the discipline accessible and meaningful for learners to assure mastery of the content **Standard #5:** Application of Content. The teacher understands how to connect concepts and use differing perspectives to engage learners in critical thinking, creativity, and collaborative problem solving related to authentic local and global issues	**Domain:** Cognition **Domain:** Scientific Reasoning

Chapter	**naeyc** NAEYC's Professional Preparation Standards	**DAP** Developmentally Appropriate Practice (DAP) Guidelines	**InTASC** Interstate Teacher Assessment and Support Consortium (InTASC)	**HS** Head Start Early Learning Outcomes Framework (HS)
			Standard #8: Instructional Strategies. The teacher understands and uses a variety of instructional strategies to encourage learners to develop deep understanding of content areas and their connections, and to build skills to apply knowledge in meaningful ways	
Chapter 10: Math	5a. Understanding content knowledge and resources in academic disciplines 5b. Knowing and using the central concepts, inquiry tools, and structures of content areas or academic disciplines 5c. Using own knowledge, appropriate early learning standards, and other resources to design, implement, and evaluate developmentally meaningful and challenging curriculum for each child	2. Teaching to Enhance development and learning	**Standard #4:** Content Knowledge. The teacher understands the central concepts, tools of inquiry, and structures of the discipline(s) he or she teaches and creates learning experiences that make the discipline accessible and meaningful for learners to assure mastery of the content **Standard #5:** Application of Content. The teacher understands how to connect concepts and use differing perspectives to engage learners in critical thinking, creativity, and collaborative problem solving related to authentic local and global issues **Standard #8:** Instructional Strategies. The teacher understands and uses a variety of instructional strategies to encourage learners to develop deep understanding of content areas and their connections, and to build skills to apply knowledge in meaningful ways	**Domain:** Mathematics Development
Chapter 11: Fine Motor and Manipulative	5a. Understanding content knowledge and resources in academic disciplines 5b. Knowing and using the central concepts, inquiry tools, and structures of content areas or academic disciplines	2. Teaching to Enhance development and learning	**Standard #4:** Content Knowledge. The teacher understands the central concepts, tools of inquiry, and structures of the discipline(s) he or she teaches and creates learning experiences that make the discipline accessible and meaningful for learners to assure mastery of the content	**Domain:** Perceptual, Motor and Physical Development

Chapter	**naeyc** NAEYC's Professional Preparation Standards	**DAP** Developmentally Appropriate Practice (DAP) Guidelines	**INTASC** Interstate Teacher Assessment and Support Consortium (InTASC)	**HS** Head Start Early Learning Outcomes Framework (HS)
	5c. Using own knowledge, appropriate early learning standards, and other resources to design, implement, and evaluate developmentally meaningful and challenging curriculum for each child		**Standard #5:** Application of Content. The teacher understands how to connect concepts and use differing perspectives to engage learners in critical thinking, creativity, and collaborative problem solving related to authentic local and global issues **Standard #8:** Instructional Strategies. The teacher understands and uses a variety of instructional strategies to encourage learners to develop deep understanding of content areas and their connections, and to build skills to apply knowledge in meaningful ways	
Chapter 12: Large Motor and Outdoor Platy	5a. Understanding content knowledge and resources in academic disciplines 5b. Knowing and using the central concepts, inquiry tools, and structures of content areas or academic disciplines 5c. Using own knowledge, appropriate early learning standards, and other resources to design, implement, and evaluate developmentally meaningful and challenging curriculum for each child	2. Teaching to Enhance development and learning	**Standard #4:** Content Knowledge. The teacher understands the central concepts, tools of inquiry, and structures of the discipline(s) he or she teaches and creates learning experiences that make the discipline accessible and meaningful for learners to assure mastery of the content **Standard #5:** Application of Content. The teacher understands how to connect concepts and use differing perspectives to engage learners in critical thinking, creativity, and collaborative problem solving related to authentic local and global issues **Standard #8:** Instructional Strategies. The teacher understands and uses a variety of instructional strategies to encourage learners to develop deep understanding of content areas and their connections, and to build skills to apply knowledge in meaningful ways	**Domain:** Perceptual, Motor and Physical Development

Chapter	**naeyc** NAEYC's Professional Preparation Standards	**DAP** Developmentally Appropriate Practice (DAP) Guidelines	**INTASC** Interstate Teacher Assessment and Support Consortium (InTASC)	**HS** Head Start Early Learning Outcomes Framework (HS)
Chapter 13: Construction: Blocks and Wood-working	5a. Understanding content knowledge and resources in academic disciplines 5b. Knowing and using the central concepts, inquiry tools, and structures of content areas or academic disciplines 5c. Using own knowledge, appropriate early learning standards, and other resources to design, implement, and evaluate developmentally meaningful and challenging curriculum for each child	2. Teaching to Enhance development and learning	**Standard #4:** Content Knowledge. The teacher understands the central concepts, tools of inquiry, and structures of the discipline(s) he or she teaches and creates learning experiences that make the discipline accessible and meaningful for learners to assure mastery of the content **Standard #5:** Application of Content. The teacher understands how to connect concepts and use differing perspectives to engage learners in critical thinking, creativity, and collaborative problem solving related to authentic local and global issues **Standard #8:** Instructional Strategies. The teacher understands and uses a variety of instructional strategies to encourage learners to develop deep understanding of content areas and their connections, and to build skills to apply knowledge in meaningful ways	**Domain:** Perceptual, Motor and Physical Development **Domain:** Mathematics Development
Chapter 14: Putting it All Together: Evaluation & Documentation	4d. Reflecting on own practice to promote positive outcomes for each child 5c. Using own knowledge, appropriate early learning standards, and other resources to design, implement, and evaluate development-developmentally meaningful and challenging curriculum for each child 6d. Integrating knowledgeable, reflective and critical perspectives on early education	NONE	NONE	NONE